THE RESTORATION CHURCH OF ENGLAND, 1646–1689

Contents

Acknowledgements

While researching and writing this book between 1980 and 1990, I incurred numerous debts which it is now a pleasure to be able to acknowledge. Some of the research was undertaken while preparing a thesis: I am grateful to the Department of Education and Science for financial support during that period. Subsequent research and writing was aided by the award of a British Academy post-doctoral Fellowship and appointment to a Fellowship by Special Election of St Edmund Hall, Oxford: I am extremely grateful to the British Academy and to the Principal and Fellows of St Edmund Hall. A grant from the Research Support Fund of University College Swansea facilitated some final improvements to the text. My work on the Restoration church has given rise to a series of essays, and I am grateful to the editors of the *Historical Journal*, the *Journal of the History of Ideas*, the *English Historical Review*, and the *Journal of Ecclesiastical History*, and to Basil Blackwell Ltd, for permission to reproduce the occasional paragraph or quotation from those pieces.

The staff of the British Library, Lambeth Palace Library, Dr Williams's Library, and the Cambridge University Library have been unfailingly helpful. The bulk of my reading, however, has been done in Duke Humfrey's Library at the Bodleian Library, Oxford. It would not have been so easy, so rewarding, or so much fun without the contributions of Russell Edwards, William Hodges, and Jean-Pierre Mialon, the staff of Duke Humfrey's. St Edmund Hall, Oxford is the other institution which made my undergraduate and graduate years so pleasurable and, I hope, profitable: I shall always be thankful.

Among the many scholars to whom I am indebted for suggestions, information, criticism and good company are Eamon Duffy, Perry Gauci, Mark Goldie, Ralph Houlbrooke, Michael Hunter, Mark Knights, Vivienne Larminie, Steven Pincus and Paul Seaward. I am also extremely grateful to the following scholars for allowing researchers to consult their unpublished dissertations: W.M. Abbott, J.A.I. Champion, R. Clark, C.E. Davies, J.C. Findon, P.W. Jackson, M.D.W. Jones, J. MacKay, A. Milton, J.I. Packer, J.L. Salter, M.G. Smith, D.A. Spaeth, J.T. Spivey, and E.A.O. Whiteman.

The final text of this book owes many of its virtues and none of its vices to Paul Seaward, Isabel Rivers, John Walsh, Anne Whiteman, John Morrill and Blair Worden, who generously read parts or all of an earlier version. I am obliged to Robert Baldock and his staff at Yale University Press for the care with which they have seen the book through the press. Over the years, and in a variety of ways, I have been sustained by my family and by many friends, pupils and teachers: John Morrill's enthusiasm and encouragement has been especially appreciated, as has Anne Whiteman's constant interest and support. My greatest debt is to Blair Worden who educates others by example and friendship; I count it as one of my greatest pieces of good fortune to have been his pupil. The friendship of Julia Barrell has been another such blessing.

J.S.
Swansea, March 1991

Abbreviations

Allestree	Richard Allestree, *Forty Sermons*, 2 vols (Oxford, 1684)
Barrow	*The Theological Works of Isaac Barrow*, ed. A. Napier, 9 vols (Cambridge, 1859)
BIHR	*Bulletin of the Institute of Historical Research*
BL	British Library
Bramhall	*The Works of the Most Reverend Father in God, John Bramhall*, 5 vols (LACT, Oxford, 1842)
Burnet	Gilbert Burnet, *History of My Own Time*, ed. O. Airy, 2 vols (Oxford, 1897–1900)
Cases	*A Collection of Cases and Other Discourses Written to Recover Dissenters to the Communion of the Church of England/By Some Divines of the City of London* (issued separately in 1683, as a collection in 1685, and as a single folio volume in 1694; 1698 edn of 1694 volume cited)
Concilia	*Concilia Magnae Britannae et Hiberniae*, ed. D. Wilkins, 4 vols (1737)
CR	A.G. Matthews, *Calamy Revised* (Oxford, 1934)
CSPD	*Calendar of State Papers Domestic*
CUL	Cambridge University Library
DNB	*The Dictionary of National Biography*, ed. L. Stephens and S. Lee, 63 vols (1885–1900)
DWL	Dr Williams's Library, London
EHR	*English Historical Review*
Evelyn	*The Diary of John Evelyn*, ed. E.S. de Beer, 5 vols (Oxford, 1952)
Farindon	*The Sermons of the Rev. Anthony Farindon*, ed. J. Nichols, 4 vols (1849)
Fuller	*The Collected Sermons of Thomas Fuller*, ed. J.E. Bailey and W.E.A. Axon, 2 vols (1891)

Gibson	*A Preservative against Popery*, ed. Edmund Gibson, 3 vols (1738)
Granville	*The Remains of Denis Granville*, ed. G. Ornsby, 2 vols (Surtees Society, 37, 1860; 47, 1865)
Hammond	*The Works of Henry Hammond*, ed. W. Fulman, 4 vols (Oxford, 1684)
Heywood	Joseph Hunter, *The Rise of the Old Dissent Exemplified in the Life of Oliver Heywood* (1842)
HJ	*Historical Journal*
HMC	Historical Manuscripts Commission
JEH	*Journal of Ecclesiastical History*
JHI	*Journal of the History of Ideas*
Josselin	*The Diary of Ralph Josselin 1616–1683*, ed. A. Macfarlane (1976)
Kennett	[White Kennett], *The Complete History of England* (1706), vol. III
LACT	*Library of Anglo-Catholic Theology*
Littleton	Adam Littleton, *Sixty-One Sermons*, 3 vols (1680)
Marvell, *Letters*	*The Poems and Letters of Andrew Marvell*, ed. H.M. Margoliouth (3rd edn, Oxford, 1971), vol. II
Patrick	*The Works of Simon Patrick*, ed. A. Taylor, 9 vols (Cambridge, 1858)
Pepys	*The Diary of Samuel Pepys*, ed. R. Latham and W. Matthews, 11 vols (1970–83)
Pocock	N. Pocock (ed.), 'Illustrations of the State of the Church During the Great Rebellion', *The Theologian and Ecclesiastic*, VI–XV (1848–54)
RB	Richard Baxter, *Reliquiae Baxterianae*, ed. M. Sylvester (1696)
SCH	*Studies in Church History*
South	*The Sermons of Robert South D.D.*, 5 vols (Oxford, 1842)
Stillingfleet	*The Works of Edward Stillingfleet*, ed. R. Bentley, 6 vols (1710)
Taylor	*The Whole Works of the Right Reverend Jeremy Taylor*, ed. R. Heber, 15 vols (1828)
Tillotson	*The Sermons of John Tillotson*, 12 vols (1757)
TRHS	*Transactions of the Royal Historical Society*
WAWD	[Richard Allestree], *The Works of the Author of the Whole Duty of Man* (Oxford, 1684)
Wing	D. Wing (ed.), *Short-Title Catalogue of Books Printed in England . . . 1641–1700* (2nd edn, New York, 1972–1988)
Wood	*The Life and Times of Anthony Wood*, ed. A. Clark, 5

vols (Oxford Historical Society, 19, 21, 26, 30, 40, 1891–1900)

WR   A.G. Matthews, *Walker Revised* (Oxford, 1948)

Note on Sources

All manuscripts cited are from the Bodleian Library, Oxford, unless otherwise indicated. In the interests of comprehensibility, I have where necessary modernized the spelling and punctuation of all sources, manuscript and printed, seventeenth-century and modern, other than the titles of published works.

Introduction

The Restoration Church of England has inevitably suffered by association with her own times. Sandwiched between the heroic era of puritanism and the eighteenth-century age of reason and stability, the Restoration period can, all too often, appear sordid, cynical, chaotic and godless; it seems as if, in the England of Charles II and James II, all genuine religious zeal was spent. And as a consequence, the national church of Restoration England is commonly perceived as lukewarm, emasculated and Erastian, as a spiritually moribund vehicle of reaction and intolerance which had little to offer the laity. Many commentators can scarcely conceal their distaste for a church which so steadfastly refused to bow to the inevitability of religious pluralism, and they turn with relief to consider instead the enobling travails of Nonconformity. The Restoration Church of England has also suffered – rather unfairly as some might think – by anachronistic association with the Hanoverian Church of England. With one eye on the enlightened eighteenth century, some historians single out those Restoration churchmen whose progressive views distinguish them as harbingers of tolerance and reason; other scholars meanwhile are at pains to stress the Church of England's ideological role in shaping and sustaining an aristocratic and authoritarian political culture in Georgian England. This book, however, is an attempt to explore the Restoration Church of England in her own right, to view her with neither hindsight nor unwarranted assumptions about her motivation and morale; while writing it, I have kept in mind the Restoration vicar of Stratford's daunting maxim that 'a true historian should be neither party, advocate, nor judge, but a bare witness'.[1]

As one of the principal political and social institutions in Restora-

---

1. *The Diary of the Rev. John Ward, A.M., Vicar of Stratford upon Avon . . . 1648–1679*, ed. C. Severn (1839), p. 216.

tion England, the church deserves the attention of all students of the seventeenth century. She was the church of the overwhelming majority of the population throughout the later seventeenth century, and her ubiquity, property and history assured her of a standing in society enjoyed by no other corporate body. The church's political fortunes are thus part of the history of Restoration England, as are the often difficult relations of individual ministers with their parishioners. The purpose of this book is not, however, simply to supply a history of the church in Restoration England, but also to make a contribution to the history of the Church of England and of Anglicanism. Recently, we have been reminded that 'the political, social and cultural context can only provide the *occasion* for a church and contribute to the shaping of its outward form: it cannot provide a *definition* of a church or its *raison d'être*.[2] In this book I have sought to go beyond the 'occasion' of the Restoration Church of England in search of her theological definition and spiritual *raison d'être*. This is to set out in pursuit of the Church of England's identity, a pursuit which has occupied the church from the sixteenth century to the present day; and while it is, perhaps, reckless of a mere historian to venture on to such terrain, it seems to me to be a necessary historical undertaking. It is necessary because without a grasp of the central theological identity of the Restoration church, much of her history in the later seventeenth century – her implacable opposition to other Protestant denominations, her insistence upon her authority as the national church, and even her moments of opposition to the Stuarts – is incomprehensible. But it is also necessary because between the 1640s and the 1690s, the Church of England came close to enjoying, perhaps for the first and only time, a single identity, a single 'Anglicanism'. I make no apologies for using the anachronistic term 'Anglican' throughout this book, nor for stretching the term 'Restoration', when discussing the church, to cover the period between 1646 and 1689, since I hope that, by the end of the book, the reader will appreciate why I use them and may even have been convinced that there was a uniqueness and integrity to this period of the Church of England's history.

What makes the Church of England's continuing search for her identity such an absorbing historical problem is that, as a church, she is particularly dependent upon her 'occasion'. She has no irreducible doctrinal core, no confession of faith nor petrine rock, upon which to rest, but must go out, armed only with her Bible, liturgy, Articles and traditions, to do battle with each new set of political,

2. The phrase is Paul Avis's, see *The Study of Anglicanism*, ed. S. Sykes and J. Booty (1988), p. 406.

social and cultural circumstances. The Restoration church was no exception to this rule of constant self-invention. She too was the creation of her own peculiar circumstances. Restoration Anglicanism was rooted in the mixed experience of the Puritan Revolution; an experience for Anglicans of dispossession and persecution, but also one of renewed piety and ecclesiological confidence. The Church of England emerged from the 1640s and 1650s with a distinct doctrinal, ecclesiological and spiritual identity, which was subsequently tempered by the challenges and disappointments of the next three decades. The hesitant search for a clerical *modus vivendi*, the awkward relationships with an aloof, if not antagonistic, monarch and a supposedly vicious laity, and the failure to reimpose religious uniformity on a nation which had tasted liberty and licence, all played their part in reinforcing the Restoration church's sense of unity and of identity. This Anglican identity was finally dissipated by the Glorious Revolution, the Toleration Act of 1689 and the schism of the Nonjurors: it is arguable, therefore, that 1689 has a claim to be considered the great watershed in the history of the seventeenth-century Church of England.

Throughout this book, I repeatedly refer to 'the church' and 'the churchmen' as if the Restoration clergy spoke with a single voice – which, of course, they did not. In my defence, I could echo Dryden and claim that 'no general characters of parties (call 'em either sects or churches) can be so fully and exactly drawn, as to comprehend all the several members of 'em; at least all such as are received under that denomination'.[3] But I would prefer to allow the book itself to explain how circumstances and policy led to the creation of an Anglican identity, a common outlook born out of compromise between different views and aspirations. At the Restoration many ministers had thrown in their lot with a church which they only slowly and grudgingly came to appreciate and value; meanwhile other, more zealously episcopalian, churchmen strained after more doctrinaire or partisan goals. Common dangers – from lay apathy and vice, from Nonconformity, atheism, and political betrayal – kept these centrifugal tendencies in check and even contributed to a sense of shared purpose among the clergy. True, many differences were disguised rather than healed, but they were well disguised, and the church could feel confident that her clergy were pulling together towards shared, practical, goals: from this point of view, it could be said that Anglican solidarity was as much a product as a cause of the attempt to reimpose religious uniformity on Restoration England.

3. John Dryden, *The Hind and the Panther* (1687), To the Reader (in *Poems and Fables of Dryden*, ed. J. Kinsley (Oxford, 1958), p. 352).

The Restoration Church of England was led, both politically and intellectually, from above. A handful of bishops steered the church through the dangerous political waters of the later seventeenth century: the lower clergy were curiously lacking in initiative, self-confidence and organization; their views had no forum since Convocation did not meet; and they created no alternative mouthpieces, nothing along the lines of the voluntary clerical associations of the early Stuart church, or the ecclesiastical parties, periodicals and societies of the post-1689 church. The tone and agenda for the church's theological and spiritual life were set by a coterie of controversialists, preachers and devotional writers, based in London and the two universities. The provincial clergy snapped up every published sermon by Anglican champions like Edward Stillingfleet or John Tillotson; they flocked to every assize or visitation sermon delivered by a dignitary of the church; and they amplified the message of the clerical leadership each Sunday in their own parish churches. Among these rank-and-file clergy there were some who would publish the occasional sermon and dedicate it, with fulsome professions of obedience and duty, to the bishop or archbishop in the hope of winning favour or preferment. This informal system, exploiting men's hunger for promotion, effectively ensured that the views of the church's leaders were reflected back to them and that, on public matters, the church spoke with one voice. It had the additional advantage, from the historian's point of view, of creating a body of published literature from which Anglican attitudes on a variety of subjects can now be gleaned. There were, of course, other clergymen, happy or resigned to live out their days in rural obscurity, who had no interest in self-advancement and so left no tracts, sermons or letters behind them. Although their world is more difficult to explore, and their views are less easily elicited, I have attempted to give due weight to this silent clerical proletariat and to their fundamental role in the church.

Finally, the identity of the Restoration Church of England was shaped by the laity. The churchmen tailored their message to suit their lay audience; castigating their vices, appealing to their better nature, and even attempting to turn their own intellectual weapons against them: the clergy took pride in their unyielding stance as messengers of the Lord, but they were intensely aware of their need for the credit and esteem of the English laity. In short – and as the following pages will demonstrate – the identity of the Restoration church is to be found somewhere between the church as she was and the church as the clergy and laity wished her to be.

I have explored the identity of the Restoration church through printed sermons, apologetical and theological works and devotional

manuals; the statistical findings of social historians on the condition
of the clergy and the religious diligence of the laity have been
pressed into service; and I have scoured the manuscript correspondence and diaries of archbishops and deans, bishops and archdeacons, and parsons and curates, for examples of what the church's
theological arguments or financial difficulties might have meant
to individuals. I hope that the resulting picture pays due regard
to the diversity of life in the Restoration church, while offering a
straightforward account of the church. I have assumed little or no
previous knowledge on the part of the reader and have preferred to
err on the side of over-simplification when explaining technicalities.
This is not meant to be a definitive study of the Restoration Church
of England since a great deal more research is necessary before that
would be possible. More could be said about almost every topic
touched on in these pages: much evidence about later seventeenth-
century religious life lies undiscovered in vestry minute books and
churchwardens' accounts; and further material on the institutional
life of the church and the condition of the clergy exists in local record
offices and diocesan archives. It is to be hoped that future work
based on such material will qualify and revise the account offered
here.

The shape of this book has been determined by its subject. Since
the Restoration church and Restoration Anglicanism were the creation of the Puritan Revolution, an introductory chapter has been
devoted to tracing the church's survival during the Interregnum; but
throughout the book I treat the church of the 1640s and 1650s as
part of the Restoration church. The next chapter offers a narrative
of the church's political and institutional fortunes between the
Restoration and the Revolution of 1688–9. Thereafter, the chapters
are thematic; if, at times, these themes seem less than obvious that is
because they have been dictated by the categories of Restoration
Anglicanism, not by those of twentieth-century secular history.
Chapter 3 is concerned with the Restoration church's ecclesiology –
the theology of the nature and purpose of the church – and argues
that the mid-seventeenth-century Church of England began to
grope towards a 'Catholic' model of the church and to renounce
'Reformed' ecclesiology. This shift entailed new and divisive views of
what it was to be a national church and of the role of the episcopate.
Fortunately, the church seems to have been able to maintain a loose
consensus which was generous enough to allow diversity of clerical
opinion on these questions and yet sufficiently coherent to give the
church a distinct identity as an autonomous, national, episcopalian
church. The practical implications of these apologetical developments, especially for Anglican attitudes towards religious unity and

Dissent, were profound. The fourth chapter shows that the Church of England was unable to ensure uniformity among her clergy or laity and that she lacked the moral authority to combat the rising tide of lay contempt for organized religion and its ministers. The fifth chapter is devoted to the clergy's understanding of apathy, irreligion and dissidence and suggests that the churchmen tended to identify all opposition, whether sanctimonious Nonconformity or witty debauchery, with sin. The Anglican theology of salvation is the subject of Chapter 6. The churchmen were consciously attempting to repair the harm done by the puritan theologies of salvation which they believed had undermined and minimized human effort. The Anglican gospel was a rigorous Protestant theology which has been grievously misrepresented as 'moralism'. Chapter 7 describes the regime of private and public piety based on the church's liturgy and sacraments which was to sustain the penitent in working out his own salvation. These chapters build up a portrait of 'Restoration Anglicanism', of an ecclesiology, theology, piety and religious culture which made the Restoration Church of England distinct from the Roman Catholic and Protestant churches and from earlier manifestations of the Church of England. The fate of this Restoration Anglicanism after the Revolution of 1688, and the story of how it became obscured by later distortions, is retailed as an epilogue in the final chapter.

Chapter 1

The Church of England and Anglicanism, 1646–60

For Anthony Blagrave, gentleman, of Bulmersh Court in Berkshire, life in the early 1650s was a convivial round of pleasure and duty. Trips to the bowling green and tavern, horse-racing and coursing, were interspersed with neighbours' marriages, christenings and funerals. Assiduous in attending his parish church, hearing sermons, and receiving communion, the devout Blagrave also found time for 'gossuping' and drinking with Mr Sexby, the vicar of Sonning. When the Assizes or Quarter Sessions opened at nearby Reading, Blagrave would be there to savour the sermon and the charge, and to dine with one of his many kinsmen; and his frequent visits to London were enlivened by the chance to hear the capital's eminent preachers or to spend some time in the tavern with old clerical friends like Dr George Wilde, minister at St Gregory's. Yet beneath the placid surface of Blagrave's life, the waters were turbulent: he was often ill and wretched; he slept badly and his dreams were all of death – once he dreamt of 'the late king', Charles I, who assured him that 'I should never want; and I hope God is the king that will see it performed'.[1] For there was no escaping the repercussions of the recent civil war and revolution. In the same month that Blagrave was sent a side of venison by his neighbour the 'retired' Bishop Juxon of London, he was also harassed by the soldiery and forced to supply a horse to the Militia Commissioners. And on his trips to London, Blagrave was careful to pay his respects to the new dignitaries thrown up by the revolution, men like his cousin Daniel Blagrave, the regicide MP, and Lieutenant-General Fleetwood. It often seemed as if two separate worlds lived in uneasy coexistence. At the prohibited festival of Christmas in 1653, while Oliver Cromwell was assuming the Protectorship of England, Anthony

---

1. Blagrave's diary for 1651–3, MS Eng Misc E 118, fo. 28 (25 June 1651).

Blagrave was busy giving dinner to sixty-nine poor folk, and serving as one of the 'godfathers' at the 'christening' of a neighbour's son. And throughout these years Blagrave was closely involved with the Church of England, a church supposedly 'abolished, and gone, and not owned by our law at this day'.[2]

That the Church of England survived there can be no doubt. The preachers that Blagrave met and heard in Berkshire and London were good Church of England men, divines stigmatized as 'Prayer Book men' by their opponents and the authorities; he heard clergy who had been thrown out of their livings by the puritans, and younger conforming divines who were to go on to make careers in the Church of England after the Restoration. Although the Book of Common Prayer was banned, it may have supplied the 'prayers' used at St Andrew's, Sonning; and on his visits to London, Blagrave could easily have attended Common Prayer services in one of several churches. While browsing among the booksellers' stalls, he might well have picked up the devotional works of George Herbert or Richard Crashaw, a copy of Charles I's *Eikon Basilike*, or one of the many other books proclaiming the continued existence of the Church of England. Thomas Fuller, for instance, prefaced his *Church History* of 1655 with the assertion that the Church of England, although 'distracted', was still in being. In the previous year, Bishop Joseph Hall had addressed the 'orthodox and genuine sons of the Church of England', while Henry Hammond had announced that 'the Church of England is not invisible; it is still preserved in bishops and presbyters rightly ordained, and multitudes rightly baptized, none of which have fallen off from their profession'. In the name of all 'that own relation, honour and adherency to the Church of England,' John Gauden, Dean of Bocking, thanked another worthy author, 'who hath not despised the low and afflicted state of his mother and brethren', for vindicating the church against her sectarian enemies. 'I hope it will not be said I seek to justify a church which is not,' wrote Dr Edward Hyde, 'for the truth and righteousness whereby it was a church, are the same they ever were'.[3]

The question is, of course, what did such claims mean? In what

---

2. William Sheppard, *A View of all the Laws and Statutes of this Nation concerning the Service of God or Religion* (1655), p. 78.
3. Fuller, *Church History* (1655), sig. a4; Joseph Hall, *Works*, ed. P. Wynter (Oxford, 1863), VII, 416; Hammond, I, pt. ii, 370 (*Of Schism*); Jeffry Watts, *A Scribe, Pharisee, Hypocrite* (1657), preface by Gauden; Edward Hyde, *Christ and his Church* (Oxford, 1658), p. 523. Also see Richard Samwaies, *England's Faithfull Reprover* (1653), pp.1–2; William Smyth, *The Safe Way to Glory* (1656); Peter Heylyn, *Ecclesia vindicata* (1657).

sense did the Church of England exist during the Interregnum? This chapter explores the church's survival as an institution, as a clergy, as a communion of Christians, and as a distinctive form of 'Anglicanism'. For it is only by examining these roots that we will be able to account for the later flowering of Restoration Anglicanism. Despite the rhetorical flights of some contemporaries, the church did not emerge like a phoenix from her own ashes in 1660–2. The persistence of the Church of England during the 'puritan rebellion', and the part she played in the lives of Englishmen and women like the Blagrave family, are an integral part of the history of the Restoration church. It is to the Interregnum that later chapters will repeatedly return to find the sources of the ecclesiology, theology and piety of the Restoration church.

In 1641, when the English Parliament began to dismantle the regime of Charles I, the most systematic and ferocious attack was not upon the political and legal agents of Stuart tyranny, but upon the Church of England. Having overturned Archbishop Laud's innovations in doctrine, discipline and ritual, and excluded the bishops from the House of Lords, Parliament began to consider a more fundamental remodelling of the national church. Her diocesan episcopacy was to be extirpated root and branch, her courts to be demolished, her parish clergy to be purged of all malignant and scandalous priests, and her wealth to be applied to more godly purposes; but then civil war overtook the nation and more urgent problems claimed Parliament's attention. Under the pressure of financing and fighting a war against the King, the parliamentarians' early enthusiasm for reform of the church gave way to *ad hoc* purges of the clergy and to a piecemeal demolition of what now appeared a largely irrelevant institution. Those bishops not in prison or in exile had long since retired, like Juxon, into rural obscurity; the last consecration of a bishop had taken place in 1644. Laud went to the scaffold in January 1645, although it was not until October 1646, when financial exigencies required the sale of episcopal and dean and chapter lands, that episcopacy was formally abolished by Parliament. On the day of Laud's attainder Parliament banned the use of the Book of Common Prayer and imposed the Westminster Assembly's *Directory of Public Worship* upon the nation. And then came the execution of Charles I on 30 January 1649. Truly, 'God had spat in their faces', observed Henry Hammond. With Charles died any hope that the Church of England, in however attenuated a form, might be negotiated back into existence; 'the church here will never rise again, though the kingdom should', concluded William Sancroft. In less than a decade

the Church of England had been deprived of her nursing father
the King, her bishops and pastors, her liturgy, her cathedrals and
chapters, her courts and her revenues.[4]

But the parish and the parochial ministry survived. And the
Church of England survived within the parish clergy of Interregnum
England. 'For you must understand,' explained the puritan Richard
Baxter,

> that when the Parliament purged the ministry, they cast out
> the grosser sort of insufficient and scandalous ones, as gross
> drunkards, and such like; and also some few civil men that had
> assisted in the wars against the Parliament, or set up bowing to
> altars, and such innovations: but they had left in near one half the
> ministers, that were not good enough to do much service, nor bad
> enough to be cast out as utterly intolerable: these were a company
> of poor weak preachers, that had no great skill in divinity, nor zeal
> for godliness; but preached weakly that which is true, and lived in
> no gross notorious sin: these men were not cast out, but yet their
> people greatly needed help; for their dark sleepy preaching did but
> little good.[5]

Baxter was by his own account a 'mere Catholic' of no denomination, but many of his fellow parish ministers were Presbyterians or
Independents. More radical than these two denominations were
those English Protestants who had renounced all but voluntary and
'congregationalist' worship; many of these trusted implicitly in 'the
leading of the Holy Spirit' and scorned a clergy or a liturgy as
'human inventions'; such libertarian thinking was rumoured to have
led the more extreme sects to an antinomian revelling in blasphemy
and licence.

The parochial structure weathered the storms of Civil War and
republican rule thanks to the protection of the landed class. During
the 1640s, authority over the parish, its officers and it affairs had
been devolved to the local gentry, who regarded the parish as an
indispensable instrument of communal order and who frequently
had a direct financial stake in the parish tithes.[6] The sectarian

4. Pocock, VI, 4; MS Tanner 57, fo. 525. Also see J.S. Morrill, 'The Attack on the
   Church of England in the Long Parliament, 1640–2', in *History, Society and the
   Churches*, ed. D. Beales and G. Best (Cambridge, 1985); J.S. Morrill, 'The Church in
   England, 1642–9', in *Reactions to the English Civil War*, ed. J.S. Morrill (1982); P.
   King, 'The Episcopate during the Civil Wars', *EHR*, 83 (1968); P. King, 'The
   Reasons for the Abolition of the Book of Common Prayer in 1645', *JEH*, 21 (1970).
5. *RB*, I, 95.
6. See A. Hughes, *Politics, Society and Civil War in Warwickshire, 1620–1660* (Cambridge,
   1987), pp. 307–9; A. Coleby, *Central Government and the Localities: Hampshire 1649–1689*

opponents of the parish were vociferous, but not numerous. All the 'gathered' congregations, even when their numbers were swollen by the advent of the Quakers in the mid-1650s, never amounted to more than a tiny proportion of the population. There was no longer any practical or legal obligation to attend the parish church, but perhaps no more than 5 per cent of the English attended other religious assemblies between 1643 and 1654.[7] Although sectarianism was a challenge to parish-based religion, it only threatened the existence of the parish once, when the radical MPs of the Barebone's Parliament prepared to abolish tithes in 1653. The forces of conservatism immediately rallied at Westminster and in the shires; the Warwickshire JPs, for example, took it upon themselves to pursue tithes owed in the parish of Bulkington so as to pay ministers to preach there while the living was vacant, 'conceiving it as a matter of necessity for upholding the service of God that there be a preaching ministry maintained'.[8]

The maintenance of the parish did not mean, of course, that the entire community, bar a few sectaries, played a full and equal role in church life: it is doubtful that the entire community had ever participated fully in the religion of the parish church. Under the decentralized, tolerant regime of the 1640s and 1650s, the degrees of involvement were many and various: Richard Baxter distinguished twelve categories of parishioner in Kidderminster and at least six of these categories were apparently God-fearing church attenders. Yet elsewhere worship at the parish church collapsed as the parishioners dispersed to different congregations and sects.[9] It may well be that the liberty of the 1650s did more harm to parish-based religion in allowing so many of the English to avoid church and worship altogether than in fostering sectarianism.

The clerical profession did their part in defending the parish system. Predictably, most were firm believers in the need for a parish-based clergy supported *faute de mieux* by the tithes or contributions of their parishioners. Even some of the Baptist and

(Cambridge, 1987), pp. 56–7; A. Fletcher, *A County Community in Peace and War: Sussex 1600–1660* (1975), pp. 114–16; Morrill, 'Church in England', pp. 97–8.

7. Morrill, 'Church in England', p. 90. An Act of September 1650 withdrew all penalties for not attending church: see C. Cross, 'The Church in England, 1646–60', in *The Interregnum*, ed. G.E. Aylmer (1974), pp. 103–5; B. Worden, 'Toleration and the Cromwellian Protectorate', *SCH*, 21 (1984).

8. Hughes, *Politics . . . in Warwickshire*, p. 308. Also see A. Woolrych, *Commonwealth to Protectorate* (Oxford, 1982), pp. 245–50; P. Styles, *Studies in Seventeenth-century West Midlands History* (Kineton, 1978), pp. 77–8.

9. E. Duffy, 'The Godly and the Multitude in Stuart England', *The Seventeenth Century*, 1 (1986), 38–40; M. Spufford, *Contrasting Communities* (Cambridge, 1974), pp. 272–6.

congregationalist churches were ready to take advantage of the parish system: in Bristol, for instance, the Baptists took the sacrament from ordained parish ministers, while also having their own preacher, who was happy to hold a corporation post as a city lecturer. In Worcestershire, Richard Baxter held the living of Kidderminster, and the neighbouring parish of Bewdley was served by John Tombes, an eminent Baptist. Approximately 130 Independent ministers accepted parish livings across the country. The Presbyterians assumed that the parish would serve as the first tier in the effective imposition of discipline.[10] And of course, Baxter's 'poor weak preachers', the lukewarm episcopalian clergy, who were able and content to stay on as parish ministers under the various regimes of the 1640s and 1650s, could envisage no other structure for the church. It is among these conforming pastors that we should begin our search for the Interregnum Church of England.

It has been claimed, both in the seventeenth century and since, that the 'authentic voice of Anglicanism' passed during the Interregnum to those who were ejected from their livings, who 'suffered' for their loyalty to church and King; the corollary is that those clergy absorbed into the parish ministry of the Interregnum had lost or abandoned their 'Anglican' identity.[11] But the claim of the 'sufferers' to embody the Church of England does not stand up to scrutiny. In reality the choice facing clergymen in the 1640s and 1650s was rarely as stark as that between 'suffering' and conformity. For instance, it is estimated that about 3,600 clergymen suffered some disturbance between 1640 and the Restoration. But that bald figure takes no account of the nature of the 'disturbance', its date or its permanence. Of the total of 3,600 only two and a half thousand were parish clergy, the rest being cathedral or university divines: and since there were about 8,600 parishes in England it is safe to conclude that the majority of parish clergy were not disturbed. Of the minority of clergymen that suffered some form of harassment, three times as many were disturbed during the 1640s as during the following decade. Even then, many of the 'sufferers' of the 1640s were later able, through equivocation or collaboration, to re-enter the ministry. If one reverses the perspective to consider the proportion escaping harassment, it emerges that perhaps 70 per cent or

10. J. Barry, 'The Parish in Civic Life: Bristol and its Churches, 1640–1750', in *Parish, Church and People*, ed. S.J. Wright (1988), pp. 158–9; M.R. Watts, *The Dissenters* (Oxford, 1978), pp. 151–63.

11. See, for example, R.S. Bosher, *The Making of the Restoration Settlement, 1649–62* (1951), esp. pp. 23–4; J.D. Tatham, *Dr John Walker's 'The Sufferings of the Clergy'* (Cambridge, 1911); Evelyn, III, 247–8.

even 75 per cent of all parish ministers were left in possession of their benefices until their death or the Restoration.[12]

Naturally, questions surround the conduct of men who continued to serve their cures. For instance, how far did they collaborate with the new regime and how far were they left to their own devices? Some conformists had presumably been dissatisfied with the pre-1640 church, although serving in it, and had gladly found themselves swept along by attempts to introduce godly preaching and discipline. But on the other hand, as Baxter pointed out, the successive puritan regimes were far from effective in purging the parish clergy of all dissidents or enforcing the ban on the worship of the Church of England. They relied upon local activists to petition against unsatisfactory clergy, but such decentralized and sporadic persecution can rarely have defined its target precisely. Thus the 'scandalous' and 'malignant' appear to have been a motley crew of zealous 'Laudians' and royalists, those unenthusiastic for the parliamentary cause, the drunken and immoral, and the inadequate preachers.[13] Although a series of political tests were demanded, most notably the Solemn League and Covenant of 1643, which required the explicit renunciation of episcopacy, and the Engagement of 1650, which required the explicit renunciation of monarchy, their patchy enforcement and the haphazard nature of accusations and investigations meant that clergymen in some parishes might never face a direct challenge to their principles or an immediate threat to their incumbency. Was this perhaps the case with conformists like John Gauden at Bocking, John Hacket at Cheam, and William Pickering at Claverdon? Others might have to decide whether it was possible to subscribe to the Covenant or the Engagement – or, like Ralph Josselin, to both – in order to achieve some greater pastoral good.[14] The conflict of loyalties – to legitimate political and spiritual authority, to their calling, to their flock, and to their family – experienced by those facing conformity are obvious; the agonies of conscience they suffered can only be imagined. One option was to seek the guidance of those with authority, moral or otherwise. When William Smyth, rector of Cotton, was confronted with the choice of acceding to the liturgical demands of his puritanical parishioners or facing ejection,

---

12. See I.M. Green, 'The Persecution of "Scandalous" and "Malignant" Parish Clergy during the English Civil War', *EHR*, 94 (1979); Bosher, *Making of Restoration*, pp. 5, 24; E.A.O. Whiteman, 'The Restoration of the Church of England', in *From Uniformity to Unity*, ed. G.F. Nuttall and O. Chadwick (1962), pp. 34–5.

13. See Green, 'Persecution'; J. Sharpe, 'Scandalous and Malignant Priests in Essex', in *Politics and People in Revolutionary England*, ed. C. Jones, M. Newitt and S. Roberts (Oxford, 1986).

14. See *DNB*, 'Thomas Lamplugh'; *WR*, p. 67, 'Francis Walsal'.

he went to Bishop Hall of Norwich 'to take his advice and order, who told me that his opinion was that I might do good service by preaching to them, omitting the use of the liturgy, excepting in the offices of the sacraments, and not keeping any thanksgivings'.[15]

There may be a distinction to be made between 'conformists', who by keeping their heads down escaped attention from the authorities, and those who offered some active, overt gesture of 'collaboration', such as taking a job from the new regime. One such act of collaboration was the practice of appearing before the committee of 'triers' to be assessed for a ministerial appointment. Even the self-proclaimed Anglican, Thomas Fuller, was prepared to be examined by this puritan committee in order to gain a new living: and among the youthful new entrants to the ministry who appeared before the triers were Simon Patrick, Laurence Womock, William Lloyd and George Hall, all of whom were to be bishops in the Restoration Church of England.[16] One has to conclude with A.G. Matthews that 'collaboration, as it is now called, was fairly general throughout the Interregnum'.[17]

So the majority of ministers remained in tranquil possession of their livings until their death: but how many of these conformists lived to see the Church of England restored? We do not know; but in any span of twenty years, the changes in the composition of the nation's clergy resulting from deaths would be significant.[18] So too would be the changes produced by recruitment to the profession. Many of the men who staffed and eventually led the Restoration Church of England had begun their ministry during the 1650s. It was an accident of their birth that 'they grew up among the sects', as one of them later wrote, yet they managed affairs so that 'it was no hurt to the church, or them, that they were educated in bad times . . . they scrupled not, because they were young, and had

15. MS Tanner 34, fo. 147.
16. In A.G. Matthew's *Walker Revised* (a list of clergy who supposedly 'suffered' during the Interregnum for their loyalty to the Church of England) I count 134 clergymen who appeared before the triers and another 15 who may have done. For Fuller and the triers see W.B. Patterson, 'Thomas Fuller as Royalist Country Parson during the Interregnum', *SCH*, 16 (1979), 308–11.
17. *WR*, p. xviii.
18. Half the incumbents in Leicestershire in 1659 had received orders in the Church of England before 1642; J.H. Pruett, *The Parish Clergy under the Later Stuarts – The Leicestershire Experience* (Urbana, Illinois, 1978), p. 15. R. Clark, 'Anglicanism, Recusancy, and Dissent in Derbyshire, 1603–1730' (unpublished Oxford University D.Phil. thesis, 1979), pp. 17–20, 133–7, suggests that the turnover of the 1640s and 1650s was not much greater than that of less disturbed decades.

been under no explicit engagements to those laws, that were then unhappily overruled'.[19] In other words, they were too young ever to have been bound personally to the monarchy and to the Church of England; they could, therefore, serve without qualm as ministers under the dubious religious regimes of the Interregnum. At the Restoration these clergy conformed to the Church of England, which now required the use of the Prayer Book, and its vestments and rituals, subscription to the Thirty-Nine Articles, and episcopal ordination. However, many of these younger men already had episcopal ordination. During the Interregnum, they had sought out ordination from the handful of functioning bishops of the Church of England. The 'general outcry' in Interregnum Cambridge 'was, that the whole university was overrun with Arminianism, and was full of men of a prelatical spirit, that had apostasized to the onions and garlic of Egypt, because they were generally ordained by bishops'.[20] The scale of covert episcopal ordinations during the Interregnum can perhaps best be appreciated by listing just some of the leading Restoration churchmen who had received such ordinations; they included Dolben, Tenison, Tillotson, Stillingfleet, Cartwright, Bull, Barrow, Kidder, Patrick, Cumberland, South, Clement Ellis, William Lloyd and John Scott. The preacher of Scott's funeral sermon described how 'when the church was covered in ruins, he discerned her beauty; and received holy orders from one of those ejected confessors, who during the devastation did secretly preserve the apostolical discipline'.[21] But what was it that led so many to discern the beauty of the Church of England and to seek out clandestine ordination by a bishop when they had no legal need of it and when, in many cases, they had already received Presbyterian orders? The answer will obviously vary with each individual, but Henry Hammond's assertion that the Church of England 'is still preserved in bishops and presbyters rightly ordained' is suggestive. As a later chapter will demonstrate, even in the midst of the 'broken times', episcopacy continued to inspire many young clergymen.

The parish clergy of the 1640s and 1650s included a large number of men who had displayed or were to display an allegiance to the episcopal Church of England. Of the 194 clergymen serving

19. Joseph Glanvil, *Essays on Several Important Subjects in Philosophy and Religion* (1676), essay 7, p. 16.
20. S.P., *A Brief Account of the New Sect of Latitude-Men* (1662), p. 5.
21. Zachary Isham in John Scott, *Works* (1718), II, 568. Also see E.H Day, 'Ordinations under the Commonwealth', *Theology*, 44 (1942); H.F. Kirkpatrick, 'Commonwealth Ordinations', *Theology*, 45 (1942–3).

the benefices of the county of Warwickshire after the 1662 Act of Uniformity, 29 had served cures continuously from the 1630s, 15 had done so from the 1640s, and 46 from the 1650s.[22] The diversity of background and outlook among these Anglican clergymen must have been wide, but the full range of what can legitimately be called Anglicanism in the Interregnum was wider still. Anglican clerical opinion stretched from the die-hard 'sufferers', who had been ejected and sequestered from their livings, through conformists and collaborators to the young, unaligned, entrants.

At one end of this spectrum stood those who 'having owned and reverenced the Church of England as a chaste matron, as a venerable mother in her lustre . . . shall not desert, nor brand her as an impure harlot in her eclipse'.[23] Yet surprisingly few bishops were to be found among this faithful remnant: fearful of the authorities, impecunious, ageing and often ill, many bishops went to ground. There were exceptions: Skinner of Oxford, and several Irish bishops, most notably Sydserf of Galloway, were responsible for large numbers of ordinations; but, in general, the episcopate had abdicated the spiritual and intellectual leadership of the church.[24] It therefore fell to Henry Hammond, former rector of Penshurst, and a small group of divines of the pre-1640 generation, who held themselves aloof from all of the usurping regimes, to take up the Anglican torch. Although geographically isolated from one another, Hammond, John Bramhall, Jeremy Taylor, Robert Sanderson, Matthew Wren and other Anglican luminaries kept up a correspondence, sharing ideas and knowledge, swopping titbits of academic and royalist gossip, and encouraging each other in the service of 'our distressed mother the church'.[25] Seclusion and enforced unemployment allowed the completion of such large-scale works as Hammond's paraphrase of the New Testament and Taylor's manuals of repentance and

22. I have produced these totals from the list of 863 serving Warwickshire clergymen in J.L. Salter, 'Warwickshire Clergy, 1660–1714' (unpublished Birmingham University Ph.D. thesis, 1975), volume II. These ministers may have served anywhere in the country before 1662.

23. William Thomas, *An Apology for the Church of England* (1679), p. 31 (written in the 1650s).

24. See King, 'Episcopate during the Civil Wars', 529–34; Bosher, *Making of Restoration*, pp. 25–7; Day, 'Ordinations under Commonwealth'; Kirkpatrick, 'Commonwealth Ordinations'.

25. The cache of their correspondence in BL, MS Harleian 6942, was published with additions in Pocock, VI–XV (1848–54). Also see *Nineteen Letters of the Truly Reverend and Learned Henry Hammond*, ed. F. Peck (1739); J.W. Packer, *The Transformation of Anglicanism, 1643–1660* (Manchester, 1969); P. Hammond, 'Thomas Smith: A Beleaguered Humanist of the Interregnum', *BIHR*, 56 (1983); J.C. Hayward, 'New Directions in Studies of the Falkland Circle', *The Seventeenth century*, 2 (1987).

casuistry. In these, and in more condensed works, Hammond and his colleagues propagated a new account of salvation which they defended, with increasing popular success, against the puritan heirs of Calvin and Perkins. Hammond exercised a stern authority over his brethren: he tutted with disapproval over some of Herbert Thorndike's writings and was perturbed by Jeremy Taylor's ideas on original sin; and he quickly brought Robert Sanderson to heel when that gentle man considered participating in a public lecture alongside Presbyterian clergymen.[26]

Yet this censorious side of Hammond should not be allowed to detract from his substantial achievement in Anglican apologetics. He was the acknowledged inspiration for the group of Anglican controversialists who responded to two separate challenges. One, of course, was Presbyterianism. Although the triumphant Presbyterians of the 1640s soon found themselves politically outmanoeuvred by the Independents and by the sects, they kept up a barrage of anti-episcopal polemic throughout the 1650s. The Anglicans' other opponent was the Church of Rome. The Roman apologists, 'who ever love to fish in troubled waters', advanced the opportunistic, but apparently plausible, argument that the judgments of divine providence had at last exposed the English Reformation as a schism and the Church of England as no true church – a claim which can have only gained plausibility from Charles II's temporary desertion to Scottish Presbyterianism in 1650–1.[27] 'What canst thou say to satisfy them that urge the present fall of this church, and sufferings and contempt of its ministry, as an argument against the truth of the profession and religion?' the churchmen asked one another.[28] Their reply embraced the rule of faith, papal supremacy and Roman infallibility, the textual history of the Ignatian epistles, the history of the Church in Apostolic times, the early history of the church in Britain and the history of England's sixteenth-century Reformation. As we shall see, this wide-ranging and resolute defence of the pre-1640 Church of England led to a more confident definition of the church. But building up the intellectual case for the Church of England was only part of the work. The Hammond circle was in close contact with the exiled royalists and Anglican go-betweens like Gilbert Sheldon or George Morley, and while steering clear of

---

26. Robert Sanderson, *Works*, ed. W. Jacobson (Oxford, 1854), VI, 377–80; Pocock, VI, 300; XIV, 156–9; cf. BL, MS Harleian 3783, fo. 165; C.J. Stranks, *The Life and Writings of Jeremy Taylor* (1952), pp. 153–4.
27. Taylor, VIII, p. ccl; Hammond, I, pt. ii, 382–4 (*A Paraenesis*). On Charles and the Scots, see Bosher, *Making of Restoration*, pp. 67–73.
28. William Smyth, *The Safe Way to Glory* (1656), p. 132.

conspiracy against the Cromwellian regime, it was party to the desperate attempts initiated by Hyde to reinvigorate the supine episcopate and to consecrate urgently needed bishops in 1655–6 and 1659.[29]

If we spread our net further, it will bring in other avowed sons of the Church of England who, while as committed to the Anglican cause as the Hammond group, were of a far more moderate and conciliatory disposition. These men inhabited a self-conscious middle ground 'between opposite parties', as George Hall put it, between 'the rigid punctilio men, both of the right hand, and of the left; unto whom, to speak of any thing tending to moderation, is the same thing, as to bring several swelling mountains together to grow into one even ground'. The conformist Hall, son of the deprived Bishop Joseph Hall, and himself to become a Restoration bishop, was able to reconcile being one of 'the legally ordained ministers of the Church of England' with a readiness to 'sacrifice himself for the unity of God's church'.[30] John Gauden was another of these Anglican conciliators. Preferred to the deanery of Bocking, Essex, in 1642, through the influence of his parliamentarian patron, the Earl of Warwick, Gauden was happy to remain there throughout the Interregnum and to succeed his hero Bishop Brownrigg as preacher at the Temple in 1659. Yet he never made any secret of his allegiance to 'the reformed Church of England'.[31] Indeed Gauden was an ardent defender of the church's rights; in 1655–6 his was one of the few voices raised against Cromwell's ordinance prohibiting the employment of Anglican ministers as private tutors or chaplains. Gauden's *Petitionary Remonstrance* made the revealing admission that while the Anglican clergy did not approve of the Cromwellian regime, nor did they actively oppose or subvert it; this, too, from a man so zealously royalist that he has long been seen as a possible author of Charles I's *Eikon Basilike*. The twists and turns of Gauden's loyalties cannot disguise the genuine sense of the country's spiritual danger which impelled him into the work of clerical reconciliation in the 1650s. These fears were widely shared: by Anthony Farindon, alarmed that 'the church was filled not with members but with names'; and by that champion of moderation and sanity, Thomas

---

29. See Bosher, *Making of Restoration*, pp. 89–99; I.M. Green, *The Re-establishment of the Church of England 1660–1663* (Oxford, 1978), pp. 81–2; D.E. Underdown, *Royalist Conspiracy in England 1649–1660* (New Haven and London, 1960), pp. 181–3, 236.
30. George Hall, *God Appearing for the Tribe of Levi* (1655), sigs A2v–A3, p. 8. For Hall see *WR*, p. 67.
31. See Gauden's entry in *DNB*, and his works, *Hieraspistes* (1653) and *Ecclesiae Anglicanae suspiria* (1659).

Fuller, who was prepared to comply with the outward requirements of the present rulers, but not with the hypocrisy of the present generation: 'let us not flatter black and say it's white, nor defame white and say it's black; let us tell Judah of their sins, and Israel of their transgressions'.[32] 'Ministers must not mutter, but publicly and strongly cry against sinners', pronounced Fuller. He lamented the prevalence of parties and sects: 'the Lord grant . . . the real and royal name of Christianity may banish and disperse the fond denominations of several factions'.[33] Although his own preference was for episcopacy, Fuller could and did pursue his pastoral vocation under Presbyterian rule: the preface to the *Church History*, which asserted that the Church of England existed still, was written in his study at Sion College, the headquarters of London's Presbyterian ministers.[34]

These, however, were all old men; Hammond died in April 1660, Fuller in August 1661 and Gauden, by then Bishop of Worcester, in September 1662. The future of the church lay with her younger men, both those who had received episcopal ordination without knowing whether the Church of England would ever be restored, and those who would conform in 1660, 1662 or even later. These younger ministers defy easy classification. Many of them were 'unaligned', disclaiming the disputes of their fathers, and they clearly were 'of a freer temper and genius' than the puritan ideologues who ran the universities of the 1650s.[35] These younger divines took to heart the nation's superficial godliness and hypocrisy.[36] Their pastoral function preoccupied them. Simon Patrick, who became a distinguished Restoration churchman and devotional writer, and who eventually rose to a bishopric, is a good example of his generation. Patrick's autobiography and his early sermons against the 'Jewish hypocrisy', or pharisaism, of the 1650s reveal a man who had renounced the speculative and fratricidal clerical divinity of his day and devoted himself to nurturing his own spirituality and studying 'learned ignorance', or the willingness 'not to know those things which our supreme master is not pleased to teach us'.[37] He drew up 'rules and admonitions' for himself which show how seriously he took the reponsibilities of ministering to souls. 'Remember thy promises when made a minister,' he wrote, 'remember the preciousness of a soul; how much we should do for its good. Read St

32. Farindon, I, 8; Fuller, II, 536–7.
33. Fuller, II, 463, 485.
34. Patterson, 'Fuller', 311–14.
35. Thomas Birch, *The Life of the Most Reverend John Tillotson* (2nd edn, 1753), p. 384.
36. See South, I, 52–3, 60–1; Clement Ellis, *The Gentile Sinner* (1661); Patrick, V, 183.
37. Patrick, IX, 425–6, 430–2; VII, 538.

Chrysostom XXIX Hom. in Rom.'[38] It comes as no surprise that in 1665 with the Great Plague raging all around him, Patrick refused to leave his parishioners.

The Church of England was more than her clergy and her apologists however, she was also a community; and 'the truth is,' admitted Hammond, 'unless some care be otherwise taken to maintain the communion of the church, it is to little purpose what any write in defence of it'.[39] The most obvious means of maintaining the identity and communion of the Church of England was to keep up worship according to her Book of Common Prayer. Anglican divines read the Common Prayer privately in gentry households up and down the land; in the aristocratic fastnesses of the remote North, in the 'dark corners' of Wales and the West, in the English heartland, Warwickshire, Worcestershire, Leicestershire, the Home Counties, and even in the metropolis itself. Men like Sir Philip Warwick, Sir Robert Bindloss, Sir Robert Shirley or Sir Henry Yelverton were the 'honest gentlemen who shall join with us in the prayers of the Church of England and the good homilies instead of their bubblings and vain repetitions', and who readily took a distressed divine into their manor houses as chaplain, tutor, or even as esteemed guest.[40] While these divines were reading the Common Prayer in gentry families, more public Prayer Book services were being conducted in various London churches – John Evelyn frequented several and Sir John Bramston casually walked into St Mary Magdalen, Milk Street, to find the old liturgy in use; in Oxford the service was used by John Fell at Dr Willis's house opposite Merton College and by Maunsell at Mr White's, and no doubt elsewhere. There is evidence of the use of the church's liturgy, or something very close to it, from parishes as far apart as Anthony Huish's at Abingdon, then in Berkshire, Robert Sanderson's at Boothby Pagnell, Lincolnshire, Francis Cook's at Yoxall, Staffordshire, Edward Rainbow's at Great Easton, Essex, John Allington's at Wardley, Rutland, and Francis Edwards's at Newtown, Hampshire.[41] Athanasius Davies of Appley, Shropshire, was applauded by Leoline Jenkins for ordering his

---

38. Patrick, IX, 424: Chrysostom's homily on Romans xv. 14–24 deals with the cares of the priestly office.
39. Pocock, XV, 186.
40. BL, MS Harleian 3783, fo. 92.
41. See J. Spurr, 'Anglican Apologetic and the Restoration Church' (unpublished Oxford University D.Phil. thesis, 1985), pp. 25–6; and for Edwards, see Coleby, *Central Government and Localities*, p. 59.

services according to the Book of Common Prayer, because 'it is of most advantage and comfort to practical and sober Christians'.[42]

The authorities of the Interregnum effectively turned a blind eye to the continued use of Common Prayer while it posed no political threat. But on 24 November 1655, in the aftermath of a royalist rising, Cromwell issued an order against the employment of Anglican ministers and the use of the Prayer Book. In mid-December Bishop Duppa acknowledged that 'we are yet suffered to offer up the public prayers and sacrifice of the church, though it be under private roofs, nor do I hear of any for the present either disturbed or troubled for doing it', but he braced himself for the coming storm.[43] A few days later, and perhaps coincidentally, Anthony Sparrow, a future bishop, published *A Rationale upon the Book of Common Prayer* which described and justified the liturgy in every detail: 'as for those that love it and suffer for the love of it,' wrote Sparrow, 'this will show the reasons, why they should suffer on and love it still more and more.[44] On 30 December Evelyn went to St Gregory's to hear Dr Wilde preach 'the funeral sermon of preaching, this being the last day, after which Cromwell's proclamation was to take place, that none of the Church of England should dare either to preach, administer sacraments, teach school etc., on pain of imprisonment or exile; so this was the mournfullest day that in my life I had seen, or the Church of England herself since the Reformation: to the great rejoicing of both papist and presbyter'.[45] But the persecution never materialized. Despite the periodic scares and the occasional swoops, like that at Christmas 1657 in which Evelyn was briefly taken prisoner, the semi-public Prayer Book services of London continued to enjoy the indulgence of the Protectorate.[46]

The use of the liturgy, even for Morning and Evening Prayer, had to be carefully tailored to the adverse circumstances. After his Prayer Book services were disrupted by troops, Robert Sanderson began to employ a selective and modified form of the liturgy, which tech-

42. William Wynne, *Life of Sir Leoline Jenkins* (1724), II, 645–6.
43. *The Correspondence of Bishop Brian Duppa and Sir Justinian Isham*, ed. G. Isham (Northamptonshire Record Society, 17, 1950–1), p. 134.
44. Anthony Sparrow, *A Rationale upon the Book of Common Prayer* (1655), preface. Also see Hamon L'Estrange, *The Alliance of Divine Offices* (1659), and BL, MS Harleian 3783, fo. 225.
45. Evelyn, III, 164.
46. Evelyn, III, 203–4. MS Tanner 52, fo. 216; BL, MS Harleian 3783, fos 178, 194, 220, 225, describe the rapid relaxation of official vigilance after this crack-down. The most balanced account of the general situation is F. Higham, *Catholic and Reformed* (1962), pp. 262–72; cf. Bosher, *Making of Restoration*, pp. 41–4.

nically absolved him from any offence, and won the approbation of Bishop Duppa.[47] In *A Case of the Liturgy*, dated 12 November 1652, Sanderson advised ministers to use in their prayers 'some such general terms, and other intimations devised for the purpose, as may sufficiently convey to the understandings of the people what our intentions are therein, and yet not be sufficient to fetch us within the compass of the ordinance', and occasionally to 'discover the weakness of the puritan principles and tenets to the people'.[48] The indefatigable Jeremy Taylor published an entire and original *Collection of Offices* (1658) which in language, structure and emphasis followed the church's prayers because it was explicitly intended 'as a charitable ministry to them, who are not permitted to use those which were formerly appointed'.[49] Though proscribed, the Prayer Book could still supply the minister with 'fit matter and proper words', with material for his own compositions. As many Anglicans pointed out, the church's liturgy was woven from scripture texts, from psalms, lessons, collects and so on, which 'we in charity conceive, though they were enjoined by the Common Prayer Book, you have not forbid to be used; and therefore without receiving the brand of obstinate, we nothing doubt of free leave for us, who are orthodox divines, to use them in our churches'.[50]

Little is known about the use made of the Prayer Book in the rites of passage, in baptism, marriage and funerals. The frequent use of godparents in christenings, such as those attended by Anthony Blagrave, might indicate that the Prayer Book was being used. In September 1652 the sequestered parson of Eltham 'christened' Evelyn's son Richard with 'susceptors' or godparents.[51] Occasionally there is more conclusive evidence of baptism in 'the old way cum signo crucis' and by sequestered Anglican divines such as Richard Drake of Radwinter, who christened his son Roger 'ex ritu ecclesiae anglicanae' while Bishop Duppa stood as a godparent.[52] These rites were, of course, performed in private: Anthony Blagrave's wife was even 'churched', a distinctly Anglican rite, at home in 1652.[53] But a

47. Sanderson, *Works*, V, 38; VI, 311–12. The modified liturgy is printed in W. Jacobson (ed.), *Fragmentary Illustrations of the History of the Book of Common Prayer* (1847). Also see Bishop Hall quoted above, p. 8.
48. Sanderson, *Works*, V, 35–57, and for Thorndike's disapproval, 58–9.
49. Taylor, VII, 241.
50. Robert Nelson, *The Life of Dr George Bull* (1713), p. 39; James Harwood, *A Plea for the Common Prayer Book* (1657), sig. A6v.
51. MS Eng Misc E 118, fos 48, 65v, 82v, 87v; Evelyn, III, 75, 63. Also see C. Durston, *The Family in the English Revolution* (Oxford, 1989), pp. 118–21.
52. Higham, *Catholic and Reformed*, p. 264, note 32; MS Rawlinson D 156 (11 June 1657); also see MS Top Oxon F 31, fo. 3.
53. MS Eng Misc E 118, fo. 53, on churching see Durston, *Family*, pp. 121–2.

baptism service of sorts was also used in public. George Bull simply memorized the baptism service and was complimented by his parishioners upon the quality and fluency of his extempore prayer.[54] In April 1652 Robert Boreman baptized 'in the open congregation' at Whethamstead the two children of a local tailor who had returned 'to our church' from the 'disorder and unseemly carriage' of a conventicle – and he took the opportunity to publish a denunciation of the moral and spiritual perils of conventicles 'congregated by men who have no calling to teach, and in opposition to the unity and uniformity of our national church'.[55] When the puritan regime instituted civil marriage by a JP in 1653, 'many would not be so married, and such for the most part who were so married, were also married in their own parish churches by their ministers'. Moreover 'a steady stream' of couples preferred the service of the Common Prayer to that of the *Directory*; it was even rumoured that when Dr Hewitt of St Gregory's conducted the religious service which followed the civil marriage of Mary Cromwell and Lord Fauconberg, he used the Prayer Book.[56] Finally, their race run, some Christians were committed to the grave while a clergymen intoned the comforting prayers of the Church of England.[57] The use of the Prayer Book was recorded on all of these occasions, but we can only guess how many more there were of which no trace remained once the baby was returned to its crib, the happy pair had gone to their wedding feast, or the mourners to their funeral meats.

The sacrament of the Lord's Supper was available for the devout and well-to-do Anglican. It appears that Anthony Blagrave took communion about three times a year, at Christmas, Easter and Whitsun. Anxious to be 'a worthy receiver', Blagrave usually heard a preparation sermon, for which he paid the parson ten shillings, before the sacrament. On Friday, 9 April 1652, 'Mr Sexby preached his preparation sermon out of the 10th to the Hebrews, the verses 21 and 22. My three sisters and my wife and I heard him.' It is possible these sermons were private affairs; preparation sermons were, in Evelyn's words, 'a very rare thing in these days', although one was

54. Nelson, *Life of Bull*, pp. 39–40.
55. Boreman, *Paideia-Thriambos* (1653), pp. 21, 28. For the author see *DNB* and *WR*.
56. B. Reay, 'Popular Religion', in *Popular Culture in Seventeenth-century England*, ed. B. Reay (1985), p. 119: Durston, *Family*, pp. 82, 72, 68; Higham, *Catholic and Reformed*, pp. 270, 283–4. Also see Fletcher, *County Community*, p. 116; *Duppa–Isham Correspondence*, p. 67; W.E. Tate, *The Parish Chest* (Cambridge, 1946), pp. 35, 46–8, 63.
57. See Evelyn, III, 76; Morrill, 'Church in England', p. 108; BL, MS Harleian 3783, fos 90, 92; several divines were buried thus, see *WR*, pp. 41, 46, 99, 115, 147, 150, 186; MS Rawlinson D 158.

delivered at his own parish church in April 1654. At Lichfield 'some more precise than wise' took offence at William Langley's preparation sermon and what had been intended as a bond of communion 'was made use of to a final separation'.[58] On average, John Evelyn received the sacrament according to the church's rite at the three great festivals and on four further occasions a year; in 1649 he had to resort to a private communion at home; but in 1659 he mentioned the 'monthly communions' held by Dr Gunning at Exeter House chapel in London.[59] It seems likely that the Prayer Book pattern of celebrating the Lord's Supper at Easter, Whitsun and Christmas was widely maintained in preference to the prescribed parliamentary pattern of monthly celebrations.[60] The pattern of celebration tells us little, however, about the parishes where the celebrations had ceased, or about the numbers receiving.

Contemporaries had the impression that the sacrament in any form, Anglican or Presbyterian, was falling into disuse in many parishes, yet the situation was complicated by the pressure to restrict the sacrament to those who were morally and spiritually 'worthy': Evelyn noted how few communicants appeared at the Easter sacrament at Deptford in 1654.[61] The Church of England traditionally admitted to the sacrament all who came unless they were notoriously and unrepentantly immoral. The puritan clergy, supported by the *Directory* and parliamentary ordinance, sought to impose more stringent tests of worthiness upon communicants and to establish 'closed' communions. The results were mixed: in Ralph Josselin's Essex parish there were only eleven celebrations of the sacrament between 1651 and 1659, and some of these were 'private'.[62] In many more parishes the bitterness engendered by such attempts at discipline, and occasionally the faint hearts of the clergy whose tithes were at stake, led to the complete suspension of the sacrament.[63] And, in the eyes of the clergy, the cost of this negligence was great; for, 'if there be any charms to be had, that may raise up our dry bones of this confused and distracted and demolished church and

---

58. MS Eng Misc E 118, fos 16v–17v, 19, 61v, 95v; Evelyn, III, 94; William Langley, *The Persecuted Minister* (1656), p. 49.
59. Higham, *Catholic and Reformed*, p. 265; Evelyn, II, 255; III, 233.
60. Morrill, 'Church in England', pp. 105–6; Coleby, *Central Government and Localities*, p. 59; D. Hirst, 'England's Third Reformation' (forthcoming in *Past and Present*).
61. Evelyn, III, 95.
62. See Josselin, *passim*; *The Autobiography of Henry Newcome*, ed. R. Parkinson (Chetham Society, 26–7, 1852), pp. 16, 20, 28; Heywood, pp. 65, 100; *RB*, I, 91–3. For a moderate Anglican view see Fuller, II, 301–27 (*The Triple Reconciler* (1654)).
63. Morrill, 'Church in England', p. 107; Spufford, *Contrasting Communities*, p. 275.

nation, they must be had, not from councils or armies, but from the devout performances of the congregations of God's people'.[64]

It is plain, then, that a religious community existed which can legitimately be labelled the 'Church of England'; but it is not clear how large that community was. The use of the Book of Common Prayer in some parishes for worship, the rites of passage, and even the sacrament, should not be taken to imply that the liturgy itself was in some sense 'popular'. Rather, it is a testimony to lay influence on worship and to the autonomy enjoyed, especially in the 1650s, by the parish. We do not know enough about either the way the laity participated in Prayer Book worship, or the motives behind opposition to the abolition of 'traditional' Prayer Book worship, to judge popular allegiance. The rebellious English could still be amenable to the example of their betters. At Kidderminster, Richard Baxter was hindered by Sir Ralph Clare, whose civility and moderation persuaded 'a great part of the parish' to follow his practice of 'coming but once a day to church on the Lord's days, and his abstaining from the sacrament etc., as if we kept not sufficiently to the old way, and because we used not the Common Prayer Book'.[65] The evidence of hostility towards puritan interference in local religious life, perhaps most glaring in the case of the ban on keeping Christmas, was less proof of a preference for the Prayer Book than an indication of ingrained conservatism and, perhaps, some vague association of the Church of England with better, merrier, times of church ales and of dancing and football on the green after the sermon. The same nostalgia underlay the frequent appeals for a return to the church of Elizabeth and James I. Reluctance, and occasionally refusal, to pay tithes to intruded ministers could have had several causes. No doubt some parishioners genuinely preferred their previous incumbent and his way of organizing their worship, while among others, respect for property rights, fear of litigation and suspicion of new clergymen with their divisive practices and rapacious demands all weighed against innovation.[66] The laity were now accustomed to exercise their muscle in religious affairs: but it was not always the same laymen, nor always to the same effect; for instance, in the early and mid-1640s the waves of parish petitions had all been against 'scandalous' and 'malignant' clergymen, while by the later 1640s there were petitions, and even risings, in favour of

64. Thomas Warmstry, *A Box of Spikenard* (3rd edn, 1660), sig. b3.
65. *RB*, I, 94.
66. D.E. Underdown, *Revel, Riot and Rebellion* (Oxford, 1985), pp. 245–6; R. Ashton, 'The Problem of Identity', in *Politics and People*, ed. Jones *et al.*, p. 135; Coleby, *Central Government and Localities*, p. 13.

the return of the Prayer Book. Assessed in this way, positive lay allegiance to the church's liturgy was a minority persuasion. The Church of England had become one denomination among many.

Interregnum Anglicanism is not to be defined in a sentence. It obviously owed much to the continuing use of the Book of Common Prayer, but it went beyond liturgical practices to encompass a pastoral approach, a spirit of personal piety, and distinctive preaching. Anglican clergymen would not forgo their preaching duty: 'I shall take no human prohibitions to be my discharge, though kings, or Parliament, or both join together therein', asserted Thomas Warmstry.[67] Laymen, like Anthony Blagrave and John Evelyn valued the continuing availability of specifically Anglican preaching. Not only were Anglican preachers to be heard, but the great Anglican sermons of the past were available in print: at Westwood, Worcestershire, George Ashwell preached 'much better than this auditory hath for a long time heard' because he read the sermons of Robert Sanderson.[68] Anglican spirituality during the Interregnum was suffused with a sombre, penitential mood, which can be attributed to one event above all others.

'The black act is done, which all the world wonders at, and which an age cannot expiate. The waters of the ocean we swim in cannot wash out the spots of that blood, than which never any was shed with greater guilt, since the son of God poured out his.' Thus William Sancroft reported the execution of Charles.[69] Men of all persuasions shed a tear for Charles I, and for themselves. 'Dies ille versus est in tenebras', exclaimed the Laudian. 'Lord lay it not as a sin to this nation', begged the puritan.[70] To many this was not simply the nadir of a cause, but the beginning of the end: God had indicated that his contest with the nation was drawing to a close; he had removed the English Josiah, and the ruin of Judah herself could only be a matter of time. For all the denunciations of this 'parricide so heinous, so horrible that it cannot be paralleled by all the murders that ever were committed since the world began, but only in the murder of Christ', and of the crime's monstrous perpetrators, the act of regicide seemed too traumatic for mere indignation or outrage; this was tragedy and beyond all words.[71] Despite their claims, many Englishmen did find a voice, a voice of lamentation and prayer: for 'now we have nothing left, but to importune God to whom

67. Thomas Warmstry, *Suspiria*, p. 185.
68. See *WR*, p. 34.
69. MS Tanner 57, fo. 525.
70. MS Rawlinson D 156; Josselin, p. 155.
71. Henry Leslie, *The Martyrdome of King Charles* (The Hague and London, 1649), p. 12.

vengeance belongs, that he would show himself forth, and speedily account with these prodigious monsters, or else hasten his coming to judgement, and so put an end to these enormous crimes, which no words yet in use can reach'.[72]

Henceforth, the lamentation for national transgressions, the wailing of Hadadrimmon in the valley, took on an even more poignant note than they had had in the 1640s. The anniversary of the regicide and the expiation of the nation's guilt now became central motifs in the prayers of intercession used by the 'mourners in Sion'.[73] The devout Anglican of the Interregnum believed in the power of prayer just as much as his puritan neighbour; indeed, the Anglican had to place more trust in the efficacy of 'prayers and tears' because these were now the only weapon left to him.[74] In allusion to the regicide, Thomas Fuller preached on Ecclesiastes vii. 15, *there is a just man that perisheth in his righteousness*, and this theme of theodicy was widely taken up. Only atheists gained from seeing the wicked prosper, and only the sectaries and papists from seeing the wrath of the Lord so hot against the sheep of his own pasture, the Church of England. Those who despaired or fell 'a-drooping' under afflictions were assured by the clergy that these tribulations were evidence of divine concern for the people's spiritual well-being. 'Notwithstanding all these distempers and disasters, God is not *un-Lorded*: he is not degraded from his dignity, but remaineth still in full possession, and power, what he was before.'[75] The Lord was the only sanctuary, he must eventually arise and vindicate his providence, but 'how long shall bloody designs and rebellious imaginations prosper? Shall not the judge of the whole earth do right?'[76]

Alongside the penitent appeal to God to rise up and scatter his enemies can be heard the still, small voice of resigned submission. The patient exercise of one's 'winter graces' in retirement from the world and its vanities held a certain attraction: the elderly Bishop Duppa could claim that 'I make it my business to forget the world'

72. MS Tanner 57, fo. 525.
73. For Hadadrimmon see Zechariah xii. 11–12; and on the nation's guilt see [Brian Duppa], *Private Forms of Prayer, Fit for these Sad Times* (Oxford, 1645); John Hewitt (also Huit), *Prayers of Intercession for their Use who Mourn in Secret, for the Public Calamities of this Nation* (1659); *Private Forms of Prayer, Fitted for the late Sad-Times* (1660), Wing H597; the textual relationship between these works is explained in Spurr, 'Anglican Apologetic', pp. 28–9.
74. See Joseph Hall, *Works*, VII, 416; Richard Gardiner, *XVI Sermons* (1659), pp. 157–76; Farindon, I, 146; cf. South, I, 66–7.
75. Fuller, I, 513–33; II, 437, 275. Also see Theophilus Wodenote, *Eremicus theologus* (1654), pp. 132, 173, 110.
76. *Prayers of Intercession*, pp. 11–12.

and to take refuge in the snug chimney corner and in the practice of his devotions; yet he was far from apathetic towards the Anglican cause. Duppa hugged to himself the gloomy thought that as the persecution intensified, the pious churchmen would be reduced to serving God as the ancient Christians did in dens and caves and deserts.[77] This was the sort of language that many Anglicans revelled in; they were 'sufferers' or 'martyrs'; metaphors of taking to upper rooms or to the catacombs, to the dens and caves of the early Christians, came easily to their lips and to their pens: but this rhetoric should not be dismissed too lightly.

Many clerical authors set a premium on the preservation of an impregnable, personal peace still attainable amidst the troubles of the Interregnum.

> We wish well to the great ship of our whole nation and will never desert it so, but that our best prayers and desires shall go with it. But however providence shall dispose thereof, we will stick to the petty pinnace of peace in our own consciences. Sure I am, no soldiers shall be able to cut the cables, I mean no forcible impression from without, shall disturb or discompose the peace which is within us.

While the ship of the church was battened down to ride out the storm of persecution, religion had to take a private refuge in the family home, the chamber, or even the conscience.[78] Personal piety was portrayed by the Anglican clergy as a valid and positive response to the tribulations of their church and nation. To have been a mourner in Sion for the foundations of religion was a consolation. The effectual mourners, the truly repentant, might only be a small fraternity, but how much better to be 'one of those ten righteous, for whose righteousness a whole Sodom might be saved; then an Achan, for whose sins an army might be routed; or a Jonah, for whose fault, a whole ship full of men was like to be broken'.[79] 'Though we cannot but confess that we are *a sinful nation, a people laden with iniquity, a seed of evil doers,*' admitted Bishop Hall, 'yet, Lord, thou knowest that thou hast thy secret ones amongst us'. The calamities visited on the nation were the providential reward for national apostasy and sinfulness; the remedy was to return to the paths of the righteousness, but such reform could only begin with the individual.[80] Hear-

---

77. *Duppa–Isham Correspondence*, pp. 139, 99, 113.
78. Fuller, II, 119, 265, 270, 272–3. Also see G.H. Jenkins, *The Foundations of Modern Wales – Wales 1642–1780* (Oxford, 1987), pp. 55–6.
79. Fuller, II, 270, 471; also see Edward Hyde, *Christ and his Church*, sigs A2–A3.
80. Hall, *Works*, VII, 422; also see Hammond, I, pt. ii, 374–81, 412–20.

ing Interregnum Anglicans speak in such tones, it becomes harder than ever to distinguish them from their pious, sober, concerned neighbours of other religious affiliations.

The Anglican concern to be among the 'people that desireth to walk close with thee their God' merged almost imperceptibly into a more widely shared anxiety about the iniquity of the times and the lack of true godliness.[81] For many, puritan as well as Anglican, the 1650s was a disheartening decade, an iron age, if not the last age, since all the judgments meted out by God and all the promises of reformation had so conspicuously failed to transform the nation into the Lord's people. At St Gregory's in London, Nathaniel Hardy sought to bring the people to repentance by keeping before their eyes 'a sad prognostic of approaching judgment; or the happy misery of good men in bad times'.[82] Henry Hammond provided a preface for *The Whole Duty of Man* (1658), a popular guide to repentance and holy living, in which he prayed that the anonymous author 'may not miss to be rewarded openly, in the visible power and benefit of this work on the hearts of the whole nation, which was never in more need of such supplies as are here afforded'.

The entire clerical profession had its back to the wall in the 1650s. Puritan divines like Ralph Josselin were just as apprehensive of a radical 'storm on the ministry' and as anxious about the mushrooming sects as were Anglican clergymen. Robert Sanderson believed that earlier attacks on the liturgy and discipline of the Church of England had unintentionally opened Pandora's box and released 'swarms of sectaries of all sorts'. Each sect was convinced that they alone were the godly and would pay heed only to their own delusion of an 'inner light'.[83] The false prophets had brought spiritual destitition to the English. There was 'scarce so much as the form of religion left in the land.'[84] And in Wales, the churches

> are become like the prophet's lodge in a garden of cucumbers, deserted, ruined; no cottage on a hill more desolate, more defaced, the people having no encouragement to resort to that place where they have neither minister to pray with, or for them, or to sing praises to God with them, nor any at all in many places, no, not so much as a gifted man (as they use to gloss it) to instruct them.[85]

81. Hall, *Works*, VII, 422.
82. Nathaniel Hardy, *A Sad Prognostick* (1658); also see Richard Gardiner, *XVI Sermons*; *RB*, I, 90; Edward Reynolds, *Sion's Praises* (1657), p. 27.
83. Sanderson, *Works*, II, pp. xi, xxiii, lv.
84. Farindon, *Sermons*, I, 257, 22–4, 289.
85. William Nicholson, *An Exposition of the Catechism of the Church of England* (1655; reissued 1661; LACT, Oxford, 1845, edn cited), p. xii. Also see DWL, Baxter Letters II, fos 128–9; Jenkins, *Foundations of Modern Wales*, ch. 2.

Anglican apologists wrote of 'whole parishes fallen off to popery, since the ministers have been cast out; and yet many men ask, what need of a clergy?'[86] Tossed to and fro by every new doctrine, led astray from or deprived of the orthodox Word and sacraments, and repeatedly disappointed by the clay feet of their new idols, many Englishmen were believed to have succumbed to doubt and despair: 'as for the apostasy of some, it is so great and general, that they seem wholly to degenerate from the profession of Christ Jesus or to atheism and utter unbelief of the truth'.[87] In 1658 Jeremy Taylor was dismayed by 'the progression of blasphemy and atheism, which are publicly professed by societies' in London and Oxford.[88]

This apostasy was, in part, a consequence of the clergy's own failings. 'The greatest abatements of religion arise,' wrote Gauden, 'from the sad divisions, which have been so pregnant among ministers, which makes many first indifferent, then loose, then profane, and at last atheistical, both in their opinion and practices'.[89] Many clergymen, especially among the younger unaligned divines, felt that the clergy had betrayed their trust: 'while they dispute of God, they do not know him; and while they wrangle about justification they remain unsanctified; and while they contend about the extent of Christ's redemption, they take care that they themselves shall have no great benefit by it.' In June 1659 Simon Patrick preached the funeral sermon for his friend, the minister Samuel Jacomb, 'whose life was a continual sermon': 'we had better begin any trade ignorantly, and venture before our time at great things in any calling, than in this divine profession undertake to teach souls, and practice godliness upon our hearers' hearts, when we have not the first rudiments of piety in our own.'[90]

This 'divine profession' was widely despised; the whole world was conspiring against 'that despised, abject, oppressed sort of men, the ministers': 'you may now spare that distinction of *scandalous ministers*, when it is even made scandalous to be a minister.' The clerical profession was badly shaken by the 'mechanicks' and 'cobblers' who were invading its office and functions – 'your ignorant, mechanick, and hedge-creeping teachers', as Gauden called them – or the blind guides 'who leap from loom to pulpit' in Fuller's disdainful phrase: 'He is a sorry fellow nowadays that cannot reproach, molest and

86. Hammond, 'Thomas Smith', 184.
87. Richard Samwaies, *England's Faithfull Reprover*, p. 195.
88. MS Tanner 52, fo. 199.
89. From a letter describing his negotiations with ministers in Essex and London in 1656; *Thurloe State Papers*, ed. T. Birch (1742), V, 599.
90. Patrick, V, 183; VII, 538.

undo a minister', claimed Richard Parr.[91] The conventionally trained clergy deeply resented the sacrilege of the preaching cobblers who, without any preparation, but claiming divine inspiration, took it upon themselves to expound the Word of God. The true minister 'was not to be inspired or blown into the ministry' like this, but painfully to attain the right to preach, pray and administer the sacraments by nurturing his gifts, educating his intellect, submitting to trial of his ministry by the proper authorities, and finally being set apart for the Lord's work by solemn ordination.[92]

Here, then, in the shape of clerical discipline and harmony was another cause around which ministers of different denominations might unite. Let the clergy appear to the world not as 'single and apart, but as a grave and venerable society', pleaded Gauden.[93] 'Why should some in the height of their zeal for the liturgy, suppose there can be no service of God, but where that is entirely used?' George Hall asked the *Sons of the Clergy* in 1655;

> Why should others again, think their piety concerned and tres-
> passed if I do proffer, and in some considerations, think fit to use a
> set form? There must be abatements and allowances of each
> other . . .[94]

Gingerly, the clergy, including a few Anglican clergymen, began to sink some of their differences with their brethren. Many of these conciliatory clerics came together in the county-based clerical associations initiated by Richard Baxter to promote a common policy and mutual aid in controlling admission to the Lord's Supper. Baxter described the clergy in his own county association as 'honest, godly, serious, humble ministers . . . not one of them (that associated) Presbyterian or Independent, and not past four or five of them episcopal; but disengaged, faithful men'. Unaligned as they may have been at the time, seventeen of these ministers conformed to the Church of England at the Restoration, and three of them were counted as Interregnum 'sufferers' for the church.[95] George Ashwell, a protégé of Henry Hammond, averred in a letter to Baxter that, although ignorant of the precise form of the association, he admired

91. South, I, 65, cf. 70–1, 82–92; John Gauden, *A Petitionary Remonstrance* (1659), sig. A3v; Fuller, I, 462; Parr, *The Judges Charge* (1658), p. 29. Also see Edward Reynolds, *Joy in the Lord* (1655), p. 31; Thomas Bradley, *Comfort from the Cradle* (Oxford, 1650), sig. A2v; Hammond, I, 375; Taylor, XIV, 415–88.
92. See South, I, 340; Hall, *God Appearing*, pp. 5, 10; Langley, *Persecuted Minister*.
93. Gauden, *Petitionary Remonstrance*, sig. A2v.
94. Hall, *God Appearing*, p. 25. The *Sons of the Clergy* was a charitable association, see E.H. Pearce, *The Sons of the Clergy* (2nd edn, 1928).
95. *RB*, I, 94; G.F. Nuttall, 'The Worcestershire Association', *JEH*, 1 (1950).

'the design in general . . . to recollect the scattered limbs of a broken church, and fortify the ministry against its common enemies . . . closing up the breaches which schism had made'.[96]

The decade wore on, and still no end could be seen to English apostasy, sectarianism and vice; the bewildered Josselin noted in his diary for April 1656, 'Quakers increase, but profaneness doth not decrease'.[97] But the Parliament called for the autumn of 1656 held out the prospect of clerical reconciliation and concerted action against religious extremism. An eirenic scheme for 'primitive' or 'reduced' episcopacy, which had first been proposed in 1641 by Archbishop Ussher in the hope of staving off the parliamentary attack on Laudian 'prelacy', now appeared in print. Although one royalist thought it 'dispersed by the Presbyterians among their friends', and Richard Baxter took an interest, it was actually promoted by Nicholas Bernard, Ussher's chaplain, and John Gauden. For several years Gauden had been recommending this dilute form of episcopal government in which the bishop was *primus inter pares*, 'ruling with joint counsel, not levelled with younger preachers and novices, not too much exalted above the graver and elder presbyters; neither despised of the one nor despising of the other'.[98] Now, presumably in the hope of erecting some sort of national church organization, Gauden began to sound out clerical sympathy for primitive episcopacy and was heartened at the response in Essex and London, where 'not only Presbyterians and Independents . . . but even episcopal men are upon a very calm temper'.[99] In January 1657 Edward Reynolds urged Parliament to heal 'the breaches amongst brethren, that men agreeing in faith, worship and obedience, may be no longer strange to one another, but join hand in hand against the dangers which are threatened from a common adversary'. The common adversary was an amalgam of irreligion, heresy and blasphemy; and MPs were beseeched to take up the power that was theirs by right to suppress 'paganism' and 'Turkism', or even worse, Socinianism, Pelagianism and Arminianism.[100] Not that this Parliament needed much encouragement to act against heretics, as it had shown by its treatment of James Naylor the Quaker. When a new, parliamentary, constitution was drawn up in 1657, it provided for a confession of faith which might serve as a standard of orthodoxy for some loose

96. DWL, MS Baxter Letters III, fo. 68 (1657). For other Anglican interest see *RB*, appendix 1; Bosher, *Making of Restoration*, p. 46.
97. Josselin, p. 366.
98. Gauden, *Hieraspistes*, pp. 273–4.
99. *Thurloe State Papers*, V, 598.
100. Edward Reynolds, *The Peace of Jerusalem* (1657), p. 33; Matthew Barker, *The Faithful and Wise Servant* (1657), pp. 26–8.

form of national church and as a measure of what was tolerable. As Reynolds reminded MPs, the peace of the English Jerusalem depended on obliging people 'to attend upon the ministry and dispensation of the gospel' in some Christian assembly, and in June the Sabbath Observance Act required attendance at a church, chapel or Christian meeting which worshipped agreeably to the new profession of faith. It was only Cromwell's reluctance which thwarted the Houses' attempt to add a compulsory Presbyterian catechism.[101] Driven on by fear of the sects and, above all, of the Quakers, the trend towards a more conservative and authoritarian religious regime continued under Richard Cromwell.[102]

As the Protectorate collapsed into 'anarchy and confusion', and the nation's danger became ever more apparent, so did the nation's need to forge its own salvation by returning to the paths of righteousness.[103] One Cheshire Presbyterian greeted the return of the Rump Parliament in May 1659 as a divine scourge deserved by a thankless, sinful, godless people.[104] 'Our sins threaten our ruin' was Josselin's observation on the 'sad confusions in England'. He pressed his parishioners to family worship and to attend catechizing, and he wrestled with God in days of prayer.[105] In October 1659 Humphrey Henchman admonished the gentry and clergy to combine 'to recover this sinful nation and oppressed church, from the miseries, spiritual and civil, under which we now groan'.[106] All was in confusion, but John Evelyn and 'the Church of England Protestants in town' kept a private fast, under the direction of Peter Gunning, 'to beg of God the removal of his judgments, with devout prayers for his mercy to our calamitous church'.[107] 'I know', wrote Gauden, 'that religious unity and national harmony, as a church, may seem useless, if not dangerous in point of policy, until there be a greater firmness and stability in civil affairs', but someone had to speak up for the Church of England.[108] None of these men were among the political actors who achieved the Restoration, but they did articulate the hope and despair, piety and hysteria, which propelled the political process. By the turn of the year, 'the misery of a deserted people' when 'the Lord forsaketh a people, and withdraws his presence from a whole church

---

101. Worden, 'Toleration and Protectorate', 226.
102. R. Hutton, *The Restoration* (Oxford, 1985), pp. 25–6, 33.
103. Evelyn, III, 228.
104. Newcome, *Autobiography*, p. 104.
105. Josselin, pp. 452, 457–8, 460.
106. Preface to [Richard Allestree], *The Gentleman's Calling* (1659), a sequel to [Richard Allestree], *The Whole Duty of Man* (1658).
107. Evelyn, III, 234.
108. Gauden, *Ecclesiae Anglicanae suspiria* (1659), p. 12.

or country', was plain to see; and so 'out of love to themselves not him', the English began to look to Charles Stuart.[109] All the divergent religious expectations and aspirations were submerged in the rush towards the old regime: the 'differences of honest Protestants' were confidently judged 'but small compared to the bonds of union in which they do agree as to doctrinals, morals, and essentials', and were relegated to a future synod and parliament.[110] Josselin confided in his diary for 6 May 1660:

> The nation runneth into the King as Israel to bring back David, Lord make him the like blessing to our England, and let God's counsel be in the work. The word and will of God is good, let it take place; my heart under this change very calm, fears on me for the ark of God, but that is under his love and care.[111]

109. Edward Reynolds, *The Misery of Deserted People* (1659), p. 16; Josselin, p. 458.
110. Gauden, *Slight Healings of Publique Hurts* (1660), p. 106.
111. Josselin, p. 463.

Chapter 2

The Church of England, 1660–89

The Miracle of Resurrection, 1660–62

Most Englishmen were less reserved than Ralph Josselin in their response to the return of Charles Stuart. Joyously, they proclaimed that the nation's prayers should now be converted into praises, her elegies into hosannas, and her lamentations into hallelujahs. The sermons exulting in the return of England's David – not all of them preached by men of 'loyal' principles and clear Church of England preferences – are full of a sense of the world coming right at last, of the vindication of divine providence. 'A Munsterian anarchy' had been averted by the return of a lawful monarchy; the tyranny was 'over-past' and a new dawn had arrived for a nation purged by affliction: 'it was the Lord's doing, *et mirabile in oculis nostris*'.[1] Whatever one's fears or hopes, the restoration of the Stuarts to their throne was too clearly the work of the Lord to be disputed. 'God has been pleased by a miracle of mercy to dissipate this confusion and chaos, to give us some new openings, some dawnings of liberty and settlement.'[2] What mattered now was what the English made of this opportunity.

A show of godliness was carefully maintained in public affairs. When Charles first stepped ashore at Dover, he was presented by the mayor of the town with 'a very rich Bible, which he took and said it was the thing he loved above all things in the world'.[3] It was soon rumoured that 'the king will prohibit all profaneness, swearing, plays etc, and that we shall be all godly and of good life, which for our own sakes, as well as the King's service, is heartily to be

1. *The Autobiography of Henry Newcome* (Chetham Society, 26–7, 1852), p. 119; Evelyn, III, 246.
2. South, I, 93.
3. Pepys, I, 158.

wished, that men of both judgements, may be both good men and good subjects.' Although such royal actions were generally interpreted as concessions to the Presbyterians, those of an episcopalian 'judgement' also hoped that the Restoration marked a new beginning in morality.[4] 'Thou that takest away the sins of the world take away for ever, from this sinful land and nation, the foul sin of rebellion, together with its monstrous offspring, the crying sins of sacrilege, of perjury and hypocrisy' pleaded an Anglican prayer of thanks for Charles's safe arrival.[5] On his deathbed, Henry Hammond prayed God to grant that 'the repentance may be national also, and that evidenced by the proper fruits of it, by zeal of restoring the rights both of thee and thine anointed.'[6] The gentry of England were exhorted to revise their notion of gentility, with all its false gallantry and gentlemanly debauchery, and to learn instead from *The Gentleman's Calling* and *The Whole Duty of Man.*[7] In May Charles issued a proclamation against 'vicious, debauched, and profane persons', pressing his subjects 'to circumspection, integrity and reformation in our lives', which Josselin greeted as 'a cut to the gentry of England, oh Lord make him a nursing father to thy people'.[8]

The King saw his role as healing and settling past animosities. As he had announced in his declaration from Breda, Charles intended to bind the bleeding wounds of his English kingdom, to abolish 'all notes of discord, separation, and difference of parties', by pardoning past crimes, extending liberty in religion to those of a tender conscience, and referring all disputed property titles to Parliament. Throughout 1660 Charles pursued policies of reconciliation, taking counsel from all quarters, offering an indemnity, and disbanding the army; and the same course was taken in the matter of religion, where Charles was uncomprehending of theological zealotry and temperamentally reluctant to adopt extremes. There was no doubt that the Church of England would return – her unswerving loyalty and the mythology surrounding Charles the Martyr made sure of that. Indeed, Charles II had told the delegation of Presbyterian ministers at Breda that 'whilst he gave them liberty, he would not have his own taken from him' and intended to have 'the good old order of the church in which he had been bred' in his own chapel. But what form would the Church of England take? And what

---

4. MS Clarendon 77, fo. 288. Paul Seaward has pointed out to me that some royalists saw this as proof that the King's mind had been poisoned against them as dissolute; see Roger L'Estrange, *A Caveat to the Cavaliers* (1661), p. 21.
5. *Private Forms of Prayer* (1660), p. 356.
6. Hammond, I, pt. ii, 638; cf. p. Hammond, 'Thomas Smith', *BIHR*, 56 (1983), 185.
7. Clement Ellis, *The Gentile Sinner* (1660).
8. Proclamation of 30 May 1660; Josselin, p. 464.

role would the church assume in the religious life of the nation?

Although some religious sects, including the Quakers and Baptists, were beyond the pale due to their perceived radicalism and republicanism, there were still many other religious parties clamouring for liberty or for accommodation. Royal agents reported that the Roman Catholics would soon attest their loyalty and their past services to the Stuart cause, while the Presbyterians came over 'with the spirit of moderation, and are no killing enemies to the church's essence in episcopacy and liturgy, though they'll divest her of her ornaments'.[9] It looked as though a viable religious settlement would have to cater for both those, such as the Presbyterians, who sought a broader national church and those, like the Independents and Roman Catholics, who hoped for the freedom to worship in their own congregations outside the parochial church structure. A broader national church would not suit the hard core of obdurate Anglican clergy, those in the Hammond mould, the former exiles, and the surviving 700 sequestered ministers; but then these were far from being the only voice of the Church of England. The conciliatory Gauden and his allies could plausibly claim to speak for a larger number of Anglican clergymen. Moreover Gauden continued to build bridges with moderate Presbyterian leaders; on 25 April, for instance, he met Baxter and Thomas Manton at Nicholas Bernard's house. And some of the leading English Presbyterians were, as they told the King, 'no enemies to moderate episcopacy'.[10] Negotiations between episcopalians and these moderate Presbyterians seem to have begun in early March 1660.[11] Towards the end of that month, Dr George Morley, Hyde's agent, arrived to steer them towards acceptance of the Church of England, and on 30 March Barwick, another of Hyde's men, reported much support in London for episcopacy and the Prayer Book.[12] Slowly the talks progressed until, by May, Morley had 'prevailed with Reynolds and Calamy, to comply as to episcopacy and the liturgy with little alteration, but as yet they cannot undertake for their brethren'.[13] Persuading their brethren and defining the 'little alteration' was to be the work of the summer. In late June, encouraged by the King, the Presbyterian clergy meet-

9. MS Clarendon 72, fo. 288.
10. *RB*, II, 268; for the disgust of their sterner Scots and Irish brethren, see I.M. Green, *The Re-establishment of the Church of England 1660–1663* (Oxford, 1978), pp. 13–16.
11. G.R. Abernathy, 'The English Presbyterians and the Stuart Restoration', *Transactions of the American Philosophical Society*, 55, pt. 2 (1965), 44.
12. Abernathy, 'Presbyterians', 44–6; MS Clarendon 71, fo. 109. For Morley's intentions see R.S. Bosher, *The Making of the Restoration Settlement, 1649–62* (1951), pp. 106–8.
13. MS Clarendon 72, fos 284, 199–200, 288; Abernathy, 'Presbyterians', 57.

ing at Sion College began to hammer out a set of proposals which, on 10 July, they offered as a basis of negotiation with 'the episcopal divines'. As these Presbyterians saw it 'the matters in difference' were three: church government, the liturgy, and the ceremonies. In church government they accepted Ussher's model of reduced episcopacy 'without a word of alteration'; they were convinced of the need for a liturgy, but only asked that since the Prayer Book 'hath in it many things that are justly offensive and need amendment', it should be revised by 'some learned, moderate, and godly divines of both persuasions'; finally, they begged that 'indifferent' ceremonies such as kneeling at the sacrament, bowing at the name of Jesus, making the sign of the cross in baptism, and the use of the surplice, should be left to the conscience of each minister. When it finally came, the reply of 'the bishops' was, in Baxter's words, nothing but 'a paper of bitter oppositions by way of confutation of our former proposals'–it certainly refused any concession, though tempering this intransigence with pleas for unity.[14] This reply flew in the face of royal policy, parliamentary opinion and much Anglican enthusiasm for reduced episcopacy. It is not clear who composed it, but it does show that the church party, just like the Presbyterians, included hardliners who would press for the restoration of the old regime at every occasion.

Royal and parliamentary policy, however, still seemed directed towards a broad-based church and a moderate religious settlement. The Convention Parliament which had assembled on 25 April included one group, led by William Prynne, that hankered after the sort of presbyterian church envisaged by Parliament in the 1640s, and a larger, but more amorphous, party of episcopalians. Almost as soon as the Convention met, religious differences came to the fore: on 27 April the overwhelming support for John Gauden as a fast day preacher, and a substantial vote against Manton and Baxter, 'did a little displease the Presbyterians'.[15] Moderate divines from both camps, like Gauden and Edward Reynolds, constantly preached up the virtues of Ussher-style reduced episcopacy. 'I confess, that I own, and ever shall do, primitive episcopacy with presbytery', preached Gauden in a sermon before Monck and the Mayor and Corporation in February 1660. Churches should be governed

> not by the dominion and pomp, luxury and tyranny of bishops,
> nor yet by the factious and refractory humours of presbyters;

14. *RB*, II, 242. Baxter is our only source for these papers; cf. Bosher, *Making of Restoration*, pp. 152–4, 166–7.
15. MS Clarendon 72, fo. 44; R. Hutton, *The Restoration* (Oxford, 1985), pp. 144–6; cf. Josselin, p. 463.

much less by the schismatic sauciness of people, who cast off both
bishop and presbyters; but by the fatherly gravity, prudence and
eminence of godly and reverend bishops; by the brotherly assistance, and son like subordination of sober and orderly presbyters,
by the service and obsequiousness of humble and diligent deacons;
and by the meek submission of Christian people to the care,
monition, counsel, and respective superiority of every order; as
sheep to their chief shepherd, and their assistants . . .[16]

The effect of this proselytizing can be seen in the interest several
MPs expressed in reduced episcopacy in the debates of July and
August 1660. On the other hand, propaganda in favour of the pre-
1640 church was also beginning to pour from the presses and to find
its mark.[17] One MP was outraged at the suggestion that 'ordination
by presbyters without a bishop is not only tolerated for the time
past, but goeth without observation of the temper of those times, and
is not restrained for the future, nor so much as discountenanced, but
left equally estimable to the ancient episcopal ordination.'[18] The
Convention was not even sure whether it was the proper forum
for decisions about church government. Should not a synod or an
assembly of divines decide on these questions of doctrine and discipline? After long and disorderly debates on 9 and 16 July, the
whole matter was referred to the King and such divines as he should
be pleased to nominate.[19]

Prynne and his supporters turned to the more practical and pressing task of providing a measure of security for those parish clergy
who held only a tenuous legal title to their livings after the changes
of the 1640s and 1650s. The increased clerical mobility of those
decades, the absence of diocesan authorities to institute, induct or
license, the seizure of advowsons from their legal owners and, of
course, the sequestration and ejection of the previous incumbent,
conspired to deprive many clergy of a title recognizable in law. In
Derbyshire, for instance, a majority of the clergy were in this ticklish
position.[20] At the same time, the sequestered ministers were clam-

---

16. Gauden, *Slight Healings of Publique Hurts* (1660), pp. 79, 78. Also see Edward
    Reynolds, *The Author and Subject of Healing in the Church* (1660), esp. p. 6.
17. *Parliamentary History*, ed. W. Cobbett (1808), IV, 82-3; Bosher, *Making of Restoration*,
    pp. 154-67.
18. *The Diaries and Papers of Sir Edward Dering*, ed. M.F. Bond (1976), p. 49; the
    suggestion to recognize non-episcopal orders was made in the bill for 'settling
    ministers'.
19. *Parliamentary History*, IV, 79-80, 82-4 (from Bowman's diary). The committee on
    religion was adjourned until 28 October.
20. R. Clark, 'Why was the Re-establishment of the Church of England Possible?
    Derbyshire: a Provincial Perspective', *Midland History*, 8 (1983), 96.

ouring for reinstatement, claiming not only that law and equity were on their side, but also that they had played 'their part in the fastings, and prayers and tears, for obtaining the blessing of the Restoration'.[21] In June 1660 Charles II issued a proclamation forbidding the ejection of any minister until Parliament had resolved the issue, and by September, Prynne, with the tacit support of the government, had pushed through the Act for Settling Ministers, which confirmed all incumbents, except those who denied infant baptism, those who had petitioned for the regicide or opposed the Restoration, and most importantly those in possession of the livings of sequestered ministers who were still alive. The effects were far-reaching: possibly as many as 700 parishes experienced a change of minister and in almost 300 of these cases this was due to the survival of the original incumbent; Richard Baxter was replaced at Kidderminster by his predecessor.[22] The vexed question of property rights also arose in the case of church lands sold off during the 1640s and 1650s. Although the 1660 Act confirming Judicial Proceedings (12 Charles II c.12) declared the sales of church and crown lands invalid (a protection which Parliament did not extend to other lands), the churchmen generally took the path of conciliation, negotiating individual compromises in which the interests of the church, the purchasers, and the former tenants were recognized.[23]

The Convention Parliament was adjourned on 13 September with a speech from Lord Chancellor Hyde urging mutual tolerance and promising a royal declaration on religion which would compose differences and indulge those of tender conscience. A series of meetings held at Hyde's residence, Worcester House, since about 4 September, had been thrashing out a declaration based on the moderate Presbyterian proposals of July. Hyde's own hostility to the reduced episcopacy at the centre of these negotiations was so pronounced that Charles replaced him as arbitrator in the final session with two leading Presbyterian MPs, Arthur Annesley and Denzil Holles.[24] The final result was the Worcester House Declara-

---

21. Robert Mossom, *An Apology in the Behalf of the Sequestered Clergy* (1660), p. 4.
22. See Green, *Re-establishment*, pp. 45, 49; J.H. Pruett, *The Parish Clergy Under the Later Stuarts – The Leicestershire Experience* (Urbana, Illinois, 1978), pp. 17–18; Clark, 'Why was Re-establishment Possible?', 97; *CR*, p. xiii; Hutton, *Restoration*, p. 140 and note 130.
23. See J.P. Kenyon (ed.), *The Stuart Constitution* (Cambridge, 1966), pp. 362, 373; Green, *Re-establishment*, ch. 5; J. Habbakuk, 'The Land Settlement and the Restoration of Charles II', *TRHS*, 28 (1978); I.J. Gentles and W.J. Sheils, *Confiscation and Restoration: The Archbishopric Estates and the Civil War* (Borthwick Papers, 59, York, 1981), esp. pp. 16–25; Hutton, *Restoration*, pp. 139–42.
24. *Parliamentary History*, IV, 129–30; Green, *Re-establishment*, pp. 210–11; Bosher, *Making of Restoration*, pp. 184–8.

tion of 25 October 1660 in which Charles reiterated the tolerant principles of the Breda Declaration, abhorred his past dalliance with the Scottish Covenant, and promised 'to promote the power of godliness', to appoint a clerical commission to review the Prayer Book, and to refer the question of ceremonial uniformity to a national synod. On the crucial issue of church government, the Declaration outlined a form of reduced episcopacy: bishops would only exercise their powers, including ordination, with the aid of a body of grave and learned clergy drawn from the cathedral chapter and the diocesan clergy.

At the same time as the Worcester House Declaration was being negotiated, the King was busy appointing bishops, most of whom were amenable to the sort of church sketched in the Declaration. Although eighteen of the twenty-seven sees were vacant at the Restoration, Charles had been in no hurry to appoint new bishops last it provoke a puritan backlash or encourage an episcopal *revanche*. But by midsummer, with his impatient episcopalian allies pressing for action and in the face of resurgent hardline Presbyterianism, the King decided to appoint a set of moderate bishops in the hope of splitting the moderate from the extreme Presbyterians. Of the Presbyterians approached in September, only Edward Reynolds was prepared to accept a bishopric, but Gauden, the leading conciliator on the episcopal side, was elevated; among the other moderates appointed were Hacket, Henchman, Sanderson and Frewen: it was striking how few 'high episcopal men', men whose promotion might awaken fears of a return of the 'Laudians', were preferred.[25]

Charles could be pleased with the work so far. The Presbyterians had given way on the return of the sequestered ministers, the episcopalians seemed for the moment to have accepted the validity of presbyterian orders, and the tricky problem of revising the Book of Common Prayer had been postponed. The religious settlement was characterized by breadth – large numbers of men who had conformed in the Interregnum were preferred or confirmed in their livings, and space had been found for the young men eager to share in the spoils.[26] The moderate episcopacy sketched in the Worcester

---

25. On the vacancies in the twenty-six English and Welsh sees and in the see of Sodor and Man, see Bosher, *Making of Restoration*, p. 92. On the new appointments, see Green, *Re-establishment*, pp. 28–30, 82–90, and appendix 6; and for the different circumstances prevailing in Ireland, where bishops were appointed in July, see pp. 17–18, 32–3. In August, Charles promised the continuation of presbyterianism in Scotland, but by December certain Scottish politicians were urging him to erect episcopacy there; see J. Buckroyd, *Church and State in Scotland, 1660–1681* (Edinburgh, 1980), pp. 25–32.

26. Indeed some of those confirmed in 1660 were to be unable to accept the terms of

House Declaration was acceptable to many within the Church of England and to many *soi-disant* 'Presbyterians': several leading churchmen, such as George Morley, assumed that this was to be the permanent shape of the restored church.[27] Yet within a few months this moderate settlement had collapsed. Why did this vision of a comprehensive church give way to the narrower Act of Uniformity and the consequent ejection of 1,700 ministers?

One factor undermining the moderate settlement was the spontaneous recovery of the Church of England in the counties, cathedral cities and parishes of England. The cautious proceedings of politicians in Westminster and Whitehall allowed a vacuum in the localities, which men rushed to fill. Clergy flocked after jobs in the cathedrals – and so the reconstruction of cathedral chapters was determined more by demand from applicants than by the conscious policy of government, and was often under way before the bishops were back on their thrones.[28] Episcopacy returned with the bishops: those who had survived since the 1640s reclaimed their sees, and the new appointees of September and October 1660 took possession of their palaces and cathedrals – although some did not get to visit their dioceses in person until the following summer. Aspiring clergymen began to acquire episcopal ordination from May 1660, long before it was legally necessary; this was, no doubt, partly because Presbyterian ordination was no longer attainable, but it is also a sure sign that some contemporaries knew which way the wind was blowing.[29] John Evelyn's parish church at Deptford was surely not the only church to resound to a sermon 'magnifying the restoration of the Church of England' in the summer of 1660.[30] Although local enthusiasm for the Prayer Book is impossible to quantify, there is abundant evidence of its uncoerced use by clergymen in 1660: Clement Barksdale told his Gloucestershire congregation in May of his intention to read the morning prayers every day; but it was only on 4 November that Pepys's minister, Mr Mills, 'did begin to nibble at the Common Prayer', and then the congregation were unsure of

1662 and were to leave the church, see Green, *Re-establishment*, p. 59, appendix 3, pt. 2.

27. Clark, 'Why was Re-establishment Possible?', 101; Green, *Re-establishment*, p. 66; E.A.O. Whiteman, 'The Restoration of the Church of England', in *From Uniformity to Unity*, ed. G.F. Nuttall and O. Chadwick (1962), pp. 67–9.

28. See the account in Green, *Re-establishment*, pp. 61–71.

29. Clark, 'Why was Re-establishment Possible?', 99; Derbyshire testimonials in 1660–2 were signed by a group of episcopalian conformists, rather than as before by Presbyterian divines; ibid., 98.

30. The vicar also read the Thirty-Nine Articles to his congregation; Evelyn, III, 253–4.

the responses.[31] The local gentry occasionally encouraged a return to the Prayer Book by prosecuting those clergy who failed to use it under Elizabethan statutes.[32] However, the extent and meaning of the gentry's support for the Church of England, her bishops and her liturgy, is a thorny question. The prosecutions of those not using the Prayer Book, the cavalcades which greeted returning and new bishops, the county petitions for the return of the liturgy and the church of Queen Elizabeth and King James, cannot be taken at face value as evidence of a *religious* commitment.[33] These laymen were welcoming back a prop of the old order, a visible sign of the restoration of the *ancien régime*, and a bulwark against sectarianism. And, since they were her old tenants and owners of tithes, they also had a very tangible interest in the church as a property-owning institution. Just as the politicians had fallen back on the old tried and trusted forms, the forms known to the law, so the clergy and the gentry had naturally turned to what they knew best, a parish-based episcopal church: the gentry's attitude may be glimpsed in the title that Peniston Whalley gave to his charge to the Nottingham Grand Jury in April 1661, *The Civil Rights and Convenience of Episcopacy*.

The provincial advocates of an old-style church were not without encouragement from the centre. Although Charles II may have been pursuing a moderate religious settlement, the same could not be said of his ministers and allies. The government's 'confusions and divisions over ecclesiastical policy' did much to shape the eventual religious settlement, and indeed much of the ecclesiastical legislation of the 1660s.[34] On 6 November the Convention reassembled and a bill was soon brought forward to enact the Worcester House Declaration. However the court, its allies and some Independents, who feared that this settlement would lessen their own chances of a

31. Barksdale, *The Kings Return* (1660), p. 16: Pepys, III, 282–3. Also see T. Harris, *London Crowds in the Reign of Charles II* (Cambridge, 1987), p. 59; Clark, 'Why was Re-establishment Possible?', 100; Bosher, *Making of Restoration*, p. 163; Hutton, *Restoration*, pp. 199–204; Evelyn, III, 251–2; CUL, MS Add. 8499, fo. 44; Robert Nelson, *The Life of Dr George Bull* (1713), pp. 52–5. Green, *Re-establishment*, p. 5, points out that the Prayer Book was not much used on the thanksgiving day of 28 June 1660.

32. See MS Clarendon 73, fos 218–19; *The Diaries and Letters of Philip Henry*, ed. M.H. Lee (1882), p. 72; A. Coleby, *Central Government and the Localities: Hampshire 1649–1689* (Cambridge, 1987), p. 130; Clark, 'Why was Re-establishment Possible?', 100.

33. See MS Clarendon 77, fo. 222; Green, *Re-establishment*, pp. 183, 184; R.A. Beddard, 'The Restoration Church', in *The Restored Monarchy 1660–1689*, ed. J.R. Jones (1979), pp. 161–2; Bosher, *Making of Restoration*, p. 156; Coleby, *Central Government and Localities*, p. 147. On the general point of lay commitment see Green, *Re-establishment*, p. 188 and ch. 9.

34. Paul Seaward, *The Cavalier Parliament and the Reconstruction of the Old Regime, 1661–1667* (Cambridge, 1989), pp. 162–3.

toleration, together scotched the bill in a vote of 183 to 157 on 28 November. In a piece of wishful thinking, Sir Henry Yelverton, one of the staunchly episcopalian MPs, reported that the 'king was troubled, that what for peace sake he connives at, should be attempted to be made a law'.[35] The Presbyterians were already divided about whether to thank the King for his Declaration, and now, in the face of this final disappointment, their unity collapsed.[36] At the same time episcopalians appeared to be going on to the offensive: the consecration of the first of the new bishops had raised old fears of 'prelacy'; criticisms were voiced of the Worcester House Declaration's implied recognition of Presbyterian ordination.[37] The rising of London Fifth Monarchy men in January 1661 played into the hands of these hardline Anglicans. The consequent royal order against conventicles produced the first severe wave of persecution against Baptists, Quakers and other 'fanatic' sectaries.[38] An atmosphere of insecurity was only heightened by the first returns in the London elections for a parliament to succeed the Convention (which had been dissolved on 24 December) – on 19 March four fiercely anti-episcopalian MPs were returned to the cry of 'No Bishops! No Lord Bishops!' Such events were bound to harden conservative political opinion in time to influence the elections elsewhere in the country.

It was on 15 April, in the midst of these inauspicious developments, that the representatives of the episcopal and Presbyterian clergy finally met at the Savoy under a royal commission to discuss what revisions and additions were necessary to the Prayer Book.[39] What had been proposed in the Worcester House Declaration as a conference between equals was already far more one-sided, with the Presbyterians reduced 'to the position of suppliants to those in authority', while Bishop Sheldon of London as one who 'knew more of the King's mind' assumed the leadership of the episcopal divines.[40] Politics and personalities had brought the conference to grief long before its official deadline of 25 July. The intransigent

35. MS Eng Letters C 210, fo. 19 (1 December 1660); Bosher, *Making of Restoration*, pp. 185–9, 195–9; Green, *Re-establishment*, p. 127.
36. N.H. Keeble, *The Literary Culture of Nonconformity in Later Seventeenth-century England* (Leicester, 1987), pp. 27–8.
37. Bosher, *Making of Restoration*, pp. 181–2; Keeble, *Literary Culture*, p. 27; Green, *Re-establishment*, p. 211.
38. M.R. Watts, *The Dissenters* (Oxford, 1978), p. 233; Coleby, *Central Government and Localities*, pp. 134–5.
39. G. Cuming, *The Godly Order* (Alcuin Club, 1983), pp. 144, 149–50; Abernathy, 'Presbyterians', 80; Bosher, *Making of Restoration*, pp. 226–30.
40. Keeble, *Literary Culture*, p. 30.

churchmen hampered the work by insisting that the exchanges should be in writing rather than verbal, and on the other side, Richard Baxter was allowed to dominate the Presbyterian case and even to spring a 'liturgy' of his own composing on the conference. The pleas of Nicholas Bernard for moderation, 'it being one of the best evidences of a true son of the Church of England, to be willing to bear with somewhat cross to his own opinion, for the peace of his Mother', went unheeded.[41] While goodwill and fraternity ran into the sands at the Savoy, the King was crowned, the new Parliament assembled, and a Convocation of the clergy gathered in the vestry of St Paul's.

The 'Cavalier Parliament' was ready and eager to take up the government's invitation to cooperate in settling religion and exercising severity against seditious preachers. The new Parliament had fewer Presbyterian MPs than its predecessor, as was soon underlined by the vote of 228 to 103 in favour of burning the Solemn League and Covenant, and the decision that all members should receive the sacrament according to the Prayer Book rite.[42] There were several loose ends to tie up in the religious and ecclesiastical field. In 1641 the bishops had been excluded from the House of Lords. The court now orchestrated the moves which resulted in the decision of June to repeal that Act so that the bishops could assume their seats at the opening of the second session in November.[43] On 25 June the Commons appointed a committee to review the laws 'confirming' the liturgy and to produce 'a compendious bill' to supply their defects and 'to provide for an effectual conformity to the liturgy of the church for the time to come'. The same committee was also to look into the legislation of 1641 which had abolished the Court of High Commission and the coercive powers of the church courts. The bill to repeal this legislation, and thus to resurrect the church courts, with the sole exception of High Commission, had passed both Houses by 27 July. In fact, some church courts had gone to work well before this legislation, but now they began to step up their activity.[44] The bill of uniformity as it had emerged in the Commons by 9 July was a return to the situation and laws existing before the

---

41. Bernard, *Devotions of the Ancient Church* (1660), preface: Thomason dates to January 1661. John Gauden, however, was concerned that the Worcester House Declaration should not be misread as a sign of royal 'dis-esteem' for the Prayer Book; see *Considerations touching the Liturgy of the Church of England* (1661), p. 1.
42. Seaward, *Cavalier Parliament*, pp. 163–4; 171–2 for anti-Quaker legislation.
43. Ibid., pp. 165–6; Bosher, *Making of Restoration*, pp. 222–3.
44. Bosher, *Making of Restoration*, pp. 223–4; Seaward, *Cavalier Parliament*, pp. 167–8; Clark, 'Why was Re-establishment Possible?', 99–100; Pruett, *Parish Clergy*, pp. 19–20; Hutton, *Restoration*, p. 173.

Civil War. It required all ministers to use the Prayer Book and to declare their 'unfeigned assent and consent' to the use of everything prescribed in the book. Yet it is plain that the government was already thinking of attaching a new version of the Prayer Book to the uniformity bill; by 9 July, with the Savoy Conference hopelessly deadlocked, the bishops had been entrusted with the task of revising the liturgy.[45] And, even more ominously, on 14 August Charles proclaimed that bishops were to be restored as 'before the late troubles' in Scotland.[46]

Meanwhile Convocation was waiting impatiently in the wings. Although Convocations of the clergy of the two archiepiscopal provinces were normally called to coincide with a Parliament, Charles had been wary of summoning Convocation in the spring of 1661. Eventually his fears were overcome and Convocations carefully screened to exclude all but loyal episcopalians met at York and London on 8 May. At first there was little work to be done because the Savoy Conference had 'an antecedent commission to ours', and so the Convocation spent the summer composing orders of service for the Stuart anniversaries of 29 May and 30 January.[47] The clerical firebrands passed the time denouncing 'the managers of the division' and reminding them that Convocation 'are the proper and authentic representatives of the ministry in whose judgement they ought to acquiesce in such matters. And not only so but to let the people that follow them know that they ought not to disturb the peace of the church under the pretence of the prosecution of expediencies since the division of the church is the great inexpedient'.[48] After a summer recess, Convocation returned to a clear field on 21 November, and launched into a rapid and well prepared revision of the Prayer Book. Yet strangely these changes were far from partisan or extreme. The suggestions of 'Laudians' like John Cosin and Matthew Wren were not taken up (except in the case of the Ordinal), and if anything the revisions, although minor in themselves, leaned towards the puritan objections, a tendency which may reflect the role of the moderates, Robert Sanderson and Edward Reynolds. Reynolds contributed the first draft of the General Thanksgiving from a eucharistic prayer which he had 'conceived' along lines suggested by the *Directory of Public Worship*. Within

45. Seaward, *Cavalier Parliament*, pp. 166–7.
46. This was the end of a lengthy power struggle between Middleton and Lauderdale, and was a victory for naked Erastianism; see Buckroyd, *Church and State in Scotland*, p. 40.
47. See Bosher, *Making of Restoration*, pp. 213–15, 230–1; Hutton, *Restoration*, pp. 174–5.
48. MS Rawlinson D 399, fo. 97, endorsed 'Dr Warmstry June 1661'.

a month, 600 revisions had been agreed, and on 20 December representatives of both Convocations – the bishops of the northern province having been previously empowered – signed the new Prayer Book.[49]

The need for the new Parliament to confirm the Convention's legislation gave Anglican MPs a chance to vent their dislike of the Presbyterian clergy.[50] The generosity of the Convention's Act for Settling Ministers rankled with some Anglican MPs, and as early as May there had been rumours that it would not be confirmed without alterations. On 29 November the Commons committee considering the Act reported a series of amendments: sequestered ministers were to be restored or compensated, incumbents were to abjure the Covenant and all resistance to royal authority, and to be instituted, inducted and ordained according to the forms of the Church of England. Describing the consequences of the bill 'which is almost passed the House of Commons', on 2 January, Sir Henry Yelverton wrote, 'all livings since '41 will be void, and so by consequence if any be presented none will be instituted and inducted unless he be ordained by a bishop and subscribe'.[51] Six days later the bill was passed by a House of Commons impatient of delay and heated by revelations of fanatic and Presbyterian plots. The court, however, would not tolerate this threat to the policy of retaining moderate Presbyterians within the restored church, and used the House of Lords to wreck the amended bill. Seven bishops, including Sheldon, Reynolds, Gauden, Sanderson and Morley, were persuaded to oppose the amendments, and finally the Lords confirmed the Ministers' Act without any of the changes suggested by the Commons. Yet it seems that some sort of trade-off had taken place, and a promise had been made to add to the bill of uniformity provisions similar to those excised from the bill confirming the Ministers' Act. So when the uniformity bill was considered in a House of Lords committee which included eight bishops, such amendments were made, drastically altering the character of the bill. On 25 February Clarendon brought the revised liturgy to Parliament and on 13 March the new version of the uniformity bill with the Prayer Book attached was reported to the House of Lords. The 1662 Act of Uniformity had achieved its final form.

It was still possible that the Act of Uniformity would be stillborn.[52] While thanking Parliament for their 'wholesome prescription',

49. Bosher, *Making of Restoration*, pp. 244–9.
50. My account is based on Seaward, *Cavalier Parliament*, pp. 172–5.
51. MS Eng Letters C 210, fo. 61.
52. This paragraph follows Seaward, *Cavalier Parliament*, pp. 175–80.

Clarendon reminded MPs that 'the application of these remedies, the execution of these sharp laws, depends upon the wisdom of the most discerning, generous, and merciful prince'. Instead of healing the nation's divisions and easing the path to conformity for moderate Presbyterians, this 'sharp act' virtually ensured that they would be forced out of the national church. 'The Presbyterian party sets up meetings, appoints days of fasting and possesses the people that now persecution is approaching and profaneness and idolatry is coming in like a flood', reported one observer on 19 March.[53] Many believed that the enforcement of the Act was bound to provoke violence, or even rebellion, and it was long tense summer as the country was swept by rumours that the 'episcopal party' were 'in the saddle' or were cast low, that the King would or would not suspend the imminent Act, and that the Presbyterians would rise in rebellion on 3 September.[54] Between 19 May, when the bill received the royal assent, and St Bartholomew's day, 24 August 1662, when the Act came into force, Clarendon made a series of proposals to moderate or postpone the Act and, each time, he was thwarted by Sheldon, the Duke of York, and the King. Events took their course; the Act of Uniformity was enforced and enforced without the feared violence. The die had been cast.

The Act of Uniformity was the work of many hands, the product of parliamentary horse-trading rather than theological self-definition; it did not create a breach within English Protestantism, for that had been growing over the preceding two decades, but it did prevent the union of moderate Presbyterians with the established church and set the legal boundaries within which a Restoration Anglicanism would be elaborated. The settlement of 1662 was a political, indeed an Erastian, solution to the religious divisions of the English; moreover, it was based on a conspicuously narrower interest than was the political settlement. None of this augured well for its stability or survival.

From Uniformity to Indulgence, 1662–72

'I see no reason upon me to change my religion, not any reason so much as to change my opinion by conforming to what the Act [of Uniformity] requires', wrote one conforming clergyman in 1662.[55] The overwhelming majority of the English parish clergy simply

53. BL, MS Egerton 2537, fo. 331. I am grateful to Dr Steven Pincus for this reference.
54. See Josselin, pp. 481, 482, 490; Newcome, *Autobiography*, p. 136; Pepys, III, 183.
55. MS Rawlinson D 361, fo. 18.

endured the changes brought about in 1660–2 as they had those of the previous decades. The 1660 Act for Settling Ministers had led to the ejection of 695 parish ministers, while the Act of Uniformity forced out 936 (59 of whom had been first ejected in 1660, but then found another living). In all, about 1,760 clergy were forced to leave their parishes in 1660–3.[56] The figures are probably less important than the standing and the motives of those who went out. The Act of 1660 indiscriminately affected both those whose religious and political convictions prevented their absorption into a revived national church and those who had no more commitment to the Puritan Revolution than the fact that they had served in the place of a sequestered divine. In Leicestershire, for example, nearly a quarter of the incumbents left their livings in 1660, but many of these were happy to conform in other parishes – the number who became Nonconformists is small. On the other hand, more than half of those finally ejected in that county were ejected before 1662.[57] In short, the bulk of the irreconcilable puritan clergy, including many of the Independents and Baptist incumbents, had been picked off in 1660. And many leading puritan divines, such as John Owen, Peter Sterry and Increase Mather, occupied no living at the Restoration from which to be ousted. So what sort of men were the 936 ministers who were forced out of the church in 1662 by the Act of Uniformity?

The bulk of this group were men who could have accepted some sort of diluted uniformity, perhaps along the lines of the Worcester House Declaration, but who jibbed at the requirements of 1662. Plainly they felt a distaste for the arbitrary and inflexible terms of communion, but the seventeenth-century mind preferred to take a stand on less abstract principles than charity and tolerance. The Act presented four specific difficulties to the scrupulous: to qualify for a clerical living it was necessary to give 'unfeigned assent and consent to all and everything contained and prescribed in and by' the Book of Common Prayer, including the sacraments and ceremonies, psalter and ordinal; to subscribe to the Thirty-Nine Articles, of which three concerned church government; to renounce the obligation of the Solemn League and Covenant for yourself and all others, and forswear 'to endeavour any change or alteration of government either in church or state'; and, finally, to have received ordination from the hands of a bishop. It is plain that in many cases – although we cannot put a figure on them – a personal difficulty, a prior

---

56. Another 200 lecturers, university dons and schoolmasters could be added to this figure, as could 120 clergy in Wales. 171 of the 1,760 are known to have later conformed.
57. Pruett, *Parish Clergy*, pp. 17–18, 23.

commitment by that individual, rather than a general theological principle, stood in the way of conformity: thus ministers who could not conform themselves, because they could not renounce their Presbyterian ordination or their oath, might countenance their sons' conformity to the church.[58] Some clergy failed to conform for what appear to be quite needless technical difficulties. Richard Kidder claimed

> I had a good title to my living, I never took the Covenant or Engagement; I was entirely satisfied in episcopacy, and with a liturgy; I had no hand in the late confusions and was so far from it that I lamented them; I had orders from a bishop at a time when it was dangerous to receive them that way. The truth is I had not due time given me to consider, and was deprived of my living for not subscribing to a book that was not (as it ought to have been) laid before me.[59]

Agonies of conscience were suffered by those considering conformity.[60] To be contemplating conformity implied that they accepted the principle of a national parochial church, but they could not accept the hierarchy's uncharitable, nay schismatic, terms of communion. Yet neither would they now compound the bishops' sin by forming their own congregations.[61] In their farewell sermons before 'black Bartholomew' and their circumspect behaviour after their 'legal death' or ejection, these peaceable ministers strove to avoid offence.[62] The sober non-conforming clergy often remained on good terms with the ministers of the Church of England, exhorted their lay followers to conformity, and themselves attended Anglican worship, albeit only a part of the service or an occasional service.[63] They also prided themselves on their loyalty: 'we will do anything

58. See G.F. Nuttall, 'The First Nonconformists', in *From Uniformity to Unity*, ed. G.F. Nuttall and O. Chadwick (1962), pp. 157–9; J. Spurr, 'The Church of England, Comprehension and the Toleration Act of 1689', *EHR*, 104 (1989), 929–30.

59. *The Life of Richard Kidder D.D. Bishop of Bath and Wells Written by Himself*, ed. A.E. Robinson (Somerset Record Society, 37, 1922), p. 11.

60. Nuttall, 'First Nonconformists', pp. 177–82.

61. See J. Spurr, 'Schism and the Restoration Church', *JEH*, 41 (1990), 409, 418; Pruett, *Parish Clergy*, p. 24; R. Clark, 'Anglicanism, Recusancy and Dissent in Derbyshire, 1603–1670' (unpublished Oxford University D. Phil. thesis, 1979), pp. 199–201; J.L. Salter, 'Warwickshire Clergy 1660–1714' (unpublished Birmingham University Ph.D. thesis, 1975), pp. 116–17.

62. Most preached for the last time on 17 August; see Evelyn, III, 321; Clark, 'Anglicanism', pp. 197–8. Some farewell sermons caused offence; see MS Tanner 48, fo. 49; P.W. Thomas, *Sir John Berkenhead* (Oxford, 1969), p. 224.

63. *RB*, II, 436–7, 440; III, 19; Matthew Henry, *The Life of the Rev. Philip Henry*, ed. J.B. Williams (1825), pp. 2, 100–3, 111–12, 121–3; C.E. Whiting, *Studies in English*

for his majesty but sin,' announced the ejected rector of St John's, Exeter. 'We could hope to die for him, but we dare not be damned for him.'[64] Several of the ejected clergy kept the anniversaries of 30 January and 29 May in their own homes, although some also kept 24 August as 'a day of humiliation'.[65] A consequence of all this was that in the 1660s a large group of respected clerical leaders were neither of the established church nor felt themselves part of Dissent – indeed they were, they claimed, the victims of a conservative, episcopal backlash provoked by the extremism of the sects.[66]

These clergymen and their followers formed a puritan penumbra around the parish churches and clergy. Without minimizing the clear legal distinctions between conformity and non-conformity, or the existence of zealous Anglican conformists, we should recognize that many Restoration clergymen and ejected ministers had common backgrounds, associations and values.[67] The uniformity demanded by the Church of England was, after all, largely outward, mainly a conformity of practice rather than subscription to detailed doctrinal orthodoxies, and so many remained certain that the church and Dissent were in agreement on the fundamentals of religion. Matthew Robinson and George Gray, his nephew and successor in the living of Burneston,

> were alike minded in all things. Both were episcopal in their judgements, yet both were highly prized by their dissenting brethren for their piety and moderation: both much wished a reformation in the church in many particulars, and in that fatal Bartholomew day which silenced so many able ministers, these two did scruple at many things with the rest of the dissenters: and the bishop of the diocese took a great deal of pains to satisfy their doubts, that they might not be deserters among the rest of the dissenters.[68]

They conformed to the Church of England, but mixed easily and frequently with leading Nonconformist clergy of the North, like Henry Newcome. In London, at the funerals of eminent Nonconformist

Puritanism from the Restoration to the Revolution (1931), pp. 18–19; P.W. Jackson, 'Nonconformists and Society in Devon 1660–1689' (unpublished Exeter University Ph.D. thesis, 1986), p. 42.

64. Quoted in Watts, *Dissenters*, p. 219.
65. *Life of Philip Henry*, p. 125; MS Eng Th D 71, fo. 64v; Josselin, pp. 475, 480, 486, 489, 495, 505, 508, 533.
66. Spurr, 'Schism', 408–10, 418; Heywood, p. 127.
67. Pruett, *Parish Clergy*, pp. 25–6; J. Spurr, '"Latitudinarianism" and the Restoration Church', *HJ*, 31 (1988), 77 note 98; Watts, *Dissenters*, p. 228; Wood, III, 36.
68. *Autobiography of Matthew Robinson*, ed. J.E.B. Mayor (Cambridge, 1856), p. 68.

clergy, such as Thomas Manton or Daniel Featley, leading church-men could be seen walking in pairs with Nonconformist ministers.[69]

The parish clergy of the 1660s were deeply tinged with past conformity – 90 out of 194 clergy serving in Warwickshire after 1662 and 236 of 383 ministers in Devon had probably been conformists.[70] Giles Moore, rector of Horsted Keynes, Sussex, from 1655 until his death in 1679, was perhaps typical of many. Moore disliked the Protectorate regime, and may even have used the Prayer Book; he instructed his parishioners with the Westminster Assembly's cat-echism but then switched quite easily back to the church's catechism at the Restoration.[71] The young unaligned men of the 1650s, men like Simon Patrick, John Tillotson, Richard Kidder, Edward Fowler or Isaac Archer, came into the church, but in some cases only after a delay. Kidder and Fowler conformed in 1664. Archer, a confused, easily swayed young man, was financially dependent while a student at Cambridge on a father with whom his relationship was difficult. In October 1660 he was persuaded by a sermon that the profane favoured conformity and that the Nonconformists were marked out by their godliness; but in March 1662, Archer's need to earn a living forced him into conformity, 'yet I examined things, as well as I could, and found none of those things we had at our ordinary service sinfull, or contrary to God's word; though even then I had rather not done any of such things'. He was duly ordained by Bishop Wren in September, and subsequently served several livings, though not without scruples and lapses from strict conformity.[72] The need to earn a living and get on in the world was apparently a common motive, and it was one disparaged by the less pliant on both sides of the divide. Richard Baxter believed most of the conforming clergy were young, penurious or hypocritical; Thomas Ken suggested that preferment was 'their only confession of faith'; and Bishop Robert Sanderson reported from Leicester, on 5 August 1662, 'I find the clergy of different constitutions; the obstinate presbyterians appear not. But of those that for their wor[l]dly interest will subscribe anything, and yet are hollow-hearted, there are I fear very many. I have discovered such palpable hypocrisy in the men of that faction, as I thought could not possibly have been found in men that pretend

69. C.F. Richardson, *English Preachers and Preaching 1640–1670* (1928), p. 31; Wood, III, 23; Tillotson, II, 91–137 (funeral sermon for Thomas Gouge).
70. Calculated from Salter, 'Warwickshire Clergy'; Jackson, 'Nonconformists in Devon', p. 75.
71. *The Journal of Giles Moore*, ed. R. Bird (Sussex Record Society, 68, 1971), 2–3, 148, 317. Also see MS Eng Th D 59, fos 33, 36, 49, cf. 27; Jackson, 'Nonconformists in Devon', pp. 74–6; Nuttall, 'First Nonconformists', pp. 175–6.
72. CUL, MS Add. 8499, fos 49–50, 68.

to godliness or tenderness of conscience.'[73] It was indeed possible to make an equivocal subscription or even evade full conformity while retaining a living in the Church of England[74].

Such a picture of a broad-based parish clergy does not sit easily with the historical reputation of the Restoration church as united in intolerant, reactionary, Tory principles. This reputed unity was at best a partial truth, for this was a façade, a public face, created and maintained by the leaders of the church. Although the figureheads of the restored church were her two aged archbishops, Juxon and Frewen, real power lay, from the outset, with Gilbert Sheldon, Bishop of London and confidant of politicians. When, in August 1662, Clarendon proposed in the Privy Council to moderate the Act of Uniformity even after it had come into force, Sheldon made his stand. The bishop's fury still blazes off the page in the bitter note he scribbled to Clarendon immediately afterwards, complaining of his 'great unkindness' in exposing Sheldon to certain ruin by Parliament or the extreme hatred of 'that malicious party in whose jaws I must live, and never giving me the least notice of it'.[75] Sir Henry Yelverton spread the news that 'resolute counsels are taken as to [the] Act of Uniformity, and that through the prudence and wisdom of my Lord of London the Presbyterians were totally foiled last Thursday at the Privy Council'. Meanwhile old friends and elder statesmen among the bishops tried to stiffen Clarendon's resolve: 'resume your old courage and your old cheerfullness,' advised Bishop George Morley of Winchester, for God will not now desert a cause he has so conspicuously favoured.[76]

The iron had entered Sheldon's soul in August 1662. The Act of Uniformity made a clear-cut legal distinction between the orthodox and the rest. No matter that it classed the sober and scrupulous Nonconforming clergyman with the inspired sectarian fanatic, all were equally beyond the pale, equally worthy of severity.

> Tis only a resolute execution of the law that must cure this disease, all other remedies serve and will increase it; and it's necessary that they who will not be governed as men by reason and persuasions should be governed as beasts by power and force, all other courses will be ineffectual, ever have been so, ever will be . . .[77]

73. *RB*, II, 386; [Thomas Ken], *Ichabod* (Cambridge, 1663), ch. 2; MS Clarendon 77, fo. 157; Spurr, 'Latitudinarianism', 63–4, 65.
74. Green, *Re-establishment*, p. 149; Josselin, p. 507; Keeble, *Literary Culture*, p. 73; and see pp. 184–90 below.
75. MS Clarendon 77, fo. 319.
76. MS Eng Letters C 210, fo. 78; MS Clarendon 77, fos 157, 340.
77. MS Carte 45, fo. 151. Also see Beddard, 'Restoration Church', p. 171.

In the pulpit and in print, Sheldon and his Anglican brethren beat the drum ecclesiastic. They insisted that the Act of Uniformity had reduced the issues surrounding religious conformity to the simple obligation of submission to the law. Schism and sedition were 'twin sisters', Nonconformity and rebellion shared the same dam; and the notion of 'peaceable' or 'loyal' Dissenters was nonsensical. The case for obedience to the church was constantly subsumed within the argument for subjection to the King. In part, this was a simple reflection of the fervent royalism of the Restoration Church of England. She had rejoiced in the return of England's David, her churches were adorned by his coat of arms (even where, as at North Walsham, they were painted on the back of the Commonwealth's arms), and her liturgy celebrated his family and their anniversaries. In 1671, a painting of Charles I 'kneeling, with a crown of thorns in his hand, his crown and sceptre lying by' was hung in St Paul's, Covent Garden.[78] The alliance of Moses and Aaron was an evergreen subject for Anglican preachers – there was even a proposal in the later 1660s for a fortieth article of religion, 'on the duty of subjects'.[79] But the equation of religious dissent with political disloyalty also played on the social and political fears of the gentry. It was a commonplace of conservative lay thinking that 'uniformity is the cement of both Christian and civil societies', and that neither society nor authority can stand without religious unity.[80]

Archbishop Sheldon (as he became in August 1663) was an astute politician and a skilled manipulator of political opinion. In the 1660s he seems to have set a group of clerical pamphleteers to work to defend uniformity and thwart any move towards the 'comprehension' or toleration of Dissent. The tracts of George Stradling, Thomas Tomkins, Samuel Parker and others were tailored to suit the secular, political terrain upon which these issues were fought. They appealed to lay values and concerns, by harping on the dangers and 'inconveniences' of religious pluralism, and in content and vitriol they matched the works of the leading lights of court propaganda, such as Sir Roger L'Estrange.[81] The disloyal, hypocritical, untrustworthy

78. *The Parish of St Paul's, Covent Garden* (The Survey of London, 36, 1970), 105 (I owe this reference to Paul Seaward).

79. R.A. Beddard, 'Of the Duty of Subjects: A Proposed Fortieth Article of Religion', *The Bodleian Library Record*, 10 (1981), 229–36.

80. Sir Roger L'Estrange, *Toleration Discussed* (1663), p. 86: also see Sir Robert Pointz, *A Vindication of Monarchy* (1661), p. 35 (I also owe this reference to Dr Seaward).

81. Stradling, Tomkins and Parker were all chaplains to Sheldon. See *RB*, III, 44; Thomas, *Berkenhead*, pp. 217 ff.; M. Goldie, 'John Locke and Anglican Royalism', *Political Studies*, 31 (1983), 66–7; R.L. Greaves, *Deliver Us From Evil* (Oxford, 1986), pp. 216–20.

and covertly anti-monarchical character of Nonconformity was 'revealed' *ad nauseam*. Simon Patrick's *A Friendly Debate* (1669), written to explode hopes of a 'comprehension', so dwelt upon Nonconformist disloyalty that it offended more conciliatory churchmen like Gilbert Burnet, but it won Archbishop Sheldon's favour.[82] Anglicans had no qualms that, in winning the political argument, they also traduced and vilified honest and conscientious Nonconformists. They shared Sheldon's belief that Nonconformists had put themselves beyond reasonable government and rational persuasion by their very refusal to conform.[83] Nor did the churchmen ever tire of warning the nation that 'there is a papacy in every sect or faction' and that they should 'take heed of the old proverb, that the Pope shall come upon the puritan's back'. 'Far from being the bulwarks against popery', the Dissenters, with their breach of Protestant unity and appeals for toleration, 'have been the great promotors of that interest; and it will be owing wholly to them, if ever it be again introduced into these kingdoms'.[84]

The need to produce this apologetic indicates the delicacy of the church's position. The defence and execution of the Act of Uniformity – and the fate of the Church of England – depended upon the gentlemen who ran the counties as JPs and who served in Parliament. Much has been made of the 'irresistible Anglican reflex' in the counties, a natural alliance of country squire and High Church parson, based on the gentry's appreciation of the social, political and proprietorial interests they shared with the church.[85] But this is to beg the question of what 'Anglican loyalty' means. Enthusiastic as they may have been about episcopacy, the Prayer Book and orderly parish religion, the provincial gentry, as we shall see, did not always go along with the divisive, persecuting policies deemed necessary at Lambeth and Whitehall. Nor was the 'Long Parliament' of Charles II, the 'Cavalier Parliament' which sat from 1661 to 1679 and enacted the 'Clarendon Code' in defence of the church, whole-heartedly and irreclaimably Anglican. The Cavalier Parliament was far from an homogeneous assembly of reactionary,

82. Burnet, I, 467; Patrick, IX, 450; cf. Thomas Pittis, *A Private Conference* (1670), pp. 156–60.

83. See Keeble, *Literary Culture*, p. 41, on the transformation of the term 'Nonconformity' into 'Dissent'.

84. South, III, 339; Francis Fullwood, *Toleration Not To Be Abused* (1672), p. 34; Patrick, V, 252–68. Also see Goldie, 'Locke and Anglican Royalism', 71–3.

85. R.A. Beddard, 'Sheldon and Anglican Recovery', *HJ*, 19 (1976), 1010; Beddard, 'Restoration Church', pp. 162, 156; Green, *Re-establishment*, pp. 142, 179, 200; S.K. Roberts, *Recovery and Restoration in an English County: Devon Local Administration 1646–70* (Exeter, 1985), pp. 165–7.

backwoods squires; it was a divided and anxious body ready to be guided by those who knew how to play upon its fears. So although only a very few MPs were zealous for the Church of England, a small clique was able to exploit the larger body's anxiety about security and stability: 'High-flying, prelatical Anglicanism was not, it seems, characteristic of the country, gentry, or even the clergy as a whole: yet parliament was deeply imbued with it, not because such men dominated it in numbers, but because they dominated it in political weight and the effectiveness of their rhetoric.'[86] The intolerant Anglican Cavalier Parliament was not then a myth so much as a creation of Sheldon and his allies. When, delighted by 'the constancy of the votes of the House of Commons, for the suppressing conventicles, and non-conformitants', Bishop Hacket of Lichfield wrote in praise of 'those prudent, and religious patriots', he recognized that this was the result of the archbishop's 'dexterity', 'prudence, and indefatigable industry', and that no other Parliament would have been so dutiful.[87]

Sheldon's dexterity and the constancy of the Commons were called upon shortly after the Act of Uniformity came into force. On 26 December 1662 Charles announced his intention of asking Parliament to find a way in which he could exercise his 'inherent' power to dispense with the penalties of the Act.[88] As widely suspected, this proposal was inspired by the Roman Catholics around the King, chiefly the Earl of Bristol, and perhaps for this reason the Nonconformists kept their distance from it. Nor would the Commons have any truck with 'indulging' religious dissidents. As they warned the King in their address of 27 February 1663, if religious pluralism is permitted 'in time, some prevalent sect will, at last, contend for an establishment; which, for aught can be foreseen, may end in popery'. The whole affair revealed that the court had no consensus on religious policy: Bristol's proposal horrified Clarendon as much as it did the churchmen. The Church of England was at the mercy of a divided court and of a King who liked to play his ministers off against one another. No wonder that Sheldon preferred to place his

86. Seaward, *Cavalier Parliament*, p. 62; also see pp. 67, 193–5, 328; P. Seaward, 'Gilbert Sheldon, the London Vestries, and the Defence of the Church', in *The Politics of Religion in Restoration England*, ed. T. Harris, P. Seaward and M. Goldie (Oxford, 1990), pp. 49–50; Hutton, *Restoration*, pp. 168–9, 174.
87. MS Tanner 45, fos 295, 278, 288.
88. This account is based on Seaward, *Cavalier Parliament*, pp. 181–5; *RB*, II, 430; Green, *Re-establishment*, pp. 219–26; J. Miller, *Popery and Politics in England 1660–1688* (Cambridge, 1973), pp. 93–102; F. Bate, *The Declaration of Indulgence 1672* (1908), pp. 38–9. Burnet believed that the Catholic strategy was to win a toleration or to provoke a general persecution (I, 249, quoting Walsh).

trust in the House of Commons, which would have been the Crown's most compliant servant, he believed, if only it had been treated properly, 'for all the disorders have arisen from the King's family and servants'.[89] The Commons was not, however, the archbishop's poodle. There were good legal and constitutional grounds for rejecting the 1662 Declaration; and while the equation of Dissent and sedition so assiduously promoted by the churchmen undoubtedly played a part in thwarting the Declaration, it was not sufficient to persuade MPs to accede to a bill against conventicles proposed by Sheldon's henchmen.[90] But then, as if on cue, the churchmen's arguments about the treasonableness of Dissent were vindicated by the Yorkshire Plot of October 1663.

Rumours of Nonconformist risings, of arms stockpiled at conventicles, of plots in league with the Scots and the Dutch, were a constant feature of life in the early 1660s, but when the abortive 1663 rising was unravelled it was found to include several Presbyterians as well as sectaries. The court now began to draw back from the Nonconformists; Clarendon echoed Sheldon's line that the laws must be executed, and endorsed severity against Nonconformist ministers.[91] In March 1664 frightened backbench MPs eagerly voted through the revived bill of 1663 against conventicles. Aimed against 'seditious sectaries and other disloyal persons', the Conventicle Act (16 Charles II c.4) imposed on conventiclers fines of up to £100 and transportation for a third offence. JPs were empowered to break into houses on information that a conventicle was taking place. The Act was to lapse three years after the end of the current session of Parliament. Sheldon also bound the fortunes of the church to Parliament by surrendering the clergy's right to tax themselves in Convocation. The financial implications of the arrangement were perhaps less important than the fact that it gave the clergy the right to vote in parliamentary elections (assuming they met the property qualifications), although the first chance for most clergy to use their vote only occurred in the general election of 1679. A second consequence was that Convocation no longer conducted business, although members continued to meet for prayers on Wednesday and Friday mornings and to choose Prolocutors.[92]

89. MS Carte 45, fo. 212 (Sheldon to Ormonde, 25 February 1667).
90. The bill was copied, however, in Scotland where an Act against Conventicles was passed on 10 July 1663; see Burnet, I, 365–6; Buckroyd, *Church and State in Scotland*, p. 54, and see p. 57 for Sheldon's influence on Archbishop Sharp.
91. Seaward, *Cavalier Parliament*, pp. 189–92.
92. Kennett, pp. 254–5, 361–2; Burnet, I, 352–3; N. Sykes, *From Sheldon to Secker* (Cambridge, 1959), pp. 41–3; *The Records of the Northern Convocation* (Surtees Society, 113, 1907), pp. 325–9.

The Conventicle Act does not seem to have curbed the insolence of Nonconformity, for eighteen months later Parliament supplemented it with the 'Five Mile Act' (17 Charles II c.5). With the nation at war and plague raging in the capital, a thinly attended Parliament met in Oxford, to be welcomed with a speech from Clarendon denouncing the Nonconformist 'scorpions' in the nation's bosom, who might yet 'sting us to death'. The government was particularly concerned about the Nonconformists who were preaching to London congregations deserted by the Anglican clergy. When a bill against Dissenting ministers was introduced into the Commons, it received support from the court and quickly passed into law. The Five Mile Act banned Nonconformist ministers from living within five miles of any corporate town unless they swore the 'Oxford oath' abhorring armed opposition to the King as traitorous and illegal and promising not to endeavour any alteration of government in church or state. Many MPs and Lords were troubled by this oath against all change, but Sheldon pressed on in his eagerness to harry Dissenters, saying that he was 'sorry to see there is such tenderness for ill men' and that, since the oath was to preserve monarchy and episcopacy, 'it did not hinder altering of what should be thought fit so this government were preserved'.[93] These two Acts were seen by supporters as necessary concomitants of the Act of Uniformity. Bishop Seth Ward supported the penal laws, his biographer tells us, because there was no other viable political means of preserving peace and government – precisely the argument used so often by the MPs.[94]

The life of the church, like that of the nation, was dislocated by the plague of 1665–6. Among its victims the plague claimed the reputation of many of the London churchmen. 'Who now, those sons of Aaron being fled,/ Shall stand between the living and the dead?' asked the balladeers.[95] Richard Baxter was assiduous in reporting the clergy's desertion of their flocks and the courage of the Dissenting pastors in ministering in their place.[96] In the country, Dean Sancroft of St Paul's received news from a physician friend

93. C. Robbins, 'The Oxford Session of the Long Parliament of Charles II', *BIHR*, 21 (1948), 222.

94. Walter Pope, *The Life of the Right Reverend Father in God Seth [Ward]* (1697), p. 69; E.A.O. Whiteman, 'The Episcopate of Dr Seth Ward, Bishop of Exeter (1662 to 1667) and Salisbury (1667 to 1668/89) with Special Reference to the Ecclesiastical Problems of His Time' (unpublished Oxford University D.Phil. thesis, 1951), pp. 99, 114.

95. *Poems on Affairs of State: I 1660–1678*, ed. G. deF. Lord (New Haven and London, 1963), p. 299.

96. *RB*, III, 2.

in London that 'the mouths of the slanderous generation are wide enough open against those that are withdrawn, both of your profession and ours'. Sancroft was kept informed of the performance of the services and the sermons preached in the cathedral and the city. In July he was told services still enjoyed 'a reverential decency and a comely congregation'; in August numbers were dwindling, but prayers were still read thrice daily and Bishop Henchman had announced that those incumbents who did not return to their places would be ousted. Sancroft recognized the 'scarcity of priests to officiate', but communion was still celebrated at St Paul's, and a team of clerics took turns in reading prayers in the most stricken parish of all, St Giles Cripplegate.[97] When, in October, Matthew Griffith, the pluralist rector of St Mary Magdalen, Old Fish Street, died at his Oxfordshire living, the candidates to succeed him at St Mary's had all served in London during the plague. John Overing, for instance, had been Griffith's curate and had taken a turn at preaching in St Paul's.[98] 'I perceive,' wrote Thomas Holbeach of his own candidate, 'he hopes by adventuring himself in these perilous times to supply a place in London, when many left theirs unprovided, may capacitate him for the favour of those, in whose power it shall be to dispose of such vacancies as this sad visitation hath brought forth.'[99]

Of course, not all clerical service was so calculated. Simon Patrick, the rector of St Paul's, Covent Garden, remained with his parishioners, urging them to hate their sins more than the pestilence itself – 'I cannot tell what good we do their souls . . . but I am sure, while I stay here, I shall do good to their bodies, and perhaps save some from perishing, which I look upon as a considerable end of my continuing'. The letters which Patrick wrote at this time to his friend Mrs Gauden reveal both his own profound belief in the dispensations of providence and his occasional gentle cynicism about his fellow sinners. 'The more incurable this disease is, and beyond the account of men, the more are they directed to acknowledge a supreme power that chastizes men and corrects their disobedience.'[100] This same message, that divine providences were calling for the nation's moral regeneration, was relayed to a wider public through the sermons preached on the monthly fast day for the plague. The preachers argued (with dubious arithmetic) that for three years and

97. BL, MS Harleian 3785, fos 26, 19, 24; MS Tanner 145, fo. 106, replies at MS Harleian 3785, fos 27, 31.
98. BL, MS Harleian 3785, fos 27, 43, 47, 48.
99. BL, MS Harleian 3785, fo. 50; cf. fos 37, 81; MS Tanner 42, fo. 44.
100. Patrick, IX, 584–5.

one further year the Lord 'expected fruit of his barren fig tree', but the people had not forsaken their sins, and now it seemed that the Lord was about their uprooting.[101] It was never too late to repent, of course: Thomas Pierce believed that 'the pestilence is the best orator in the world, to speak the frailty and filthiness of human nature' and to prompt the repudiation of our 'crying sins'.[102]

However, as Richard Perrinchief observed, the miseries which used to come singly now fell upon the nation 'with as much speed as hasty messengers, one treading upon the heels of another; that we have had scarce time to survey the wastes which one hath made, ere another come to call for our tears and wonder'.[103] On 2 September 1666 fire laid waste 89 of London's parish churches and 13,000 houses. The three sixes in the date of the year had not been a good omen, and now the entire nation began to speculate about why God had allowed this further judgment to befall the metropolis:

> The Quakers say, it is for their persecution. The fanatics say it is for banishing and silencing their ministers. Others say, it is for the murder of the King and rebellion of the city. The clergy lay blame on schism and licentiousness, while the sectaries lay it on imposition and their pride. Thus do many pretend to determine the sin aimed at in this punishment.[104]

But most were agreed that 'Popish incendiaries' had set the fire, and a French watchmaker was executed for the crime, amid a frenzy of anti-Catholic anxiety, much of which centred on the debauchery and Catholicism rampant at the court.[105] For the churchmen, the fire, 'that horrid theatre of divine judgment', served primarily as a weapon in their rhetorical campaign to 'awaken our consciences, melt our hard hearts'. An order of service to acknowledge the fire was designed as 'a mixed confession of severe judgments and almost miraculous mercy'.[106] One Anglican author reviewed the self-delusion of the nation as it had disregarded each successive sign of divine wrath. Now with the fire, he suggested, 'God appears to avow

101. Richard Perrinchief, *A Sermon Preached . . . 7 November* (1666); Seth Ward, *Six Sermons* (1672), p. 392; Allestree, I, 148; Josselin, pp. 518, 521.
102. Thomas Pierce, *A Collection of Sermons upon Several Occasions* (Oxford, 1671), pp. 156–7.
103. Perrinchief, *Sermon . . . 7 November*, p. 48.
104. Quoted in M. McKeon, *Politics and Poetry In Restoration England – The Case of Dryden's 'Annus Mirabilis'* (Cambridge, Mass., 1975), p. 138.
105. Marvell, *Letters*, p. 42; Harris, *London Crowds*, pp. 78–9.
106. G. D'Oyly, *The Life of William Sancroft* (1821), II, 367; C. P., *Christian Devotion* (1679), p. 128; MS Tanner 45, fo. 101 (Henchman to Sancroft, 10 September 1666).

the enmity as openly as we have done': the loss of so many churches to the flames was 'a sad testimonial that our very religion was provoking'. Surely 'if this brings us not to sense we are like to sleep on to destruction'?[107] In private Sheldon hoped that the nation had learned its lesson, for he was impressed by the patience with which the citizens bore their loss, 'I presume from a general persuasion they had so well deserved it'.[108]

While the clergy struggled to bring their flocks to a true sense of their spiritual danger, the 'Clarendon Code' was failing to reduce the Dissenters to uniformity. The Conventicle Act was 'discretionary legislation par excellence', of limited lifespan and to be enforced as needed; like the Five Mile Act, it placed the burden of enforcement on the local gentry, and increasingly upon the single JP acting outside the Sessions or upon the borough court. This decentralization and the consequent lack of records has obscured the impact of the Clarendon Code at a local level. Of course, the Nonconformists held on to local office – despite the Corporation Act and the re-modelling of the Commissions of the Peace – and were a serious obstacle to the enforcement of the legislation.[109] Thus many of those charged with enforcing the penal laws were at best indifferent to the cause of uniformity and at worst active sympathizers with Non-conformity. For the first year of its life the Conventicle Act was probably enforced quite effectively, but as the fears of fanatic sedition began to fade, so too did enthusiasm for persecuting convent-iclers. In the later 1660s there was little effective prosecution of the Nonconformists and what there was, was heavily dependent upon the heroic efforts of one or two zealous JPs.[110] The churchmen were often near despair at the lack of cooperation from the lay magistracy. In 1666 Bishop Nicholson of Gloucester admitted that he was 'very

107. Richard Allestree, *The Causes of the Decay of Christian Piety* (1667), preface; cf. Stillingfleet, I, 4; Nathaniel Hardy, *Lamentation, Mourning and Woe* (1666), p. 8; Henry Killigrew, *A Sermon Preached before the King* (1666), p. 31.
108. MS Carte 45, fo. 200.
109. Coleby, *Central Government and Localities*, pp. 133–4; A. Fletcher, 'The Enforcement of the Conventicle Acts 1664–1679', *SCH*, 21 (1984), 236; A Fletcher, *Reform in the Provinces* (New Haven and London, 1986), pp. 19–20; G.C.F. Forster, 'Government in Provincial England under the Later Stuarts', *TRHS*, 33 (1983), 30–1; Jackson, 'Nonconformists in Devon', pp. 122–9; P.J. Norrey, 'The Restoration Regime in Action: The Relationship between Central and Local Government in Dorset, Somerset and Wiltshire, 1660–1678', *HJ*, 31 (1988), 805–6; P.J. Challinor, 'Restoration and Exclusion in the County of Cheshire', *Bulletin of the John Rylands Library*, 64 (1982), 363.
110. Hutton, *Restoration*, p. 208; Coleby, *Central Government and Localities*, p. 136; Fletcher, 'Enforcement'; C. Holmes, *Seventeenth-century Lincolnshire* (Lincoln, 1980), pp. 229–30.

much perplexed at the many impudent conventicles in every part of
this county, and the numbers that openly appear at them, and justify
their meetings to my face. They do it, and say they will do it.
Complaints have been made to Justices of Peace, but they will not be
heard, I have proceeded in my court against them, but that was so
far slighted'.[111] Sheldon had the governor of Dover Castle enforce
the Five Mile Act against 'a factious Nonconformist minister' in the
town.[112] The civil courts, the JPs, the Quarter Sessions and the
Assizes had increasingly taken over responsibility from the church
courts for enforcing uniformity. The church courts could and did
proceed against Nonconformists, but as Bishop Nicholson found, the
ecclesiastical authorities lacked the muscle to enforce attendance or
obedience.

Although 1666 had been 'a year of nothing but prodigies in this
nation: plague, war, fire, rains, tempest, comets', and rebellion in
Scotland, God's quiver was not yet empty.[113] As the bitterly cold
spring of 1667 gave way to a summer of drought, the regime and
even the nation approached the nadir of their fortunes. These 'sad
and troublesome times' were capped by the national humilation
of the burning of the English fleet at anchor in the Medway, and
the capture of its flagship, the *Royal Charles*. As the Dutch fleet
blockaded the Thames, and ready money disappeared, the government disintegrated into mutual recrimination. In desperation,
Clarendon was heard to talk of forced loans and billeting, and even
began to make overtures to the Dissenters. But, in the nick of time,
other courses were taken, Parliament was recalled, a hasty peace
made, and the jackals began to circle the stricken Chancellor.
Although their relations with Clarendon were already strained,
the bishops had been too closely associated with him not to suffer
by his fall. Ormonde was shocked by Sheldon's attitude towards
Clarendon: 'I wish him innocent,' wrote the archbishop, 'but if he
proves guilty, let him suffer, I am sure we owe that confusion we are
in, to his ill management of our affairs and of himself . . . God knows
for these divers years I have had little reason to be fond of him'.[114]

Charles II was now free to follow more daring policies. Rumours
circulated through the winter of 1667–8 that some form of liberty
would be extended to the Nonconformists. Negotiations were undertaken, hints were dropped in public, the King's speech to Parliament

111. MS Add. C 302, fo. 71.
112. MS Add. C 308, fo. 66; cf. Challinor, 'Restoration in Cheshire', 362–3.
113. Evelyn, III, 477. Reflecting on these evil times, Pepys's cousin opined that
      'nothing but a union of religious interests will ever settle us'; Pepys, VIII, 305.
114. MS Carte 45, fo. 232; also see fos 228, 230; Seaward, *Cavalier Parliament*,
      pp. 318–19; Harris, *London Crowds*, pp. 81–2.

spoke of religious 'union and composure', bills were prepared, but nothing was ever brought before Parliament.[115] Although this hesitation may have been based on a correct reading of parliamentary opinion, it is plain that the Nonconformists enjoyed a degree of sympathy among Londoners and that their episcopal opponents were not popular. Throughout the rest of 1668 and into 1669 – 'these not very happy times,' as one churchman described them – the Nonconformists continued to meet openly, and even to build meeting houses, apparently sharing the widespread assumption that they enjoyed royal favour and would not be punished.[116] The churchmen were despondent. 'The misfortunes of the church which you complain of are not peculiar to your town, but too universal throughout the whole kingdom,' wrote Sheldon to a concerned correspondent in Ipswich,

> And such things are not to be wondered at wherever there wants power and zeal in the magistrates and justices to do their duty. How heavily so ever the storm seems to threaten, I have hope yet it may not fall so fatally, as the enemies of the church desire, and that after a while we may see better order among us. But however let us do our duty in our several places and learn patience by what we have formerly suffered.[117]

Sheldon himself was out of favour at court. In July 1670 he had to tell one suitor for the deanery of Norwich that his 'advice is seldom asked of late in any promotions'.[118] He and his fellow bishops had been compelled to endure the appointment of the detested John Wilkins, a promoter of comprehension in 1668 and a protégé of the Duke of Buckingham, to the see of Chester.[119] A further blow to the church was the loss in Parliament of the intended successor to the 1664 Conventicle Act. Nor did anything come of the various schemes for reforming the church courts and improving clerical stipends which were drawn up by Sheldon and Sir Leoline Jenkins in the hope of diverting the criticisms of the pro-comprehension lobby.[120]

In the spring of 1669, however, the government began to adopt a tougher policy towards Nonconformity. The Conventicle Act had

115. Spurr, 'Comprehension', 933–4; Marvell, *Letters*, p. 69; MS Tanner 45, fos 249, 272, 276; *CSPD 1667*, p. 437; Heywood, pp. 200–1; Bate, *Indulgence*, p. 61.
116. MS Tanner 44, fo. 15; Keeble, *Literary Culture*, pp. 72–3.
117. MS Add. C 308, fo. 130.
118. MS Tanner 44, fo. 215.
119. Beddard, 'Sheldon', 1011; MS Tanner 44, fos 37, 196, 161; Evelyn, III, 517–18. In 1669, however, the more acceptable Bishop Isaac Barrow of Sodor went to St Asaph and William Sancroft was offered, but declined, Chicester.
120. See pp. 193–4, 217–19 below.

lapsed on 1 March, and the King and his councillors were receiving disturbing reports of Nonconformist arrogance. 'I always said that the insolencies of the sectaries would prove to our advantage', crowed Bishop Henchman of London, on the news in April of an order to the Lord-Lieutenants to act against conventicles.[121] On 8 June Sheldon sent Henchman a letter for distribution to the other bishops in which he reminded him of the King's recent criticism of conventicles and his 'expressing an indignation against all the reports of him as if he either favoured or connived at them'. 'After he had laid some blame on the bishops for want of care in this affair', continued Sheldon, the King had promised the assistance of the civil authority in the suppression of conventicles and the investigation of any justice who neglected the King's service. Sheldon called upon his bishops to play their part by enquiring into the number of conventicles, the number and status of those who attended, and the names of their pastors. Finally, he exhorted them to prosecute all Dissenters and to squash their false 'hopes of immunity'.[122] On 16 July a royal proclamation demanded the prosecution of conventicles and reminded the nation that the Five Mile Act was still in force.

But Sheldon did not let down his guard. He was justifiably suspicious of the King, who had issued this proclamation, and rightly pessimistic about its likely effect given the 'unreliability' of the lesser magistrates.[123] In August, writing about the prosecution of Dissent and the Act of Uniformity, he commented,

> those who should assist the laws, and help us in our duty, have already upon that very Act, declared the meaning of it, to the destroying the law it self. And when there shall be occasion again, may again do the same, as well as they have before. So that unless the Parliament when they meet will give us better remedies, we must (I think) yield up the cudgels.[124]

The churchmen went off to Parliament in October hoping, as did Bishop Hacket, 'to concur in some strict Act against Nonconformists and conventiclers'.[125] To stiffen Parliament's resolve against 'toleration', the church launched a pamphlet campaign – although the virulence of these tracts, especially Samuel Parker's *Discourse of*

121. MS Tanner 44, fo. 101. Also see R. Hutton, 'The Making of the Secret Treaty of Dover, 1668–1670', *HJ*, 29 (1986), 315–16.
122. *Concilia*, IV, 588; BL, MS Add. 34769, fo. 70.
123. The effects of the proclamation in the provinces were short-lived, see Bishop Hacket's letters, MS Tanner 44, fos 108, 121, 125, 127, 140; Coleby, *Central Government and Localities*, pp. 136–7.
124. BL, MS Harleian 7377, fo. 4v.
125. MS Tanner 44, fo. 149.

Ecclesiastical Politie, almost backfired on the church.[126] At home in Lichfield for Christmas 1669, Bishop Hacket prayed that 'God confirm our great and royal master in noble and firm resolutions to execute strict laws against Nonconformists. There is no other course to be taken with such turbulent people to preserve the peace, nay the being of kingdom as well as church.'[127] His prayer was answered in the shape of the second Conventicle Act, the 'quintessence of arbitrary malice', in Marvell's famous phrase, which after a difficult passage through Parliament became law on 12 April 1670. It 'is a good bill and is perpetual,' reported Sir Henry Yelverton. 'When the King passed it the House of Commons gave such a hum as was not very acceptable to divers sectaries that heard it.'[128] From the Anglican point of view, the Act did remedy the defects of its predecessor. It increased the penalties facing the Nonconformist minister and reduced those for his congregation; it made conviction easier, by allowing a single justice to convict; and it introduced a £5 fine for constables and churchwardens who did not present and a £100 fine for justices who did not prosecute. The King also inserted a proviso reasserting his inherent rights in ecclesiastical affairs – a clause which left him (and his successor) the loophole of dispensing with the Act in individual cases. The Act may have been the price of money bills. This session of Parliament also considered a bill to prevent Roman Catholics from holding office which closely foreshadows the 1673 Test Act.[129] The bill for the divorce of Lord Roos, which may have been a kite for a royal divorce, was vehemently opposed by the bishops in the Lords – except that, as usual, the pusillanimous Bishop Wilkins let the church down.[130]

For all the talk of Moses and Aaron, ministry and magistracy, alliance of altar and sword, the Church of England did not enjoy the committed support of the governors of England in the 1660s.

---

126. See R. Ashcraft, *Revolutionary Politics and Locke's 'Two Treatises of Government'* (Princeton, 1986), pp. 43–4; Andrew Marvell, *The Rehearsal Transpros'd* (1672; ed. D.I.B. Smith, Oxford, 1971). For Sheldon's role see Whiting, *Studies*, p. 502. Other tracts published to coincide with this session of Parliament include an enlarged edition of Roger L'Estrange's *Toleration Discussed* (1670) and William Assheton's *Toleration Disapprov'd and Condemn'd* (Oxford, 1670). Professor Ashcraft's suggestion (pp. 23–4, 41–74) that Parker's tract set the agenda is unconvincing; cf. Sheldon's view of 1663, quoted above p. 47.
127. MS Tanner 44, fo. 183.
128. MS Eng Letters C 210, fo. 181. Also see Fletcher, 'Enforcement', 236–7; Burnet, I, 489–94; MS Tanner 44, fo. 196.
129. D.T. Witcombe, *Charles II and the Cavalier House of Commons 1663–74* (Manchester, 1966), pp. 120–3.
130. MS Eng Letters C 210, fo. 141; MS Tanner 44, fo. 196; see Burnet, I, 493–4, for Wilkins's opposition to the second Conventicle Act.

Her leaders had wed the church to a policy of maintaining her monopoly through persecution. The political adroitness of the hierarchy supplied the legislation; but the church did not have the means nor always the will to put it into effect. She depended upon Moses. Prosecution fluctuated: at different times it was inspired by local initiative and instructions from the centre. A large proportion of the English gentry had no stomach for enforcing uniformity by means of the Clarendon Code.[131] Those who had the stomach were zealots like Thoroton in Nottinghamshire, Daniel Fleming in Westmorland, or Sir Henry Yelverton in Northamptonshire.[132] Yelverton exulted in the strictness of the Act of Uniformity, and told the incumbent of a living to which he held the presentation, that

> I should choose rather to present him than anybody else; yet I cannot in conscience do it unless he be conformable and doth it out of conscience, not to keep the living. Now I count not him a conformable person, that reads the Book of Prayer by patches, but doth use it all, and that out of a conviction, that it is most advantagious to the people, since those that govern in the church, and understand what is best for people enjoin it. I look upon my self as somewhat concerned in the good of that people, and I am sensible of how much they have been torn in pieces by deceitfull men, and am resolved to do my utmost to reduce them to principles of sobriety.[133]

Yelverton bombarded Sheldon with complaints of 'the extreme negligence that reigns here' – the fanatic schoolmasters, the unchecked conventicles, the partially conforming clergy, the insufficent curates – 'as for the Act of Uniformity I know not who regards it'. Sir Henry blamed Northamptonshire's trouble on the attitude of Bishop Henshaw of Peterborough.[134] Matters came to a head when Yelverton ejected Mr Wells, the schoolteacher of Wellingborough, in April 1669. Yelverton complained that Henshaw had licensed this ignorant fanatic and that he had then written 'in a very lofty style, not as if he had been Bishop of Peterborough and might want the assistance of gentlemen, but as if he had been the Pope himself, taxing us in effect for fools that we meddled'.[135] Henshaw, however, believed

131. Seaward, *Cavalier Parliament*, pp. 59–61; Coleby, *Central Government and Localities*, pp. 138–9; Forster, 'Government', 32–3.
132. Fletcher, 'Enforcement', 244; Coleby, *Central Government and Localities*, p. 139; Jackson, 'Nonconformists in Devon', pp. 130–5.
133. MS Eng Letters C 210, fo. 62 and fos 70, 74.
134. MS Add. C 302, fos 221–2.

that Sir Henry had been misled by his 'great friend and favourite', Archdeacon Palmer – in fact, as Henshaw told Sheldon, Wells had conformed before being licensed. 'My Lord, our business is to bring over as many of these Nonconformists to the Church of England as we can, but if after they have renounced their Nonconformity they shall be discountenanced because they were once Nonconformists, it will very much discourage others.'[136] Dealing with Dissent required fine judgement. Churchmen continually found themselves between Scylla and Charybdis, between the excessive zeal of their own fanatical supporters and the negligence or manipulation of their own Supreme Governor. But the King was just about to spring his greatest surprise yet on the Church of England.

New Opportunities and Old Enemies, 1672–81

The Declaration of Indulgence issued by the King on 15 March 1672 suspended 'the execution of all and all manner of penal laws in matters ecclesiastical, against whatsover sorts of nonconformists or recusants'. Nonconformists were allowed freedom of public worship if their ministers and meeting places were licensed, and Roman Catholics were allowed to worship in private; meanwhile the Church of England 'as now it stands established by law' was to be preserved as 'the basis, rule and standard of the general and public worship of God'.[137] This reversal of the religious policy of a decade was sprung on an unsuspecting nation. 'Many thoughts of heart there were about it, and various; we being surprized with it', wrote Henry Newcome on 19 March.[138] Not that the dilemma posed for Presbyterians like Newcome was unforeseen. Since the Five Mile Act they had been debating whether their future lay in eventual reunion with the established church or in accepting the status of a sect – debates which the government was aware of and which it was ready to exploit.[139] The argument, which tended to divide the older generation from the younger, was not just strategic, but ecclesiological: it hinged upon the legitimacy of a congregationalist church and the

---

135. Ibid., fos 206, 211, 217–220.
136. Ibid., fo. 213. Also see evidence of Sheldon's attitude in MS Add. C 308, fos 29, 76, 79, 80.
137. Bate, *Indulgence*, pp. 76–8.
138. Newcome, *Autobiography*, p. 199.
139. *CSPD 1671*, p. 496; *CSPD 1671–2*, pp. 27–9; R. Thomas, 'Comprehension and Indulgence', in *From Uniformity to Unity*, ed. G.F. Nuttall and O. Chadwick (1962), pp. 204–5.

implications of past conformity for those who now separated to form a sect. Older Presbyterians remembered the success that they had had as parish ministers in the 1650s and prized their 'principles of anti-separation'. Philip Henry feared lest 'the allowing of separate places help to overthrow our parish-order, which God hath owned, and to beget divisons and animosities among us'.[140] Anglican apologists were quick to play upon this fear, claiming that the issue was simply whether the Nonconformists might take advantage of the Indulgence 'to deny or rebate their communion with our parochial congregations and to gather themselves into distinct and separate churches?' In reply, the moderate Nonconformist had to acknowledge that if he recognized parish churches as true churches and aspired to reunion with them, then to take out a licence under the Indulgence would appear to be a schism.[141] Equally troubling for Dissenters were the suspicions that the Declaration was unconstitutional – the 1663 Parliament had already denied the King's power to use his prerogative to suspend the laws of the land – and that it was intended to help the papists. Oliver Heywood found it a 'cause of grief that papists and atheists enjoy so much liberty' under the Declaration.[142] Whatever their misgivings, many of these moderates seized the chance to exercise their ministry – although they took care to ensure that their congregations were loyal in politics 'and not rigid or schismatical in their separation, but willing to attend ... upon those administrations which they found most lively and edifying, and most helpful to them, in the great business of working out their salvation'.[143] Other Nonconformists, including the Independents and Baptists, had no qualms about separating from the parish and eagerly applied for a licence. In all, between 1,400 and 1,600 licences were issued.[144] The inevitable result was to give a sharper definition to Nonconformity, to encourage the *rapprochement* of Presbyterian and congregationalist wings, and to give a fillip to the Nonconformist ministry which had been declining in numbers during the preceding decade.[145] After the Declaration of Indulgence,

---

140. See Heywood, p. 224; *Life of Philip Henry*, p. 125.
141. Francis Fullwood, *Toleration Not to be Abused* (1672), title-page and pp. 8–9; Richard Baxter, *Sacrilegious Desertion of the Holy Ministry Rebuked* (1672); *RB*, III, 99–100. Also see Whiting, *Studies*, p. 61; South, II, 161–81.
142. Heywood, p. 224.
143. *Life of Philip Henry*, pp. 132–3; Heywood, pp. 228–37; Newcome, *Autobiography*, p. 200.
144. For the figures see Bate, *Indulgence*, p. 98; *CR*, p. xv; Watts, *Dissenters*, p. 248.
145. Watts, *Dissenters*, p. 243; Heywood, pp. 238–9; Nuttall, 'First Nonconformists', p. 205. A.G. Matthews suggests an active Nonconformist ministry of 1,200 in the 1660s; *CR*, p. xv. Also see Jackson, 'Nonconformists in Devon', p. 55; Heywood, pp. 244–5.

contemporaries were convinced that the Dissenters would never again be brought to heel.[146]

The Indulgence of 1672 was 'to the extreme weakening [of] the Church of England'. It 'hath made the church empty,' wailed the rector of Somerford Magna. 'I warn communion and none appears and often times [I] read prayers to the walls'. Bishop Sparrow of Exeter felt helpless: 'I see daily to my heart's grief the poor sheep committed to my trust snatched out of the fold by cunning wolves, and I know not how to bring them back', he wrote to Sheldon.[147] The fluidity of religious allegiance during the 1660s, and the indiscriminate attendance of both the church and Nonconformist meetings, was now exposed. Parishioners who had been lukewarm conformists or 'neutralists between Presbyterians and conformists' threw off the trammels and set up 'prayers, preaching and sacraments apart' from the parish church.[148] Elsewhere, however, the imprecise and obscure boundaries of the established church might have helped to stave off the attractions of separation. The Cambridgeshire parishioners of the puritanical vicar, Isaac Archer, were apparently happy enough with his loose conformity, since Archer recorded of the Indulgence, 'with us it signified nothing, for none forsook the public' worship; while Ralph Josselin in Essex simply noted the Indulgence without reference to any local effects.[149] This latest royal betrayal seemed to break the nerve of some bishops. Bishop Fuller meekly enquired whether he still had the power to prosecute unlicensed Dissenters. An exasperated Sheldon assured him that he had, but advised that there was little time to achieve anything before Parliament met: 'what can be done to heal that sore we shall be able to give some guess when our Parliament meets', wrote the archbishop, and he sought to mobilise 'all the force we can' for 'so critical' a session.[150]

Parliament assembled in February 1673, with Charles's plans all in ruins. He was strapped for cash, the war against the Netherlands had gone badly, and he had been left high and dry by his French ally. There could be little hope of saving his religious toleration. In March, after a frosty exchange of messages with his Parliament, the

146. Sir John Reresby, *Memoirs*, ed. A. Browning (Glasgow, 1936), pp. 84–5.
147. Evelyn, III, 328; D.A. Spaeth, 'Parsons and Parishioners: Lay–Clerical Conflict and Popular Piety in Wiltshire Villages, 1660–1740' (unpublished Brown University Ph.D. thesis, 1985), p. 34. Also see Wood, II, 244; MS Tanner 44, fo. 183; Watts, *Dissenters*, p. 249.
148. See Spurr, 'Schism', 408–10; Evelyn, IV, 39.
149. CUL, MS Add. 8499, fo. 161; Josselin, p. 562.
150. MS Tanner 43, fo. 11; BL, MS Harleian 7377, fos 38, 37, 39.

King cancelled the Declaration of Indulgence.[151] The demise of the Indulgence 'made many rejoice', observed Isaac Archer, and although it had had no effect in his own parish, 'if 'twas dangerous as to the growth of Popery, I am glad 'tis at end, though I could wish indulgence to sober, and peaceable, men. Twas because of a war with Holland that 'twas granted; and as the King said, it kept peace at home. What the limitations will be I know not, but something is promised by the Parliament, by way of comprehension'.[152] It was the unconstitutional nature of the Indulgence which most upset Parliament, and so 'to let him see that we did not dislike the matter of his declaration but the manner, and did not doubt the prudence, but only the legality of it', MPs began to draw up a bill 'for the ease of dissenters'.[153] In their eyes, the beauty of this bill was that, while it respected the constitutional proprieties, it did not pander to the papists. It was proposed to remove the penal laws from the Nonconformists and to offer terms which would allow the 'comprehension' or reunion of ministers who differed from the church 'only in some circumstance, or ceremonial point'.[154] The Anglican MP Sir Edward Dering 'did not like the bill as thinking it a very great blow to the Church of England, and not easy to be recovered', but the House had gone too far to draw back, and so although many others shared Dering's doubts, 'it passed with little opposition, and as little approbation'.[155] The bill went up to the Lords and was handed over to a committee, which included Bishops Ward, Dolben, Crew, Mews and Pearson, where it was still under discussion at the adjournment of Parliament. The loss of the bill was greeted with delight by Sheldon, Morley and Sterne.[156]

It was apparent to all that the years 1672–3 were a watershed. The Cavalier sentiment that had been nurtured and exploited so well by Sheldon in the 1660s began to wane. We had 'lived in peace, plenty and happiness' for a decade, commented Dering, 'but this blessing was too great to be continued long to those who deserved it so ill as we, and then the nation began to think that the court inclined to favour popery and France'.[157] Fear of popery, France and

---

151. See Bate, *Indulgence*, ch. 6; Witcombe, *Charles II and Cavalier Commons*, pp. 128–36.
152. CUL, MS Add. 8499, fo. 161.
153. Sir Edward Dering, *Diary* (1940), p. 145. Also see MS Rawlinson Letters 50, fo. 103; Newcome, *Autobiography*, p. 204.
154. Spurr, 'Comprehension', 935.
155. Dering, *Diary* (1940), p. 145 (19 March). For more enthusiastic support, see Bate, *Indulgence*, pp. 126–7.
156. MS Tanner 43, fos 189–194 is a draft of the bill. For episcopal reaction, see MS Tanner 42, fos 7, 46; BL, MS Harleian 7377, fo. 44.
157. Sir Edward Dering, *Diaries* (1976), pp. 125–6.

arbitrary government was beginning to replace fear of Dissent and sedition as the ruling anxiety of the gentlemen who ran the counties and crowded on to the back benches of the Commons. The anti-popish reflexes of seventeenth-century English Protestants were well developed: when the Indulgence was withdrawn, Oliver Heywood, who had taken out a licence as a Nonconformist preacher, pro-claimed this a 'rich mercy' because it meant that papists would now be prosecuted once more.[158] The paradox of this 'anti-popery' was that the English Catholicism was quiescent. The Roman Catholic community was introspective, gentry dominated and politically loyal, its numbers remained stable at about 60,000, and the mission which served it was only just beginning to revive under the influence of the secular clergy. These were the inescapable facts of parish life.[159] Yet to Restoration Englishmen popery was a many-headed beast. In the popular imagination, 'popery' conjured up lurid visions of bloody risings and the massacre of Protestants, and was often only dimly associated with the local recusant family. The popish plots, real and imagined, which punctuated the seventeenth century, were based on the Jesuit 'statecraft' that permitted, in the name of religion, cities to be fired, monarchs deposed and murdered, and subjects absolved of their allegiance. So subtle were the papists, who 'take all shapes upon them, and all disguises, of Agitator, Ranters, Levellers and Quakers', that they had made the Protestant sects their Trojan horse. Now that the 'puritan' revolution had failed, they hoped to win freedom for themselves through the toleration of Dissent. 'Tush (say the popelings) let us level this, the mushroom sectaries will either fall in the ruins of it, or else into our hands.' Robert South was not alone in deciding that 'puritanism ... is only reformed Jesuitism, as Jesuitism is nothing else but popish puritanism'.[160]

The year 1673 saw the greatest outburst of anti-popery since the early 1640s. This was a consequence of, first, the suspicions raised about royal intentions by the Declaration and the alliance with

---

158. Heywood, p. 250.

159. See *RB*, III, 25; MS Tanner 39, fo. 114; *Episcopal Visitation Returns for Cambridgeshire*, ed. W.M. Palmer (Cambridge, 1930), p. 78; Holmes, *Lincolnshire*, pp. 39–41; J. Bossy, *The English Catholic Community 1570–1850* (1976). On the revival among secular clergy see E. Duffy, 'Peter and Jack: Roman Catholics and Dissent in Eighteenth-century England' (Friends of Dr Williams's Library Lecture, 1982); E. Duffy, 'The English Secular Clergy and the Counter-Reformation', *JEH*, 34 (1983); on the regular clergy see D. Lunn, *The English Benedictines 1540–1688* (1980).

160. George Stradling, *Sermons* (1692), pp. 383, 393; John Shaw, *No Reformation* (1685), pp. 9–10; South, III, 189.

Catholic France, and second, the dawning public realization that James, Duke of York, brother to the King and heir to the throne, was a Catholic. The Duke had been a covert Catholic since 1670; but in 1673, 'to the amazement of every body', he failed to make his Easter communion in the Church of England, and then in June he resigned his office as Lord Admiral rather than take the 'test' stipulated by the recent Test Act.[161] Under this statute all office-holders were required to receive the sacrament in the Church of England and to declare against the Roman Catholic doctrine of transubstantiation. Popery became the dominant issue of English politics. On the instructions of the bishops 'Popery was every where preached against, and the authority of the laws much magnified'.[162] Partly in response to parliamentary pressure, Charles ordered the enforcement of the penal laws against Roman Catholic laymen and priests throughout 1674 and 1675. Although much of this prosecution was merely token, some Catholics began to suffer harassment, particularly in those regions where they were numerous or where Catholic aristocrats held sway.[163] Catholic houses were searched for arms and reports of papist assemblies investigated. In London especially, the fear of popery was fanned into a central theme of popular politics by the preachers, by pope-burnings, and by the Green Ribbon club.[164] The country was alive with rumour. In November 1675, a French Jesuit, de Luzancy, who had converted to Protestantism and taken refuge in England, complained that the Duchess of York's Jesuit confessor, St Germain, had threatened his life. Whatever the truth of his allegations, they confirmed existing prejudices that the royal court and the Society of Jesus were at the heart of sinister designs to subvert the English state and church.[165]

Some Protestant gentlemen even began to wonder whether, in view of the mounting threat from popery, it was wise to persecute fellow Protestants rather than try to woo them back to the church.[166]

161. In September 1673 James married a Catholic princess, Mary of Modena. See Evelyn, IV, 7; Bate, *Indulgence*, p. 128; Miller, *Popery and Politics*, pp. 55–6, 125; Witcombe, *Charles II and Cavalier Commons*, pp. 134–7.
162. Burnet, I, 555.
163. For accounts of this persecution see Miller, *Popery and Politics*, pp. 132–3; Coleby, *Central Government and Localities*, p. 138; Challinor, 'Restoration in Cheshire', 383; P. Jenkins, 'Anti-popery on the Welsh Marches in the Seventeenth Century', *HJ*, 23 (1980), 282; Jenkins, *The Making of a Ruling Class – The Glamorgan Gentry 1640–1790* (Cambridge, 1983), pp. 121–4, 126–7; R. Clifton, *The Last Popular Rebellion – The Western Rising of 1685* (1984), pp. 56–7.
164. Harris, *London Crowds*, pp. 92–4.
165. Marvell, *Letters*, p. 171; Kennett, p. 307; J. Stoughton, *History of Religion in England* (1881), IV, 446–7; J.P. Kenyon, *The Popish Plot* (1972; Harmondsworth, 1984), pp. 21–2.
166. Fletcher, 'Enforcement', 236–7; Witcombe, *Charles II and Cavalier Commons*, p. 134.

These doubts were as yet only straws in the wind; they did not amount, either in Parliament or the shires, to a change of heart towards Dissent. The prosecution of Dissent was resumed, but once again it depended heavily upon the enthusiasm of local JPs, on zealots like Dr Thoroton in Nottinghamshire or Edmund Bohun in Suffolk. Often only the presence of the bishop or a zealous arch-deacon like Denis Granville on the bench, or even the encourage-ment of a local parson, could ensure efficient prosecution of Dissent. Although the Declaration had been withdrawn, the licences issued under it were not recalled until 1675; most prosecution was under the 1670 Conventicle Act with its detested informers.[167] While wild rumours of another Indulgence circulated among Dissenters, the bishops gleefully reported the collapse of conventicles under the strict enforcement of the law, leaving 'religion on tiptoes', as Newcome put it. The persecution gave rise to seditious talk, to mutterings against bishops and parliaments, but it neither sup-pressed Dissent nor drove Dissenters into rebellion; it simply inten-sified the religious divisions within English society.

Charles II began to shift his ground in the light of his humiliation in 1673. He cast around for new ministers and new options – by the end of 1673, the Cabal ministers, including Lord Chancellor Shaftesbury, were out of power and the Earl of Danby was moving towards the centre of the political stage.[168] Danby believed that while the present Parliament wanted the execution of laws against both Nonconformists and Roman Catholics, a new Parliament would demand the comprehension or toleration of all Protestants. Cal-culating how best to manage the King's business in Parliament, which was mainly raising money, Danby decided 'to keep up Parliament, to raise the old cavaliers and the church party and to sacrifice papists and presbyterians'.[169] He ruthlessly undermined the rival policy of the Duke of York, who was busy courting the Nonconformists. Danby's allies, the bishops, went through the charade of discussing terms of comprehension with Baxter and others, and even moving bills in Parliament, in order to divide 'the

---

167. The rest of this paragraph draws on Fletcher, 'Enforcement', 240–3; Harris, *London Crowds*, pp. 72–6; Holmes, *Lincolnshire*, pp. 228–30, 232–4; Jackson, 'Nonconformists in Devon', pp. 135, 138, 245, 251–308; Norrey, 'Restoration Regime', 803, 808; Miller, *Popery and Politics*, pp. 118–19; Granville, II, 13–14; Josselin, p. 584; MS Tanner 42, fos 119, 137, 167; Bate, *Indulgence*, ch. 8; Newcome, *Autobiography*, p. 207; Coleby, *Central Government and Localities*, pp. 137–8; Stoughton, *History*, IV, 421–2; Watts, *Dissenters*, pp. 249–50.

168. Sir Thomas Osborne became Lord Treasurer in October 1673 and was created Earl of Danby in May 1674.

169. A. Browning, *Thomas Osborne, Earl of Danby* (Glasgow, 1944–51), II, 63; *The Essex Correspondence*, ed. C.E. Pike (Camden Society, 24, 1913), p. 1.

Presbyterians from the rest of the sectaries' and so weaken York's Nonconformist dependants.[170] Several of the bishops also met in conference at London in October 1674 to advise the King on the dangers facing the church.

Here at last was the prospect of real political power if only the church would grasp it; Danby's ministry offered the church the chance to give substance to the shadowy Anglican ascendancy. Not that at the time it was perceived as an opportunity to build a confessional state, for the churchmen could see only the dangers facing the church – from factious Dissent, from subversive popery, and above all from irreligion. The bishops told the King that despite all efforts

> atheism and profaneness daily abound more and more, and defections are frequently made on the one side to the superstitious and idolatrous practices and usurpations of Rome, on the other to the pernicious and destructive novelties of the various sects raised in the worst of times . . . nothing is more necessary than the suppressing of atheism, profaneness and open and professed wickedness without the amendment or punishment of which nothing can avail to the preservation of a church which God has threatened for such sins, unrepented and unpunished, to destroy.[171]

The war against profanity and godlessness took precedence over all else, even the threat from popery. Anglican clergymen from Ralph Josselin, who barely conformed, to Denis Granville, the High Church Dean of Durham, agreed that 'licentiousness [was] like to be our ruin. i. cause of sects. ii. cause of atheism'.[172] The vicar of West Ham believed that London had sunk to the level of another Amsterdam, a city of all religions and none; and an address to Parliament in 1675 demanded the urgent suppression of 'men that set their mouth against heaven, and with a masterful impudence affirm that there is none to behold or judge them'.[173] At one level this great surge of Anglican anxiety about atheism and profanity was a reaction to the lingering effects of the 1672 Indulgence, which had compromised the church's ideal of national religious uniformity, but at another level it was a reaction to the cult of 'wit', of intellectual scepticism and fashionable scoffing at religion, which seemed so

---

170. For details see Spurr, 'Comprehension', 935–6; Thomas, 'Comprehension and Indulgence', p. 219.
171. *CSPD 1673–5*, p. 549. Also see Browning, *Danby*, II, 54–5; I, 147; J.R. Jones, *Charles II – Royal Politician* (1987), pp. 116–17.
172. Granville, II, 12; cf. Josselin, pp. 558, 562.
173. Richard Hollingworth, *A Modest Plea for the Church of England* (1676), sig. b2; *The Voice of the Nation* (1675).

prevalent in the later 1660s and the 1670s. A succession of best-selling pamphlets deriding the clergy or advancing 'rationalist' criticism of the church and her intolerance had thrown the churchmen on the defensive. The embattled Church of England drew up her own political agenda which, in alliance with Danby, she would come near to achieving.

At the beginning of 1675 the alliance of church and minister was proclaimed by several symbolic actions. The rebuilding of St Paul's Cathedral was taken in hand; a brass statue of Charles I was erected at Charing Cross; and it was proposed, and not for the last time, that the body of the Martyr King should be 'reinterred with great magnificence'. But all this 'pageantry', as Marvell called it, was window-dressing; 'principally the laws were to be severely executed, and reinforced, against fanatics and papists'.[174] In April Danby introduced into the Lords a bill reviving the proposal of 1665 that members of Parliament and office-holders should declare resistance to the King unlawful and swear not to 'endeavour' any alteration of the government in church or state. The aim was to 'institutionalize and perpetuate' both the alliance of church and court and the sitting Cavalier Parliament. Charles and Danby fought hard for the Test and only a jurisdictional dispute between the two Houses prevented its enactment.[175] Here then was proof, if it was needed, that Charles was attempting to base his regime upon the narrow interest of Cavalier churchmen and that the court was beginning to look upon Parliament as a tool to be managed for more effective government rather than as a forum for independent debate. A substantial number of MPs deplored this 'corruption' of Parliament and the growing authoritarianism of the government and its supporters. In the Commons, Henry Powle spoke scathingly of 'the convention at Lambeth, and . . . a few lords and bishops advising that which the Parliament never yet desired and which in very truth was plain persecution'. The Earl of Shaftesbury took up this conspiracy theory as a means of harnessing 'Country' disaffection to his attack on Danby. In his *Letter from a Person of Quality*, Shaftesbury blamed the 'high episcopal men and cavaliers' for a deep-laid plot to establish absolute government, a standing army, and immutable *iure divino* episcopacy. He took particular exception to those dignified divines

174. Browning, *Danby*, I, 149; Marvell, *Letters*, pp. 341–3; D.R. Lacey, *Dissent and Parliamentary Politics in England 1661–1689* (New Brunswick, N.J., 1969), pp. 71–2; *Concilia*, IV, 595; Jones, *Charles II*, pp. 117–18; R.A. Beddard, 'Wren's Mausoleum for Charles I and the Cult of the Royal Martyr', *Architectural History*, 27 (1984).

175. Jones, *Charles II*, pp. 117–18; Browning, *Danby*, I, 152–5; HMC, 9th Report, pt. 2, appendix, p. 51; cf. Witcombe, *Charles II and Cavalier Commons*, pp. 92, 94–5.

who advanced the Laudian notion of divine right monarchy: 'I am sure they are the most dangerous sort of men alive to our English government'. Elsewhere, he asserted that the bishops 'neither are nor can be otherwise than creatures to prerogative, for all their promotions, dignities, and domination depends upon it'. And the attacks were carried into Parliament; as Marvell observed, 'never were poor men exposed and abused all the session as the bishops were by the Duke of Buckingham'.[176] The cost of the church's alliance with Danby and his master was that her bishops too were now tarred with promoting 'popery' and arbitrary government.

As it was plain that neither the Test nor supply would be forthcoming, Parliament was prorogued on 9 June until October. The new hard line taken by the court, and the strength of opposition, led to careful preparations by both sides for the next session. In pursuit of his campaign against Danby and for a fresh Parliament, Shaftesbury published his *Letter* and began to muster his forces. Foremost among his allies were the Dissenters, who had been taught the need for greater political involvement by the fate of the Indulgence and by the signs that any reunion with the Church of England was fast becoming impossible. The church's leaders had thrown in their lot with Danby, and her younger theologians were also travelling away from Dissent – the 1674–5 controversy over William Sherlock's views on salvation had brought it home to many that the church and Dissent were no longer agreed on fundamental doctrines. Nonconformity was eager to demonstrate that in the past Dissenters had sympathizers even among the churchmen and bishops, 'and the reason they have had no more friends, has certainly been a misrepresentation of them to the world as seditious and turbulent persons, enemies to Caesar and all good government and order in church and state'.[177] There was an awareness on all sides that the middle ground between church and Dissent was slowly disappearing; but this only spurred the moderates and conciliators to greater efforts.

For the parliamentary session of October 1675, the indefatigable John Humfrey prepared *The Peaceable Design*, a tract which explained the Dissenters' scruples about conformity and sketched bills for comprehension and toleration. Humfrey's plea received support from a most unexpected quarter, a bishop of the church. The maverick Bishop Herbert Croft of Hereford intended his anonymous pamphlet

176.   Browning, *Danby*, I, 152–3; [Anthony Ashley Cooper, 1st Earl of Shaftesbury], *A Letter from a Person of Quality* (1675), p. 34; Lacey, *Dissent and Politics*, pp. 80–1; Marvell, *Letters*, pp. 341–3; Miller, *Popery and Politics*, pp. 140–2.
177.   *Certain Considerations Tending to Promote Peace* (1674), p. 8.

The Naked Truth for distribution among MPs, probably in the autumn session, but his ultimate goals are not clear.[178] This free-wheeling pamphlet appealed for moderation, church reforms, and even comprehension, while undermining the case for regarding bishops as a separate order of the ministry. Croft's scepticism about religious convictions, and the power of reason or coercion to affect them, led the Nonconformists to greet him as another John Hales. The tract was suspicious of the church as a theological authority and a persecutor, and therefore, despite a brief final admonition to the Dissenters to exercise humility and obedience, all of the suggested concessions seem to come from the church's side. The rest of the clergy, however, were busy demolishing the case for 'a comprehensive church'; 'it might have been better called a dragnet, that will fetch in all kinds of fish, good or bad, great or small, there will be room enough for Leviathan . . . lay all common, and then no doubt there will be room enough for all', as one bishop told the King.[179] In the short-lived session of Parliament itself, the Duke of Buckingham did gain permission to introduce a bill for the Dissenters in the Lords, but the bill was never presented. Meanwhile the Lords petitioned the King for a meeting of Convocation. However, these moves were overshadowed by the vote of 20 November in which an address calling for a dissolution of the Cavalier Parliament was defeated in the Lords by two votes. Two days later a prorogation was announced.[180]

The Church of England worked to strengthen her position and her alliance. In the spring and summer of 1676 a series of sermons and pamphlets refuted Bishop Croft. Gilbert Burnet argued that change in 'indifferent things', such as the liturgy and ceremonies, was only permissible if it brought the schismatics back to the church, but that this was neither likely nor the goal of *The Naked Truth*. Francis Turner thought Croft aimed at subverting the authority of the visible

178. For the authorship, timing and purpose of the tract see [Herbert Croft] *The Naked Truth* (1675), pp. 270–1; Evelyn, IV, 83 and note 181 below. Although this tract has been dated to April 1675, it is more likely that it appeared during the autumn session because the sudden prorogation prevented the tract's distribution among MPs, and because the replies are all from the spring of 1676; see MSS Rawlinson Letters 99, fo. 72; 93, fo. 114.

179. Benjamin Laney, *A Sermon Preached Before the King* (1675), p. 26 (Laney died in January 1675); Thomas Tomkins, *The Modern Pleas for Comprehension* (1675); Tomkins died in 1675, see *DNB*. On 24 July 1675 Bishop Mews reported to Sheldon that his clergy thought a comprehension unnecessary if only the laws were enforced; MS Tanner 42, fo. 167.

180. Buckingham's speech was later published with Shaftesbury's speech for a dissolution, see Spurr, 'Comprehension', 936, note 4; Lacey, *Dissent and Politics*, p. 80; on Convocation, see Sykes, *From Sheldon*, pp. 43–4.

church with the ulterior motive of gaining a full-blown toleration. Bishop Gunning believed that the pamphlet contained things contrary to the law of the land. And the popular reputation of the work was as a Presbyterian attack upon episcopacy.[181] Meanwhile the Canons were reprinted and in July the bishops caballed to decide on political priorities.[182] But the greatest task undertaken by the church was a census of religious conformity. Archbishop Sheldon had made enquiries in 1665, and in 1669 – when the information was used to argue for the Conventicle Act – and now, in January 1676, he initiated another national investigation of religious affiliation. But the ailing, aged Sheldon lived in retirement from the court, and 'from a concern in all state-affairs', and since Henry Compton, Bishop of London, shouldered much of the administrative burden, his name has become attached to the survey.[183] The Compton Census showed that, although the percentages varied from diocese to diocese, the Nonconformists were usually less than 5 per cent of the population, and the Roman catholics less than 1 per cent.[184] Those who compiled the final figures from the 1676 returns commented that the 1672 Indulgence had depleted the church and that the present enquiry had brought people back. Anabaptists, Quakers, Independents and Presbyterians were said to be equal in numbers, although the last two categories shaded imperceptibly into that of occasional conformity. Indeed, as the statisticians commented, many Dissenters were of no sect. But even more importantly perhaps, from the church's perspective, many who attended church did not receive the sacrament. The census confirmed once again that the 'profane and unstable', the irreligious and apathetic, were a growing party in the nation and a long-term threat to the Church of England.[185] The immediate consequence of the census was to confirm Danby and his allies in their belief that the Anglican interest was indeed the strongest in the nation and should be maintained.

181. Burnet, *A Modest Survey* (1676); Turner, *Animadversions on the Naked Truth* (1676); Peter Gunning, *Lex talionis* (1676); also see Marvell, *Letters*, pp. 345–6; Anthony Wood, *Athenae Oxonienses*, ed. P. Bliss (1813–20), IV, 313; and note 178 above.
182. *The Essex Correspondence*, p. 62.
183. In a letter of 7 December 1676 Sheldon referred to cataracts in both eyes, MS Tanner 40, fo. 41; Kennett, p. 361; Edward Carpenter, *The Protestant Bishop – Being the Life of Henry Compton* (1956), pp. 31–2. Carpenter's biography contains a wealth of detail on Compton's energetic pastoral role as well as on his political activities. As bishop of London Compton had oversight of the Church of England in the colonies; see Carpenter, *Protestant Bishop*, ch. 14; P.S. Haffenden, 'The Anglican Church in Restoration Colonial Policy', in *Seventeenth-century America*, ed. J.M. Smith (Chapel Hill, 1959).
184. E.A.O. Whiteman (ed.), *The Compton Census of 1676* (1986).
185. Thomas Barlow, *Remains* (1693), pp. 312–23.

After a prorogation of fifteen months, Parliament reconvened in February 1677, and Shaftesbury and Buckingham played straight into Danby's hands by arguing that Parliament was technically dissolved, for which they were committed to the Tower by their peers. Meanwhile the government proposed a bill for 'the more effectual conviction and prosecution of popish recusants'. This distinguished between loyal and disloyal Catholics, the former paying the old twelve-pence fine, while the full severity of the penal laws was restricted to those who disguised their popery. As one MP complained, the bill 'puts but twelve pence a Sunday difference betwixt the best Protestant and severest Papists'. It was summarily dismissed by the Commons as 'much different from the title'.[186] Another bill, introduced into the Lords by Archbishop Dolben of York, was designed to secure the Protestant religion in the event of the accession of a Catholic monarch. The children of such a monarch were to be brought up as Protestants; but far more contentiously, the bill provided for the bishops to assume control of the church or, as its critics saw it, for the King to divest himself of his supremacy and hand it to the bishops. On 27 March a lengthy silence greeted the second reading of the bill in the Commons, to be finally broken by Mr Mallet's denunciation of a bill which 'sets up nine mitres above the crown – monstrum horrendum!'[187]

The furore over this bill has tended to obscure the Church of England's legislative programme of 1677–8. A series of proposals in the parliamentary sessions of 1677 and January to March 1678 were designed to strengthen the church by reforming glaring abuses and providing the machinery to curb atheism, profanity and vice among the laity. That the church had been toying with some of these reforms for years is attested by the many draft bills to be found among the papers of Sheldon and Sancroft. In 1677 the detested and redundant writ *de haeretico comburendo* was abolished along with 'all punishment by death in pursuance of any ecclesiastical censures'. In March 1678 yet another bill to regulate clerical pluralism was read in the Lords, and the Commons read a bill to prevent clandestine marriages sent down from the Lords.[188] Parliament considered means of helping the clergy recover their small tithes, and once again failed to find a solution: it was not until 1696 that a measure was enacted. Another attempt to improve the clergy's financial position, the 1677 Act

186. Miller, *Popery and Politics*, pp. 145–7.
187. *Parliamentary History*, IV, 853–7; for the bill see Andrew Marvell, *The Growth of Popery and Arbitrary Government* (1677), pp. 85–100; HMC, 9th Report, pt. 2, appendix, pp. 81–2.
188. HMC, 9th Report, pt. 2, appendix, p. 109; cf. pp. 90–1; MS Tanner 447, fos 39–41.

confirming the augmentation of small stipends, was no more than cosmetic.[189] In March 1677 a bill was proposed to enforce baptism, catechizing and sabbath observance, and although the first two components fell by the wayside, an Act for Better Observance of the Lord's Day was hurried through as the session closed.[190] In January 1678 the House of Lords passed a bill 'for the better suppressing of those crying sins of atheism and blasphemy, and the turning away of God's wrath and his judgements from this land and nation'. Although MPs had considered such legislation in the 1660s, and the bishops and Lords had been recommending legislation since at least 1675, it was laid aside by the House of Commons after a first reading.[191] Abortive though they may have been, the breadth of these proposed reforms suggests that the church's leaders were not only conscious of the dangers, but prepared to meet them head on when afforded the opportunity and the necessary political support.

On 9 November 1677, in his seventy-ninth year, Archbishop Sheldon died at Croydon. The choice of his successor was hotly contested. And, as with other episcopal appointments during the 1670s, the free play of political patronage and royal inattention made for a wide and diverse field of contenders. Bishop Compton of London had been carrying much of the political and administrative burden in Sheldon's last years, and he enjoyed the support of Danby; but the Duke of York disliked his anti-popish stance, and proposed instead Nathaniel Crew, Bishop of Durham. There were other unlikely candidacies. Morley of Winchester suggested that, after the Bishop of London, there was no man so fit for the place as Bishop Ward of Salisbury.[192] The eventual victor, William Sancroft, Dean of St Paul's, was another of the Duke of York's protégés. Sancroft's name was being noised about Cambridge by Compton's own chaplain as early as November; he was finally appointed in late December and consecrated on 27 January.[193] Yet public reac-

---

189. See pp. 193–4 below.
190. HMC, 9th Report, pt. 2, appendix, p. 83: partial drafts in MS Tanner 447, fos 85–99, 100–8; Marvell, *Letters*, p. 199.
191. HMC, 9th Report, pt. 2, appendix, p. 98; cf. p. 43; *CSPD 1673–5*, p. 549; HMC, 8th Report, pt. 1, appendix, p. 111a; *The Diary of John Milward*, ed. C. Robbins (Cambridge, 1938), pp. 14, 18, 24–5.
192. Morley curiously went on to deny unspecified 'misprisions' under which Ward lay; see BL, MS Add. 17017, fo. 159 (Morley to the Earl of Clarendon, 25 Sept? 1677); Kennett, p. 361; HMC, Ormonde, IV, 381–91. The elevation of such men as Thomas Barlow, Henry Compton and Nathaniel Crew during the 1670s had resulted in a rather disparate episcopal bench; see R. Hutton, *Charles the Second* (Oxford, 1989), pp. 340–1.
193. MS Tanner 40, fo. 113; cf. HMC, Ormonde, IV, 385.

tion was enthusiastic at 'so excellent a choice', for Dean Sancroft was a strong and worthy candidate, who had been respected by Sheldon and Henchman, and had been offered a bishopric on previous occasions.[194] To judge from the not disinterested letters of congratulation which he received from his clergy, Sancroft was popular and was expected, in the words of Laurence Womock, to rescue the church 'from the attempts of such persons, as (either by too stiff, or too lax set of principles) have lately been in a fair way to betray the constitution of it'.[195] But events were to overtake the new primate for the political life of the nation was about to lurch into crisis.

Danby's position had become progressively less secure. For all his use of pensions and offices to create a court party in Parliament, he could count on only a handful of dependants, and his policies had provoked a 'Country' opposition which increasingly felt itself to be the protector of traditional religious, political and moral values against the arbitrary, decadent, francophile court. Accordingly, in 1677 Danby took out insurance by initiating an alliance with the Dutch and making military preparations against France, even though he was still negotiating with the French. Although it is unlikely that Charles would ever have gone to war against Louis XIV, an army was assembled, the Duke of York made bellicose noises, and in response the French set about stirring up the opposition to Danby. To coincide with the meeting of Parliament in 1678, Andrew Marvell published *An Account of the Growth of Popery and Arbitrary Government*, which supplied chapter and verse for the allegation of a well-established plot to convert the lawful government into 'absolute tyranny' and the established religion into 'downright Popery'. The parliamentary opposition pressed for discussion of the state of the nation, the growth of popery, the existence of a 30,000-strong army, and the influence of evil councillors. Danby struggled to obtain inadequate war supplies, while the opposition fought in vain to have the army disbanded and to bring in a bill to relieve Dissenters from the penalties meant for popish recusants. This fruitless Parliament was prorogued on 15 July. Then, at the end of the summer, came the first revelations of a 'plot' to kill Charles as the prelude to a Catholic rising and invasion.

The crises which engulfed England between September 1678 and April 1681 were just as dangerous for the Church of England as they were for the monarchy. At first the scare was all of papist rebellion and massacre, an hysteria which throve on a huge literature devoted

---

194. Marvell, *Letters*, pp. 208–9 (formal letter to Hull corporation); BL, MS Harleian 3784, fos 77, 190, 191, 195; MS Tanner 44, fo. 161; 43, fo. 139.
195. MS Tanner 40, fo. 153.

to exposing the nefarious principles and monstrous practices of the Romanists. Although the clergy occasionally took a hand in such titillating works, they reserved their sharpest barbs against popery for the pulpit. In his funeral sermon for that Protestant Abner, Sir Edmundbury Godfrey, William Lloyd laid his murder at the door of Jesuit doctrines, and this theme was taken up and embroidered in hundreds of sermons preached subsequently: on 5 November, recorded Anthony Wood, the 'preachers generally in their sermons at London were bitter against the papists'.[196] Shortly after reconvening on 21 October, Parliament asserted 'that there hath been and still is a damnable and hellish plot contrived and carried on by the popish recusants for the assassinating and murdering the King, and for subverting the government, and rooting out and destroying the Protestant religion'.[197] And now Parliament set off in pursuit of the plotters. Ominously one of the first to be identified, tried and convicted was Edward Coleman, a former secretary to the Duke of York. The King played for time by ordering the prosecution of recusants and giving his assent to a second Test Act to exclude Roman Catholics from Parliament – a proviso waiving the Test for the Duke of York was passed by two votes. At this stage, however, the parliamentary opposition still identified Danby as their greatest enemy, and when in December authentic information of his secret dealings with Louis XIV was laid before the House, articles of impeachment were immediately drawn up. To protect himself as much as his minister, Charles first prorogued and then, on 24 January 1679, dissolved the Cavalier Parliament.

The new Parliament, which met on 6 March, had perhaps twice as many anti-court members as its predecessor, but its goals were the same – impeaching Danby, disbanding the army, and limiting the powers of a Catholic successor. But late in April full details of the plot and more of Coleman's papers, apparently implicating the Duke of York in negotiations with Rome, were made public, and this spurred the House to contemplate Exclusion. On 21 May a bill to exclude James from the succession in favour of his daughter Princess Mary passed its second reading; Charles moved swiftly to prorogue Parliament. The character of the crisis had begun to change: not simply because Exclusion had replaced investigation of the plot as the focus of opposition activity, but also because, as Bishop Francis Turner put it,

196. Wood, II, 422. Wood, who was suspected of popery, regarded many of those divines who now talked boldly against Catholicism as 'poor spirited men' or even 'Presbyterians'.
197. Kenyon, *Popish Plot*, p. 94; Evelyn, IV, 154.

the republican plots and conspiracies to destroy the government were so transparent that as one nail drives out another they had put the danger of popery out of men's heads and scarce left room in our thoughts but how to preserve the monarchy and the church against their machinations, some of the most zealous prosecutors when the plot first lift up its head . . . now said there was a wheel within a wheel, a conspiracy within a conspiracy.[198]

The necessity of preserving the Church of England from the Exclusionist party, or Whigs as they were known, rather than the papists had probably first become apparent to many during the controversy over the bishops' right to vote in Danby's trial in the House of Lords. If the bishops voted in the preliminaries of the trial they would allow the pardon which Danby had already received from the King, and Danby would escape.[199] The resulting deadlock between the two Houses was held by many to have precipitated the dissolution of the Parliament. According to Burnet, the King could not risk losing the vote of the bishops in Danby's trial, and 'he told the bishops that they must stick to him, and to his prerogative . . . by this means they were exposed to the popular fury'.[200] In May Bishop Morley observed 'with what an evil eye those of our order and all their actions (especially such as are of public concernment) are now looked upon', and advised caution. The printing presses worked day and night to produce an avalanche of polemic – all of it legal now that the Licensing Act had expired and most of it 'very licentious, both against the court and the clergy'.[201] The churchmen decided that their best means of defence was attack.

The bishops and the clergy, apprehending that a rebellion and with it the pulling the church to pieces were designed, set themselves on the other hand to write against the late times, and to draw a parallel between the present time and them: which was not decently enough managed by those who undertook the argument, and who were believed to be set on and paid by the court for it. The chief manager of all those angry writings was one Sir Roger L'Estrange.[202]

198. MS Rawlinson Letters 99, fo. 111; Wood, II, 448 (11 April 1679).
199. On the controversy surrounding the bishops and Danby's trial see M. Goldie, 'Danby, the Bishops, and the Whigs', in *The Politics of Religion in Restoration England*, ed. T. Harris, P. Seaward and M. Goldie (Oxford, 1990).
200. Burnet, II, 220.
201. MS Tanner 38, fo. 20; W. Mason, 'The Annual Output of Wing-listed Titles, 1649–84', *The Library*, 29 (1974), 219–20; Burnet, II, 221. For the sinking reputation of the clergy see DWL, MS Morrice P, fos 158–9.
202. Burnet, II, 221.

L'Estrange, one of the most influential shapers of Restoration political discourse, was in fact rather more restrained in 1679–80 than he became after the Oxford Parliament. But his achievement was still considerable – he helped to fashion a Tory anti-popery.[203] A by-product was a new breed of highly politicized and aggressive churchmen, all too ready to wield their pen in support of the royal prerogative and indefeasible divine right of hereditary monarchy. This was a message that the majority of churchmen echoed in an attempt to remedy the 'very ill understanding 'twixt the Court and Country' caused by Charles's refusal to allow Parliament to meet.[204] But beneath all the pamphleteering and bravado, churchmen of different outlooks shared 'the dismal apprehensions we generally had of our approaching ruin'. The canons of Gloucester Cathedral were alarmed by 'the very bad face of affairs which looked with a dismal aspect towards the church'. Even Archbishop Sancroft carefully copied into one of his notebooks an anonymous paper of 'thoughts concerning the ways for uniting our church into a body for preserving itself independent on [of?] the state'.[205]

The church was in danger, too, from the 'threat' of Protestant union. With the ubiquitous Jesuit plotters apparently preparing to deliver up England to the bondage of Rome, Protestant unity became attractive. The Dissenters believed that they should be offered terms to re-enter the fold. Richard Baxter, emboldened by the freedom of the press, published *The Nonconformists Plea for Peace* in 1679, and repeated his demands in *A Proposal for Union among Protestants* addressed to Parliament in the same year. Although the church herself had repeatedly demanded that English Protestants should close ranks against the threat of popery, she envisaged the submission of Nonconformity rather than the widening of her own terms of communion. Indeed churchmen pleaded for enforcement of the laws, especially the Conventicle Act, as the most effective means of 'uniting' Protestants and of thwarting papist manipulation of the sectaries.[206] Nevertheless when Parliament was finally allowed to meet on 21 October 1680, it seemed to many that 'union and moderation were coming into fashion'.[207] The first step towards

203. R. Willman, 'The Origins of "Whig" and "Tory" in English Political Language', *HJ*, 17 (1974), 254; Miller, *Popery and Politics*, pp. 177–9; Harris, *London Crowds*.

204. Evelyn, IV, 192–3.

205. Kidder, *Life*, p. 36; C. Clay, ' "The Greed of Whig Bishops"?: Church Landlords and their Lessees 1660–1760', *Past and Present*, 87 (1980), 148; MS Sancroft 64 (of a date after 5 March 1680).

206. See Edward Stillingfleet, *The Mischief of Separation* (1680); Joseph Glanvil, *The Zealous, and Impartial Protestant* (1681), pp. 4–9; Timothy Puller, *The Moderation of the Church of England* (1679), p. 538; MS Cherry 23, fo. 317.

207. *Moderation a Vertue* (1683), p. 16; MS Tanner 37, fo. 234.

reunion would be the removal of the penal laws from moderate Nonconformists. The effective prosecution of dangerous religious dissidents had long been hampered by the failure of these laws to discriminate between Protestants and Roman Catholics, or between different sorts of Protestant Dissenter. The government had already signalled its willingness to secure Nonconformists from prosecution under laws intended against papists, and now a bill was introduced to repeal one of the most frequently used such statutes.[208] The King's friends, the Tory Anglicans, like Daniel Finch, were also behind the comprehension and toleration bills considered in this Parliament. Greeted with stony indifference from the Nonconformists, these proposals were still under discussion when Parliament was prorogued, with only fifteen minutes' notice, on 10 January 1681. The quarrel had reached a stalemate; the King would not accept Exclusion, and this Parliament would not grant supply until an Exclusion bill was passed.[209] Yet there were also signs in the second Exclusion Parliament that the political tide was on the turn. On 15 November, in the presence of the King, the Lords had voted to reject the Exclusion bill. Although the Whigs still enjoyed a majority in the Commons, some of their less committed supporters, alarmed by Whig tactics and suspicious of where they might lead, now began to draw back. Among the undecided and the 'trimmers', the backlash had begun.

Although another Exclusionist majority was returned to the Parliament which met at Oxford on 21 March 1681, the King was ready to call the Whigs' bluff. He had planned this Parliament purely and simply as an opportunity to outmanoeuvre and discredit his opponents – now he paid out the rope with which the Whigs were to hang themselves. Their increasing extremism and populism ensured that the faint hearts would fall away, and the determined core of Whigs withdrew rather than resort to violence.[210] For nearly three years, Charles had been fighting a war of nerves and propaganda. His eventual victory was assured once a majority of political opinion had decided that the Whigs represented a greater threat to stability than did the monarch and his Catholic heir. Not long

---

208. DWL, MS Morrice P, fo. 263; Spurr, 'Comprehension', 936.
209. See H. Horwitz, 'Protestant Reconciliation in the Exclusion Crisis', *JEH*, 15 (1964); Spurr, 'Comprehension', 936–7; Burnet, II, 278–9; Lacey, *Dissent and Politics*, p. 147.
210. See Challinor, 'Restoration in Cheshire', 372–6; R.A. Beddard, 'The Retreat on Toryism: Lionel Ducket, Member for Calne, and the Politics of Conservatism', *Wiltshire Archaeological Magazine*, 72–3 (1980). Parliament raised the subject of accommodating Dissent and enquired into the fate of earlier bills, but could do no more; see HMC, 9th Report, pt. 2, appendix, p. 269; Horwitz, 'Protestant Reconciliation', 214.

after the Oxford Parliament broke up, Bishop Fell wrote to Richard Newdigate, assuming (wrongly it seems) that Newdigate had favoured the comprehension proposals. Fell's attempt to explain his own opposition to comprehension became a statement of the Anglican outlook, with its burden of history and its appropriation of true Protestantism.

> We both aim at the same thing, though we differ in the methods of procuring them. The preservation of the Protestant religion, and established government, is our common care, but we are so unhappy, that you think we desert and betray both, while we adhere to the present constitution; and you imagine the nation can only be preserved, by letting in all dissenters into your church; and on the other side, we are most firmly persuaded that your proceedings must draw after them the alteration of government, and popery: toleration being certainly destructive of our reformed religion, whether procured by a Lord Clifford, or a popular pretence to the uniting of Protestants. Your zeal for your country and religion is exceedingly commendable; but I pray consider, that every one who seems to have the same honest aims with you, is not sincere as you are. We remember very well the time, when blood and rapine put on the mark of godliness and reformation; and we lost our king, our liberty and property and religion, by fighting for them. As it then appeared that we poor cavaliers were Protestants, though scandalled with the names of malignants and papists; so I hope we shall still continue: and be as willing to suffer and die for our religion, as others are to talk of it.[211]

A Kingdom Divided Against Itself, 1681–89

In a declaration read from the pulpits of the parish churches on 24 April, Charles blamed his recent troubles on 'the restless malice of ill men' and he called upon the nation to unite in submission to royal authority and the rule of law.[212] Royal hopes were all in vain, however; far from being the King of all his people, Charles was fast becoming the prisoner of his old friends of the mid-1670s, the Cavalier Anglicans, now led by Archbishop Sancroft and the two Hyde brothers, Lawrence, soon to become Earl of Rochester, and Henry, the second Earl of Clarendon. These old Tory friends were

---

211. Warwickshire County Record Office, CR 136, B413; this transcript was very kindly supplied by Dr V.M. Larminie.
212. See Kennett, pp. 398–9; Holmes, *Lincolnshire*, pp. 245–6.

also a 'Yorkist' clique: Francis Turner, who was with the Duke of York in Scotland, reported to Sancroft that the Duke

> places his hopes altogether upon that interest we call the Church of England, upon the episcopal party, and mainly upon the bishops themselves, your Grace especially, wishing and desiring that your Grace will take all opportunities of encouraging the King (that was the Duke's own word) to be steady in well-chosen resolutions, and laying before his Majesty how fatal a thing it would be now to draw back again the ground he has gained and how mighty safe to stick by his old friends and the laws.[213]

The King's old friends in the church vied with one another to proclaim their loyalty to the Stuart dynasty and to heap indignation upon Exclusion, that 'design full of ingratitude'; as one clergyman observed, 'we were mad with loyalty', but then loyalty was well rewarded.[214] The Ecclesiastical Commission, erected in February 1681, restricted preferment to clerics of known zeal for Crown and church. Although occasionally thwarted by the vagaries of patronage and influence, the commissioners – Sancroft, Compton, Lawrence Hyde, Lord Halifax, and Radnor (Edward Seymour, although nominated, never served) – exercised a control over clerical preferment that can rarely have been matched in the seventeenth century.[215]

The requisite 'loyalty' might be displayed in different ways. An acknowledged route to preferment was polemical service. When Laurence Womock was pressing his claim for the see of 'my beloved Ely' in 1684, he promised Sancroft that if translated, 'I shall sit down with all imaginable contentment to pray and preach and (as occasion serves) to write in defence of the crown and church; and to gratify younger expectants, 'twill not be long e're I deposit my mitre upon a hearse to make way for them.'[216] The 'revelation' of the Rye House Plot in 1683 supplied the loyal preachers with yet more evidence (as if they needed it) that neither church nor Crown were safe from 'the sinister practices and opinions of the Jesuits and Presbyterians' concerning rebellion.[217] Although papists and puritans were brethren in iniquity, it was the latter who now received

213. MS Tanner 36, fo. 31v. Also see Beddard, 'Restoration Church', pp. 174–5.
214. Kidder, *Life*, p. 36.
215. R.A. Beddard, 'The Commission for Ecclesiastical Promotions, 1681–84: An Instrument of Tory Reaction', *HJ*, 10 (1967).
216. MS Tanner 32, fo. 89v.
217. William Bolton, *Core redivivus* (1684), p. 2; John Turner, *A Sermon Preached at Epsom upon the 9th of September* (1683), pp. 5–6. Also see Goldie, 'Locke and Anglican Royalism', 73.

most attention from the Anglican authorities.[218] Policy and pragmatism dictated that, in many places, this was not just a drive
against Dissent and popery, but for conformity to the Church of
England. So occasional conformists were flushed out: Bishop Ward
reported from Salisbury the suppression of 'a Samaritan conventicle
of persons pretending themselves friends of our church, partakers of
the public service and sacraments, and afterwards resorting to an
exercise of a presbyterian'.[219] Unsure of jurors' willingness to convict
at the Quarter Sessions, the Norfolk justices 'promised to execute the
laws against Dissenters in their several parts and to begin with the
statute of twelve pence a Sunday for absence from church'.[220] In
many counties the Elizabethan recusancy statutes were the favoured
means of bringing Nonconformists to heel, and they had the additional advantage of applying to all who absented themselves from
church whatever their motive.[221] The nation was being dragooned
into church attendance as a by-product of political vendettas between local Whigs and Tories. Few of the bishops or clergy appear
as remorseless as their congregations; in Norwich Bishop Sparrow
found 'some clamouring loud against me for prosecuting schismatics,
and some who profess great loyalty and zeal for the church, as loud
complaining because we do not proceed violently beyond the rule of
law'.[222] Nevertheless, the churchmen urged on the prosecution of
Dissent, arguing that 'unless the blow be pursued, it would have
been better we had never stirred'.[223]

At first sight the unanimity of the Anglican clergy throughout the
later 1670s and early 1680s is striking.[224] 'My clergy are entirely
unanimous in their respect and assistance to me', reported the
Bishop of Peterborough, a touch smugly, in May 1683.[225] Had a sect
of High Tory zealots, fanatically loyal to the Stuart monarchy and
intent on prosecuting Dissent into extinction, replaced the broad
church of the 1660s? There are grounds to believe so. A new genera-

---

218. On prosecution see Miller, *Popery and Politics*, pp. 162–9, 189–95; Coleby, *Central
     Government and Localities*, pp. 199–202; Forster, 'Government in Provincial
     England', 33; Sancroft demanded 'wholesome severity' against Roman Catholics,
     see *Concilia*, V, 606.
219. MS Tanner 36, fo. 196.
220. MS Tanner 35, fo. 107 (Bishop Sparrow of Norwich, 11 October 1682); also see
     Granville, II, 51.
221. Jackson, 'Nonconformists in Devon', pp. 160–1; G.V. Bennett, 'The Seven
     Bishops: A Reconsideration', *SCH*, 15 (1978), 268–9.
222. MS Tanner 35, fo. 170.
223. MS Tanner 36, fo. 173.
224. See J.R. Jones, *Country and Court – England 1658–1714* (1978), pp. 88–9.
225. MS Tanner 34, fo. 39.

tion of clergymen, raised in the Restoration universities, was beginning to succeed the reluctant conformists of the 1660s. And many of the latter had over the years grown fonder of the church in which they served and less indulgent to the irreconcilable Dissenters: as Isaac Archer noted complacently in his diary for 1673, 'I am more satisfied in the Church of England than ever'.[226] Peer pressure was intense, especially during the Tory reaction. 'Such of the clergy as would not engage in that fury were cried out on as the betrayers of the church, and as secret favourers of the dissenters,' observed Burnet. 'The truth is, the numbers of these were not great. . . . The scent of preferment will draw aspiring men after it.'[227] Yet the dissidents were never far beneath the surface of parish and cathedral life. During Lent 1682, Samuel Bolde, vicar of Shapwick in Dorset, preached against the persecution of Dissenters, knowing it would arouse the criticism of those who 'cannot understand how a man can except against their violent proceedings against some Dissenters, and yet be himself a thorough conformist'.[228] The sermon was duly presented at the Sherborne Assizes. Bishop Gulston of Bristol took notice of the prosecution and persuaded the Grand Jury to draw up an address thanking the King for the execution of laws against Nonconformity, 'which may be of great concern, if other counties would do the like, both in answering further objections against prosecutors of the laws, and for prevention of any sort of toleration'.[229] Despite a disappointing legal opinion that Bolde's sermon was 'a virulent libel in the main against the ground of our church discipline, yet no particular passage directly impugns any one canon of the Church of England', Bishop Gulston now proceeded against him in the church courts. But Bolde was not easily intimidated and in *A Plea for Moderation towards Dissenters* (1682) he repeated the call for Protestant unity against popery. Gulston was equally dogged, however, tracking Bolde through the courts until he read three recantation sermons. Yet it would be wrong to conclude that Gulston was an extremist: while he pursued Bolde, he was also engaged in a bitter struggle with the High Tory zealot, Dr Richard Thompson, minister of St Mary Redcliffe, Bristol, and briefly dean of Bristol. 'I am resolved,' wrote Gulston, 'to keep out fanaticism on one hand, and Popery, simony and atheism on the other hand.'[230]

226. CUL, MS Add. 8499, fo. 161.
227. Burnet, II, 290.
228. Samuel Bolde, *A Sermon Against Persecution. Preached March 26* (1682), sig. A2.
229. MS Tanner 35, fo. 67, cf. fos 55, 63; Spurr, 'Comprehension', 943.
230. MS Tanner 34, fo. 123. On Thompson also see J. Barry, 'The Politics of Religion in Restoration Bristol', in *The Politics of Religion in Restoration England*, ed. T. Harris, P. Seaward and M. Goldie (Oxford, 1990), p. 173.

Daniel Whitby, precentor of Salisbury Cathedral, was another dissident churchman who was shouted down by his brethren. In 1682 Whitby published *The Protestant Reconciler, humbly pleading for Condescention to Dissenting Brethren, in Things Indifferent and Unnecessary, For the Sake of Peace*, an even-handed, and massively documented, argument against 'the stiff imposers of unnecessary things' on one hand and the disobedient Dissenters on the other. 'What should put him on this work I cannot guess unless discontent for want of preferment answerable to his expectations,' commented Andrew Allam, 'but I suppose that he was never looked upon as one of the most prudent and discreet men in all the world.'[231] Whitby was harried by Dean Pierce of Salisbury and by the scribblers of the Tory press, especially Laurence Womock, a close friend of Pierce, who had been set on by the second Earl of Clarendon.[232] Bishop Ward of Salisbury seems to have done nothing to help his chaplain Whitby, partly perhaps because of his own quarrel with Dean Pierce. And so in June 1683 Whitby appeared before the Consistory Court and eventually, on 9 October, he recanted the *Reconciler*.[233] Although the terms of this recantation were submitted for Sancroft's approval, they failed to satisfy firebrands like Womock, who told the archbishop that it 'signified nothing' and that 'upon this gentle acquittal, the Whigs rejoice and the trimmers gravely approve of it: but the loyal Church of Englandmen lament',[234] When Edward Fowler preached at Gloucester Cathedral on 19 August 1683, the Common Council charged him with preaching sedition and faction. His offence appears to have been that he laid the responsibility for the Rye House Plot on the doctrines of Roman Catholics like Suarez, Parsons and Mariana, without mentioning king-killing Calvinist and Presbyterian principles.[235] Bishop Frampton of Gloucester had no idea 'how to salve' the situation, since both sides of the dispute were indubitably loyal, if too 'hot'. Frampton did his best to defuse the situation, but when Fowler visited the city the following summer, his preaching led to a fracas and to an accusation against him of assault. The exasperated bishop wrote to Sancroft, 'I am almost weary of my life, but most certainly of my office, were there any way for me to lay it down with decency'.[236] The bishop caught between Whigs

---

231. BL, MS Lansdowne 960, fo. 107.
232. MS Tanner 35, fo. 215. For this episode see Whiteman, 'Ward', ch. 9.
233. MS Tanner 34, fo. 182; MS Ballard 62, fo. 54.
234. MS Tanner 34, fo. 199 and see fos 133, 141, 226, 240.
235. MS Tanner 34, fos 114, 156. Fowler published his sermon in *A Discourse of Offences* (1683).
236. MSS Tanner 34, fo. 125; 32, fos 73, 143.

and Tories, between extremists, was a familiar story. According to Bishop Sparrow of Norwich, some of the loyal party there 'are so hot and eager, that nothing will please but what is come by their method' and as a result the King's friends were divided.[237] It was a similar story in Cheshire where Dean Arderne of Chester set himself to combat the 'deep infection of Whiggism' allegedly promoted by local clergy like Zachary Cawdrey at the weekday lectures at Knutsford, Nantwich and Tarvin.[238] Bishop Pearson of Chester explained that the lectures were opposed by 'those of the gentry who have been more than ordinarily entrusted with the management of the affairs of the government'. Conflicts like those between Arderne and Cawdrey, the bishop concluded, 'could be no otherwise in a county so divided, and must continue so long as the divisions last at this height'.[239]

Since the mid-1670s English society had become deeply politicized and polarized. The Church of England was not immune to this process; she too had her zealots and her trimmers, but it is plain that the hierarchy, while staunch Tories, had little sympathy for extremists of either ilk. Partial clerical conformity was a perennial problem, but in the 1680s its antithesis, excessive political 'loyalty', began for the first time to appear as a threat to the church's interests. Sancroft was worried by the growing prominence of divines like Pierce, Womock, Parker and Arderne, divines whose enthusiasm for the royal prerogative knew no bounds, not even the 'the restraints of law'. Such men formed an 'extravagant, ultra-Tory wing of the Church, which, in the course of the 1680s, not only grew in importance, but also repeatedly threatened to subvert the stability of the Anglican Establishment from within'.[240] At present Sancroft could direct the energies or thwart the ambitions of these enthusiasts – but for how much longer?

The Church of England meanwhile took steps to convince, as well as convict, her Protestant opponents. The *Collection of Cases and Other Discourses Written to Recover Dissenters to the Communion of the Church of England/ By Some Divines of the City of London* was regarded by contemporaries as the high-water mark of Restoration Anglican apologetic against Dissent.[241] Many of the cases had originally

237. MS Tanner 35, fo. 170.
238. MSS Tanner 32, fo. 15; 34, fos 18, 26; 35, fo. 117. For another Exclusionist cleric, see Clifton, *Last Popular Rebellion*, p. 65.
239. MS Tanner 34, fo. 27. Also see Newcome, *Autobiography*, p. 241.
240. R.A. Beddard, 'Bishop Cartwright's Death-Bed', *Bodleian Library Record*, 11 (1984), 220.
241. William Clagett, *The Present State of the Controversie* (1687), pp. 3–4; John Rawlett, *A Dialogue betwixt two Protestants* (1685), sig. b.

appeared separately and anonymously, but in a uniformly plain format and from the same publishers, during 1683 and 1684: it was suggested that they 'were imposed as tasks by the Bishop of London on several divines of that city'.[242] They were reissued by their publishers as a *Collection* in two volumes in 1685, and reprinted as a folio in 1694 and in three volumes in 1718. Each *Case* was given over to a different Nonconformist objection to the national church. The Anglicans laid out their own position confidently and, in measured and moderate terms, urged the Dissenters, and especially the Dissenting laity, to forsake their schism. The churchmen made no concessions whatsoever. There was no need to: they seemed to be winning the war against Nonconformity in the early 1680s. The bishops could not but be heartened by the 'very full communions' which were reported from the parishes – even if it was 'the fear of punishment more than love of God makes many in this juncture of time appear in our assemblies'.[243] But persuading or coercing the people into coming to church was only half the battle; once there they then had to be offered attractive and meaningful worship. The campaign of the early 1680s for a weekly celebration of the sacrament in the cathedrals – described by Dean Granville as the bishops' 'late noble and heroic expression of their pious zeal in the seasonable restoring of the eucharist' – inspired churchmen of all degrees and of all political complexions.[244] As always, there were practical difficulties: several cathedrals did not have the resident clergy required for the correct administration of the sacrament; while in the parishes, a revival of worship depended upon the quality, conformity and diligence of the clergy. Sancroft had taken this in hand almost as soon as he arrived at Lambeth, by requiring more careful testimonials for those seeking ordination.[245] The Ecclesiastical Commission enabled the archbishop to prevent or mitigate pluralism, especially among the dignified clergy.[246] The drive for more zealous worship was heavily dependent upon extracting greater conformity and more diligent performance from the clergy themselves: thus Compton began to devote his clerical 'conferences' to the subject of the clergy's conformity, Lloyd of St Asaph agreed 'certain orders' with his clergy to obtain more stringent performance of their

242. BL, MS Lansdowne 937, fo. 39; also see Evelyn, IV, 418.
243. MS Tanner 35, fo. 9; *Bishop Fell and Nonconformity*, ed. M. Clapinson (Oxfordshire Record Society, 62, 1980), p. 13. Also see J.T. Evans, *Seventeenth-century Norwich* (Oxford, 1979), pp. 306–7; ch. 7 below.
244. MS Rawlinson Letters 93, fo. 192. See pp. 191, 364–6, below.
245. D'Oyly, *Life of Sancroft*, I, 154; *Concilia*, IV, 600; MS Tanner 39, fo. 92.
246. Beddard, 'Commission for Ecclesiastical Promotions', 14, 33–4.

duties, and a similar contract was agreed by Sancroft and other bishops.[247] In several other dioceses the bishops demanded reports and surveys, undertook visitations and exhorted their clergy to greater pastoral efforts. Archbishop Sancroft backed his bishops. He engineered a metropolitical visitation of Salisbury diocese, which took place in July 1686, in order to resolve the long-running dispute between Bishop Ward and Dean Pierce.[248] Although always respectful of episcopal rights, Sancroft was prepared to discipline the bishops: he held a metropolitical visitation of Barlow's see of Lincoln in 1686 and suspended the notorious Bishop Wood of Coventry and Lichfield in July 1684.[249]

The political alliance of Halifax and the Hydes, which had sustained the ascendancy of the Church of England since 1681, was in jeopardy by the autumn of 1684. A political reshuffle was already under way, with the Earl of Sunderland assuming power, and the abolition of the Ecclesiastical Commission, when a fatal stroke felled Charles II in March 1685. The moment had come to see whether James really did put his hopes and trust in the Church of England. On their side, the churchmen loyally played their part in easing his accession to the throne. The bishops took their place in their robes alongside the magistracy in their scarlet and the paraded militia, and with drums beating and trumpets sounding, James II was proclaimed with 'as loud and hearty acclamations as could possibly be imagined'.[250] From their pulpits the parish clergy assured the nation that the two royal brothers were so alike 'that we are scarce sensible even of a change', and that 'whatever the persuasions of our gracious sovereign are, in some particular points of faith, or modes of worship different from us; yet when we deserve it, God shall make him *wholly* ours'.[251] A wave of loyal addresses from the clergy to their new monarch were published in the *Gazette* – all carefully orchestrated from London and even from Lambeth. Archbishop Dolben wrote from York on 16 February that 'our gentlemen have already taken the hint' and their address 'will make it necessary

247. Carpenter, *Protestant Bishop*, p. 208; *Concilia*, IV, 608–10 (4 July 1683), 612–14 (1685).
248. See R.A. Beddard, 'The Church of Salisbury and the Accession of James II', *Wiltshire Archaeological Magazine*, 67 (1972), 143–4; Whiteman, 'Ward', ch. 10.
249. MS Tanner 31, fos 277, 297; *Documentary Annals of the Reformed Church of England 1546–1716*, ed. E. Cardwell (2nd ed, Oxford, 1844), p. 352.
250. MS Tanner 32, fo. 216.
251. William Jegon, *The Damning Nature of Rebellion* (1685), p. 5; [Thomas Manningham], *A Short View of the Most Gracious Providence of God in the Restoration and Succession* (1685), p. 18. This last passage was copied into a notebook by White Kennett, see BL, MS Lansdowne 960.

for the clergy either to fall in with them, or [make] addresses by themselves'; the clergy of Bristol felt obliged by the four addresses being offered from the laymen of their city. In Salisbury, the ultra-Tory Dean Pierce used the occasion to stigmatize former Exclusionists and to upstage his bishop.[252] The Commons followed the clergy's suit when they voted on 27 May that they 'acquiesce, entirely rely, and rest wholly satisfied in' James's promise to defend the Church of England as established by law 'which is dearer to us than our lives'. There were few voices to be heard counselling caution, at least in public. Preaching to the Commons on 29 May, William Sherlock daringly criticized the new King's religion, while professing complete trust in his person; it was only with hindsight that this sermon came to be seen as the opening shot in the Church of England's campaign against Rome and their Romish Supreme Governor.

In the summer of 1685 the church dutifully came to James's aid against the Argyle and Monmouth rebellions. Bishop Mews actually directed the artillery at Sedgemoor, while the scholars of Oxford drilled in preparation under Bishop Fell. More significantly perhaps, on 26 July, the day of thanksgiving for Monmouth's defeat, the nation's churches resounded to denunciations of rebellion and to assertions of divine right and the duty of passive obedience. But unease was growing at the 'insolence' of Roman Catholics.[253] James had still not disbanded his army, in which Catholic officers were employed, by the time Parliament met in November 1685. When Bishop Compton protested at this in the Lords – claiming that he spoke for all of the bishops – he promptly lost his seat in the Privy Council. Over the winter of 1685–6, alignments began to change at court: Sunderland was in cahoots with a Catholic cabal and was outmanoeuvring the King's old friends. By the spring, with the guidance of these ministers, 'all engines' were 'now at work to bring in popery amain' – or so it appeared to Evelyn. The main 'engine' was the dispensation of certain individuals from the requirements of the Test Acts and the penalties of other laws, allowing them to hold various offices 'contrary to 20 Acts of Parliaments [and] . . . repugnant to his Majesty's own declaration at the beginning of his reign'. On 21 June, the hand-picked judges of the test case of 'Godden versus Hales' decided that the King had the right in law to dispense with statutes. The effect of their decision was succinctly noted by Evelyn: 'the Test was abolished. Times of great jealousies

252.   MSS Tanner 32, fos 223, 226, 236; 31, fo. 18; Beddard, 'Church of Salisbury and James II'.
253.   See MS Tanner 31, fos 123, 246.

where these proceedings would end.'[254] Meanwhile in March, the King had torpedoed the efforts of the church to ensure conformity by issuing a general pardon which annulled many legal proceedings. Gradually, James began to grant personal dispensations from the penal laws to Quakers, Baptists and other Dissenters.[255]

Things were beginning to look bleak for the church. All that praise of monarchs was coming home to roost as 'the dispirited clergy' recognized that 'we are cramped in our temporal' power.[256] Several of the bishops died that year: Dolben of York in April, Pearson of Chester and Fell of Oxford in July – 'an extraordinary loss at this time to this poor church'[257] – and the choice of their successors might be crucial to the fate of the church. It did not bode well that the apostate Obadiah Walker, provost of University College, Oxford, busied himself in the choice of a successor to Fell – and the final choice of Parker for Oxford and Cartwright for Chester was a blow to the churchmen. Sancroft did not mince his words when he told Clarendon that Parker 'hates me'.[258] Even more significantly the archbishopric of York was left vacant until the hurried nomination of Lamplugh in 1688.[259]

The anti-Roman preaching of the Church of England infuriated James. In February 1686 he reissued Charles II's 1662 injunctions against seditious preaching, and began exerting pressure. But the church stood firm; as Bishop Compton explained:

> a modest latitude must be allowed in this point, whilst we are permitted to assert our own religion: because many of our doctrines do necessarily engage us to it. Besides that at present the behaviour of the Romish priests in many places constrains our ministers to say more in this particular for the settling of men's minds, than otherwise they would do.[260]

Needless to say, this was not the King's opinion. In June, John Sharp and George Tully were ordered to be suspended 'for preaching against Popery'. Even worse, on 14 July, a new Ecclesiastical Commission was established, which Evelyn compared to 'the late High Commission Court'. This body had the wide-ranging powers of

254. Evelyn, IV, 517.
255. Miller, *Popery and Politics*, pp. 210–12.
256. MS Tanner 30, fo. 104.
257. Warwickshire County Record Office, CR 136, B418 (I owe this reference to Dr Larminie).
258. *The Correspondence of Henry Hyde, Earl of Clarendon*, ed. S.W. Singer (1828), I, 150.
259. Miller, *Popery and Politics*, p. 208: James had uses for the see's revenues.
260. MS Tanner 31, fo. 268.

a vicar-general to visit, examine and order, 'but the main drift was to suppress zealous preachers'. The Commission was indeed intended, in the words of Sunderland, 'to regulate the licence of the Protestant ministers and to curb the audacity of the bishops', above all Bishop Compton of London, who had failed to suspend John Sharp.[261] The commissioners – Sunderland, Rochester, Bishops Crew of Durham and Sprat of Rochester, Lord Chancellor Jeffreys, Lord Chief Justice Herbert, but not Sancroft, who refused to serve – met on 3 August. Their first act was to summon Bishop Compton to appear before them on 9 August.[262] After some initial skirmishes over the legitimacy and jurisdiction of the Commission, Compton's trial came to centre on whether the King could require a subject to act unlawfully, in this case to suspend a clergyman without proper judicial proceedings. On 6 September, for his 'disobedience and contempt', Compton was suspended from the function and exercise of his episcopal office and jurisdiction during His Majesty's pleasure. Compton was not the only victim. Sancroft's refusal to serve cost him his place on the Privy Council and he gave up attending court.[263] The suspension of Compton also marked Rochester's final political defeat by Sunderland and the Catholic faction – before the end of the year Rochester too was out of office.[264] After one last attempt to browbeat MPs individually, James gave up on his Parliament, which was first prorogued, and then dissolved. The new royal strategy was to woo Dissent and to appoint Roman Catholics in central and local government so that, by the time the next Parliament met, opposition to repeal of the penal laws would have been overcome. On 4 April 1687 a Declaration of Indulgence was issued, which suspended 'the execution of all and all manner of penal laws in matters ecclesiastical', and ordered that the oaths required of office-holders by the Test Act should no longer be imposed.

The propagandists joined battle. Confident Anglican apologists, flushed with the success of their *Cases* against Dissent, had just begun a similar set of tracts against Rome when James's accession threw them on the defensive. James too recognized the value of propaganda and supported the Roman Catholic controversialists and their printers. John Gother's *A Papist Misrepresented and Represented* (1685) was the first Catholic sally and it provoked yet another collaborative response from the London clergy.[265] Led by William

261. Evelyn, IV, 516, 519–20; Miller, *Popery and Politics*, p. 210.
262. For the trial see Carpenter, *Protestant Bishop*, pp. 89–99.
263. See MS Tanner 30, fos 123, 14.
264. *Correspondence of Clarendon*, II, 116–18, 132–3.
265. See Miller, *Popery and Politics*, pp. 208, 256–7; MS Tanner 31, fo. 190; W.A. Speck, *Reluctant Revolutionaries – Englishmen and the Revolution of 1688* (Oxford, 1988), pp. 179–82.

Sherlock, and including William Wake – who was described by George Hickes as 'the young David, which providence seemeth to have raised up to conquer the giants, which defy our church' – these metropolitan churchmen were coming to monopolize the argument with Rome.[266] They had acquired a taste for dividing the work among themselves and they went on to produce two further series: one in which each of Cardinal Bellarmine's fifteen 'notes' of a true church was minutely scrutinized, and another entitled *The Texts Examined which the Papists cite out of the Bible* – after which, as Wake remarked, 'I do not see what more can be desired in order to our full satisfaction'.[267] The church rallied her own followers, calling for zealous attendance at her prayers and sacraments, and exhorted the Nonconformists to swallow their scruples for the sake of Protestant unity. Halifax's famous warning to the Nonconformists that they were being duped by the papists, whose policy was to 'hug' them now, so that they could 'squeeze' them later, was typical of prudential Anglican arguments. There is, indeed, some evidence to suggest that Nonconformists preferred the Anglican devil they knew. From Yorkshire, Sir John Reresby reported that 'the generality in these parts seem very firm and very quiet of the Church of England, and the only Dissenters that seem pleased with their toleration are the Quakers and Independents, the number of either not very considerable, for notwithstanding they have meeting houses, the churches are observed not to be less full in York, Leeds, Sheffield'.[268] Yet in the same region Oliver Heywood heard 'Papists and Quakers complain nobody is a gainer by this liberty but Presbyterians' and he exulted in the fact that 'we [the Presbyterians] have sacraments, solemn ordination of ministers, conferences, and exercises set up on weekdays, discipline, and no disturbance in any thing.'[269] On the other hand, many of the Dissenters were in the same dilemma as they had been in 1672. They were reluctant to give thanks for or use an Indulgence which was so transparently designed to liberate popery, but on the other hand they had no reason to trust the Church of England. In May 1687 Roger Morrice the Nonconformist noted that for over twenty years the Church of England had turned down union with Dissent, repeatedly arguing that it was impossible while the Dissenters perpetuated schism, and yet even now the churchmen sought to blame Dissent for having brought in popery.[270]

266. MS Ballard 12, fo. 23v
267. William Wake, *A Continuation of the Present State of the Controversy* (1688), p. 75; cf. Clagett, *Present State of Controversy* (1687); Edward Gee, *A Catalogue of all the Discourses* (1689).
268. Reresby, *Memoirs*, p. 582.
269. Heywood, pp. 349–50.
270. DWL, MS Morrice Q, fo. 116.

James believed that the English would eagerly embrace Catholicism if only they were given the chance. He hoped to establish the Roman Catholic Church on an equal footing with the Church of England.[271] Yet, with hindsight, the Catholic mission had little chance of success: with too little time, too few priests and a restricted appeal, the Romish missionaries reaped a disappointing harvest of souls before the whole enterprise collapsed about their ears. Only ten Anglican clergymen transferred their allegiance to Rome.[272] The King blamed the Church of England for prejudicing the people against his religion and tried to cow the churchmen. Although he managed to create a climate of fear among Anglican preachers, the work of exposing the pitfalls of popery never stopped; virulently anti-Catholic sermons were heard across the land.[273] The London clergy 'universally' refused to subscribe the address of thanks for the 1687 Declaration of Indulgence signed by Bishops Crew, Sprat, Cartwright and Parker.[274] Next James tried to force a Catholic president on Magdalen College, Oxford, and when that failed, instructed the college to overturn its own election in favour of Bishop Parker of Oxford. Although James succeeded in forcing Parker, and subsequently a Roman Catholic, into the presidency, it was at the cost of ejecting the entire fellowship and alienating public opinion. The King had trespassed against the president and fellows' consciences, property and religion. 'We have a religion to defend,' the ejected president told William Penn, James's Quaker courtier, 'and I suppose that you yourself would think us knaves if we should tamely give it up.'[275] But the church was steadily being undermined from within. The universities were salted with Roman Catholics or with compliant Anglicans. The ultra-Tories of the early 1680s, men like Parker and Cartwright, were coming into their own, and as Sancroft had feared, they were betraying the church. Late in 1687 an informed observer believed that the Bishops of Durham, Chester, Oxford and St David's – the last three all appointed by James – were prepared to vote for the repeal of the Test Acts.[276] And who

271. Miller, *Popery and Politics*, pp. 199–200; Speck, *Reluctant Revolutionaries*, p. 126.
272. Miller, *Popery and Politics*, p. 240 and ch. 13; but on Roman Catholic missionary work see E. Duffy, 'English Secular Clergy and the Counter-Reformation'; E. Duffy, '"Poor Protestant Flies": Conversions to Catholicism in Early Eighteenth-century England', *SCH*, 15 (1978).
273. See MSS Tanner 30, fos 7, 176; 33, fo. 7; 31, fos 271, 275; Evelyn, IV, 507-8; HMC, 14th Report, appendix 2 (Portland MSS, III), p. 405.
274. DWL, MS Morrice Q, fos 114, 118.
275. L. Brockliss, G. Harriss and A. Macintyre, *Magdalen College and the Crown* (Oxford, 1988), p. 54.
276. D.H. Hosford, 'The Peerage and the Test Act: a List, c. November 1687', *BIHR*, 42 (1969), 119.

knew who might be appointed to the vacant see of York or, even worse, who might fill the 'next vacancy at Lambeth'?[277] In matters ecclesiastical the King now took advice from Nonconformists like Penn, Stephen Lobb and Vincent Alsop, or from timeservers like Sunderland. But his guiding star was the interest of the Roman Catholic Church, which was beginning to assume the role of the nation's official church. In May 1688 the four bishops appointed by Rome to govern England's Catholics issued a pastoral letter, in which they announced that divine providence and royal piety had restored episcopal authority to the Catholics of England.[278] Although little more than a gesture, this letter deeply shocked the Church of England, whose sense of her own identity was bound up with the royal supremacy. There was, however, very little that the spurned Church of England could do: the laity were once more warned against popish seducers and were exhorted yet again to Protestant unity, while the bishops took legal advice 'what method to be used to obviate the invasion of our jurisdiction' by the four 'titular' bishops.[279]

By the spring of 1688 James was confident that regulating the corporations and sounding out the gentry had paid off, and that a new Parliament would emancipate his co-religionists. On 27 April the Declaration of Indulgence of 1687 was reissued, with the addition of a promise of a Parliament in November. On 4 May, in a move which still mystifies, James ordered that the Declaration should 'be read at the usual time of divine service' on 20 and 27 May in the churches of London, and on 3 and 10 June in the rest of the country.[280] Over the following week the London clergy consulted their political allies. Halifax, Nottingham and Rochester prevaricated, but seemed to think the clergy should comply with the royal instruction – only Clarendon advised a refusal; and the clergy conferred among themselves, meeting at Ely House, London residence of the Bishop of Ely, on 7 and 8 May. It had become apparent that reading the Declaration had to be the last ditch. The church could not afford to appear pusillanimous, especially when so many of their lay supporters had recently lost office for refusing to countenance the abolition of religious laws. If the clergy complied in this, wrote Sir John Lowther,

277. BL, MS Lansdowne 937, fo. 94; MS Ballard 12, fo. 36.
278. *A Pastoral Letter from the Four Catholic Bishops to the lay Catholics of England* (1688).
279. MS Tanner 28, fos 147–52, Henry Maurice's draft reply to the *Pastoral Letter*, and fos 153–4, Sancroft's notes on this draft.
280. The following account is based upon *Correspondence of Clarendon*; Patrick, IX, 510–14; DWL, MS Morrice Q, fos 255–9; Sir John Lowther, *Memoir of the Reign of James II*, ed. T. Zouch (York, 1808).

something worse would certainly be imposed upon them to ruin them, and having lost their reputation, they should fall unpitied; that they could never take an opportunity of refusing upon a point more justifiable; that their consenting to this, made their condition as precarious as that of any other Dissenters, who having no legal establishment, were forced to fly to the Declaration for protection.

On 11 May the leading London clergy met at William Sherlock's house in the Temple and decided to ask the bishops to petition the King. The next day an uneasy dinner party took place at Lambeth Palace. The presence of Bishops Cartwright and Watson rendered conversation stilted, but once they had left, Clarendon, Sancroft and the Bishops of London, Ely and Peterborough got down to business. They resolved that the Declaration should not be read and that the clergy should petition the King; 'in order thereunto' the Bishops of Winchester, Norwich, Gloucester, St Asaph, Bath and Wells, Bristol and Chichester were summoned to town. The next day, Sunday 13 May, the Bishops of Ely and Peterborough and fifteen leading clergy met at the Temple to organize the widest possible support for the defiance of the King. 'Near twenty of us, as I remember . . . were desired to feel the pulse of all the ministers in London, how they stood affected', wrote Simon Patrick. There now took place 'divers meetings of the clergy in divers places and they generally inclined to a refusal', according to Morrice the Nonconformist. His account suggests that the clergy were concerned to know how the Dissenters would react to their refusal and that it was a 'great encouragement' to them to gather that the Dissenters 'would be very well satisfied with the refusal if they would come up to a national temperament, and keep the Papists out of the government, and concur to a due liberty to others'. The leading London clergymen had reasonably good contacts with the leaders of Dissent, and were adept in leading them on, hinting at, without ever promising, a degree of emancipation. And that is what they now did. Included in the final petition to the King was the statement that the refusal to read the Declaration did not spring 'from any want of due tenderness to Dissenters; in relation to whom they are willing to come to such a temper, as shall be thought fit, when that matter shall be considered and settled in Parliament, and Convocation'. The more pressing task was to ensure that the clergy of the Church of England were behind the refusal to read the Declaration. By Thursday 17 May Patrick and the other clerical canvassers could be sure of 'near seventy' who would not read; Patrick wrote out a list of them and it was taken that night to Lambeth by Bishop White of Peterborough. Next day, Sancroft, Compton, White, Lloyd, Turner of Ely, Ken of Bath and Wells,

Trelawney of Bristol, Lake of Chichester, and Stillingfleet, Patrick, Tillotson, Tenison and Grove drew up the final petition to the King. That evening the six bishops crossed the river and handed it to the King. Sancroft 'did not go with it, because he has not been at court almost these two years . . . for the King told him long since that he need not come thither'.

The Church of England had made her stand. The activity of May can be seen as orchestrated by the old Yorkist party of Sancroft and Clarendon – the role of Bishop Turner of Ely as intermediary is particularly striking – or it can be seen as a campaign mounted from among those London clergy who had figured so prominently in the recent pamphleteering campaigns against Dissent and Rome.[281] More likely, it was a result of the coming together of these two groups. There was now no point in being half-hearted in defiance of the King. The churchmen were keen to harness the support of Dissent if fair words would achieve it; and they were determined that the clergy in the provinces should follow suit when their turn came to read the Declaration. Thousands of copies of the anonymous *Letter from a Clergy-man in the City, to his Friend in the Country* (dated 22 May) were distributed around the dioceses. This tract argued that reading the Declaration was the same as teaching it, that the clergy would be censured for it by their flocks, and that the 'wise and considering' Dissenters would not want a religious liberty purchased at such cost to church and state.

Only a handful read the Declaration in their churches in London, and 'far more than a majority refused to read it in the country within ten miles of London'.[282] Bishop Sprat had it read in Westminster Abbey, confirming Clarendon's opinion of him as a 'poor-spirited man', but later excused his action by admitting to 'dreadful apprehensions' that the Abbey might fall into Jesuit hands.[283] The rest of the country followed the capital's suit: Anthony Wood guessed that only 400 read it in the entire country.[284] On the other hand, Bishop Lamplugh of Exeter obliged his clergy to read the Declaration, much to the disgust of his neighbour Trelawney of Bristol – subsequently the vacillating Lamplugh added his signature to the bishops' petition of 18 May.[285] Herbert Croft, Bishop of Hereford, who had been both

281. Compare Bennett, 'The Seven Bishops' and R. Thomas, 'The Seven Bishops and their Petition, 18 May 1688', *JEH*, 12 (1961).
282. DWL, MS Morrice Q, fo. 261.
283. HMC, 15th Report, appendix 8 (Buccleuch MSS), p. 32; BL, MS Lansdowne 1024, fo. 49.
284. Wood, III, 267; Speck, *Reluctant Revolutionaries*, p. 222; MS Ballard 12, fo. 3.
285. MS Tanner 28, fo. 109.

an advocate of religious charity and a zealous Jesuit-hunter in the 1670s, now penned a reply to the *Letter from a Clergy-man*, explaining that he felt obliged to obey the King in all things not contrary to the law of God, and although the dispensing power had been declared illegal by Parliament in 1662 and 1672, it was not contrary to the word of God. Although he suffered 'a perfect agony' at breaking ranks with the other bishops, Croft felt God would forgive anything done 'out of pure obedience to my King, upon God's command'.[286]

Meanwhile the confrontation between church and monarch was moving to its climax. The very night that the bishops presented their petition, a pirated version of an earlier draft was being hawked around the streets of London, and within days the final version of the petition had appeared in print. At the beginning of June, Sancroft and the six bishops were charged with publishing a false, malicious and seditious libel; their trial was to be a watershed. The seven bishops managed to outmanoeuvre the King at every step. On 8 June they refused to give recognizances and so forced James to choose between remanding them in custody or dropping the case. They went to the Tower. There they were visited by their fellow clergymen, including a deputation of London Nonconformists, and by their aristocratic supporters. Clarendon told them of his interview with Lord Chancellor Jeffreys in which Jeffreys made 'many professions of service for them'. According to Jeffreys and others, the King wished things had never gone this far.[287] With an impressive array of gentlemen and nobility prepared to stand surety for them, the bishops were released on bail on 15 June: Clarendon found Lloyd of St Asaph surrounded by a crowd, who all thought 'it a blessing to kiss any of these bishops' hands or garments', so he snatched Lloyd up in his coach and took him home to dinner. The trial opened on 29 June and the prosecution immediately found themselves on the defensive, sidetracked into debating the 'falsehood' of the petition or, in other words, debating whether the Crown really did enjoy a suspending power in ecclesiastical causes.[288] When, on Saturday 30 June, Sir Roger Langley, foreman of the jury, brought in a verdict of 'not guilty', 'there was a most wonderful shout, that one would have thought the hall had cracked'. This glorious noise 'went out of the hall, which was crowded with people, and was taken up by the watermen, and in a moment, like a train of gunpowder set

---

286. Herbert Croft, *Discourse Concerning the Reading his Majesties Late Declaration* (1688); cf. MS Tanner 28, fos 72–4, for anonymous criticisms; and fo. 167, for Croft's own explanation.
287. *Correspondence of Clarendon*, II, 177; Reresby, *Memoirs*, p. 499.
288. Speck, *Reluctant Revolutionaries*, pp. 223, 142–3.

on fire, went both up and down the river, and along the streets, to the astonishment even of those that contributed to it'. The city was jubilant, there were 'multitudes of bonfires' that night, and more celebration as the news spread across the country; 'very few villages throughout all England' did not rejoice at the bishops' acquittal.[289]

The support for the seven bishops indicated that the church was popular, perhaps more popular than it had been before – Lowther writes of 'people, that upon other occasions had perhaps but little religion, and less veneration for that office' falling upon their knees to ask for the blessing of the acquitted prelates. In mid-June Bishop Levinz found 'vast numbers desiring confirmation' in Kent: he was met outside Canterbury by the clergy and laity and they 'made a very pretty cavalcata into the city' where he confirmed 5,000.[290] In July, Sancroft sent instructions down to the bishops to urge their clergy to apply themselves to their ministry, to catechize, read daily prayers and exhort their flocks to frequent communions. The clergy should preach against papal authority, while persuading the people to loyalty and obedience to their monarch. They should guard their flocks against the wiles of 'Romish emissaries', maintain 'a fair correspondence' with the gentry, and 'walk in wisdom towards those, who are not of our communion'. Protestant Dissenters should be gently persuaded to a full compliance with the church, or at least to appreciate that 'we may all walk by the same rule, and mind the same thing', and all opportunities should be taken to dispel the mistaken notion that the bishops were popishly affected.[291] At the same time Sancroft had general discussions with Nonconformist leaders and allowed a small committee of Anglican divines to draw up revisions of the liturgy in case there should be a need to 'bring in the honest, and moderate dissenters' to the church.[292]

Through July and August, his confidence strengthened immeasurably by the birth of a son on 10 June, James II pursued his self-destructive course. On 12 July the Ecclesiastical Commission ordered chancellors and archdeacons to inform them, before their meeting of 16 August, which clergymen had not read the Declaration; on 15 August Sprat of Rochester wrote to his fellow commissioners to explain that as they were going to proceed against non-readers 'it is absolutely impossible for me to serve his Majesty any longer in this Commission'. He had submitted, as his brethren had refused, on the grounds of conscience, and he could not now sit as a judge 'upon so

289. Lowther, *Memoir*, pp. 31–2.
290. MS Tanner 28, fos 84, 85.
291. Cardwell (ed), *Documentary Annals*, pp. 370–6.
292. Spurr, 'Comprehension', 437–8.

many pious, and excellent men: with whom, if it be God's will, it rather becomes me to suffer than to be in the least accessory to their suffering'.[293] No doubt Sprat, who took care that his 'very honest and handsome letter' was published, was emboldened by the news that the archdeacons had decided to ignore the Commission's instructions and to boycott the meeting of 16 August.[294] An humiliated Commission was forced to change tack, and instruct chancellors and archdeacons to include the inquiry among their visitation articles and to report by 6 December. Clearly the issue had been shelved.[295]

Late in August, with fears of a Dutch invasion growing, James decided to call a Parliament to meet on 27 November; and in a declaration of 21 September he set out his aims: although he would still 'endeavour a legal establishment of an universal liberty of conscience for all his subjects', he was determined to preserve the Church of England, and was happy that Roman Catholics should be barred from the House of Commons. In conversation with Clarendon, Jeffreys claimed to have penned this declaration with the agreement of Sunderland and others; 'he further told me, that the King intended to send for my Lord of Canterbury, my brother, myself, and some others of his old friends, to discourse with us upon the whole state of his affairs.'[296] Bishop Mews of Winchester had already met the King, and James now embarked on the slow and agonizing process of climbing down. On Monday 24 September James admitted to Clarendon that the Dutch were going to invade England 'in good earnest':

> 'And now, my lord,' said he, 'I shall see what the Church of England men will do.'
> I answered, 'And your Majesty will see they will behave themselves like honest men; though they have been somewhat severely used of late.'[297]

James summoned a group of bishops to meet him that Friday (28 September), and in the meantime forced an unwilling Bishop Turner of Ely to meet him privately, although they 'discoursed only of generals'. James and the bishops were playing cat and mouse.[298] On

293. MS Tanner 26, fo. 164; also see Evelyn, IV, 596.
294. The description is Evelyn's, IV, 596; A.T. Hart, *The Life and Times of John Sharp* (1949), pp. 108–9.
295. Kennett, p. 486.
296. Ibid., p. 489; Evelyn, IV, 597; *Correspondence of Clarendon*, II, 188.
297. *Correspondence of Clarendon*, II, 189.
298. 'Extraordinary consternation' reigned at court, according to Evelyn, IV, 598–607; James changed his mind about concessions on several occasions; see *Correspondence of Clarendon*, II, 191.

the Friday, Sancroft was too ill to attend, and Compton and Turner were out of town, but James would still only speak in general terms. The disappointed bishops 'entreated my Lord of Canterbury to procure for us a second and more particular audience; wherein we might all deliver our plain and sincere sense of things'.[299] So on Sunday, Sancroft met the King privately and tactfully told him that the bishops needed to hear more from him. That same day Bishop Compton's suspension was rescinded. Finally, the bishops had their 'full audience' with the King on the morning of Wednesday 3 October, and that afternoon Bishop Turner returned to the King with their conclusions drawn into heads. The urgency of the situation demanded that royal policy be immediately thrown into reverse. The churchmen's proposals turned back the clock to the halcyon days of the early 1680s. James was urged to return local government to the hands of the traditional Anglican rulers; to quash *quo warranto* proceedings; to desist from further dispensations; and to curb the Roman Catholic bishops. The Ecclesiastical Commission should be abolished; the principal and fellows of Magdalen restored; the vacant sees filled – and Sancroft here made a personal plea that one of the bishops present might be elevated to the see of York – and a free Parliament called 'in which the Church of England may be secured according to the Acts of Uniformity; provision may be made for a due liberty of conscience, and for securing the liberties and properties of all your subjects'. Finally, the King was urged to allow his loyal bishops to offer him some arguments for returning to the Church of England in which he had been born and bred.[300] James seemed to digest several of the demands. On 5 October the Ecclesiastical Commission was dissolved. On the 8th, James met the bishops and, having considered their paper, 'at which he seemed displeased', he announced that the business of Magdalen College was to be put into the hands of its Visitor, Bishop Mews.[301] But these gains were not secure. On 15 October the Prince of Wales was baptized according to the Roman rite. Timothy Hall, 'one of the meanest and most obscure of the city-divines', but also one of the few who had read the Declaration, was preferred to the see of Oxford and consecrated on 7 October. A month later the timid Lamplugh, rather than Turner, White or Lloyd, was translated to the see of

299. BL, MS Lansdowne 1024, fo. 51.
300. See MS Tanner 28, fo. 189; Kennett, pp. 490–1; N.N., *An Account of the Late Proposals of the Archbishop of Canterbury, with some other Bishops to his Majesty. In a Letter to M.B.*(1688).
301. Deputy Lieutenants and JPs were restored on 12th, and charters on the 17th. Sunderland was dismissed on 27 October.

York. The bishops had little cause for confidence when they dispersed to their dioceses in mid-October: even Princess Anne believed they were wasting their time, 'the King will not harken to them'.[302] Roger Morrice felt that the government was 'like a vessel tossed up and down at sea, and ready to sink. The bishops have now given the vessel a twig to take hold on whereby it may draw it self to land, but they seem yet to keep the hatchet in their own hand, by which they can cut off that twig at their pleasure.'[303]

All these developments were overshadowed by the greater events which were already in train, events which were to attain a momentum of their own once William of Orange had landed on 5 November.[304] Yet still James did not grasp the twig held out to him by the churchmen. On 17 November, Sancroft, Sprat, Lamplugh and Turner petitioned the King to call a free Parliament as the only means of averting bloodshed – and received a very dusty answer.[305] Only ten days later, after sacrificing his military advantage and on the advice of a Council of Peers, James had to agree to call a Parliament and send commissioners to William. William and the commissioners hammered out a truce, despite Whig attempts to wreck it. It was James himself who wrecked the plan when, unnerved by the publication of William's 'Third Declaration', a bogus ultimatum, and by the growth of anti-popish disorder, he fled for safety on 11 December. Rochester and Bishop Turner of Ely, the old Yorkist politicians, immediately stepped into the breach and summoned a Council of Peers to meet at the Guildhall in London. In their Declaration of 11 December these notables applied themselves to William to obtain a free Parliament which might secure the laws of the land, the liberty and property of the subject, and 'the Church of England in particular, with a due liberty to Protestant Dissenters'.[306] The Lords continued to meet until James returned to London on 16 December. Over the next few days, James was encouraged to withdraw to Rochester, William entered London and called another meeting of peers, and finally on 23 December James fled to France. By Christmas the peers had asked the Prince of Orange to issue writs for a Convention and to assume the government until that assembly met, and on 28 December he agreed.

302. *Correspondence of Clarendon*, II, 194.
303. DWL, MS Morrice Q, fo. 303.
304. This paragraph follows the narrative of R.A. Beddard, *A Kingdom without a King* (Oxford, 1988). Also see J. Miller, 'Proto-Jacobitism? The Tories and the Revolution of 1688–9', in *The Jacobite Challenge*, ed. E. Cruickshanks and J. Black (Edinburgh, 1988).
305. *Correspondence of Clarendon*, II, 205.
306. Beddard, *Kingdom*, pp. 71–2.

The Church of England could not flee from her responsibilities as easily as her Supreme Governor. Since the 1640s the church had made a substantial emotional and intellectual investment in the Stuart family and in the doctrines of divine right and passive obedience. Throughout the troubled 1680s she had repeatedly asserted the duty of passive obedience. The clergy were 'loyalist' almost to a man. In the spring of 1688, Stillingfleet and Lloyd had advised Daniel Finch not to consider rebellion.[307] The only churchman who conspired against James was Compton who – perhaps with good reason – signed the invitation to William to 'rescue the nation'; although one should note that Gilbert Burnet had been at the Hague since 1686. In general, the churchmen dreaded a return to civil and religious strife. 'I hope by this time the danger of invasion is over,' wrote one optimistic clergyman from the sticks on 17 October;

> This place [Worcester] affords no news, but that there is some danger of being distinguished by names and parties again, which God prevent and give us all one heart to do our duty, and stick to our principles of loyalty in the strictest manner, as I hope, we of the Church of England shall ... pray let me know, if the London clergy do not in this juncture unanimously preach up loyalty.[308]

Several of those who played a leading part in opposing the King in May sought to save him in December. Although Sancroft had succumbed to a 'strange, obstinate passiveness', Bishops Turner and Mews tried to keep James's kingdom for him during his first flight by organizing the assembly of peers at the Guildhall, and when he returned they urged him to stay, to maintain his rights and attend the Council of Peers. But all was in vain. James's final flight on 23 December hit Turner and Clarendon 'like an earthquake'.[309]

In the New Year, with the King gone, the unity of the Church of England began to collapse. On 21 January a meeting at Ely House was reported, where 'some high words passed between Dr Sherlock and Dr Burnet. There are four opinions among the members, viz 1. for recalling the King, 2. for a regency, 3. for crowning the princess, and 4. for crowning the prince.'[310] Confusion reigned among the clergy and the members of the newly convened Parliament. Preaching to Parliament on 30 January, John Sharp 'talked against deposing' and prayed for James II, which led the house into 'extravagant heats' as some MPs wished to thank him and others to pack him off to the Tower. 31 January was a day of thanksgiving,

307. Henry Horwitz, *Revolution Politicks* (Cambridge, 1968), pp. 52–3.
308. MS Ballard 12, fo. 40.
309. Beddard, *Kingdom*, pp. 63–4.
310. MS Ballard 45, fo. 24.

a day of bonfires and sermons[,] our parsons some preached obedience and others magnified the deliverance[.] Dr Lake before the Lord Mayor and Court of Aldermen not only prayed lengthily for the King: but preached obedience to the higher powers. Dr Sherlock said: He could not find any text in the Bible that would make that King absolute that was not so by the constitution but said subjects ought not to rebel and that God keep us sober.[311]

As it became apparent that James was not to be restored to his throne, the problem of allegiance became acute for all churchmen, but especially perhaps for the King's old and sorely tried 'friends'. Sancroft refused to wait upon William, or to act without a commission from James II or before a Convocation met. The archbishop and his allies were already on the path which led to their refusal of the new oaths of allegiance, their suspension from office in August and their deprivation at the end of January 1690.

Meanwhile the pressure for some amelioration of the Nonconformists' position was inescapable. The church had seen the danger of a Nonconformist–Catholic alliance, while Dissenting hopes had been raised by the 1688 negotiations with the churchmen. In addition, it had long been known that the Calvinist William was inclined towards religious liberty for sober Dissenters, and when he arrived in England his favour towards the Presbyterians was remarked upon. And so percipient and pragmatic Anglican clergy and politicians moved quickly to propose their own measure of reunion in 1689. While the succession was still under discussion, Tillotson, Sharp, Patrick, Tenison and Bishop Lloyd of St Asaph met on 14 January to draft a bill 'to be offered by the bishops' in the forthcoming Convention Parliament.[312] Daniel Finch, the Earl of Nottingham, who had been responsible for the comprehension and toleration bills in 1680, now took control of these proposals and refined them in a series of meetings with unknown 'bishops', and other clergymen, before introducing them into Parliament. Since Sancroft had made his refusal to act in this matter plain to Thomas Tenison on 3 January, and later withheld his approval, Nottingham relied heavily upon the group of London divines who had encouraged the seven bishops, had been involved in revising the liturgy in the late summer of 1688, and had attended the meeting of 14 January 1689. Some of these clergy, such as John Tillotson, were prepared to make extensive concessions to win over Nonconformists, but the majority were zealous Anglicans, with proven records of

311.　Ibid., fo. 25. Also see Evelyn, IV, 620; Hart, *Sharp*, pp. 117–18.
312.　Patrick, IX, 516–17.

opposition to Dissent and comprehension; they were reinforced by the presence of bishops like Lloyd of St Asaph and Compton of London, whose loyalty to the church was equally indisputable. What had changed were the circumstances, not the men.

The bills brought forward by Nottingham were designed to embrace most of moderate Dissent within the church and to allow restricted liberty of worship to the recalcitrant Protestant minority who defied comprehension. The bills were intended to complement each other, which is why the apparently deliberate sacrifice of the comprehension bill is so difficult to explain. At a hint from Nottingham, the Tory Anglican MPs petitioned William to support and defend the Church of England and to call a Convocation to consider the comprehension proposal.[313] Everyone recognized that this spelt the end for comprehension. With the comprehension bill lying on the table, the toleration bill was unenthusiastically advanced through Parliament and received the royal assent on 24 May.[314] Thus the toleration covered many more English Protestants than had been intended. Although many observers were mystified by the Tory motive in virtually ensuring the passage of toleration at the expense of comprehension,[315] it may have reflected no more than their unwillingness to allow the extension of political rights which would go along with a wider definition of the established church. William had not yet finally thrown in his lot with the Tory church party, and so the King and his Secretary of State, Nottingham, sometimes found themselves working at cross purposes. On 16 March William had proposed to abolish the Anglican sacramental test for office-holders. Parliament rejected the proposal angrily and parliamentary opinion rallied to the defence of the church as a political establishment.[316] This Parliament, like most of its recent predecessors, understood Anglicanism as a badge of political and ideological trustworthiness; widening the terms of communion meant widening access to office; but a toleration would simply allow freedom of worship, while restricting political power to safe hands. The cost to the Church of England was incalculable.

In 1689 the Church of England was denied a valuable transfusion of talent and enthusiasm, which went instead to strengthen rival

313. H. Horwitz, *Parliament, Policy and Politics in the Reign of William III* (Manchester, 1977), p. 25.
314. Spurr, 'Comprehension', 927, 938–9, 946; Horwitz, *Parliament*, pp. 28–9.
315. See DWL, MS Morrice Q, fo. 558; MS Rawlinson Letters 48, fo. 98.
316. Horwitz, *Parliament*, p. 22; G.V. Bennett, 'King William III and the Episcopate', in *Essays in Modern English Church History*, ed. G.V. Bennett and J.D. Walsh (1966), pp. 115–16.

Protestant denominations. But far more importantly, the Glorious Revolution's religious settlement reduced the Church of England from the *national* to merely the *established* church. In many ways this was simply a legal and political recognition of a situation which had prevailed since the early 1640s, but it cut the Church of England to the quick, since the claim to be the national church had been her *raison d'être* for the last forty years. She was about to enter a period of profound reassessment, prompted by the realization that for many the churches represented little more than rival interest groups. This crisis of Anglican confidence was deepened when six bishops and four hundred clergy were ejected from the church because they could not swear the oaths of allegiance to William and Mary. These 'Nonjurors' were affronted by the breach of the divine right of succession, by the Toleration Act (which was seen as a virtual licence for irreligion as well as sectarianism), by the illegal and uncanonical deprivation of bishops, and by the moves afoot to dilute the liturgy. And they had many sympathizers among the parish clergy, sympathizers who would soon find a voice in the Lower House of Convocation. During the 1690s, the clergy of the Church of England became divided along political, ideological and ecclesiological lines in a way that would have been scarcely conceivable to their predecessors in the Restoration church. It is true that, with hindsight, one can discern in the façade of the Restoration church some of the hairline cracks which were to become great fissures in the Augustan church; but the Revolution of 1688 and its repercussions opened up far more animosities and differences. For the history of the Restoration Church of England is essentially a tale of clerical coherence and unity; the nature, achievements and limitations of that unity form the subject of the next chapter.

Chapter 3

The Unity of the National Church

The Toleration Act of 1689 marked the end of the Church of England's claim to be the national church, the single all-inclusive church of the English people, after almost thirty years of struggle. But why had the Church of England for so long set her face against religious pluralism, opposed reunion with sober Nonconformists, and hounded Dissenters and recusants? And why had the churchmen clung so doggedly to the Stuarts, and to the ideal of a strict alliance between church and Crown, when experience had repeatedly proved the Stuarts untrustworthy and the state at best a fair-weather friend? Self-interest presumably played a part, as did the clergy's conviction that religious pluralism was quite simply 'destructive of the common peace and amity of mankind'. 'Toleration and liberty of conscience in the church are as plausibly cried up as liberty and property in the state, and indeed each from the same cause and with the same effect, a stiff, unwieldy, restless, humour hurrying to disorder, anarchy and confusion.'[1] But the churchmen also had a less worldly appreciation of the national church. To state a simple truth – and one which is too easily and too often overlooked – the clergy were convinced that the Church of England was the best constituted church and the safest path to heaven. Even those who had conformed un-enthusiastically in 1660–2 were committed by their conformity to the proposition that the church offered a better route than her opponents: the majority of churchmen sincerely believed the Church of England 'to be most comely in discipline, most retentive of good antiquity, most certain of fundamental truth, and of all churches in the world to have the least disagreement with all Christian churches throughout the world'. She was 'a lily among thorns', for William Sancroft, 'the purest certainly upon earth'.[2]

1. Samuel Parker, *Discourse of Ecclesiastical Politie* (1670), p. vi; BL, MS Lansdowne 960, fo. 69v.
2. John Hacket, *A Century of Sermons* (1675), p. 947; G. D'Oyly, *The Life of William Sancroft* (1821), I, 166–7; N. Sykes, *From Sheldon to Secker* (Cambridge, 1959),

This confidence in the church was more than ecclesiastical chauvinism, it was a product of the Restoration church's 'ecclesiology' or her theology of the nature and purpose of the church. Since 'the Christian Church is nothing else but such a society of men as is in covenant with God through Christ', all ecclesiology is founded on the person and office of Christ.[3] But when one goes beyond this Christological foundation to consider the nature of *churches* and their relationships to each other, ecclesiology becomes subject to debate and refinement. It has long been apparent that the mid-seventeenth century was a turning point in Anglican ecclesiology, that the Church of England's understanding of herself, her Reformation, and her Nonconformist and Roman Catholic rivals, was transformed – yet historians have fought shy of describing this change too precisely. It had much to do with clarifying both the church's relationship to the universal Catholic Church and the role of the bishop in constituting a church. One recent commentator has suggested that for the first century of the Church of England's existence 'Anglicanism was a state religious monopoly and its symbol was sacred kingship', but that from the mid-seventeenth century the church had embarked on 'a long and reluctant retreat' towards the 'apostolic paradigm' of the nineteenth century in which the bishop had replaced the King as sacred symbol.[4] This shift had vital implications for the idea of a national church. For if the Church of England was the territorial church of a godly prince then her claim to be the national church was well founded; but if the Church of England was constituted by her bishops, why should she be coterminous with the realm of England?

Although, when viewed in this long perspective, the seventeenth-century developments appear reluctant and confused, a sort of ecclesiological half-way house between fully elaborated models of the church, they can, and perhaps should, be seen in the more positive light shed by contemporary concerns and priorities. The Church of England had been bedevilled by ecclesiological ambiguities since the Reformation, and now, in the difficult years of the mid-seventeenth century, a small group of Anglican divines proposed a route out of this morass, a route which depended on the office of the bishop *and*

pp. 223–4. Also see Hickes in Gibson, I, pt. i, 214; Tillotson, II, 268; Evelyn, III, 303; IV, 73.

3. William Sherlock in *Cases*, p. 18.
4. P.D.L. Avis, *Anglicanism and the Christian Church – Theological Resources in Historical Perspective* (Edinburgh, 1989), pp. xv, 158, 308–9. On the significance of the mid-seventeenth century, see pp. 17, 90, 93, 94; J.W. Packer, *The Transformation of Anglicanism* (1969); H.R. McAdoo, *The Spirit of Anglicanism* (1965).

the authority of a national church. These apologists vindicated the autonomy of national churches under their bishops without surrendering a jot of the royal supremacy. The attraction of this ecclesiology was that it simultaneously, and elegantly, made sense of the church's relations with the Church of Rome and with Protestant Dissenters. Consequently, this may have been the moment when the Church of England could be said to come of age, when she realized her potential for 'Anglicanism', for something distinct from both her Protestant sisters and her Catholic heritage. Some churchmen, of course, had reservations about the new ecclesiology since it seemed to cut the Church of England off from other Protestant churches and to elevate episcopacy to an unacceptable height. But, as I shall show, the second great achievement of the Church of England between 1662 and 1689 was to maintain a semblance of unity among the clergy. This was achieved by a realistic acceptance of the tensions and ambiguities within a body of shared Anglican belief, by allowing ecclesiological arguments to be pitched at a variety of levels to suit different audiences and different advocates, and by a pragmatic willingness to live with intellectual anomalies, confusions and evasions.

'Out of this Ark . . . ': The Church, Schism and Separation

The Catholic Church is but one, and can be but one; because all the Christians in the world belong to it: and that is the Church which we profess to believe in our creeds. But particular churches are many, as many as the nations are that own and profess the Christian religion: nay, as many as are the dioceses into which the Christian people are distributed under their several bishops. But yet all these churches, whether they be diocesan, or provincial, or national, they are all parts of the universal Church, just as our several limbs and members are parts of our body.[5]

Now as our Christianity obliges us to be members of that body of Christ the Catholic Church: so the eternal reasons of peace and order bind us to communicate with that part of the Catholic Church, in which our lot hath placed us, except it can manifestly appear, that that part is so corrupted that we cannot communicate with it without evident hazard of our salvation.[6]

5. John Sharp, *Sermons* (1735–48), VII, 118.
6. Robert Conold, *The Notion of Schism Stated* (2nd edn, 1677), pp. 23–4.

The term 'Church' has several simultaneous meanings.[7] At its simplest, 'the Church' is the people of God. The 'invisible Church' comprises the whole company of God's chosen people, those ordained to eternal life in all churches and all ages, past, present and future. The term 'visible Church' refers to the fellowship of Christian believers both in a particular place and everywhere on earth; and can be used, by extension, of the bishops, pastors and governors of a church. The Church, then, has a corporate nature and a spiritual life; she is separate from and transcends the world, yet her spiritual reality also has a physical manifestation. Traditionally, the four 'notes' or marks of the Church are unity, holiness, catholicity and apostolicity: Christ founded one Church, set her apart as sacred and intended her to be universal; this Church teaches the doctrine of the Apostles and is historically descended from them. The membership and unity of the Church depend upon participation in the visible sacraments of baptism and holy communion.

This traditional understanding of the nature of the Church was overturned by the Reformation of the sixteenth century. For the Reformers, Christ was present in the Church through the gospel.[8] These evangelicals saw the Church more as the creation of the Word of God than the product of sacramental relationships. Possession of the Word was paramount, and the true comprehension of the saving doctrine of the gospel lay at the heart of the Church. The 'notes' of the Church, as taught by Luther, still included the two sacraments and discipline, but the Protestant churches defined themselves doctrinally, by the pure, evangelical, exposition of the Word, and they rooted their identity in, and guaranteed their unity by, a confession of faith or a statement of belief binding on laity and clergy alike. So in these 'confessional' churches, the Word – a common profession of right doctrine and, above all, of the doctrine of justification – came to be regarded as the predominant note of the true Church: the Church became identified with the community of professors or the gathering of the visible godly; and the clergy took on the role of prophets of the Word. This emphasis on the Word had two further consequences. One was that it subverted the visible Church: the workings of the Word of God are a mystery, that which saves an individual and makes him a member of the Church is the inward act of faith, and so the 'invisible Church' rather than the visibly godly are, in the last resort, the true Church. More importantly for the present argument, the emphasis on the Word in confessional churches meant that it was the common profession of right

7. E.G. Jay, *The Church – Its Changing Image through Twenty Centuries* (London, 1977), I.
8. See P.D.L. Avis, *The Church in the Theology of the Reformers* (1981).

doctrine which bound such churches to the true Church of the Apostles and Fathers: a church was Apostolic because it taught the faith delivered by the Apostles, not because it was founded by an Apostle. Catholicity was seen to reside in the continuity of true doctrine, in comparison with which institutional continuity, visible clerical succession, and the mediation of the church (through what might be called 'sacramental grace'), were of minor or even negligible importance. In ecclesiology, then, the Reformation can be seen as establishing a series of polarities, between visible and invisible, continuity and reform, the sacrament and the Word, Catholic and Reformed.

In ecclesiology, however, as in so much else, the Church of England fell between two stools. Unlike the foreign Reformed churches, the English church was not constituted afresh at the Reformation, but simply continued as a purified version of the medieval church. The historical accident of her politically inspired Reformation left the English church with vaguely Reformed doctrine, a medieval church government, and a royal Supreme Governor. Her Thirty-Nine Articles were a statement of what the church held to be true doctrine, but they were not a confession of faith.[9] In defining what she believed, the Church of England laid as much weight upon her Prayer Book as upon the Articles or Homilies. The royal supremacy had replaced papal supremacy over the English church: although the bishops, archdeacons, and deans and chapters remained in day-to-day control of the church, the clergy could not gather in a synod nor could the church issue Canons without royal leave; the ordering of the church became the province of the godly prince or magistrate, who guaranteed the primitive, pure pattern of ministry and ecclesiastical government. The magistrate, however, laid no claim to spiritual or sacerdotal power and the church accorded him none: 'we commit the keys of the kingdom of heaven only unto the priest'.[10] In theory, the non-confessional Church of England faced a problem of identity. What made her a separate and distinct church? Did one become a member of the Church of England by virtue of being a subject of her godly prince or through the sacraments of the church? In practice, such questions were virtually unthinkable; church and state were inseparable: in Hooker's famous phrase, 'there is not any man of the Church of England but the same man is a member of the

9. W.P. Haugaard, *Elizabeth and the English Reformation* (Cambridge, 1968), ch. 6.

10. John Jewel, *Works* (Parker Society, Cambridge, 1845–50), III, 356. On the royal supremacy see Haugaard, *Elizabeth and Reformation*, pp. 270–1; C. Cross, *The Royal Supremacy in the Elizabethan Church* (1969); P. Collinson, *The Religion of Protestants* (Oxford, 1982).

commonwealth, nor a member of the commonwealth which is not also a member of the Church of England.'

The Church of England's mixed heritage was not initially a source of much pride. The Erastianism of her Reformation left her ecclesiology looking superficial and even confused; the sacramental tradition of the Roman Catholic Church had been displaced, but the proclamation of the Word as a means of bringing Christians to salvation was curiously muffled in the Reformed English church. For the first century of her existence, the cry from Protestant activists was that the church was but 'halfly reformed' and the pressure was to bring her into line with the continental Reformed churches by making the Word more central to her being. This argument drew support from the Lutheran overtones of Article 19, 'Of the Church';

> The visible Church of Christ is a congregation of faithful men, in the which the pure Word of God is preached and the Sacraments be duly ministered according to Christ's ordinance in all those things that of necessity are requisite to the same.[11]

Elizabethan puritans sought to make doctrine the 'foundation' of the church: from St Paul, these divines had learned that the Church of Christ is built of living stones and timber, of those born to new life in Christ through faith; and from Calvin and his successors, they took the predestinarianism which linked personal salvation to membership of the godly community and which identified the true visible church with the godly community. Historians of puritanism have quite rightly made much of the 'existential' significance of right doctrine, of the puritan idea that the church grew out of a common profession of doctrine, out of 'edification', and a common experience of the Word; and they have emphasized the tension which necessarily exists between this conception of the church as a godly community and the ideal of a national church.[12] For example, unlike a national church, the godly community did not need to seek its forebears in previous churches for it was a creation of the living Word of God. The Word of God had never been tied to any one visible church or succession of churches, for all particular churches are liable to error or failure; had not the visible church of the Middle Ages, the papal Church of Rome, become so corrupt that true religion had taken flight? It was Luther 'whom the Lord did ordain

11. See Jay, *Church*, pp. 184–5; Avis, *Church*, pp. 66–7
12. The classic work on this theme is J.S. Coolidge, *The Pauline Renaissance in England – Puritanism and the Bible* (1970), esp. ch. 2; Coolidge's insights have been further developed by Peter Lake in a series of works, particularly, *Anglicans and Puritans? Presbyterianism and English Conformist Thought from Whitgift to Hooker* (1988), see chs 1, 2 and p. 241.

and appoint, through his great mercy, to be the principal organ and minister under him, to reform and re-edify again the desolate ruins of his religion'.[13] The Reformed tradition regarded the Papacy and Church of Rome as the Antichrist, the antithesis of the true Church of Christ, and denied any continuity between the Church of Rome and the Reformed English church. Indeed, for many English puritans religious truth necessarily lay at the opposite pole to the teaching and practice of the Roman Antichrist. This identification of Rome with the Antichrist was part of the unspoken consensus of the Elizabethan and Jacobean church, not least because it justified the Reformation: the 'charge of God' (in Revelations xviii) to separate from the Antichrist 'freeth us from schism: for there is no sin, no schism in that which God commandeth to be done'.[14]

The embarrassment was that the Church of England, as constituted in the sixteenth century, had undeniable continuities with the Church of Rome. This was not simply a matter of 'popish' vestments and rites, or 'prelatical' government, for the connection was recognized even in her formularies: Article 19 asserted that the Church of Rome had erred in matters of faith, just as the churches of Jerusalem, Alexandria and Antioch had, but it did not deny that Rome was part of the Church of Christ. In the sixteenth century one or two churchmen were prepared to concede that salvation was possible within the communion of Rome.[15] But in the first decades of the next century some of the church's leading divines acknowledged that the Church of Rome was a true, if corrupt, church: an acknowledgement perhaps prompted by the need to account for the salvation of their forefathers in the Roman church; or by their desire to escape the impasse which had been reached in the controversy with Presbyterianism; or by an ecclesiological re-evaluation which led to the rejection of 'anti-popery' and its identification of Rome with the Antichrist.[16] These churchmen were equally prepared to admit to

13. Foxe quoted by R.H. Fritze, 'Root or Link? Luther's Position in the Historical Debate over the Legitimacy of the Church of England, 1558–1625', *JEH*, 37 (1986), 290.
14. Richard Bernard, *Looke beyond Luther* (1623), p. 45, quoted by A. Milton, 'The Laudians and the Church of Rome c. 1625–1640' (unpublished Cambridge University Ph.D thesis, 1989), p. 39; also see chs 1 and 2. Also helpful on this subject are P. Lake, 'The Significance of the Elizabethan Identification of the Pope as Antichrist', *JEH*, 31 (1980); H.F. Woodhouse, *The Doctrine of the Church in Anglican Theology, 1547–1603* (1954), p. 146; Lake, *Anglican and Puritans?*, pp. 157–8; Avis, *Anglicanism*, pp. 52–3.
15. See Avis, *Church*, pp. 67–8; Woodhouse, *Doctrine*, pp. 145–6.
16. On these putative motives see Lake, *Anglicans and Puritans?*, pp. 155–7, 229; Avis, *Church*, p. 69; Milton, 'Laudians and Church of Rome'; C.M. Dent, *Protestant Reformers in Elizabethan Oxford* (Oxford, 1983), p. 232.

the Church of England's continuity with the medieval Church of Rome, and thus to spike the persistent Roman gibe, where was your church before Luther? 'Before Luther, the religion we profess was in our own church, though loaded and obscured with Romish errors and superstitions; and we have now no new religion, nor no new church, but the old religion, and the old church reformed and restored to its first beauty and lustre.'[17] As the Church of England matured, her Catholic inheritance increasingly came into its own. The judicious Richard Hooker, for instance, offered a generous and inclusive definition of the church 'by its outward profession of faith taken at face value', the profession of one Lord, one faith, and one baptism; and it has been argued that this amounted to a synthesis of the Reformed doctrine of justification in the context of a visible Catholic society, a synthesis which has been dubbed 'a reformed Catholicity'.[18]

Yet this intellectual synthesis was far from being 'Anglicanism', far from a self-conscious and widely held identity for the Church of England; in the early seventeenth century the Church of England remained torn between the Reformed and the Catholic, rather than united in a 'Reformed Catholicity'. If, as some have suggested, Hooker was mounting a full-scale attack on Reformed piety under the guise of a simple refutation of Presbyterianism, and was inching his way towards a distinctive 'conformist' style of piety, built on the sacraments, then he may well have been a forerunner of the Laudians. The Laudians certainly stressed the mediation of the church and her sacraments, and could justifiably claim to be re-asserting neglected elements in the Church of England's ecclesiological, theological and devotional heritage. Yet they did not create a new ecclesiology, but rather, in the words of one scholar, they 'effectively widened the ecclesiological options available'.[19] Theologically they were principally *anti-Calvinists*, critics of the theology of their fellow Protestants, a force of opposition rather than construction, a disruptive group whose fate indicated just how small a minority they were in the Early Stuart Church of England.[20] The elaboration of a true 'Anglicanism', rooted in ecclesiology and

---

17. Freeman in Gibson, I, pt. iii, 8; for examples from the earlier seventeenth century, see Fritze, 'Root or Link?', 299–301; Milton, 'Laudians and Church of Rome', ch. 6.
18. Avis, *Anglicanism*, p. 48.
19. Milton, 'Laudians and Church of Rome', p. 296.
20. See Lake, *Anglicans and Puritans?*, ch. 4; N.R.N. Tyacke, *Anti-Calvinists* (Oxford, 1987); J.S. Morrill, 'The Religious Context of the English Civil War', *TRHS*, 34 (1984), 163; D. Hoyle, 'A Commons Investigation of Arminianism and Popery in Cambridge on the Eve of the Civil War', *HJ*, 29 (1986).

theology, with a compelling vision of personal and communal piety, and widely disseminated among the churchmen, was the work of the next generation, the generation of the Interregnum and Restoration.

One of the first steps in this work was a shift in the Church of England's ecclesiological centre of gravity towards a more Catholic understanding of the nature of the church. Surprisingly, perhaps, this shift was particularly visible in the debate with Rome, which by mid-century had largely succeeded the controversy with English Presbyterianism as the force shaping the church's ecclesiology. The English church had always justified her breach from Rome by claiming that the Church of Rome was corrupt: Anglican apologists charged Rome with introducing 'errors and superstitions'; in his famous 'challenge sermon' of November 1559, Bishop Jewel challenged the Romanists to justify from scripture and the Early Church twenty-seven separate beliefs and practices. Bishop Joseph Hall's *The Old Religion* (1628) examined each of the new points of faith which the Church of Rome has sought to obtrude upon her adherents and showed that they had neither scriptural, nor traditional, nor rational justification. Although Hall did refute Rome's claims to be the universal church and to make new points of faith, he based his case against the Church of Rome and, by implication, his defence of the English Reformation, on the corrupt innovations introduced by Rome.[21] Yet if Hall's book is compared with a typical work of apologetics from the Restoration, such as Samuel Freeman's *A Plain and Familiar Discourse* of 1687, a striking difference emerges. Freeman, too, denounced Rome's errors; he complained of the twelve new Articles of Faith introduced in the creed of 1564, and traced the very recent origin of doctrines such as purgatory, transubstantiation, indulgences, lay communion in one kind, the seven sacraments, and papal supremacy and infallibility. But the crux of his argument had little to do with these innovations; rather it lay in the Church of England's authority, 'as she was a free independent church as well as the Roman', to separate from Rome in order to move closer to the Catholic Church.[22] It seems then that, in the earlier part of the century, most Anglican apologists concentrated their fire upon the

21.   To an extent, the Anglicans were merely replying to Roman accusations of heresy in repudiating vital points of faith and practice. For instance, Lancelot Andrewes argued on ground chosen by Bellarmine that the Church of England was Catholic despite her rejection of transubstantiation, the invocation of saints, and the temporal authority of the Pope. See P.A. Welsby, *Lancelot Andrewes* (1964), ch. 5. Hall's *The Old Religion* was criticized by Henry Burton and others for its apparent admission that Rome was a true church, see Milton, 'Laudians and Church of Rome', pp. 43–4.

22.   Freeman in Gibson, I, pt. i, 4–7.

novelties of faith and pratice introduced by Rome, but in the second half, they were questioning the authority by which these errors were imposed. The authority of churches, rather than their innovations and corruption, had moved to the centre of the stage in the controversy between Anglicans and Romanists.[23]

In a corresponding development, 'schism' was replacing 'heresy' as Rome's principal charge against the Church of England. In the sixteenth century, Bishop Jewel had complained that the Romanists 'slander us as heretics, and say that we have left the Church and fellowship of Christ'; in other words, Rome made the greater charge of heresy, or the profession of false doctrine, which by definition must always include the sin of schism, the 'voluntary and causeless separation from the Christian Church of which one is a member'.[24] Late seventeenth-century churchmen believed that the topic of schism had been neglected by their forebears because Rome's apologists had preferred to level the charge of heresy against the English church.[25] But the Roman Church had now come to regard the schism as a much greater obstacle to reconciliation with the Church of England than their differences over doctrine.[26] Where the Catholic Church 'is to be found, and what are the measures of our obligation to it, hath been a long and great debate, especially between us and the Romanists', wrote William Cave in 1684. 'In most of their late controversial books they have seemed ready to waive disputes about particular points, in hopes of greater advantage, which they promise themselves from this venerable name, and that bold, though most false and presumptuous claim which they lay to the thing itself, even exclusive to all others.'[27] Or, as Edward Stillingfleet told the Romanists, 'the truth is, all that you have in effect to say for your church is, that she is infallible, and the Catholic Church, and by this means you think to cast the schism upon us'.[28]

23. A similar trend can be seen in contemporary French controversy; see A. Rébelliau, *Bossuet* (Paris, 1892) pp. 24–44; W.E. Rex, *Essays on Pierre Bayle and Religious Controversy* (The Hague, 1965), ch. 1. For signs of this shift among Laud and his acolytes in the first half of the century see Milton, 'Laudians and Church of Rome', pp. 106, 109–16, 240–6.

24. Jewel, *Works*, III, 77, 91–2; Grove in *Cases*, p. 3; Michael Altham in Gibson, I, pt. i, 154; William Clagett in Gibson, III, pt. i, 439.

25. Sharp, *Sermons*, VII, 146; Henry Dodwell, *Separation of Churches from Episcopal Government, as practised by the present Non-Conformists, proved Schismatical* (1679), p. 34.

26. Altham in Gibson, I, pt. i, 54; *The Correspondence of Isaac Basire*, ed. W.N. Darnell (1831), pp. 61–7; *The Rawdon Papers*, ed. E. Berwick (1819), p. 102.

27. Cave in Gibson, I, pt. i, 134; the Roman priests insist 'as their main artifice' on the impossibility of salvation outside the Catholic Church, according to Freeman in Gibson, I, pt. i, 4.

28. Stillingfleet, *A Rational Account* (1664; Oxford, 1844 edn cited), II, 84.

Religious controversy tends to accumulate new arguments without discarding older lines of attack: throughout the Restoration, churchmen criticized Roman errors and innovations, as Freeman did; and in 1686 it was still thought worthwhile to republish Bishop Hall's *Old Religion*. In 1679 Bishop Compton of London conducted a clerical conference on the well-rehearsed topics of communion in one kind, prayers in an unknown tongue, and prayers to saints.[29] Thomas Comber answered *The Plausible Arguments Of a Romish Priest* in 1686 by pitting the Word of God against Roman 'Tradition'. Meanwhile the London clergy collaborated on a work in which all fifteen of Cardinal Bellarmine's 'notes' of the church were scrutinized. But beneath these reminders of past battles, there had been a discernible shift in the central argument – the controversy now turned on the question of the churches' authority and relationship with the Catholic Church – and that shift can be precisely pinned down to the mid-century, to a group of Anglican apologists writing on schism in the 1640s and 1650s.

During the Civil War and Interregnum, the Church of England found herself taunted by Roman Catholic controversialists, who alleged that her present troubles were a divine judgment upon a schismatical nation. They repeatedly invited Englishmen, including Charles Stuart, to abandon the sinking Anglican ship for the secure haven of the infallible Roman Church.[30] Yet in Anglican eyes the plight of their church was not a condemnation of her doctrine, constitution or worship, 'but of those sins by which we provoked this wrath'.[31] Nevertheless while bringing the English to a sense of their own sinfulness, Anglican apologists had also to reply to their adversaries and vindicate the church from the slur of schism. At first, the Church of England's right to separate from the Church of Rome was demonstrated within the well-worn terms of the 'rule of faith' debate.[32] The debate turned on whether all we need to know for salvation was contained in scripture alone or, as the Romanists claimed, in scripture complemented by the equally authoritative tradition of the universal Catholic Church. Since the Church of

29. E. Carpenter, *The Protestant Bishop – Being the Life of Henry Compton* (1956), p. 208. For the range of anti-Roman apologetics in the 1680s see *A Catalogue of the Discourses for and against Popery*, ed. T. Jones (Chetham Society, 48 and 64, 1859 and 1865).

30. See Bramhall, I, i, pp. cxix, 23–81; *The Works of the Right Reverend Father in God John Cosin* (LACT, Oxford, 1843–51), IV, 242; P. Hammond, 'Thomas Smith', *BIHR*, 56 (1983), 183–4.

31. Henry Ferne, *Of the Division between the English and Romish Church upon the Reformation*, (1655 edn), sig. A7v; cf. Hammond, I, pt. ii, 368.

32. The best account remains L.I. Bredvold, *The Intellectual Milieu of John Dryden* (Chicago, 1934), ch. 4.

Rome was the repository of tradition and an authentic exponent of scripture, she could claim to be infallible on matters of faith. The 'fundamental questions of Rome's infallibility, and universal pastorship (on which the case of schism depends) comprehend all lesser debates', asserted Henry Hammond.[33] And these were the questions tackled by the Anglican champions of the Interregnum, authors like Hammond, Henry Ferne and John Bramhall, whose books were 'then in everybody's hands, wherein they had fully vindicated the Church of England from any imputation of schism'.[34]

Ferne, a future bishop, was first into the fray with *Of the Division between the English and Romish Church upon the Reformation* (1652). He seems to have been particularly stung by the Roman gibe that the Church of England was now reaping a sectarian and enthusiastic whirlwind sown by her own principle of allowing the individual the liberty to determine the 'rule of faith' from scripture. The Church of England was proud, retorted Ferne, to leave men the use of their reason as Christ and the Apostles had done and to assert the sufficiency and clarity of scripture for salvation, yet she had never abandoned the helpful interpretative skills of the pastors and guides appointed by God in his Church. There was neither licence nor infallibility within the Church of England: the individual Anglican was responsible for working out his own salvation, but his speculations were carefully guided and contained by the morally certain (rather than infallible) teaching of the church. Ferne also sought to show that the sects did not possess the same justification for separating from the Church of England as she had for departing from the Church of Rome. A justifiable separation required 'just cause' and 'due authority'. The autonomous national church of England was able to prove from scripture and antiquity that remaining in communion with the Church of Rome would oblige her to err and sin. But such proof had not been, and could not be, produced by the sectaries, nor had they, as mere individuals, the authority to leave the Church of England's communion.[35] In a further work devoted to the parallel cases of the English church's separation from Rome and the sectarians' breach from the Church of England, Ferne

33. Hammond, II, pt. ii, 65 (*The Disarmers Dexterities Examined*).
34. William Saywell, *The Reformation of the Church of England Justified* (Cambridge, 1688), sig. A3v; cf. *The Minor Theological Works of John Pearson*, ed. E. Churton (Cambridge, 1844), I, pp. xxiv–xxvi. Saywell also mentions Peter Heylyn in this context, for whom see J.A.I. Champion, 'The Ancient Constitution of the Christian Church' (unpublished Cambridge University Ph.D. thesis, 1989), ch. 3. I am grateful to Dr Champion for sending me a copy of his thesis.
35. Ferne, *Of the Division*, pp. 28–32, 35–47, 53, 57–63, 90, 119–25, 150; cf. Ferne, *Certain Considerations* (1653), sig. A5, and his other, historical, works.

blamed misconceptions of 'the rule of faith' for leading men to leave a true church. He drew out the lessons to be learned from the third-century Novatian schism and endorsed Bishop Cyprian of Carthage's rule that church unity lies in having one bishop in a city.[36]

This question of the authority and autonomy of national churches such as the Church of England receives careful treatment in Hammond's tract *Of Schism* (1653). Hammond too was responding to Roman arguments about the 'rule of faith', but he refuted Roman supremacy and infallibility by demonstrating the equality of the Apostles and the consequent equality of bishops within the Catholic Church.[37] The Early Church was comprised of local churches each governed by her own bishop. Although these churches were grouped into larger units under archbishops or metropolitans and these in turn were subject to primates and patriarchs, this hierarchy simply reflected the needs of the civil administration, and in the final resort all bishops were of equal authority.[38] Schismatics were those who 'reject the ministry of the deacons or presbyters in any thing wherein they are ordained and appointed by the bishop' or his superior.[39] For a church to be schismatic she would have to offend not against the authority of a superior, for there was none, but against that mutual charity which should exist between Christians and between churches. The Church of England displayed no lack of charity towards the Church of Rome and her adherents; it was the Church of Rome which imposed unwarranted innovations and stigmatized those who found them unacceptable; it was the Church of Rome which destroyed the unity of faith and thus bore the guilt of schism.[40]

Contemporaries often bracketed Hammond's Interregnum writings on schism with those of Bishop John Bramhall, although they were of 'a different nature', Bramhall's being 'more historical, fuller of matter of fact' and more concerned to vindicate royal and episcopal jurisdiction over the native church.[41] The autonomy of the ancient 'Britannic churches', for example, was attested by the existence of British bishops under the primacy of the Bishop of Caerleon-on-Usk long before St Augustine landed in Kent. Bramhall trots out the famous story of Dionothus, Abbot of Bangor, and his refusal to submit to the Bishop of Rome at Augustine's behest because of his

36. Ferne, *A Compendious Discourse* (1655), pp. 132, 85–9.
37. See Hammond, I, pt. ii, 335, and the sequels in vol. II; Pocock, XIII, 324–6; XIV, 159.
38. Hammond, I, pt. ii, 339–44.
39. Ibid., 338.
40. Ibid., 364–8.
41. Henry Holden, *The Analysis of Divine Faith* (Paris, 1658), p. 449.

obedience to the British primate. And where is the evidence, asks
Bramhall, of ecclesiastical courts held by Roman bishops or their
legates in Britain during the first 600 years of Christianity, of British
subjects excommunicated or summoned to Rome, or of British
bishoprics conferred by Rome?[42] For his part, Bramhall can demonstrate the continuity of ecclesiastical legislation by English monarchs
from the Saxons onwards, while 'those former kings who reigned in
England about the years 1200 and 1300, might properly be called
the first reformers; and their laws of Provisors and *Praemunire's* . . .
the beginning of the Reformation. They laid the foundation, and
Henry the Eighth builded upon it.' The Reformation, initiated after
all by Roman Catholics, was based on laws which were 'declarative'
of the existing legal position, rather than 'operative' in putting forth
new laws.[43] All this not only proves the Church of Rome guilty
of exaggerating her jurisdiction, but allows Bramhall to find her
'actually' and 'causally' guilty of schism. The schism was caused by
Rome's 'rigid censures, and new creeds, and exorbitant decrees',
which were in turn based upon her alleged 'universality of jurisdiction, or rather sole jurisdiction, *jure divino,* with superiority above
general councils, with infallibility of judgement, and temporal power
over princes'.[44] The Bishop of Rome usurped the 'supreme ecclesiastical authority' that is 'episcopacy, or a general council: for as
single bishops are heads of particular churches, so episcopacy, that
is, a general council, or oecumenical assembly of bishops, is the head
of the universal church'.[45]

All three authors insist on the right of a national church to reform
herself, they emphasize the authority and autonomy of particular
churches, and they associate this emphasis with the equality and
autonomy of all bishops. In doing so, they had shifted the weight of
the Anglican case a little further away from the Word and the
Christian magistrate. But nothing was renounced. The Church of
England continued to hold that that which makes a church Apostolic
is her Apostolic doctrine: 'the formal reason for any particular
church's having the denomination Catholic, must come not from any
communion with the Church of Rome: but from owning the Catholic
and apostolic faith, and joining in with those churches which did
own and acknowledge it.'[46] When repudiating the claims of Rome to
decide on matters of faith, the church took her stand on Apostolic

42. Bramhall, I, 162–4, 158–9, 95, 132–6; II, 166–75, 404–9, 525–46.
43. Bramhall, I, 151; II, 125, 449.
44. Bramhall, I, 97.
45. Ibid., 248–52, 104.
46. Stillingfleet, *Rational Account*, II, 15. Also see Thomas Comber, *The Plausible
     Arguments of a Romish Priest Answered* (1686), p. 8.

doctrine: 'the truth is not built upon the church, but the church upon the truth'.[47] The Church of England continued to pay due respect to the godly prince and to his duty in reforming the church in his lands; the 'visible company of faithful people, who here under the dominion of our sovereign lord the king, call themselves Christians, and profess the faith of Christ . . . are the Church of England'.[48] But there was an undeniable implication in these apologetics that, at the level of *What makes a church a church,* bishops were somehow more significant than the sovereign – a not unnatural sentiment during the 1650s, even among those who yearned for the return of the Stuarts. During the Interregnum a shift had begun in Anglican ecclesiology: a shift which was confirmed as a significant and permanent development in the church's understanding of herself during the Restoration, when the Anglican case against Rome came into conjunction with her case against Dissent.

Every point of the Anglican case marshalled against Rome during the 1650s was repeated *ad nauseam* in the anti-Roman apologetics of the Restoration church, in great set pieces like Isaac Barrow's *Treatise of Papal Supremacy* and in hundreds of occasional tracts or thousands of sermons. The English church had been forced to separate from Rome to avoid being contaminated by the 'unlawful unscriptural impositions' of that church.[49] As the fact of a breach of communion was indisputable, 'a criminal schism lies at the door of some party or other' – in this case, at Rome's door, for 'this usurping, momopolizing church is, in all reason, the schismatic'.[50] The autonomy of the English church was a reflection of the equality of the episcopate. 'Our bishops (as to their just authority) stand upon the same level with the bishops of Rome, and so do all the bishops in the world beside'.[51] The authority of the national church to break from Rome was demonstrable from the history of the Early Church, of the ancient British church, and of the English Reformation.[52] So far as Anglicans were concerned, the Church

47. John Sudbury, *A Sermon preached before the King* (1676), p. 21.
48. Timothy Puller, *The Moderation of the Church of England* (1679), p. 35; Puller proceeds to quote Richard Hooker.
49. Sharp, *Sermons*, VII, 132. Also see William Sherlock, *A Short Summary of the Principal Controversies* (1687), pp. 114–33; Clagett in Gibson, III, pt. i, 440; Cave in Gibson, I, pt. i, 142, 145; John Rawlett, *A Dialogue betwixt two Protestants* (1685); William Lloyd, *A Sermon Preached before the King* (1679), pp. 66–7.
50. John Sharp, *Sermons*, VII, 133, 138.
51. Edward Pelling, *The True Mark of the Beast* (1685), p. 25. Also see Isaac Basire, *The Ancient Liberty of the Britannick Church* (1661), pp. 60–1; Evelyn, III, 303; Rawlett, *Dialogue*, pp. 49–52, 227–9; Gilbert Burnet, *A Vindication of the Ordinations of the Church of England*, (1677), preface, sig. xx7v; Barrow, VIII, 344.
52. See Francis Fullwood, *Roma ruit* (1679; Oxford, 1847 edn cited), pp. 29–33, 247–6,

of Rome was indubitably guilty of schism, and the *via tutior,* the safer path to salvation, lay in the reformed Church of England and Catholic Christianity. That said, the Restoration church also exhibited signs of hesitancy, and even doubt, about her relationship with the Church of Rome. For example, the history of the English Reformation ought to have been an important field of anti-Roman apologetics, yet Anglican authors were surprisingly half-hearted about tackling the subject: as Gilbert Burnet asked, where was the Sleidan, Thuanus or Sarpi of the English Reformation?

Very careful footwork was necessary when approaching the subject of England's Reformation. While the church needed ammunition against Roman claims that the English Reformation was an Erastian affair, 'totally carried on by worldly interest', this could not be easily provided without trespassing against the canons of historical veracity and scholarly accuracy.[53] Peter Heylyn's history of the Reformation, *Ecclesia restaurata* (1661), fell into this trap. Designed to influence the Restoration settlement by describing the original intention of the Henrician and Elizabethan Reformation, and the subsequent efforts of 'puritan' innovators to subvert it, Heylyn's book inevitably stressed episcopal succession and the continuity between the medieval Catholic Church and the Church of England. While Roman Catholics mined the book to bolster their own case against the English schism, Heylyn's intemperate history only provoked his Protestant opponents and earned the contempt of more dispassionate Anglican historians.[54] Thomas Fuller's *Church History* (1655) was a far more even-handed account, which is one reason why Heylyn was so scathing about it. In his own *History of the Reformation of the Church of England* (1679), Gilbert Burnet also strove for objectivity, admitting Henry VIII's 'great enormities' for instance, but within an apologetical context. Burnet was responding to a recent French translation of a Catholic work on the English Reformation, Nicholas

and ch. 4; Cave in Gibson, I, pt. i, 139–41; William Cave, *Primitive Christianity* (1673), pp. 225–31; William Falkner, *Christian Loyalty* (1679), pt. i, chs 6, 7; Edward Pelling, *The Good Old Way* (1680), pp. 25–48; John Evelyn, *The History of Religion,* ed. R.M. Evanson (1850), I, 322–4; William Cave, *A Dissertation concerning the Government of the Ancient Church* (1683), pp. 244–55; Puller, *Moderation,* pp. 423–54; Conold, *Notion,* p. 27; [William Lloyd], *Papists No Catholicks* (1679), pp. 4, 7–9. There is also an account of debates surrounding the Early British church in Champion, 'Ancient Constitution', ch. 4.

53. [George Touchet], *Historical Collections* (1674), preface.

54. The Catholic Touchet's *Historical Collections* drew heavily on Heylyn. Henry Hickman used Bishop Jewel to rebut Heylyn's account; see H. N., *Plus ultra* (1661), pp. 13, 16–34, 48. For a churchman's dismissal of Heylyn's history of Presbyterianism see MS Add C 304b, fo. 79v. For a different and fuller account of Heylyn now see Champion, 'Ancient Constitution', ch. 3.

Sanders' tract of 1585, and his history was alive to the threats from both popery and sectarianism; indeed, the first volume earned him a formal vote of thanks from the House of Commons at the height of the Popish Plot.[55]

In general, however, Anglican attitudes towards Rome were perceptibly softening in the mid- and late seventeenth century. More and more churchmen were coming to believe that for all her faults, her novelties and her tyranny, the Church of Rome remained a 'true church' in fundamentals: 'we grant to it a true metaphysical being, though not a true moral being; we hope their errors are rather in superstructures, than in fundamentals.'[56] There was always room for doubt, of course: several Roman practices such as the Mass, the 'excess' sacraments, and the invocation of saints, raised the question whether Rome practised idolatry, a sin which should logically have condemned her as a false church; 'where other things are subtle and nice, tedious and obscure,' wrote Stillingfleet, 'this lies plain to the conscience of every man; if the Church of Rome be guilty of idolatry, our separation can be no schism either before God or man, because our communion would be sin'.[57] When the Duke of York heard of Stillingfleet's attack on the Roman idolatry, he is said to have asked Archbishop Sheldon, 'if it was the doctrine of the Church of England that Roman Catholics were idolators: who answered him it was not; but that young men of parts would be popular, and such a charge was the way to it'.[58] The church was genuinely divided on the question, however: the Test Act (1678) declared Rome to be idolatrous, but Bishop Gunning of Ely denied this in the House of Lords, possibly with the support of Sancroft and Dolben of Rochester, and certainly in the face of opposition from Bishop Barlow of Lincoln.[59] In the margin of an Anglican work purporting to show that the

---

55. Further volumes appeared in 1685 and 1715; see J.E. Drabble, 'Gilbert Burnet and the History of the English Reformation', *Journal of Religious History*, 12 (1983); A.G. Dickens and J. Tonkin, *The Reformation in Historical Thought* (Oxford, 1985); W.B. Patterson, 'The Recusant View of the English Past', *SCH*, 11 (1975). The next great historian of the Reformation was John Strype (1643–1737), whose first work was published in 1693; see R. O'Day, *The Debate on the English Reformation* (1986), pp. 41–7.
56. Bramhall, I, 43; also see 47, 298, 278; Ferne, *Of the Divisions*, ch. 12, pp. 22–3; Sharp, *Sermons*, VII, 131–3; Fowler in *Cases*, p. 305; Rawlett, *Dialogue*, pp. 231–3, 10–12; William Lloyd, *A Sermon Preached before the House of Lords on November 5 1680* (1680), pp. 12–16; Tillotson, II, 265–7; Puller, *Moderation*, p. 538; Evelyn, *History of Religion*, I, 306–9, 355–9.
57. Edward Stillingfleet, *A Discourse concerning the Idolatry practiced in the Church of Rome* (1671), sig. B3v.
58. Burnet, II, 30–1.
59. Ibid., 175; Evelyn, IV, 159; HMC, Ormonde, IV, 473.

Church of England had always recognized that Rome was a true church 'in fundamentals', Barlow scrawled that since she was formally idolatrous, she must err fundamentally.[60] In his copy of *Reasons why a Protestant should Not Turn Papist* (1687), Barlow noted that there should have been a further 'reason in this book (as in mine) about Popish idolatry but [it] would not be licensed at Lambeth'.[61] Equally unfashionable was Barlow's belief that the Pope was Antichrist. Although this had been the opinion of the generality of English divines 'down from the Reformation till the end of King James [I]'s reign', it was not the view of Archbishop Sheldon and his generation.[62] Attitudes towards Rome varied in the Restoration church and, naturally, they fluctuated according to the threat posed by 'popery'. It was perhaps not surprising that the congregation took offence when Dr Lloyd 'seemed to say, the Church of Rome was a true church' in a sermon before the court at the height of the Exclusion crisis.[63] Yet the impression given to outsiders, such as Nonconformists, was that the Church of England was smiling on, if not advancing towards, the Church of Rome. Indeed, attitudes towards Rome were becoming a touchstone for distinguishing Nonconformists from Anglicans. The Nonconformists tended to see it as a black-and-white issue, one was either for or against Rome; but then they were still obsessed with Rome's doctrinal errors, and less concerned with questions of the inherent authority of churches. From the Church of England's point of view, however, the errors of Rome were of only secondary importance, since what counted was her own authority as a properly constituted church under her own episcopate and godly prince to separate from the communion of Rome.

It was not only the persistence of Roman opposition which ensured that Anglican arguments about schism remained pertinent during the Restoration. The Protestant Nonconformists alleged that their separation had the same cause and justice as the Church of England's separation from Rome.[64] An Anglican case originally

60. Puller, *Moderation*, p. 453, Barlow's copy, now in the Bodleian Library, shelfmark 8° K 72 Linc.
61. *Reasons Why A Protestant should Not Turn Papist* (1687), Bodleian shelfmark, C 11.7. Linc (7), p. 30. This work was licensed by Henry Maurice, chaplain to Sancroft, on 9 July 1687.
62. BL, MS Lansdowne 960, fo. 41; Thomas Barlow, *Remains* (1693), pp. 190, 224 (back in 1628 the young Sheldon was the very first whom Barlow had ever heard deny the Pope to be the Antichrist).
63. Evelyn, IV, 187 (November 1679). Also see John Milton, *Of True Religion* (1673), in *Complete Prose Works of Milton: VIII* (New Haven and London, 1982), pp. 429–31.
64. [T. Carter], *Non-Conformists No Schismaticks, No Rebels* (1670), pp. 12–13; Thomas De Laune, *De Laune's Plea for the Non-Conformists* (1704 edn).

developed against Rome had now also to be deployed against schismatical Dissenters, to show 'the difference of the case between the separation of Protestants from the Church of Rome and the separation of Dissenters from the Church of England'.[65] The difference between the two cases, in the opinion of Anglicans, hinged upon the autonomy and authority of a national church: the Church of England had divided from the Church of Rome 'as one particular constituted church from another', but the Dissenters merely withdrew as individuals from the national church.[66] As the churchmen had said so often, individuals simply did not have that authority. In response, many sectaries and some Nonconformists brushed off the charge of schism as no more than a 'theological scarecrow'.[67] But the churchmen knew better: schism was a deadly sin, and they strove to convince their dissident parishioners of this truth. 'At last I desired him seriously to consider of it as a weighty business which concerned the welfare of his soul,' wrote one Oxfordshire minister of his wrangle with a local Quaker, 'that schism is a work of the flesh and excludes from the kingdom of heaven; and that without sin he could not separate from the Church of England, unless he could prove the said church to be idolatrous, or teach any doctrine contrary to the Word of God; to which he said nothing to the purpose, but returned again to his conscience.'[68] Invoking one's conscience was, of course, the simplest and most fundamental defence against the accusation; as one Anglican admitted, the Dissenters left the Church of England, as that church had separated from Rome 'in a *full persuasion of conscience,* that so we ought to do'.[69] Fruitless exchanges between parish ministers and local sectaries about separation and conscience were probably a daily event, for the sin of schism touched every parish, and every Anglican minister, in Restoration England.

The arguments of the Restoration church against schism ranged from the pragmatic and understated to the doctrinaire and assertive. A first line of approach was an appeal to the schismatics' better nature, backed by a firm but gentle reminder that schism from the national church was an offence against charity, common sense

---

65. The title of a tract by Clagett in Gibson, III, pt. i, 438–60.
66. Ibid., 443.
67. *Separation yet no Schisme* (1675); Carter, *Non-Conformists No Schismaticks*, p. 16; John Barrett, *The Rector of Sutton Committed with the Dean of St Paul's* (1680), p. 33; *Plea for Nonconformists* (1674), p. 13; Lewis Du Moulin, *The Several Advances of the Church of England towards the Church of Rome* (1680), pp. 39–40. To the chagrin of the Anglicans, John Hales was the source of this tag; see Conold, *Notion*, p. 59.
68. *Bishop Fell and Nonconformity*, ed. M. Clapinson (Oxfordshire Record Society, 62, 1980), p. 31.
69. Clagett in Gibson, III, pt. i, 442.

and prudence. That 'the sin of schism woundeth the very vitals of religion, is obvious unto any that shall consider how destructive it is of charity, which is the life, spirit, and soul of all'.[70] To separate from the church was to asperse those who remained in communion with her. Even worse, to divide Protestantism could only play into the hands of the papists and harden the hearts of the atheistically inclined.[71] Nor, of course, could it be prudent for the separatists to 'run themselves into a known sin, for dark and disputable advantages', 'leaving a certainty for an uncertainty, which no wise man would do in any thing, much less in a matter upon which his eternal happiness and salvation depends'.[72] When the Dissenters suggested 'that they leave us upon the same ground, as we ourselves left the Romish church', churchmen like Adam Littleton reminded them of their obligations to authority:

> We only flung off an unjust power (as it concerned and became us to do) which they had usurped over us; but these desert a church of which they are members, into which they were baptized, and were by their very birth engaged in an obedience to her supreme moderator and governor; and for them to deny this supremacy is (I must tell them) neither better nor worse than that which they would seem so utterly to detest, rank down-right Popery.[73]

Moderate Nonconformists, who recognized the need for and aspired to play a full part in a national church, indignantly blamed the Church of England for dividing English Protestants: 'the grand schismatics of the world are the engineers that fabricate needless, impossible dividing terms and conditions of unity and communion'.[74] As John Fell claimed in a sermon to the House of Lords, 'schism is so severely branded in the holy scripture, that even they who place their religion in separation acknowledge the guilt of it; and lay the blame of their dissent on those from whom they differ; alleging either

---

70. Pelling, *Good Old Way*, p. 105.
71. Robert Grove in *Cases*, pp. 1, 3; William Cave in *Cases*, pp. 505–6; Clagett in Gibson, III, pt. i, 439.
72. Gregory Hascard in *Cases*, p. 459; William Beveridge, *The Theological Works* (LACT, Oxford, 1842–8), II, 439; cf. Thomas Comber, *The Autobiographies and Letters*, ed. C.E. Whiting (Surtees Society, 156 and 157, 1941 and 1942), II, 4.
73. Littleton, II, 111.
74. Richard Baxter, *Richard Baxters Answer to Dr Edward Stillingfleet's Charge of Separation* (1680), pp. 43, 47, 36, 82, 14, 53; John Corbet, *An Account given of the Principles & Practices of Several Nonconformists* (1682), p. 7; Carter, *Non-Conformists*, p. 12; John Humfrey, *The Peaceable Design* (1675), pp. 6–7, 69–70; Barrett, *Rector of Sutton*, p. 18; N.H. Keeble, *The Literary Culture of Nonconformity in Later Seventeenth-century England* (Leicester, 1987), p. 35.

the immorality of their lives, or errors in the faith: and in fine, resolve their separation is therefore innocent because 'twas necessary.'[75] According to the churchmen, these moderate Dissenters 'chose to justify their separation upon the account of the unlawfulness or suspected unlawfulness of the things imposed, or upon the preference of a better communion than ours is'.[76] 'Our Dissenting brethren are wont to plead,' noted Robert Grove,

> That there is a liturgy, or set form of public worship prescribed; that there are certain ceremonies enjoined; that the use of these controverted things gives great scandal to the weak; that they cannot safely join in our mixed communion; that they leave our assemblies for the sake of greater edification, which they find elsewhere; and for these reasons they think they are necessitated to depart from ours and to set up churches to themselves, according to the best models that everyone is able to draw.[77]

In the conventicles of Ipswich 'they teach for doctrines that their separation is not from, but for the ordinance, and that separation is a sign of true grace'.[78] In short, moderate Dissenters believed that their separation was justified and not schismatic because of the Church of England's unlawful impositions and because of the opportunities for greater 'edification' outside the church.

The first of these claims – that the Church of England's impositions were unlawful – provoked Anglican apologists to rehearse their arguments for the church's authority to decide 'indifferent' matters. The cry of 'unlawful impositions' had been the Church of England's own justification for separating from Rome and it had been advanced – erroneously in the church's opinion – since the 1550s by those who would not conform to the external forms and government of the Church of England.[79] Robert Grove claimed that it was 'a very dangerous adventure' to leave the church on such shaky grounds since 'none of these things against which the exceptions are made are unlawful; and therefore they cannot make our communion unlawful; and if that be not unlawful, it must be unlawful to divide from it.'[80] But what is it to be 'unlawful'? While the

---

75. John Fell, *A Sermon preached before the House of Peers on December 22 1680* (Oxford, 1680), p. 12.
76. Clagett in Gibson, III, pt. i, 441.
77. Grove in *Cases*, p. 7. For the Dissenters' own view of their case, see *RB*, III, 388–420; J. Spurr, 'The Church of England, Comprehension and the Toleration Act of 1689', *EHR*, 104 (1989).
78. MS Add. C 308, fo. 130v.
79. For the earlier debates see J.H. Primus, *The Vestments Controversy*, (Kampen 1960).
80. Grove in *Cases*, p. 7.

Church of England could show that the practices imposed by Rome were repugnant to scripture and thus justify her separation from Rome, the Dissenters (claimed the churchmen) could only complain that Anglican practices 'are unlawful, because they are not necessary to worship, nor commanded by any express law of God'.[81] And there were indeed Dissenters who believed that scripture was the sole and sufficient rule of worship and that the use of human additions was a breach of the Second Commandment. To these the Anglicans could only protest that 'the purest church imaginable cannot produce scripture for all circumstances.' The Church of England required nothing 'which is plainly forbidden in Gods word, and so is sinful', and therefore if there was no sin in communion with the church, it must be a sin not to communicate with her.[82] The things enjoined by the church which were neither forbidden nor expressly commanded by God were simply 'indifferent' matters left to human judgement. This was where the Nonconformist might object that the Church of England was elevating 'indifferent' into 'necessary' things by making them terms of communion with her; one complained of 'those things which I have showed before I cannot find in my Bible to be instituted by God as necessary parts of his worship, but I find them instituted as necessary by the Church of England'.[83] When the clergy patiently explained that none of these human institutions were regarded as immutable or essential by the church, the Dissenters demanded to know why then they were imposed, since they excluded thousands of ministers from the church and, by the Anglicans' own admission, endangered the salvation of Nonconformists?[84]

Was the Church of England not 'crying up that great Diana of the Papists, the church's authority'?[85] Even the Catholic Duke of York complained to Burnet that the Anglicans made much use of the church's authority in their controversies with Dissent 'and then took it all away when we [the Anglicans] dealt with the papists'. Burnet spotted the drift of the Duke's argument 'and quickly convinced him that there was a great difference between an authority of government in things indifferent and a pretence to infallibility'.[86] The church, it

81. Clagett in Gibson, III, pt. i, 445–6.
82. Comber, *Autobiographies*, II, 5, 7; cf. Grove in *Cases*, p. 4; John Williams in *Cases*, pp. 111–13; *The Works of Robert Sanderson*, ed. W. Jacobson (Oxford, 1854), II, pp. xxxii–xl; Robert Grove, *A Short Defence of the Church and Clergy of England* (1681), pp. 48–9.
83. Comber, *Autobiographies*, I, 105.
84. Barrett, *Rector of Sutton*, p. 66; [John Howe], *An Answer to Dr Stillingfleets Mischief of Separation* (1680), p. 39; cf. Francis Fullwood, *The Case of the Times* (1683), pp. 113–15.
85. Edward Bagshaw, *A Brief Enquiry* (1662), sig. c.
86. Burnet, II, 28.

was claimed, needed 'a double power and authority' of jurisdiction and legislation. Once she had legislated on matters neither commanded nor prohibited by God, the private Christian was 'obliged to silence and peace' – whatever his private convictions or doubts – because 'the professing of such a controverted truth is not necessary, but the preservation of the peace and unity of the church is. This is not to assert infallibility in the church, but authority.'[87] As her Articles stated, the Church of England was free, indeed obliged, to decide on indifferent and controverted matters, provided that she imposed nothing repugnant or contrary to the Word of God.[88]

In the opinion of Anglican authors, to question the permissibility of the church's impositions was to stray from the point at issue, the schism of the Dissenters. Whatever some Nonconformist apologists might fondly imagine, no alteration of the laws governing church attendance nor parliamentary modification of the church's worship or discipline would remove the stain of schism from the Dissenters.[89] After establishing that the church constrained only outward practice and not belief, the disagreement between her and the Dissenters became 'very narrow', in Robert South's words; 'either the Church of England enjoins something unlawful, as the condition of her communion, and then she is schismatical; or there is no unlawful thing thus enjoined by her, and then those who separate from her are and must be schismatics'. South warned that altering the constitution of the church to humour the Dissenters would be 'a tacit acknowledgement of the truth and justice' of their case and, by representing their reasons for separation as lawful, would shift the responsibility for schism 'from their own door to ours'.[90] The proposals – against which South was preaching – to 'comprehend' moderate Dissenters within the church were repeatedly denounced by churchmen as importing schism into the church.[91] To relax the terms of communion with the church would create a double standard of clerical subscription and conformity. Even worse, such a relaxation would be tantamount to recognizing the Dissenters'

87. Anthony Sparrow, *A Collection of Articles, Injunctions, Canons* (1661), preface; also see Littleton, II, 311–4.
88. See Article 20; Williams in *Cases*, pp. 106–7, 117–8; Fowler in *Cases*, pp. 308–9; Beveridge, *Works*, VI, 369–70. To extend this freedom to private individuals 'would not be so much liberty as libertinism'; Littleton, II, 311; also see 314–15; I, 311–12; Grove in *Cases*, p. 15.
89. See Conold, *Notion*, p. 46; William Saywell, *Evangelical and Catholick Unity* (1680), p. 139; Sherlock in *Cases*, p. 48; cf. Humfrey, *Peaceable Design*, p. 70; *The Diary of John Milward*, ed. C. Robbins (Cambridge, 1938), p. 221.
90. South, III, 352; cf. Cave in *Cases*, pp. 497–8.
91. See Spurr, 'Comprehension', 941–4.

case for separation and to admitting that the church had imposed schismatic terms – an admission that was patently nonsense in view of the church's entitlement to order indifferent matters. Some churchmen urged that any alterations should be accompanied with a declaration 'that such change is not made upon the grounds pretended by those of the separation' for fear that the Dissenters might otherwise conclude that their schism had been justifiable.[92]

The Nonconformists were caught in the same double bind. Although many Dissenters accepted the principle of things left 'indifferent', it seemed to the churchmen that they always denied the application of the principle to any of the disputed parts of the liturgy.[93] There was, of course, good reason for such a denial, since just as the Church of England could not modify her constitution without accepting responsibility for the schism, neither could the Dissenters acknowledge that the sign of the cross in baptism or the wearing of a surplice was in itself indifferent, without effectively admitting that they had breached the communion of the church over impositions which involved no sin.[94] Neither side could give way when accusations of schism had been made, because it was in the nature of the offence that one side must be in the wrong.

The second general ground of the Nonconformists' separation was their claim to be pursuing greater 'edification' than was possible within the national church. 'Edification' was a nebulous process which was understood in different ways by Nonconformists and churchmen. In the Reformed tradition, the 'edification' of individuals in the knowledge of Christ grew out of their faith and experience of grace. The Restoration churchmen, however, tended to see edification as a corporate exercise of the whole church or congregation. Fundamentally different conceptions of the church underpinned these different notions of edification. The Reformed tradition saw the church as the creation of the living Word of God working through the faith of individual believers; while the Restoration Church of England increasingly saw the church as constituted by her episcopate and sacraments as well as by her faith.[95]

The final and, perhaps, the strongest Anglican argument against Nonconformist schism was the ecclesiological argument drawn from

92. Peter Samwaies, 13 December 1661, *Records of the Northern Convocation* (Surtees Society, 113, 1907), p. 320.
93. Richard Baxter, *The Second Part of the Nonconformists Plea for Peace* (1680), pp. 38–9; Corbet, *Account*, pp. 9–12; cf. Clagett in Gibson, III, pt. i, 446; Calamy in *Cases*, p. 219.
94. Baxter, *Second Part*, pp. 40, 84; cf. Williams in *Cases*, pp. 66–7.
95. See pp. 110 above and 374 below; J. Spurr, 'Schism and the Restoration Church', *JEH*, 41 (1990), 421–3.

the autonomy and authority of a national church. Here, the teaching of Ferne, Hammond and Bramhall that the autonomy of a national church was derived from her episcopate came into its own. Isaac Basire, for instance, was at pains to prove the ancient liberty of the British church by demonstrating her original status as an autonomous patriarchate.[96]

> The Britannic church, such as she was lately under episcopacy rightly constituted, was no way schismatical, neither materially, nor formally, since that she neither erected unto her self chair against chair, which is the foul brand of schismatics, in St Cyprian; nor did that church cut her self off from episcopacy, or made a congregation at any time unto her self against her canonical bishops (which ever is the formal character of schismaticks, by the definition of the Constantinopolitan Council) much less did she shake off her bishops, and with the continued succession of bishops, by consequence, the succession of her priests, not interrupted (as I may say) from the very cradle of her Christianism.[97]

'The ancients did assert to each bishop a free, absolute, independent authority . . . in the administration of affairs properly concerning his particular church', explained Isaac Barrow. 'This is most evident in St Cyprian's writings, out of which it will not be amiss to set down some passages.'[98]

St Cyprian, Bishop of Carthage, stood out among the early Fathers of the Church as one 'who had as well considered the nature of schism, and as diligently armed the Christians of his age against it, and given us as sure rules to judge by, in this matter, as any'.[99] The shadow of Cyprian stood behind the teachings of Hammond, Bramhall, Ferne and the others. Restoration churchmen drew on Cyprian's *De catholicae ecclesiae unitate* (251), which existed in two versions; one, the so-called 'primacy text', seemed to favour the supremacy of St Peter and the Bishop of Rome, while the other presented the episcopate as the entire and equal successor to the Apostles. But St Cyprian's single most important phrase, 'episcopatus unus est, cuius a singulis in solidum pars tenetur', was

96. Isaac Basire, *The Ancient Liberty of the Britannick Church* (original Latin edn, Bruges, 1656; translation 1661), p. 59; J. Spurr, 'Anglican Apologetic and the Restoration Church' (unpublished Oxford University D.Phil. thesis, 1985), pp. 263–4; and for earlier uses of the argument by Bramhall, Laud and others, see Milton, 'Laudians and Church of Rome', pp. 55–7, 113–15, 227, 256–7.
97. Basire, *Ancient Liberty*, pp. 60–1; cf. Rawlett, *Dialogue*, pp. 49–52, 227–9; Burnet, *a Vindication of Ordinations*, sig. xx7v.
98. Barrow, VIII, 344; also see 259, 352, 355.
99. Hammond, I, pt. ii, 367.

found in the common text.[100] This gnomic statement was held to assert that the universal government of the church is one episcopal office, committed in different parts of the church to particular bishops, each of whom enjoys 'full right and power' over his flock to the exclusion of any external authority.[101] It followed that any invasion of the bishop's rights, whether by another bishop or by rebellious presbyters and laity, was schismatic. If only the errant would read St Cyprian, claimed Bishop Fell, his Restoration editor, then 'it would be impossible for them to continue in their opinions, and be either Papists or separatists'.[102] John Bramhall quoted Cyprian at length against the pretended Roman supremacy,

> He liked not the swelling title bishop of bishops, nor that one bishop should tyrannically terrify another into obedience; no more do we. He gave a primacy, or principality, of order, to the Chair of St Peter, as *principium unitatis*; so do we: but he believed that every bishop had an equal share of episcopal power; so do we. He provided apart, as he thought fit, in a provincial council, for his own safety and the safety of his flock; so did we.

Bramhall concluded, in a denunciation as suited to the Non-conformists as to the Roman Catholics, 'in St. Cyprian's sense, *you* are the beam that separated yourselves from the body of the sun; *you* are the bough that is lopped from the tree; *you* are the stream that is divided from the fountain. It is *you*, principally *you*, that have divided the unity of the church.'[103]

In the Ancient Church 'presbyters who rejected the authority of their bishop, or affected separate meetings, where no fault could be found with the doctrines of a church, were condemned of schism'.[104] Schism is a 'recession from the bishop'; the Nonconformists who left their parochial congregations would have been schismatic even if 'the churches of this kingdom had not been united as they are into a

100. Of help on St Cyprian are H. Bettenson (ed.), *The Early Christian Fathers* (Oxford, 1956; 1969 edn cited), pp. 22–4, 263; M.F. Wiles, 'The Theological Legacy of St Cyprian', *JEH*, 25 (1963).

101. See Stillingfleet, *Rational Account*, II, 21 and pt. 2, ch. 1 *passim*; William Sherlock, *A Discourse about Church Unity* (1681), pp. 568–9, 208–15; Pelling, *True Mark of Beast*, pp. 16–25; Clagett in Gibson, III, pt. i, 439–40; Barrow, VIII, 178, 295; Lloyd, *Sermon*, pp. 12–16; Conold, *Notion*, pp. 62–3; John Norris, *A Discourse concerning the Pretended Religious Assembling in Private Conventicles* (1685), pp. 68, 83–4; Milton, 'Laudians and Church of Rome', pp. 281–3.

102. [John Fell], *Of the Unity of the Church ... written ... by Cyprian Bishop of Carthage and Martyr* (Oxford, 1681), pp. 39–40; Cave in *Cases*, pp. 510–11; Cave in Gibson, I, pt. i, 136; Conold, *Notion*, p. 16; Barrow, VIII, 344, 352, 355.

103. Bramhall, I, 61.

104. Stillingfleet, I, 288.

national form; but each bishop with his presbyters had made rules for religious assemblies independently upon the rest'.[105] 'There must be one church in one place; according to that ancient rule of the Catholic Church that there must be but one bishop in a city', explained William Sherlock; thus 'the Presbyterian and Independent churches, and those other conventicles of sectaries, which are among us . . . they are churches in a church, churches formed out of the national church, by which means Christians who live together, refuse to worship God in the same assemblies'.[106] The Anglican case could simply not allow the existence of two churches in one place and so it followed that occasional conformity was just as nonsensical and schismatic as outright separation.[107] Those who left the church, most notably those who left in 1672, stood self-condemned as schismatics because their previous conformity had been an acknowledgement of the lawfulness of the church and nothing had since changed in the church or in her terms of communion.[108]

The argument about the autonomy of a national episcopal church equipped the Church of England with a new weapon in her contest with Dissent – not that all churchmen were ready to deploy it given the unsettling claims it made for episcopacy. More importantly – and irrespective of whether all churchmen were willing to recognize it – the ecclesiology of the Church of England had gained an extra dimension. The Anglican cases against Rome and against Dissent had now been brought into alignment. The Church of England could now present the same argument against both of these adversaries, and in doing so she asserted her own unique identity as both Reformed in doctrine and episcopal in government. The Restoration church remained firmly committed to the principles of royal supremacy, a national church, and Apostolic doctrine as the foundation of a true church; but she was increasingly frank about the Catholic nature of the Church of England and her conviction that Christian communion begins with the church and ends in Christ, or that 'the union of particular Christians to Christ is by means of their union to the Christian church'.[109] To quote William Sherlock once again:

105. Simon Lowth, *Of the Subject of Church Power* (1685), p. 301; also see Lloyd, *Sermon*, p. 69; Conold, *Notion*, 18, 47–8; Clagett in Gibson, III, pt. i, 443.
106. Sherlock in *Cases*, p. 24; idem, *Discourse concerning Unity*, pp. 208–16, 577–8; Francis Fullwood, *The Necessity of Keeping Our Parish Churches* (1672), p. 129.
107. Sherlock in *Cases*, p. 32; Clagett in Gibson, III, pt. i, 449.
108. See Grove in *Cases*, p. 2; William Saywell, *A Serious Inquiry into the Means of an Happy Union* (1681), p. 22; Fullwood, *Necessity*, pp. 9–10; cf. Williams in *Cases*, p. 64.
109. William Sherlock, *A Discourse concerning the Knowledge of Jesus Christ* (1674), pp.

Our obligation to maintain communion with a particular church, wholly results from our obligation to Catholic communion ... so that there is no choice what church we shall communicate with, for there is but one Church all the world over, with which we must communicate; and therefore we have nothing else to do, but to judge whether that part of the Church wherein we live be so sound and orthodox that we may communicate with it according to the principles of Catholic communion; and if it be, we are bound to communicate with it, under peril of schism from the Catholic Church if we do not.[110]

And no one should gamble with their membership of the Catholic Church, 'for out of this ark there is no prospect given to us of any escape from the universal deluge'.[111]

The Blessing of Episcopal Government

As for our parts, we believe episcopacy to be at least an apostolical institution, approved by Christ himself in the revelation, ordained in the infancy of Christianity as a remedy against schism; and we bless God that we have a clear succession of it.[112]

'Our Church of England hath had the peculiar happiness of a monarchical Reformation, and retains the blessing of episcopal government', wrote one Restoration churchman, unconsciously exposing the nub of the question about authority in the national church; did it, in the last resort, rest with the King or the bishops?[113] Not that seventeenth-century Anglican apologists pitted the royal supremacy against episcopal authority; for they did not doubt that the King was Supreme Governor of their episcopal church, nor that the English Reformation had been achieved by the legitimate authority of King *and* bishops. Yet unsettling changes were in the wind: Interregnum Anglican apologists like Hammond, Bramhall and Ferne were suspected of regarding the episcopate as the more fundamental authority in the church; and at the Restoration, 'that happy clause' of the Act of Uniformity requiring episcopal ordination, and the revision of the Ordinal to distinguish the episcopal ministry, seemed to indicate that the church's attitude towards episcopacy had reached

143–4; also see Edward Hyde, *Christ and His Church* (1658), p. 395; Spurr, 'Schism and Church', 416–17.

110. Sherlock in *Cases*, p. 23.
111. Cave in Gibson, I, pt. iii, 135.
112. Bramhall, I, 271.
113. Puller, *Moderation*, p. 419.

some sort of turning point.[114] With hindsight, the change of emphasis becomes 'both sinister and unprecedented', according to Hensley Henson; 'the Church of England had always been episcopal; it now became episcopalian, that is, what had been a matter of practical policy became the requirement of religious principle.'[115] These are the partisan fears of the nineteenth and twentieth centuries, however; the situation at the Restoration was far more complex. Many regarded the new obeisance to episcopacy as primarily a legal requirement or a political necessity. The following decades saw valiant attempts on the part of many Anglicans to avoid the elevation of episcopacy into a 'requirement of religious principle', and to prevent the tensions implicit in the Church of England since the Reformation from wrenching her apart.

The English Reformation had indeed been monarchical. The King had succeeded to the Pope's authority in all matters 'spiritual and temporal', and had assumed the mantle of the 'godly prince' of scripture; but he had no spiritual powers himself. Episcopacy, on the other hand, was merely a happy historical survival, an office which had stood the test of time and was retained due to its proven administrative utility. So the Tudor monarchs governed the church under God, and their agents were the bishops. Although these agents could stand up to their prince in the name of the church (as did Archbishop Grindal), their own authority was carefully limited to the sphere of preaching and doctrine – certainly no one in the mid-sixteenth century suspected that the episcopal office was or could be central to the very being of the church. Bishops shared their preaching and teaching functions with the other clergy, but they alone were permitted to ordain men to the ministry. It was generally assumed that the legal authority to ordain came from the civil authority, and as yet few ventured beyond this to discuss the origin of the power of ordination itself.[116] It was the claims of English Presbyterianism which eventually provoked a re-evaluation of episcopacy. Chafing against 'prelacy' – as they dubbed the style of episcopal government established in 1559 – the Presbyterians of the 1570s and 1580s demanded further institutional reform of the English church to bring her into line with the continental Reformed

---

114. Bishop Francis Turner, MS Rawlinson Letters 99, fo. 101; P.F. Bradshaw, *The Anglican Ordinal* (Alcuin Club, 1971), pp. 87–95.
115. H.H. Henson, *The Church of England* (Cambridge, 1939), p. 123. Also see A.J. Mason, *The Church of England and Episcopacy* (Cambridge, 1914), p. 167; N. Sykes, *Old Priest and New Presbyter* (Cambridge, 1956), p. 117.
116. See Bradshaw, *Anglican Ordinal*, pp. 43–7. The assumption was that all ministers were equal in their ministry; see Avis, *Church*, pp. 119–23; *Study of Anglicanism*, ed. S. Sykes and J. Booty (1983), pp. 148–9.

churches, especially in the areas of clerical parity and lay participation in church government. In reply to their insistent criticism of English episcopacy as unscriptural, unnecessary and ungodly, a handful of churchmen asserted that episcopacy was the form of government appointed by God in the church.[117] This position is commonly described as a belief in the *ius divinum*, the divine right, of episcopacy; but this is a term fraught with difficulty. 'The truth is,' observed the sage Bishop Sanderson, 'all this ado about *ius divinum* is in the last result no more than a verbal nicety; that term being not always taken in the one and the same latitude of signification.'[118]

The debate about the divine or other appointment of episcopacy is a morass of verbal niceties. It is evident from scripture, says the Prayer Book Ordinal, 'that from the Apostles' time, there hath been these orders of ministers in Christ's Church; bishops, priests, and deacons'. But what offices do these terms denote? Have the terms changed meaning since the Apostles' time? How and by whom were these offices created? In particular, what distinguished the bishop from the priest? Did the first bishops devolve some of their power to other grades of the ministry: or did other grades of the ministry evolve as required by the Church? Are the offices of bishop and priest different degrees of a single order of the ministry – and if so, which is the original? Or are they different orders? The difference of order or degree was the crux of the matter. Unfortunately, the scriptures could not resolve the matter. The evidence of the Apostolic Church, as recorded in Acts, is confusing since the names of offices are not confined to one use, but are 'ambulatory':[119] presbyteros and episcopos are not always clearly distinguished (Acts xx. 17, 28); nor are presbyter and deacon or elder (Acts vi. 1–7; xiv. 23). Christ as the archetype of a bishop may have instituted separate orders of bishop and priest when he commissioned twelve Apostles to the work of his church and distinguished them from the seventy disciples (Luke x. 1). Or the Apostles may have instituted episcopacy by appointing Timothy in Ephesus and Titus in Crete with authority over ordinary elders in those churches (Titus i. 5–7).

The argument from scripture is unending. For many it was enough to look to 'the next age to the apostles' for the first evidence of bishops in the Church.[120] So after referring to the Apostles' appointment of 'bishops' to rule over the churches which they had planted, Anglican apologists for episcopacy tended to dwell upon the sub-

---

117. For references see Avis, *Church*, pp. 125–7; Lake, *Anglicans and Puritans?*, pp. 3–4.
118. Sanderson, *Works*, V, 151.
119. John Templer, *The Reason of Episcopall Inspection* (Cambridge, 1676), p. 43.
120. William Cave, *Primitive Christianity* (1673), p. 221.

sequent, continuous, succession of bishops in these churches: bishops 'were derived from the apostles and confirmed by them, and may not be reversed and repealed after 1,500 years, unless we challenge to be wiser and better able to govern and order the church of Christ than the apostles were'.[121] However, more extreme episcopalians, such as John Bridges, Matthew Sutcliffe, Hadrian Saravia, and Bishops Bilson and Bancroft, apparently accepting 'the Presbyterian premise that there was one form of church government contained in and commended by scripture', matched Presbyterian pretensions with episcopal claims that were every bit as exalted. Bishop Bilson, for instance, was allegedly the first to state that grace was transmitted through Apostolic succession and that only bishops can ordain, thus casting doubt upon the ministry and sacraments available in the continental Reformed churches.[122] A similar hard line was later exhibited by Archbishop Laud, who insisted to Bishop Hall that 'episcopacy is not so to be asserted to apostolical institution, as to bar it from looking higher, and from fetching it materially and originally, in the ground and intention of it, from Christ himself'; little wonder that many contemporaries suspected Laud of 'unchurching' the foreign non-episcopalian churches.[123] Such uncompromising episcopalianism has been presented as 'a significant staging post on the long road back from the brutal Erastianism of the Edwardian and early Elizabethan Reformations . . . now the godly bishop had joined the Christian prince'.[124] As yet this was a minority viewpoint in the English church, which for the main part continued to look to the historical, rather than scriptural, justifications for episcopacy, and to assume that its 'divine right' was an Apostolic recommendation rather than an immutable or perpetual divine prescription. This view of 'divine right' commanded widespread support in the late Elizabethan and Early Stuart church, mainly because it was based upon a common respect for the authority of the Early Church, the traditions of the Catholic Church, and human reason.[125] It was easily squared with the reality of the English situation and it settled

---

121. Thomas Bilson, *The Perpetual Government of Christ's Church* (1593; Oxford, 1842 edn cited), p. 333. Also see *Study of Anglicanism*, ed. Sykes and Booty, p. 301.
122. P. Lake, 'Presbyterianism, the Idea of a National Church and the Argument from Divine Right', in *Protestantism and the National Church in Sixteenth-century England*, ed. P. Lake and M. Dowling (1987), p. 208; Bradshaw, *Anglican Ordinal*, pp. 45–6.
123. William Laud, *Works* (LACT, Oxford, 1847–60), VI, 573, quoted by Avis, *Anglicanism*, p. 140, also see pp. 139–42; Dent, *Protestant Reformers in Oxford*, p. 233.
124. Lake, 'Presbyterianism, National Church and Divine Right', p. 211.
125. See Sanderson, *Works*, V, 11–12; Sykes, *Old Priest*, p. 26; M.R. Sommerville, 'Richard Hooker and his Contemporaries on Episcopacy: an Elizabethan Consensus', *JEH*, 35 (1984).

the nagging question of what status should be accorded to the non-episcopalian, Reformed churches of the continent.

Generally, early seventeenth-century Anglicans were agreed that in cases of 'necessity', such as the tumultuous European Reformations, episcopacy was not always, absolutely, required, but where it already existed or could be obtained it was the mandatory form of church government. For, although episcopacy is 'indispensable by any voluntary act; what inevitable necessity may do in such a case we now dispute not: necessity hath dispensed with some immediately divine laws. Where then that may be justly pleaded, we shall not be wanting both in our pity and our prayers'.[126] In the terminology of Hooker and Andrewes, episcopacy was part of the well-being (*bene esse*) rather than the being (*esse*) of a true church. Whatever the aberrant views of Laud, this 'necessity' proviso was the Church of England's standard solution to the problem of whether to recognize the non-episcopalian Reformed churches. In his correspondence with the Huguenot Pierre Du Moulin, Lancelot Andrewes invoked 'necessity' to excuse the French Reformed Church while simultaneously arguing for an Apostolic, or even dominical, institution of episcopacy. If episcopacy is of divine right, 'it doth not follow from thence that there is no salvation without it, or that a church cannot consist without it. He is blind who does not see churches consisting without it; he is hard-hearted who denieth them salvation. We are none of those hard-hearted persons'.[127]

Similar obfuscation enveloped the episcopate's relationship with the godly prince or magistrate. The suggestion that the episcopate had a mandate and authority separate from that which they received from the temporal ruler was a *prima facie* challenge to the ruler's sovereignty. Although puritan adversaries repeatedly denounced this episcopal threat to the royal supremacy, there was no serious conflict of interests between the bishops and their Supreme Governor under Elizabeth and the first two Stuarts – indeed divine right episcopacy was elaborated as a way of combating the quasi-democratic impulse of Presbyterianism, and its partisans were often coincidentally the keenest supporters of the royal prerogative, as the career of Archbishop Laud demonstrates.[128] Only in the 1640s did episco-

126. Joseph Hall, *Works*, ed. P. Wynter (Oxford, 1863), IX, 254. Also see Woodhouse, *Doctrine of Church*, pp. 175–6; *Rawdon Papers*, p. 95.
127. *Anglicanism*, ed. P.E. More and F.L. Cross (1935), p. 403; Andrewes's letter was republished in 1647, and is quoted by, among others, Bramhall, II, 69–71.
128. See Collinson, *Religion of Protestants*, ch. 1; J.P. Sommerville, 'The Royal Supremacy and Episcopacy "Jure Divino", 1603–1640', *JEH*, 34 (1983); Lake, 'Presbyterianism, National Church and Divine Right', 213, 218–19.

pacy come into conflict with the secular ruler, in this case, a godly Parliament.

The petitions and pamphlets accompanying the parliamentary debates of 1641–2 threw up a variety of 'episcopalianisms'. In *Episcopacy Asserted* (1641), Jeremy Taylor claimed that the church depended upon episcopacy for its very being.[129] Others attempted a compromise; a catena of moderate opinion published in 1641 maintained both 'the primitive institution of episcopacy' and 'the lawfulness of the ordination of the Protestant ministers beyond the seas'.[130] And despite its title, Joseph Hall's *Episcopacy by Divine Right* (1641) in fact contains a textbook account of the Anglican qualifications surrounding the *ius divinum* of bishops:

> First, our position is only affirmative; implying the justifiableness and holiness of an episcopal calling without any further implication. Next, when we speak of divine right, we mean not an express law of God, requiring it upon the absolute necessity of the being of a church, what hindrance so may interpose; but a divine institution, warranting it where it is, and requiring it where it may be had.[131]

Among much hazy talk of 'primitive' and 'reduced' episcopacy, schemes and bills were circulating which would have radically altered diocesan episcopacy. 'Sir, I praise God I am no separatist nor have I any spawn of schism in me', wrote one of Sir Edward Dering's correspondents, and then proceeded to advise, 'Make bishops Timothies by lopping off their temporal honours and employments and paring away their superfluities. Then will they be more apt to teach and be watchful and able to rule the ministry. So let them be bishops still.'[132] Dering was the architect of just such a scheme, while another was proposed in the Lords in July 1641 which, among much else, would have deprived the bishops of secular office and have appointed a dozen ministers in each county to assist them in excommunications and ordinations.[133] Yet insufficient political will existed to push through any of these reforms: there was

129. Taylor, VII, 232–3.
130. *Certain Brief Treatises* (Oxford, 1641).
131. Hall, *Works*, IX, 291.
132. Anthony Fletcher, *The Outbreak of the English Civil War* (1981), pp. 221–2.
133. *Constitutional Documents of the Puritan Revolution*, ed. S.R. Gardiner (Oxford, 1936), pp. 167–79. Also see W.M. Abbott, 'The Issue of Episcopacy in the Long Parliament, 1640–1648: The Reasons for Abolition' (unpublished Oxford University D.Phil. thesis, 1981); J.S. Morrill, 'The Attack on the Church of England in the Long Parliament, 1640–1642', in *History, Society and the Churches*, ed. D. Beales and G. Best (Cambridge, 1985).

simply too much suspicion of the bishops, of those 'great remoras at which all our pious endeavours for the nation's welfare stop'.[134]

Within a few months episcopal government had ground to a halt, and within a few years the office of bishop had been abolished; but then, surprisingly, when the institution was at its lowest, the intellectual case for episcopacy was revived and reinvigorated. It is not easy to be precise about this new vigour since it had as much to do with reawakening self-confidence as with the breaking of new intellectual ground. Apologetics is often most useful when it provides a fillip to morale, an authority which inspires the embattled adherent and which, in its psychological effect, far outweighs its ability to bring the controversy to a definitive conclusion. Thus it was with the episcopalian apologetics of the 1640s and 1650s. The apologetics restated and synthesized existing positions, brought the debate on episcopacy into conjunction with the anti-Roman 'schism controversy', reinforced the patristic case, and wove episcopacy further into the Anglican understanding of the constitution of a church. The sum was much greater than the parts and the cumulative effect on Anglican self-confidence was dramatic.

Once again, Henry Hammond was at the forefront of this Anglican resurgence. In a slim tract of 1644 on church government, Hammond asserted the apostolic institution of episcopacy, the existence of three clerical orders of bishop, presbyter and deacon as foreshadowed in the hierarchy of Christ, Apostles and disciples, and the bishop's exclusive power of ordination.[135] Three years later, Hammond argued that

> the church was by the apostles put into the hands of bishops, that ordinarily the consent of the bishop was required to enable a presbyter for any ecclesiastical act, the plenitude of power being by Christ delivered down to the apostles, and through them to their successor-bishops, and by them dispensed out to others in that measure, and those portions, which they should think fit.[136]

This exalted view of the institution of the bishop's office did not prevent Hammond from recognizing the value and prudence of 'a moderate episcopacy, with a standing assistant presbytery', or in other words, the sort of 'primitive episcopacy' under discussion in 1641.[137] But his primary concern was with the origin of the office.

---

134. Fletcher, *Outbreak*, p. 213.
135. Hammond, I, pt. ii, 186–91. Also see Packer, *Transformation*, ch. 5.
136. Hammond, I, pt. ii, 217 (*Of the Power of the Keyes*).
137. Hammond, I, pt. ii, 197; cf. Richard Parr, *Life of Ussher* (1668), p. 68. Hammond also had a hand in 'The Proposals of the Clergy: A Scheme for Toleration Propounded at Uxbridge in 1645', ed. S.R. Gardiner, *EHR*, 2 (1887), 340–2.

In *Dissertationes quatuor* (1651) and its English sequels, Hammond revised his earlier opinion that there were originally three distinct orders of clergy. Now he argued that the New Testament referred only to the two orders of deacon and bishop; the bishop or 'episcopos' was also referred to as 'presbyteros'. As the churches grew, however, the need arose for 'secondary presbyters' to take on part of the episcopal function. Hammond was confident that his demonstration of the original equivalence of the offices or names of bishop and presbyter had not strengthened the Presbyterian case since he had shown both terms meant 'bishop' and that the modern office of priest was a devolution of some episcopal functions. Yet in a letter he confided that while the Presbyterians could not prove from the scriptures or from ancient writings that presbyters existed in scripture times, neither could he prove from the scriptures or ancient writings that they did not exist.[138]

The worth of patristic evidence was a delicate question. In 1644 Hammond pointed out that the opaque scriptural evidence for bishops was rather like that for the obligation to observe the Lord's Day, yet

> the obscure mentions of that in the scripture were explained in the writings and stories of the first age of the church, particularly in the Epistles of Ignatius; and the obscurities of the sacred texts concerning episcopacy, are as clearly explicated and unfolded by the same Ignatius, even in every one of those epistles of his which Vedelius (as great an enemy of this order as Geneva hath produced) after his fiery trial of that author hath acknowledged to be his.[139]

The first-century epistles of Ignatius, Bishop of Antioch, are excellent testimony to the authority of bishops in the Early Church, full of bold and even extravagant claims for episcopal power, and of warnings against any separation from the bishop. As the churchman Andrew Allam later observed, 'if these epistles and canons so much controverted are not spurious and supposititious [*sic*], episcopacy stands on a very sure, firm and primitive bottom'.[140] The controversy to which Hammond and Allam referred turned on the authenticity of the epistles. In 1623, the Genevan Calvinist, Vedelius, produced a critical edition of the epistles which rejected more than

---

138. See Hammond, II, pt. iii, 26, 36 (*Vindication of Dissertations concerning Episcopacy*); (Pocock, VII, 122; Packer,) *Transformation*, pp. 120–6.
139. Hammond, I, pt. ii, 188–9; also see Edward Wetenhall, *A Sermon against Neutrality* (1663), pp. 32–5.
140. BL, MS Lansdowne 960, fo. 39v.

half of the canon; Joseph Hall depended on this edition for his *Episcopacy by Divine Right* (1641), and found himself battling against the editor's doubts.[141] Three years later, however, in 1644, Archbishop Ussher published a new collation of the epistles in Latin based on manuscripts discovered in Cambridge and in Bishop Montagu's library. As a result, apologists such as Hammond were able to mount a far more confident argument for episcopacy based on the practice of the Early Church.[142]

The Anglican case for episcopacy was gaining a new coherence – the patristic evidence for its use in the first-century Church seemed to be on a firmer footing than before. The controversy over schism had reaffirmed its continuous use in the Church thereafter and had emphasized the role of the episcopate in guaranteeing the visible unity of a true Catholic church. The Romanists, however, continued to snipe at the Church of England and to question the validity of her ordination. They alleged that the episcopal succession had been broken at the Reformation and, in particular, that Archbishop Parker had been irregularly consecrated in the Nag's Head Tavern at Cheapside. Although repudiated as 'a senseless fabulous fiction, made by a man of a leaden heart and a brazen forehead', the story of the Nag's Head consecration long remained a thorn in the Church of England's side.[143] The more profound debate with Rome centred upon the form and matter of ordination and consecration, upon what part of the ordination rite was essential and whether the Church of England possessed it. John Cosin debated this at length with Father Robinson, Prior of the English Benedictines at Paris, in the summer of 1645, but the exchanges continued throughout the 1650s: and some of the Roman sallies, such as the charge that the English Ordinal made no clear distinction between ordaining to the priesthood and consecrating to the episcopate, seem to have struck home, if we are to judge by the revisions of the Ordinal in 1661.[144] The doctrine of papal supremacy lay behind Roman attempts to cast doubt on the succession of English bishops; but then, it was clear to Anglican eyes that Rome was an enemy to episcopacy. To claim to be the universal bishop, argued the Anglicans, is 'to trample upon

141. See Hall, *Works*, IX, 216–26.
142. Isaac Vossius published an edition of the epistles in Greek in 1646; see editor's note 'O' at Joseph Hall, *Works*, IX, 216; Packer, *Transformation*, pp. 58–9, 106–10; R. Buick Knox, *James Ussher, Archbishop of Armagh* (Cardiff, 1967), pp. 119–26; J.P. Hammond Bammel, 'Ignatian Problems', *Journal of Theological Studies*, 33 (1982).
143. Bramhall, I, 270. Also see Ferne, *Certain Considerations*, pp. 252–64.
144. Cosin, *Works*, IV, 241–318; Bramhall, I, 270; Bradshaw, *Anglican Ordinal*, ch. 5; *Study of Anglicanism*, ed. Sykes and Booty, pp. 287, 289; cf. Sykes, *From Sheldon*, pp. 125–31.

episcopacy, and to make them equivocal bishops; to dissolve the primitive bonds of brotherly unity, to overthrow the discipline instituted by Christ, and to take away the line of apostolical succession'.[145] It was in the Papacy's interest 'to cry down the *jus divinum* of episcopacy'.[146] It seemed that every manifestation of papal disdain for episcopacy provoked Anglicans into a further assertion of the rights and powers of the episcopate; yet, strangely, none of this negated their earlier argument from 'necessity'.[147]

In Paris in 1650, John Cosin advised that communion with the French Reformed church was permissible because the Presbyterian orders of their ministers were valid. The power of ordination was 'restrained' to bishops by 'apostolical practice and the perpetual customs and canons of the church', not 'by any absolute precept, that either Christ or his apostles gave about it'.[148] He later amplified this: there was not 'such an absolute necessity and precept in that *ius divinum*' as to render invalid Presbyterian ordination in cases of necessity, as in France and Germany, but he could not see that this 'either hurts the *ius divinum* of episcopacy, or excuseth their voluntary and transcendent impiety, that hath endeavoured to destroy it in the Church of England, contrary to the laws of God, and his universal Church, the mother of us all'.[149] Of course, the argument from 'necessity' came much closer to home during the Interregnum. In 1657 Anthony Farindon wrote to Bishop Brian Duppa, asking whether, since episcopal discipline and government had long since collapsed, bishops were really essential to the being of the church? 'I call that absolutely necessary to a church without which a church cannot subsist, nor salvation be had'. Surely to define episcopacy as 'necessary' would be to 'unchurch' foreign non-episcopalian churches? In response Duppa claimed that Christ had chosen episcopacy as the government of his Church and so 'I can no more deny the absolute necessity of this government than I can call in question the wisdom of God and the love of Christ'. He would, however, acknowledge that salvation was possible 'in such a case where no bishops might be had, and consequently no priests ordained, no sacraments administered'. But, he repeated, this was not the case in England where there were bishops still alive and willing to ordain

---

145. Bramhall, I, 253.
146. Cosin, *Works*, IV, 448; also see Conold, *Notion*, p. 110; Templer, *Reason of Episcopall Inspection*, p. 18; MS Walker C 7, fo. 177.
147. See Hammond, I, 217; *Nineteen Letters of the Truly Reverend and Learned Henry Hammond*, ed. F. Peck (1739), pp. 49–50; Bramhall, II, 69.
148. Cosin, *Works*, IV, 402.
149. Ibid., 448–50 (Cosin to Gunning, 26 May 1657).

and so they must be attended and their rights must be asserted.[150] Bishop Thomas Morton was equally unwilling to 'un-church' foreign Protestants for their lack of episcopacy and equally certain that their case did not apply to domestic schismatics:

> as for our perverse Protestants at home, I cannot say the same of them, seeing they impiously reject that which the other piously desire. And therefore I cannot flatter those in this church who have received ordination only from mere presbyters, so far as to think them lawfully ordained. St Jerome himself reserved to the bishop the power of ordination. Seeing therefore I have been (as I hear) so far misunderstood by some among us, as to be thought to approve of their ordination by mere presbyters, because I once said, it might be valid in case of necessity: I do here profess my meaning to be, that I never thought there was any such necessity in the Church of England as to warrant it, where (blessed be God for it) there be so many bishops still surviving.[151]

These were not simply brave words. There were bishops willing to ordain in Interregnum England and there were, as we have seen, many young men anxious to receive ordination from them; indeed, one Presbyterian minister took pride in *not* being 'Jack on both hands, ordained by bishops and presbyters too'.[152] But what motivated those who received covert ordination from the hands of the bishop? The emotional attraction of episcopacy stemmed from a variety of factors, including human contrariness; never had the excellency of episcopal government been so obvious, remarked Jeremy Taylor, as now when it was lacking.[153] Episcopal ordination was a way of distancing oneself from puritan orthodoxy; it was an assertion of something older and more traditional in an age of tottering religious certainties; and it was an insurance policy to guarantee both the divine sanction of one's ministry and one's career in case the Church of England should ever be revived. But what could episcopacy mean to the younger divines who had little or no personal experience of the pre-1640 church? We can only make an occasional guess at how these ordinands imagined the episcopal office. Not long after his Presbyterian ordination, Simon Patrick 'met

---

150. MS Tanner 52, fos 210–11. Also see Edward Martin, *Doctor Martin, Late Dean of Ely, His Opinion* (1662), pp. 101–7.
151. John Barwick, *IEPONIKHΣ, or The Fight, Victory and Triumph of S. Paul accommodated to . . . Thomas, late Lord Bishop of Duresme* (1660), pp. 48–9 (Morton's last will and testament, dated 15 April 1658).
152. *The Autobiography of Henry Newcome*, ed. R. Parkinson (Chetham Society, 26–7, 1852), pp. 106–7.
153. Taylor, XV, p. iv (*The Golden Grove* (1655), To The Reader).

with Dr Hammond upon Ignatius' Epistles and Mr Thorndike's *Primitive Government of the Church*; whereby I was fully convinced of the necessity of episcopal ordination', and thus inspired he sought out Bishop Hall and received ordination in Hall's parlour at Higham.[154] Patrick was intellectually convinced by two books – and very different books at that; for while Hammond was making out the case for a sort of 'monarchical' episcopacy, Thorndike argued that bishops governed with the advice and cooperation of their presbyters. Although Thorndike was convinced that bishops were successors to the Apostles in governing the Church, he was anxious to emphasize the collaboration of the presbyters in order to exclude lay elders from any active part in ordination and excommunication.[155]

Convincing as such apologia might be about the legitimacy of episcopacy, they were vague about what a bishop actually did; and although past experience of episcopacy could hardly have faded from men's memories so soon, one encounters time and time again in the Interregnum, and especially among the younger men, a great uncertainty about the nature of the episcopal office. Men were free to imagine bishops as they wished them to be, and one of the most seductive visions of episcopacy to fill this vacuum was Archbishop Ussher's scheme of 'primitive' bishops, pastors governing the church as *primus inter pares* through consultation and committee. Ussher's sketch was brief and deliberately vague, its aim was conciliatory, and it positively invited men to read into it what they wanted. Richard Baxter was a great enthusiast for Ussher and his works; he strenuously supported the idea of reduced or 'Ignatian' episcopacy, and when he met Ussher to discuss the scheme they came to agreement in half an hour (or so Baxter claimed). Later, Baxter alleged that Ussher had told him that bishops and presbyters were the same order of the ministry.[156] Certainly John Gauden and Nicholas Bernard, Ussher's former chaplain, stressed the archbishop's 'puritan' credentials when recommending reduced episcopacy. In 1658 Thomas Hodges, an Oxfordshire rector, cited Bernard's recent biography of Ussher to prove that the archbishop, like Hodges, doubted that bishops were 'essential, or absolutely necessary to the very being of a church or ministry'. Hodges's scruple was familiar: 'I dare not so easily unchurch those of the reformed religion abroad, who have no bishops, name or thing'. Predictably, in 1662, this

---

154. Patrick, IX, 423.
155. Herbert Thorndike, *Works* (LACT, Oxford, 1854), I, pt. 1.
156. *RB*, II, 387; Bradshaw, *Anglican Ordinal*, p. 63.

potential supporter of reduced episcopacy left his living and the church.[157]

Between 1660 and 1662 politicians and divines were confronted by the need to find an acceptable form of episcopacy and of episcopal practice. Although the political constraints were probably narrower than many realized, the debate over episcopacy at the Restoration was wide-ranging, exhilarating and innovative. Everyone knew that the Church of England would return, and that she would be 'episcopal', but what that 'episcopacy' would entail seemed negotiable. In 1660, with the ground carefully prepared by Gauden and Bernard – who brought out another edition of Ussher's scheme in June – it seemed that the tide was running in the direction of 'moderate episcopacy'; on all sides ministers pronounced themselves willing to accept an episcopal church shorn of 'excresencies', built on 'Ignatius's episcopacy, but not the English diocesan frame'.[158] Such heady times encouraged the bolder spirits among the clergy to speculate; Edward Stillingfleet's *Irenicum*, for instance, explored the ideas of Grotius, Hooker, Hales, Amyraldus and even Hobbes to establish a case for prudence in the organization of religious life. But *Irenicum*, which appeared in November 1660, was also designed to show that no divine right or prescription exists to prevent men from adopting the form of church government 'as may bear the greatest correspondency to the primitive church' and most tends to peace and unity; and Stillingfleet could not resist the chance to put in a plug for Ussher's 'excellent model' of reduced episcopacy.[159] In such a liberal and optimistic intellectual climate, it must have seemed that the moment for 'primitive' episcopacy had finally arrived.

It was only when the negotiations for the Worcester House Declaration attempted to define 'primitive' episcopacy in all its detail, that the inherent feebleness of the Ussher platform was revealed and the chimera was finally exposed. On seeing the first draft of the Declaration in September, Richard Baxter petitioned the King, saying that 'the bishop which your Majesty declareth for, is not *episcopus praeses*, but *episcopus princeps*; indued with sole power both of ordination and jurisdiction.'[160] The Presbyterians pleaded in vain that bishops should ordain with the *consent*, not just the assistance, of their clergy, and that these clergymen should be drawn from across

157. Thomas Hodges, *A Scripture Catechisme* (1658), sig. D5.
158. See John Lloyd, *A Treatise of the Episcopacy, Liturgies, and Ecclesiastical Ceremonies of the Primitive Times* (1661), dedicated to Gauden, pp. 13, 29, 55, 63–4; anon., *Terms of Accommodation* (1661), pp. 5–6; *RB*, I, 387–408.
159. See Stillingfleet, II, 153, 416–17. Thomason's copy is dated 21 November 1660.
160. See *RB*, II, 106; Bradshaw, *Anglican Ordinal*, pp. 67–70.

the diocese, not simply from the dean and chapter. The other great obstacle was reordination. George Morley had warned at the beginning of 1660 that this would be a stumbling block to reconciliation with those who believed that any reordination would cast doubt on the validity of their past ministry. And so it proved. The episcopal representatives appear to have stonewalled the Presbyterians on this question throughout 1660: the Worcester House Declaration was almost deliberately vague and confusing, citing 13 Elizabeth c. 12, and conceding nothing about the validity of Presbyterian orders. Someone meanwhile was driving on the plan to proscribe all but episcopal ordination in the church. The Ordinal was not discussed at the Savoy Conference, but it was comprehensively rewritten by Convocation in November and December so as to make the distinction between bishops and priests crystal clear. This was the one instance in which the liturgical preparations of Wren, Sancroft and other 'High' Churchmen paid off, and it is plain that the clergy were determined to counter both Presbyterian and Roman Catholic taunts about the incoherence of the Anglican Ordinal.[161] At precisely the same time, the Cavalier Parliament was undoing the work of the Convention and making episcopal ordination essential to preferment in the national church. And to rub home the point, when the first Scottish bishops were consecrated in December, the two who possessed only Presbyterian orders were ordained first in private by a bishop.[162] By the beginning of 1662, episcopacy was clearly enthroned in the church. But, once the legal position had been settled, once the blessing of episcopal government had been established, the church drew back and did not press the issue. Reticence – disturbed only occasionally by some extravagant claim – was the hallmark of Anglican episcopalianism during the Restoration.

One glaring reason not to press exalted claims for episcopacy was the bishops' transparent dependency upon the Supreme Governor of the church. It was the King who made bishops. The royal *congé d'élire* and letters of nomination told the dean and chapter who they were to elect as their bishop, and that election was then confirmed by the royal writ of assent and mandate for consecration. It was the King and his Parliament who had brought the bishops back to the House of Lords, and who had made the Act of Uniformity; it was the

---

161. Bradshaw, *Anglican Ordinal*, pp. 87–96; E. Cardwell, *A History of Conferences and other Proceedings connected with Revision of the Book of Common Prayer* (3rd edn, Oxford, 1849), pp. 386–8; E.C. Ratcliff, 'The Savoy Conference', in *From Uniformity to Unity*, ed. G.F. Nuttall and O. Chadwick (1962), pp. 137–8.
162. J. Buckroyd, *Church and State in Scotland, 1660–1681* (Edinburgh, 1980), p. 43; Bradshaw, *Anglican Ordinal*, p. 70.

King who had issued the commissions for the Savoy Conference and for Convocation. Nor did the Church of England shy away from this dependence. It was the glory of the Christian religion that it reconciled the fear of God and the honour of the King, 'and these precepts which God hath joined together, let no man separate'; the Church of England revelled in the fact that she was the best friend of monarchy, and her ministers regularly told their flocks that all authority came from the King.[163] To their opponents this was naked Erastianism or even cynical flattery of potential tyrants: but Anglicans knew that the Church of England was more than the religion of her Supreme Governor, and that royal supremacy over the church was carefully circumscribed. The bishops were the spiritual governors of the church, for their spiritual powers, such as ordination, consecration and excommunication, were derived from God. As Supreme Governor of the church, the monarch had the right to control the clergy's exercise of their spiritual powers, but he did not have these powers himself.[164] The clergymen told themselves that the secular authorities could not 'deprive our church of its essential rights given us by God, but only lay temporal punishments on us for the use of them without their permission'.[165] 'Every sovereign Christian prince is a head of that church, which is in his dominions, as the head signifies the principal member', but Christ was the head of the universal Church of which each national church was a branch.[166] This division of the church and of the ministry into a spiritual and a civil sphere allowed the clergyman to think of himself as Aaron in partnership with Moses, but the exact distribution of power between the partners remained ill-defined. When an Oxford student asked his tutor how far the jurisdiction of the English bishops 'derived from the civil supreme magistrate', he was directed to Bishop Sanderson's *Episcopacy not Prejudicial to Regal Power*, where Sanderson 'tells you in what sense he takes the divine right of episcopacy, which may possible be the truest notion thereof, though contrary to the sentiments of some high-flying men'.[167] It was only when William III began to deprive clergymen and bishops that some Anglicans realized that in the past 'our own great men . . . have

---

163. Falkner, *Christian Loyalty*, sig. a3; J[ohn] D[owell], *The Clergies Honour* (1681), Wing C4646, p. 57; John Shaw, *No Reformation* (1685), p. 66.
164. See Cosin, *Works*, IV, 371–3; Pocock, VI, 167; John Copleston, *Moses next to God, and God next to Moses* (1661), p. 20; BL, MS Lansdowne 960, fos 41v–42v; Falkner, *Christian Loyalty*, pp. 13–15.
165. Samuel Hill, *The Catholic Balance* (1687), p. 99.
166. John Sudbury, *Sermon Preach'd before the King* (1677), p. 28.
167. BL, MS Lansdowne 960, fos 37v, 39v.

carried the supremacy so far, as to let it in upon the ancient rights of the church, and . . . too much in favour of the civil magistrate's usurpations upon the bishops. It will little avail us to say now when they make against us, that they were ill done, since we condemned them not whilst they seemed to make for us.'[168]

The Church of England was forcibly reminded of the 'underlying resources' she possessed in episcopacy every time the Stuarts let her down; the events of 1649, 1650–1, 1662–3, 1672–3 and 1686–9, each pushed the high-flying clergy a little closer towards an assertion of the church's independence from the monarchy and state.[169] The church could never relax her guard. The fortunes of the Scottish church under Lauderdale's Erastian regime were, for instance, a constant warning to Sheldon. A church commission had been imposed on the Scottish church in 1663–5; the 1669 Act of Supremacy had been used to crush episcopal resistance to the indulgence of dissenting clergy; and, most spectacularly, Archbishop Burnet of St Andrew's had been forced to resign in 1669, only to be reappointed in 1674: and, of course, much worse was later to befall the Scottish episcopate under James II and VII.[170] If the Church of England was to avoid such humiliations, vigilance and, on occasion, blatant political pressure were necessary. Despite Whig complaints of an Anglican ascendancy, the churchmen perceived the reign of Charles II as bringing subservience, contempt and humiliation upon the church, as an era of captivity relieved only by the years of hope in 1675–8 and 1681–5. In 1677 the Church of England was brought to the point of protecting the prerogative and the church by undermining the royal supremacy. Archbishop Dolben's bill would have removed from a Roman Catholic monarch the power to appoint bishops. Throughout the 1680s, the churchmen repeatedly offered this drastic proposal as a means of avoiding the exclusion of James II from the throne. But all the time the threat was growing that the church would have to find some way 'for preserving itself independent of the state' – 'the more we are cramped in our temporal, the more stress should be laid in the exercise of that spiritual power by which the church subsisted so many ages before Constantine'. Or, as Samuel Hill stated in the spring of 1687, if any heretic or infidel prince 'should design to dissolve our succession, we have a canonical

168. MS Rawlinson Letters 94, fo. 203v.
169. The phrase is Professor Collinson's, see *Religion of Protestants*, p. 8.
170. Buckroyd, *Church and State in Scotland*, pp. 55, 72–85, 115–116. For the situation under James see I.B. Cowan, 'The Reluctant Revolutionaries: Scotland in 1688', in *By Force or Default? The Revolution of 1688–1689*, ed. E. Cruickshanks (Edinburgh, 1989), p. 72.

right to preserve our orders, and can but suffer penalties, which may oppress, but not null or vacate the validity of our ordination'.[171]

The old problem of the Church of England's relationship with other Protestant churches was a further constraint on the trumpeting of episcopacy. The 'necessity' claim remained in force for benighted foreigners. The 'trans-marine churches' were exculpated because bishops are part of a church's well-being, not her being:

> it may fall out also, that all the bishops of a well-formed complete church may die, or by persecution be so scattered that they dare not appear, or by an infidel conquerour be banished, or murdered: but if the remaining Christians in this distressed condition keep their first faith, they are in a salvable state, and continue true members of the universal Church.[172]

These foreign churches were 'true tho' imperfect' and the Act 'was fully designed against our home Dissenters, who had opportunities of episcopal orders at home; not against those who could not have them at home'.[173] In 1683, when ministers of the French Reformed Church in England petitioned Sancroft for the freedom to exercise their ministry, they enrolled one of the English bishops in support.[174] Thomas Turner was deputed to consider the unnamed bishop's arguments:

> His notion I perceive is that tho' the French orders are now allowable in the church, but in a case of necessity, as theirs is supposed to be, yet their submission to our church, and licenses from our bishops, authorizes them as ministers in our church, without the formality, as I may call it, of an ordination.[175]

The anonymous bishop apparently argued that the essence of ordination lies in the authorization of an individual to perform the offices of a minister by the governor of the church. Archbishop Laud had recognized the orders of French ministers by authorizing them to officiate as priests, a practice which might still be followed 'if the Act of Parliament did not now expressly require it [i.e., episcopal

---

171. MS Sancroft 64 (quoted p. 78 above); MS Tanner 30, fo. 104 (Bishop Turner of Ely, 16 August 1686); Hill, *Catholic Balance*, p. 127.
172. John Shaw, *Origo protestantium* (1677), pp. 72, 70.
173. Edward Gee, *Veteres vindicati* (1686), pp. 48–9; cf. Gilbert Burnet, *A Modest Survey* (1676), pp. 26–7; Timothy Puller, *The Moderation of the Church of England* (1679), p. 307; Samuel Parker, *The Case of the Church of England* (1681), pp. 267–8; William Saywell, *Evangelical and Catholick Unity* (1682), p. 300; Henry Maurice, *A Vindication of the Primitive Church, and Diocesan Episcopacy* (1682), pp. 373–4.
174. MS Rawlinson Letters 93, fo. 223.
175. Ibid., fo. 255 (Turner to ?, 22 April 1684, Fulham).

ordination]; and therefore 'tis a thing which the state only, not our church as such, nor our religion, do require'. As Turner observes, 'there seems to be some what of truth in this notion'. That is a striking admission on Turner's part – and an even more astonishing argument for an Anglican bishop to advance – yet the suspicion that, in Turner's words, 'ordination is only a civil constitution' was a natural outcome of the Church of England's refusal to jettison the principle that 'necessity' could justify non-episcopalian ordination and government. There was, however, no such 'necessity' in England. Francis Turner, Bishop of Ely, reported that one 'ancient Minister of Montpellier', now in exile in England, 'understands our church so well, that purely out of reverence to episcopal ordination, he desires to waive his classical [orders], and next Sunday to be made a deacon'.[176] The availability in England, and indeed the legal requirement, of episcopal ordination was taken by the churchmen to absolve them from making any concession to those Dissenting clergy who feared that a 'reordination' would impugn the validity of their past ministry. The Restoration church would have no truck with 'promiscuous ordinations'.[177]

Wherever possible, churchmen discussed episcopacy pragmatically, emphasizing the utility of bishops, and the circumspection, learning and diligence required by this 'primitive', 'apostolic' office; 'unless you give some prerogative of power to *one bishop in a diocese*, to examine external order, and to maintain sound doctrine, you will have so many fashions as there are men, and so many faiths as there are parishes'.[178] At the first Restoration consecration, on 28 October 1660, John Sudbury preached on the office and dignity of a bishop, claiming that the bishop 'is so necessary to the peace and safety of the church, that the opposing of one must needs beget disorder and confusion in the other. But I will pray, that God, who hath restored us to a better understanding of the royal office and dignity, will likewise give us a right apprehension of the episcopal'.[179] Sudbury's sermon was a paean to unity and discipline, and to the naturalness of authority being centred in one person. After describing the bishop

176. MS Tanner 30, fo. 192; also see fos 95, 99, 182. On the Huguenots, and especially the French-speaking 'Anglican' church at the Savoy, see R.D. Gwynn, *The Huguenot Heritage* (1985), ch. 6.

177. See John Pearson, *Minor Theological Works*, II, 231–7; Spurr, 'Comprehension', 940.

178. John Hacket, *A Sermon Preached before the Kings Majesty [22 March 1660–1]* (1660), p. '16'; also see Benjamin Laney, *Five Sermons* (1668), 'The Shepherd'.

179. John Sudbury, *A Sermon Preached at the Consecration of . . the Bishops of London, Sarum, Worcester, Lincoln and St Asaph* (1660), epistle dedicatory, pp. 5, 35. Also see D'Oyly, *Sancroft*, II, 305–53.

as 'a prince, or principal pastor in God's church' at a 1663 consecration, Isaac Barrow preached on the divine promise of protection
and salvation to the priesthood.[180] The same year, at the consecration of Seth Ward, Robert South made a pragmatic claim for episcopacy, portraying bishops as a fence against schism and sects, and
trying to bolster the courage of the present hierarchy.[181] Three years
later, at Dolben's consecration as Bishop of Rochester, South's text
was Titus ii. 15, a text which could be expected to 'engage me in a
discourse about the nature, original, and divine right of episcopacy',
but instead he chose to discuss the duties of teaching and governing
which belonged to the office of a bishop.[182]

At John Fell's consecration, Adam Littleton stressed that the office
of the bishop was good works.

> I shall waive the controversy, whether episcopacy be *iure divino*, as
> having at my entrance shown partly, how episcopal government
> was grafted on the apostolical stock, and so is not (as enemies
> cavil) *a plant, which God hath not planted*. However it be, by divine or
> only apostolical right, all lawful powers are the ordinances of God,
> and our obedience to them is obliged by divine precept.
>
> Nor shall I dispute, whether bishop and presbyter be distinct
> orders or no; for the promiscuous use of the words in scripture
> signifies little, but the humility and condescension of superior
> officers, in taking up the inferior's appellation; as St Peter, though
> an apostle, calls himself... their fellow-presbyter; and St Paul
> goes even lower, when he styles himself... a deacon.

If St Jerome is brought forward to witness to an original single order
of clergy, then we are to reply with St Paul 'we have no such custom,
neither the churches of God. We appeal to the universal practice of
all Christian churches, down along from the apostles' time for fifteen
hundred years together. In law, an estate of so many descents would,
by so long a prescription, certainly gain an unquestionable right'.[183]
Edward Young, preaching at Thomas Ken's consecration on II
Timothy i. 6, said that his text offers 'to our consideration the charge
or office conferred by this solemnity, and that is the office episcopal;
St Paul consecrating a bishop and investing him with such rights
and powers as we never find committed to a simple priest'. He then
proceeded to devote the sermon to a discussion of the grace being
conferred on the person being consecrated.[184]

180. Barrow, I, 485–6 (consecration of Bishop of Sodor and Man, 4 July 1663).
181. South, IV, 42–55, esp. pp. 49, 55.
182. South, I, 94–113.
183. Littleton, I, 293–4.
184. Edward Young, *A Sermon Preached at Lambeth* (1685), p. 2.

There were, of course, more forthright descriptions of bishops as 'the principles of unity, or that which makes a church'.[185] Jasper Mayne told the bishops gathered at Herbert Croft's consecration of their pedigree, 'God sent his son, his son sent apostles, the apostles made bishops, and those bishops made their successors'. He expounded the Epistles to Timothy to show that Timothy was ordained by St Paul with the assistance of bishops, not presbyters, for ordination belonged solely to the bishop.[186] William Jane was equally confident of the superiority of episcopacy when preaching at Henry Compton's consecration as Bishop of Oxford in 1674.[187] In print, other churchmen came out strongly in defence of 'our episcopacy, the thing that is such an eye-sore to papists, atheists, and schismatics', and piled up the evidence of scripture, the Apostolic age, and the first centuries.[188] But there is less of this assertive episcopalianism in print than one might expect, indeed there were surprisingly few consecration sermons published, which may in itself be revealing.[189] Such reticence does not lend itself to measurement, let alone to quotation. Very occasionally, a clergyman might admit to self-censorship. When preaching to Dissenters, the vicar of St Stephen's, Coleman Street, did not press episcopacy as an Apostolical institution, although he was convinced of it, because 'this controversy has so much of obscurity and perplexity in it, that it is not easy to convince such of this, who are under considerable prejudices against it'.[190] From the Anglican point of view, 'this controversy' was complicated by the need to reply to several different opponents at once and to preserve the 'necessity' argument. As a consequence, the pragmatism, and what one suspects to be the evasion, of Restoration churchmen cast a veil of ambiguity over the subject of episcopacy.

Yet there were hints of a divergence in Anglican views on episcopacy. All churchmen recognized a 'divine right' of episcopacy, yet for some this simply meant that bishops were warranted by Apostolical practice and the perpetual custom of the Church; while

---

185. John Gaskarth, *A Sermon preached before...John Lord Bishop of Bristol* (1685), p. 28, quoting Cyprian of Carthage.

186. Jasper Mayne, *A Sermon Preached at the Consecration of...Herbert, Lord Bishop of Hereford* (1662), p. 41.

187. William Jane, *A Sermon preached at the Consecration of Henry, Lord Bishop of Oxford* (1675).

188. Edward Pelling, *Good Old Way*, p. 26; also see pp. 26–48; Robert Grove, *Short Defence*, ch. 2; Hill, *Catholic Balance*, p. 62 and *passim*.

189. I have found eleven sermons preached at ten of the fifty consecrations between 1660 and 1688.

190. Richard Lucas, *Unity and Peace* (1683), p. 8.

for others it implied some constitutive, and therefore indispensable, role for the bishop in the Church. As yet this difference only betrayed itself in the nuance of a sermon or the tone of a tract; it can be detected, for instance, in discussions of episcopal 'succession'. In making the case for episcopacy, most Restoration churchmen relied upon the argument that bishops were a perpetual custom of the Church and, almost inevitably, they referred to some sort of succession of bishops in the Church. Richard Allestree spoke of 'that apostolical and divine dignity, which the chief priests are acknowledged to be possessed of by right of succession'.[191] Virtually all churchmen recognized the centrality of episcopal succession in defining the Church, but not all of them meant the same thing by 'succession'. Often they meant something quite prosaic – as in Adam Littleton's example of 'an estate of so many descents' and a right in law.

Edward Stillingfleet expressed his own understanding of succession in an appendix to the 1662 second edition of *Irenicum*;

> Whatever practice is founded upon grounds perpetual and common, that practice must continue as long as the grounds of it do, and the church's capacity will admit; (which hypothesis is the only rational foundation on which episcopal government in the church doth stand firm and unshaken, and which in the former discourse I am far from undermining of, as an intelligent reader may perceive) ... [192]

Stillingfleet never did acknowledge the need to recant *Irenicum*, although it is clear that from 1662 onwards he believed that the Apostolic succession was demonstrated by 'the universal consent of the church' and the 'general consent of the Ancient Fathers who were the most competent witnesses in this case'. He agreed with the Church of England 'that since the apostles' times there hath been three orders, of bishops, priests and deacons; and in a regular, well constituted church, are to continue to the world's end'.[193] Here the idea of succession is completely empty, it means nothing in itself. Compare the idea of succession underlying Henry Dodwell's huge tract on schism, which argued that the Dissenters were obliged to conform to all unsinful conditions of the episcopal communion imposed by the ecclesiastical governors in the place where they lived. Dodwell first establishes the necessity for the Christian to receive the

---

191. Allestree, I, 214 (quoting Photius); also see Nathaniel Bisbie, *The Bishop Visiting* (1686), pp. 8–10; Barrow, IV, 5–11; VIII, 178–83, 216–21,
192. Stillingfleet, II, 436.
193. Stillingfleet, I, 374 (ordination sermon of 15 March 1685).

sacraments, from which it follows that the validity of the sacraments must be assured.

> The act of the minister does not give possession of the spiritual benefits of them; but the giving of the symbols by the minister confers a legal right, and obliges God to put well-disposed communicants in actual possession of those spiritual graces, where the symbols themselves are validly administered, that is, where the person who administers has received a power from God of acting in his name in their administration.[194]

This ecclesiastical authority could not have come down to the present age without a continued succession of personal acts transferring that power. At a stroke Dodwell has cut the ground from beneath his Presbyterian opponents. Whether presbyters had ever originally enjoyed the power of ordination was immaterial to the *present* situation. All that is now relevant is which order of clergy can prove a continuous succession to the present day: and, of course, only the episcopate can do so. In effect, Dodwell argues that by persisting in an unbroken succession episcopacy has created its own form of indispensability and divine right. Dodwell's notion of succession was a guarantee of the sacraments, indeed of the Christian's eucharistic union with Christ. He amplified this theme in *A Discourse concerning the One Altar and the One Priesthood* (1683). Under the Old Dispensation the Jewish sacrifices caused a mystical union with God, dependent upon the external communion of the Jews with their high priest. Dodwell traces the evolution of the Jewish idea of sacrifice through the Hellenized and Neoplatonic vocabulary and thinking of the Apostles and the first Christians to its formulation as 'koinoinia' (fellowship) in I John i. 3. Thus he can argue that the Christian bishop is answerable to the Jewish high priest, 'and this seems also very agreeable with the absoluteness of episcopacy so much insisted upon by St Cyprian'.[195] In short, those not in communion with their bishop were not in communion with the Church or with God.

Samuel Bolde, the Anglican opponent of persecution, attacked Dodwell and his allies for insisting on the divine right of episcopacy and 'keeping such a stir as they do about succession (whereas I cannot find that any of the first Fathers did insist on any other succession than a succession in faith)'. Until he sees a convincing answer to 'Dr Stillingfleet's most rational and elaborate *Irenicum*', Bolde will not admit that recognizing the divine right of episcopacy

194. Henry Dodwell, *Separation of Churches from Episcopal Government ... proved Schismatical* (1679), p. 407.
195. *A Discourse* (1683), p. 252.

is 'necessary to conformity'.[196] Bolde, of course, was wrong, since even Stillingfleet acknowledged that the continuous succession of episcopacy amounted to some form of divine prescription. (But he was right to draw attention to the difficulties of proving a continuous episcopal succession in the church.)

The range of views within the church and her determination to maintain a united front were never more apparent than in the great controversy provoked by Edward Stillingfleet's sermon on *The Mischief of Separation* preached at the Guildhall on 2 May 1680. The sermon may not have been intended to give offence at that dangerous moment for the church, but that was its effect; by October, one correspondent could report, 'there are no less than six answers against Dr Stillingfleet's sermon and about eight small pieces in defence of him', and the final tally was far greater.[197] Stillingfleet denounced the Nonconformist separation as unwarranted, irrational, harmful and schismatic, and made a very heavy-handed plea for Protestant unity. Dissenters, and some churchmen, were incensed by Stillingfleet's 'Erastian' account of how the national church was constituted.

> Just as several families uniting making one kingdom, which at first had a distinct and independent power, but it would make strange confusion in the world to reduce kingdoms back again to families, because at first they were made up of them. Thus national churches are national societies of Christians under the same laws of government and rules of worship. For the true notion of a church is no more than of a society of men united together for their order and government according to the rules of the Christian religion.[198]

Stillingfleet's comments were aimed at the Nonconformist assumption that a church is first constituted by the bonds which arise from within the congregation. He saw church unity as something external or imposed: 'if there be one Catholic Church consisting of multitudes of particular churches consenting in one faith; then why may there not be one national church from the consent in the same articles of religion, and the same rules of government and order of worship.'[199]

196. Samuel Bolde, *A Plea for Moderation towards Dissenters* (1682), p. 16.
197. MS Wood F 39, fo. 25. There are selective accounts of the controversy in Spurr, 'Anglican Apologetic', pp. 297–304; C.E. Whiting, *Studies in English Puritanism from the Restoration to the Revolution* (1931), pp. 522–8; H. Horwitz, 'Protestant Reconciliation and the Exclusion Crisis', *JEH*, 15 (1964); J. Marshall, 'The Ecclesiology of the Latitude-Men 1660–1689: Stillingfleet, Tillotson, and "Hobbism"', *JEH* 36 (1985).
198. Stillingfleet, I, 283.
199. Ibid.; cf. Barrow, VIII, 748.

The process by which national churches were created was historical. At 'the decay of the Roman Empire' national churches 'resumed their just right of government to themselves, and upon their owning Christianity, incorporated into one Christian society'.[200] In *The Unreasonableness of Separation* (1680), a vindication of his sermon, Stillingfleet wrote

> If they ask, how it comes to be one national church? I say, because it was received by the common consent of the whole nation in Parliament, as other laws of the nation are; and is universally received by all those that obey those laws . . . all bishops, ministers and people, taken 'together, who profess the faith so established, and worship God according to the rules so appointed, make up this national Church of England.[201]

In a rather jaundiced aside, one Nonconformist suggested this argument was needed 'to acquit us from the imputation of schism in our separating from the Church of Rome'.[202] But to Richard Baxter it was 'somewhat worse' than Erastianism, for how did this national church differ from a Christian kingdom? Where were the 'constitutive essential relations of pastor and flock'?[203]

Stillingfleet had little to say about the role of the episcopate in constituting a church: in *The Mischief*, he simply asserted that 'the notion of a church was the same with that of a diocese; or such a number of Christians as were under the inspection of a bishop'.[204] In *The Unreasonableness*, he again confuted Dissent by simply expanding upon the congruency between the diocesan episcopacy of the Early Church and the Church of England; the bishops had succeeded to the ordinary part of the Apostles' power in governing the Church; English episcopacy is not repugnant to any institution of Christ.[205] Taken together with his Erastianism, Stillingfleet's lukewarm attitude towards episcopacy was enough for Samuel Parker, Archdeacon of Canterbury, to pillory him as one of those

> learned and moderate divines, both at home and abroad, that grant indeed the necessity of some kind of government in the

200. Stillingfleet, I, 283.
201. Stillingfleet, II, 605, 606.
202. John Howe, *Answer to Mischief of Separation* (1680), p. 26.
203. Richard Baxter, *Richard Baxters Answer*, pp. 43, 37. Also see W.M. Lamont, *Richard Baxter and the Millennium* (1979), ch. 4.
204. Stillingfleet, I, 288. The passage continues, 'those presbyters who rejected the authority of their bishop, or affected separate meetings, where no fault could be found with the doctrines of the church, were condemned of schism'.
205. Stillingfleet, II, 567–92.

church, but deny it to have been settled and fixed by our Saviour in any one form, or upon any certain order of men, and leave it wholly at somebody's disposal (though who that somebody is they have not as yet clearly determined) to appoint officers and governors . . .[206]

Before it was published, Parker told Henry Dodwell that *The Case of the Church of England* (1681) was designed to rebut 'Dr Stillingfleet's notion of no *ius divinum*', and despite his reluctance to join in the cry when the 'presbyterian hounds' were upon Stillingfleet, it was absolutely necessary for the church's peace that she should be established upon a divine form of government.[207] The archdeacon later admitted that another target was also intended, the reunion schemes under discussion in 1680. 'The chief design of my book being to blow up Dr Stillingfleet's *Irenicum*, upon whose principles the whole project was erected.'[208] Elsewhere Parker railed against the prestige being accorded to Stillingfleet on account of *The Unreasonableness of Separation*.

The book is as pernicious a book as ever was written, being the extract of all puritanism, it takes away all the power of the church, it justifies all the fanatics' pretences against the laws, it makes us guilty of the same schism in reference to the Dissenters as the Church of Rome is in reference to us, in short it is the whole mystery of Independency.[209]

To churchmen like Parker and his protégé, Simon Lowth, any diminution of the role of the bishop in constituting and governing the church must necessarily undermine the case against the Nonconformists. To represent the form of church government as mutable, argued Lowth, is to make nonsense of the idea of schism. Schism is 'recession from the bishop' and to suggest that 'this church-sense of it, is a mere chimera' is to contradict 'all the ancient Fathers, Doctors and teachers of the Church of God, and the whole current of theology'.[210]

The majority of churchmen and the hierarchy took a very different line towards Stillingfleet's works. Parker himself admitted that Stillingfleet's book was 'in mighty vogue', and one correspondent

---

206. Samuel Parker, *The Case of the Church of England* (1681), p. 4.
207. MS Eng Letters C 28, fos 3–4 (13 November 1680).
208. MS Tanner 31, fo. 170.
209. MS Tanner 36, fo. 255, Parker to Simon Patrick, ?1682. It is possible, but unlikely, that Parker was referring to *Irenicum*.
210. Simon Lowth, *A Letter to Edward Stillingfleet* (1687), pp. 74–5. Also see Lowth's *Of the Subject of Church Power* (1685), an attack on Stillingfleet and Tillotson.

urged Sancroft that every parish church 'might be pleasured with Dr Stillingfleet's book against separation'.[211] Sancroft warned Parker that 'if I would be meddling I must look to myself' and publication of his work was 'hindered first by the advice, and then the command of my Lord of Canterbury, my Lord of London, and my Lord of St Asaph, after they had perused it'.[212] Leading churchmen threw themselves into the fray in support of the 'excellent Dean of St. Paul's' and 'his late incomparable book'.[213] William Clagett, for instance, explained that while the churchmen did not believe that a man could be 'Head' of the Church as Christ is, they did allow a role to the bishop and the sovereign. The 'being' of a national church is easily understood by common sense, it is the result of an organic union under the same rules of government and worship of the several churches of a kingdom sharing a common faith.[214] While the Erastian flavour of Clagett's ecclesiology marks him out as a natural ally for Stillingfleet, the same could not be said of William Sherlock, whose two long defences of the Dean of St Paul's argued, from the authority of Cyprian among many others, that unity in faith is insufficient without unity in sacraments and church government. It is startling to find, in an avowed defence of *The Unreasonableness of Separation*, the following account of how particular churches unite into one national church:

> (1.)The obligation to Catholic communion . . . is the foundation of this union (2.) Every particular bishop is the supreme governor in his own diocese: (3.) That yet every bishop has a relation to the whole Christian Church, and [is] concerned as far as he can to take care of the whole, especially of neighbouring churches . . . and therefore (4.) That those bishops, especially whose vicinity and neighbourhood makes them capable of such a union, should govern their churches by mutual advice and counsel, and observe the same laws and rules of worship, discipline and government.[215]

Those churchmen who had earlier criticized *Irenicum*, now rushed to defend Stillingfleet or to press home his indictment of Non-

---

211. MS Tanner 36, fos 255, 231; also see fo. 144.
212. MS Tanner 31, fo. 170; also see MS Eng Letters C 28, fo. 5.
213. Richard Hollingworth, *Christian Principles* (1681), epistle dedicatory; William Saywell, *A Serious Inquiry into the Means of an Happy Union* (1681), pp. 42–8; idem, *Evangelical and Catholick Unity*, sig. A4.
214. [William Clagett], *A Reply to a Pamphlet called the Mischief of Impositions* (1681): the *Mischief of Impositions* (1680) was by Vincent Alsop.
215. William Sherlock, *A Discourse about Church Unity* (1681), p. 568; also see Sherlock, *A Continuation and Vindication of the Defence* (1682).

conformity.[216] William Saywell, one of Bishop Gunning's acolytes and a reputed 'High-Church-Man' (sic), was lavish in his praise of Stillingfleet's 'great and elaborate book', and saw no difficulty in citing Stillingfleet and Dodwell as joint authorities against the Nonconformist schism.[217]

The historical testimony of the Catholic Church was of importance to the Stillingfleet controversy, as it was to the whole Catholic trend of Anglican ecclesiology. Henry Maurice's *A Vindication of the Primitive Church, and Diocesan Episcopacy* (1682) cited Ignatius, Theodoret, and even Jerome to prove the present necessity of episcopacy from primitive *practice*; at one point, Maurice's extended discussion of the testimony of Cyprian of Carthage became a defence of Stillingfleet's presentation of Cyprian in *The Unreasonableness of Separation*. From the first-century authorities for episcopacy, Edward Pelling cited Ireneus, Hegesippus, Dionysius of Corinth, Clemens Romanus, the Apostolical canons, and above all the Ignatian epistles. The Ignatian texts were still the target of criticism from those 'who have been schismatics from the Catholic Church in this particular of government'. In 1666 Jean Daillé, a Huguenot, had attacked Ussher's dating and recension of the Ignatian epistles, only to be roundly dismissed by another Anglican bishop, John Pearson, whose *Vindiciae epistolarum S. Ignatii* (1672) held the field for many years afterwards.[218] Pearson also worked with Bishop Fell on the texts of Cyprian, while George Bull's controversy with the Jesuit Petavius led to *Defensio fidei Nicaenae* (1685), his vindication of the trinitarianism of the pre-Nicene Fathers. These historical enquiries into the government and doctrines of the Early Church count among the great jewels of English scholarship, yet it is often said that they also represent a deterioration of Anglican theological thought, as the patristic past became seen simply as 'the norm or model to which the present [Church of England] had to conform'.[219] Differences of theological principle were evaded or lost just as surely in the appeal to history as they were in the ambiguities of religious controversy.

It is tempting, but unwise, to make generalizations about the predominant understanding of episcopacy in the Restoration Church of England. Henry Dodwell's view of the episcopate and the church

---

216. Thomas Long, *A Second Part of the Unreasonableness of Separation* (1682), is a lacerating attack on Baxter; cf. Long, *The Character of a Separatist* (1677).
217. Saywell, *Serious Inquiry*, pp. 42–8; cf. pp. 10–12, for Dodwell-like sentiments on episcopacy; *Evangelical and Catholick Unity*, sig. A4.
218. Pelling, *Good Old Way*, p. 27.
219. See G.V. Bennett, 'Patristic Tradition in Anglican Thought, 1660–1900', *Oecumenica* (Gütersloh, 1972), 74–5.

may have been idiosyncratic – certainly Nonconformists asserted that he was the only Anglican who believed that non-episcopally ordained ministers were not true ministers.[220] Yet the times demanded circumspection. Initially, Dr Anthony Dopping was an enthusiastic supporter of Dodwell, discounting Stillingfleet 'because his reputation is concerned the other way and is for the peace of the Reformed churches abroad. I do not think that it [peace] is to be bought at the loss of an important truth: especially since some eminent men among them have declared in favour of episcopacy, and ascribe their want of it to the infelicity of their affairs.' But Dopping grew colder as he came to realize 'that churchmen have their fears and policies as well as others', and to suspect that Dodwell's denunciation of Dissent and the tendency of his arguments 'to the unchurching of the Reformed churches abroad' might prevent the licensing of his work for publication.[221] Dodwell's views were to come into their own after 1688 when there was no longer any pretence of an Anglican consensus, and when he became the chief architect of Nonjuring churchmanship and a proponent of the Cyprianic 'spiritual monarchy' of the episcopate. But their practical implications during the Restoration gave many churchmen cause for thought. To take one example: in 1680 Bishop Gulston of Bristol sought advice from Sancroft about a young woman who had been baptized before the Restoration by a Presbyterian minister:

> This young woman hearing a city vicar preach up the necessity of baptism by a priest in episcopal orders, and warmly asserting the nullity of all other baptism . . . reflects upon herself as one still unbaptized, and therefore passionately desires to receive baptism from a person lawfully ordained, and will not easily be satisfied without it, tho' she hath been confirmed by my predecessor, and hath received the sacrament of the Lord's Supper.

Presumably on the archbishop's advice, Bishop Gulston persuaded the young woman that her baptism was valid – a concession no less striking than the bishop's own uncertainty about the matter.[222] At the other extreme from Dodwell, there were some Anglican voices, like Bishop Croft's, to be heard asserting that bishops were simply elevated from the single order of presbyters by human authority for purposes of good order in the church. Somewhere between these

220. John Cheney, *The Conforming Non-conformist* (1680), p. 119.
221. MS Eng Letters C 29, fos 43, 46 and 47b.
222. MS Tanner 37, fos 40, 82. It is likely that the 'city vicar' was Richard Thompson; see p. 83 above and p. 192 below.

extremes lay the mainstream Anglican view of episcopacy, a view which was far less precise than might be expected.

Scholars often overestimate the effect of scholarship even upon other scholars and students. Most Restoration churchmen were concerned with invoking the authority of the church's champions, not with tracing the subtleties of their arguments and proofs. In private or in print, churchmen took little heed of fine points of interpretation and theological difference, and blithely classed together some very different works on episcopacy. The Oxford tutor Andrew Allam recommended the work of Bishops Hall, Taylor, Bilson, Downham, Andrewes and Gauden, and of Hammond and Dodwell, all of which 'irrefragably defends our episcopal government'.[223] Edward Eccleston adduced the works of Hammond, Sanderson, Stillingfleet and Edward Fowler in vindication of bishops against Richard Baxter; while Jeremy Taylor recommended to the novice student his own work, that of Hammond, and Andrewes's letter to Du Moulin. According to Robert Conold, 'that episcopacy is *jure divino* hath been learnedly asserted by Bishop Taylor, Dr Hammond, and Bishop Hall; and I never saw an answer to those elaborate discourses, and therefore the Church of England is yet in full possession of that doctrine'.[224] *Ius divinum* remained as nebulous as ever. 'Touching the institution of episcopacy I find among those who assert it some make it established *jure divino* in the strictest sense, others *apostolico* [by the Apostles], some *ecclesiastico* [by the church], and others only *regioni* [by the state], our English Erastians Mr Selden and Mr Hobbs, but all of the true sons of the Church of England honour it with the defensible title of *jure divino*.'[225] Bishop Lucy believed his office was *iure divino*, 'or more properly, *iure apostolico*'. Sir Henry Yelverton, that stringent critic of lax bishops, published Bishop Thomas Morton's old-fashioned vindication of episcopacy, with his own dedication to Sheldon in which he asked, 'is not there as sufficient assurance, that that government was settled by the apostles, and so in some sense of divine right, and so unalterable, as we have to admit for scripture'.[226] Perhaps the best one can say is that many Restoration churchmen plainly thought episcopacy the preferable,

223. BL, MS Lansdowne 960, fo. 35.
224. DWL, Baxter Letters II, fo. 205 (Eccleston to Baxter); Taylor's advice quoted in Jeremy Taylor, *Works*, ed. Heber and revised by C.P. Eden (1847–52), I, p. lxxxix; Conold, *Notion*, p. 111.
225. BL, MS Lansdowne 960, fo. 44v.
226. William Lucy, *A Treatise of the Nature of a Minister* (1670), p. 95 (written against congregationalists in the 1650s); Thomas Morton, *Episkopos Apostolikos* (1670), p. xxv; also see pp. 11, 25, 150, for the views of Bishop Morton (1584–1659).

but not the prescribed form of government; not *iure divino* but *iure humano*, yet not, punned John Ward, *iniuria humana* either.[227]

Learned discussion of the episcopal office could never be abstracted from men's day-to-day experience of English bishops. Contemporary perceptions of the episcopal office were shaped by diverse cultural and social models; the notion of the bishop as a 'right reverend father in God' to his flock sat easily with patriarchal assumptions. The Restoration bishop was also a prince of the Church of England, a baron of the realm and a member of the House of Lords, a feudal lord with his own courts and jurisdiction, a courtier and government agent, and in consequence, all too often, a venal and negligent pastor. This medieval model was married to theological, scriptural and patristic notions of what it was to be a bishop. Bishops knew that they 'stood in St Paul's place'; they identified with Early Christian figures like Cyprian or Ambrose; and these patristic fantasies were further promoted by biographies with titles like *Cyprianus Anglicus*.[228] The primitive model was particularly appealing – as William Cave's account suggests:

> The first and principal officer of the church was the president or bishop, usually chosen out of the presbyters. I shall not here concern myself in the disputes, whether episcopacy as a superior order to presbytery, was of divine institution (a controversy sufficiently ventilated in the late times) it being enough to my purpose, what is acknowledged both by Blondel and Salmasius, the most learned ᵈefenders of presbytery, that bishops were distinct from, and superᵢᵤᵣ to presbyters in the second century, or the next age to the apostles. The main work and office of a bishop was to teach and instruct the people, to administer the sacraments, to absolve penitents, to eject and excommunicate obstinate and incorrigible offenders, to preside in the assemblies of the clergy, to

227. John Ward, *Diary* (1839), p. 208. Also see Joseph Glanvil, *Essays*, essay 7, p. 40; [Edward Fowler], *Principles and Practices* (1670), p. 323; and Conold, *Notion*, p. 110, where the *ius divinum* is equated solely with immutability.

228. MS Tanner 35, fo. 189. Heylyn's life of Laud was entitled *Cyprianus Anglicus* (1668). Cyprian was a popular exemplar: Whitgift had identified with him, as did Bishop Fell; BL, MS Sloane 1008, fo. 266. The church took a keen interest in how the lives of her pastors and bishops were represented; Bishop Morley spent much time and effort overseeing the composition of Isaac Walton's *Lives*, which included subtly biased and idealized portraits of Richard Hooker and Robert Sanderson. See D. Novarr, *The Making of Walton's 'Lives'* (Cornell, 1958), chs 7–8, 11; BL, MS Lansdowne 937, fo. 72; John Fell, *Life of Richard Allestree* in Allestree; MS Tanner 30, fos 114, 137 (Sancroft's interest in Hacket's life of Archbishop Williams); the life by Thomas Plume prefixed to Hacket, *Century of Sermons*; John Barwick's life of Morton in *ΙΕΡΟΝΙΚΗΣ*.

ordain inferior officers in the church, to call them to account, and to suspend or deal with them according to the nature of the offence, to urge the observance of ecclesiastical laws, and to appoint and institute such indifferent rites, as were for the decent and orderly administration of his church. In short . . . a watchman and sentinel.[229]

There were a variety of personal episcopal styles in the Restoration church. The return of prelatical pomp along with the episcopacy was not always to everyone's taste: while John Evelyn commended the 'decent solemnity' of Bishop Monck's funeral, when a silver mitre and episcopal robes were carried in procession, he was less taken with Bishop Wren's blessing 'very pontifically' at the end of service.[230] At the other extreme from Wren were bishops like John Gauden, the proponent of reduced episcopacy, or Edward Reynolds, the former Presbyterian, who hoped he would not offend his clergy

> if after the example of the ancient bishops in the primitive and purer ages of the Church, who were wont to sit with their clergy and preside in an ecclesiastical senate, I shall in matters of weight and difficulty intreat the advice and assistance of you who are presbyter urbis . . .[231]

Such 'primitive' synods did not always indicate the bishop's humble view of his own office. Both Compton of London and Lloyd of St Asaph used such conferences as a way of keeping their diocesan clergy up to the mark; and whereas some bishops 'were wont to sit with their clergy', others took a far more autocratic line, reflecting in the case of men like Sir Jonathan Trelawney, Bishop of Exeter, or Nathaniel Lord Crew, Bishop of Durham, a confidence born of inherited social standing. Disparity of social background, of income, of intelligence, drive and ambition, meant that there was no typical Restoration bishop nor a typical episcopal style. Even in death, the bishops went their own way. Compare the the tombs of Accepted Frewen (died 1664) and John Dolben (died 1686) in York Minster, the former recumbent in black gown and cap, with hands together in prayer, while the latter in his mitre is half rising, surrounded by angels and facing the east, 'as if waking to the Last Trump'.[232]

229. William Cave, *Primitive Christianity* (1673), pp. 221–2.
230. Evelyn, III, 307, 271. For some later evidence of mitres being worn on state occasions, see F.C. Mather, 'Georgian Churchmanship Reconsidered', *JEH*, 36 (1985), 258–9.
231. Reynolds, *The Preaching of Christ* (1662), epistle dedicatory; also see *RB*, II, 283.
232. See G.E. Aylmer and R. Cant (eds), *A History of York Minster* (Oxford, 1979), pp. 443–5; also see *The Journeys of Celia Fiennes*, ed. C. Morris (1947), pp. 77–8.

At first sight the difference between these two episcopal effigies, Frewen's harking back to the sixteenth century if not earlier, and Dolben's a harbinger of the eighteenth, seems instructive of some deep change in clerical attitudes, but on reflection it may tell us more about changing tastes in funerary monuments. We know too little of the personal dress, deportment and managerial style of late seventeenth-century bishops to make any meaningful assessment of changes. And such assessment may well be otiose, for the Restoration church had precious little interest in exploring the episcopal office. Above all, it was the possession of bishops, the blessing of episcopal government here and now, which mattered to Restoration churchmen.

The Restoration Church of England's *via media* between Catholic and Reformed was a broad path, wide enough to accommodate those who wished to hug either side and those who yawed from one to the other. The justification of this *via media* lay in the unquestionable authority of the national church. The Restoration church continued to associate her own authority with that of her Supreme Governor, the King, just as the church had in the sixteenth century. But some churchmen had begun to suggest that the episcopate sustained the authority of the national church, a principle which simultaneously repudiated Rome's accusations and condemned the Nonconformists, while also remaining compatible with the royal supremacy. To a hostile witness like Richard Baxter, these were 'high prelatists', innovators who believed episcopacy to be 'of divine institution and perpetual usage in the church, and necessary to order among the clergy and people, and of experienced benefit to this land, and most congruous to civil monarchy; and therefore not to be altered by any, no, not by the king and parliament'.[233] This was indeed what they believed, but they did not see themselves as innovators, and they did not rule the Anglican roost during the Restoration. It should be stressed, once again, that there is no reason for thinking that the 'new episcopalianism' of Hammond and his friends was responsible for the political decision in 1662 to make episcopacy a touchstone of the church, whatever it may have later contributed to the enhancement and elaboration of that decision. Meanwhile those Restoration churchmen unable to accept such an elevated view of episcopacy, for fear of 'unchurching' foreign Reformed churches, were obliged to no more than a prudential recognition of bishops as a useful and lawful form of church government. So, although the Anglican 'apostolic

233. *RB*, ii. 388.

paradigm' of the mid-nineteenth century appears to be a logical outcome of the 'new episcopalianism' of the Restoration church, the Restoration church did not seek to develop her episcopalianism to its logical outcome. What she sought to do, and succeeded in doing, was to pause at the brink and to hold in tension several ideas about episcopacy and church authority. By resisting the pressure to precise definition, the church did not foreclose avenues of communication with other Protestant churches or with the Catholic Church, nor did she throw down a challenge to her royal Governor.

This balancing act was brought crashing down by the Revolution of 1688 and the actions of the church's new Supreme Governor, William III. The exercise of naked royal power and the deprivation of the Nonjuring bishops and clergy drove many churchmen to new conclusions about authority in the church. The Nonjurors took refuge in the principle that the church relied solely on the independent succession of the episcopate and accordingly began to consecrate their own bishops. Soon this conception of the bishops' 'spiritual monarchy' and ecclesiastical autonomy began to filter back into the disillusioned 'High Church' ranks of the national church, but it would take another century or more, and another crisis in church-state relations, before the idea that episcopacy was essential to the being of a church was widely accepted in the Church of England; and even today it remains a moot point in some quarters.[234]

The Restoration Church of England was a broad church: her clergy included Interregnum collaborators and Anglican 'sufferers', zealots who demanded that every rubric be performed to the letter and the indulgent who pandered to the semi-conformists among their parishioners; the theological variety to be found among her clergy was a standing joke.[235] Yet she was also a united church. There were few opportunities for the clergy's private differences to spill over into public quarrels; the church's leaders kept a tight rein on the expression of theological or ecclesiological opinions. Far more importantly, the Anglican clergy of the Restoration were united by their fundamental belief in the principle of a national church.

---

234. My interpretation owes a great deal to the important arguments of J.C. Findon, 'The Nonjurors and the Church of England, 1689–1716' (unpublished Oxford University D.Phil. thesis, 1978); also see *Study of Anglicanism*, ed. Sykes and Booty, p. 305; Bradshaw, *Anglican Ordinal*, p. 164; P.A. Welsby, *A History of the Church of England, 1945–1980* (1984), pp. 60–1; J. Kent, *The Unacceptable Face – The Modern Church in the Eyes of the Historian* (1987), pp. 102–3. Dr Avis refers to episcopacy as an Anglican 'house rule'; see *Anglicanism*, pp. 136, 308.

235. See *Poems on Affairs of State: I 1660–1678*, ed. G. deF. Lord (New Haven and London, 1963), p. 312; Sykes, *From Sheldon*, p. 146; Horwitz, 'Protestant Reconciliation', 212.

And slowly, this principle was maturing into an appreciation of the Church of England's uniqueness; the second half of the seventeenth century saw the creation of an Anglican consciousness among the clergy. There was nothing mysterious about this wider sense of Anglican identity; it was partly imposed from outside by the clear legal distinctions between church and Dissent, and it was partly a product of the generous consensus established within the church. As this chapter has shown, an important contribution was made by the development of an 'Anglican ecclesiology', a sense of being both Catholic and Reformed, episcopalian and yet in charity with non-episcopalian churches. The burgeoning Anglicanism of the later seventeenth century also drew upon a series of specifically Anglican teachings on the theology of salvation, on Christian duty, on piety and worship. But before we can examine these other components of Restoration Anglicanism, we must first investigate the authority of the Restoration Church of England.

Chapter 4

Christian Unanimity: The Authority of the National Church

> In matter of religion there is nothing so worthy of memory as the Christian unanimity of the parish of Brightwell, where through the exemplary piety and prudent conduct of that worthy gentleman, the worshipful John Stone Esq., lord of the town and the Revd. Mr Fiddes then rector of the place, and their predecessors, and the good dispositions of the people themselves, all matters both of spiritual and temporal concern, have been so effectually pressed and prudently managed, that there has not been known any such thing as an ale house, a sectary, or suit of law commenced within the whole parish (which is of a large extent) in the memory of man; which being more for ought I know, than any parish in England can say beside, and so worthy the imitation of all other places, I thought fit (for the eternal honour of its inhabitants) to recommend it accordingly.[1]

The ideal of Christian unanimity spoke to the hearts of many Restoration Anglicans. In practice, the intellectually coherent case for a single, all-inclusive, national church, came down to a happy little parish community, free from vice and dissent, under the benevolent, paternalistic government of squire and parson. It was an harmonious, but authoritarian vision. Indeed without authority, without the power to command obedience and create obligation, there could be neither harmony nor order. Authority descended from God, and his vicegerent the King, down through the hierarchy to every squire, justice, patriarch and parson. And it seemed that spiritual and political authority went hand in hand, that ministry and magistracy, Aaron and Moses, bolstered each other at every turn.

In the spiritual realm the authority of the parson was complete:

---

1. Robert Plot, *The Natural History of Oxfordshire* (Oxford, 1676), pp. 203–4.

he was responsible for all the souls in his parish, whether conformists or not, and his authority sat easily in a larger patriarchal scheme of social order. As spokesmen for the ultimate source of all authority, the clergy taught their flock to fear God and the King: 'we perceive plainly that there is a lasting obligation laid upon by Christ for [us] to submit, and yield a cheerful and ready obedience to all our governors'. Submission was required by divine precept and by 'the comfortable end of government'. Churchwardens could report that 'our minister doth yearly, if not weekly, declare the sole interest of authority in all cases ecclesiastical and civil to be in the King'.[2] Royal declarations and Acts of Parliament were read from the pulpit; prayers for the King were offered up from the desk; and the principles of patriarchy and submission were instilled into the children at the catechism class. Symbols of authority cluttered the parish church. With reserved pews for the aldermen or vestrymen and their wives, a niche for the mayor's mace, a chest full of royal proclamations and statutes, and with the walls crammed with the ornate funerary monuments of the well-to-do, the table of affinity, benefactor's board, the Ten Commandments, and the King's coat of arms, the church was a theatre of social and political precedence. Even today, the sight of a gloriously gilded and painted royal coat of arms, such as that adorning St Mary Redcliffe, Bristol, can impart something of the immense political faith which seventeenth-century England placed in the authority of the national church and the ideal of religious unanimity.[3]

Yet the reality seems to have eluded Restoration England. In the following pages there are many examples of disunity and indiscipline within the church; of disorder, apathy and Nonconformity among the laity; and of the mockery and anti-clericalism so prevalent in Restoration society. But it could be argued, of course, that these instances of the collapse of authority are, by their very nature, out of the ordinary. When authority commands obedience and respect, it leaves little trace; few think to do what Robert Plot did for the village of Brightwell Baldwin, and memorialize uneventful unanimity. So, beyond noting that these were exceptional cases, we can only guess at their likely effect on the morale and reputation of

2. MS Eng Th F 63, fos 99, 98; *Episcopal Visitation Returns for Cambridgeshire*, ed. W.M. Palmer (Cambridge, 1930), p. 94. Also see Evelyn, IV, 135, 336–7.
3. This point can be pursued in C. Russell, 'Arguments for Religious Unity in England, 1530–1650', *JEH*, 18 (1967); R. Harvey, 'The Problem of Socio-Political Obligation for the Church of England in the Seventeenth Century', *Church History*, 40 (1971); G. Schochet, *Patriarchalism in Political Thought* (Oxford, 1975); S. Staves, *Players' Scepters – Fictions of Authority in Restoration England* (Lincoln, Nebraska, 1979).

the churchmen; for, as the churchmen knew all too well, 'where our credit is concerned, it is not what we are, but what we are represented, and believed to be, that either greatens or lessens it.'[4]

'Labourers to this Work': Authority within the Church

The Restoration was a Heaven-sent opportunity to re-establish the moral authority of the ministry. In June 1660 Thomas Hodges implored the peers to make the nation 'a temple for the Lord to dwell in; to this end, promote not loiterers, but labourers to this work, that have both skill and will to promote it: that bear both Urim and Thummim in their hearts and lives, and are like *John Baptist* shining in ability, burning in zeal, and sanctity'.[5] John Barnard urged that, when 'rebuilding our spiritual Temple', care should be taken not to employ ministers who had been shown to be scandalous and negligent simply because they had been sequestered from their livings by the usurpers.[6] And in a petition of June 1661, John Davis and other graduates lamented the employment of so many 'raw youths' and besought Parliament to improve clerical stipends, restrict the ministry to graduates, and eject the idle and debauched among the clergy.[7] These high-minded assertions that piety must take precedence over property rights, and pastoral zeal should be the sole qualification for the ministry, also pressed the claims of those who were tarred by their compliance with the puritan regimes. Despite the 'peevish talk of some few', a generation of young pastors, who had devoted themselves to exposing the hypocrisy of puritans and to preaching practical religion, were now to find a place in the church.[8] It was the hireling shepherd, the loose-living pastor and the negligent drone who would find no room in the restored Church of England.[9]

The authority of these labourers in God's harvest was guaranteed by the strict qualifications for entry to the ministry. The church's

---

4. W.S., *An Answer to a Letter of Enquiry* (1671). p. 20
5. Hodges, *Sions Halelujah* (1660), p. 20. Also see Samuel Gardner, *A Sermon Preached at the Visitation* (1672), p. 6; Thomas Hodges, *The Necessity, Dignity and Duty of Gospel Ministers* (1685), p. 17.
6. J. Barnard, *Censura cleri* (1660), p. 21; cf. Edward Reynolds, *Divine Efficacy* (1660), pp. 22–3, 29.
7. *CSPD 1661–2*, p. 18.
8. S.P., *A Brief Account of the New Sect of Latitude-Men* (1662); [Thomas Ken], *Ichabod, Or the Five Groans of the Church* (Cambridge, 1663).
9. See John Riland, *Doom's-Day Books Opened* (1663), p. 68; Thomas Smith, *A Sermon of Conforming and Reforming* (Cambridge, 1662); P. Hammond, 'Thomas Smith', *BIHR* 56 (1983), 185–6.

Canons stipulated a minimum age of twenty-three for ordination as a deacon and twenty-four for a minister. It was forbidden to receive both orders on the same day or to be ordained a minister without evidence of immediate preferment to a living or curacy; ordinands had to supply a testimonial from the head of their college or from three 'grave Ministers' as to their abilities, worthiness and orthodoxy; they had also to submit to further examination by the bishop or his chaplain, and to subscribe to the Act of Uniformity, the Book of Common Prayer and the Articles. The aim was to select – in the words of one testimonial – those who were 'for life blameless, for doctrine orthodox, for the present government loyal, for ecclesiastical discipline conformable'. The regulations were buttressed by the image of the ideal minister as a man 'slipt off the common stock of mankind' and 'mortified to the motions of the flesh'.[10]

The model cleric was an educated man with sufficient Latin, Greek and Hebrew to sustain his exegesis of the scriptures and to harvest the pure Catholic teaching of the Early Church. Although it was a source of pride that the Church of England had nurtured a succession of scholars capable of defending her *via media* against Rome and puritanism, not all churchmen were expected to be suited to apologetics. Yet each churchman was to be a plain preacher of the truths of Christianity and was to eschew the speculative and vainglorious lest his sermons lose sight of their primary purpose – the edification of the flock in the first principles of faith. And every cleric was to be a personal example to his flock: 'let your ministry first manifest its power in making your selves good.'[11] For unless the clergy's office and persons were respected by the laity, there was little hope of success in their preaching or pastoral work. Barnabas Oley republished George Herbert's *A Priest to the Temple* with an exemplary life of the author, and pleaded with his young clerical readers to

> bethink themselves what stock of learning and prudence, the occasions of these times (conference with sectaries and disputations with Papists) will require: what an habit of gravity in attire, and of retiredness in conversation is necessary to make a clergyman exemplary to the loose and vain conversation of these days: what an adult degree of virtue and godliness it must be, that must withstand the incursion of profaneness in this age. And there will not be so much need to beseech them, to buy Fathers, Councils,

10. W.M. Marshall, 'Episcopal Activity in the Hereford and Oxford Dioceses, 1660–1760', *Midland History*, 8 (1983), 111; Laurence Womock, *Moses and Aaron* (1675), p. 44.

11. Lancelot Addison, *A Modest Plea for the Clergy* (1671), p. 155.

and other good classic books; to mortify the flesh, with study, fasting, and prayer, and to do every thing becoming a curate of souls: using this book, as a looking-glass, to inform them what is decent.[12]

The cure of souls was not to be undertaken lightly. 'Take heed that you may never hear that fearful sentence, "I was hungry and ye gave me no meat." If you suffer Christ's little ones to starve, it will be required severely at your hands.'[13]

This ideal has, of course, to be measured against what is known of the realities of the Restoration clergy and of their insecure and overcrowded profession. The Restoration ministry was a graduate profession; in Leicestershire in 1670, 95 per cent of incumbents possessed degrees.[14] Indeed the universities produced so many aspirant clerics that the nation was 'perfectly overstocked with professors of divinity, there being scarce employment for half of those who undertake that office'.[15] Those 'professors' with only a bachelor's degree were at a disadvantage, since it was admitted that the secular BA course offered a poor preparation for the ministry – employment prospects in the church were much better for those who stayed on at university to study theology in the MA course. Most Restoration clergy did acquire a master's degree – 67 per cent of Leicestershire incumbents were MAs, while 23 per cent were only BAs – and almost inevitably those clergymen without an MA began to form a clerical proletariat.[16] The authorities were concerned that candidates for ordination should have used their time at university and since graduation to prepare themselves – this was

12.   George Herbert, *A Priest to the Temple*, ed. Barnabas Oley (1671), sigs v–vi. Also see Granville, I, 132; II, 48.
13.   Taylor, VI, 327.
14.   J.H. Pruett, *The Parish Clergy under the Later Stuarts – The Leicestershire Experience* (Urbana, Illinois, 1978), pp. 23, 39–48; cf. J.L. Salter, 'Warwickshire Clergy, 1660–1714' (unpublished Birmingham University Ph.D. thesis, 1975), pp. 49–54; E.A.O. Whiteman, 'The Episcopate of Dr Seth Ward, Bishop of Exeter (1662 to 1667) and Salisbury (1667 to 1688/89)' (unpublished Oxford University D.Phil. thesis, 1951), p. 358. Other helpful studies of the clerical profession include G.A. Holmes, *Augustan England* (1982); R. O'Day, 'Anatomy of a Profession: the Clergy of the Church of England', in *The Professions in Early Modern England*, ed. W. Prest (1987); I.M. Green, 'Career Prospects and Clerical Conformity in Early Stuart England', *Past and Present*, 90 (1981); G.V. Bennett, 'University, Society and the Church 1688–1714', in *History of the University of Oxford: V The Eighteenth Century*, ed. L.S. Sutherland and L.G. Mitchell (Oxford, 1986); C.F. Richardson, *English Preachers and Preaching 1640–1670* (1928).
15.   John Eachard, *The Grounds and Occasions of the Contempt of the Clergy* (1670), p. 115; Pruett, *Parish Clergy*, pp. 52–3.
16.   Bennett, 'University, Society and Church', pp. 371–7, 386–9.

one reason for setting the minimum age of twenty-three – and they frowned on those who were ordained before they were of age.[17] But, of course, for young men in a hurry, there was no time and often no money to allow quiet years of reading and contemplation before joining in the scramble after clerical preferment. At the Restoration, Isaac Archer of Trinity College, Cambridge, was 'involved ... in a necessity of conforming' when his Nonconformist father refused to support him any longer; 'because without orders I could have no considerable place' (and encouraged by his college), Archer presented himself for ordination as deacon on 21 September 1662, when, with the connivance of the Master, and because he was tall for his years, his age went unquestioned. Three days later he was presented to the college vicarage of Arrington, and a week after 'I went and read prayers and preached having never before performed any duties either in a family or in public'. Small and poor as the vicarage was, it was 'very convenient for a young beginner' like Archer, who now took up the study of divinity. Archer was ordained priest at Ely House in London on 21 December 1662, when he was still two days short of being twenty-one years old. He eventually took his MA in 1664.[18]

Young ordinands chased all sorts of jobs, from vicarages and rectories to university and cathedral posts, from chaplaincies and lectureships to stipendary curacies. Eventually most of them obtained a permanent post, but it took time: the median interval between graduating with a BA and landing a permanent position in the church has been estimated at six years.[19] While waiting for their soliciting and talents to win them a vicarage or rectory, it was the fate of most ordinands to eke out a miserable existence as a curate. On average, curacies were worth between £20 and £30 a year, although some curates earned very much less – several Worcestershire curacies were worth only £10 – and others very much more. The curate at Clayworth in Nottinghamshire received £120 for three years' service; and curates at St Giles in the Fields, a populous and prosperous London parish, were paid £120 a year.[20] Other

17. Ken, *Ichabod*, ch. 2, 'Undue Ordination'; Granville, II, 169–70; Whiteman, 'Ward', p. 217; Pruett, *Parish Clergy*, p. 50
18. Details from CUL, MS Add. 8499, fos 68, 73, 75–6, 93.
19. Pruett, *Parish Clergy*, p. 54. There was perhaps a total of 13,000 permanent posts and several hundred ancillary posts in the English church; see Green, 'Career Prospects', 95–9.
20. See Pruett, *Parish Clergy*, p. 56; Whiteman, 'Ward', p. 355; *Inspections of Churches and Parsonage Houses in the Diocese of Worcester in 1674, 1676, 1684 and 1687*, ed. P. Morgan (Worcestershire Historical Studies, 12, 1986), 14, 75, 84, 91, 92, 94, 96; Salter, 'Warwickshire Clergy', p. 22; *The Rector's Book, Clayworth*, ed. H. Gill and E.L.

courses were open to a lucky few. The university offered its own routes to clerical preferment. Isaac Archer's was one path, but if a college fellowship could be obtained, then ordination usually followed as required by college statutes, and eventually a successful fellow might be elected to a rich college living. A chaplaincy to a noble or gentry family was also a very good stepping-stone for an ambitious young cleric, especially if the living of the local parish was attached or the position offered the chance of influencing political or ecclesiastical affairs.[21] On the other hand, some chaplaincies were demeaning, reducing the divine to a household servant and child-minder. A chaplaincy to a bishop was regarded, quite justifiably, as an almost certain path to a prebendal stall.[22] When Sancroft was first elevated to the primacy, William Turner wrote to the archbishop's chaplain, 'no doubt he is much sought to for servants, especially chaplains, for there are no such warm solicitors as clergymen, when they are in chase of preferment, which is not the primitive way' – the censorious Turner then proceeded to recommend his own candidate for a chaplaincy![23]

However, most of the clergy's soliciting for preferment was addressed, directly or indirectly, to the laity, for the church did not have control of the majority of her own appointments. The right to nominate a clergyman to a benefice, the patron's right of presentation or the 'advowson', was a property right which could be bought and sold, and the majority of patrons were laymen or lay institutions. In Warwickshire the clergy were patrons of only 13.5 per cent of livings; in Leicestershire only 15 per cent of advowsons were in clerical hands. In the diocese of Salisbury, the Crown was patron of 40 livings, and other laymen were patrons of 221 livings, while the clergy held 104 advowsons: these clerically owned advowsons were distributed widely: the bishop held 26, while the Bishop of Winchester held ten, Oxford colleges seventeen, and Cambridge colleges six, and the rest were divided between several clerical dignitaries, incumbents and institutions.[24] The clergy resented the way in which 'a rich shoe-maker, rope-maker, or ale-draper, who hath a son to prefer' could buy the right of presentation and ride roughshod over the interests of the church and needs of the com-

Guilford (Nottingham, 1910), p. 13; A.T. Hart, *The Life and Times of John Sharp* (1949), p. 80.

21. See Patrick, IX, 426–8; Thomas Watts, *The Christian Indeed, and Faithful Pastor* (1714), p. 14; BL, MS Harleian 3785, fo. 109.
22. MSS Tanner 41, fo. 51; 40, fo. 147.
23. MS Tanner 41, fo. 54.
24. Salter, 'Warwickshire Clergy', p. 33; Pruett, *Parish Clergy*, p. 60; Whiteman, 'Ward', p. 351.

munity.[25] The opportunities for abuse were legion. Simony – receiving payment to present a particular candidate – was widely suspected, but difficult to prove, especially given the resort to legal fictions such as the right to next presentation and that 'stratagem of Satan', the bond of resignation.[26] The unwary clergyman could quickly come to grief in these waters: Jabez Brideoake, an Oxfordshire rector, took a living in the diocese of Chichester, 'but finding the patron had a design to ensnare him into a simonaical contract, he forbore to be inducted', only to discover that the patron of this original living was now trying to oust him in order to preserve his own right of presentation. Bishop Fell sympathized. 'Mr Brideoake being low in the world, and having a numerous family, I have thought it hard that he should lose his whole livelihood upon a nicety of law.'[27] It was ' the most pernicious' cause of the country's religious divisions 'that so many parochial minister enter not at the door into the sheepfold, (though they use a silver key) but climb up another way'.[28] The nepotism and favouritism which pervaded the system of preferment seemed perfectly natural to those who practised or benefited from it; excessive consideration of one's nephews or godsons seems to have been a particularly clerical vice, although not a shameful one; Bishop Sanderson of Lincoln preferred one incumbent on the strength of 'his abilities, former sufferings, present necessities, and near relation to me'.[29]

Entering upon the ministry was, then, a finely judged career decision; there is very little to suggest that ideas of vocation played a part in the careful calculations of young clergymen – although, as we shall see, the clergy were often deeply conscious of the dignity and duties of their office.[30] A rectory or vicarage was a valuable piece of property; indeed even the terms 'rector' and 'vicar' are principally descriptive of property relations rather than spiritual functions. A rector was the incumbent of a parish who received all of the revenues or tithes of that parish. The office of vicar had emerged out of the medieval habit of 'appropiating' parish churches

25. Zachary Cawdrey, *A Discourse of Patronage* (1675), p. 28.
26. Cawdrey, *Discourse of Patronage*, pp. 24–6; Ken, *Ichabod*, pp. 47–56; G.F.A. Best, *Temporal Pillars – Queen Anne's Bounty, the Ecclesiastical Commissioners and the Church of England* (1964), pp. 53–9.
27. MS Tanner 33, fo. 23.
28. Cawdrey, *Discourse of Patronage*, p. 37. Also see Pruett, *Parish Clergy*, pp. 57–8.
29. Quoted by Pruett, *Parish Clergy*, p. 62. Also see Whiteman, 'Ward', ch. 9; Granville, I, 195; MS Tanner 31, fo. 118.
30. See Bennett, 'University, Church and Society', pp. 389–90; *The Oxinden and Peyton Letters*, ed. D. Gardiner (1937); chapter 5 below.

to institutions like monasteries which received the parish tithes. In return the monastery sent one of its monks as a substitute or 'vicarius' to perform the duties of the nominal rector. One third of the tithes was set aside to support the vicar, while the rest were reserved for the monastery. At the dissolution of the monasteries in the 1530s, approximately one in three of the country's benefices were 'appropriate' in this way, and the Crown promptly granted these appropriated tithes to laymen. These laymen are said to have 'impropriated' the tithes, and are described as lay impropriators or lay rectors; it was their duty to retain a vicar to serve the parish, and since the vicarial or 'small' tithes were often inadequate to support him, the impropriators were obliged to pay an extra stipend out of their tithes. The vicar held the freehold of the church, the churchyard, the vicarage house and the glebe or farmland attached to the vicarage. As a parish priest, the clergyman who was a vicar had exactly the same spiritual status as a clergyman who was a rector. It seems probable that there were more clerical rectors than vicars across the country: Leicestershire had 115 rectories, 76 vicarages and 14 'perpetual curacies' – where the incumbent received a stipend and none of the tithes – while the diocese of Salisbury had 219 rectories, 145 vicarages and 14 perpetual curacies.[31] What were these properties worth?

According to Bishop Seth Ward's own notes there were in his diocese of Salisbury 255 livings worth less than £100, 91 worth between £100 and £200, and 26 worth more than £200.[32] In Leicestershire in 1706–7, there were 136 parishes in the first category (and 67 of them were worth less than £50 p.a.), 53 in the second, and only twelve in the last.[33] Seventy per cent of all Warwickshire livings were worth less than £60 a year.[34] To place these figures in perspective we should recall that an annual income of £50 placed someone in the wealthiest fifth of the nation, at about the same level as a yeoman or freeholder. This was suggested as the minimum stipend for curates, as in effect the clerical poverty line, by the King

---

31. Pruett, *Parish Clergy*, p. 7; Whiteman, 'Ward', p. 287; but cf. Salter, 'Warwickshire Clergy', p. 22. For perpetual curacies see Green, 'Career Prospects', 83.
32. Forty parishes are of unknown value; see Whiteman, 'Ward', p. 321.
33. And four livings of unknown value, see Pruett, *Parish Clergy*, p. 84. These figures are based on those collected as part of the scheme known as Queen Anne's Bounty in 1705–6 and 1707–8. For the details and an explanation of the difficulties involved in using the figures see I.M. Green, 'The First Five Years of Queen Anne's Bounty', in *Princes and Paupers in the English Church 1500–1800*, ed. R. O'Day and F. Heal (Leicester, 1981). In 1664–5 Sheldon had a survey made of values, the 'Notitia Episcopalia'; Lambeth Palace Library, MS 923.
34. Salter, 'Warwickshire Clergy', p. 24.

and the church; an incumbent, however, was thought to need more, perhaps somewhere between £80 and £100 a year.[35] This level of income was necessary to maintain the minister's authority in the parish: for 'which way is it possible that a man shall be able to maintain perhaps eight or ten in his family, with £20 or £30 per annum, without a intolerable dependence upon his parish; and without committing himself to such vileness as will, in all likelihood, render him contemptible to his people?' And how should 'men of knowledge, prudence, and wealth' be expected to take such small and contemptible livings?[36] John Bradshaw, rector of Cublington, Buckinghamshire, complained that the 'fanatics' of Bedford exulted over his poverty, and he pleaded with Sancroft for a sinecure or prebendary 'which having no great burden annexed may bring me in about a £100 p.a., which added to what I have will enable me to fund an assistant, to uphold and make more sightly my house, and to keep hospitality more to my desire'.[37]

The paper value of a living was only remotely related to the sums received by the incumbent. His income would inevitable fluctuate according to the value of the various sorts of tithes and dues he received, and in response to the agrarian economy of which he was a part. The yearly receipts of William Sampson, rector of Clayworth in Nottinghamshire, varied significantly between £150 and £200, and reached an all-time low of £109 in 1688, but their average was about £185 a year between 1676 and 1701. Even more significantly, many clergymen were 'pluralists', holding two or more livings at the same time and serving them with the aid of curates. The Canons of the church allowed this only in the case of learned men with MAs and in livings no more than thirty miles apart. But in the diocese of Exeter in the 1660s, 80 to 100 of the 530 livings were held in plurality, and 60 to 78 of these contravened the canonical restrictions; in the see of Salisbury in the 1670s, between 106 and 117 of the 380 livings were held in plurality, and 86 to 97 of these were uncanonical. Something like 12 per cent of Warwickshire's incumbents were pluralists, as were about a quarter of Leicestershire's, and one third of that county's 205 parishes were held in plurality.[38] Pluralism clearly did something to alleviate clerical poverty. In Leicestershire, where one third of livings were worth less than £50 p.a., and a half of them were worth between £50 and £100, less

35. *Concilia*, IV, 556–7, 580, 605–6; 17 Charles II c.3; 29 Charles II c.8.
36. Eachard, *Grounds*, pp. 92–3, 119; cf. Best, *Temporal Pillars*, p. 15.
37. MS Tanner 39, fos 101–3.
38. Whiteman, 'Ward', pp. 330–5; Salter, 'Warwickshire Clergy', pp. 134–6; Pruett, *Parish Clergy*, p. 53.

than 20 per cent of the county's incumbents actually received under £50 a year. On the other hand, half of the county's pluralists managed to combine two livings each worth over £50, thus doing rather well for themselves while reducing other ministers 'to small contributions, poor dependencies'.[39] Out of a sample of twenty-nine pluralists who held both of their livings in the diocese of Salisbury, it appears that four had a total income of between £50 and £100, seven received between £100 and £150, six between £150 and £200, seven between £200 and £250, and five over £250. Fortune had smiled indeed on a clergyman like Dr Francis Mundy who held Hinton Waldrist, worth £200, in plurality with the living of Welford which brought him £300 a year.[40]

The churchmen complained that parish priest 'live upon such small pittances, in such skeletons of mangled benefices, that they feed upon listernum juice, and wear away their lifeless lives for want of maintenance to support them'.[41] Such plaints gain credence from cases like that of Claverdon in Warwickshire where the vicar received an annual stipend of £12 from the rector, small tithes of £19 5s. 8d., £5 from the vicarage, churchyard and five acres of glebe, and 15 shillings from a tithe of wood; after deductions his annual income came to the princely sum of £36 18s. 10½d.[42] Isaac Acher's stipend as vicar of Arrington was £20 p.a. and as vicar of Chippenham £28 p.a. In many towns the incumbent's position was even worse since the tithes had long since been commuted into a fixed payment, and there were usually far too many parish churches for the citizens to maintain each minister adequately. However, in general terms, it seems that while a third of the parish clergy earned less than £50 a year and did endure grinding poverty, the remaining two-thirds earned more than £50 a year, some of them considerably more, and were on a par with their wealthiest resident neighbours: in general terms, therefore, the parish clergy as a class were prosperous. And, in comparison to these parish clergy, the dignified clergy were distinctly affluent, and even greater pluralists. In 1670 Dean Ralph Brideoake was estimated to receive

39. Ken, *Ichabod*, p. 62. Also see Pruett, *Parish Clergy*, pp. 7, 132–3, 175–6; D.A. Spaeth, 'Parsons and Parishioners: Lay–Clerical Conflict and Popular Piety in Wiltshire Villages, 1660–1740' (unpublished Brown University Ph.D. thesis, 1985), pp. 326–30.
40. Whiteman, 'Ward', p. 335.
41. MS Eng Th E 171, fo. 146.
42. P. Styles, *Studies in Seventeenth-century West Midlands History* (Kineton, 1978), pp. 83–4; cf. *Inspection of Churches . . . in Diocese of Worcester*, ed. Morgan, p. 92, which shows Pilkington paying out £5 a year for a fortnightly preacher.

£400 p.a. as rector of Standish in Lancashire, and another £94 in tithes, £90 in rents from the glebe and £15 in 'perquisites' each year as rector of St Bartholomew Exchange, London – in addition, Brideoake was a prebendary of Windsor, dean of Salisbury and a chaplain in ordinary to the King.[43] As dean of Canterbury, John Tillotson enjoyed an income of over £600 a year. This was far more than the value of some bishoprics – Bristol, for instance, was valued at £300, and Exeter at £500 – although ancient sees such as Durham and Canterbury were worth £4,000 or more a year.[44] In 1683 William Lloyd, Bishop of Peterborough, carefully calculated his income: manors and rents brought in £580, appropriated rectories produced £22, the clergy's triennial dues came to £49, and the parsonage of Castor which Parliament had 'annexed' to the bishopric was worth £100. The final figure after deductions was £692 1s. 1d.[45]

Such pluralism was undoubtedly forced on the church by financial exigencies, but it made the hierarchy uneasy. 'I am known to be no friend to pluralities', declared Sancroft, and a petitioner acknowledged 'how tender a point this is to touch upon'; Bishop Fell believed that it threatened the 'ruin' of our church.[46] On occasion both Sheldon and Sancroft demurred at the 'learning' of the pluralist or the distance between his livings: Sancroft refused John Sharp the deanery of Norwich 'till he could take up his parish of St Giles [in the Fields, London] and set it down at the gates of Norwich', but Sharp's patron, Lord Chancellor Finch 'is very powerful and prevailed for his chaplain against us'. Nothing could be done in the face of royal commands such as that of 13 August 1678 requesting a dispensation for Robert South, rector of Islip outside Oxford, to hold the rectory of Llanrhaidar in Denbighshire.[47] The non-residence which accompanied pluralism was its worst feature.

---

43. *Vestry Minutes of St Bartholomew Exchange*, ed. E. Freshfield (1890), p. 112.
44. J. Mackay, 'John Tillotson, 1630–1694: A Study of his Life and of his Contribution to the Development of English Prose' (unpublished Oxford University D.Phil. thesis, 1952), pp. 175, 136; M.G. Smith, *Fighting Joshua – A Study of the Career of Sir Jonathan Trelawney* (Redruth, 1985), pp. 20–1; D. Hirschberg, 'Episcopal Incomes and Expenses, 1660–c.1760', in *Princes and Paupers*, ed. R. O'Day and F. Heal (Leicester, 1981); B.J. Shapiro, *John Wilkins 1614–1672* (Berkeley and Los Angeles, 1969), pp. 180–1.
45. MS Rawlinson D 1163, fos 1–6.
46. MSS Tanner 38, fo. 141; 41, fo. 67; 32, fos 158–9; and 33, fo. 25 for Fell's disapproval. In one case Sheldon refused a dispensation 'the livings being a mile or two distant above thirty'; MS Add. C 308, fo. 86v.
47. MSS Tanner 36, fo. 52; 39, fo. 81; also see fo. 105, MSS Tanner 49, fo. 125; 41, fos 21, 149; BL, MSS Harleian 7377, fo. 18; 3785, fo. 102.

Isaac Barrow traced a series of 'grievous mischiefs and occasions of offence' which flowed from non-residence. First was the problem of curates: 'many great places are supplied by young men, ill-qualified for knowledge, discretion, good manners; who are also poor and have no authority with the people'. The impoverished and insufficient curate was indeed a familiar figure in the Restoration church.[48] Barrow feared that the inability of curates to provide the moral authority, good example and hospitality necessary to bind parishioners to the church would leave parishes 'exposed for a prey to nonconformists and seducers from the church; especially there where there are persons who are affected to religion; many well meaning people thence enticed to conventicles'. And the parishioners of Stokenchurch in Oxfordshire drew a connection between the non-residence of their minister and the growth of 'a factious people amongst us'.[49] Non-residence also demonstrated to the laity that the clergy were 'greedy of sordid gain', preoccupied with Mammon and the prizes of this world. 'Men of parts and abilities are diverted from their study and holy employments by running about after the world; after this prebend, that parsonage, etc.' But while 'so many worthy men are spoiled, being withdrawn from the study, and entangled in secular cares',[50] the reverse was also true and pastoral duties were neglected by the studious. One price of Ralph Cudworth's massive treatise on the *True Intellectual System of the Universe* seems to have been the neglect of his Hertfordshire parish. 'We have not met with so great complaints of any man as of Dr Cudworth,' reported the visitation of 1686,

> whose church and chancel lie in a ruinous condition, without a communion table, or with such a table as does not deserve that name, without a settled curate, but served sometimes by a young man that gallops over from Cambridge on Sunday mornings, and returns at night, and sometimes wholly neglected. I have written to him, acquainting him with the complaints of the whole country, gentry, clergy, parishioners, and desired him to take care that these great neglects may be reformed.[51]

Non-residence also blighted the life of the cathedrals which suffered from a lack of clerical manpower. There were two types of

48.   Barrow, IX, 581–2; Ken, *Ichabod*, pp. 77–80. Also see MS Add. C 308, fo. 101; BL, MS Harleian 7377, fo. 18; MS Tanner 41, fo. 215.
49.   M.D.W. Jones, 'The Ecclesiastical Courts before and after the Civil War: The Office Jurisdiction in the Dioceses of Oxford and Peterborough, 1630–1675' (unpublished Oxford University B.Litt. thesis, 1977), p. 210; *Bishop Fell and Nonconformity*, ed. M. Clapinson (Oxfordshire Record Society, 62, 1980), p. 37.
50.   Barrow, IX, 581–2.
51.   MS Tanner 30, fo. 45.

cathedral: those of the 'old foundation', such as Salisbury, Lincoln, London and York, which had been 'secular' or non-monastic cathedrals in the Middle Ages; and those of the 'new foundation' which were either monastic houses 'refounded' by Henry VIII, such as Winchester, Ely and Durham, or one of the five new cathedrals created by Henry and endowed from the estates of dissolved monasteries.[52] Both sorts of cathedral were governed by a body of canons organized in a chapter: but whereas those of the new foundation had received constitutions and statutes from the Crown at their 'refounding', those of the old foundation had only slowly codified their customs into governing statutes. One consequence was a great variety in the constitutions of cathedrals and in their relations with their bishop.[53] Another consequence was financial. Secular clergy were those who could own property; therefore in most of the secular cathedrals of the old foundation each canon had long since been assigned lands from the cathedral estates and the right to collect rents, fees and tithes from parish churches. This formed the canon's 'prebend' and such a canon was usually called a 'prebendary'. York Minster had thirty prebends worth almost £1,000 in total, while Salisbury had forty. In cathedrals of the new foundation, however, the canons, although now secular, did not hold estates individually; instead the chapter enjoyed a corporate endowment from which the canons were paid a stipend – so despite the fact that contemporaries often called them 'prebendaries' these clerics were technically canons. Cathedrals of the new foundation tended to have far fewer canons than those of the old foundation; Peterborough and Bristol had only six major canons apiece. In short, then, the attractions and profit of cathedral canonry could vary considerably. However, most canonries were sinecures for clergymen with parishes elsewhere; such canons might come to the cathedral once a year to preach their turn or occasionally to vote in the chapter. Meanwhile the life of the cathedral depended upon its resident officers, the dean, chancellor, treasurer and precentor, and upon the vicars choral who performed the majority of the ser-

---

52. There is no study of seventeenth-century English cathedrals. This paragraph is based on A.H. Thompson, *The English Clergy and their Organization in the later Middle Ages* (Oxford, 1947), pp. 76–8; K. Edwards, *English Secular Cathedrals in the Middle Ages* (2nd edn, Manchester, 1967); S.E. Lehmberg, *The Reformation of the Cathedrals – Cathedrals and English Society 1485–1603* (Princeton, 1988); the chapters by C. Cross and D.M. Owen in *A History of York Minster*, ed. G.E. Aylmer and R. Cant (Oxford, 1977); A.C. Miller, 'Herbert Astley, Dean of Norwich', *Norfolk Archaeology*, 38 (1982).

53. An impression of the variety can be gained from the entries for each diocese in *A Dictionary of English Church History*, ed. S.L. Ollard and G. Crosse (1912).

vices. The number of resident canons was small. Cathedral statutes usually restricted the number of these 'residentiaries' – to five, including the dean, at York and Chichester, for instance, and to six at Norwich – and stipulated their period of residence and other duties. Limiting numbers in this way had to be done if the income which was divided between the residentiaries was to be sufficient to support them. Nevertheless even resident canons failed to fulfil their obligations. The absence of the residentiaries was a constant problem in most cathedrals. Fines for non-residence were rarely a deterrent; even the commands of the hierarchy, such as Sheldon's instruction of June 1670 that residentiaries should personally perform divine service on Sundays and holy days, had minimal effect.[54] When the cathedrals were ordered to celebrate weekly communions in 1684, several deans reported that they lacked sufficient resident priests to fulfil the command.[55]

Those who spoke for the clergy urged not that pluralism be banned, but that more consideration be given to the requests for dispensations and that they be granted, as the church intended, only to men of note.[56] The solution to the problem was to make pluralism unnecessary by ensuring that all benefices provided the minister with an adequate income. But the obstacle here was the laity.

The clergy were convinced that 'the church is every one's prey, and the shepherds are pilled, and polled, and fleeced by none more than their own flocks'. The root of clerical poverty lay with 'greedy impropriators or fraudulent parishioners'.[57] The prevalence of impropriation is difficult to assess: the author of *Ichabod* (1663) claimed that 3,000 out of a total of 12,000 livings in England and Wales were impropriate, but neither of these figures is particularly trustworthy. Behind every vicar stood an impropriator of some sort, either clerical or lay. Little is known of lay impropriators as a class; although their names occasionally appear in the records – for instance when they were presented in the church courts for neglecting the upkeep of the chancel[58] – no systematic or central record was kept and the practice of leasing tithes further complicates the picture.

54. See *History of York Minster*, ed. Aylmer and Cant, pp. 226–30; Lehmberg, *Reformation of the Cathedrals*, pp. 169–72; Whiteman, 'Ward', pp. 79–81, 445–6; Miller, 'Astley', 151, 159; *Concilia*, IV, 590.
55. See pp. 364–5 below.
56. Addison, *Modest Plea*, pp. 116–20.
57. South, III, 307; MS Eng Th E 171, fo. 146.
58. As was the case with lay patronage, the possession and ownership of impropriate tithes was complicated by the sale and leasing of tithes. See Whiteman, 'Ward', pp. 284–6.

Clerical 'appropriators' may be easier to identify, but they were no more generous than their lay counterparts; the archdeacon of Worcester was the rector of Claverdon; the Bishop of Peterborough drew £100 from the parsonage at Castor, yet paid the curate at Eye only £16. But they might be more amenable to pressure from above. On 1 June 1660 Charles II wrote to the bishops exhorting all clerical appropriators to augment small vicarages to between £80 and £100, or failing that, to at least half the clear profits of the rectory. By the 1670s Anglican apologists were claiming that the church had done her part, that the bishops and the deans and chapters had augmented the majority of small vicarages in their gift, but this was an overstatement. In 1677 a statute 'for confirm-ing and perpetuating augmentations made by ecclesiastical persons to small vicarages and curacies' gave teeth to the pious wish of 1660 by providing incumbents with a legal remedy to recover the revenues due to them. Yet in February 1680 Sancroft was still re-proving the bishops for their failure to live up to their promises.[59]

The tithes which maintained the parson were begrudged by the laity and were frequently the cause of unseemly squabbles – not least because their details were customary. The parishioners of Croydon endeavoured 'by pretended customs' to reduce their vicar 'to a very poor pittance'.[60] To make matters worse, there was no effective legal remedy for the minister who was denied his 'small tithes' other than recourse to the church courts; only tithes commuted into money payments were recoverable in the secular courts. 'There are few tithes paid any farther than it please the humour of the people', asserted one Restoration churchman, while another be-lieved that any incumbent who managed to extract all of his tithes would automatically become in the eyes of his parishioners a 'cater-pillar, a muck-worm, a very earthly-minded man'.[61] The church had fallen among robbers, wailed the clergy, and even the lay mor-alists advised their readers to 'grudge not tithes to the teachers of the gospel, assigned for their wages by the divine legislator'.[62]

The Restoration clergy fell short of the ideal in other ways besides pluralism and non-residence. Despite her strict regulations the Restoration church was commonly believed to offer 'promiscuous

59. *Concilia*, IV, 556–7, 605–6; 29 Charles II c.8; *A Vindication of the Clergy, from the Contempt Imposed* (1672), p. 29. For the response to the royal letter of 1660 see I.M. Green, *The Re-establishment of the Church of England, 1660–1663* (Oxford, 1978), pp. 109–10; I.J. Gentles and W. Sheils, *Confiscation and Restoration: The Archbishopric Estates and the Civil War* (Borthwick Papers, 59, York, 1981), pp. 25–7.
60. MS Tanner 30, fo. 172; also see Pruett, *Parish Clergy*, p. 90.
61. *A Representation of the State of Christianity* (1674), p. 15; Eachard, *Grounds*, pp. 114–15.
62. Francis Osborne, *Advice to a Son* (Oxford, 1656), p. 180.

ordination' to all comers, and there appears to have been sufficient truth in this charge for Sheldon to warn the bishops against ordaining those who were 'to the scandal of the church and dissatisfaction of good men'.[63] Similar suspicions were expressed of the testimonials borne by ordinands. Although Anglican apologists might deny 'that hands and seals to letters testimonial are common as stones in the streets, and never denied to the most incorrigible dunces', Sancroft still felt the need to issue orders in 1678 against granting testimonials 'only upon the credit of others, or out of a judgement of charity, which believes all things, and hopes all things'; and in 1685, he and several bishops agreed articles regulating ordinations and institutions.[64] The regulatory system was not foolproof; occasionally ministers without episcopal ordination were discovered officiating in the Church of England.[65] The facts of such cases easily became clouded when the suspect clerics prevaricated over or ignored demands to present their orders at a visitation. Several ministers resorted to this stratagem at the Canterbury visitation of 1682, including one, a Mr Lodowick, who seems to have aroused Archdeacon Thorp's sympathies. Lodowick had been asked to produce his orders at the 1663 visitation, but the matter had not been pursued, and now he claimed that his papers had been destroyed in the Fire of London. Thorp believed, however, that this 'very honest man' had only ever been ordained as deacon by Bishop Sanderson. As the archdeacon found when he compared the list of those who failed to produce thier orders in 1682 with a list of those who had shown full orders in 1663, the non-production of orders did not necessarily mean that their orders had never existed. It was a relief to Thorp's bureaucratic tidy-mindedness to find that those clergy who had shown their orders in 1663, but not in 1682, had since become 'disturbed in mind' or simply old and infirm – the archdeacon was either oblivious or resigned to the implications of this admission for the standard of pastoral care in the diocese.[66] The hierarchy were also troubled by the prevalence of forged letters of orders, especially among the roving clergy of the borders and the Welsh dioceses.[67]

---

63. Eachard, *Grounds*, p. 254; *Vindication*, p. 47; Herbert, *Priest to the Temple*, sig. ix; for Sheldon see *Concilia*, IV, 581–2; cf. MS Add. C 308, fo. 30.

64. *Vindication*, p. 62; *Concilia*, IV, 600, 612–14; cf. Bishop Ward's reply, MS Tanner 39, fo. 92; Francis Turner, *A Letter to the Clergy of the Diocess [sic] of Ely from the Bishop of Ely* (Cambridge, 1686), pp. 19–23.

65. See cases in MSS Tanner 37, fo. 147 (1680); 290, fos 141, 181; BL, MS Harleian 7377, fo. 24v; cf. MS Add. C 308, fo. 101.

66. MS Tanner 33, fos 176, 171, 177, 178.

67. See cases in Tanner MSS 35, fos 113, 119–20; 42, fos 11, 133; BL, MS Harleian 7377, fo. 19v.

Not that the problem was restricted to the darker corners of the land: the vicar of Croxton Kerrial, Leicestershire, was deprived in 1701, after having officiated with forged orders since the Restoration; and William Crouch was licensed to serve as curate at Keevil, Wiltshire, and served in the diocese for eight years, before his fraudulent orders were exposed.[68] These shortcomings reflect the inadequate administrative techniques of the Restoration church and the poor communications of the period. All documents were laboriously written out and copied by hand and all administration centred upon the cathedral city and bishop's registry. Since clergy were usually ordained in the diocese in which they were to serve, there was no national record of them or their qualifications. As men moved from living to living their papers became disordered or lost, and letters of recommendation or denunciation followed them from diocese to diocese. To an extent, the universities and the two archbishops functioned as clearing houses for general information, character references and clerical vacancies; and compared to secular administration, the ecclesiastical bureaucracy was sophisticated and ambitious. Nevertheless, the church was not equipped to exercise any strict day-to-day control over her own clergy.[69]

The 'notorious offender', whose life and lips mocked the very religion he professed, could never be totally excluded from the ministry. In 1670, 'having often complaints made unto me in general, of the offensive lives of some of the clergy', Bishop Reynolds of Norwich entreated his clergy to be

> very tender of the credit of religion, of the dignity of their function, and of the success of their ministry, and endeavour by their sober, pious, and prudent conversations, to stop the mouths of any that watch for their halting; to bear witness to the truth of that doctrine which they preach, to be guides and examples of holiness of life to the people over whom they are set, and to lay up for themselves a comfortable account against the time that we shall all appear before the great shepherd and bishop of souls.[70]

Those who led offensive and scandalous lives were often denounced by their own churchwardens or parishioners: John Gey, vicar of Antony in Cornwall, was alleged to be 'a frequenter of alehouses, a brawler, a fighter and a challenger of the field for duels'. Another Cornish incumbent was charged with everything from brawling and negligence to consorting with a conjurer and fortune teller, wearing

68. Pruett, *Parish Clergy*, p. 74; Whiteman, 'Ward', p. 359.
69. See D.M. Owen, *The Records of the Established Church of England* (1970), pp. 17-18.
70. Lambeth Palace Library, MS 674, fo. 46.

lay clothes, going armed, and trading in pilchards at St Ives.[71] Yet despite all the innuendo and rumour about drunkenness and fornication, despite the swiving vicar of popular imagination, the statistical evidence, at least from ecclesiastical prosecutions, suggests that moral offences by ministers were scarce: between 1662 and 1714, only 20, or 2 per cent, of Leicestershire's clergy were reported for moral offences.[72] Such figures, of course, take no account of the offensive behaviour that was never reported, of the drinking and bawdiness which parishioners tolerated, or of the uncharitable and quarrelsome behaviour they were forced to endure for want of legal recourse.

Scandal was not the only clerical offence reported to the church courts. Laity and clergy alike took a dim view of 'clandestine marriage', that is, marrying individuals without banns or a licence, which was usually performed for the sake of the fee.[73] Clergymen were repeatedly chastised for the offence by their superiors; but bills against clandestine marriage were proposed in the Commons in 1666 and 1667, and in 1677 another threatening clerical culprits with deprivation passed the Lords, only to fail in the Commons. Eventually, and prompted by fiscal considerations, and Act of 1696 imposed a £100 fine on clergy who performed clandestine marriages.[74] The church spent much time monitoring her own clergy, ensuring that they paid their dues to the bishop and attended his visitations; that their qualifications were in order; that they did their part in maintaining the fabric of the church and parsonage; and that they were not 'negligent'.

This clerical 'negligence' took many forms, from non-residence and not exercising proper care and control over curates to not catechizing, omitting all or part of the services, and not administering the sacraments of baptism and the Lord's Supper; in Restoration Leicestershire, 7 per cent of parsons were summoned to answer charges of neglecting church services.[75] But somewhere this negligence about worship, these omissions of the rites of the Prayer Book, shade into something more deliberate and sinister. 'The shortness of the days and coldness of the weather are very good reason for not reading both the entire services,' acknowledged one

71. See Whiteman, 'Ward', pp. 347–9.
72. Pruett, *Parish Clergy*, pp. 130–2; cf. Jones, 'Ecclesiastical Courts', p. 199.
73. See MSS Tanner 30, fos 134, 135, 158v, 168, 169, 178; 38, fo. 108.
74. See *The Diary of John Milward*, ed. C. Robbins (Cambridge, 1938), pp. 5–6, 8, 117–18; HMC, 9th Report, pt. 2, appendix, pp. 90–1; Whiteman, 'Ward', pp. 343–6; Pruett, *Parish Clergy*, p. 131; 7&8 William III c.35.
75. Pruett, *Parish Clergy*, pp. 131–2.

pious Anglican gentleman, 'but I am acquainted with too many which do it on purpose, as I doubt some of Norton do. Certainly them that omit words, and phrases, and whole prayers constantly can come under no other notion but partial conformists, of which number I am afraid many with you are.'[76]

The clergy failed in a variety of ways. Very occasionally, they erred in doctrine. A handful of Anglican clergy evidently held views which tended towards Roman Catholicism; the occasional minister was reported for angrily asserting when in his cups that worship was due to the Virgin Mary or that things would never be well 'till the Pope did come and scourge them in with his whip'.[77] Others strayed in a different direction; Stephen Nye, an Essex rector from 1679 until his death in 1719, was a Unitarian. Although most churchmen were resolute Protestants, the vagueness of the church's doctrine and of the Thirty-Nine Articles allowed plenty of room for personal theological emphases and idiosyncracies. Clerical deeds and statements, not thoughts, were what really alarmed the authorities. The church could not tolerate any preaching or action which threatened the Christian unanimity of the parish, diocese or kingdom. In 1671, the rector of Hittisleigh, Devon, was ordered to read a paper of penance in church before his flock on Christmas eve. Judging by the penance which he was required to read, the minister, Mr Bull, seems to have offended against all that the Restoration church held dear.

> I, Abraham Bull . . . have several times since his Majesty's happy restoration in my sermons, by me here preached, used and uttered divers words and passages unbecoming a subject much more a minister of the Church of England, thereby aspersing both the government and governors thereof and particularly in saying that the sins of England were greater than the sins of Sodom and Gomorrah, and that idolatry was set up in the King's own palace, and that [the] silenced ministers were his anointed, and the fire of London was a judgement upon this land for that the King and Council had stopped their mouths – thereby insinuating faction and disaffection to the government into the hearts of my auditors; and whereas I have behaved myself careless, negligent and disobedient in my function and duty, frequently omitting upon Sundays and holy days the prayers appointed to be read for the preservation of the King's and Queen's Majesties and their bishops, as also the use of the sign of the cross in baptism, thereby

76. MS Eng Letters C 210, fo. 65.
77. MS Rawlinson D 399, fo. 319; Whiteman, 'Ward', p. 351.

giving example of disobedience, and whereas I have uttered divers
wild opinions and ungodly tenets, saying that preaching was more
acceptable to God than prayers . . . and have for the most part, or
very frequently, delivered my sermons from the desk and not the
pulpit contrary to the appointment and usage of the Church of
England, and have once caused rhythms of my own making to be
sung in my own church instead of the Psalms allowed to be sung,
and have sometimes made very unhandsome reflections upon the
persons of my parishioners in the midst of my sermons to their
great grief and offence and the scandal of my ministerial function and contrary to the canons and discipline of the Church of
England.[78]

Although Bull refused to read this paper and was suspended from
office, he died in full possession of his living in 1682.

At least the hierarchy knew where they stood with Mr Bull; other
disaffected churchmen were less forthright and, in the eyes of the
self-appointed guardians of orthodoxy, more dangerous for 'they
conform with duplicity of mind, and do as little as they can'. The
zealots castigated the 'false friend' to the church: 'he that inveighs
privately against what publicly he hath sworn to, and in his visits
sighs and mourns for those impositions which under his own hand,
he hath declared his full satisfaction in. This is the man indeed
that nurses faction.'[79] Ralph Josselin, vicar of Earls Colne, Essex,
from 1641 until his death in 1683, was perhaps such a man. He did
not usually wear the surplice or read the entire service; he only
administered the sacrament at Easter and then only to a handful
of communicants; he identified himself emotionally with the Nonconformists and attended a private prayer group. Josselin's diary
suggests very strongly that his ministry reached only a select group
of his parishioners.[80] And his semi-detached attitude was clearly
not unique among the clergy. Mr Cloube, chaplain to the 'presbyterian' Lady Brooke, officiated in a parish church in Laurence
Womock's archdeaconry while it was without an incumbent. When
challenged by the archdeacon in 1665, Cloube readily admitted that
the 'episcopal ordination' which he had received in 1660 had not
involved any subscription to the Articles, Canons or Prayer Book.
Yet he was, wrote Womock,

78. Quoted and discussed in P.W. Jackson, 'Nonconformists and Society in Devon
    1660–1689' (unpublished Exeter University Ph.D. thesis, 1986), pp. 89–92
79. Barnabas Oley, preface to Herbert, *Priest to the Temple*, sig. vi; Richard
    Hollingworth, *A Modest Plea for the Church of England* (1676), p. 44.
80. Josselin, pp. 508, 548–9, 588 and *passim*.

a good scholar and a sober man so far from being a promoter of the faction, that he reads always a good part of the prayers, and as far as I can perceive, there are none of them but he says some time or other, though not all at once; he is earnest for kneeling at the sacrament and hath justified the Church of England in that particular and persuaded several to receive in that posture. He chooses to converse with as able and worthy men as are in Norwich amongst the conformable clergy. I find him unsatisfied in nothing but the surplice and not obstinate against that. He gives fair hope that he may be perfectly reconciled to all our establishment.[81]

The spring afternoon Womock spent in conversation with Cloube afforded the archdeacon (and affords us) a glimpse of an East Anglian world of the 1660s where the boundaries between churchman and Dissenter were vague and unimportant, and where half-hearted conformity seemed less dangerous than it did to the heated imaginations of many Restoration preachers and pamphleteers.

'Nothing is a more common trespass, them omitting or curtailing divine service', complained Bishop Hacket of Lichfield to Sheldon in May 1670.[82] Robert South agreed that

> the wounds which the church of England now bleeds by, she received *in the house of her friends* (if they may be called so) viz. her treacherous undermining friends, and that most of the nonconformity to her excellent constitutions, have proceeded from nothing more than the false, partial, half conformity of too many of her ministers. The surplice sometime worn, and oftener laid aside; the liturgy so read, and mangled in the reading, as if they were ashamed of it; the divine service so curtailed, as if the people were to have but the tenths of it from the priest, for the tenths he had received from them. . . . These and the like vile passages have made some schismatics, and confirmed others; and, in a word, have made so many nonconformists to the church, by their conforming to the minister.[83]

There were indeed innumerable cases across the kingdom of clergymen giving the sacrament to those who remained seated, or 'mangling' the Prayer Book, or evading the letter of the Act of Uniformity, or not wearing the surplice.[84] Reporting on the state

---

81. MS Add. C 304a, fo. 16; also see fos 18, 58, 60.
82. MS Tanner 44, fo. 206.
83. South, III, 349.
84. MSS Tanner 32, fos 98, 142; 31, fo. 273; 37, fos 82, 139; MS Rawlinson D 1163, fo. 11; C.E. Whiting, *Studies in English Puritanism from the Restoration to the Revolution* (1931), pp. 28–9, 32–9; Salter, 'Warwickshire Clergy', I, 107, 140; Granville, II,

of the diocese of Durham after his visitation of 1675, Archdeacon Denis Granville suggested that it was the most 'conformable' in the land and yet it was plagued with every sort of neglect and breach of the services of the church.[85] Granville claimed that many of the Nonconformist ministers would willingly have assented to the Prayer Book, 'had they expected to have been indulged half so far as most of us indulge our selves . . . and of all Nonconformists, I confess I have most indignation against those that can accept of a fat benefice and preferment upon pretences of conforming' to the liturgy. The churchmen were convinced that the Nonconformists had prevailed with some Anglican ministers to 'abate' the rigour of the Prayer Book rubrics and the Canons, and the Dissenters in turn tried to exploit this incipient Anglican division by claiming the support of the most 'moderate' and pious churchmen.[86]

In the face of this lack of conformity – as in the face of so many other clerical deficiencies – the hierarchy could do little; witness the Archdeacon of Chichester's joyful announcement to Sancroft that the vicar of Framfield, 'who could never be brought to conform whilst vicar, was at last persuaded to resign'.[87] The parish clergy seem to have been governed primarily through admonition and exhortation. The history of Ralph Josselin's dealings with the hierarchy is instructive. In the summer of 1662 Josselin was bracing himself for the effects of the Act of Uniformity, to which he could not conform, but nothing happened. When, in October, he was cited to the Archdeacon of Colchester's visitation, he simply did not go, but he did read part of the Prayer Book on the following Sunday. Regarding himself as one of the Nonconformists, he disdained the Prayer Book and the surplice, and yet 'my public liberty [was] strangely continued unto me'. Then, in May 1664, he was presented for not having administered the sacrament for a whole year, but to little effect, the 'court except a little, not meddling with me'; in June he was cited again for the same offence; and in September he was called to Bishop Henchman's primary visitation and there 'through mercy met with no rubs, but my path clear'. His diary for 9 July 1669 records, 'rid to court whither summoned for not wearing the surplice, dismissed', and at the episcopal visitation

101–7 (possibly a concoction by Granville); there were more than 33 ministers who did not wear the surplice in Peterborough diocese in 1680; see MS Rawlinson D 1163, fo. 11.

85. Granville, II, 23–4.
86. Ibid., 42–3; James Fawkett, *Account of Seignior* (1681), p. 24; Addison, *Modest Plea*, p. 143; William Gould, *Conformity according to Canon Justified* (1674); cf. William Ramsay, *The Julian Ship* (1681).
87. MS Tanner 41, fo. 57. Also see Pruett, *Parish Clergy*, pp. 74–5.

of September he 'appeared with quiet'. Throughout the 1670s, Josselin attended the visitations and, despite the complaints from neighbouring ministers of his unconformity, he escaped censure; at the 'court' in May 1680, he 'avoided receiving articles, through God's goodness . . . the matter is the surplice'.[88] How did Josselin get away so apparently scot-free – save a little 'meddling' – and was he exceptional?

It seems not. Restoration bishops and archdeacons were unable to enforce the attendance of the clergy at their visitations or courts. In the diocese of Oxford between 1664 and 1675, an average of 13 per cent of the clergy cited to appear in the diocesan courts did not attend. Although this may be because they were given insufficient warning of their appearance, some undoubtedly did as Josselin did in 1678 and arranged to be away when the summons arrived or the visitation took place.[89] Once the clergy arrived, they might simply receive an informal warning or exhortation; in September 1678 Josselin was 'but coarsely used by the bishop', yet he 'came off well' at a later session from which the bishop was absent.[90] These private interviews between the parish clergy and their superiors were fundamental to the management of the church, but scant trace survives of the archdeacon's little chats with peccant incumbents or of the bishop's admonitions to those 'appearing' in his 'Court of Audience'.[91] If the offender or offence merited more severe chastisement, then the authorities could demand that the minister perform penance or recant his errors before his congregation. And if incorrigible, the clergyman could be temporarily suspended from his office and his income, as Ralph Josselin apparently was in April 1667. The effectiveness of suspension is difficult to gauge. It seems to have had no effect whatsoever on Josselin's preaching ministry, yet Bishop Hacket could 'hit of no better remedy' to combat partial conformity than to send apparitors and spies to suspect parishes and upon proof of neglect 'to suspend the incumbent ab officio et beneficio for six months, and to assure to that spy or informer the fourth part of the profits; which punishment, being executed upon a few, will startle the rest'.[92] Permanent deprivation of a minister was rare. Since rectors and vicars held the freehold of their livings, depriving them was a difficult and messy business, which the church

88. Josselin, pp. 507, 508, 512, 548, 549, 628.
89. Jones, 'Ecclesiastical Courts', pp. 211–15; Josselin, p. 609.
90. Josselin, p. 614; Jones, 'Ecclesiastical Courts', pp. 215–16.
91. Whiteman, 'Ward', pp. 350, 176; Jones, 'Ecclesiastical Courts', p. 200.
92. Josselin, p. 535; cf. p. 609; MS Tanner 44, fo. 206. Also see Whiteman, 'Ward', p. 176; MS Rawlinson D 1163, fo. 27.

avoided if at all possible.[93] Prosecution in the diocesan courts was at best an uncertain remedy for clerical unconformity. Theophilus Hart, rector of Wappenham, Northamptonshire, who refused to read the Common Prayer, wear the surplice or keep the holy days, was 'rich and stubborn,' in Sheldon's words, 'and therefore fitter to be made an example'; but even after conviction and sentence on seven charges of nonconformity, Hart still managed to obtain an inhibition against the sentence from the higher ecclesiastical court, the Court of Arches.[94]

The church's whole creaking disciplinary machine had to be animated from the top; it simply would not work without the cajoling and threatening, the charges to incumbents and churchwardens, and the visitations of the bishops and their officials. Therefore the calibre and enthusiasm of those who led the church was all-important. Yet the quality of the episcopate was decidedly varied, as might be expected in a body of men appointed for such diverse reasons. Some, no doubt, were capable of being both father and mother to their diocese, governing their clergy and laity with a firm, yet tender, hand, and offering a personal example of piety and diligence. But others were promoted to the episcopal bench in recognition of different strengths, not least their political loyalty or utility – such were Nicholas Monck, Nathaniel Crew, Laurence Womock and Jonathan Trelawney. That is not to say that they were ineffective diocesan bishops, but it might mean that they did not always pull in the same direction as their archbishops: few would claim that Bishop Wilkins of Chester or Bishop Parker of Oxford advanced the church's best interests as they were perceived by Sheldon or Sancroft. Other bishops, however, did not seem to be pulling their weight at all. In some cases this was due to ill-health or old age – for their last five years Seth Ward of Salisbury was senile and William Lucy of St David's was housebound – but in others there was little excuse. Thomas Barlow, Bishop of Lincoln from 1675, governed his diocese from afar, but his failure to confirm, to ordain, or even to visit his diocese, brought upon him the public humiliation of a metropolitical visitation, conducted by the energetic White of Peterborough in the summer of 1686.[95] Thomas Wood, the rich and well-connected dean of Lichfield, spent years quarrelling with Bishop Hacket – in 1668 he even had the Court of

93. Whiteman, 'Ward', p. 338; Pruett, *Parish Clergy*, pp. 74–5.
94. MS Add. C 304a, fo. 50: MS Add. C 308, fos 76, 79v, 80. On the Court of Arches see MSS Add. C 308, fo. 114; Add. C 302, fo. 71; M.D. Slatter, 'The Records of the Court of Arches', *JEH*, 4 (1953).
95. See Tanner MSS 30, fo. 131; 31, fo. 265; 32, fo. 54; Wood, II, 312.

Arches excommunciate the bishop 'to the joy and laughter of all Nonconformists' – and yet still succeeded him at Lichfield and Coventry thanks to the Duchess of Cleveland. Eventually, in July 1684, Sancroft suspended Bishop Wood, but only after carefully preparing his ground at court. Bishop Turner of Rochester was detailed to mention Wood's case to the King, who 'well approved what had been done, and spoke of the man with the utmost contempt. All this was aloud, and openly in the circle; then followed a great deal of raillery upon the sordidness and refractoriness of this unhappy man.' Turner was confident that Wood would now find no 'relief' at Whitehall or Windsor, and Sancroft, before filing his letter away, meticulously endorsed it, 'the King and Duke abandon the bishop as sordid and refractory'.[96]

In general, the Restoration episcopate was at its energetic best in the 1660s – when the bishops had thrown themselves into reconstructing the church – and in the early 1680s, when, their energies unleashed by the Tory reaction, a new generation of bishops sought to reinvigorate the organizational and religious life of the church. Efforts were made to turn the cathedrals into the centres of liturgical and preaching inspiration which they should have been; the bishops began to consult their deans and chapters and even their diocesan clergy; and campaigns for more celebration and reception of the sacrament were launched.[97] Bishop William Lloyd's account of his work in the diocese of Peterborough between 1679 and 1683, while no doubt self-serving, suggests improvements in almost every field of endeavour. The diocese's 'twenty-nine capital conventicles' had been entirely suppressed with the help of the justices; and the threat of widespread presentations for not receiving the sacrament 'brought in a vast number of persons throughout the whole diocese'. In four years, Lloyd had confirmed 7,864 and ordained 47 priests and deacons; across the see £982 had been collected on various royal briefs or appeals for charity; and, in short, through judicious use of suspensions and penance, the clergy and the laity had been brought to a very good order.[98]

Bishops could only be as effective as their administration and officials allowed. Few bishops were fortunate enough to enjoy the unstinting support and cooperation of their deans, archdeacons,

---

96. Turner to Sancroft, Windsor, 21 July 1684, MS Tanner 32, fo. 97. On Wood see MSS Tanner 45, fo. 265; 104, fos 137–44, 311–13; W.G. Simon, *Restoration Episcopate* (New York, 1965), pp. 62–5.
97. See Granville, II, 45, 171–3; pp. 86 above and 364–6 below.
98. See MS Rawlinson D 1163. For the vigorous approach of Fell of Oxford and Trelawney of Bristol, see *Fell*, ed. Clapinson, *passim* and MS Tanner 30, fo. 49.

chancellors and registrars; indeed several had stormy relations with these dignitaries. The clash between Dean Pierce and Bishop Ward at Salisbury resulted in a metropolitical visitation. Bishop Gulston of Bristol was troubled by Samuel Crossman, briefly dean of Bristol in 1683–4, and 'his creature' Richard Thompson, who preached against Gulston in his own cathedral and spread erroneous theological opinions.[99] Although the Ecclesiastical Commission extracted Thompson's recantation of these errors, he was able to succeed Crossman as dean thanks to the Duke of Beaufort's influence, and much to Sancroft's disgust.[100] Thompson was no less amenable under the subsequent rule of Bishop Lake – 'the dean (if I may call him so) neither acts, nor appears'.[101] Bishop Lamplugh of Exeter complained of his chancellor and at Chichester Bishop Carleton came to blows with his; while Bishop Lloyd of Norwich was affronted by the archdeacon of Sudbury and 'his huffing humour of trampling upon the Canons and the statutes of this church'.[102] Jealous of their jurisdictions, bishops stubbornly resisted all invaders; in 1663–4 Lucy of St David's fought a bitter campaign against the claims of William Nicholson, Bishop of Gloucester and Archdeacon of Brecon, to hold visitations in the archdeaconry.

The harm done by these quarrels was immeasurable. They exposed the church to ridicule. The archbishops incessantly exhorted the clergy 'to embrace one another in love, and live together in peace and unity'. Although the archbishop might privately take sides, as Sheldon did with Bishop Hacket against his 'most untractable and filthy natured dean', Thomas Wood, he was more generally concerned that these quarrels should not become 'a public flame' or be 'spread up and down' or appear 'upon the stage in an open court' since that only 'made sport for those that love you not'.[103] Dissension also impeded diocesan administration. The channels of communication between the governors of the church and the parishes all too easily became choked by personal animosi-

99. MS Tanner 34, fo. 89; cf. MS Tanner 35, fo. 45. Crossman had been ejected at the Restoration (see Josselin, p. 493), but later conformed.

100. R.A. Beddard, 'The Commission for Ecclesiastical Promotions, 1681–84: An Instrument of Tory Reaction', *HJ*, 10 (1967), 34.

101. MS Tanner 32, fo. 239 (Lake to Sancroft, 7 March 1685). Thompson died in November 1685.

102. MS Tanner 35, fo. 29; C.E. Davies, 'The Enforcement of Religious Uniformity in England, 1668–1700, with Special Reference to the Dioceses of Chichester and Worcester' (unpublished Oxford University D.Phil. thesis, 1982), pp. 84–9; MSS Tanner 104, fo. 258; 30, fos 37, 159.

103. BL, MS Harleian 7377, fos 7v, 8v, 9v, 11; MS Tanner 48, fo. 65; MS Add. C 308, fo. 38v.

ties and the truculence of officials. The diocesan courts were in the hands of lay officials such as chancellors and registrars who were appointed by the bishop's letters patent for life, so not to have them on your side was fatal to the attempt to discipline the clergy; the chapter at Norwich resisted Bishop Reynolds's candidate for chancellor for over a decade.[104] The same was true of the exempt jurisdictions where the diocesan's authority did not run. All too often a dean or archdeacon who defended his jurisdiction in a 'peculiar' against his bishop, might also be sheltering a partially or nonconforming clergyman from episcopal censure.[105] One way of bypassing such blockages in the system was to revive the office of rural dean, a sort of direct agent of the bishop.[106] After his first visitation of Peterborough diocese, Lloyd appointed 'one of the most loyal and confiding clergymen that I could think of' as rural dean in each deanery, with the hope of combating the 'falseness and perjury of the churchwardens' and their returns of *omnia bene* or 'all's well'.[107] When Bishop White visited Bedfordshire (in pursuit of the metropolitical visitation of Lincoln diocese), he found one part of the clergy vicious in their manners and the other 'very unconformable in the discharge of their office . . . and the churchwardens generally so hardened in their foolish obstinacy that they will confess nothing of either'.[108] Nor were churchwardens any more amenable to the authority of the bishops than the clergy: in the diocese of Oxford, an average of 12 per cent of parish officers summoned to visitations between 1662 and 1675 did not appear.[109]

No one was more aware of the deficiencies and abuses of the church than the churchmen themselves. The clergy were their own harshest critics, and although they might agree that the problems were 'not peculiar to this age or church', few seem to have thought them 'remediless'.[110] Both Sheldon and Sancroft had plans drawn up for statutory reform of the church.[111] Pluralism was to be 're-

---

104. Whiteman, 'Ward', pp. 162–7; Miller, 'Astley', 157.

105. See Tanner MS 30, fos 83, 51.

106. MS Rawlinson D 1163, fo. 8. Seth Ward used rural deans in Exeter and Salisbury; see Whiteman, 'Ward', pp. 184–9.

107. MS Rawlinson D 1163, fos 8–9.

108. MS Tanner 30, fo. 45.

109. Jones, 'Ecclesiastical Courts', p. 225.

110. Barrow, IX, 586; cf. Granville, II, 45; J.J. Hughes, 'The Missing "Last Words" of Gilbert Burnet in July 1687', *HJ*, 20 (1977).

111. MS Tanner 300 includes Sancroft's drafts for legislation which draw on Sheldon's drafts in MS Tanner 447; also see N. Sykes, *From Sheldon to Secker* (Cambridge, 1959), pp. 188–92; Beddard, 'Commission for Ecclesiastical Promotions', esp. 12, 14, 20. Much of this reform was bound up with reform of the church courts, see pp. 217–19 below.

strained' and the stipends of curates to be raised to £80; lay impropriators were to make adequate financial provision for a minister to serve the cure of souls ('which are many times very large and considerable parishes'); smaller parishes needed to be amalgamated, while larger parishes should be divided; and poorly endowed livings should be 'augmented' to ensure their incumbents a tolerable income.[112] The church courts were to be overhauled; the exempt jurisdictions of peculiars were to be abolished; and bishops were to regain direct control over their own officers, the commutation of penalties and the excommunication of clergymen.

All of these schemes harked back to earlier models, and especially to the Canons of 1640. They seem to have been revived in about 1664 and to have been seriously prepared for Parliament in 1668, no doubt partly in the hope of heading off the threat of comprehension or toleration. Several of them were resuscitated in the heady years of the Danby alliance in the later 1670s, and Sancroft carefully reworked the plans at some stage in the 1680s; they may, for instance, have contributed to the proposals for church reforms discussed with Dissenters in the summer of 1688.[113] The successes, however, were few: in 1665 an Act was passed 'for uniting churches in cities and towns corporate', which was clearly intended to save impoverished ministers from 'the temptation of too much complying in their doctrine with the humour of the people before whom they depend, which is an occasion of faction and schism', or in other words to shore up the establishment against Dissent;[114] and a 1677 statute confirmed clerical augmentations which the clergy had not in fact yet established. But the near-misses also deserve recognition; legislation to ease the recovery of small tithes, to ban clandestine marriages, and to enforce baptism and catechizing, was laid aside in 1677–8.[115]

Clearly, the Restoration Church of England did not enjoy the sort of unanimity which was idealized by her own ecclesiology and apologetics. Too many of the clergy failed to live up to the vision

112. See MSS Tanner 300, fos 143–4; 447, fos 127–8; Milward, *Diary*, pp. 117, 222 (1667, 1668); HMC, 9th Report, pt. 2, appendix, p. 109 (1678).
113. See the sources indicated in J. Spurr, 'The Church of England, Comprehension and the Toleration Act of 1689', *EHR*, 104 (1989), 934 note 1 (1668), 938 note 1 (1688).
114. Quoted from a draft for the Act, MS Tanner 447, fos 55–6.
115. Proposals for the recovery of small tithes were a feature of almost every session of Parliament; see Milward, *Diary*, pp. 90, 95; MS Tanner 447, fos 21–4; *The Diaries and Papers of Sir Edward Dering*, ed. M.F. Bond (1976), pp. 169–71, 180, 171–5; HMC, 9th Report, pt. 2, appendix. p. 95.

of a united national church; but it should be recognized that, in general, these clergy fell short of the governing principles of the Restoration church rather than opposed them: and so, to her rivals, the church was still able to present a single public face. That this was so is a testimony to the intellectual leadership of a metropolitan clerical elite, and perhaps to the parish clergy's readiness to sink their differences and unite against the common enemy. For many churchmen, however, this enemy was the laity. When the bishops asked their clergy to account for their neglect of their pastoral duties, the clergy blamed the laity. 'If I require a constant diligence in offering the daily sacrifice of prayer for the people,' complained an exasperated Bishop Fell, the clergy's 'usual answer is, they are ready to do their duty, but the people will not be prevailed with to join with them'.

> If I call for catechizing 'tis said the youth are backward and have no mind to come, and parents and masters are negligent to sent them.
> If I insist on frequent sacraments, the devotion of the people is objected; they are not willing to communicate, or they are not fit.[116]

It seemed to many churchmen that it was the laity who connived at clerical unconformity or negligence by failing to present it at the visitations. The clergy believed that lay impropriators and patrons obstructed the augmentation of clerical incomes, tempted churchmen into simony, and preferred unsuitable, unconforming and insufficient clergy.[117] If authority in the church was not what it should be, that was because authority in society was not. The root of the problem lay in the relations between the laymen and the churchmen.

Authority over the Laity

'The serviceableness of the clergy does much, very much depend upon the credit and esteem that we can have in the world.' The churchmen knew that, at bottom, their authority was based on lay respect.[118] But the respect of the laity was difficult to earn and

---

116. Tanner MS 31, fo. 156.
117. Hollingworth, *Modest Plea*, pp. 70–2; Cawdrey, *Discourse of Patronage*; Granville, II, 45; MS Tanner 33, fos 21, 23.
118. *An Answer to a Letter of Enquiry* (1671), sig. A4.

harder to keep in the parishes of late seventeenth-century England. 'Many people are glad to meet with anything ill done by or ill reported of a minister nowadays', observed the churchwarden of Wylye in Wiltshire. Another warden, from East Hendred in Oxfordshire, was presented in 1683 as, among other things, 'a scoffer at his minister and [the] authority of the ecclesiastical court'.[119] Robert South was in no doubt about the credit of the clergy: 'I do, from all that I have read, heard or seen, confidently aver that there is no nation or people under heaven, Christian or not Christian, which despise, hate and trample upon their clergy or priesthood comparably to the English.'[120]

The parish clergy were in an awkward position: they were both part of the workaday rural world of their neighbours and set apart by their education and their spiritual function. Many were weekday farmers, whose accounts and records of seed corn and cattle were jotted in the same notebook as their sermons.[121] Since the clergy were drawn from all ranks of society, it was not always clear who were their social equals and superiors in the parish. While a substantial rector might be on terms of equality with the most prosperous yeoman or even the resident gentry, the impoverished curate was treated with disdain. The wife of the squire of Steeple Ashton, begrudging the curate his board, would give him only his dinner; 'he must search his breakfast and his supper where he could, or (as they said) get him a loaf and cheese and keep it in the parsonage'.[122] The clergy's income rarely lived up to their needs, their status or their pretensions. Although the average glebe attached to a rural living was a substantial landholding – about the same size in Leicestershire as that of the average yeoman farmer – most clergymen depended principally on their tithes and hence on their lay parishioners. In towns, especially, where tithes had often been commuted into various forms of fixed and inadequate stipend, the clergy found their dependence upon the laity galling. Even when the parishioners were generous and made up their minister's stipend to a handsome wage, it rankled with the churchmen: 'it will never be well,' wrote Bishop Ward to Sheldon, 'till such men shall cease to depend upon voluntary contribution'.[123] Insufficient provision for the clergy gave

119. Spaeth, 'Parsons and Parishioners', p. 315; Whiteman, 'Ward', p. 308.
120. South, III, 311.
121. See for instance *Rector's Book, Clayworth*; *The Journal of Giles Moore*, ed. R. Bird (Sussex Record Society, 68, 1971); the sermon notes of Richard Immings, rector of Holdgate, Herefordshire, MS Eng Th E 171, esp. fos 170–166 reversed.
122. Whiteman, 'Ward', p. 340.
123. Ibid., p. 325. Also see J. Barry, 'The Parish in Civic Life: Bristol and its Churches, 1640–1750', in *Parish, Church and People*, ed. S.J. Wright (1988), pp. 154–5; J.

the people the power 'to corrupt an easy and necessitous man, or to starve out a worthy and inflexible one; and so whatever the humour of the place shall be, it is uncontrollable and incurable'.[124] In many urban parishes, power had become concentrated in the hands of a 'select vestry' or parish oligarchy, which easily succumbed to factionalism and to bullying the incumbent.[125]

In the pulpit, the clergy made much of their role as exemplars – 'a minister must not undo on the week day, what he hath builded on the Lord's day' – as local arbitrators, and as spiritual physicians.[126] But there was a cost to assuming this role. The minister was the subject of the parish's searching and continual scrutiny – indeed this close attention was officially sanctioned by the bishop's articles of visitation. In 1662 the wardens of Hungry Hatley reported that their minister 'doth usually wear a gown with a standing collar, and sleeves straight at hands. In journeying he doth wear a cloak with sleeves called a priest's cloak . . . he doth not at any time wear in public any wrought night cap nor coif, nor go abroad in his doublet and hose without a coat or cassock, nor wear any light coloured stockings, deep bands, long hair, nor great ruffled boots, nor any other undecent thing, neither is he nor his wife excessive in apparel' – but they still presented him for not usually wearing a 'square cap' and for frequenting the alehouse.[127] Even in the best-ordered parish, such as Hungry Hatley appeared to be, or as Brightwell Baldwin was alleged to be, tensions arose between the interests and expectations of the laity and those of their minister, and between those of different laymen. Some parishioners expected their parson to show his face in the alehouse – Roger Lowe invited the vicar to a drink – while others were horrified if he was seen anywhere near the place. And ministers marooned in their dilapidated parsonages at the end of miry lanes, bereft of cultivated company and with no hope of advancement, occasionally succumbed to despair. Richard Luce, the vicar of Chardstock, proclaimed that if his parishioners heard him 'all the days of their lives, they should

Barry, 'The Politics of Religion in Restoration Bristol', in *The Politics of Religion in Restoration England*, ed. T. Harris, P. Seaward and M. Goldie (Oxford, 1990), p. 166.

124. John Goodman, *A Serious and Compassionate Inquiry* (1674; 1675 edn cited), p. 41.

125. See P. Seaward, 'Gilbert Sheldon, the London Vestries and the Defence of Church', in *The Politics of Religion in Restoration England*, ed. T. Harris, P. Seaward and M. Goldie (Oxford, 1990); Barry, 'Parish in Civic Life', pp. 155–6.

126. MS Eng Th D 59, fo. 15; *Visitation Returns for Cambridgeshire*, ed. Palmer, p. 99; Pruett, *Parish Clergy*, p. 179; MS Tanner 104, fo. 74; Spaeth, 'Parsons and Parishioners', ch. 9.

127. *Visitation Returns for Cambridgeshire*, ed. Palmer, p. 87.

not be a fart the better for his preaching', and throwing his bible to the ground, he trampled on it, while swearing that he would burn all his books. Poor Parson Luce later took to drink.[128]

The antagonisms of parish life – the layman's grudging resentment of the grasping, negligent or officious man in black, and the clergyman's frustration with his slatternly, ignorant, tight-fisted parishioners – are probably perennial. From the days of Enoch, 'it hath ever been the practice of unreasonable men' to despise and condemn those whose duty it is to admonish sinners and urge the exercise of virtue and godliness.[129] Some clerics brought the laity's scorn upon themselves; even the exemplary parish of Brightwell Baldwin suffered from an overbearing rector – 'the Bishop of Brightwell', as a neighbouring minister described him.[130] Clashes of personality, disputes over tithes and dues and quarrels over precedence were certainly a feature of parish life in the Restoration, as they had been for centuries before and would continue to be.[131] But other factors, factors peculiar to the age, were also at work to sour the relationship of the clergy and laity.

The authority of the clergy and their church was compromised by the marked lack of Christian unanimity in Restoration England. Religious diversity had become a fact of English life. After 1660 the religious alternatives which had emerged from the religious liberty of the Interregnum, although now illegal, had been consolidated. Many of the preachers and pastors of the Interregnum continued to live and work in the same parish or neighbourhood, often enjoying the protection of lay patrons and inevitably serving as a focus for religious dissidents. Ministers ejected from their livings, who continued to be a thorn in the side of their Anglican successors – men like William Bagshawe, 'the apostle of the Peak district', William Bridge of Great Yarmouth, Oliver Heywood of Halifax, Christopher Fowler of Reading, John Stalham of Terling, or the fathers of Cambridgeshire Congregationalism, Francis Holcroft of Bassingbourn and Nathaniel Bradshaw of Willingham – created a virtual 'shadow ministry' in their own districts.[132] At Hertford in

---

128. Spaeth, 'Parsons and Parishioners', pp. 335, 349.
129. Addison, *Modest Plea*, pp. 76, 3; Gardner, *Sermon Preached at Visitation* p. 10.
130. MS Tanner 30, fo. 45v.
131. Whiteman, 'Ward', p. 288; Spaeth, 'Parsons and Parishioners', pp. 311–19, 26–47; R.A. Beddard, 'Church and State in Old St Paul's', *Guildhall Miscellany*, 4 (1972), 161–74; MS Tanner 35, fo. 87.
132. M.R. Watts, *The Dissenters* (Oxford, 1978), pp. 280–1; Whiteman, 'Ward', p. 411; K. Wrightson and D. Levine, *Poverty and Piety in an English Village* (New York, 1979), p. 164; M. Spufford, *Contrasting Communities* (Cambridge, 1974), pp. 225–7,

1669 religious meetings of Baptists and of Quakers took place at the same time as the services of the established church. In London in the same year, meeting houses were purpose-built for the Presbyterian congregations of Thomas Doolittle in Monkwell St, Thomas Vincent in Bishopgate St ('spacious ... with galleries'), for Nathaniel Vincent in Southwark, and for Samuel Annesley in Spitalfields ('with pulpit and seats'); and others were to be erected after the 1672 Indulgence.[133] In a marvellous piece of self-deception, Bishop Lucy of St David's argued that were the dissident civic leaders who maintained these preachers 'forced to pay such sums to the amendment of poor vicarages in market towns, I durst say I would make this a happy diocese free from such scandalous schisms'.[134]

In their anxiety to grasp the number and nature of their adversaries, the leaders of the church launched a series of statistical enquiries into religious affiliation, the most thorough of which was the Compton Census of 1676. According to this survey, Nonconformists were less than 5 per cent and Roman Catholics less than 1 per cent of the population of most dioceses.[135] But as statistics these figures can only be approximate; for instance, 343 Catholics and 1,170 Nonconformists were returned for the diocese of Oxford in 1676, while nine years later Bishop Fell's survey found only 148 Catholics, 332 Nonconformists and 270 Quakers or Anabaptists.[136] The enquiries of the Restoration church were undertaken in the vain hope that what could be enumerated could be understood and even controlled.

Roman Catholics were quite easily identified by their recusancy and their tendency to gather around an eminent Catholic family; Bishop Lloyd of Peterborough found that 'Popish recusants are not very numerous in these parts especially since the Lord Cardigan's family is removed out of that country.' In 1686 the vicar of Brailes complained that the parsonage was impropriated by a gentleman

293; G.H. Jenkins, *The Foundations of Modern Wales – Wales 1642–1780* (Oxford, 1987), pp. 192–3.

133. N.H. Keeble, *The Literary Culture of Nonconformity in Later Seventeenth-century England* (Leicester, 1987), p. 73.

134. MS Tanner 146, fo. 113.

135. E.A.O. Whiteman (ed.), *The Compton Census of 1676* (1986), pp. lxxvi–lxxix, appendix F.

136. Jones, 'Ecclesiastical Courts', p. 145. One estimate puts Warwickshire's population at 37,000 in the early 1680s, of whom 2,200 or 6 per cent were Catholics and 4,000–5,000, 11–13 per cent, were Protestant Dissenters (500 Baptists, 900 Quakers and between 2,600 and 3,500 (7–9 per cent) Presbyterians and Independents); see J.J. Hurwich, 'Dissent and Catholicism in English Society: a Study of Warwickshire, 1660–1720', *Journal of British Studies*, 16 (1976), 31. Also see Watts, *Dissenters*, pp. 346–53, appendix.

who kept a popish priest and chapel in his house. As yet few had been converted by this priest, 'but to this chapel the papists in the town go publicly, even through the churchyard in companies whilst we are at divine service, as if they meant to outface authority and the laws of the land'.[137] These adversaries were at least visible; but what of the secret Catholics, the 'church-papists' who attended the Church of England?[138] Even more difficult to quantify and comprehend were the varieties of Protestant Nonconformity; contemporaries talked of 'neutralists between presbyterians and conformists', of 'fanatics' and 'sober Dissenters', of 'partial conformity'. In 1682 the parson of Adderbury complained to his bishop that 'though we have very few indeed that wilfully and constantly absent themselves from the offices of the church . . . yet they, many of 'em, will straggle one part of the day thither [to the Presbyterian conventicle outside the town], when they duly attend the public worship of God on the other, and they seem to be like the borderers betwixt two kingdoms, one can't well tell what prince they are subject to'.[139] The 1676 Census asked each parish minister for the number of inhabitants in the parish, the number of popish recusants, known or suspected, in the parish, and the number of 'other Dissenters . . . (of what sect soever) which either obstinately refuse or wholly absent themselves from the communion of the Church of England at such times as by law they are required'. The third question confused many churchmen, such as the vicar of St Lawrence in Thanet: 'if by this last expression be meant joining in the public worship with the congregation in hearing the prayers of the church in the parish church on the Lord's day', then there was not above 50 of the 1,200 adult parishioners who 'wholly absent themselves from the church[;] but if by communion be meant the holy sacrament of the Lord's supper, then our answer is that there are not two hundred that receive the holy sacrament once in a year and not one hundred persons that receive thrice in a year as is so commanded by the canons. For though the most part of the said 1,200 come constantly to the church to prayers and sermon, yet few of them will be induced to receive the communion by any arguments or persuasions.'[140]

The fluid religious situation meant that the church could never

---

137. MS Rawlinson D 1163, fos 14–15; the vicar of Brailes is quoted in Hurwich, 'Dissent and Catholicism', 33; also see Whiteman, 'Ward', pp. 412–13.

138. See MS Tanner 33, fo. 162, a request for clarification of the meaning of 'recusancy'. The 14,000 recusants found in 1676 may only have been the tip of an iceberg; see J. Miller, *Popery and Politics in England 1660–1688* (Cambridge, 1973), pp. 11–12; J.P. Kenyon, *The Popish Plot* (1972; Harmondsworth, 1984), pp. 28–34.

139. *Fell*, ed. Clapinson, p. 2; also see p. 14.

140. Whiteman (ed.), *Compton Census*, p. xxxix. See *Fell*, ed. Clapinson, p. 22; *Church-*

be sure where the boundary with Dissent or Catholicism lay, or indeed whether her own flock was what it seemed. The church was concerned that in their hearts many of her followers might be Dissenters or church-papists. The neglect or 'general apostasy' from the Lords's Supper alarmed the churchmen: 'how know we that there are not more papists among us than protestants, and more that offer up strange fire, and partake of other altars than ours, if they eat not of the sacrifice?'[141] 'Church-Papists and Church-Puritans do undermine the church, whilst others profess an open hostility against it; but a declared enemy without is not so dangerous as a pretended traitorous friend within.'[142] The churchmen yearned for greater clarity. From one point of view, prosecution helped to clarify the battle lines, to identify those for and those against the church. But on the other hand, persecution may simply have driven people to church, without winning their hearts and minds. Was not the constrained nature of the large Anglican congregations of the 1680s revealed when the Indulgence of 1687 left the parish churches 'exceeding thin'?[143]

Against the statistics, with their false promise of solidity and precision, and against the fears of the churchmen, we have to place the untidy history of individuals – of men like John Gratton of Derbyshire, who progressed from 'following the presbyterians and hireling priests' as a youth in the 1650s, through Anglican conformity at the Restoration, and a subsequent dalliance with the Independents at Chesterfield, to a period of 'walking alone . . . like one that had no mate or companion', sustained only by the belief that 'God had a people somewhere, but I knew not who they were, and was now afraid to join with any, lest they should not worship God aright, and then I might be guilty of idolatry'. Eventually Gratton found God's people in the shape of the Quakers, but where he might have been pigeon-holed in any religious survey *en route* is not at all clear. Gratton's account of his progress from sect to sect also warns us against a common misperception: we tend to think of the seventeenth century's religious history in denominational terms, and to define denominations by their theology or church structure, but Gratton was in search of meaningful worship, of

    wardens' Presentments: II Archdeaconry of Lewes, ed. H. Johnstone (Sussex Record Society, 50, 1948–9), p. 18.

141. Henry Compton, *Episcopalia* (1686), p. 9.
142. John Shaw, *No Reformation of the Established Reformation* (1685), sig. a.
143. Evelyn, IV, 546–7; D.R. Lacey, *Dissent and Parliamentary Politics in England, 1661–1689* (New Brunswick, 1969), pp. 25–7; cf. *The Uncollected Verse of Aphra Behn*, ed. G. Greer (Stump Cross, Essex, 1989), p. 12.

a way of 'worshipping God aright'. He complained that written prayers reduce the scriptures to 'a dead, empty sound', and found 'nothing at all of any life or power of God' in the services of the church.[144] In a similar vein, the Lancashire apprentice Roger Lowe described how in the alehouse one day, he and John Potter 'began to discourse concerning the manner of God's worship. He was for episcopacy and I for presbytery. The contention had like to have been hot, but the Lord prevented. It was two or three days ere we spoke, and I was afraid lest he should do me some hurt.'[145] Lowe and his quarrelsome friend used 'episcopacy' and 'presbytery' as shorthand for different modes of worship. Slowly but surely, religious preferences were becoming one more cultural option, in which religious affiliation was determined by one's taste in preaching, worship and piety and by social status. As one Nonconformist put it, 'some contract a kindness for a pompous and ceremonious religion, and way of worshipping God, others contract a fondness for a very plain and simple way and method of worship and devotion'.[146] Much to his chagrin, Roger Lowe was publicly chastised by his vicar in church for not standing at the gospel. Lowe did not mince words in replying:

> I told him my mind to the full; that standing at gospel, with other ceremonies now in use, was a mere Romish foppery and I should never do it, but sith I could not come to the public ordinances without public disturbance for a ceremonial failing, I should thence forward betake my self to such recepticles [sic] where I could, to my poor ability, serve God without disturbance.[147]

The ease with which one could move between forms of religion – 'going from one church to another hearing a bit here and a bit there'[148] – clearly depended upon a series of contingent factors – whether one lived in a town or a village, the disposition of local magistrates, the direction of government policy, the zeal of the local Anglican clergy. And there was often a price to be paid for religious dissidence in terms of employment prospects, social life, political ambitions and petty harassment; but, besides the unfortunate Quakers and the victims of the Popish Plot, few died for their religious beliefs or preferences in Restoration England.[149]

144. John Gratton, *A Journal of the Life of that Ancient Servant of Christ, John Gratton* (1720), pp. 16, 11–13: Gratton was also a Muggletonian at one time.
145. *The Diary of Roger Lowe*, ed. W.L. Sachse (1938), p. 52.
146. [Edward Polhill], *The Samaritan* (1682), p. 20. Also see Barry, 'Parish in Civic Life', pp. 160–1.
147. Lowe, *Diary*, p. 121.
148. Pepys, III, 47 (describing his own activity in 1662).
149. Other historians would make more of the sufferings of religious dissidents, see

At the parish level, the Church of England was unable to defend herself against this trend towards religious choice. The hierarchy might pore over national statistics in the hope of detecting a decline in Dissent, but they knew that every parish minister faced the uncomfortable truth of religious pluralism. At Ashton-in-Makerfield Roger Lowe debated religion with Anglican laymen and papist friends in the alehouse, and risked a joke with John Lowe, the vicar of Huyton: 'we began in disputing about episcopacy and presbytery. He said they were apostolical. "Yea," quoth I, "they are apostatical from the truths of God"; and he seemed to be displeased.' Every incumbent had his Roger Lowe to confront, and had few real allies to support him.[150] The clergy were beset with 'false friends' who 'sometimes for their own ends will talk loud in the behalf of the church, as if they were the only defenders of the faith, when they can run counter to it in all public votes and employments'.[151] When the parson of Congestone, Leicestershire, announced his intention to catechize, his parishioners 'shut the church door and would not suffer him to come in, but went many of them to a conventicle held in Mr Palmer's house at Temple Hall, the pretended patron of Congeston'.[152] Lay patrons could be a thorn in the church's side. They either presented partially conforming incumbents or forced conformist ministers to allow Dissenting preachers to use the church.[153] And when the parishioners had a say in appointments things were, if anything, worse. Bishop Henchman of London was pathologically suspicious of many London parishes: he suspected the parishioners of St Martin Orgars of having got their minister to resign 'by some indirect means ... in hope to obtain the church for some man whom they would commend'; when the living of Tottenham became vacant, he warned Dean Sancroft that 'it is necessary to send one of your own choice, not of the commendation of the parishioners, they are not to be trusted'.[154] The church kept a close eye on the appointment of clergy in notoriously Nonconformist towns like Plymouth.[155] In some parishes, the right of patronage had been gained by the parishioners during the Interregnum and they often proved reluctant to give it up after the Restoration.[156]

Watts, *Dissenters*, pp. 227–38; Spufford, *Contrasting Communities*, pp. 289–97; G.R. Cragg, *Puritanism in the Period of the Great Persecution* (Cambridge, 1957).
150. Lowe, *Diary*, p. 67; *Fell*, ed. Clapinson, *passim*.
151. MS Tanner 37, fo. 5; cf. Hollingworth, *Modest Plea*, pp. 103–6; South, III, 308.
152. Pruett, *Parish Clergy*, p. 116.
153. Whiting, *Studies*, pp. 34, 37–8; Jackson, 'Nonconformists in Devon', pp. 102–3.
154. BL, MS Harleian 3785, fos 216, 161.
155. See MS Tanner 37, fos 145, 149, 152, on the appointment of Nicholas Clagett at St Andrew's Plymouth in 1680.
156. Jackson, 'Nonconformists in Devon', pp. 98–100.

Bishop Trelawney of Bristol was outraged when the churchwardens and parishioners of Wareham called on Mr Howson, incumbent of Poole, to preach 'as agreeing with them in fanatical doctrines and principles'.[157]

There were disconcerting signs that the parish as a civil institution was no longer automatically and exclusively identified with the Church of England in men's minds. The parish had long been both spiritual and secular, clerical and lay. It was the basic unit of civil administration with a right to make parish rates and choose parish officers, 'which officers with the incumbent, by order of the vestry, have the direction and management of all the parish affairs and business'.[158] The vestry was made up of the incumbent, the churchwardens, and a number of parishioners; the officers, whether primarily ecclesiastical, like the churchwardens, or secular, like the constable, were all laymen. Some Restoration Nonconformists could not see why their religious dissent should exclude them from parish office. In Terling, Essex, eleven Nonconformists served as churchwardens, eight as overseers of the poor, and four as vestrymen, between 1662 and 1688.[159] When the son-in-law of the leading local Nonconformist was proposed as churchwarden at Aston in Oxfordshire, the vicar's refusal to accept his nomination led to a churchyard showdown: 'after I came out of the church the ring-leading Dissenter came to me and insolently asked what my reason was to oppose the parish: I told I did only vindicate my own right, and that I would never give my vote for any man to be a church officer who did not frequent the church and sacrament.'[160]

Religious diversity was at work within the Anglican congregation too. It was perhaps only natural for parishioners to take a proprietorial interest in their parish church and to develop their own customs about such incidentals as seating – it was quite common for men and women to sit separately – wearing hats, or singing.[161] In country churches the parish clerk would lead the congregation

---

157. MS Tanner 30, fo. 83.
158. Joseph Shaw, *Parish Law* (1733), p. 7. Also see Seaward, 'Sheldon, London Vestries and Defence of Church'; C. Hill, *Society and Puritanism in Pre-revolutionary England* (1964), ch. 12.
159. Wrightson and Levine, *Poverty and Piety*, p. 168; cf. Whiteman, 'Ward', p. 308.
160. *Fell*, ed. Clapinson, p. 3; cf. Whiteman, 'Ward', p. 305. In 1682 the vicar of Rye was preparing to go to law with his Whig parishioners over the choice of churchwarden and parish clerk; see MS Tanner 35, fo. 115.
161. *Rector's Book, Clayworth*, pp. 26–7; BL, MS Egerton 3358, item A; C.E. Whiting, *Nathaniel Lord Crewe Bishop of Durham (1674–1721)* (1940), p. 272; *Visitation Returns for Cambridgeshire*, ed. Palmer, p. 96; J. Wickham Legg, *English Church Life from the Restoration to the Tractarian Movement* (1914), pp. 171–2; Pepys, II, 215.

in a slow, ponderous singing of a psalm of their choice in the middle of the service – and often the presiding clergyman would take this opportunity to stretch his legs, or change his surplice.[162] In the 1680s, William Turner, the newly arrived incumbent of a Sussex parish, found that it was a local custom that the women did not sing in church, and if one did, the congregation would all turn to stare. He had to learn how to manage his flock.

> When I call to catechism and sacrament, and expound the one and urge the frequency of the other, and am importunate in my exhortations to those duties, and in admonishing about some faults concerning public worship, as staying in the churchyard talking (in service time) and sitting all prayer-time and wearing hats all service-time (which I am apt to resent with more sharpness than perhaps they expected from me), they at first suspended their approbation and favour; but when I recollected myself and endeavoured to temper my admonition with a softness of spirit and accommodate myself to their case with more mildness and less satire, I found and still do their affections coming.[163]

Although they refused to kneel in prayer or to remove their hats, these were perfectly sober, orthodox, conforming parishioners of the Church of England, who simply had their own way of doing things when it came to religious worship. In the 1720s, the parishioners of Somerford Keynes in Wiltshire shocked their new curate by singing at a burial 'as they always do on such occasions'.[164] Local habits easily intruded upon the performance of religious duties, and lay preferences could have a very direct effect on the nature of parish Anglicanism.

What the laity sought from their religious service was not always what the clergy were prepared to provide. In the 1670s the curate of Weltham in Suffolk preached an additional sermon on a Sunday afternoon, only to find that he became unpopular with the neighbouring clergy 'because their people would come sometimes'. In another parish, the same zealous curate had been discouraged from this afternoon preaching by his vicar 'because it was unusual, and it would be expected from him [the vicar]'.[165] But elsewhere, parishioners disliked too much preaching or catechizing and denounced sermons which went over their heads: Evelyn grumbled at one

162. N. Temperley, *The Music of the English Parish Church* (Cambridge, 1979), pp. 88–9; also see ch. 7 below.
163. MS Eng Letters E 29, fo. 178.
164. Spaeth, 'Parsons and Parishioners', p. 129.
165. CUL, MS Add 8499, fos 153, 121.

'metaphysical discourse of the perfections of God, altogether unintelligible to most of our plain auditors'.[166] They expected to be able to work on Sundays if they needed to – despite the fact that, except for works of 'necessity' like milking, this was an offence under the injunctions of 1559 and the statute of 1677 – and some apparently attended only one of the two Sunday services, choosing whichever fitted in best with the work they were doing that day.[167] The main 'neglects' discovered by Bishop Trelawney on his primary visitation of the diocese of Bristol in 1686,

> were the backwardness of people to be confirmed, occasioned by the neglect of constantly instructing the children in the words and meaning of the church catechism: the ill customs of private christenings, through the ministers' compliance with the richer sort of their parish: the disuse of visiting the sick at their houses, proceeding chiefly from the custom which is very frequent of reading most part of the form of the visitation of the sick when they are prayed for in the church; the confused and irregular way of reading the prayers in some ministers, either through their own dissatisfaction at them, or fear of others dissatisfied with them[;] and the ill condition which most of the churches were in by reason the parishes are not put in mind, or else unwilling to assess themselves for their reparation.[168]

At some point the clergy's pandering to such lay pressure becomes indistinguishable from partial conformity or even compliance with Nonconformity. As a young vicar in Cambridgeshire in the early 1660s, Isaac Archer was very 'tender of the Nonconformists', who all loved him, and he explained that in baptizing according to the Prayer Book 'I did not sign with the cross, because it gave offence'. Indeed his general attitude towards liturgical conformity was to do 'as little as was possible, without incurring danger [prosecution from the church authorities], and so [I] kept myself very moderate, and displeased, I think, none by so doing'.[169] Information was passed to Bishop Reynolds of Norwich by the Bishop of London in 1670 that 'there is a practice taken up in Suffolk towards Essex side, that the Nonconformists pressure some to read parts of the Common Prayer, and then they preach and carry on the duty of the day.'[170]

166. Evelyn, IV, 291, also see 4–5, 109; MS Rawlinson D 399, fo. 184; *Fell*, ed. Clapinson, pp. 2–3, 6, 9.
167. Spaeth, 'Common Prayer?', in *Parish, Church and People*, ed. S.J. Wright (1988), p. 141; A. Fletcher, *A County Community in Peace and War* (1975), p. 87.
168. MS Tanner 30, fo. 50.
169. CUL, MS Add. 8499, fo. 81.
170. Lambeth Palace Library, MS 674, fo. 48.

In the 1660s Richard Kidder found that many parishioners at St Helen's Bishopsgate, London, 'kneeled not at the sacrament, but were otherwise very devout and regular'. He knew what the Canon required, but 'on the other hand I considered the mischief of dismissing such a number of communicants and sending them to the Nonconformists' and the precedent of compliance established by his predecessor. Eventually he decided to give them the sacrament whether they knelt or not; subsequently he consulted Bishop Henchman, who told him to proceed, but 'that I should never preach up kneeling in the pulpit; for then (said he) those who kneel not will think you aim at them. But that I should in private conversation endeavour their satisfaction.'[171] By the 1680s official Anglican attitudes had hardened against such collusion or 'trimming' – the church's apologists repeatedly denounced those who undermined their own church in this way and the authorities attempted to crack down on laxness – but how much of this covert compliance continued as before will never be known.

So local customs and preferences influenced local religious practices. But the influence of the laity over the local church and clergy could be quite naked – it was after all the laity who paid the piper, and it would be surprising if they did not occasionally attempt to call the tune. The lay patrons of parish livings could do much to dictate the sort of Anglicanism practised in a parish. In 1683 Sir Robert Atkins wrote on behalf of the parish of Stow on the Wold to the Bishop of Oxford, entreating him to send a pious, resident, conscientious minister, but hoping that the parish would be allowed to approve any candidate before he was 'imposed on us ... we are well content to have a conformable person, so he be prudent and moderate, not too rigid and severe in ceremony. We love to have all decent and to have his work done with love and meekness: and if it please God to bless us with such a minister we shall love and honour him, and he shall not want for encouragement.'[172] What love, honour and encouragement a strict ceremonialist might expect from this parish is not specified. Like their forebears, Restoration laymen demanded value for money and were quite prepared to present to the church courts clergy who failed to live up to their expectations.[173] The churchwardens of Kerdford, Sussex, presented

171. *The Life of Richard Kidder D.D. Bishop of Bath and Wells Written by Himself*, ed. A.E. Robinson (Somerset Record Society, 37, 1922), pp. 19–20.
172. MS Rawlinson D 399, fo. 279.
173. *Churchwardens' Presentments ... Lewes*, ed. Johnstone, p. 31; *Episcopal Visitation Book for the Archdeaconry of Buckinghamshire 1662*, ed. E.R.C. Brinkworth (Buckinghamshire Record Society, 7, 1947), p. 10; MS Rawlinson D 384; Jones, 'Ecclesiastical Courts', p. 210; *Fell*, ed. Clapinson, p. 37; MS Tanner 35, fo. 57.

Edward Holt in 1664 'for his absence, that we have had no prayers but every other Sunday any time these ten weeks; and for neglecting to bury the dead, for we have had dead corpses to be buried and have been brought to the church and have been set down for three or four days together before he came to administer burial'. One of the wardens of Northmarden had obviously had enough by 1664, when he reported 'that for the space of a year and three quarters of a year last past there hath been no service nor sermon in the morning of any Lord's day said in our church by the rector or any others for him. And many whole days service and sermon there have been omitted. And in the afternoon, when any service is said or sermon preached, it is done unseasonably, and so late that people cannot conveniently come and return.' A year later the parish was still complaining that their minister, Mr Smith, does 'not officiate according to the canons of the Church of England, for he never since he was our minister did read divine service in the morning, neither did he ever warn or give the sacrament or read the litany or ten commandments since he was our minister'.[174]

If some clergymen did too little to suit their parishioners, others did far too much. The account left by Isaac Archer of a brush with some of his Cambridgeshire parishioners in August 1663 still resonates with his sense of indignation and powerlessness:

> in harvest time I observed that men used to frequent the alehouse on the Lord's day; I asked the constable to assist me, but he said he should get the ill will of his neighbours, I asked him if that should hinder him from doing his office etc, but he would not go, and so I went alone, and found several there, some went away. But one of my own parish, for the others were most strangers, asked me if he might not drink upon the Sunday. I told him he must not fuddle (as I perceived he was it [in?] that case) upon any day much less upon that; and so inquiring his name, when the hostess would not, he told it me himself, and I left him at his pots and pipes. When I was gone he railed on me for meddling where I had nothing to do (though 'twas out of the bishop's articles to look to the strict observing the Lord's day, and so did belong to me, if not upon an higher account) and said he could read the Lord's Prayer better than I, and that I could not read Common Prayer well, meaning because I stammered.[175]

174. *Churchwardens' Presentments: I Archdeaconry of Chichester*, ed. H. Johnstone (Sussex Record Society, 49, 1947–8), pp. 130–1, 132, 137.
175. CUL, MS Add. 8499, fo. 85.

William Sampson, rector of Clayworth, refused to register private baptisms, and William Bradford refused to baptize without god-parents since 'it was against the canons of the church'.[176] In 1682 the curate of Caversham wrote to the bishop, explaining that he had made enquiries into the numbers of local Dissenters and re-cusants, but 'the parish are much displeased with me about it, thinking it the effect of my too forward zeal, rather than the obliga-tion of your Lordship's commands'.[177] Caught between the demands of their superiors and the obstinacy of their flock, the position of many parish ministers was unenviable. But if all else failed, they could invoke the authority of the archdeacon and the bishop, of the diocesan and national church beyond the parish.

The authority of the diocesan and national church was embodied in the ecclesiastical courts; but these courts were not simply auth-oritarian, they also served society and much of their business was brought to them by the laity. The church courts dealt with three areas of business – matrimonial and testamentary matters; ecclesi-astical cases, such as disputes about church seating, tithes or the church rate; and moral and spiritual offences. The lay community had an interest in all of these areas; in the administration of their estates, the resolution of local disputes, and the preservation of parochial order through moral regulation. The probate of wills was the work first taken up by the church courts when they were revived as part of the reconstruction of episcopal administration in 1660; with the Ecclesiastical Causes Act of the following year, the courts' traditional coercive machinery was resurrected, and they could be-gin to enforce their authority in tithe or church rate cases; and finally, after the Act of Uniformity, the church could once again prosecute breaches of religious observance.[178] However, despite the deliberate resurrection of this apparently useful judicial system, its subsequent history seems to be a story of shrinking business and declining authority.

This, at least, is the impression created by our present knowledge, for although shafts of scholarly light have illuminated the workings of some courts in a few dioceses, most of the church courts of Restoration England remain unstudied and consequently all gener-alizations about them remain fragile.[179] No doubt one reason for

176. *Rector's Book, Clayworth*, pp. 35–6; Spaeth, 'Parsons and Parishioners', p. 101.
177. *Fell*, ed. Clapinson, p. 9.
178. Green, *Re-establishment*, pp. 131–5.
179. For what follows I am particularly indebted to Whiteman, 'Ward'; Jones, 'Ecclesiastical Courts'; D.M. Owen, *The Records of the Established Church of England*

this neglect by historians is the difficulty of the work; the church courts did not keep neat records, nor did they all follow the same procedures, and the protracted cases are difficult to trace to a conclusion through the surviving documents. As a result even such basic issues as the volume of business conducted in the church courts are unclear. Causes before the church courts fell into two categories: instance causes, begun by an aggrieved party and with written pleas and evidence – matrimonial, defamation and tithe cases are of this sort – and office causes, brought by the judge of the court for the public good and *pro salute animae* (for the sake of the soul) of the defendant, in which the evidence was oral and the proceedings summary. Office cases included moral offences and breaches of religious observance. Information about such faults usually came to the notice of the ecclesiastical courts through the presentments of offenders made by the churchwardens and minister of each parish at the bishop's or archdeacon's visitation. Since both the minister and the wardens were involved, and since they were responding to a set of visitation articles or enquiries issued by the bishop, the system could fairly claim to reflect the values and anxieties of both the church and the community. The visitation was usually based at a local centre to which the wardens and clergy could travel; it was rare for each parish church to be visited, although Archdeacon Granville attempted it in Durham in 1680 and claimed that the clergy 'were soon sensible that the archdeacon's appearance in their parishes did them many real services'.[180] Those whose names and offences were presented at the visitation would usually be 'cited' or summoned subsequently to the archdeaconry or consistory court, but there is some evidence of the authorities exercising discretion and summoning only a proportion, presumably the recalcitrant or notorious offenders, of those presented.

Vigorous diocesan campaigns for religious observance were conducted through some church courts in the 1660s. Perhaps 75 per cent of office business before the courts of Oxford and Peterborough dioceses in the early 1660s concerned religious observance. Yet from about 1667, the impetus began to fade in Oxford, where office

(1970), pp. 36–45; M.G. Smith, 'A Study of the Administration of the Diocese of Exeter during the Episcopate of Sir Jonathan Trelawney, bart., 1689–1707' (unpublished Oxford University B.D. thesis, no year); idem, *Pastoral Discipline and the Church Courts: the Hexham Court 1680–1730* (Borthwick Papers, 62, York, 1982); idem, *Fighting Joshua*; and Davies, 'The Enforcement of Uniformity', which takes an exceptionally optimistic view of the efficiency and vitality of the church courts in the dioceses of Chichester and Worcester. J. Addy, *Sin and Society in the Seventeenth Century* (1989) is a useful survey of the work of the courts of Chester diocese.

180. Josselin, p. 593; Granville, II, 46–7.

business declined by 40 per cent, and in Peterborough the courts increasingly concerned themselves with moral regulation. This faltering effort was dealt a further blow by the 1672 Declaration of Indulgence and the 'general pardon' of 1673.[181] In the dioceses of Chichester and Worcester, however, prosecutions of religious observance offences soon recovered and in 1675 formed 45 per cent and 55 per cent respectively of the total office business of the two Consistory Courts.[182] After a decline during the years of the Exclusion crisis, religious observance prosecutions revived; at Worcester they formed 22 per cent in 1681 and 50 per cent in 1682 of total office business; and while they were only 3 per cent of business at Chicester in 1682, they had risen to 31 per cent in the following year.[183] But the policies of James II, especially the 'general pardon' of 10 March 1686 and the Indulgence of 1687, seem finally to have put paid to such prosecutions.

The phrase 'religious observance' covers a multitude of sins, some of omission and some of commission, and it would be extremely misleading to suggest that these were prosecutions of Nonconformists and recusants. Offences included in this category were failure to receive the sacrament, failure to attend the sermon, or the prayers, or any of the services, and failure to have one's children baptized and catechized, as well as the more active offences of disrupting services by profane, blasphemous or drunken behaviour, abusing the minister, and attending conventicles. Where it has been possible to break down 'religious observance' cases into further categories, it has been shown that the vast majority, between 75 and 80 per cent, of these presentments were for non-attendance at church.[184] Yet the historian's abiding difficulty is that, in the words of one authority, 'a presentment does not distinguish between a wilful offender and one who is merely lazy or indifferent'; absenteeism or the failure to have your child baptized may be expressions of a theological scruple or may simply be evidence of apathy, but the records do not allow us to decide which.[185]

Meanwhile, of course, the secular judges and courts, the Justices

181. Jones, 'Ecclesiastical Courts', pp. 47–50, 59.
182. Davies, 'Enforcement of Uniformity', p. 28; also see Jackson, 'Nonconformists in Devon ', p. 245.
183. Davies, 'Enforcement of Uniformity', p. 287, but cf. appendices; also see Smith, 'Administration of Diocese of Exeter', pp. 182–3.
184. Jones, 'Ecclesiastical Courts', pp. 130–5; see R.A. Marchant, *The Church under the Law* (Cambridge, 1969), table 32, for the situation at the beginning of the century. (Cambridge, 1969), table 32, for the situation at the beginning of the century.
185. Whiteman, 'Ward', p. 131.

of the Peace, Quarter Sessions and Assizes, were on the advance against religious dissidence. As early as 1660 the justices had begun to appropriate prosecutions for recusancy, and the Clarendon Code further encouraged the secular courts and justices especially to assume responsibility for the enforcement of religious uniformity. But there was nothing dramatically new in this, and it appears that ecclesiastical and secular courts tended to reinforce one another's efforts in the field of religious observance.[186] Their jurisdictions and even their personnel overlapped since several clergymen sat as JPs. In March 1668, the sidesmen and churchwardens of St Thomas, Salisbury, were instructed to make a regular monthly report to the city's JPs of those who usually absented themselves from Common Prayer especially on the Lord's Day.[187] In 1664 the vicar of Rothwell presented 59 parishioners for not making their Easter communion to the justices at Northampton rather than the Consistory Court at Peterborough.[188] During the Tory reaction, the bishops once again used the church courts to prosecute Nonconformity: 'there is not a separatist (as far as I can learn) in this diocese, who is not under prosecution', reported Bishop Lloyd of St Asaph. 'Only those that come to me for information I proceed with the more leisurely. All the rest are under excommunication.'[189] And they were encouraged by the secular courts. The Grand Jury at the Salisbury Sessions of January 1683 requested the bishop to order the ecclesiastical courts 'to proceed to an excommunication against all sorts of dissenters within their diocese that they may have no share in the government of this kingdom unless they will conform to the laws in church and state'.[190] At the Epiphany Quarter Sessions of 1681 the Exeter JPs instructed that all should be reported who absented themselves from church, or attended only part of the service, or had not received the sacrament 'for one or two or more months'.[191] At the Bedfordshire Sessions of January 1685 the Earl of Ailesbury, the Custos Rotulorum, ordered churchwardens to present all those who arrived late at church and did not kneel and stand as appropriate during the service; this speech was published with a letter from Bishop Barlow commanding the clergy to publish the earl's order from their pulpits.[192]

186. See Jones, 'Ecclesiastical Courts', p. 137; Jackson, 'Nonconformists in Devon', p. 216.
187. *Churchwardens' Accounts of S. Edmund and S. Thomas, Sarum*, ed. H.J.F. Swayne (Salisbury, 1896), p. 339.
188. Jones, 'Ecclesiastical Courts', p. 4.
189. Tanner MS 35, fo. 162.
190. Whiteman, 'Ward', p. 416.
191. Jackson, 'Nonconformists in Devon', pp. 140–2.
192. *Order to the Sessions of Peace at Ampthill, 14 January 1684 [1684/5]*

The contribution of the church courts to the Restoration's drive for religious uniformity should not be overestimated. Although religious observance cases formed a significant proportion of the office cases of the ecclesiastical courts, the number of individuals actually before each court was never very large, varying from a few dozen one year to a couple of hundred the next. In 1663, 144 individuals were prosecuted in the church courts of Exeter for observance offences – this was the diocese's largest annual total of such prosecutions during the decade – and these individuals came from 53 out of the 630 or so different parishes or chapelries of the diocese.[193] The Bristol Consistory Court summoned 213 individuals, six of whom were clergy, in the three years between August 1683 and July 1686; Chichester Consistory Court heard 84 religious observance cases in 1668, eight in 1669 and 181 in 1670; in the 1680s, the numbers of cases heard at Chichester varied from two in 1682, forming just 3 per cent of the year's cases, to 115 in 1685, which accounted for 70 per cent of that year's business.[194] In short, only a very few individuals were ever cited into the church courts on religious observance charges; but to make matters worse, even fewer bothered to turn up.

Just like the clergy and parish officials, the laity had a very poor record of attendance at the church courts. Only one in three of those cited to appear before the Oxford diocesan courts in 1667–9 actually appeared, and only one in twenty-five attended every session of his or her case; of the 213 cited to Bristol in 1683–6, only 59 attended; and figures from other courts suggest non-attendance rates running quite routinely at 60 per cent.[195] Non-attendance, which had been just as much of a problem before the Civil War, had several causes, including conscientious scruples, fear of excessive fees, and resentment at the dilatory proceedings, but it also stemmed from the fact that the church courts could not enforce their will, either administratively – in 13 per cent cases the apparitor of Exeter archdeaconry could not find the defendant to deliver the citation personally – or judicially.[196]

The church courts exercised an authority derived from Christ, not from man. But this meant that the church had very few sanctions against offenders; her sanctions were spiritual, she had no power

---

193. Whiteman, 'Ward', pp. 131–5.
194. Smith, *Fighting Joshua*, p. 34; Davies, 'Enforcement of Uniformity', p. 174, but also see appendices 1–3 which include totals of persons.
195. Jones, 'Ecclesiastical Courts', pp. 91–100; Smith, *Fighting Joshua*, p. 34; Davies, 'Enforcement of Uniformity', appendices 1–3; cf. P. Collinson, *The Religion of Protestants* (Oxford, 1982), pp. 214–15.
196. Jackson, 'Nonconformists in Devon', p. 218. The usual solution was to leave the citation on the defendant's door.

over life, limb or property, and no means of coercing obedience other than the scripturally based church censures of admonition, penance and excommunication. Admonition and penance were only effective for those who valued their communion with the church. Penance, which in many dioceses was reserved for offences of sexual immorality, was frequently commuted either to private penance, performed in ordinary clothes before the churchwardens and minister, or to a money payment.[197] But on occasion full penance was exacted. In the diocese of Peterborough, 39 men and women did penance between 1679 and 1683, mainly for fornication, adultery and defamation; and in 1668 an Oxfordshire man was required 'at the toll of the last bell immediately before morning service [to] be ready in the church porch ... standing there with his schedule in his hand and audibly desire the people particularly as they pass into the church to pray God to forgive him'.[198] In February 1683 a Quaker who had admitted double adultery performed penance at Llanroost, in the diocese of St Asaph. Bishop Lloyd described how the penitent 'stood very demurely' in 'a very full church', without his hat, dressed in a sheet, and holding a white staff, 'and then read the schedule of penance, though not without a little demur at the word good people in the beginning of it'. The penance was repeated on the following two Sundays at Denbigh and St Asaph, although in view of the cold weather Lloyd would not require that he did this 'bare legged and bare-foot as he did at Llanroost without my order for it'. Bishop Lloyd hoped that 'this severity on one of that sect' would do much good in the region.[199]

Excommunication was attended with spiritual and civil disabilities which were far from negligible. Besides being denied the sacraments and worship of the church, excommunicates could not plead at law, nor act as executors, and their fellow parishioners were inhibited from all 'manner of converse ... by buying, selling, eating, drinking, conversing or talking with them.'[200] Lloyd described another penalty imposed on excommunicates:

It was ordered at the last convocation in this diocese that whosoever dies excommunicate shall want burial in the church or churchyard unless the bishop order contrary in any particular case. This indeed is a punishment to the relations and therefore where the relations are good conformable people I have suffered

197. Jones, 'Ecclesiastical Courts', pp. 103–12.
198. MS Rawlinson D 1163, fos 28–9; Jones, 'Ecclesiastical Courts', p. 109.
199. MS Tanner 35, fo. 190.
200. C. Holmes, *Seventeenth-century Lincolnshire* (Lincoln, 1980), p. 10.

them to bury their dead in the churchyard (but by no means in the church) and that by night without prayers or any other solemnity. Yesterday some Papists came to me for leave to bury one of their dead that died under excommunication. I endeavoured by that handle to bring them to church but after long discourse with them found them obstinate and therefore refused them the use of holy ground for their dead. If I did amiss I submit to your Grace's censure for this. But I thought it the best way of dealing with a people so much led by their senses as they are, and I hope to do them good by it.[201]

Excommunication ostensibly cut the offender off from his or her community, but the reality was rather different.

The clergy lamented that 'the power of the keys, excommunication, or church-censures, are become very contemptible, and sunk so low in some men's opinions, that they rise not above the estimate of artificial fire or mere noisy thunder'.[202] Although such complaints had a long history, there are indications that church censures carried less weight than they had earlier in the century.[203] Two reasons for this contempt were the promiscuous imposition of the penalty and its lack of effect. Excommunication had been 'prostituted, by inflicting it for small offences or neglects' and had been used to line the pockets of lay court officials.[204] The recourse to excommunication for matters such as unpaid tithes and non-attendance at church had swollen the number of those who were officially cut off from the church: in the archdeaconry of Stowe in 1664 there were 377 excommunicates; in the church courts of Exeter, 85 of the 144 individuals cited in 1663 were excommunicated, as were 52 of the 115 cited in 1665 and 61 of the 107 summoned the year after; nearly half of those who were cited to appear before the church courts of Oxford and Peterborough were eventually excommunicated.[205] A vicious circle was operating: the generous imposition of the penalty meant that many preferred not to answer their citation to the church court and to suffer the near-automatic excommuni-

---

201. MS Tanner 35, fo. 190.
202. Addison, *Modest Plea*, pp. 130–1. Baxter suggested that 'a popish interdict, or mock excommunication, by the sentence of a prelate or lay chancellor, may pass against multitudes, and have no considerable effect (but it is enforced by the sword)'; *RB*, I, 93.
203. More cases were ending in excommunication than had in the 1630s; see Jones, 'Ecclesiastical Courts', pp. 118, 236.
204. Barrow, IX, 579.
205. Holmes, *Lincolnshire*, p. 225; Whiteman, 'Ward', pp. 132–4; Jones, 'Ecclesiastical Courts', p. 118.

cation for non-attendance or 'contumacy'. At one Derbyshire visitation 478 individuals were excommunicated for non-attendance.
Many of those excommunicated in Exeter, Oxford or Peterborough
courts were contumacious. With an increasing air of desperation,
the Restoration church issued more and more excommunications
for contumacy, which simply exposed the penalty for the hollow
threat that it was.[206]

Excommunication did not ostracize the individual as it was supposed to do. For all the talk of excommunicate corpses being ex-
humed from churchyards, and of individuals being presented for
consorting with excommunicates, there is very little evidence that
this happened.[207] Indeed the numbers involved and the weak administration meant that few knew exactly who was excommunicate
or absolved. When, in 1683, Bishop Lloyd of St Asaph and his
diocesan clergy drew up rules to make excommunication more effective, they stipulated that 'the minister of every parish is to keep a
book by him both of excommunications and absolutions, that he
may know who are and who are not in church communion among
his parishioners', and that if an excommunicate moved away, information of his status should be passed to his new parish or to
the bishop.[208] Once excommunicated the delay before absolution
could vary from a few months to several years, and a large number
died excommunicate. On the other hand, some individuals rushed
to have themselves absolved, perhaps out of sincere devotion to the
church or perhaps from a concern to protect their property. It has
been suggested that excommunication primarily affected the prop-
ertied or those approaching death.[209] This seems plausible, as does
the suggestion that the penalty was most effective when used most
selectively: in 1673, Mr Aske, rector of Somerford Magna, presented
'some of the chief of the parish who will not stand excommunication . . . and therefore the fees are the more certain[;] I would not
present too many at a time lest it should encourage them all to be
contumacious.'[210]

More than anything else, it was the rise of Nonconformity which
undermined excommunication, since those who had cut themselves

206. R. Clark, 'Anglicanism, Recusancy, and Dissent in Derbyshire, 1603–1670'
     (unpublished Oxford University D.Phil. thesis, 1979), pp. 236, 238.
207. Jones, 'Ecclesiastical Courts', pp. 116, 136; Davies, 'Enforcement of Uniformity',
     pp. 181–3; Smith, 'Administration of Diocese of Exeter', p. 73; Whiting, *Crewe*,
     p. 364; MS Tanner 38, fo. 111.
208. *Concilia*, IV, 609.
209. Jones, 'Ecclesiastical Courts', pp. 119–20. Also see *Fell*, ed. Clapinson, p. xxii;
     Jackson, 'Nonconformists in Devon', pp. 221–3.
210. Whiteman, 'Ward', p. 431.

off from the church would hardly resent being cut off by the church –
excommunication was 'but a cloak for their not coming to church'
or, in the words of an MP, it 'was of no force at all with some men,
especially those that did willingly absent themselves from the
church'.[211] Many ecclesiastical officials were, like the Archdeacon
of Canterbury, troubled by 'Quakers and Anabaptists' who were
already excommunicate 'of which they have no regard, so that a
new sentence of the same without somewhat farther doth but expose
the censures of the church to new contempt'. The archdeacon sought
directions from Sancroft on how to 'proceed with them that refuse
to come to church and will not appear at court tho cited . . . I know
not what sentence we can proceed to, but excommunication, which
I know your Grace would avoid as much as possible.'[212]

One way of making excommunication bite was to seek a writ *de
excommunicato capiendo* from Chancery, by which the sheriff could
seize and imprison an excommunicate. But the writ was expensive
to obtain and difficult to serve in some towns and regions. The
limited evidence suggests that the writ was a measure of last resort:
only one was sought in the Oxford courts and thirteen in the Peterborough courts between 1660 and 1675; it was used against 21 of
the 85 excommunicated in Exeter in 1664; and in 1683 Bishop Lloyd
of Peterborough reported twelve individuals 'now in gaol' on such
writs. The writ was probably only worthwhile against troublesome
Nonconformist clergy or patrons, and may well have been intended
in many cases as a warning shot to bring the culprit scurrying for
absolution before the sheriff caught up with him.[213]

The courts of the Restoration Church of England simply did not
have the moral authority to bring errant parishioners to heel. Unfortunately, the ineffectiveness of the church courts did not mean
that they were inoffensive. 'You cannot but have heard (at least
somewhat) of the great clamours that are made against the ecclesiastical courts for delay of justice and other abuses in their proceedings', wrote Sheldon to Sir Giles Sweit, Dean of the Arches, when
instructing him to 'sit down and seriously consider what is amiss
in your courts and profession, and how to regulate and rectify the
same'.[214] To many the church courts seemed to have run out of
control, to have escaped from effective episcopal discipline; as one

---

211. Spaeth, 'Parsons and Parishioners', pp. 210–11; Milward, *Diary*, p. 240.
212. MS Tanner 33, fos 176, 171.
213. Jones, 'Ecclesiastical Courts', pp. 120–2; Whiteman, 'Ward', pp. 135–6, 415;
     MS Rawlinson D 1163, fo. 29; Smith, *Fighting Joshua*, pp. 34–5; Jackson, 'Non-
     conformists in Devon', pp. 224–9, 237.
214. MS Add. C 308, fo. 114.

MP commented in 1672, 'the ecclesiastical courts in some things have too much power; in others, too little and the bishops usually the least'.[215] The inefficiency of the courts in matters like probate, the lengthy suits, with litigants dragged back and forth to distant courts, and then the crippling fees – which in John Aubrey's breach of promise case came to a total of £13 13s. 4d. – all fuelled lay hostility.[216] But, inevitably, the courts also looked repressive; the writ *de excommunicato capiendo* was a breach of Magna Carta; the 'exorbitancies' of the courts, their lay chancellors, and the use of excommunication, were deplored even by those accounted 'severe son[s] of the church', never mind by determined opponents like William Prynne.[217] In March 1668, in response to a royal invitation, the House of Commons considered the problem of religion, and with the possibility of comprehension or toleration looming, some speakers proposed the reform of the church courts 'to take away the exceptions of the Dissenters'. This is what prompted Sheldon's letter to Sir Giles Sweit, and the threat behind it is what the archbishop alluded to when he told Sir Giles, 'nor can you be ignorant what a shock the church is at this time likely to undergo upon that account, if you mend not your ways'.[218]

Although the storm was averted in 1668, the danger was not, and the clergy remained only too aware that the church courts would have to mend their ways. A chorus of clerical voices demanded that the solemn and awful sentence of excommunication be restricted to serious spiritual offences and be imposed and lifted only by clergymen.[219] But if excommunication was restricted, what would replace it as the penalty for lesser offences? Resurrecting an earlier proposal, Sheldon and Sir Leoline Jenkins considered the creation by statute of a new sentence of 'contumacy' which would carry the civil, but not the spiritual, disabilities of excommunciation. This remedy also interested Sancroft, but it was never to be instituted because to enact it would be a recognition that the penalties and even the authority of the church courts were derived from the state.[220] This

215. Smith, *Fighting Joshua*, p. 26.
216. Whiteman, 'Ward', p. 180; Jones, 'Ecclesiastical Courts', pp. 85–90; Jackson, 'Nonconformists in Devon', pp. 238–41.
217. Milward, *Diary*, pp. 150, 191.
218. Ibid., p. 215; MS Add. C 308, fo. 114; Spurr, 'Comprehension', 933–5.
219. See *A Vindication*, pp. 108–19; [Herbert Croft], *The Naked Truth* (1675); Hamon L'Estrange, *The Alliance of Divine Offices* (1659; LACT, Oxford, 1846 edn cited), p. 489; John Stileman, *A View of Church Government* (1663), epistle dedicatory; Addison, *Modest Plea*, p. 132; Hughes, '"Last Words" of Burnet', 224.
220. See Sykes, *From Sheldon*, pp. 40–1, 188–92; Jones, 'Ecclesiastical Courts', p. 250; Smith, *Pastoral Discipline and Church Courts*, p. 8.

fear did not however prevent efforts to impose excommunication more selectively and with greater solemnity, nor did it stop the hierarchy drawing up draft legislation to control fees, to improve the bishop's direct control over his own officials and courts, and to restore to him sole control of disciplining the laity by prohibiting excommunications or commutations without his personal approval.[221]

The authority of the Restoration church was undermined by the deficiencies of the clergy, the weakness of her discipline, and the religious diversity of English society, all of which are discernible, even quantifiable, institutional and social trends; but another force, more pervasive, perhaps more corrosive, and certainly less tangible, was eroding the moral standing of religion and of the Church of England in particular. This was the spirit of the age, an age given over to the pleasure of wit, the exercise of reason, the jeering of anticlericalism, and the self-indulgence of libertinism.

A World Grown Saucy

It was observed in 1661 that 'many of the gentry of late are grown more inquisitive in religious things' and would no longer be constrained in what they thought by the clergy. 'The world is grown saucy, and expecteth reasons, and good ones too, before they give up their opinions to other men's dictates,' wrote Halifax. 'The liberty of the late times gave men so much light, and diffused it so universally amongst the people, that they . . . are become so good judges of what they hear that the clergy ought to be very wary before they go about to impose upon their understandings, which are grown less humble than they were in former times.'[222] Divinity became 'the frequentest table-talk in England', as gentlemen exercised their freedom to debate doctrine and ethics, to draw up their own spiritual *vade mecum* or to compose a *religio laici*.[223] The 'most esteemed' works of the day, Sir Thomas Browne's *Religio medici* (1642), Francis Osborne's *Advice to a Son* (1656) and Samuel Butler's *Hudibras* (1663), all exhibited this inquisitive and independent

221. *Concilia*, IV, 608–9; MS Tanner 447, fos 175–83; MS Tanner 300, fo. 143 (most of these MSS are printed in Sykes, *From Sheldon*, pp. 188–92); Jones, 'Ecclesiastical Courts', pp. 245–51; Sir Edward Lake, *Memoranda* (1662), pp. 123–32.

222. [Pete]R [Pet]T, *A Discourse concerning Liberty of Conscience* (1661), pp. 47–9, 55; *Halifax – Complete Works*, ed. J.P. Kenyon (Harmondsworth, 1969), p. 73. Also see J.F. MacLear, 'Popular Anticlericalism in the Puritan Revolution', *JHI*, 18 (1956).

223. See M. Hunter, *Science and Society in Restoration England* (Cambridge, 1981), p. 163; C.D. Atkins, *The Faith of John Dryden* (University of Kentucky Press, 1980), p. 5.

streak.[224] Laymen were keen critics of sermons and of the abilities of preachers. Nor would they be denied the pleasure of debating the Church of England's shortcomings: after all, 'does not the church consist of lay-men as well as clergy-men'?[225] There was, for instance, 'much discourse' at Samuel Pepys's dinner table one Sunday in 1668 'about the bad state of the church, and how the clergy are come to be men of no worth – and, as the world doth now generally discourse, they must be reformed'.[226] Such talk, and the independent, critical frame of mind which spawned it, threatened to erode the authority of church and clergy.

The churchmen naturally loathed this rooting up of the hedge around their vineyard. Although there was little they could do to control the laity's conversation, they made their feelings plain; Bishop Wren of Ely asked the churchwardens at his 1662 visitation whether they knew of any in their parishes who presumed to make matters of divinity their ordinary table-talk or to debate the scriptures at their trencher meetings.[227] If anti-clerical table-talk was an annoyance, criticism of the church in print was an outrage. Or so it seems from the furore provoked by the most famous, and most successful, analysis of the church's ills, John Eachard's *The Grounds and Occasions of the Contempt of the Clergy and Religion Enquired Into. In a Letter Written to R.L.*. This anonymous tract appeared in the late summer of 1670 and had gone into eight editions by 1672. Although Eachard joked that his respondents composed their books by bundling up some old sermons with 'an hundred or two of names for me, and all the curses in the Bible', and that another eight or ten answers might appear if it was a warm spring, he was clearly taken aback at the storm he had aroused.[228] Eachard's offence was less what he said, however, than how he said it.

'You have reproved divers things worthy of reproof,' admitted Archdeacon Barnabas Oley, 'but in a manner worthy to be reproved: i.e. scepticé, sarcasticé, with wit satirical'.[229] The clergy had difficulty in separating the substance from the tone of this attack. The *Letter* 'will probably do us this unkindness, to make us more obnoxious and contemptible than yet we are,' wrote a churchman.

224. See Pepys, V, 27; II, 22, 199; III, 294; Wood, I, 257, 185; Samuel Butler, *Prose Observations*, ed. H. De Quehen (Oxford, 1979).
225. See Evelyn, III, 295; IV, 9, 197, 243, 560; *A Seasonable Treatise* (1678) [Wing S2246], sig. B.
226. Pepys, IX, 72–3. Pepys was habitually disdainful of the 'men in black'; see III, 127, 134–5.
227. Wren, *Articles of Enquiry* (1662), ch. 4, art. 32.
228. Eachard, *Mr Hobbs's State of Nature* (1672), Letter 1, pp. 12, 14.
229. Herbert, *Priest to the Temple*, p. ix.

The style and manner of it is enough to provoke willing readers to make us their table-talk, not in order to our amendment, but to our farther disgrace. There are many of our country neighbours, who seldom or never see any plays: but I fancy his *Letter* looks like such a piece of merriment sent among them into the country.

No dry-as-dust theological critique of the church could compete with Eachard's 'lofty and swaggering style' which turned 'divinity into drollery (the peccant humour of the times)'.[230] The great design of the *Letter* 'is to magnify your own way of talking (or wit as you call it)'. His critics could identify precisely the dangerous milieu from which this book sprang and to which it was addressed. 'As some things in your book were matter of chat in coffee-houses at Cambridge before it was printed; so now since it was printed, they be matter of pastime in taverns in London where wit, and wine, and profaneness, *sport themselves in their own deceivings*: and make the faults of God's ministers (for which, all that fear God, do grieve) the matter of unhallowed mirth.'[231]

The Restoration was an age with 'somewhat of mockery for its particular genius', a scoffing age in which nothing was sacrosanct, certainly not the clergy. 'This folly of laughing at [things worthwhile] continued worse and worse until 1679 and from thence', complained Wood; it was 'an age given to brutish pleasure and atheism'. While improving religious works lay unsold on the booksellers' stalls, only 'plays, poems, and drollery [were] in request'.[232] The scoffers spared neither virtue, nor religion, nor even God, for atheism was 'esteemed a piece of gallantry, and an effect of that extraordinary wit in which we pretend to excel our ancestors'. Where once only the fool had denied God, now the wit rushed to follow him.[233] The outward duties of religion were treated with a flippancy bordering on contempt: Charles II complained of the 'disease of sermons', but comforted himself with the thought that sleep 'is a great ease to those who are bound to hear them'.[234] And the clergy were treated worse. Trotting to the spa at Tunbridge Wells, the poet and rake John Wilmot, Earl of Rochester, came upon 'a tribe of curates, priests, canonical elves,/ Fit company for

230. *An Answer to a Letter of Enquiry* (1671), sigs a5–a6, pp. 22–3; *An Answer to Two Letters of T.B.* (1673), p. 64; D.I., *Hieragonisticon* (1672), p. 11.
231. *An Answer to Two Letters*, p. 35; Herbert, *Priest to the Temple*, sig, av.
232. John Fell, *The Character of the Last Daies* (Oxford, 1675), p. 5; Wood, I, 465; II, 56.
233. S.L., *Remarques on the Humours and Conversation of the Gallants of the Town* (2nd edn, 1673), p. 69; Goodman, *Serious Inquiry*, p. 225.
234. J.H. Wilson, *The Court Wits of the Restoration* (Princeton, 1948), p. 77.

none besides themselves,' who all complained of their diseases, 'but none had modesty enough t'complain/ Their want of learning, honesty, and brain,/ The general diseases of that train.'[235] Such witty attacks on the clergy are principally evidence of wit and nothing more; they were designed to amuse, as when Sir William Petty entertained John Evelyn to an imitation of preaching styles; or when John Aubrey, who was no friend of the clergy, railed against Bishop Fell:

> Could a man have imagined that such a ghostlike-ghostly father, so continual and assiduous in the prayers of the Church of England that made *Almighty and most merciful father* nauseous to his lodgers (viz. six times a day); that upheld the ark in the late times, that wore a countenance so pompous in its sanctity, I say could one have thought that this great practiser of piety, and walking common-prayer book, could have made such a breach in the morals and justice? ... who can pardon such a dry bone? a stalking, consecrated engine of hypocrisy etc.[236]

The joke was the point, and no opportunity for wit was to be passed up, whatever the damage or injustice, which was precisely what so scandalized the clergy about Eachard's droll little book.[237] It was bad enough that 'the great lights of deportment, and the refined and philosophical persons of the age' should mock the church and revile the clergy, but what the churchmen feared was that their example, mediated by works like Eachard's, would infect the entire nation. It was 'the strange progress of vices' to descend from 'persons somewhat above the vulgar ... as fast as the capacities of instruments can carry them down' to the young, uneducated and poor.[238]

There was no worse example than that set by Rochester and his dissipated cronies, the so-called 'court wits', who gave themselves over to fornication and drink, to drollery and random violence, heedless of either temporal or divine authority. Scandal magnified their sordid debauchery, embroidering events like the 'frolic' at the Cock Tavern, when a drunken and possibly naked Sir Charles

---

235. Rochester, *Tunbridge Wells*, lines 43–4, 49–51 (in *The Complete Poems*, ed. D.M. Vieth (New Haven and London, 1968), p. 75).

236. Evelyn, IV, 59; M. Hunter, *John Aubrey and the Realm of Learning* (1975), p. 35. Aubrey was writing to Anthony Wood whose *History of the University* had been censored by Fell.

237. *A Vindication of the Clergy*, sig. A8; cf. Sir Thomas Culpeper, *Essayes* (1671), p. 112.

238. Addison, *Modest Plea*, p. 4; Wood, II, 95–6, 400; S.L., *Remarques on Humours and Conversation of Gallants*, p. 87 (on the vices of swearing and deriding marriage).

Sedley may have 'abused' scripture and preached a 'mountebank sermon'.[239] Rochester clashed with the church over his *Satyr against Reason and Mankind*, which lampooned the Christian or clerical notion of 'Reason, by whose aspiring influence/ We take a flight beyond material sense,/ Dive into mysteries, then soaring pierce/ The flaming limits of the universe.' 'And 'tis this very reason I despise:/ This supernatural gift, that makes a mite/ Think he's the image of the infinite.' How much more preferable, suggests the poem, to be governed by a rational appetite, as are animals when they kill for food. The clerical response came in a sermon before the King on 24 February 1675, when Edward Stillingfleet alluded to the *Satyr*, and lamented that when the scoffers found themselves unable to defend their 'extravagant courses by reason, the only way left for them is to make satirical invectives against reason'. Rochester replied with the question. 'Is there a churchman who on God relies;/ Whose life, his faith and doctrine justifies?'[240] Here Rochester's nihilistic wit momentarily matches the widespread contemporary nostalgia for those imaginary 'pious times, e'r priest-craft did begin'.[241]

Many Restoration laymen yearned for a tranquil, practical religion, free of the divisive speculation and belligerent zeal which had carried the nation over the precipice into civil war; and they were suspicious of the domineering clerics who propagated such zeal as a means to ensure their own power. Among the more cynical it became a commonplace that the world contains mainly 'fools and knaves', and that the clerical knaves had usurped power 'over the folly and ignorance of the others' by turning religion into a mystery, trade or craft.[242] Francis Osborne warned that the curious questions of school divinity had been 'devised to puzzle the laity, and render the clergy no less necessary than honourable'.[243] All that the wits sought was the freedom to go their own sweet way. 'I have ever enjoyed a liberty of opinion in matters of religion,' announced Sir George Etherege. ''Tis indifferent to me whether there be an other

---

239. Pepys, IV, 209; also see IX, 335–6, 435–6; Wood, I, 476; II, 335; Evelyn, III, 365; Josselin, p. 501; Wilson, *Court Wits*, pp. 40–2 and *passim*.

240. See K.F. Paulson, 'The Reverend Edward Stillingfleet and the "Epilogue" to Rochester's *A Satyr against Reason and Mankind*', *Philological Quarterly*, 50 (1971).

241. Dryden, *Absalom and Achitophel*, line 1 (in *Poems and Fables*, ed. J. Kinsley (Oxford, 1958), p. 190)

242. *The Genuine Works of His Grace George Villiers, Duke of Buckingham* (Edinburgh, 1754), p. 407; cf. [Albert Warren], *An Apology for the Discourse of Human Reason* (1680), p. 127.

243. Osborne, *Advice*, I, 153–4; cf. *The Petty–Southwell Correspondence 1676–1687*, ed. Marquis of Lansdowne (1828), pp. 186–7.

in the world who thinks as I do. This makes me have no temptation to talk of the business, but quietly following the light within me, I leave that to them that are born with the ambition of becoming prophets or legislators.'[244] The problem was that the ambitious divines would not leave men alone, and so they had to be brought down a peg, to be humbled by superior wit and reason. "Tis not amiss to see an humble clergy,' opined Etherege, 'they are more like the primitive time'; while Dryden's *Religio laici* (1682) was greeted as a resounding blow for freedom from 'the holy cheat' and the tyranny of the priest.[245] The crew of poets, rationalists, rakes and dissidents who gathered beneath the banner of opposition to 'priestcraft' in the 1670s, and again in the mid-1680s, had diverse motives, but most were concerned with the defence of both political and intellectual freedoms.

Political resentment of the narrow religious settlement of 1662 and revulsion at the subsequent persecution of peaceable Dissenters fuelled criticism of the church, the clergy and, above all, the bishops. Sancroft received a report in 1675 that the Norfolk MPs courted the Nonconformists and promoted comprehension, while aspersing 'many of our worthy clergymen with the opprobrious terms of drunken clergymen and high Church of England men'.[246] Meanwhile, Shaftesbury was denouncing the 'high episcopal men and cavaliers', and Buckingham was abusing the bishops in the House of Lords. Buckingham told the peers that a man's safety ought to depend upon his adherence to the laws, not 'upon his being transported with zeal for every opinion that is held by those who have power in the church then in fashion', and he begged their favour for a bill of indulgence for all Protestant Dissenters.[247] From the mid-1670s, the Nonconformist rhetoric of persecution became a prominent part of the political opposition's case. Opposition and Whig propaganda took up the theme of proud prelates and censorious clerics with gusto – Shaftesbury's *Letter from a Person of Quality* was not simply a denunciation of Danby and arbitrary government, it was a full-scale exposé of the churchmen's deep-laid plot to gain all political power.[248] And the intransigence and arrogance of the

---

244. *Letters of Sir George Etherege*, ed. F. Bracher (Berkeley, 1974), p. 168.
245. Dryden, *Religio laici*, lines 10–11, (in *Poems*, p. 282); Atkins, *Faith of Dryden*, pp. 5–7; cf. Rochester, *Satyr*, line 177; A. Powell, *John Aubrey and his Friends* (1963 edn), p. 147.
246. MS Tanner 42, fo. 148.
247. Buckingham, *Works*, p. 439.
248. See T. Harris, *London Crowds in the Reign of Charles II* (Cambridge, 1987), pp. 81–2, 94; M. Goldie, 'Danby, the Bishops and the Whigs', in *The Politics of Religion in Restoration England*, ed. T. Harris, P. Seaward and M. Goldie (Oxford, 1990), p. 83.

Anglican clergy lent substance to the opposition's interpretation. The intemperate violence of some Anglican apologetic against Dissent, of Simon Patrick's *Friendly Debate*, Parker's *Ecclesiastical Polity*, or the replies to Croft's *Naked Truth*, played into the hands of adversaries like Marvell: 'these are the divines in mode, who, by their dignities and preferments plumped up beyond human proportions, do whether for their pride or ignorance, neither understand themselves, nor others, (men of nonsense) much less do they understand to speak of God, which ought to be their study, with any tolerable decorum.'[249] The bishops' association with Danby in the 1670s, and the church's subsequent stance during the Exclusion crisis, only confirmed the opposition's account of the growth of 'popery and arbitrary government' in England. In May 1679 Bishop Morley lamented the 'evil eye' with which the bishops and all their actions were now viewed; and at some of the parliamentary elections of these years, the 'blackcoats', or 'Baal's priests', were jeered and jostled, while Whigs raised their glasses to the toast of 'confusion to the bishops'.[250]

In the eyes of their adversaries, the churchmen were not only a danger to the nation's political liberties, they were a threat to her intellectual liberty. The clergy sought to 'impose' on men's understandings, to restore the 'former times, when the men in black had made learning such a sin in the laity that for fear of offending they made a conscience of being able to read'. A despotic and obscurantist clergy could hold the laity in tutelage by stifling intellectual freedom and by the 'preclusion of enquiry'.[251] Much was made of the threat posed to independent thinkers by heresy charges: Aubrey believed that there was a parliamentary move to have Hobbes burnt for his ideas; and Marvell claimed that 'some of our ruling clergy, who yet would be content to be accounted good protestants, are so loath to part with any hank they have got, at what time soever over the poor laity, or what other reason, that the writ *de haeretico comburendo*, though desired to be abolished, is still kept in force to this day'.[252] More was made of the church's control of the press. Under the 1662 Licensing Act, the church and universities were legally obliged to license publications on 'divinity, physic, philosophy or whatsoever other science or art'. Both Nonconformist and Catholic authors wailed that licensing denied them a right of reply; 'by this

---

249.   Andrew Marvell, *Mr Smirke, or the Divine in Mode* (1676), p. 33.
250.   MS Tanner 38, fo. 20; Goldie, 'Danby, Bishops and Whigs', pp. 97–9.
251.   Halifax, *Complete Works*, p. 73; Warren, *Apology for Discourse of Humane Reason*, p. 47; cf. Miles Barne, *A Sermon Preached before the King* (1675), pp. 21–2; Hunter, *Science and Society*, p. 172.
252.   Powell, *Aubrey*, p. 266; Marvell, *Mr Smirke*, p. 23.

means they license or not license what they list,' grumbled the Dissenters, 'books of Arminians and Socinians can be licensed, but orthodox books cannot pass'. Charles Blount, the deist, condemned censorship as 'an old relic of Popery' that 'reflects upon our church and clergy, of whose labours we should hope better, and of the proficiency which their flock reaps by them; than after all this light of the Gospel, all this continual preaching, they should be still frequented with such an unprincipled, unedified and laic rabble, as that the whiff of every new pamphlet should stagger them out of their catechism and Christian walking'.[253]

These opponents protested too much. True, some churchmen believed that the free debate of ideas could subvert religion and the status quo. A few took delight in hunting down or 'preventing' dissident publications; and the University of Oxford did make the dramatic gesture of burning books in 1683.[254] But this was an example of the classic pattern of limited repression provoking opposition which it could not silence; the church suffered by being part of a regime that looked more repressive than it was. The bishops' refusal to permit a reprinting of *Leviathan* merely had the effect of pushing up the price of second-hand copies.[255] The writ *de haeretico comburendo* was quietly repealed in 1677. The Licensing Act expired in May 1679, and was not re-established until 1685. And it had never ensured pre-publication censorship anyway: few works of the period carry the imprimatur of a licensing chaplain – it was said that booksellers disliked the imprimatur because it was a sure sign of a dull and slow-selling book. Repression was mainly after the event and involved the seizure of materials, machinery and people; its motives were often political and frequently commercial, but rarely hierocratic.[256] The Restoration church did not take the repression of dissident ideas seriously because, as the next chapter will show, she did not take the ideas seriously.

253. *RB*, III, 41, 86–7, 142; Hugh Cressy, *Fanaticism fanatically Imputed* (1672), preface; MS Carte 77, fo. 616; T. Crist, 'Government Control of the Press after the Expiration of the Printing Act in 1679', *Publishing History*, 5 (1979); Blount, *A Just Vindication of Learning* (1679) quoted by Keeble, *Literary Culture*, p. 97.
254. E. Carpenter, *The Protestant Bishop – Being the Life to Henry Compton* (1956), p. 67; Fawkett, *Account of Seignior*, p. 29; for the book burning, see p. 261 below.
255. Pepys, IX, 298.
256. See Keeble, *Literary Culture*, pp. 82–175; Crist, 'Government Control of Press'; A.B. Worden, 'Literature and Political Censorship in Early Modern England', in *Too Mighty to be Free* (Zutphen, 1988); D. McKenzie, 'Bibliography and History in Seventeenth-century England', unpublished Lyell Lectures, delivered in the University of Oxford, Trinity Term 1988.

What the Restoration churchmen took very seriously was their own reputation. Ever mindful that their authority depended upon their credit, the churchmen were determined to rebuke the wits, prevent the spread of 'scoffing', and rebut the slanderous misrepresentation of their own calling as 'priestcraft'.[257] This was no easy undertaking, as they found when responding to John Eachard. Some of the Anglican replies flailed wildly at a range of targets; the *Hieragonisticon*, for instance, accused Eachard of being an atheist, 'a Bartholomew-gentleman' and 'some *à la mode* spark'.[258] Others saw why Eachard had adopted his witty style – 'sportiveness and drollery is so much the humour of the times, that if you had written after another fashion, some hundred of copies might have lain upon the bookseller's hands' – but then perversely chose to overlook his drollery and answer his points seriously.[259] The churchmen could not respond in kind for they abhorred 'this gibing, jingling knack called wit'. They detested satire, 'the easiest kind of wit. Almost any degree of it will serve to abuse and find fault'; and they renounced the use of 'sharpness' and 'satire' in their own ministry, since 'satirical virulency may vex men sorely, but it hardly ever soundly converts them.'[260] Yet even if principle had been no obstacle, the clergy might still have failed to match their witty adversaries, for the sad truth was that few of them had any facility for wit. Their education and vocation stifled the necessary cynicism, irreverence and lightness of touch. Eachard, who refused to be 'mathematically grave and serious' or to find a rope of onions 'to carry on the work of crying' over the clergy, was clearly atuned to popular taste.[261] Anglican attempts to play Marvell or Rochester at their own game were rarely successful and often embarrassing.[262] Comparing replies to Dryden's *Hind and Panther*, Etherege claimed to be able to distinguish a verse satire 'by an angry clergymen' from one 'writ by a gentleman who has dipped his hands in satire e're

---

257. Roger Hayward, *A Sermon Preached before the King* (1676), p. 29; Thomas Sprat, *A Sermon Preached before the King* (1677), pp. 29, 31; cf. pp. 28–30 and T.A., *Religio clerici* (?2nd edn, 1681), pp. 82–7.
258. D.I., *Hieragonisticon*, p. 65.
259. W.S., *Answer to a Letter of Enquiry*, pp. 79, 3.
260. Rochester, *Satyr*, lines 49, 54; Tillotson, I, 91; MS Eng Letters E 29, fo. 178. Also see D. Trotter, 'Wanton Expressions', in *Spirit of Wit*, ed. J. Treglown (Oxford, 1982).
261. Eachard, *Some Observations* (1671), pp. 107–8, 103; idem, *Mr Hobbs's*, Letter 5, p. 114. In his own defence Eachard cited the 'pleasant' style of Patrick's *Friendly Debate* and Parker's *Ecclesiastical Politie*; these were exceptional works for clergymen and were aimed at Dissent.
262. See Marvell, *Mr Smirke*, p. 33; Wilson, *Court Wits*, pp. 140–1.

now'.[263] Satire, wit and drollery were a language from which the clergy were largely excluded.

On the other hand, the clergy were not entirely helpless before the new mores of Restoration England. Their most spectacular coup in the war against wit was the reclamation of the Earl of Rochester. In October 1679, a failing Rochester, exhausted by hard living, venereal disease and by its treatments, began to discuss religion and morality with Gilbert Burnet. That this was a soul worth winning was beyond doubt. The beau monde looked on with bated breath: on 25 June 1680, Rochester wrote from Woodstock to Burnet detailing his repentance, and remarking incidentally, 'I begin to value churchmen above all men in the world'; by 7 July Sir Thomas Browne in distant Norwich had seen a copy of this letter.[264] On 25 July Rochester died, and Burnet wrote, 'he was the greatest penitent I ever saw, and died a sincere Christian, but of this I shall say no more because he gave me in charge to publish an account how he died'.[265] Encouraged by Halifax, Burnet rolled up his sleeves and produced his account of Rochester's dreadful life and edifying death, knowing that while some would resent the mention of Rochester's impious maxims, 'others will censure it because it comes from one of my profession, too many supposing us to be induced, to frame such discourses for carrying on what they are pleased to call *our trade*.' But then the charge of priestcraft was one of Burnet's targets. Rochester, according to Burnet, was so possessed of the 'general conceit' that fools and knaves had foisted belief in the 'extraordinary things' of revealed religion on the world, that he had never examined the historical evidence for the truth of Christianity. What price now the pose of intellectual scepticism maintained by so many of Rochester's emulators? Burnet's artful account repeatedly uses Rochester's own vices to undermine his objections to religion. Rochester is reported as arguing that the mysteries of religion 'made way for all the jugglings of priests' and then offering as an example of such priestcraft the restriction of monogamy and the prohibition of divorce. 'I was sure,' confided Burnet, 'if his mind were once cleared of these disorders, and cured of those distempers, which vice brought on it, so great an understanding would soon see through all these flights of wit that do feed atheism and irreligion.'[266]

---

263. Etherege, *Letters*, pp. 137–8.
264. Gilbert Burnet, *Some Passages of the Life and Death of the Right Honourable John, Earl of Rochester* (1680), sig. A5.
265. 'Some Unpublished Letters of Burnet', ed. H.C. Foxcroft (Camden Society, 11, 1907), p. 41.
266. Burnet, *Some Passages*, sig. A3v, pp. 78, 100–1, 126–7.

Plainly, the church was learning how to manipulate the image of the 'wit', and how to exploit the figure of the 'atheist', in order to rule the conforming, god-fearing laity. And at the same time, the wits and rakes were on the retreat. The harder school of politics after 1678 was no place for these ironists; and the 1680s ushered in a new world, a world safer for monarchy, Anglicanism, and the clergy. Vice continued, but not the pseudo-intellectual posturing which had sought to justify it, and the Church of England felt more confident in dealing with vice among the leaders of society. One summer evening in 1682 two drunken sons of Lord Wharton vandalized the church at Barrington, Somerset, cutting the bell-ropes and tearing the church's bible. When, allegedly stricken with remorse, they submitted themselves to Bishop Frampton of Gloucester, he grasped the opportunity to make an example of them so far as was 'prudent, practicable and sufficient'. They appeared on the appointed day 'each of them confessing, lamenting, and asking pardon, first in private, afterwards in public, before three of the clergy and three of the laity. By way of commutation for their penance, they laid down fifty guineas, ten of which I returned to them, the forty I gave in their presence towards the repairs of Stow Church.' As Frampton reported to the archbishop, 'they assured me, that it was neither atheism, popery, nor fanaticism that led them to it, but mere drunkenness of which they said they are ashamed'.[267]

How are we finally to assess the authority of the church and her clergy in Restoration England? It has become fashionable to suggest that the Restoration saw the 'triumph of the laity' or the 'end of the clerical world', but such sweeping generalizations do not do justice to the complexity of the period. We should not assume that the gallants of London reflect a single, prevailing spirit of the age, nor confuse metropolitan with village culture, nor indeed take on trust all we hear from the critics of priestcraft or the clerical victims of contempt. Indeed, it is the lack of religious unanimity which most forcibly strikes the observer of Restoration England; this was a society which enjoyed a plural, competitive, religious culture.

Religious publishing is just one instance of this diversity and competition, for despite all the hand-wringing over national frivolity, this was still a booming business. While drollery and science, plays and poetry, the writings of Hobbes and translations of Descartes and Spinoza were in vogue, they did not crowd out works by clerical authors or on religious subjects. 'Every book-seller's stall groans

---

267. MS Tanner 35, fos 73, 111, 168, 172, 178; cf. G.F.T. Jones, *Saw-Pit Wharton* (Sydney, 1967), p. 264.

under the burden of sermons, sermons,' observed one contemporary, 'sermons as common (and as commonly cried about the streets) as ballads'.[268] In November 1678 the whole impression of 4,000 copies of a sermon preached by Stillingfleet on the Plot was sold out in a day.[269] Bookseller publishers, such as Walter Kettilby, Brabazon Aylmer, Richard Royston, Thomas Basset and Benjamin Tooke, knew the value of their clerical authors. In 1681 Aylmer paid £470 for the manuscript of Isaac Barrow's sermons and Tillotson's manuscript sermons were bought for £2,500 after his death. In his will, Royston left money for mourning rings to 'my worthy authors', including John and Simon Patrick, John Goodman, Ralph Cudworth and William Cave, all Anglican clergymen.[270] The most popular, in the sense of the most widely distributed, books of the age were the manuals of practical devotion and piety, exemplified by *The Whole Duty of Man*, which achieved a saturation of the market equal to that of modern bestsellers. Richard Baxter's *Saints Everlasting Rest* went through twelve editions between 1650 and 1688, and John Rawlett's *Christian Monitor* went through nineteen. Clearly, the religious co-existed with the secular; the same people who read sermons and edifying tracts also bought scurrilous satires and profane plays.[271] It also seems likely that the market was expanding to accommodate the denominational publishing of the new sects such as the Baptists and Quakers.

In the teeming city or the bustling towns, where central parishes were often too small and suburban parishes too large to serve as effective religious communities, the Church of England struggled to compete with the attractions of her myriad rivals. Among these 'competitors' were counted not only other Christian denominations and the fledgling polite culture of the urban middle classes, but profane pastimes, worldliness and, worst of all, apathy; the church-men had constantly to disabuse the laity of the notion that con-formity to the religion of the land was no more than 'going to church once a month'.[272] The churchmen also strove to capture the loyalty of the upper classes before they could be corrupted by the manners of the age and town. The church's dignitaries assiduously courted

268. Edmund Hickeringill, *The Horrid Sin of Man-Catching* (1680), epistle.
269. C.J. Sommerville, *Popular Religion in Restoration England* (Gainesville, 1977), p. 10.
270. P.H. Osmond, *Isaac Barrow* (1944), p. 147; I. Simon (ed.), *Three Restoration Divines* (Paris, 1976), II, 353; G. Pollard, 'The English Market for Printed Books', *Publishing History*, 4 (1978), 26. Also see Sommerville, *Popular Religion*; M. Spufford, *Small Books and Pleasant Histories* (Cambridge 1981), ch. 8.
271. See, for instance, Pepys's collections, discussed in Spufford, *Small Books and Pleasant Histories*.
272. *The Works of Thomas Otway*, ed. J.C. Ghosh (Oxford, 1932), II, 301.

the gentry and aristocracy, writing letters of spiritual and practical advice, acting for them in marriage negotiations and other confidential business, visiting them at their country seats, and arranging for the education of their children. The close relations that Bishop Fell, for example, enjoyed with several leading families attest to the success of the clergy's strategy.[273]

Humbler souls lived out their lives within narrower horizons, and in communities where the ideal of unanimity, although challenged and occasionally compromised, retained more appeal. In a rural parish where all the parishioners were tenants of a single resident lord and in the care of a diligent, resident, conformable but not unrealistically rigid parson, Christian unanimity was attainable – as the example of Brightwell Baldwin perhaps shows. But subtract any of these ingredients, or add a disruptive schoolmaster, a tradition of Dissent, or a minister of doubtful orthodoxy or partial conformity, and a recipe for parochial strife and religious apathy had been created.[274] The clergyman may well have been the single most important factor in the creation of Christian unanimity – certainly the absence of a minister told. The visitation of the archdeaconry of Ely in 1685 pronounced Oakington 'the most scandalous parish and worst in the diocese for the people are most vile'. Unanimity, order and authority were in ruins: 'the church lies in great neglect like a barn or dovehouse. The King's arms and the ten commandments [are] taken down'; the schoolmaster was a 'fanatic', several parishioners were excommunicate, and there were three or four Quaker families. A root cause of this situation was the non-residence of Mr Palmer, the vicar; 'a stranger comes every Lord's day so there can be no catechizing or holy days'.[275] The parlous condition of Bucknell, Oxfordshire, in the 1670s, under its non-resident, pluralist parson, underlines the minister's importance in creating and maintaining the Christian unanimity of the parish. The parson hired a young man under the age of twenty-four 'who is also chaplain at the hall of St Edmund in Oxford, and is resident there all the week and comes to Bucknell on Saturday night or the Lord's day and returns the same day often or on Monday morning'. According to the churchwardens, this arrangement gave rise to a series of ills: the services on holy days and fasts were not performed; and parish-

---

273. See Warwick County Record Office, CR 136 (Fell to Newdigate); BL, MS Add. 11046 (letters from Fell to John, second Lord Scudamore, 1672).

274. See Spufford, *Contrasting Communities*, ch. 12.

275. *Notes of the Episcopal Visitation of the Archdeaconry of Ely in 1685*, ed. H. Bradshaw (Cambridge Antiquarian Society Communications, 3, Cambridge 1879), pp. 356–7.

ioners were inconvenienced by being called to church at 11 or 12 o'clock, their 'dinner time', or for evening prayer 'before we or our servants had dined'.

> By reason of all which the younger sort are not instructed in the principles of religion nor the older sort put in mind of their duty, nor the sick visited, nor the poor relieved or set on work, nor vagrants punished or passed according to law (no minister being resident to join with the churchwardens etc. in making such passes), the better sort discouraged, the profaner sort encouraged by such evil examples, and occasions many to go to other churches.[276]

The ideal of unanimity was perhaps most long-lived among the clergy themselves. It was, after all, the goal at which their labours were aimed, and it played an important point in justifying their efforts, in creating their sense of corporate identity through common endeavour. The churchmen thought of themselves as beleaguered by the forces of evil; they were, in the words of one admirer, 'now exposed as the ancient Christians were, amongst the beasts in the amphitheatres, without any guard but their own generous courage and innocence'.[277] But the churchmen took courage from their leaders; Thomas Fiddes, rector of Brightwell Baldwin, besought Heaven that Archbishop Sancroft might be 'a successful pilot at the helm of that well-built ship our Anglican-church now threatened by the surges of schism, sacrilege and simony'. The clergy of Oxford diocese were told by their bishop that 'as bad as times are, they are not worse than they were at the first planting of the gospel. . . . Events are in the hands of God, but duty is in ours'.[278] The churchmen seemed to draw strength from the contempt in which they were held. It was, as countless visitation sermons asserted, almost their duty to be hated; we are 'persons who have an office devolved upon us to tell men of their faults, to awaken a thing called conscience, which the luxury and affected liberty of the age hath no mind to hear'.[279] Ministers are not 'wits' to please men by telling them what they want to hear; good ministers 'are salt, their sermons are full of acrimony, they make men's wounds smart'.

> To cry down the ways of sin, which corrupt nature cries up; and to promote righteousness, holiness and sobriety, and all the

---

276. MS Rawlinson D 384, fo. 19.
277. A.M., *Plain-Dealing* (1675), p. 76.
278. Tanner MSS 40, fo. 157; 31, fo. 157.
279. Edward Wetenhall, *Miserere cleri* (1668), p. 16; also see Joshua Bonhome, *A New Constellation* (1675), p. 20.

virtues which men's lusts have such an antipathy against must needs prove an ungratefull work.[280]

It was this profound sense of their own office which inspired the clergy of the Restoration Church of England to develop a coherent and powerful diagnosis of the nation's spiritual and moral malaise.

280. Thomas Hodges, *The Necessity, Dignity and Duty of Gospel Ministers* (1685), p. 19; Thomas Lodington, *The Honour of the Clergy Vindicated* (1674), p. 51.

Chapter 5

The Causes of the Decay of Christian Piety

Anglican churchmen were obsessed with the decay of Christian piety in Restoration England; they devoted much of their time, and thousands of their sermons and tracts, to the pathology of national piety. So widespread was this preoccupation that it can be confidently identified as one of the fundamental components of Restoration Anglicanism. Two points should be borne in mind, however: this preoccupation was not an intellectual conviction or opinion, but rather a cast of mind or a moral stance; and, precisely because it was such a deep-seated attitude, this outlook did far more than inform the clergy's estimation of national piety and morality, it coloured their view of the world and, above all, of their opponents. Although this aspect of the churchmen's mentality will be discussed at length in this chapter, some preliminary remarks on its motives and its effects may be of help here.

The Restoration churchmen were on the defensive; they were keenly aware that their 'holy function is esteemed nowadays vile and contemptible' by the laity, and so whenever they could, they turned the tables on their lay adversaries.[1] When the deficiencies of the clergy were raised, the churchmen countered that 'there is nothing more frequent, than for the laity to patronize their sins upon the example of others, and to fortify their profaneness from the infirmities of their teachers ... a minister's life is bad, therefore his doctrine is false. O this is an harsh *non sequitur*.'[2] When the church was criticized, the clergy began to talk loudly of 'false friends', and sought to stiffen their allies' spines by referring to the enemies on all sides: the fox and the wolf who first try 'to make the silly sheep hate their shepherds'; and the Dissenter who taught that it was 'the most

---

1. Malachi Conant, *Urim and Thummim* (Oxford, 1669), p. 6.
2. Samuel Gardner, *A Sermon Preached at the Visitation* (1672), p. 29.

certain sign of saintship and grace' to hate and despise a minister.[3]
John Eachard was asked why he did not criticize the Nonconformists, the atheists, the profane? 'Could you not have jerked the laity a
little, and told them of their faults?'[4] The clergy were quick to
conclude that if they and their church were under attack, then so too
was the authority of religion; 'who is so blind as not to see that
irreverence and disrespect for the Lord's clergy, hath been accompanied with a manifest decay of piety, and a notorious contempt of
the most essential parts of religion?'[5]

What better method of defence than to take the fight into the
enemy's camp? The Restoration churchmen did not shrink from
their mission to rebuke the troublers of Israel and chastise sinners in
the name of God. 'If the whole nation be grown sermon-proof, sitteth
still and is at rest, settled on the lees, profane, atheistical; should not
we be false prophets to cry nothing but peace?' the Restoration
clergy asked themselves. 'Certainly we must now cry with Isaiah,
Woe to a sinful nation. When men's lives proclaim wars against
God, we must not denounce God's judgements against them.'[6] Since
the seventeenth-century English were 'a people whom God hath
exercized with wondrous judgements and deliverances', it fell to the
Anglican Jeremiahs to expound 'the mysterious texts of God's holy
providence'.[7] There were countless preaching opportunities, both
on extraordinary days of humiliation and thanksgiving and in the
course of the church's calendar, to spread the message of repentance
and reform. These clerical messengers identified themselves with
their message and with its divine source, to the point where those
who remained deaf to the clergy were presumed to be deaf to the
Lord.

This rhetoric of complaint and exhortation bound together
Anglican clergymen who otherwise had little in common; and it
enunciated and reinforced their instinctive belief that bad opinions
are the result of a bad life. It followed, all too obviously, that the bad
opinions of their opponents did not merit serious consideration.
Time and time again, the clergy's preaching and writing betrays
their assumption that, at bottom, all of the church's enemies, atheists, Dissenters and papists, were associated in sin. To put it bluntly,

---

3. A. M., *Plain-Dealing* (1675), p. 78; *A Representation of the State of Christianity* (1674), p. 13.
4. W. S., *An Answer to a Letter of Enquiry* (1671), p. 6.
5. Miles Barne, *A Sermon Preached before the King* (1675), p. 40.
6. Gardner, *Sermon Preached at Visitation*, p. 10.
7. John Scott, *A Sermon Preached . . . 2 September 1686* (1686), p. 18; G. D'Oyly, *The Life of William Sancroft* (1821), II, 373.

the Restoration churchmen regarded their opponents and critics as morally deficient. Such a blanket denunciation left little ground for compromise or tolerance. It also suggested that the church was edging ever closer to a dangerous anti-intellectualism; the clergy's condescending attitude towards the laity and their intellectual pretensions was out of place in a critical, rationalist era like the Restoration. On the other hand, few of the clergy's adversaries were in church to hear these denunciations or can have bothered to read them, so perhaps they were designed for another, less hostile, audience. It is arguable that the clergy's rhetoric was designed less to convince their enemies than to edify their own congregations by presenting them with the reverse image of true religion. In harping on sin, vice and error, the churchmen revealed not only their anxiety about national profligacy, but also their positive aspirations for the Church of England.

'A Controversy with the Land'

Are our peers and nobles renowned for their advancement and protection of true honour and vertue, as their great ancestors have been? Sit down, and think upon it. The reverend sages of the law, are their minds set upon righteousness? And do they judge the thing that is right with courage and integrity? Sit down and think upon it. The portion and tribe of God, the holy clergy, do they remember or can they forget, how they were lately trodden down, reviled, and cast out of all they had for twenty years? And doth it stir us up to be burning and shining lights more than ever? And to double our diligence now in prayer, in preaching, and administring the holy sacraments? Sit down and think upon it. For the gentry, are they not addicted to waste and riot; Do they not crowd themselves into our enlarged suburbs, where they have no calling, but to emulate one another in excess of feminine pride, and rude debauchery? Sit down and think upon it. As for what concerns the great city, not to rub it with salt and satyrs, is it not as palpable as God's light, that it did poison the whole land with rebellion, and still infects it with gaudiness, gluttony, whoredoms, and falsehoods? Sit down and think upon it. Do the country villages deserve the old commendations of simplicity and innocency? But how ignorant are they in the knowledge of salvation? How unthankful to God in all seasons? How hath Satan bewitched them of late years into dissolute lives, and drunkenness? Sit down and think upon it.

This was how, in 1665, John Hacket sought to warn his fellow countrymen of the 'ocean of ungodliness breaking in upon us'.[8] At a visitation in Essex that spring, Ralph Josselin found 'the countenances of many ministers sad to eye, Lord heal our manners, sermon was pressing to labour and holiness'.[9] The high hopes which had accompanied the Restoration lay in ruins, and the churchmen were convinced that the nation had given itself over to wantonness and impiety, that a 'flood of atheism, prophaneness and irreligion' was sweeping the realm; 'the whole land is overwhelmed with impiety and licentiousness, all manner of debauchery and profaneness; drunkenness, lying, swearing, oppression, etc.' The majority of the nation 'openly commit the most horrid sins; monstrously swearing, as if they would dare God to his face, scoffing at the practice of piety, making no scruple of deceiving, spending their times in drinking, prodigally wasting their estates by luxury and the like'.[10] The nation's 'crying sins' were sacrilege and simony, perjury and profanity, 'and impatience of the cross, schism, and faction, and an itch after changes'.[11] 'We live in an age, when there is an universal complaint (and God knows, there is too much reason for it) of an universal corruption of good manners.'[12] In particular, drunkenness – 'the abuse of good wine and the use of bad women' – was 'a vice strangely epidemical' which stood out as 'a sad indication of national impiety'.[13] Predictably, this impious nation either entirely neglected religious duties and the Lord's Day or grudgingly gave them only half their attention; 'how do they tacitly chide the slow-paced sands in the preacher's glass, and grow angry with him if he exceeds his hour, when the time spent on sports, and pleasures, and business of the world is thought too swift of foot? An hour spent at a sermon, yea and upon God's day too, is thought too long, when a play of three or four hours is done too soon. If this is not an evidence of an atheistical and worldly spirit I know not what is.'[14] The debauched and the worldly were joined in the neglect of religion by the 'scoffers'

8. John Hacket, *A Century of Sermons* (1675), p. 853.
9. Josselin, p. 517.
10. Charles Gibbes, *XXXI Sermons* (1677), pp. 148–9, also see pp. 52–5, 272–4, 415–20; Richard West, *The Profitableness of Piety* (1671), p. 7; South, I, 287; William Outram, *Twenty Sermons* (1682), pp. 319–25; Benjamin Calamy, *Sermons* (1687), sermon 8.
11. Thomas Pierce, *A Collection of Sermons upon Several Occasions* (Oxford, 1671), p. 156.
12. Thomas Sprat, *A Sermon preached at the Anniversary Meeting of the Sons of the Clergy* (1678), p. 28.
13. MS Eng Th E 168; William Smythies, *The Norfolk Feast* (1671), p. 31; *WAWD*, I, 293 (*The Causes of the Decay of Christian Piety* (1667))
14. Matthew Bryan, *A Perswasive to the Stricter Observations of the Lords Day* (1686), p. 20.

– the would-be intellectuals who posed as sceptics and infidels – and in these, the last days, they all walked after their own lusts.[15] On every side the waters of irreligion were rising. Profanity 'is an epidemical distemper that has infected all sorts of men, as well knowing as ignorant, orthodox as schismatical'.[16] 'The enormities that now abound, notwithstanding the good laws of God and man, bespeak an *unruly* age', lamented one divine. And an unruly age gave 'just cause to fear, that God hath a controversy with the land, the issue whereof may be some fearful judgment'.[17]

Of course, all clergymen think that they live in an unruly, disordered age. Their ministry is to be a remembrancer of the Lord, to discover to the people their spiritual state and dangers. Sweet words become a clergyman: 'the ministers are spiritual surgeons, and they must dress the wound faithfully with a tender hand. The preacher must study acceptable words and seasonable words.' But 'if the songs of Sion cannot mollify, the thunders of Mount Sinai must terrify'.[18] The jeremiad, declaimed from the pulpit with a stern voice and accusing eye, was a clerical stock in trade. Similarly, the tract of moral complaint, exemplified in the Restoration by the works of Richard Allestree, and especially his *The Causes of the Decay of Christian Piety* (1667), was a well established literary genre, of which many earlier examples, such as Lewis Bayly's *The Practice of Piety*, were still read in Restoration England. Nevertheless, as any reader of Evelyn's diary will agree, there was a distinctive quality about the Restoration clergy's denunciation of the national malaise.[19] Rarely before had the church's rhetoric of moral reform been inflected with such urgency; rarely had it conveyed such a strong sense of the imminent dissolution of society and nation; and rarely had it been so persistently, closely and uniformly tied down to the dispensations of divine providence, to the moral message of history. But then, never before had history, in the shape of rebellion, civil war, regicide and usurpation, pointed so clearly to the urgent need for national reformation.

Intestine war, civil war, was in itself a chastisement, an obvious punishment sent from on high to correct a backsliding nation; but 'war makes a nation more wicked', it destroys harmony and discipline, and unleashes malice and contention, error and vice.[20] Dur-

15. II Peter iii. 3. See John Fell, *The Character of the Last Daies* (Oxford, 1675).
16. William Saywell, *A Serious Inquiry into the Means of an Happy Union* (1681), p. 32.
17. Richard Allen, *Insulae fortunatae* (1675), epistle dedicatory.
18. MS Eng Th D 59, fos 15–16; Gardner, *Sermon Preached at Visitation*, pp. 10–11; also see Thomas Hodges, *The Necessity, Dignity and Duty of Gospel Ministers* (1685), p. 19.
19. See Evelyn, III, 275, 295, 311–12, 415–16, 418; IV, 330.
20. Fuller, I, 243.

ing the Interregnum, 'Almighty God had a controversy with this nation, for our ingratitude, schism, sedition, and rebellion; which he severely punished by sheathing that sword in our own bowels, that was so causelessly, and unlawfully, drawn against his anointed; and making us captives in our own land; yea we were slaves, to the worst of conquerors, even our lusts.'[21] For the churchmen, nothing confirmed this quarrel with God and national captivity to sin better than the execution of Charles I. As Robert Brown preached in 1649, 'calamity like the flood is now lifted up above our earth, and hath almost covered the highest hills of our temporal felicity; could our sorrow swell as high as that, the sense of our present, and impending miseries would drown us; if we search into the causes of them, we shall find those in our selves, (*our sins*)'. As Josiah was sacrificed for the sins of Judah, even as Christ atoned for the sins of mankind, so had Charles been martyred for his people: 'the sins of every one of us hath added force unto this great stroke and wound given unto these kingdoms in His Majesty's death.'[22] And still the heavy judgments continued, still 'the bloody vials of his fiercest wrath are daily poured down upon us'.[23] 'God now begins to cut England short, short in men, short in meat, short in money, short in wealth, so that it is to be feared that Great Britain will be a little Britain, and remain great only in her sins and sufferings,' observed Thomas Fuller in the mid-1650s.

> And is this a time for men to lengthen themselves, when God doth shorten them! Is this a time for people to affect fond fashions, when it is to be feared that we shall all be brought into the same fashion of ruin and desolation? A strange people! Who can dance at so doleful music, as the passing bell of a church and commonwealth? Take heed, atheism knocks at the door of the hearts of all men, and where luxury is the porter it will be let in. Let not the multiplicity of so many religions as are now on foot, make you careless to have any, but careful to have the best.[24]

The 'licentious libertines, Independent usurpers, and profane atheists' who stalked Interregnum England were simply the agents by which God punished the English.[25] The world is the theatre of God's

---

21. Matthew Griffith, *The King's Life-Guard* (1665), sig. A4.
22. [Robert Brown], *Subjects Sorrow* (1649), p. 1; Henry Leslie, *The Martyrdome of King Charles . . . preached at Breda on 3/13 June 1649* (The Hague and London, 1649), pp. 21–2.
23. Thomas Fettiplace, *The Sinner's Tears* (1653), epistle.
24. Fuller, II, 437.
25. Peter Bales, *Infirmity Inducing to Conformity* (1649), p. 1.

judgments, and the clergy knew that eventually God would avenge their offences and raise the church up again; yet to resign oneself to God's will was not to surrender to 'stoical apathy', for while waiting for divine deliverance it was the task of the faithful to look to their own sins.[26] The churchmen's most pressing task was to teach the people how to go about personal amendment and private devotion.

In these dark days 'true piety is absolutely necessary, because none can hinder me from that but myself; but it is not always in every man's power to bring himself to the font, or approach the Lord's table.'[27] And personal piety has its part to play in redeeming the nation from slavery and impiety, since 'the way to amend all, is every one to amend one'.[28] In *England's Faithfull Reprover* (1653), Richard Samwaies, 'a sequestered divine' and ousted fellow of Corpus Christi College, Oxford, laid about the Church of England, the nobility and gentry, the universities, the lawyers, the City of London, those who had separated from the parish churches, and the whole body of the 'sinful English people'. Nothing less than a national revival was the goal of these divines. Henry Hammond hoped to see the 'visible power and benefit' of *The Whole Duty of Man* 'on the hearts of the whole nation'; in October 1659, Humphrey Henchman, soon to be Bishop of London, admonished the gentry and clergy to combine to aid the recovery of 'this sinful nation and oppressed church'; Clement Ellis, Simon Patrick, Richard Allestree, and many others lectured the English on their transgressions. Many years later, Clement Barksdale claimed that the zeal and constancy of those loyal to the church during the Interregnum had led them to hope and expect that if law and liberty were returned, 'England would really become a nation of saints, an holy nation, Christian not in name only, but in deed and truth'.[29]

England in the summer of 1660 was England reborn. This was to be 'England's season for reformation of life' because 'the reformation of our manners will be the properest answer to such a blessing'.[30] The Restoration was the most admirable of 'the wonderful revolutions and intricate riddles of God's providence' in which the hand of God could be seen 'punishing us justly for our sins, yet relieving us mercifully from our sufferings'.[31] The Restoration intervened be-

---

26. Peter Samwaies, *Devotion Digested* (1652), pp. 126, 85–6.
27. Farindon, I, 146.
28. Richard Gove, *The Saint's Honeycomb* (1652), p. 191; see *WR*, p. 313.
29. Clement Barksdale, *A Sermon Preached upon the Fifth of November 1679* (Oxford, 1680), p. 8.
30. Pierce, *Sermons*, p. 22.
31. John Gauden, *Gods Great Demonstrations* (1660), sig. A2v.

tween the writing and publication of Simon Patrick's tract against the hypocrisy of 'the present generation', so the optimistic Patrick simply announced that what had been intended as a remedy, now 'must serve as a preservative from the like mischiefs in time to come'.[32] The more realistic William Sancroft observed that while 'we have a Jerusalem (it is true) and the hill of Sion in our eyes: yet many look back to Babel, and multitudes sit captives still by those waters, increasing them with their tears'.[33] To ensure that the people did not forget their good resolutions made in adversity, nor the tribulations which had prompted them, 'the piety of the state' set apart 30 January and 29 May for perpetual anniversaries, which joined 5 November as 'three grand solemnities' in the liturgical calendar of the Church of England.[34] Although it would be unrealistic to assume the universal observance of these anniversaries, especially in rural parishes, they formed part of the experience of most of the population.[35] Carefully composed forms of Morning and Evening Prayer gave voice to the nation's guilt and her sense of the 'unspeakable mercies' she had received from a 'long-suffering' God, who had delivered her 'from the unnatural rebellion, usurpation and tyranny of ungodly and cruel men, and from the sad confusions and ruin thereupon ensuing'. On 30 January the minister was instructed to read parts of the homily against disobedience and rebellion or to 'preach a sermon of his own composing upon the same argument'. The vicar of Impington, Cambridgeshire, who 'doth preach to the people their obedience to the King and especially on 29th May and 30th January' was probably typical of parish clergymen.[36] One

32. Patrick, V, 3; IX, 431.
33. D'Oyly, *Sancroft*, II, 349.
34. Allestree, I, 149; Edward Sparke, *Scintillula altaris* (1678 edn), p. 373. 30 January and 29 May were added to the calendar by 12 Charles II c.30 and 12 Charles II c.14, and repealed with 5 November by 22 Victoria c.2.
35. For an impression of the observance of these anniversaries see Wood, II, 215; Evelyn, IV, 204, 513; *The Diary of Samuel Newton*, ed. J.R. Foster (Cambridge Antiquarian Society, 23, 1890), esp. pp. 11, 12, 40, 46–7, 98; but cf. Pepys, III, 95; IV, 29, 163; VI, 25; X, 163–4. Also see D.A. Spaeth, 'Common Prayer?', in *Parish, Church and People*, ed. S.J. Wright (1988), pp. 139–40; J. Spurr, ' "Virtue, Religion and Government": The Anglican Uses of Providence', in *The Politics of Religion in Restoration England*, ed. T. Harris, P. Seaward and M. Goldie (Oxford, 1990); B.S. Stewart, 'The Cult of the Royal Martyr', *Church History*, 38 (1969), 177; H.W. Randall, 'The Rise and Fall of a Martyrology: Sermons on Charles I', *Huntington Library Quarterly*, 10 (1946–7), 145; B.S. Capp, *Astrology and the Popular Press* (1979), pp. 49–50. Some Nonconformists kept these and other anniversaries, such as 24 August, St Bartholomew's Day; see Heywood, pp. vi, 119, 152–3, 162; MS Eng Th D 71.
36. *Episcopal Visitation Returns for Cambridgeshire*, ed. W.M. Palmer (Cambridge, 1930), p. 113.

preacher guessed that over 3,000 sermons were delivered each 30 January, and, of course, many of these found their way into print and so could be read in private.[37] These sermons aimed at more, however, than simply inculcating 'obedience to the King'.

On 30 January 1667 John Milward heard Nathaniel Hardy preach at the Temple on Matthew x. 39, *he that findeth his life shall lose it: and he that loseth his life for my sake shall find it*, on which text Hardy 'made a very good sermon and moved many to tears in applying it to our late King's sufferings'.[38] But these weren't simply tears of sympathy, they were tears of contrition. 'Did not God take away our good King in his wrath?' asked James Duport, 'and were not the sins of the nation the fuel that kindled and fed the fire of his wrath? and have not we contributed some sparks at least, yea and some fuel too to this fire?'[39] 'All Israel suffered for the sin of Achan. Beloved the murder of King Charles may be an Achan in England, to bring down the curse of God upon it; unless we acquit our selves by serious humiliation from the guilt thereof.'[40] The regicide stained the land and all who dwelt in it with blood. 'Public sins', which 'like the first rebellion of man, may remain a debt upon posterity', were not only the rebellion and regicide, but the 'provoking sins' which had led a wrathful God to take away England's Josiah.[41] Many preachers, including Dr Hardy, distinguished between the 'instrumental' causes of the King's murder, such as schism, sedition, rebellion and treason, and the 'meritorious' causes, such as 'swearing and drunkenness, chambering and wantonness, pride and profaneness'.[42] It would take too long, thought Adam Littleton, 'to draw up a catalogue of *national sins*, which might be the occasion of this great sin and judgment [the regicide]. Let every one reflect upon his own, that those were the actions, which troubled the camp, and brought this great evil upon the land.'[43]

The sermons on 29 May and 5 November hammered home the same message. 'Let us consider,' suggested Bishop Lamplugh on 5

---

37. Francis Turner, *A Sermon Preached* (1685), p. 26. Also see BL, MS Harleian 6621, fos 37v–38; *The Diary and Autobiography of Edmund Bohun*, ed. S. W. Rix (Beccles, 1853), p. 47; Pepys, VI, 54.

38. *The Diary of John Milward*, ed. C. Robbins (Cambridge, 1938), p. 75.

39. James Duport, *Three Sermons* (1676), p. 24; cf. Evelyn, III, 624.

40. John Paradise, *Hadadrimmon* (1660), p. 13.

41. Henry Maurice, *A Sermon Preached* (1682), pp. 12–14.

42. Nathaniel Hardy, *A Loud Call* (1668), p. 32, also see Duport, *Three Sermons*, p. 24; Benjamin Calamy, *A Sermon Preached* (1685), p. 26; *Diary and Correspondence of John Evelyn*, ed. W. Bray (1906), p. 616; *The Autobiography of Mrs Alice Thornton* (Surtees Society, 62, 1873), p. 57.

43. Littleton, I, 243.

November 1678, 'how much the public peace and safety of the nation may be furthered in the reformation and amendment of a few.' Although God might with justice pursue these 'national sins' to 'a universal national repentance' and chastise us 'until we were all of us either consumed or reformed', he might in his mercy be content with less: after all, he would have saved Sodom for the sake of even ten righteous people.[44] A further opportunity to amplify this call for national reform was provided by fasts and thanksgivings appointed in *ad hoc* response to natural and man-made events, such as plague, fire, war, plot and rebellion; there were fourteen such days appointed in Charles II's reign.[45] William Sancroft seems to have been expert in composing these special forms of prayer to avert dearth, pestilence or defeat.[46] 10 October 1666 was appointed as a fast day for the recent judgments which, in Evelyn's opinion, 'we highly deserved for our prodigious ingratitude, burning lusts, dissolute court, profane and abominable lives under such dispensations of God's continued favour in restoring church, prince and people from our late intestine calamities . . . this made me resolve to go to our parish assembly, where our Doctor preached on Luke xix. 41. piously applying it to the occasion'.[47] It is unlikely, however, that congregations were large for these special fasts and thanksgivings; on Wednesday, 5 April 1665, Roger Lowe arrived early for a funeral at Standish church and found to his surprise, Mr Bowker preaching 'for it was a day of humiliation for the King's navy'.[48] Anthony Wood suggested that a Sunday had been appointed as the thanksgiving day for the discovery of the Rye House Plot so that those busy on the harvest would still attend.[49] In 1685, another Sunday was chosen to mark the nation's deliverance from Monmouth. But when a community felt the rod of the Lord smite them directly as, for instance, in the Southwark fire of 26 May 1676 or the Northampton fire of 20 September 1675, then it was perhaps a more chastened congregation

---

44. Thomas Lamplugh, *A Sermon preached before the House of Lords on the Fifth of November* (1678), p. 42.
45. See Spurr, 'Virtue, Religion and Government', esp. note 4.
46. BL, MSS Harleian 3785, fos 6, 8; 3784, fo. 296; 7377, *passim*. Forms of prayer were usually printed in runs of over 12,000; see the printers' accounts in MSS Tanner 29, fo. 21; 33, fos 29, 30. It was often difficult to get them to remote parts of the kingdom, such as Brecon, in time for the fast day; see MS Tanner 42, fo. 84; BL, MS Harleian 7377, fo. 51v.
47. Evelyn, III, 464.
48. *The Diary of Roger Lowe*, ed. W.L. Sachse (1938), p. 82; also see Evelyn, III, 404 (this day was appointed on 6 March as a fast for the Dutch war); and, more generally, Spaeth, 'Common Prayer?', p. 140.
49. Wood, III, 72.

that gathered to hear their own minister roundly denounce them and their sins as the cause of their tribulation, and assert that God had punished them less than they deserved.[50]

Contemporaries remarked upon how quickly the professions of piety and amendment made at the Restoration were forgotten; but the clergy knew that 'we seldom care for our physician, until the time that we are sick; and then as soon as recovered, are very glad rather than thankful.' In this case, however, ingratitude might prove to be a fatal error. 'The pleasant effects of a deliverance (which are peace and plenty, living securely, and at ease) are apt to make us turn atheists, provoking the author of our deliverance to correct us once more in the house of bondage.'[51] 'Any sense of religion will tell us, that our sinning again after such judgments, and such deliverances, will cause a worse thing to happen to us, will aggravate our guilt, and heighten divine wrath, provoke God to change our rods into scorpions, and the milder corrections into exterminating judgments.'[52] As catastrophe succeeded disaster during the 1660s, as the tempo of divine chastisements quickened, the clergy were convinced that the nation was moving towards its final destruction. Every respite was an invitation to reform – for 'whilst the rod is removing, 'tis also hanging over our heads'.[53] 'Let us not flatter ourselves,' said Sancroft after the Fire of London, 'nor think that God hath now emptied his quiver, and spent all his artillery upon us'.[54] In *London's Calamity by Fire Bewailed and Improved*, Robert Elborough, 'minister of that parish that was lately St Lawrence Pountney, London', warned the nation that 'if we continue acting such comedies, God will be sure to act a severer tragedy upon us, than ever yet hath been acted'.[55] Adam Littleton explained that God 'doth not pour out all his indignation at once; but gives people a time of probationership for judgment, to see whether they will repent. I wish poor England be not upon such a probation.' With each progressive display of national ingratitude and impenitence the danger grew not only of further, but of heavier, afflictions from on high: 'who knows how soon our provocations may precipitate our ruin? how near our destruction may be? and how soon an offended God may *un-Church* us, *un-people* us?'[56]

50.   See the sermons preached by Richard Martin at St Saviour's, Southwark, MS Eng Th E 168, fos 11v–21, 22–9; and John Conant of Northampton's *Sermons* (1693), sermons 10 and 11, esp. p. 569.
51.   Pierce, *Sermons*, pp. 58, 53.
52.   Henry Hesketh, *A Sermon preached ... September the 2d. 1682* (1682), p. 26.
53.   Pierce, *Sermons*, p. 124 (on the Plague).
54.   D'Oyly, *Sancroft*, II, 397.
55.   Elborough, *London's Calamity* (1666), pp. 15–16.
56.   Littleton, II, 237.

The uneasy peace between God and the English in the 1670s was shattered by the 'discovery' of the Popish Plot – *another* Popish Plot, which suggested to Clement Barksdale that the neglect of the 5 November anniversary in rural parishes had been noted in Heaven.[57] On 13 November 1678, the fast day for the discovery of the plot, Stillingfleet preached at St Margaret's Westminster, and took as his text I Samuel xii. 24 – 5, *only fear the Lord, and serve him in truth with all your heart: for consider how great things he hath done for you. But if ye shall still do wickedly, ye shall be consumed, both ye and your King.* The plot was proof in Stillingfleet's eyes of 'the influence which continuance in sin hath upon a kingdom's ruin'. Or, as William Jane told the House of Commons,

> a general dissoluteness of manners, an impudent boldness in the practice of iniquity, a neglect and contempt of all the duties of religion, the loosing the joints of government by treasons and conspiracies, divided interests and dissensions among the people, confusions and divisions in the church are as infallible symptoms of a dying state, of the dissolution of a commonwealth and the funeral of a kingdom, as if a flaming sword had hung over it, or a voice from heaven had revealed its doom.[58]

On the fast day appointed for the Popish Plot, the congregation and minister were to implore God: 'deprive us not of the light of thy gospel, of the purity, the regularity of thy worship, because we have not walked upright and suitably to it; whilst strict and reformed in our doctrines, having been lewd and licentious in our conversation.'[59] We should all beware 'of those privy conspirators in our own bosoms, our carnal lusts, and unruly passions, and our presumptuous sins proceeding thence'.[60]

'How long,' asked the clergy, 'have we slighted his judgments, abused his mercies, and turned his grace into wantonness?'[61] Although as the Exclusion crisis developed, the preachers devoted more time to expositions of passive obedience and to assertions of Stuart legitimacy, they continued to use anniversary and fast sermons primarily as a platform for their moral crusade. 'We may also be instrumental in a reformation,' suggested a preacher on 29 May 1680, 'but we should begin it at the right end, our own wicked hearts

57. Barksdale, *Sermon ... on 5 November*, p. 9; also see Gregory Hascard, *A Sermon preached upon the Fifth of November, 1678* (1678), p. 30.
58. Stillingfleet, I, 236; William Jane, *A Sermon preached on the Day of the Publick Fast* [11 April 1679] (1679), p. 10.
59. *A Form of Prayer to be used on Wednesday November the Thirteenth* (1678).
60. Barksdale, *Sermon ... on 5 November*, p. 24.
61. Thomas Jekyll, *Popery a Great Mystery of Iniquity* (1681), p. 2.

and lives, and not at the heads of our superiors'.[62] Even the increasingly partisan tone of Anglican preaching in the years of Tory reaction could not drown out the persistent demand for moral reform. The 'eminent' providence of Charles and James's escape from the Rye House Plot gave preachers and poets 'a noble subject to enlarge on'; and the sermons preached on 9 September 1683, the day of thanksgiving, castigated the traitors, while warning the loyal that 'profane and ungodly subjects may, by their wicked lives, work great mischief to their sovereign, though they may mean it not in their minds'.[63] On 26 July 1685, the day of thanksgiving for the defeat of the Monmouth rebellion, Henry Hesketh did 'not come to preach up loyalty' but religion, the best grounds of loyalty. Indeed, in the eyes of the clergy, there was little to choose between the two: 'loyalty to the king will not excuse from piety to God, and piety to God excludes not loyalty to the king. Never was man the worse subject for being a good Christian.'[64]

The moral message of the Restoration church was essentially what it had been in the 1650s, a message of personal piety and political quiescence. It began from the axiom that it is our Christian duty to 'turn . . . over the diaries of our lives' for the evidence of divine care, so 'that from every event, whether national or personal, we may still infer the obligation and necessity of turning from our sins; that gratitude for past mercies may allure us to good, and fear of impending judgments may drive us from evil'.[65] But these were the only lessons to be drawn safely from the dispensations of providence. The churchmen denounced the presumption of those who tried to fathom the secret intentions behind providences, who wrested them to support a particular line of action or a self-serving evaluation of their own spiritual state. The general rule was that scripture, the revealed will of God, should determine the interpretation of all providences, while in practice the clergy themselves sought to dictate through their preaching the permissible readings of providence.[66] Providences were directed at reforming the individual: 'every one of us should first and chiefly mind his own private duty, that belongs to him in

62. Thomas Long, *A Sermon against Murmuring* (1680), p. 12.
63. Burnet, II, 363; William Hughes, *Two Sermons Preach'd on the Ninth of September 1683* (1684), p. 34.
64. John Meriton, *Curse not the King* (1660), p. 24. Also see Henry Hesketh, *A Sermon . . . on September the 9th [the Rye House thanksgiving]* (1684), p. 30. More political sermons were preached by, among others, Miles Barne, *A Sermon Preached before the University of Cambridge* (Cambridge, 1683), and Francis Bridge, *A Sermon Preached before the Lord Mayor . . . 5 November 1684* (1685).
65. Littleton, II, 67; Allestree, *Causes* (1668 edn), 'Private Devotions', p. 445.
66. See Spurr, 'Virtue, Religion and Government', pp. 33–4.

that station God's providence hath placed him in here; and to be sure to amend and reform himself, before he goes about to reform others, or the public.'[67] The sinner was to apply providences to himself, to 'improve' them to their intended ends, to make a good 'use' of them in becoming truly penitent. Such penitence was not to be measured by the day; as one 29 May preacher explained, 'in vain do we observe this day as a thanksgiving-day, except we labour to keep every day of our life henceforward a holy-day'. 'It is not fasting and prayer, alms and prayer, tears and prayer, but prayer and holiness, prayer and a general reformation that will avail. Repentance is the best argument to move God to mercy, and a holy life is a continual intercession.'[68] Under divine chastisements it was generally acknowledged 'that prayer and general reformation were the best averters of God Almighty's wrath against a people'.[69] 'Work out your own salvation,' urged Archbishop Sancroft (quoting St Paul), 'and so the salvation of the nation too'.[70] For every private individual does have an interest in and responsibility to 'the public'; society cannot subsist without divine providential care and hence there is an obligation upon each of us to engage and retain God's care over the nation by making ourselves worthy of such a guardian.[71]

The nation appeared to be deaf to this message; the constant round of divine chastisement and deliverance was surely proof that this was 'an age not over prone to admire and take notice of any remarkable instances of divine providence either in our preservations from dangers or our deliverances out of them'.[72] Although everyone deplored the nation's moral and religious degeneracy, the complaints were 'far more general, than the endeavours to redress it. Abroad every man would be a reformer, how very few at home?'[73] The magistracy showed little sign of having taken the clergy's message to heart. Occasionally a Grand Jury might be told from the bench that profanity, swearing, perjury and atheism were 'the sins which stand as a partition wall betwixt God's mercies and us, therefore wonder not nor complain of his judgements, 'till you forbear by remissness

---

67. Benjamin Calamy, *A Sermon Preached* (1682), p. 17; cf. *WAWD*, I, 276; Long, *Sermon against Murmuring*, p. 12.
68. Clement Ellis, *A Sermon preached* (Oxford, 1661), pp. 37–8; John Cave, *A Sermon Preached . . . January 30* (1679), p. 16.
69. Evelyn, III, 424.
70. D'Oyly, *Sancroft*, II, 425.
71. William Pindar, *A Sermon of Divine Providence* (1679), pp. 4, 34–8; cf. Gilbert Sheldon, *David's Deliverance and Thanksgiving* (1660), p. 23; Littleton, I, 243.
72. Stillingfleet, I, 232.
73. Thomas Sprat, *A Sermon preached at the Anniversary Meeting of the Sons of Clergy-men* (1678), pp. 28–9.

and neglect of your duty to make these sins your own'.[74] Or a notorious debauchee, like Sir Charles Sedley, might be told by a judge that it was for 'such wicked wretches as he was that God's anger and judgements hung over us'.[75] Now and again, Parliament might bestir itself. After the Fire, and apparently inspired by the sermons of Dolben and Outram, the Commons appointed a committee to prepare a bill 'for the suppressing of atheism, swearing, cursing, lying, profaneness and luxury'; this bill was dropped, but revived briefly in the next session. A similar measure was initiated in the House of Lords in 1674, and another in 1677–8, all presumably spurred on by the bishops who, in their conference of 1674–5, had identified atheism as the major threat to the church.[76] Unfortunately, the chief magistrate offered only a bad personal example. Several clergymen blamed Charles II's own sins for the tribulations of his realm, and one or two even hinted at this gently in court sermons and elsewhere.[77] However, in 1678, when Francis Wells, minister of Tewkesbury, denounced the King from the pulpit for adultery, whoredom and fornication, he was suspended from office.[78]

If the English were to be reformed, then the clergy would have to take the job on. Although their sermons denounced fanatics, enthusiasts, rebels and Jesuits, the churchmen preached to pews full of conforming Anglicans, and it was only natural that they should direct their rhetoric principally against the sins of their parishioners. As one preacher pointed out, it was the concern of the historian, not the divine, to lay the guilt on one particular party.[79] But too often the message of a sermon aimed at the sins of its conforming audience must have been deflected by the laity's desire to cast the blame on to puritans or papists. John Allington preached the same 30 January sermon in a city and a town, 'in the one it was censured thus, "he came hither to make us guilty of the King's death!" In the other, "it were well to be preached oft, that men might become sensible of their *latent* guilt".[80]

---

74. MS Rawlinson C. 719, fo. 114 (probably delivered at Hertford in the 1670s).
75. Pepys, IV, 209; also see Wood, II, 213; Sir Peter Leicester, *Charges to the Grand Jury at Quarter Sessions 1660–1677*, ed. E.M. Halcrow (Chetham Society, 5, 1953), pp. 46–8.
76. See Milward, *Diary*, pp. 12–14, 75, for the effect of the preaching in 1666; and pp. 73–4 above for details of the bills.
77. See Pepys, III, 60; Evelyn, IV, 478; Burnet, II, 299; Stillingfleet, I, 215–31.
78. MS Tanner 147, fo. 128; HMC, 13th Report, appendix 2 (Portland MSS, II), p. 300; also see the case of Abraham Bull quoted above at p. 185.
79. [Thomas Manningham], *A Solemn Humiliation for the Murder of King Charles I* (1686), p. 2.
80. John Allington, *The Regal Proto-Martyr* (1672), sig. A3.

The clergy raged against their godless nation, threatening them in the name of God: 'you that are profane scoffers that deride the word and service of God; or close hypocrites, that counterfeit godliness, know that God will not be mocked and cannot be resisted.'[81] But, for the churchmen, there was a terrible, and inevitable, circularity about the fate of a nation so unheeding of divine providences. 'It was laid down in holy scripture,' observed Henry Hesketh, 'as a sure character of an evil man, to be regardless and unobservant of God's common judgements, but it is a rank sign of irreligion, and next to an atheistical contempt of God, not to be deeply affected, when his hand is lifted up in greater chastisements, and not to entertain a very humble sense of his severer inflictions'.[82] 'Study providence,' pleaded Stephen Charnock, a Nonconformist, ''tis part of atheism not to think the acts of God in the world worth our serious thoughts'.[83] Ignoring or denying providence was a hallmark of atheism. The 'prodigious humour of atheism, scepticism, and infidelity, which so abounds in this nation,' said William Jane, 'is both a real cause of men's impenitency under judgments, and a dreadful symptom, that God will go on to judge and afflict them still'.[84] How did the clergy combat this humour of atheism, scepticism and infidelity?

The Folly of Atheism and Superstition

Religion stood on tiptoe ready to flee Restoration England. An ungrateful nation threw divine mercies back in God's face in the belief that they were throwing off the shackles of a morose, constraining religion and the toils of priestcraft; but the churchmen knew that it was God who was withdrawing his candlestick.[85] Aghast, the clergy watched as atheism, an old, but surreptitious, enemy, became dangerously brazen. 'Sure I am,' wrote William Cave,

> the thing it self is too sadly visible, men are not content to be modest and retired atheists, and with the *fool* to say only *in their hearts, there is no God*; but impiety appears with an open forehead, and disputes its place in every company, and without any regard

81. Gibbes, *Sermons*, p. 16.
82. Henry Hesketh, *Sermon . . . on January 30th 1677/8* (1678), p. 2.
83. Stephen Charnock, *Works* (1684), I, 47.
84. Jane, *A Sermon preached . . . April 11th 1679*, p. 37. Also see Littleton, II, 292; B. Worden, 'Providence and Politics in Cromwellian England', *Past and Present*, 109 (1985), 66–7.
85. John Goodman, *A Serious and Compassionate Inquiry* (1674; 1675 edn cited), pp. 53–4; John Sharp, *A Sermon Preached* (1676), pp. 5–6.

to the voice of nature, the dictates of conscience, and the common sense of mankind, men peremptorily determine against a supreme being, account it a pleasant divertisement to droll upon religion, and a piece of wit to plead for atheism.[86]

The 'high assumers and pretenders to reason' and 'that profane, atheistical, epicurean rabble' had grown to a 'daring height here of late years', warned Robert South in 1667.[87] Atheism had 'got strange ground, and made many proselytes' by the early 1680s, with the country 'infested by such swarms of deists, Socinians, atheists, and others'.[88] The distinguishing feature of these adversaries was their pretence to reason.

In this unruly, scoffing age it was only to be expected that the vain coffee-house wit and those with pretensions as 'rational men' should attempt to cast doubt on the principles of Christianity. But 'do they think,' asked Stillingfleet, 'that we are all become such fools to take scoffs for arguments and raillery for demonstrations?'[89] The churchmen knew these opponents all too well; they were the exponents of wit, the practitioners of drollery and buffoonery, who believing themselves 'above the drudgery of thinking', reject the principles of Christianity without having scrutinized them, a neglect which 'savours neither of a gentlemen, nor a scholar'; and the clergy were prepared for them.[90] The Christian of the Church of England owes his God a 'reasonable service', not the sacrifice of fools.[91] Not only was reason on the side of revealed religion – and of the Church of England in particular – but many of the Anglican clergy had flirted with the daringly 'rational' ideas of Hobbes and Descartes, only to discard them once their hidden errors and dangers had become apparent.[92] As a consequence, the clergy often adopted a faintly

---

86. William Cave, *Antiquitates Christianae* (1675), epistle dedicatory.

87. South, I, 286–7.

88. Benjamin Calamy, *A Sermon Preached before the Lord Mayor* (1682), p. 29; T. A., *Religio clerici* (1681), p. 113.

89. Stillingfleet, I, 19, 34–5. On the craze for reason see M. Hunter, *John Aubrey and the Realm of Learning* (1975), pp. 47, 52; J. Spurr, ' "Rational Religion" in Restoration England', *JHI*, 49 (1988).

90. Seth Ward, *An Apology for the Mysteries of the Gospel* (1673), pp. 15, 17; cf. John Scott, *The Works* (1718), I, 288; John Goodman, *The Old Religion* (1684), pp. 3–8; Goodman, *Serious Inquiry*, pp. 53–4; Gilbert Burnet, *Some Passages of the Life and Death of the Right Honourable John, Earl of Rochester* (1680), p. 78.

91. See *WAWD*, I, 231; Miles Barne, *A Sermon preached before the King* (1675); T. A., *Religio clerici*, pp. 81, 104; James Lowde, *The Reasonableness of the Christian Religion* (1684), p. 25; Timothy Puller, *The Moderation of the Church of England* (1679), pp. 161–5.

92. This large and understudied topic can be approached from several angles; see M.H.

condescending tone towards the 'virtuosi' and made it plain that they would have the better of them even on their own favoured ground of 'reason'; added to such confidence in their own rational case was the clergy's conviction that most of this 'rational atheism' was no more than drollery and arrogance. It is little wonder, then, that they took the field in high spirits, 'prepared to batter the atheists and then the Arians and Socinians'.[93]

Most easily disposed of were the atheists proper, the arrogant fools who denied the principles of religion, which are 'that there is a God, and a providence, that our souls are immortal, and that there are rewards to be expected after this life'.[94] In reply the clergy merely pointed to the existence of '*natural religion*, which men might know, and should be obliged unto, by the mere principles of *reason*, improved by consideration and experience without the help of revelation'.[95] These self-evident and rational arguments for the existence of God were threefold: that the design and course of the created world argued for a supreme creator; that it was the universal consent and practice of mankind to recognize a supreme being; and that each individual enjoyed an innate sense of God. So clear and certain, so impossible to deny, were these truths about God, that the defenders of Christianity preferred to doubt whether an intellectually based atheism actually existed. They meticulously rehearsed the arguments from design and universal consent, while simultaneously professing their disbelief 'that there ever was such a monster as a thorough-paced, speculative atheist in the world'.[96] They believed rather that intellectual or 'speculative' atheism, where it existed, was simply a

Nicholson, 'The Early Stages of Cartesianism in England', *Studies in Philology*, 26 (1929); S.I. Mintz, *The Hunting of Leviathan* (Cambridge, 1970); R.T. Carroll, *The Common-sense Philosophy of Religion of Bishop Edward Stillingfleet* (The Hague, 1975); J.C. Hayward, 'New Directions in Studies of the Falkland Circle', *The Seventeenth Century*, 2 (1987); Spurr, 'Rational Religion'.

93. Roger North, *Lives of the Norths* (1890), II, 313.
94. Tillotson, I, 61.
95. John Wilkins, *Of the Principles and Duties of Natural Religion* (1675), p. 39.
96. John Evelyn, *The History of Religion*, ed. R.M. Evanson (1850), I, 89. Also see Tillotson, I, 13–14, 59–60, 78–9; South, I, 286; R[obert] S[harrock], *De finibus virtutis Christianae* (Oxford, 1673), pp. 14–15, 18–20. Even Rochester claimed never to have met an 'entire atheist', according to Burnet's *Life and Death of Rochester*, p. 22. Charles Blount dismissed 'atheist' as a term of abuse. On the extent of true 'speculative atheism' see M. Hunter, 'The Problem of "Atheism" in Early Modern England', *TRHS*, 35 (1985), esp. 144; M. Hunter, 'Science and Heterodoxy: An Early Modern Problem Reconsidered', in *Reappraisals of the Scientific Revolution*, ed. D.C. Lindberg and R.S. Westman (Cambridge, 1990); G. E. Aylmer, 'Unbelief in Seventeenth-Century England', in *Puritans and Revolutionaries*, ed. D. Pennington and K.V. Thomas (Oxford, 1978); D.C. Allen, *Doubt's Boundless Sea* (Baltimore, 1964); David Berman, *A History of Atheism in Britain from Hobbes to Russell* (1988).

mask or justification for the vice of those who lived as if there were no God, the 'practical atheists'.[97] 'When men once indulge themselves in wicked courses,' explained John Tillotson,

> the vicious inclinations of their minds sway their understandings, and make them apt to disbelieve those truths which contradict their lusts. Every inordinate lust and passion is a false bias upon men's understandings which naturally draws towards atheism. And when men's judgments are once biassed they do not believe according to the evidence of things, but according to their humour and their interest. For when men live as if there were no God it becomes expedient for them that there should be none . . .[98]

As Clement Ellis told 'a witty gentleman', 'it was not any strength of reason that prevailed upon you to dislike our faith; but that opposition which it now makes against your darling lusts.'[99] The 'unanswerable doubts and difficulties, which, over their cups or their coffee, they pretend to have against Christianity' are a blind: 'men are atheistical, because they are first vicious; and question the truth of Christianity, because they hate the practice.'[100] For the churchmen, at least, the decay of piety and morality tended to explain the rise of atheism, and not vice versa.

As early as the 1680s those who pleaded 'only for a natural religion in opposition to any particular mode or way of divine revelation; and hence though they profess to acknowledge a God and providence, yet have withal a mean and low esteem of the scriptures and Christianity' were being called deists.[101] These freethinkers questioned the very purpose and rationality of God making a revelation of his will.[102] The deity, who was by definition perfect and absolutely good, must be presumed to give all of his creatures the chance to

---

97. [Clement Ellis], *The Vanity of Scoffing* (1674), p. 30. Also see Matthew Barker, *Natural Religion* (1674), pp. 37–9, 49, 53, 60; Joshua Bonhome, *The Arraignment and Conviction of Atheism* (1679), p. 144; Fell, *Character of Last Daies*, pp. 3–5; Allestree, I, 141; Calamy, *Sermons*, pp. 485–7; Hunter, 'Atheism', 139.

98. Tillotson, I, 78.

99. Ellis, *Vanity*, p. 30; cf. Fell, *Character of Last Daies*, pp. 3–5.

100. South, I, 130–1.

101. George Rust, *A Discourse of the Use of Reason in Matters of Religion* (1683), preface by Henry Halywell. On the history of the word 'deist' see P. Harth, *Contexts of Dryden's Thought* (Chicago, 1968), pp. 77–80; Hunter, 'Atheism', 156; and, for a further reference to the 'anti-scripturists', see Seth Ward, *Six Sermons* (1672), sermon 2.

102. See 'Of Natural Religion', BL collection of MS tracts, shelfmark *873 b. 3*. This MS was first printed in Charles Blount's *Oracles of Reason* (1693), pp. 195–209, and there ascribed to an 'A. W.' (possibly Albert Warren); also see pp. 88–96; Harth, *Contexts*, pp. 85, 87.

attain eternal happiness. But since God's revealed will had only been published to a minority of mankind, it seemed that revealed religion was not intended to be the necessary route to future bliss. For that route had to be available and accessible to all mankind; it had to be a common standard by which all men, whether Christians or not, could be judged.[103] The only such standard available was the law of nature, that nebulous conception which embraced our ideas of God and of our duties to him and to others as they are 'manifested to us by our reason'. The natural and rational religion established by the law of nature contains two cardinal articles, that men should practice virtue and revere the deity.[104] Nothing more is necessary. What could the supporters of revealed religion reply to this objection that it was irrational, as well as uncharitable, to believe that those millions who had been denied divine revelation were beyond the pale of salvation? They did make the lame response that the salvation of pagans was a possibility not revealed by God and one which 'therefore ought not to be pryed into by the rules of Christianity'.[105] But their real defence against the charge that revealed religion was irrational, unnecessary and unfair was rationally to demonstrate that it had indeed been revealed by God: 'our faith is grounded upon the scriptures, as divine, which to be so, may be proved by sound and solid reason; and upon that account, grounded upon reason'.[106] Miracles, prophecy and the preservation of the scriptures through the centuries were advanced as the rational proof of their divine origin. Those who possessed the Bible, and did not recognize that the assurance of its divine authorship was the main foundation of Christianity, were guilty of incredulity. In short, deists were nothing more than atheists.[107] And atheists were nothing more than fools and sinners.

103. Blount, *Oracles*, pp. 196, 208; others raised the same difficulty while claiming to be Christians, see Martin Clifford, *A Treatise of Human Reason* (1674), pp. 29–34; [Albert Warren], *An Apology for the Discourse of Humane Reason* (1680), pp. 48–9.

104. Blount, *Oracles*, pp. 195, 197, 199.

105. *Nineteen Letters of the Truly Reverend and Learned Henry Hammond*, ed. F. Peck (1739), pp. 31–2; Sir George Blundell, *Remarks upon . . . A Treatise of Humane Reason* (1683), p. 39; cf. pp. 36–9; A. M., *Plain-Dealing*, p. 53.

106. Meric Casaubon, *Of Credulity and Incredulity; In Things Divine* (1670), p. 13. Also see A. M., *Plain-Dealing*, pp. 12–13, 27–30, 38–41, 84–5; Warren, *Apology*, p. 12; Thomas Sprat, *A Sermon Preached before the King* (1677), pp. 7–10; Goodman, *Serious Inquiry*, pp. 86–92; James Arderne, *Directions concerning the Matter and Stile of Sermons* (1671), p. 17; Puller, *Moderation*, pp. 97, 146–61.

107. Casaubon, *Credulity*, p. 28; Goodman, *Old Religion*, p. 20. Had anyone, it was asked, ever heard of a 'theist' who lived according to those principles of natural religion which he said obliged him: William Outram, *Twenty Sermons* (1682), sig. A5v; cf. pp. 258–9; Thomas Smith, *A Sermon of the Credibility of the Mysteries of the Christian Religion* (1675), p. 8.

The Anglican response to Socinianism was only a little less dismissive. Socinianism was perceived by the churchmen as both a detestable doctrinal heresy and a presumptuous scepticism. The heresy involved was anti-trinitarianism – 'Socinianism being nothing else but Arianism cultivated and improved'.[108] And the presumption behind the heresy was a sceptical rationalism. The Socinian was prepared, wrote Richard Allestree, 'to admit nothing into his faith but what agrees with that which he counts reason, which in a Socinian's faith is judge of all points in the last resort'.[109] The rationalist impulse in Socinianism rejected the dubiously supported and incomprehensible doctrine of the trinity, while the ethical tendency asserted human free will and renounced the vicarious sacrifice of Christ.[110] After emerging in sixteenth-century Italy, this highly intellectual heresy soon spread to groups in Poland and the Netherlands, and to the cosmopolitan elite of other countries, including England. But it was brought to a wider public in Interregnum England by John Biddle, whose propagation of Socinianism sorely tried and finally surpassed the limits of the Cromwellian religious toleration.[111] Pockets of Socinianism survived on the fringes of Restoration Nonconformity in Gloucestershire and London. In the 1660s, leading continental Socinians visited England; Christopher Crell raised funds for Polish Socinian refugees, and left two of his sons to be educated here; Sand spent time working in the Bodleian Library and rummaging among the stocks of the Oxford booksellers. Thomas Firmin, a London merchant and philanthropist, was a keen Socinian and yet also a faithful pillar of St Mary Woolnoth and friend to several churchmen including Wilkins, Fowler and Tillotson. Churchmen feared that the heresy was on the advance in Restoration England; they worried that the availability of Socinian books might corrupt the younger generation of ministers. There was Socinianism and Pelagianism abroad in the University of Oxford in 1667, according to Anthony Wood, while the 'whimsys' of Henry More were blamed for the spread of 'Socinianism' in Cambridge in 1664. Bishop Hacket complained in 1669 of the publication of 'a rank Arian piece' and of the spread of the heresy, especially at the Inns of Court.[112]

---

108. BL, Lansdowne MS 960, fo. 96v; also see William Jane, *A Sermon Preached at the Consecration of Henry [Compton]* (1675), p. 5.
109. Allestree, II, 12. Also see Francis Osborne, *Advice to Son* (Oxford, 1656), p. 155; and pp. 261–2 below.
110. For this and much of what follows see H.J. McLachlan, *Socinianism in Seventeenth-century England* (1951).
111. B. Worden, 'Toleration and the Cromwellian Protectorate', *SCH*, 21 (1984).
112. BL, Harleian MS 3784, fo. 117; Wood, II, 97; Tanner MS 44, fos 149, 151. Also see BL, Lansdowne MS 937, fos 38v, 26, 57; CUL, Add. MS 1, fo. 14; W. S.,

And in 1687, Stephen Nye, rector of Little Hormead, Hertfordshire, published at the behest of Thomas Firmin, *A Brief History of the Unitarians, also called Socinians*, a catena of the arguments for the unity of God and the humanity of Jesus. Inevitably, the question arose whether the church herself could be insulated from these 'rationalist' trends.

Roman Catholic apologists had long accused the Church of England of fostering Socinianism; the charge had been a mainstay of the 'rule of faith' controversy and much used against Chillingworth. In the absence of any religious certainties, argued the Romanists, faith had to be guaranteed by the Papacy or the Church: 'without such a judge, every man's reason is reason, and every man's scripture is scripture, and he is left to run wild after his own imaginations.'[113] Yet the Church of England was proud of the role she gave to reason. In contrast to the papists' 'tyranny of implicit faith' or the sectaries' 'inner light', the Anglican had only to follow his own reason until he was persuaded of the truth of the scriptures. 'But there is a wide difference betwixt instrument and contriver, betwixt service and authority', and once human reason has demonstrated that scripture is truly the Word of God, its work is done, scripture becomes the rule of the Protestant's faith and the mysteries which it contains remain beyond the ken of reason.[114] The vital, but limited, role of reason in religion meant that the emphasis given to reason could be varied to suit the needs of controversy: it could be elevated against enthusiasts, fideists and reasoning atheists, and played down against 'Socinians'.[115] So it was asserted that the 'right reason' demanded by the Socinians was 'as diverse in men, as their fancies or faces', and it was asked, 'is it not then the ready way to the introduction of all sects, of libertinism, yea (at last) of atheism it self, to bring all points of religion to the censure and tribunal of this conceitedly blind judge?'[116] Among Francis Turner's objections to *The Naked Truth* was that its author 'would have the several parties to express themselves in the very words of scripture only, but be permitted to use them in their own sense' in order to achieve religious peace and union. The

Answer to a Letter of Enquiry (1671), pp. 47–8 (on the expense of Socinian books); George Ashwell, *De Socino et socinianisme dissertatio* (Oxford, 1680); *Catalogue of the Plume Library*, ed. S.G. Deed (Maldon, Essex, 1959), pp. 45–6, 152; *Catalogus librorum . . Gulielmi Outrami* (1681), p. 4.

113. Thomas Tension, *The Difference Betwixt the Protestant and Socinian Methods* (1687), p. 57; also see *A Supplement to Burnet's History of My Own Time*, ed. H.C. Foxcroft (Oxford, 1902), p. 306.

114. James Arderne, *A Sermon Preached at the Visitation* (1677), pp. 6–8.

115. See G. Reedy, *The Bible and Reason* (Philadelphia, 1985), pp. 16–17, 119–141.

116. George Ashwell, *Fides apostolica* (Oxford, 1653), sigs Av, A6.

abolition of any guarantee of the meaning of scripture beyond the individual's own reason and conscience was 'Arian', 'Socinian', and even 'Mahometan'.[117]

The two most dangerous heresies 'abetted' by the Socinians, as one divine explained to a pupil, were the denial of the divinity of Christ and the Holy Ghost and, secondly, 'their denial of the necessity of Christ's satisfaction for expiating the sins of mankind, such necessity of our Saviour's satisfaction being as they pretend inconsistent with God's gratuitous remission of the sins of men'. Although the Dutch scholar Grotius had refuted these errors, he himself had been tarred with Socinian sympathies, and 'some of our own divines', who in turn had defended Grotius, had also been accused of leaning towards Socinianism.[118] Gilbert Burnet believed that 'they read Episcopius much, and the making out the reasons of things being a main part of their studies, their enemies called them Socinians.'[119] But there was more to it than this. Churchmen like Stillingfleet and Tillotson defended the doctrine of Christ's 'satisfaction' for our sins against Crell and other Socinians, but they could not disguise the fact that their scheme of salvation, with its emphasis upon the individual's responsibility for his own salvation, was marginalizing the 'righteousness of Christ' as that notion had been understood in the Reformed tradition. To Nonconformists, and indeed some churchmen, this theological development appeared as an 'Arminian' and a 'Socinian' tendency among the churchmen.[120] Suspicions about the trinitarian orthodoxy of leading members of the Restoration church were also raised by their views on the Athanasian creed. There was growing disquiet among churchmen about the Platonic terminology which had been laid over the doctrine of the trinity in an attempt to express ineffable mysteries. The Athanasian creed not only tried to define the relationship within the trinity – in terms which the Orthodox Church had never accepted – but it contained 'damnatory clauses' against all who refused to acknowledge these 'truths'. The Church of England required her clergy to subscribe to the Athanasian creed, damnatory clauses and all, but several leading churchmen wished that the church was rid of this creed. In the liturgical commission of 1689, Edward Fowler proposed that it be dropped from the liturgy.[121] The ground was being prepared for the

117. MS Rawlinson Letters 93, fo. 114.
118. BL, Lansdowne MS 960, fo. 95v. Grotius's *De veritate* had made no reference to the trinity.
119. Burnet, I, 334–5 (from a description of the latitudinarians).
120. See pp. 325–6 below.
121. T.J. Fawcett, *The Liturgy of Comprehension 1689* (Alcuin Club, Southend, 1973), pp. 200–1.

storm of controversy – most of it futile – which was to surround the doctrine of the trinity in the 1690s.

The attacks on revealed religion came not only from reason, but from other quarters such as pagan history and physics.[122] 'That proud triumvirate of atheists, the Grecian Epicurus, the Latin Democritus, and our English Hobbes' espoused a materialist physics; in other words, they argued that the world contained only matter or atoms, and not 'spirit'; but, for the clergy, 'not believing . . . the real existence of incorporeal essences, is the most immediate, and intrinsic . . . cause of atheism'.[123] Building on the atomism of Democritus, Epicurus taught that random 'concourse' or concatenation of falling atoms created the world.[124] Although the works of Epicurus and his famous follower, the 'atheistical poet', Lucretius, were already known in England thanks to continental editions, the unsympathetic commentary of Cicero, and modern authors like Montaigne and Gassendi, there was a sudden surge of English translations and commentaries on Epicureanism in the 1650s. In part this was due to the interest of the new scientists in materialist physics, although these 'natural philosophers' asserted loudly and repeatedly that they found the physics implausible and its atheistical implications abominable.[125] Thomas Hobbes, of course, was 'Lucretius enlarged' to his enemies, a materialist who scarcely bothered to disguise his atheistical leanings; his earliest critics, like the churchman Thomas Tenison, repeatedly applied Cicero's criticism of Epicurus to Hobbes's atomism.[126] It undoubtedly was the case that, for the orthodox Christian, 'a labyrinth of difficulty' arose from atomism.[127]

For a clergy who spent so much time expounding the immediate moral messages contained in divine providences, the idea that the world had its origin in a random collision of atoms and that God took no part in its government was patently absurd and irrational. 'That work of providence whereby the world and all creatures are continually upheld, provided for, and governed, doth lead us to a deity.' The preachers beheld 'the goodly frame and structure of the world, and the variety of all those curious and useful parts contained

---

122. Stillingfleet, *Origines sacrae* (1662) was a reply to the three 'most popular pretences of the atheists of our age', that Christianity did not accord with reason, with the chronology of heathen history, or with other accounts of the origin of things.

123. BL, Lansdowne MS 960, fo. 82; Casaubon, *Of Credulity*, p. 192.

124. T.F. Mayo, *Epicurus in England* (Dallas, 1934), pp. 67–8; my account of Epicureanism draws heavily on this book.

125. Ibid., pp. 43, 67–9.

126. In fact, Hobbes and Epicurus disagreed over the existence of empty space, see Mayo, *Epicurus*, pp. 119–20.

127. BL, Lansdowne MS 960, fo. 91v.

in it', and were satisfied that 'all these things, my brethren, came not by chance. Let atheists blaspheme as they please, there is the hand of providence in it.'[128] Equally absurd was the materialists' denial of spirit, since it was so obvious that 'there are some beings in the world which cannot depend on matter and motion, i.e. that there are some spiritual and immaterial substances or beings'.[129] Leaving aside the existence of spiritual beings like God and the angels, the problem of human imagination, or even thought – the mind's ability to reflect upon itself – posed substantial difficulties for Hobbes's mechanical materialism.[130] Moreover, if only matter exists and all motion is purely mechanical, it seems to follow that everything is determined and that there is no such thing as free will. The clergy were horrified at 'the ridiculous folly of imposing a fatal necessity on the infinitely free God' and rendering 'men to be but the tennis balls of destiny'.[131] In a series of exchanges with Hobbes, John Bramhall argued that his determinism dishonoured human nature by making men unavoidably good or evil and dishonoured God by making him the author of sin. It was not coincidental that these complaints echoed those of the churchmen against the iron law of necessity enshrined in the double decree predestinarianism of the Calvinists. Bramhall asked where Hobbesian determinism leaves prayer and repentance, for 'if all things be necessary, our devotions and endeavours cannot alter that which must be'. The implications of this enquiry suggest how fast the churchmen were travelling away from their theological inheritance in the 1650s – such a question would not have troubled the reformers of the sixteenth century or the Calvinists of the early seventeenth.[132]

In fact, Epicureanism taught free will, but its denial of the soul's immortality, and its assertion of divine indifference, left man with little reason to exercise his freedom to be virtuous. In orthodox eyes, Epicureanism – especially when commonly misconceived as hedonism – stoic fatalism, and Hobbesian egoism, all sapped morality. The good held out by these moral philosophies – the pursuit of pleasure, the contentment that comes from embracing the inevitable – were laughably insubstantial in comparison with the everlasting joys promised by Christianity.[133] Even more ridiculous, and offen-

128. Paul Lathom, *God Manifested by his Works* (1678), p. 9; Sharrock, *De finibus*, pp. 6, 8; also see John Goodman, *The Interest of Divine Providence* (1683), p. 16.
129. Stillingfleet, *Origines sacrae* (1662; Oxford, 1847 edn cited), I. 469.
130. Mintz, *Hunting of Leviathan*, pp. 71–2.
131. BL, Lansdowne MS 960, fo. 90; Mintz, *Hunting of Leviathan*, p. 115.
132. Mintz, *Hunting of Leviathan*, p. 120; also see L. Damrosch, 'Hobbes as Reformation Theologian: Implications of the Free-will Controversy', *JHI*, 90 (1979).
133. Sharrock, *De finibus*, p. 156.

sive, was Hobbes's ethical relativism, his argument that good and evil were merely names, not absolute and immutable values, and that there was no natural law written in the hearts of men by their creator, only the positive laws of a specific lawgiver in a particular society.[134] The state of nature – in which the life of man is solitary, poor, nasty, brutish and short – may have been only a theoretical construct in Hobbes's system, but the cynicism it displayed about human nature, and the egotistical, appetite-driven psychology which underpinned it, were abhorrent to the churchmen.[135] The 'monster of Malmesbury' went on to assert that law is what the magistrate decrees, even to the exclusion of the laws of the New Testament, and that the subject's obligation to his sovereign lasts only as long as the sovereign's power to protect him. Such views touched a raw nerve in those who had experienced the Interregnum or who later squirmed under the religious policy of their hereditary monarch, James II. Understandably, the clergy were no fonder of 'the suspicion of atheistical men that religion is but a politic trick to catch silly persons with, whilst those that are privy to the plot, keep out of the bondage of it'; nor of Hobbist insinuations that God and the possibility of eternal torments had been invented 'to uphold states'; all of which simply proved that 'these atheists are fanatics . . . in politics'.[136]

The clergy enjoyed pointing out that the wits and atheists could only revive ancient and implausible errors, rejecting God on 'lamentably weak' grounds and substituting 'precarious, obscure, and uncertain' hypotheses. 'Acquaint me in your next,' they would write smugly to one another, 'which hypothesis savours most of absurdity, the Aristotelian eternity of the universe or the Epicurean atomical concourse?'[137] Since 'the great business of religion, is to oblige its votaries to present duty by the awe and expectation of future retribution', the clergy gave short shrift to any hypothesis which cast doubt on the eternity of hell's torments or the immortality of the soul.[138] The churchmen were content to say with Stillingfleet 'that

134. See Mintz, *Hunting of Leviathan*, pp. 28, 154.
135. See Samuel Parker, *A Demonstration of the Divine Authority of the Law of Nature* (1681). pp. 2, 20; Casaubon, *Of Credulity*, p. 195.
136. Goodman, *Old Religion*, p. 311; Allestree, I, 134–5; also see John Barnard, *Censura cleri, or, A Plea against Scandalous Ministers* (1660), pp. 6–8; South, I, 193; Stillingfleet, *Origines sacrae*, I, 436.
137. Stillingfleet, *Origines sacrae*, I, 428; BL, Lansdowne MS 960, fo. 84. On Aristotle's view of an eternal world, see Sharrock, *De finibus*, pp. 11–13; South, II, 547–8; Tillotson, I, 15–16.
138. Fell, *Character of Last Daies*, p. 1; also see Sharrock, *De finibus*; George Stradling, *Sermons and Discourses* (1692), sermon 12. For the unorthodox ideas of Tillotson, Rust and Henry More on these topics, see D.P. Walker, *The Decline of Hell* (1964).

we need no other argument to prove the reasonableness of religion, than from the manifest folly, as well as impiety, of those who oppose it'.[139] This disdain for their antagonists, this belief that a debased nature, rather than an independent intellect, was the spur for sceptical opinions, may have a been a comfort to the clerical defenders of orthodoxy, but it was eventually to prove their Achilles' heel.

The clergy, it seemed, had only to look around them to find corroboration of their understanding of the relation between a bad life and bad opinions. When Daniel Scargill recanted his Hobbism at Cambridge in 1669, he confessed that 'agreeably unto which principles and positions, I have lived in great licentiousness; swearing rashly, drinking intemperately; boasting myself insolently; corrupting others by my pernicious principles and example'.[140] While Scargill spent the rest of his life bemoaning his misrepresentation as a Hobbist, he escaped the sorry fate of the libertines and sceptics allegedly driven to self-destruction by their dreadful views.[141] It was not only the vicious who cloaked their ill-living in 'atheism'; so did many who were more foolish than wicked. The virtuoso who passed himself of as an Epicurean, the libertine who posed as a Stoic fatalist, or the fop who postured as a man of wit and reason, knew little of their 'philosophies', but blindly followed the vagaries of fashion. The 'town gallant's religion is pretendedly Hobbist', but he never saw a copy of *Leviathan*, it was the coffee-house which had 'taught him to laugh at spirits, and maintain that there are no angels but those in petticoats'.[142] Even Scargill was regarded by Sheldon as 'a foolish fellow', a man who had acknowledged that 'a foolish proud conceit of my own wit' had led him astray.[143] It is as if heterodox ideas were seen as somehow less harmful than the wickedness or folly of those who pretended to espouse them. Admittedly, the churchmen realized that 'if we desire to suppress atheism and immorality we must suppress licentious doctrines and principles', most of which they traced back to *Leviathan*, since 'not one English infidel in a hundred is any other than a Hobbist'.[144] Hobbes 'hath exceeded the atheism not only of the ancient heretics in philosophy, but of all pretenders to

139. Stillingfleet, *Origines sacrae*, I, 428.
140. Mintz, *Hunting of Leviathan*, pp. 50–2; also see BL, MS Harleian 7377, fo. 1; BL, MS Add. 38693, fos 127–32.
141. Mintz, *Hunting of Leviathan*, p. 147.
142. *The Character of a Town Gallant* (1680), p. 4.
143. J. Axtell, 'The Mechanics of Opposition: Restoration Cambridge v. Daniel Scargill', *BIHR*, 38 (1965), 107–8.
144. Robert Hancocke, *A Sermon Preached before the ... Mayor* (1680), pp. 10–12; Sir Charles Wolseley, *The Reasonablenesse of Scripture-belief* (1672), sig. A4; Richard Bentley (1692), quoted in Berman, *History of Atheism*, p. 50.

it, in this last and most atheistical age', claimed Robert Sharrock.[145] But Hobbes was also 'a godsend to orthodox writers' for publishing views which were elusive, but whose existence the clergy inferred from the scoffing, vice and secularism that surrounded them.[146]

The churchmen marshalled their arguments and launched their treatises against atheism and deism, materialism and Hobbism; but they could not shake off the worry that they might be helping to disseminate the very principles that they were opposing; that atheists and Hobbists learned more from the sermons and books denouncing those errors than from the rare and expensive works of atheists and Hobbes. 'More might be spoken to heighten and improve the objection, but I am afraid to persist further therein,' wrote Thomas Fuller. 'It is not only dangerous to be, but even to act an atheist, though with intent to confute their error, for fear that our poisons pierce further than our antidotes.'[147] Even as they wrestled with the arguments of the 'reasoning' atheists, the churchmen also sought cruder means of suppressing licentious doctrines and principles. Daniel Scargill was deprived of his fellowship and expelled from the University of Cambridge; and, in deference to the bishops, Hobbes was prevented from publishing his views on Scargill's case.[148] The University of Oxford was also busy attempting to suppress, or even deny, heterodoxy: Henry Wilkinson exhorted Anthony Wood to omit the heretics, Hobbes, Biddle and Sancta Clara from his history of Oxford; in the 1680s, the university consigned works of Hobbes, along with those of Milton, Owen, Goodwin, Baxter and others, to the flames of a bonfire in the Schools quadrangle.[149]

It is difficult to avoid the conclusion that the churchmen wanted to obliterate, rather than convince, their atheistical opponents. But then the clergy did not believe that rational argument could convince these opponents, for these were not reasonable men, but evil, foolish and proud sinners. 'I know not one objection or doubt against the being of a deity and providence but what is thus raised only by pride, and an arrogant opinion of our own understanding, as if nothing could be either true or reasonable, but what is perfectly within our own ken and cognisance.' It was pride that had betrayed

145. Sharrock, *De finibus*, p. 117.
146. Hunter, 'Science and Heterodoxy', p. 450.
147. Fuller, I, 251.
148. Aubrey alleged that to please the bishops Sir John Berkenhead refused Hobbes a licence to publish; see Mintz, *Hunting of Leviathan*, p. 152; Berman, *History of Atheism*, p. 61.
149. See Wood MS F 45, fo. 128 (Wilkinson was a moderate Nonconformist); *The Judgement and Decree of the University of Oxford* (1683).

Epicurus and Aristotle into error. It was the sin of Simon Magus and of Satan which lay at

> the bottom of the great veneration some have paid to reason, which they have set up in the throne, not only in defiance of blind implicit assent, but even of divine revelation...'tis not reason in general, the common excellency of our nature that is thus advanced, but every man's own private and individual...[150]

The scoffing rationalists and the blatantly irreligious were not, however, the only promoters of atheism.

'The atheism that is at present so rife among us,' wrote Richard Hollingworth, 'owes its growth to the changeableness of many men's principles who pretend to more than ordinary godliness.' The hypocrisy of the Pharisees was a sore trial for sincere religion: 'the life is derided for the deformity of the picture, the truth is prejudiced by the counterfeit, the faults and basenesses of hypocrisy ascribed to true religion itself, and this I take to be one reason of the infidelity and prophaneness that reign at present in this nation.'

> Men are generally very strangely charmed by the shows and pretences of religion, yet when it appears, as it doth at last where it is not real, that all these shows are void of truth, that they are but shows and nothing more, this makes the very name of religion despicable, odious and abhorred, it brings profaneness and infidelity, and makes the very profession of piety, vile and contemptible in the world, a dangerous and destructive issue, as we ourselves have plainly found by our own experience in this nation.[151]

The experience of the Civil War and Interregnum had been a salutary example of the effects of religious hypocrisy; effects which were still with the English.

The 'licentious preaching' of the 'reforming' puritans had unleashed such 'legions of heresies', observed William Jackson, 'that it hath been by wise men of late thought a necessary work to prove that there is a God; and to resume the primitive employment of writing apologies, and defences for the truth and excellency of the Christian religion, as if we had been reformed into the heathenism of our forefathers'.[152] Englishmen were so corrupted by the liberty and

150. Calamy, *Sermons*, p. 108; Sharrock, *De finibus*, p. 16; *WAWD*, I, 331.
151. Hollingworth, *A Modest Plea* (1676), p. 88; William Outram, *Twenty Sermons*, pp. 214, 215; cf. *WAWD*, I, 279; Scott, *Works*, I, 230–1.
152. William Jackson, *Of the Rule of Faith* (Cambridge, 1675), pp. 3–4.

licentiousness of the late broken times that they were ready to throw off the gentle hand of the orthodox clergy and to receive the most startling ideas, even those of Hobbes.[153] Scattered through the works of Restoration churchmen was the maxim that 'the follies and divisions of one age, make way for atheism in the next', or as John Goodman had it, apparently from Lord Bacon, 'superstition in the fore-going age, usually becomes atheism in the succeeding generation'.[154]

Superstition, folly and hypocrisy had been the characteristics of the self-proclaimed 'godly' during the Interregnum. These sons of Belial, 'a generation as dark as hell', had been much castigated by moderate and Anglican clergy in the 1640s and 1650s. Simon Patrick wrote extensively on the 'Jewish hypocrisy' of 'the present canting, talking and not doing Christians'. In a pointed parallel, Patrick described how the Jews made a fetish of worship, and 'their great zeal in these matters, and their forwardness to introduce the true religion made them overlook these little trifling things of justice and equity, of mercy and compassion, and to hope that God would do also, and not be angry with such a reformed people.'[155] The form of godliness, but not its power, was everywhere apparent; the only preaching to be heard was speculative and notional – nothing practical, 'or that pressed reformation of life', was taught – so the people were left without 'principles and grew very ignorant of even the common points of Christianity'.[156] Many Anglicans were convinced that Calvinist predestinarianism was at the heart of puritan hypocrisy. 'Because they read of election, they elect themselves; which is more indeed than any man can deny, and more, I am sure, than themselves can prove', suggested Anthony Farindon. Convinced of their election, applying I Corinthians xv. 55–6 to themselves, these saints fear neither death nor sin,

> for sin itself shall turn to the good of those elect and chosen vessels. And we have some reason to suspect, that, in the strength of this doctrine, and a groundless conceit that they are these particular men, they walk as all the days of their life in fraud and malice, in hypocrisy and disobedience, in all that uncleanness and pollution of sin which is enough to wipe out any name out of the book of life.[157]

153. See Burnet, I, 334; and p. 219 above.
154. Joseph Glanvil, *Some Discourses, Sermons and Remains* (1681), p. 183; Goodman, *Serious Inquiry*, p. 226 (Bacon says something similar, but not in these words, in his essays on atheism and superstition); Parker, *Demonstration*, sig. iii.
155. Peter Bales, *Infirmity Inducing to Conformity* (1649), p. 17; Patrick, VII, 407, 436.
156. Richard Gardiner, *XVI Sermons* (1659), p. 292; Evelyn, III, 184, 160.
157. Farindon, II, 20.

But they had the appearance of sanctity – and that was what captured the popular imagination. The people were 'bewitched with the seeming sanctity of the scribes and Pharisees, their painted sepulchers and washed pots, their hypocritical zeal of prayer in the streets', and so if the orthodox were to win back popular affection at the Restoration, they must outshine these hypocrites in sincere piety.[158]

Hypocrisy and superstition were far from exhausted in 1660. 'If true godliness be thus a likeness to God, where, O where, is it to be found?' asked one divine in 1671, 'betwixt the atheists in heart, dissembling hypocrites on the one hand, and atheists in practice, the profane hectors on the other; betwixt scribes and pharisees here, and publicans and sinners there, how is sincere piety decayed and lost'.[159] While the Dissenters 'gloried in themselves as the only godly and sober part of the nation', the Anglican clergy could only lament 'the credulity and easiness of the common people to take in whatsoever is suggested to them, by men pretending more than ordinary sanctity and holiness'.[160] According to Robert South, Nonconformist 'fanaticism' was based on a pretence of a more pure and spiritual worship of God than 'the national established church' provided; 'a pretence so utterly false and shamefully groundless, that in comparison of the principle which makes it, hypocrisy may worthily pass for sincerity, and pharisaism for the truest and most refined Christianity'.[161] According to the churchmen, the Nonconformist clergy were guilty of the 'preaching up of an empty, formal, notional kind of religion, and causing and encouraging men to build their hopes of heaven upon very easy and pleasing conditions'. Although these Pharisees were scrupulous about the formal petty matters of religion, 'this exactly suits with a man's humour; for while the one (i.e., strictness) may a little quiet his conscience, so it being but in the other (i.e., small, trifling things) secures his other interest also'.[162] 'This was the hypocrisy the scripture so much speaks of,' thundered Simon Patrick, 'the finer sort of hypocrisy, that carries so many to hell in a pleasing belief that they are going to heaven'.[163] Pharisaical formalism and superstition ran like 'a vein of Judaism' through Dissent. The Dissenters made it 'the great point of sanctity to

158.   John Barnard, *Censura cleri*, p. 13.
159.   Richard West, *The Profitableness of Piety* (1671), pp. 8–9.
160.   Henry Hesketh, *A Sermon Preached . . . 26 July 1685* (1685), p. 27; Richard Hollingworth, *Modest Plea*, p. 82.
161.   South, II, 549.
162.   *A Free and Impartial Inquiry* (1673), pp. 36, 52.
163.   Patrick, V, 47.

scruple every thing'; their itching ears led them into a 'superstitious doting upon sermons'; and their preachers flattered them with talk of election, marks of grace, the perseverance of the saints, and other shibboleths: in short, their difference from the church 'amounteth to no more but this, stand off, for I am holier than thou'.[164] 'Out of a high conceit of their own transcendent purity', the Dissenters refused church fellowship with those who did not share their 'sainthood'. They had become models 'of such an artificial religion, that not only the outside and the garb of piety is represented by it, but there is an imitation also of inward motions of the soul in such affections of fear and love and joy as are in truly religious hearts'.[165] This self-delusion could be traced back to 'enthusiasm' or 'a false conceit of inspiration' by which the fancies of an overheated imagination were cried up as divine inspiration and true godliness, 'making all religion to consist in airy notions and nice speculations'.[166] This enthusiasm has a natural, indeed physiological, explanation, since it arose 'either from a constant heat of constitution, or a casual agitation of the spirits, occasioned either by vapours of heated melancholy, or an intermixture of sharp and feverish humours with the blood; which, as all men know, who understand any thing of the nature and composition of human bodies, naturally heightens and impregnates the fancy'.[167] From the Quakers with their 'indwelling of the spirit' to the Presbyterians' extempore preaching and prayer, all of the Nonconformists were the victims of melancholy and enthusiasm. But the churchmen did not believe that this could excuse 'the rankest of all ill qualities', spiritual pride.[168]

Spiritual pride blinded its victims to the truth, so obvious to the churchmen, that genuine godliness would not cry up a party or a faction to the detriment of Christian unity. The differences between English Protestants could never be healed, argued Benjamin Calamy, 'till we learn humility and modesty, till pride and self-conceit, and all imperious affectation of imposing our own singularities upon others be rooted out of the world, till we learn to submit to our betters, and in indifferent things not to oppose our private opinions to the public determinations of the church. . . . Whatever is the cause of the error, pride is always the cause of the quarrel that makes the

164. Goodman, *Serious Inquiry*, p. 62, sig. c2v; William Assheton, *The Danger of Hypocrisie* (1673), p. 17; Nathaniel Bisbie, *The Modern Pharisees* (1683), p. 22.
165. Thomas Bradley, *A Sermon ad clerum* (1663), pp. 30–1; Patrick, IV, 155.
166. Joseph Glanvil, *Essays on Several Important Subjects in Philosophy and Religion* (1676), essay 4, p. 17; Lowde, *Reasonableness*, p. 45.
167. Scott in *Cases*, p. 244. Also see P. Harth, *Swift and Anglican Rationalism* (Chicago, 1961); J.I. Cope, *Joseph Glanvill, Anglican Apologist* (St Louis, 1956), pp. 57–8.
168. South, II, 151.

breach and forms the party.'[169] It was the great failing of the Non-conformist clergy that instead of winning souls to heaven, they were more concerned with winning proselytes to their party.[170] The temerity of the Nonconformists in assuming the name of 'the godly' did not just offend the Anglicans, it convinced them that even if reunited with the national church, these proud and headstrong men would maintain a separate identity. To 'comprehend' sober Dissenters in the Church of England would be to import a schism into the bowels of the church, 'for their enthusiastical way will be only admired by the vulgar, and all the sober judicious divines will be slighted as unprofitable preachers'. 'Every petty sect amongst us seems wonderfully devout in their way, even to superstition, and are inflamed with a blind zeal in their errors.'[171]

Popery was equally superstitous. 'I have ever looked on popery as a gross corruption both of Christianity and morality,' declared Gilbert Burnet, 'and as a religion made up of superstition and idolatry that is easy to the greatest sins but cruel upon the smallest oppositions to its own authority'.[172] Anglicans denounced the superstition and idolatry of 'the papists relying upon their indulgences, their saints' merits, and superogations, and other such fopperies'. Defining superstition as 'the unpleasing worship of God', the Anglicans excoriated Rome for her idolatrous ritual, her contemplative life and mystical tradition, and her moral theology. The moral theologians of the Roman church, and especially the Jesuits, seemed to 'have framed their casuistical divinity to a perfect compliance with all the corrupt affections of a man's nature'.[173] The individual Roman Catholic had surrendered his intellect and his moral autonomy to the church, he had espoused a blind implicit faith in an infallible institution, 'and withall may be seen, how necessary an implicit faith is for those that will be of the Romish communion; since did they use but half an eye, they must needs discover, instead of a guide in controversies, an endless maze, wherein, it is no wonder, that many, even of the greatest wits, lose all religion, and take up in atheism'.[174] Anglicans tended to blame the institution rather than the individual,

169. Calamy, *Sermons*, pp. 129–30.
170. William Assheton, *The Cases of Scandal and Persecution* (1674), p. 4.
171. Spurr, 'Comprehension', 941–3; Saywell, *Serious Inquiry*, p. 38; John Goodman, *A Sermon Preached before the ... Mayor* (1685), p. 33.
172. J.J. Hughes, 'The Missing "Last Words" of Gilbert Burnet in July 1687', *HJ*, 20 (1977), 223–4.
173. Stillingfleet, I, 330; South, II, 22; also see John Patrick, *Reflexions upon the Devotions of the Roman Church* (1674); Littleton, I, 311; George Hickes, *The Spirit of Enthusiasm Exorcized* (1680).
174. William Jackson, *Of Rule of Faith*, p. 17.

to indict the ambition of popes, cardinals and the Society of Jesus rather than the errors of the individual Roman Catholic. Burnet saw 'a great difference between the governing spirit which rules in that church particularly among the Jesuits and the individual members that are in that communion, but though I have great charity for many papists I have none at all for popery'.[175] Popery is 'a religion (such a one as it is) that all loose and licentious people are already prepared for; 'tis the most pleasant and easy, the most gay and pompous religion in the world; 'tis such a one as they would devise, were they to make a religion for themselves'.[176]

The Church of England discerned several parallels and connections between popery and Protestant 'fanaticism'. Superstitiously repudiating any belief or practice associated with the Church of Rome, the Nonconformists' 'very opposition to one usurpation makes them deliver themselves up to another'.[177] Popery and enthusiasm shared a concern for establishing absolutes, for claiming infallibility, although the former at least limited this to one person, the Pope, and so gained in South's eyes 'the poor commendation of being the less evil of the two'. Some Dissenters had careered through Nonconformity and sectarianism to end up as Quakers, 'from whence being able to advance no further, they are in a fair way to wheel about to the other extreme of popery; a religion and interest the most loudly decried, and most effectually served by these men, of any other in the world besides'.[178] It was a commonplace that the Church of Rome was the puppetmaster of English sectarianism and that both perverted 'religions' taught that princes could be resisted by their subjects.[179] The theological bonds between popery and Dissent lay in their pandering to the 'forms' of religion, in spiritual pride, and in a basic mistake about justification:

> How full is the scripture against all self-justitiaries, Pharisees, philosophers, votaries, Pelagians, Quakers, and other perfection-

175. Hughes, 'Last Words of Burnet', 224.
176. Robert Hancocke, *A Sermon preached before the Lord Mayor* (1680), pp. 5–6.
177. *WAWD*, I, 348. Also see Bisbie, *Modern Pharisees*, p. 20; William Wray, *Loyalty Protesting against Popery* (1683), pp. 20–1; Joseph Glanvil, *The Zealous, and Impartial Protestant* (1681), p. 45; Patrick, I, 219.
178. South, III, 147–8; II, 550.
179. See W. S., *Answer to a Letter of Enquiry*, pp. 14–17; Goodman, *Serious Inquiry*, p. 235; Allestree, II, 56; South, III, 285, 535; Miles Barne, *A Discourse* (1682), pp. 20–1; George Hickes, *A Sermon Preached before the Lord Mayor ... 30th of January 1681/2* (1683), p. 30. Also see E. Duffy, 'Peter and Jack: Roman Catholics and Dissent in Eighteenth-century England' (Friends of Dr Williams's Library Lecture, 1982), pp. 4–5; M. Goldie, 'Sir Peter Pett, Sceptical Toryism and the Science of Toler-

ists, that boast of their own good works, and their being free from sin? No marvel that they that think they have no need of pardon, should find none. God *filleth the hungry with good things: the rich he sendeth empty away.* The proud Pharisee, that talked of his own well doings, the boasting papist, that is confident of his own merits from God, are not capable of justification.[180]

The Anglican conviction that the papists and fanatics were 'sworn brethren in iniquity' was unshakeable.[181] The clergy liked to describe their church as being crucified between the two thieves of superstition and enthusiasm, or as being ground between the two millstones of Rome and Dissent, and themselves as 'always persecuted by the papists, those pseudo-Catholics on the one hand, and their instruments, the anti-prelatical sects on the other'.[182]

The Restoration Church of England had little time for her opponents. Atheism was a pretence to reason, or a pride in the intellect, which fed of and masked a vicious life; Dissent was marked by spiritual pride and an unhealthy interest in delusions of 'inspiration' and 'election'; and popery was a superstitious abdication of individual moral responsibility. These were nothing but different paths to the same destination. 'What is the difference betwixt a seduced Quaker, that would serve God if he could tell how; and a profane Epicure, that is satisfied how he ought to serve God, but will not?' asked the blunt country parson, before beseeching the judges at the Assizes: 'O kill this atheism, these gross abominations, that will else undoubtedly be the disturbers of our peace.'[183] Occasionally, the churchmen suggested that their opponents had formed an unholy triple alliance. William Outram believed that the nation was threatened by a 'confederacy' of papists, libertines and Dissenters, but especially by 'the first, who imploy the two latter to work under them, and to weaken the Church of England, one by profaneness and the other by separation, that so they may argue against the sufficiency of our constitution to maintain good life, and preserve unity, and dispose those who are of no religion and no church to become proselytes to theirs'.[184] The churchmen strengthened their

ation in the 1680's', *SCH*, 21 (1984), 254–5; M. Goldie, 'John Locke and Anglican Royalism', *Political Studies*, 31 (1983), 71–3.

180. Gibbes, *Sermons*, p. 139, also see pp. 71, 149–50.
181. Nathaniel Bisbie, *Prosecution no Persecution* (1682), p. 2.
182. See John Scott, *The Christian Life* (1681), sig. A3v; Puller, *Moderation*, p. 44; South, III, 123; George Hickes, *Spirit of Enthusiasm*, sig. a2v.
183. Henry Glover, *An Exhortation to Prayer* (1663), pp. 18–19.
184. Outram, *Twenty Sermons*, 'Publisher to reader'.

resolve with Christ's promise that the church would withstand the gates of hell.

> Let us not be disquieted with rumours of the strength and number of its enemies. Though *Ammon* and *Amalek*, the *Philistines* and inhabitants of *Tyre*, I mean, though atheist, sceptick, papist, fanatic, all combine against it, the prediction of our Saviour shall stand. . . . So let us do our work undauntedly and courageously, that neither the scoffs of atheists abash us, nor the rude follies of ignorant persons move us, nor the conspiracy of all together tempt us to such meanness of spirit, or weakness of faith, as to grow despondent.[185]

However, the association between atheist, sceptic, papist and fanatic went deeper than a mere tactical alliance. Something more fundamental than the folly of atheism and superstition united the church's enemies, and their common bond even reached into the Church of England herself: they were united by sin.

The Common Cause of Evil

> Thus sin, you see, is the common cause of evil, the fruitful womb of all kinds of mischief; for I doubt not but to one of these three heads most of the miseries of mankind may be reduced, that they are either the natural effects, the just punishments, or the necessary preservatives of sin. Hence therefore let us learn under all our calamities to acknowledge our sins to be the cause of them, to trace up our evils to their fountain head, which we shall find is in our bosoms. From hence spring all those wasting wars, those sweeping plagues, those devouring fires that make such devastations in the world.[186]

> *Parishioner*: Since the Christian doctrine more strictly than ever any before, binds all its professors to unity, and love, and peace, how come so many disputes and dissensions and animosities to arise among them?
> *Minister*: They proceed from whence all other evils come, from men's lusts and passions. That which makes some men to be of no religion, makes others of any, and, as occasion serves, of many. They have a lust to gratify, or an interest to serve, and they will be

185. John Goodman, *A Visitation Sermon* (1677), pp. 29, 30.
186. John Scott, *A Sermon Preached before the . . . Mayor . . . 2 September 1686 being the Anniversary Fast for the dreadful Fire in the Year 1666* (1686), pp. 10–11.

of that sect that can best comply, or best pay them for it. I need not tell you from what root most of the Romish errors and superstitions grow; and because the name of scripture is venerable, and carries authority with it, that many times is pressed into the service, and by an unnatural construction forced to bear witness against it self. So long as there is vice in the world, there will be error; no church or religious society can be wholly exempt from either; that is the best and purest that has the fewest of both.[187]

Sin was the common cause of evil in the world. Sin was the cause of divine chastisements, civil strife, religious divisions, atheism and irreligion. Archbishop Sheldon spoke for many when he explained that the Civil War was a result of sin, of the years of impiety when, in Robert South's words, 'a long sunshine of mercy had ripened the sins of the nation'; unfortunately, there was 'still the same reigning inquity' after the Restoration 'that was the occasion and commencement of our late unhappy broils'.[188] 'Sin then,' concluded a preacher on the Fire of London, 'is a nation's greatest enemy'.[189] Yet when the churchmen described sin as a social or national problem, they were not talking of some impersonal, abstract sin, but addressing each individual's personal sins; the transgressions of every private subject threatened the stability of the realm, the cohesion of the nation and the survival of true religion. Worse still, sin was the radical connection between the papists, the dissenting fanatics and the debauched, profane atheists, those 'three squadrons' confronting the Restoration Church of England.[190] The glaring simplicity of this attribution of all error and opposition to sin should not obscure its importance in explaining Anglican attitudes towards religious dissidence and the piety of conformists.

Sin – the ascendancy of the will in fallen man – was understood within a 'psychological' framework. 'This is that which religion aims at,' pronounced Richard Allestree, 'to make us men, teach us to live according to our nature, to put reason in the throne, and vindicate the spirit from the tyranny of its own vassal flesh'. The soul possesses 'a power of discerning betwixt good and evil; the understanding: and a power of choosing the good, and refusing the evil, the will', and so man is at his best and most 'rational' when his will and under-

187. Samuel Freeman, *A Plain and Familiar Discourse By Way of Dialogue betwixt a Minister and his Parishioner concerning the Catholick Church* (1687) in Gibson, I, pt. iii, 25.
188. Sheldon, *David's Deliverance*, p. 35; South, III, 102; Richard Burd, *A Sermon Preached . . . on May 29. 1684* (1684), p. 11.
189. Elborough, *London's Calamity*, p. 22.
190. *A Vindication of the Clergy* (1672), p. 106.

standing work in unison.[191] When applied to the psychology of religious error and moral deficiency, the message was predictable: 'the government of the soul must be altered from the rule of popular opinions, and the tyranny of fancies and imaginations, to the sole command of Christian reason.'[192] But altering the government of the soul was not easy. Adam and Eve knew what was good until they embraced the Devil's promise of the knowledge of evil, explained William Gould. 'This knowledge of evil was the introduction of ignorance, the understanding being baffled, the will became foolish, and both conspired to ruin each other; for the will beginning to love sin, the understanding was set on work to commend and advance it.'[193] Although there are 'laws which eternal reason obligeth us to, and which of our selves we should choose to live under, were we freed from the intanglements of the world, and interests of flesh', since the Fall these are no longer accessible or sufficient. If we are to subordinate the passions and appetites of our will to the direction of our understanding or reason, if we are to regain 'the state of integrity, in which we were first made', the laws of eternal reason require the additional guidance of the revealed laws of God.[194] The revelation of the divine will supplied man with the promises which motivated him to be virtuous, to enthrone his enlightened reason above his will. 'God did not intend by an irresistible act upon the minds of men to over-rule them into a compliance with the gospel': the individual's struggle to subjugate the passions and will was the core of human free will.[195] The effort was what differentiated between good and evil men, 'between those who maintain the empire of reason assisted by the motives of religion, over all the inferior faculties, and such who dethrone their souls and make them slaves to every lust that will command them'.[196]

This, then, was the charge against all of the religious dissidents. The Nonconformist had sacrificed the Protestant religion to his 'lusts and passions'. Sensuality and appetite, the manifestations of an unbridled will, had gained the upper hand over his reason, and 'when reason it self, as well as the irascible and concupiscible facul-

191. Allestree, I, 183; Thomas Willis, *The Excellency of Wisdom* (1676), p. 14. Also see T. A., *Religio clerici*, pp. 15–18; Wolseley, *Unreasonablenesse of Atheism*, p. 44; Wolseley, *Reasonablenesse of Scripture-Belief*, pp. 128, 131; South, I, 223–4; J. Morgan, *Godly Learning* (Cambridge, 1986), pp. 46–7.
192. Patrick, III, 543; also see Seth Ward, *Six Sermons*, p. 350.
193. William Gould, *The Primitive Christian Justified* (1682), pp. 4–5.
194. Glanvil, *Essays*, essay 5, p. 5; Glanvil, *Discourses*, pp. 64, 67.
195. William Clagett, *Seventeen Sermons* (1689), p. 62.
196. Stillingfleet, I, 23; cf. Wolseley, *Reasonablenesse of Scripture-Belief*, pp. 85, 131.

ties of the soul, are acted by the sensual and fleshly appetite, no beast is more hurtful and brutish than a man.' Heresy and schism were 'both works of the flesh, the wicked product of a depraved nature, forged in an ill head and a naughty heart'; 'though every sinner is not a professed heretic, yet in every apostate conscience there are seeds of heresy'.[197] The atheist was similarly 'irrational' – less because he denied the proof of God and Revelation than because he refused the power of 'right reason' to command his errant will.[198] It is not 'contradiction to reason, but to appetite, that makes things of religion so incredible'.[199] The 'ground' of all atheism is the 'irregularity of our fleshly appetites and passions,' preached Daniel Whitby, 'a dissolute and sensual life being the cause as well as the result of atheism'. 'The power of godliness consists in the due regulation of our passions and affections, and the subjection of them to the rules of reason enlightened by the word of God.'[200] The gospel can only obtain 'a free admission into the assent of the understanding, when it brings a passport from a rightly disposed will'.[201] This was why 'the difficult work of religion is not in the understanding, but in the affections, and will.'[202]

Since religious dissidence sprang from the will and affections, from men's 'naughty hearts' and sinfulness, it could be allowed no latitude or indulgence. The Restoration Church of England did not believe that religious differences were simply differences of taste and upbringing, nor that all religions were equally valid; for the church to tolerate alternative opinions and practices in substantial matters of religion would be for her to condone moral deficiency and to connive at sin. The clergy were well aware of 'atheism creeping in by insensible degrees, from indulging too great a latitude in matters of religion'. During the Interregnum, when men were free to follow their own enthusiasms, 'the witty people of the nation became athe-

---

197. Richard Hollingworth, *Modest Plea*, p. 124; Thomas Long, *The Character of a Separatist* (1677), p. 48; Richard Parr, *Christian Reformation* (1660), p. 85; [Samuel Hill], *Necessity of Heresies*, p. 9.
198. Ellis, *Vanity*, p. 30; Tillotson, I, 78, 79; Wolseley, *Unreasonablenesse of Atheism*, pp. 9, 193; T. A., *Religio clerici*, p. 39; Calamy, *Sermons*, p. 108.
199. Allestree, I, 157.
200. Whitby, *Three Sermons Preach'd at Salisbury* (1685), sermon on II Timothy iii. 5, p. 15. Also see Lowde, *Reasonableness*, p. 48; Roger Hayward, *A Sermon Preacht before the King* (1673), pp. 11, 24; Hayward, *Sermon* (1676), pp. 11–12; Edward Sermon, *The Wisdom of Public Piety* (1679), pp. 1–2; Burnet, *Life and Death of Rochester*, p. 81.
201. South, I, i, 130–1, 116. Also see Hayward, *Sermon* (1673), p. 13; Burnet, *Life and Death of Rochester*, pp. 69–70, 126–7; Casaubon, *Of Credulity*, pp. 191–2.
202. William Bates, *The Divinity of the Christian Religion* (1677), p. 202; cf. pp. 201–9, 42–3.

ists, and the inconsiderate turned papists'.[203] If she allowed the English to go to hell in their own way, the church would be failing in her appointed mission. However illiberal it may now seem, her refusal to contemplate religious pluralism, like her stern attacks on vice, was inspired by the church's concern for the souls entrusted to her. Even the penal laws served this greater end: 'penalties in matters of religion are designed to remove such evil obstructions as lie in the passage to a man's right reason, that it may judge more equally and impartially of that which is laid before it.' The clergy denied that they were persecuting their opponents and argued that the penalties were designed only to rescue the judgement 'from the sluggishness and teachlessness it had contracted, and from that slavery into which the will and passions, its own natural subjects, had reduced it'.[204]

Yet it would also seem to follow from the clergy's understanding of religious error as a failure of the will rather than the intellect, that their arguments were doomed to failure. Prejudice and passion blinded their adversaries to the force of reason, 'the malady lying more in the perverseness of the will, than the mistake of the intellect'.[205] What could rational argument achieve against such wilful error? As South wrote of the Quakers, 'there being but little of argument to be expected from men professing nothing but inspiration, and the impulse of a principle discernible by none but themselves'.[206] Yet the clergy and the orthodox persevered; they churned out sermons, pamphlets and books to refute the arguments of atheists, 'fanatics' and papists. Anglican apologists continued to swap biblical texts and historical evidence with their religious opponents, and to offer 'rational' defences of revealed religion against the sceptics and atheists. Yet all the while they were convinced that their adversaries were wilfully and sinfully resisting the power of their arguments. In truth, these sermons and books were as much, if not more, for the benefit of the conforming, orthodox laity, 'who are obliged to converse with the literati of atheism' or enthusiasm, as for the atheists and enthusiasts themselves; by rehearsing the rational arguments for the existence of God, the apologists were arming their flock against hectoring atheists; by expounding providences and revealing hypocrisy and superstition, the churchmen were equipping their

---

203. Miles Barne, *Sermon*, p. 41; Josias Pleydell, *Loyalty and Conformity Asserted* (1682), p. 34.
204. [Henry Maurice], *The Antithelemite* (1685), pp. 40–1.
205. T. A., *Religio clerici*, p. 39. Also see the slightly later views reported by Hunter, 'Science and Heterodoxy', pp. 18–19.
206. William Assheton, *Cases of Scandal*, p. 6; South, II, 549.

congregations against plausible Jesuits or deluded fanatics. Equally, this literature was designed to keep conformists on the straight and narrow, to chastise the profane among Anglican congregations, and to warn the godly of the perils of going astray.[207]

The churchmen lived in fear of a fifth column of the dissolute and indifferent undermining the church. The bishops in conclave agreed that 'atheism' and vice were the greatest dangers threatening the church, the Compton Census confirmed that many who attended church never received the sacrament, and every visitation seemed to turn up apathetic communities like Bassingbourn, Cambridgeshire, where there were, in the laconic official phrase, '150 families, no dissenters, many sluggards'.[208] The Church of England 'has always been invulnerable against all darts, but what have been taken out of its own quiver ... the vice of professors undermines her very foundation'.[209] Sin and error knew no boundaries after all, and the Devil was no respecter of denominations. Consequently, the Anglican preachers spared neither schismatics outside the church nor sluggards within it; they moved easily from denouncing the dissidents who disputed the very principles of religion and civil government, to deploring the half-hearted obedience, piety and repentance of nominal Anglicans. The partially obedient were constantly reminded that at any time Satan could 'convert their *hypocrisy* to *profaneness*, their *partial* piety to *universal* ungodliness'.[210]

The church was to be strengthened by redeeming the lukewarm and restoring the partially pious to a whole-hearted piety, but rational argument alone would not achieve these laudable transformations. Men needed to be exhorted, frightened, cajoled and lulled into piety. Therefore many sermons and moral tracts drew portraits of the 'vicious atheist', the 'deluded enthusiast' and the 'egoistical Hobbist', packed with lurid detail about their sins and their fate, in the hope of terrifying any who had been toying with such heterodoxy. At the same time, these portraits served as a positive recommendation of all that was lacking in the damned souls, as a spur to sobriety, altruism, reasonableness and benevolence. The churchmen displayed an inexhaustible confidence in the power of example. 'We are concerned to confute the atheists and to defend the

207. James Arderne, *Directions concerning the Matter and Stile of Sermons* (1671), p. 18. This was also true of the earlier literature, see Hunter, 'Atheism', 147.
208. See Thomas Barlow, *The Genuine Remains* (1693), pp. 312–33; *Notes of the Episcopal Visitation of the Archdeaconry of Ely in 1685*, ed. H. Bradshaw (Cambridge Antiquarian Society Communications, 3, 1879), p. 338.
209. *WAWD*, I, 210.
210. Ibid., 252.

excellent religion which our Lord hath left us against gainsayers,' wrote Richard Kidder. 'But there is not a more effectual way of doing this than by an exemplary and pious life.'[211] 'Examples with the common people are more prevalent, usually, than arguments and demonstrations.' Dispute and controversy was but 'vain and fruitless'; 'the best expedient for the defence of truth, and preventing the growth of gross errors, is the enforcement of a good life by the precepts and practice of it.'[212] Restoration sermons are full of disavowals of theological speculation, religious controversy and clerical strife; the clergy readily admitted that their brethren had spent more time 'in arguing, than in teaching the principles of Christianity', and they exhorted one another to feed their flocks on the milk of the catechism rather than the red meat of controversy.[213] How many clergy have perplexed their flocks by searching into the abstruse mysteries of faith? How many have traded in subtle questions? asked Bishop King at his visitation in 1662. 'I have lived and shall die in this opinion, that there can be no greater danger to a settled church than liberty to dispute and call in question the points and articles of an established religion.'[214]

The Anglican clergy were particularly concerned that the popular reaction against fanaticism, superstition and hypocrisy should not betray members of the church into indifference. Every 30 January brought a reminder of 'the terrible effects of furious zeal, when it mistakes providence'; yet because puritan 'zeal hath set the world on fire,' the clergy asked their flocks, 'shall we be key-cold in piety, and serve God, as if we served him not?'[215] The churchmen lamented the 'want of true Christian zeal, and of a deep and serious sense of piety'. The Early Christians had possessed true zeal, but it had decayed as it became confused with 'the fancies and affections', with passion and self-interest.[216] For, as the churchmen stressed, 'zeal in it self is indifferent and made good, or bad, as its objects, and incentives are.' It was not a duty in itself, but only 'a forwardness

211. Richard Kidder, *Convivium coeleste* (1674), sig. A3.
212. Richard Hollingworth, *Modest Plea*, pp. 74–5; Roger Hayward, *A Sermon Preacht* (1673), pp. 24–5.
213. Lancelot Addison, *The Primitive Institution* (1674), pp. 217, 220.
214. Henry King, *A Sermon preached at Lewes in the Diocess [sic] of Chichester . . . Octob. 8. 1662* (1663), pp. 36–7.
215. Thomas Sprat, *A Sermon preached before the . . . Commons* (1678), p. 2; Richard West, *Profitableness of Piety*, p. 10; also see Goodman, *A Sermon Preached* (1685), p. 33; Gibbes, *Sermons*, p. 148.
216. John Goodman, *Serious Inquiry*, p. 80; *Free and Impartial Inquiry*, p. 120. Also see Littleton, III, 28; *WAWD*, I, 335, 376; Patrick, IV, 742; George Seignior, *God, the King and the Church* (1670), p. 160.

or circumstance of another duty', such as charity. Anglicans were exhorted to 'refine ever their zeal, and make it serve to kindle not consume their charity'.[217] Zeal was just one of the many words and phrases which had to be reclaimed from the puritans by the Church of England. 'It is now high time to redeem truth from the slavery and cheat of words,' explained Robert South, 'and certainly that can never be imagined to be *the spirit* or *power of godliness*, which teaches either to rob or desert the church, and shows itself in nothing but sacrilege and separation'.[218] Puritan cant in the service of puritan hypocrisy had debased the language of religious commitment and had fuelled cynicism. Those whose God is their belly, whose heaven is the tavern, and whose religion is debauchery, 'ease themselves from the trouble (as they take it) of holiness' by persuading themselves and others 'that religion is only an engine of state, that zeal is but an implement of ambition, that the precisest saints are but insinuating hypocrites, who disguise the basest and bloodiest designs under the mortified countenance of sanctity and humility'.[219] If on one side lay the danger that puritan excesses might smother Anglican religious zeal, on the other was the threat that Anglicans might mistake anti-puritan zeal for real piety. John Sharp argued that the identification of religion with party zeal 'was everywhere too much in fashion', among Anglicans as much as Dissenters:

> If I be a member of the Church of England, I am too often apt to think my self in a fair way to heaven, if I be but stout for the church, and zealous against the sectaries, and punctual in observing the ceremonies of the liturgy, and now and then come to the sacrament; Though it may be I have nothing of the true life and spirit of Christianity in me, nothing of that sobriety and meekness, and charity, and inward devotion that our Saviour doth indispensably require of all his followers. Nay so far from that it may be I think 'tis no matter how I live, if I be but a good subject to the king and a true son of the church. Nay it is well if I don't go further, it is well if I don't make vice and debauchery an essential character of a man that is right in his principles; it is well if I don't brand seriousness of conversation, and a care of one's words and actions with the name of fanaticism, and reproach every one as a puritan, that will not swear and drink and take those unChristian liberties that I do.[220]

---

217. Glanvil, *Essays*, essay 1, p. 28; Taylor, IV, 202; *WAWD*, I, 379.
218. South, III, 155.
219. Arthur Bury, *The Bow* (1662), pp. 29–30.
220. John Sharp, *A Sermon Preached ... April 11th 1679*, p. 15.

There was an unmistakably 'puritan' tang to this aspect of the Restoration Church of England. One may not be surprised to encounter such puritanism with a small 'p' in, say, Ralph Josselin's diary entries for the plague months of 1665: 'the season dry, profaneness common, piety very rare'; 'medicaments used, but no public call to repentance'; 'oh how few mind this hand of God that is lifted up, but go on in their vain ways'. But the same spirit fills the moving letters of Simon Patrick, a far more committed churchman, from his Covent Garden parish at the height of the plague:

> You see how desirous all are for some token of good, and how they catch at the smallest shadows for it: but the best sign of all, I doubt, is much wanting, and that is the reformation of men's manners; of which I hear little, unless that those come to church who did not come before. I think often of a saying in the 2nd Book of Esdras, which describes the temper of the world exactly, ch. xvi, v. 19, 20, *Behold famine and plague, tribulation and anguish, are sent as scourges for amendment: but for all these things they shall not turn from their wickedness, nor be allway mindful of thy scourges.*

And so it commonly falls out, reflected Patrick, that men soon forget their pains and their good resolutions, but 'I hope, my friend, the hand of God shall not be without its instruction to us; and that we shall be careful, if he lets us live, to improve it as we ought.'[221] What the churchmen preached in their fast and thanksgiving sermons, they believed; and what they preached could transcend denominational barriers. The Cheshire clergyman, Zachary Cawdrey, thanked God that there were 'more than fifty righteous in every city, both conformists and Nonconformists, who cry night and day for the averting of God's wrath, the reforming our manners, the healing our divisions, and the continuance of the public profession of his truth amongst us'.[222] Nonconformists and churchmen shared the same detestation of luxury and profanity, the same obsession with providential mercies and punishments, and 'improving' or making a 'use' of them, and the same Old Testament rhetoric.

If sin was the nation's illness, then the promotion of godliness was the remedy – and where better to begin than in the Church of England, which was already the best and purest of churches. The lives of the sons of the Church of England should be as holy as her doctrine, as divine as her discipline, and as reformed as her liturgy.[223] Only Anglican piety would silence the church's critics and

221.   Patrick, IX, 584–5.
222.   Zachary Cawdrey, *A Preparation for Martyrdom* (1681), p. 8.
223.   West, *Profitableness of Piety*, p. 11.

rivals. 'Our profaneness and contempt of religion, begets in them a contempt of authority and the laws; and the neglect of that holy service we pretend to extol, adds greater numbers to our enemies, than all their arts and industry can pervert', warned Henry Maurice.

> If we could weaken that faction, let us take away the support they have among our selves, the open scandal and viciousness of our lives: and then they are left without pretence, and fall without our trouble. Let us confute their reproaches by a reformation of our manners, and detect their hypocrisy, not by washing off the paint with satire, but by confronting their pretence and form with solid and sincere piety: without this, all other means will be to little purpose.[224]

Solid and sincere personal piety would transform the church into a bulwark of reformation which might then serve to shore up the defences against the sea of sin which was overtaking the entire nation – atheists, Dissenters, papists and apathetic Anglicans alike. But exhortation alone would not bring men to repentance; they needed the gospel preached and piety explained, they needed rules to live by, 'the rules of our holy religion, which *teach us to deny ungodliness and worldly lusts, and to live soberly, and righteously, and godly in this present world, in expectation of the blessed hope, and the glorious appearance of the great God, and our Saviour Jesus Christ*'.[225] Enshrined in these rules was the whole duty of man.

224. Henry Maurice, *A Sermon Preached . . . on January the 30th, 1681* (1682), p. 33.
225. Tillotson, II, 268–9.

Chapter 6

The Whole Duty of Man

God hath sent his son to establish a better covenant in his blood, to preach repentance, to offer pardon, to condemn sin in the flesh, to publish the righteousness of God, to convince the world of sin by his Holy Spirit, to threaten damnation, not to sinners absolutely, but absolutely to the impenitent, and to promise and give salvation to his sons and servants.[1]

Seventeenth-century English Christians knew that they were born into a wretched condition, that as the children of wrath they were all lost and cast away, condemned to death and eternal fire, but they consoled themselves that God had not left them quite without remedy. Out of his mere mercy, it had pleased God to make a bond with fallen man, a covenant that freed the sinner from the dominion of sin and promised him life and salvation. This was the covenant of the gospel, or the covenant of grace, 'wherein God engages himself of his mere grace upon the conditions therein mentioned, to forgive us our sins, and to be our God, and we to become his people'. The conditions required of sinners 'are repentance, conversion, holiness of life'.[2] Christ is the mediator of the covenant; he ratified it in his blood, and confirmed and sealed it with the sacraments. The Christian applied the covenant to himself through faith in Jesus Christ and the pious service which flowed from a lively faith. Thus the sacrament of baptism was 'only the applying to our particulars the covenant by God in Christ with all mankind in general, and the Lord's Supper was a 'federal rite' which reinforced that covenant.[3]

The Christian's sense of the mercy and benefit of the gospel covenant was heightened when he compared it with the prior 'na-

---

1. Taylor, VIII, 290.
2. MS Eng Th E 168, fos 91v, 93.
3. *WAWD*, I, 22–6; cf. Allestree, II, 31–5; I, 18.

tural' covenant between God and man.[4] Although the covenant of grace was repeatedly promised and foreshadowed in the Old Testament, the people of Israel had laboured under God's law of works, the strict law of Moses. The requirements of this law were beyond human capabilities.[5] The 'arbitrary impositions' of the Mosaical law tended to the destruction, rather than perfection, of man: 'it threatened sinners with death, it inflicted death, it did not promise eternal life, it ministered no grace, but fear and temporal hope: it was written in tables of stone, not in their hearts'.[6]

Christ had freed mankind from the curse of the law of works. Although grace was freely given to mankind, it would contradict the principle of divine justice to pardon our sins without some reciprocation. Under the covenant of grace God accepts sinners as if they were righteous on account of Christ's death on the cross. This acceptance is our 'justification'. Three components come together in our justification: 'upon God's part, his great mercy and grace; upon Christ's part, justice, that is the satisfaction of God's justice . . . and upon our part, true and lively faith in the merits of Jesu Christ; which yet is not ours but by God's working in us'.[7] Through faith in Jesus Christ our Saviour 'we embrace the promise of God's mercy and of the remission of our sins'.[8] By faith, Christians 'grasp', 'appropriate' or 'apprehend' Christ and the great thing he has done for them: by faith, they are incorporated into Christ, they live and grow in Jesus Christ. This union with Christ through faith was the crux of seventeenth-century religion. It provided the theological and emotional assurance of the Christian's salvation as a sinner; it united theology and piety by connecting a logical account with a religious experience.

Seventeenth-century Protestants presumed that theology was 'practical'. All clergymen were agreed that 'the way to judge of religion is by doing of our duty: and theology is rather a divine life

---

4. The covenant between God and Israel is at the heart of the Old Testament. For Reformed Christians, the covenant served the hermeneutical function of uniting Old and New Testaments and the soteriological function of establishing a basis upon which men might be saved. The law or covenant of works was obviously stressed as a means of highlighting the mercy and opportunity of the covenant of grace. See A.E. McGrath, *Iustitia Dei – A History of the Doctrine of Justification II* (Cambridge, 1986), ch. 6; Taylor, VIII, 289–90, 303–5; William Nicholson, *An Exposition of the Catechism of the Church of England* (1655: Oxford, 1844 edn cited), pp. 12–13.
5. Littleton, III, 72. Our justification 'must have been made out by our own personal exact obedience to every tittle of our obligations'.
6. Taylor, VIII, 289.
7. *Certain Sermons or Homilies Appointed to be Read in Churches* (1914 edn), p. 22.
8. Ibid., p. 29.

than a divine knowledge'. Or, as Edward Reynolds put it, 'theology is not a bare speculative science, which ultimately terminateth in the understanding, but ... is a doctrine ordered and directed unto practice.'[9] All laymen were familiar with theology, not in the form of abstruse technical arguments, but as the common scriptural coin of sermons, moral tracts and devotional manuals. Week after week, the parish minister would climb into his pulpit and hold up the same text or doctrine before his congregation while exploring it from every angle for their edification; sometimes, of course, the preacher returned to his subject 'without material addition' and simply bored his auditors;[10] but, slowly and surely, these long series of practical sermons instructed the laity in doctrine. The cumulative nature of Anglican preaching has another important consequence. A single sermon rarely tells the full story, and single passages can rarely epitomize a preacher's whole message. To grasp either the common ground or the novelties of seventeenth-century Protestant theology, it is necessary to survey the whole range of the preachers' work.

This chapter concentrates upon describing the new theological approach taken by the Restoration Church of England. This reorientation of the theology of salvation complemented the church's Catholic ecclesiology, matched her earnest pulpit pleas for reform, and inspired her emphasis on the practice of and aids to a holy life. Although it involved little more than a change of theological emphasis, the new Anglican preaching incurred the disdain or wrath of many Nonconformists, and of some conformists, because it jeopardized their conception of the sinner's union with Christ. Inevitably, the argument degenerated into an apparently arid contest over 'justification', the 'imputation' of 'personal righteousness' or 'Christ's righteousness', and 'antinomianism'. But this was no scholastic quarrel. Caught up in the denouement of a drama which had begun at the Reformation, the protagonists were fighting as much for their conceptions of what it was to be religious, for their notions of piety, as for their doctrines.

'The Whole Duty of Man': The Practical Theology of the Restoration Church

In 1658 there appeared a short anonymous devotional work entitled *The Practice of Christian Graces, or The Whole Duty of Man*. *The Whole Duty* took its title from Ecclesiastes xii. 13, 'fear God, and keep his

9. Taylor, VII, 379; Reynolds, *The Rich Mans Charge* (1658), sig. A2.
10. Evelyn, IV, 382; also see 529–30.

commandments: for this *is* the whole *duty* of man', but the book was organized according to

> the words of the Apostle *Titus* ii. 12. *That we should live soberly, righteously, and godly in this present world*; where the word soberly, contains our duty to our selves; righteously, our duty to our neighbour; and godly, our duty to God. These, therefore, shall be the heads of my discourse, our duty to God, ourselves, and our neighbour.

These duties were described in seventeen chapters, one of which was to be read each Sunday so that the whole book would be read through three times in a year. The first five chapters are taken up by our duty towards God, beginning with our faith in the commands and promises contained in his revealed Word – 'this belief of the promises must therefore stir us up to perform the condition, and till it do so, we can in no reason expect any good by them'. The third chapter is given over to a discussion of the duty of receiving the sacrament of the Lord's Supper; the fourth to the dangers of swearing, blasphemy and perjury; and the fifth to the duty of prayer. The sixth to ninth 'Sundays' expound man's duty to himself and entire chapters are devoted to covetousness and envy, and to temperance both in drinking and sleep. The remaining chapters detail our obligation to be righteous in our dealings with our neighbours and discuss murder, injury, theft, slander, civic and familial relations, and charity. Appended to the main text is a series of 'devotions', prayers, intercessions, thanksgivings, and a catalogue of 'breaches of our duty' to aid the devout in the task of self-examination.

The Whole Duty of Man managed to be both singular and typical. It became the most successful book of the age, in the possession of perhaps one out of every ten households, and was being read well into the eighteenth century.[11] Prefaced by Henry Hammond and promoted and protected by the bishops, *The Whole Duty* had the character of a semi-official publication of the Church of England. It spawned a number of sequels by the same anonymous author – who was almost certainly Richard Allestree, Oxford Professor of Divinity – and many imitations; several writers claimed to be 'the same author that wrote *The Whole Duty of Man* who it seems must countenance books to the world's end', observed Bishop Croft.[12] The tract

---

11.　C.J. Sommerville, 'On the Distribution of Religious and Occult Literature', *The Library*, 29 (1974), 221–5. Also see W.M. Spellman, *John Locke and the Problem of Depravity* (Oxford, 1988), pp. 68–9.

12.　Hammond also wrote to friends about 'two excellent pieces', *The Whole Duty* and *The Gentleman's Calling*; see *Nineteen Letters of the Truly Reverend and Learned Henry Hammond,*

and its successors were read by Restoration churchmen, recommended by them in print, and distributed to their parishioners.[13] In tandem with Jeremy Taylor's *Holy Living* or Hammond's *Practical Catechism*, or later perhaps with Simon Patrick's devotional works, *The Whole Duty of Man* came to be seen as one of the few indispensable books required by the devout Anglican, to be found in the student's chamber or in the prisoner's cell; the condemned prisoner, Sir Thomas Armstrong 'read all the way, as he was drawn, in the *Whole Duty of Man* until within sight of Tyburn.'[14] 'I do most heartily wish,' wrote John Eachard, 'that such as have spent their time in reading of books and sermons about *experiences, getting of Christ*, and the like, would change them all away for *The Whole Duty of Man*, that abound with very pious and intelligible rules of godly living, and useful knowledge tending to salvation.'[15] Intended as 'a short and plain direction to the very meanest readers', its clear delineation of Christian virtues and systematic devotional apparatus are undoubtedly one explanation for the success and longevity of this manual. It is thanks to *The Whole Duty*, says one authority, that 'Anglicanism had at this time, what it has not always had since, a closely integrated system of teaching and an interlocking way of life in which the performance of each duty assisted the performance of all the other'.[16]

The Whole Duty epitomized the commonsensical, non-controversial,

ed. F. Peck (1739), p. 53. For the church's attempt to stop pirate editions in Ireland, as the Bishop of London had in England, see MS Carte 45, fo. 144b. Bishop Fell later took over the publication of *The Whole Duty* at the Oxford press; see the preface to the *WAWD*; P. Elmen, 'Richard Allestree and *The Whole Duty of Man*', *The Library*, 6 (1951–2); Herbert Croft, *Legacy* (1679), sig. B2v.

13. See Patrick, I, 628; VI, 453; Clement Ellis, *The Gentile Sinner* (Oxford, 1661), sigs A4v–A5; John Rawlett, *The Christian Monitor* (1688 edn), p. 53; Edward Boughen, *A Short Exposition of the Catechism of the Church of England* (1673 edn), p. 90; Richard Kidder, *Convivium coeleste* (1674), p. 60; Tillotson, III, 420; John Scott, *The Works* (1718), I, sig. A3; Granville, II, 43; Edward Wetenhall, *Enter into thy Closet* (1672 edn), pp. 239, 371; Edward Lake, *Officium eucharisticum* (1673; Oxford, 1843 edn cited) pp. 60–1; *CR*, 'Thomas Gouge'; *DNB*, 'John Kettlewell'.

14. HMC, 14th Report, appendix 2 (Portland MSS, III), p. 380. Richard Hollingworth, *An Account of the Penitence of John Marketman* (1680), p. 7, relates how this convicted murderer prepared himself before his execution by reading *The Whole Duty*. Also see Robert Nelson, *The Life of Dr George Bull* (1713), p. 435; MS Top Oxon F 31, fo. 101; *The Flemings in Oxford: II*, ed. J.R. McGrath (Oxford Historical Society, 62, 1913), p. 100; R. Cave, 'Thomas Cradock's Books: A West Indian Merchant's Stock', *The Book Collector*, 25 (1976); J.L. Salter, 'The Books of an Early Eighteenth-century Curate', *The Library*, 33 (1978), items 45, 116.

15. John Eachard, *Some Observations upon the Answer to an Enquiry* (1671), p. 140 (Eachard was posing as a staunch churchman in this pamphlet).

16. C.J. Stranks, *Anglican Devotion* (1951), p. 132.

brand of theology on offer in the Restoration Church of England. It was typical of a certain practical ethos which had emerged in reaction to the speculative and 'experiential' religion of the Interregnum. 'Certainly there is no want of faith,' the clergy had observed during the 1650s; 'there is nothing more talked of . . . faith is become the language of good and bad, of the pure in spirit and the hypocrite, of the saint and the Devil that taketh his name, of the whole world'.[17] The Restoration churchmen's aim was to reconnect morality and godliness, to repair the moral damage done to the nation by the 'solifidian' sectaries who had severed virtue from piety, and had elevated the first table of the Ten Commandments above the second. 'The very life of religion consists in practice', but for too long, the churchmen believed, practical religion had been subordinated to formal, notional religion.

> Profession is only the badge of a Christian, belief the beginning, but practice is the nature, and custom the perfection. For it is this which translates Christianity from a bare notion into a real business; from useless speculations into substantial duties; and from an idea in the brain into an existence in the life. An upright conversation is the bringing of the general theorems of religion into the particular instances of solid experience; and if it were not for this, religion would exist nowhere but in the Bible. The grand deciding question at the last day will be, not, What have you said? or, What have you believed? but, What have you done more than others?[18]

Anglicans were urged to take up holy living in conjunction with a lively faith, to add the power of godliness to its form, to emulate the piety of the primitive Christians. They were reminded that 'godliness is in some sense an art or mystery, and we all know that it is practice chiefly that makes the artist.'[19]

Belief, then, was not enough. John Tillotson pointed out that 'a bare assent to the truth of the gospel, without the fruits of holiness and obedience, is not *a living but a dead faith*, and so far from being acceptable to God, that is an affront to him.' Faith as an intellectual assent can only ever be 'a notional thing', explained Adam Littleton, and it must therefore find expression in terms of repentance and new obedience. William Clagett argued that faith could not be separated from these two other qualities and that the confusion about justification by faith alone arose from a failure to recognize that 'where

17. Farindon, III, 249.
18. South, II, 145, also see Littleton, II, 132–3.
19. South, II, 144.

forgiveness and salvation is promised to one single condition, there the presence of all the rest is supposed'.[20] South agreed that wherever in the scriptures justification is ascribed to faith alone, 'there the word *faith* is still used by a metonymy of the antecedent from the consequent, and does not signify abstractedly a mere persuasion, but the obedience of an holy life performed in the strength and virtue of such a persuasion'.[21] On Easter Day 1670, Dr Breton of Deptford preached on the resurrection, and on the subsequent Sundays on 'how we are justified by Christ's rising again', 'how justification has reference to works as well as faith', and 'how faith was more than a firm belief or strong persuasion'.[22] Saving faith was not to be abstracted from the process of regeneration, from the repentance and obedience of the new creature.

It was the task of the Restoration preacher 'to remove the lazy mistakes, and to convince how unavailable, a solitary speculative faith is, and what a killing peril there is in delays of a thorough reformation'.[23] And a determination to do just this can be seen in churchmen of all ideological hues. John Rawlett was an hesitant conformist and an associate of John Wilkins and Richard Baxter; yet, in his successful devotional writings, he insisted upon the manifestation of saving faith.

A right belief leads a man to holiness of life. And therefore in holy scripture do we find so much mention made of faith, or of believing in God and in Christ. This is in many places highly extolled, and most strictly required of us, as the very sum of our duty; insomuch as we are often said to be justified or pardoned on account of our faith, and to be saved by faith, and all this chiefly, as I suppose, because true faith produces obedience; and makes a man become an humble and sincere disciple of Jesus Christ, and so makes us fit for the mercies of God in and through our blessed Saviour. But when faith does not bring forth the fruit of holiness, and good works, it's of no value with God, nor will stand us in good stead, as you may see at large in the second chapter of St. James, to name no other place.[24]

Richard Sherlock, who had impeccable credentials as a royalist and an Interregnum 'sufferer', also emphasized the mutual dependence of faith and a good life. 'Have you not been mistaken in the nature of

---

20. Tillotson, VI, 456; Littleton, II, 28; William Clagett, *Eleven Sermons* (1693), p. 80.
21. South, II, 147.
22. Evelyn, III, 546.
23. James Arderne, *Directions concerning the Matter and Stile of Sermons* (1671), p. 19.
24. Rawlett, *Christian Monitor* (12th edn, 1688), p. 31.

a true Christian faith making it to be a presumption upon the *promises* of the gospel abstract from obedience to the *precepts* thereof? And hath not thy faith been rather *notional* in the brain than *practical* in the heart and life? been more in talk and dispute, and verbal profession, than in life and good works, and holy conversation? for the *kingdom of God is not in word, but in power of holy actions.*'[25] At court, in the City and in his own parish church at Deptford, John Evelyn heard sermon after sermon denouncing 'speculative faith' and insisting that practice must go along with knowledge, that the power of godliness must accompany its form.[26] 'Showing the necessity of an holy life' was the main preoccupation of the church's preachers, catechists, theologians and moral writers.[27] As a slogan, and as a book, 'the whole duty of man' stood for a single pastoral and theological enterprise to restore the wholeness of Christian profession.[28]

The whole duty of man was promoted in a profusion of different publications; in sermons, in small tracts 'fitted for the pocket' or the 'closet', and in large folios for the well-to-do and educated. These works are straightforward moral guides, or homilies about the correct attitudes and conduct of a Christian, or works of spiritual exhortation and inspiration, or paraphrases of the church's catechism, or devotional manuals with prayers and pious meditations, or all of these things at once. Such breadth of approach and diversity of format were necessary because these books were attempting to fill a gap in the church's pastoral discipline. The Church of England lacked an effective instrument of personal spiritual direction: she had no means, beyond the pulpit and liturgy, of working for individual repentance; she had no way of tailoring spiritual examinations, exercises and comforts to the individual; and the discipline she could exercise over her flocks was limited.[29] This was, of course, a problem common to many Reformed churches since the Protestant repudiation of the sacrament of penance precluded the use of the Roman Catholic tool of confession. During the Interregnum, the puritans' favoured solution, to exercise discipline by controlling access to the sacrament, had been tried and found wanting. The sacrament had been allowed only to those who would submit to 'discipline', which usually meant examination and admonition and promises of amend-

25. Richard Sherlock, *Mercurius Christianus: The Practical Christian* (1673), p. 18. Also see Sherlock's entry in *DNB*.
26. See Evelyn, III, 339, 538, 564; IV, 37, 164, 167, 258–9, 288, 291, 355, 451, 463, 521, 630.
27. Evelyn, IV, 490, also see 18, 82, 84, 414, 475; III, 574, 630.
28. See Evelyn, III, 552; IV, 190, 375, 379, 384, 536.
29. See *A Vindication of the Clergy* (1672), pp. 108–15.

ment from the communicant. But such discipline could only ever be voluntary; and while it was perfectly feasible within the gathered congregations of the various sects, it was unworkable within a parochial ministry. When Richard Baxter resolved to exercise discipline over all of his Kidderminster parishioners, only 600 submitted. At least a thousand parishioners of communicable age chose rather 'to withdraw than live under discipline'; some of these were 'honest' but forbidden to submit by masters, parents or husbands, others were profane and scandalous, and yet others refused because they followed the 'prelatical divines'.[30] The Church of England would have no truck with such schemes to deny sinners access to the sacrament; indeed, she had her work cut out to ensure that parishioners made their obligatory three communions a year.

The Restoration church preferred to think of spiritual direction in terms of individual instruction by the parish minister. It was certainly needed; the clergy observed 'the gross ignorance of many, which cries aloud for personal instruction; the open profaneness of others, which stands in need of the most serious admonitions, and seasonable reprehensions from their spiritual guides'. And experience had shown that personal instruction was effective, that 'half an hour's close discourse' worked 'more knowledge and remorse of conscience' in a sinner than could years of preaching.[31] The enthusiastic Restoration rector of Hanwell was determined

> either to send for or to visit at their own homes, all such under my change, whom I judge . . . to need my personal conference in private, namely, the sick and weak, the sad and distressed, who lie under the sore burden of any affliction or temptation, the poor and needy, those who are at difference, the scandalous and extravagant, the gross neglecters of religious duties, the slanderers and injurers of their neighbours, the ignorant and seduced, with the seducers of others either by their mispersuasions, or ill examples.[32]

The difficulty, however, was getting parishioners to submit to instruction.

Catechizing, 'the key of knowledge, which readily opens the door into the great mystery of godliness', at least brought the young

---

30. *RB*, I, 91.
31. John James, *Ad clerum* (1678), p. 39. Also see John Eachard, *The Grounds and Occasions of the Contempt of the Clergy* (1670), p. 108; Nathaniel Bisbie, *The Bishop Visiting* (1686), p. 29; Richard Baxter, *The Reformed Pastor* (1656; abridged edn, Edinburgh, 1974 cited), p. 175.
32. *Bishop Fell and Nonconformity*, ed. M. Clapinson (Oxfordshire Record Society, 62, 1980), pp. 18–19.

within the clergy's reach.[33] The work of inculcating the first principles of Christianity never ends, and like their predecessors, Restoration churchmen competed with one another to produce ever more effective catechisms.[34] There was a well-established tradition of unofficial catechisms, usually described on their title-pages as 'first drawn up for the author's private use', but from the mid-seventeenth century, the number of paraphrases and expositions of the Prayer Book catechism seems to have increased. Such works were not intended to remedy the deficiencies of the official catechism, but to recommend its sound and uncontroversial doctrines, and to promote the liturgy of which it was a part. It is tempting to identify this development as a reaction to the increasingly partisan tone of many denominational catechisms, not least the popular Westminster Assembly catechisms. Certainly, many catechists were consciously seeking 'to heal the distempers of this church' by feeding their flocks on the milk of fundamental truths rather than the red meat of speculative preaching and theological controversy; and it was all the better that catechizing 'will not a little redound to the credit of the clergy'.[35] Nor did the catechetical writers of the Restoration church limit themselves to writing for children; they believed that the Prayer Book catechism was 'improvable to a more diffusive use in the church, than only to capacitate youth for the rite of confirmation', and so addressed a range of audiences in a variety of ways.[36] While the massive works of Thomas Comber or Gabriel Towerson can only have been aimed at the clergy themselves, Comber and Bishop Ken were adept at broadening the catechism into a series of devotional exercises. Yet, paradoxically, at precisely the same time that the clergy were publishing so many catechisms, the church found it difficult to get the laity to send their children and servants to be catechized. The hierarchy exhorted the parish clergy to diligence and considered legislation to enforce lay attendance.[37] But to no avail. Even the dissemination of expositions of the official catechism seemed only to cause confusion. When Bishop Fell sent out an

---

33. Boughen, *Exposition of the Church Catechism*, sig. A3.
34. See I.M. Green, '"For Children in Yeeres and Children in Understanding": The Emergence of the English Catechism under Elizabeth and the Early Stuarts', *JEH*, 37 (1986); I.M. Green, 'The Changing Form and Content of Religious Instruction in Early Modern England', unpublished paper given at Oxford, 20 January 1987.
35. Lancelot Addison, *The Primitive Institution* (1674), pp. 67, 163 and *passim*; also see John Worthington, *A Form of Sound Words* (1674), preface by Edward Fowler.
36. Thomas Marshall, *The Catechism Set Forth* (Oxford, 1679), sig. A2v.
37. E. Cardwell (ed.), *Documentary Annals of the Reformed Church of England* (2nd edn, Oxford, 1844), p. 337; Granville, II, 100–1; MS Tanner 447, fos 85–99. Also see *Fell*, ed. Clapinson, p. 23.

exposition to his diocesan clergy, they were puzzled: 'some are of opinion that you require it to be learnt by the younger people of the parish, who are to render us an account thereof; others that your lordship expects only, it should be a rule for our expounding of it.'[38]

The church's catechism was intended to pave the way to confirmation and reception of the sacrament. There were undoubtedly some in the Restoration church who looked upon confirmation as an examination of the catechumen's faith and knowledge, but there were others for whom the rite of confirmation was a blessing, an invocation of the Holy Ghost, or even a sort of sacrament; and in practical terms, the rite did appear to most participants more like a bishop's blessing than an examination.[39] Once confirmed the English parishioner was effectively emancipated from the personal instruction of his minister. When the Lord's Supper was to be celebrated, the clergy could attempt to prepare their parishioners by preaching on the strict qualifications required of a communicant, as Isaac Archer did before the first celebration held at Chippenham after the Restoration. Archer also visited the homes of 'such as would receive, to speak with them concerning so weighty a business; I found them generally honest in their way but ignorant, wherefore I told them what I could of the grounds of religion, and particularly about the sacrament, and showing the great dangers they incurred by unworthy receiving, I left it to their own consciences what to do'.[40] In tract after tract, the clergy urged their flocks to consult a spiritual guide before receiving the Lord's Supper.[41] While denying absolutely that the church held auricular confession to a priest to be 'an integral part of repentance, and necessary condition of absolution', the clergy did advise 'the disburdening of a troubled conscience . . . to some knowing, discreet, spiritual person for his advice and resolution . . . as a sovereign expedient'.[42] The only provision made for such private 'confession' and 'absolution' in the Church of England's liturgy was in the Office for the Visitation of the Sick. Comforting the sick and afflicted was a crucial pastoral duty in the eyes of both the clergy and many of their parishioners.[43] But getting

38. *Fell*, ed. Clapinson, p. 24.
39. See *RB*, I, 93; E. Cardwell, *A History of Conferences and other Proceedings connected with the Revision of the Book of Common Prayer* (3rd edn, Oxford, 1849), pp. 327–30, 358–60; Hamon L'Estrange, *The Alliance of Divine Offices* (1659; LACT, Oxford, 1846).
40. CUL, Add. MS 8499, fo. 81.
41. See *WAWD*, I, 33; Thomas Comber, *The Plausible Arguments of a Romish Priest Answered* (1686), pp. 37–8; Patrick, IV, 30; Kidder, *Convivium coeleste*, pp. 128–9.
42. South, III, 364–5. Also see Taylor, XIV, 503–4; Littleton, II, 45–6; Pocock, VI, 216; Simon Lowth, *Catechetical Questions* (1673), p. 83; Evelyn, IV, 36.
43. *Vindication of the Clergy*, p. 112; Taylor, XIV, 504–5; [John Martin], *Go in Peace*

the hale and hearty to open their hearts to the clergy may not have been as easy. Since the laity were so reluctant to look upon the clergy 'as a kind of parents to whom they should go in all their needs', the catechisms, moral guides and little manuals of devotion had to serve as spiritual directors to the laity.[44] The Restoration clergy set great store by these publications – despite their lack of evident success in reforming the nation. When helping to prepare the young people at Easington for the Easter sacrament, Denis Granville advised 'all that can read, and are able, to buy a Bible, Common Prayer Book, and *Whole Duty of Man*', while to his own nephew, he recommended Hammond's '*The Practice of Piety*'.[45] Even the Roman Catholics grudgingly admitted that *The Crumbs of Comfort* and *The Practice of Piety* were 'for the substance good innocent books, with store of pious affections' and that the more recent *Whole Duty* was 'yet better'.[46] In Wales, an inter-denominational group of charitable persons distributed 500 Welsh translations of *The Whole Duty* and 2,500 'of a tract called *The Practice of Piety*' in 1674–5.[47] The enthusiasm of Restoration churchmen for these moral and devotional works was a legacy of the experience of the 1640s and 1650s, when books of practical divinity, of consoling private devotion, and uplifting moral exhortation were apparently popular.[48] It may also reflect the characteristic over-confidence of the literate in the persuasive power of print.

As a pastoral enterprise the whole duty of man was suffused with the penitential spirituality that had predominated in Interregnum Anglicanism and in the providentialist preaching of the Restoration. The whole duty had a single starting point in 'the necessity of repentance and a pungent sorrow for sin'.[49]

> This repentance is, in short, nothing but a turning from sin to God, the casting off all our former evils, and instead thereof constantly practising all those Christian duties which God re-

(1674); Eachard, *Grounds and Occasions*, p. 108; D.A. Spaeth, 'Parsons and Parishioners: Lay–Clerical Conflict and Popular Piety in Wiltshire Villages, 1660–1740, (unpublished Brown University Ph.D. thesis, 1985), pp. 117–21.

44. Sherlock, *Mercurius*, sig. A4.
45. Presumably *The Daily Practice of Devotion*; Granville, II, 43–4, 62–9.
46. Hugh Serenus Cressy, *Fanaticism Fanatically Imputed* (1672), p. 90. Cressy is discussing the dearth of Anglican works of help in the contemplative life. For Catholic appreciation of such printed manuals see E. Duffy, 'The English Secular Clergy and the Counter-Reformation', *JEH*, 34 (1983), 228–30.
47. M.G. Jones, 'Two Accounts of the Welsh Trust, 1675 and 1678 (?)', *Bulletin of the Board of Celtic Studies*, 9 (1939).
48. See Wood, II, 56.
49. Evelyn, IV, 66.

quires of us. And this is so necessary a duty, that without it we certainly perish. We have Christ's word for it (Luke xiii. 5), '*Except ye repent, ye shall all likewise perish.*'[50]

'At the very entrance of her liturgy' the church quoted Ezekiel's plea that men should turn from their wickedness and save their souls.[51] Repentance was probably the most common theme of Anglican sermons on ordinary Sundays.[52] Repentance was *unum necessarium*, the one necessity, for salvation, because it embraced both faith and the repudiation of sin; repentance was the application to ourselves of the covenant of grace.[53] Better still a benevolent deity had issued a standing invitation: 'how infinite is the goodness of God that excludes no sinners from the hopes of pardon who have a heart to repent sincerely of their sins!' marvelled Stillingfleet. 'And how just is God in the final punishment of those sinners, who still go on in their sins, and refuse to repent; after all the invitations and encouragements which are given them to that end!'[54]

Repentance was a process: it requires our sorrow for sin and our forsaking sin; 'it must be a repentance *from* sin as well as *for* sin'.[55] One broke free of sinfulness in stages, beginning with 'consideration' and self-examination.[56] The Christian was to take a strict search and severe scrutiny of his life, to 'ravage into' himself: we should examine ourselves not by 'the Lesbian rule of our own deceitful appetite, or corrupt reason; but some superior law, the revealed will of God, according to which he would have us walk in order to salvation, both for practice, and that summarily in the ten commandments, the abridgement of the moral law; and for faith, in the doctrine of the gospel'.[57] On reaching his sixtieth birthday, John Evelyn closeted himself away for a whole week to take a solemn survey of his life and sins and to make his peace with God.[58]

50. *WAWD*, I, 48; also see William Clagett, *Seventeen Sermons* (1689), sermon 12.
51. Littleton, II, 22.
52. For some examples see Evelyn, III, 257, 302, 304, 353, 356, 368–72, 586, 588; IV, 3, 5, 33, 36, 44–5, 52, 61, 89, 94, 165, 204, 206, 224, 238, 239, 249, 277, 283, 386, 389, 402, 523, 528, 536, 570, 573.
53. For typical accounts of repentance see Patrick, IV, 537–79; Littleton, I, 132–42; II, 189–91, 255–67; Taylor, VIII, 307–35; IX, 221.
54. Stillingfleet, I, 387.
55. Littleton, I, 142.
56. On the importance of 'consideration' or sober self-assessment, see Tillotson, I, 301–22; *WAWD*, I, 220, 225; Anthony Horneck, *The Great Law of Consideration* (1677).
57. Littleton, II, 83.
58. Evelyn, IV, 223–4; Evelyn often used his birthday and the New Year for such pious purposes.

'Labour for true brokenness of heart,' urged the preachers, 'labour to have your hearts broken for sin, and broken from sin'.[59] Face your sins and lusts in all their ugliness and deformity, and let the punishments they deserve spur you on. 'If that heart of thine be hard and stony, strike it with Moses his rod, with legal terrors; and let the waters of thy penitential tears gush out and flow, to wash off the filth and refresh the scorchings of thy guilty conscience.'[60] Mourning the lack of discipline in the Interregnum church, one cleric advised that 'the absence and want of it must be made up in this present distraction, by the private humiliation and secret revenge of every cordial penitent in the serious crucifixion of every member of the old man . . . all other courses of reforming, are but delusions of the Devil'.[61] Crucifying the old man required the confession of past sins until 'gnawen at the very heart by that viper sorrow'. But even such heartfelt sorrow for sin was useless if it was inspired simply by fear of the Almighty. Sorrow had to be transmuted into 'contrition', a sincere and voluntary penitence and repudiation of all the ways of sin. 'God loves such a pungent sorrow as pricks to the very heart, and gives a deadly wound to all our sins.'[62] The clergy emphasized 'the benefit of penitential tears; the mourning here expressed importing godly sorrow and contrition'.[63] Once the penitent's heart was broken from and for sin, then he could begin to take comfort by laying hold of Christ, who alone can sooth the bruised reed of a contrite heart – 'bathe thy soul in his blood, the sovereign balsam of a wounded conscience'.[64]

The culmination of the whole process was 'the transition which the penitent makes from acts of contrition to the acts of resolution for amendment of life, without which all sorrow for sin is in vain'. The true penitent resolves to bring forth fruits meet for repentance, to amend his life and follow the path of righteousness.[65] The infallible signs of evangelical repentance were internal mortification and external reformation. True repentance made the outward man conformable to the inward man.[66] As John Sharp reminded the court in a Lenten sermon, 'tears and even transports and satisfaction in holy performances are not that repentance God requires, without a per-

59. MS Eng Th D 59, fo. 11.
60. Littleton, II, 190.
61. Peter Samwaies, *Devotion Digested* (1652), p. 219.
62. Patrick, V, 32.
63. Evelyn, IV, 249.
64. Littleton, II, 190.
65. Patrick, IV, 563.
66. MS Eng Th D 59, fo. 8; Littleton, II, 87.

petual progress, an entire reformation, an holy, useful and innocent life'.[67]

In their sermons and tracts the clergy demolished the impediments to effective repentance. They took special care to correct what they saw as the errors spread by puritan and Nonconformist mishandling of the doctrine of repentance.[68] For the puritan, the experience of conversion was a crucial turning point in this process of regeneration, but the Restoration clergy treated the question of conversion with extreme caution, fearing that it was open to misinterpretation as either a 'universal necessity' or 'a mere momentaneous act, a kind of qualm or fit of religion'.[69] The churchmen also directed their scorn against those who cheated themselves by deferring their repentance, by promising themselves that they would eventually return to the way of righteousness before their earthly course was run.[70] Deathbed repentance was rarely sincere or sufficient; 'for if repentance on our deathbed seem so very late for the sins of our life, what time shall be left us to repent of the sins we commit on our deathbed?'[71] At the other extreme were those who made repentance too easy a duty; it was the tragedy of the Roman Catholic church to sell salvation too cheaply as if mere attrition in the sinner was enough.[72] But papists were not the only ones who made this mistake; 'we go round like men enchanted, in a circle of repenting and sinning,' preached Allestree, 'now repentance are [sic] but dislikes, little short unkindnesses at our sins, and wouldings to do better'.[73] Benjamin Calamy complained that

> There are some men of that facile temper, that they are wrought upon by every object they converse with, whom any affectionate discourse, or serious sermon, or any notable accident, shall put into a fit of religion, which yet usually lasts no longer, than till somewhat else comes in their way, and blots out those impressions, and these men are good or bad as it happens.[74]

67. Evelyn, IV, 573.
68. Patrick, V, 23–33, 281; Gibbes, *XXXI Sermons* (1677).
69. John Goodman, *The Old Religion* (1684), p. 106. Also see Tillotson, I, 315; Littleton, II, 22–36; J.S. McGee, *The Godly Man in Stuart England – Anglicans, Puritans, and the Two Tables 1620–70* (New Haven and London, 1976), pp. 55–9.
70. See Littleton, II, 35–6; Benjamin Calamy, *Sermons Preached upon Several Occasions* (1687), pp. 351–9, 225–6; Barrow, III, 301–43; Evelyn, IV, 32, 109, 127, 136, 244, 308, 333, 370–1, 502, 578.
71. Taylor, XIV, 505; also see Calamy, *Sermons*, p. 219–54; Tillotson, I, 322.
72. See Allestree, I, 35; Tillotson, I, 260–1; Evelyn, IV, 538, 562.
73. Allestree, I, 33; also see Evelyn, IV, 283, and the many sermons on repentance recorded in his diary, *passim*.
74. Calamy, *Sermons*, p. 342.

While such debased notions of repentance arose from a lack of consideration, other mistakes, with lamentably antinomian consequences, were rooted in the misreading of various scriptural metaphors as if they taught a totally extrinsic regeneration of the converted sinner. 'It is the greatest and justest discouragement in the world to all endeavours of repentance and reformation,' said John Tillotson, 'to tell men that they can do nothing in it'. Against the texts cited to prove that God alone works regeneration, Tillotson pitted

> *Work out your own salvation* [Phil. ii. 12]; *repent and turn your selves from all your evil ways* [Ezekiel xiv. 6]; *Make ye new hearts and new spirits* [Ezekiel xviii. 31]. These are more than a thousand metaphors to convince a man, that we may and ought to do something towards repentance and conversion.[75]

It was not possible to repent in part or in stages; 'there is no *medium* between living in sin and forsaking of it; and nothing deserves the name of repentance, that is short of that.' Repentance was to be the business of our whole lives.[76]

Some seasons and some occasions in our lives, however, are particularly suited to the work of repentance. It is only fit that we confess and repent our sins in times of affliction, illness, approaching death and, above all, before approaching the altar to partake of the eucharist. Under the heading of 'the preparation to the Lord's Supper', the manuals and catechisms urged communicants to particularly examine 'the truth of our (1) repentance and new obedience (2) faith (3) thankfulness (4) and charity'.[77] The Lord's Supper was of paramount importance in structuring the regime of repentance and the holy life: 'the communion is the most sublime duty of Christianity, the compendium of religion, the best opportunity for repentance, the highest exercise of faith, and the strongest engagement to our charity'.[78] The churchmen stressed the relationship between the Lord's Supper and the sacrament of baptism; the eucharist was 'an office reinforcing that baptismal covenant, an holy rite and symbol by which we reassume the same vow as before with new resolution and more considerate purpose of mind'.[79] Patrick

---

75. Tillotson, VI, 411, 427.
76. Stillingfleet, I, 230. Also see Calamy, *Sermons*, p. 323; South, I, 431; Thomas Pierce, *A Seasonable Caveat against the Dangers of Credulity* (1679), p. 17.
77. Thomas Comber, *The Church Catechism with a Brief and Easie Explanation* (1681), p. 31.
78. Thomas Comber, *A Companion to the Temple: Or, A Help to Devotion in the Use of the Common Prayer* (1684), III, epistle dedicatory.
79. Edward Wetenhall, *Two Discourses for the Furtherance of Christian Piety and Devotion* (1671), pp. 315–16; South, I, 46; Lancelot Addison, *An Introduction to the Sacrament*

believed that a proper application of religious duties produced a spiral of religious endeavour in the communicant's life:

> As our knowledge and obedience increases, so doth likewise the favour of God and his testimonies of that favour: and the more his mercies are assured unto us, the more are we engaged and confirmed in our resolution of persisting in obedience. So that it is but one and the same thing that it is thus frequently ratified, first in baptism, and afterward in confirmation, and lastly in the sacrament of the Lord's Supper.[80]

Even those Anglicans who maintained the absolute necessity of the Lord's Supper as a means of grace, admitted that regeneration began with baptism, 'but the continuance of this grace, and the daily assistances of the Holy Spirit' depended upon diligent attendance at the Lord's Supper.[81] The mystery of the sacrament was eminently practical in effect. 'It matters not where we begin,' wrote Jeremy Taylor,

> for if I describe the excellencies of this sacrament, I find it engages us upon matters of duty, and inquiries practical: if I describe our duty, it plainly signifies the greatness and excellency of the mystery: the very notion is practical, and the practice is information: we cannot discourse of the secret, but by describing our duty: and we cannot draw all the lines of duty, but so much duty must needs open a cabinet of mysteries.[82]

'A little epitome of the whole gospel', was Patrick's definition of the sacrament; 'it increases our love to God and our love to man, which is the sum of all our duty.'[83]

The vision of the whole duty of man was a vision of the wholeness of the Christian life, of 'an entire compliance of the whole man'. The aim was to overcome the separation of virtue from religion, of faith from works, theology from piety, and of the first from the second 'table' of the decalogue. The goal and the medium were perhaps deceptively straightforward; anyone could use these manuals of moral duty and all men aspired to be pious and virtuous – but the church's

(1682), pp. 1–2, 119–21; Anthony Horneck, *The Crucified Jesus* (1686), pp. 308–20; Allestree, II, 31–5.

80. Patrick, I, 77; and see Daniel Brevint, *The Christian Sacrament and Sacrifice* (Oxford, 1673), pp. 1–2.

81. William Sherlock, *A Practical Discourse of Religious Assemblies* (1681; 1682 edn cited), p. 357.

82. Taylor, XV, 403.

83. Patrick, I, 174–5.

demands were not negligible. Let everyone that nameth the name of Christ depart from iniquity, says the Apostle (II Timothy ii. 19); 'our religion must be a vital principle inwardly to change and transform us'.[84] Holy living involved a transformation: 'it must be a full assent and constant practice, in a turning of the whole heart, a complete engagement of the will and affections, of all the faculties of the soul and members of the body, in an universal and impartial obedience'.[85] It was up to the individual to work out his own salvation with fear and trembling.[86]

'Mere Moral Men': Salvation, Moralism and Moral Theology

Several of our most eminent divines, after the Restoration, [In the margin: Dr Wilkins, Barrow, Tillotson, Scott] set themselves both by preaching and writing to enlarge upon the importance of moral duties, and to recommend them with great earnestness to the regard of the people; to such a degree, as to stand charged by others with too great a disregard of the doctrines and duties peculiar to Christianity. Whereas, the case in reality was this. During the times of confusion, many of the preachers had not only forborn to inculcate the duties of morality, but had laboured to depreciate them; to persuade the people that faith was all, and works nothing. And therefore the clergy after the Restoration in order to take off those unhappy impressions, found themselves obliged to inculcate with more than ordinary diligence, the necessity of moral duties in the Christian life, and to labour to restore them to their proper share in the Christian scheme. But those of them, who with the honest view I have mentioned, laboured the most zealously in that way, were at the same time as zealous to explain to the people the great work of our redemption by *Jesus Christ*, as the means of salvation which God has appointed . . . [87]

The churchmen's presentation of the 'wholeness' of the Christian life looked suspiciously like the recommendation of a good life, as if, in the words of one Nonconformist, they regarded the Christian faith as no more than 'a hearty assent to the truth of the Gospel and endeavouring to live according to it'.[88] It was complained that the

84. Tillotson, I, 187.
85. Littleton, I, 140–1.
86. See p. 294 above; Evelyn, IV, 131, 166, 449.
87. Edmund Gibson, *The Bishop of London's Three Pastoral Letters* (1732), p. 64. I am grateful to Isabel Rivers for pointing out this source to me.
88. Lewis Du Moulin, *A Short and True Account of the Several Advances the Church of England hath made towards Rome* (1680), p. 34.

Restoration churchmen gave too much weight to 'these moral actions' of repentance, sobriety and virtue, and reduced Christianity to pious practices and virtuous performances.[89] And even today the impression lingers that the Restoration church was moralistic, complacent and prudential, in short, that she was drifting towards latitudinarian indifference.[90] Perhaps it was inevitable that the church should bring such strictures down upon herself when she attempted to break away from the theological shibboleths of the Reformed tradition. Yet, as we shall see, for all her promotion of piety and virtue, the Restoration church never lost sight of justification by faith or the saving grace of God.

During the Interregnum, several divines had self-consciously asserted 'good works', in the full knowledge that they were being provocative and ran the risk of being stigmatized as 'mere moral men'.[91] Simon Patrick had eulogized a brother minister at his funeral for maintaining 'good works, as the necessary fruits of Christian faith; and such works as are due to men, as well as those that have a more immediate respect to God: good morality was part of his Christianity'.[92] In the early 1660s John Tillotson experienced 'disrelish' of his preaching, both in London and in the Suffolk parish of Keddington, when he urged his congregations not to neglect that part of Christianity which goes 'under that contemptuous name of morality'. And later William Assheton made a robust defence of the duties of the second table of the decalogue 'which if they must neither be preached up by us, nor practised by them, lest thereby we should too much exalt a moral state; I must tell them, and I do it with some dread upon my spirits, we may come to roar in hell for not being moral men'.[93] The clergy believed that in standing up for 'morality' they were asserting the importance of a fruitful faith, of charity, and of the human side of the covenant of grace. 'A strange

89. Littleton, II, 35; Thomas Pierce, *A Collection of Sermons upon Several Occasions* (Oxford, 1671), p. 294.
90. See D.D. Wallace, *Puritans and Predestination – Grace in English Protestant Theology 1525–1695* (Chapel Hill, 1982), p. 189; C.F. Allison, *The Rise of Moralism – The Proclamation of the Gospel from Hooker to Baxter* (1966); J.S. McGee, *Godly Man in Stuart England*, esp. pp. 59–63, 94–5, 208–34, 251–3; I. Rivers, 'Grace, Holiness, and the Pursuit of Happiness: Bunyan and Restoration Latitudinarianism', in *John Bunyan Conventicle and Parnassus*, ed N.H. Keeble (Oxford, 1988); I. Rivers, *Reason, Grace and Sentiment* (Cambridge, 1991).
91. Farindon, I, 149. Also see Walter Pope, *The Life of the Right Reverend Father in God Seth [Ward]* (1697), pp. 46–7.
92. Patrick, VII, 585, 428.
93. Thomas Birch, *The Life of the Most Reverend John Tillotson* (2nd edn, 1753), pp. 28–9, 407; Assheton, *The Danger of Hypocrisie* (1673), p. 5. Also see Littleton, I, 305; Tillotson, IX, 21; X, 374–94; Evelyn, III, 405; IV, 463.

and unpardonable crime, that a minister of the gospel should preach up good works!' expostulated William Sherlock in 1675, 'and yet this is the great reproach that is cast upon the city-clergy'.[94] Their critics, of course, cast no such reproach; yet they did disdain Anglican preaching. Indeed Robert South described how the Dissenters 'look down upon all others as Christians of a lower form, as moral men, and ignorant of the mysteries of the gospel: words which I have often heard from these imposters'.[95] What was meant by this charge of being 'moral men'?

The charge of 'moralism' was – and still is, for it colours much recent writing on seventeenth-century theology – a very precise theological criticism about proclaiming the 'mysteries of the gospel'. Moralism was the promotion of an unwarranted trust in moral works, or works performed by the natural powers of men without the grace of the gospel. Those who protested against moralism took Romans xiv. 23, *whatsoever is not of faith is sin* , quite literally – as well they might, for it figures in the ninth of the Thirty-Nine Articles, which states that all human works before faith and justification are not only worthless, but have the nature of sin. However, the heritage of English Protestantism was ambivalent on these questions. There was much in the general tenor of sixteenth-century English Protestantism, such as its strongly covenantal thinking and emphases on duty and obedience, which could be seen as potentially 'moralist'; only its doctrinal stress on free grace and predestination had saved English Protestantism from the danger of moralism.[96] But the same could not be said of the gospel according to the Restoration church. The Anglican divines of the Restoration offended against the tenets of the Reformed Protestant tradition in their teaching on justification, faith and salvation.

Justification confers entrance into the covenant of grace.[97] Justification is a doctrinal description of how God accepts sinful men as righteous, of how the atonement made by Christ is applied to sinners. The traditional Protestant view was that justification was freely given by God, without any human works or merit, and was apprehended only by faith. It became the basis of sanctification, the growth in grace through a life of obedience and good works, and although sanctification is a consequence of justification, they remain

94. William Sherlock, *A Defence and Continuation of the Discourse concerning the Knowledge of Jesus Christ* (1675), p. 7.
95. South, II, 176.
96. See Wallace, *Puritans and Predestination*, pp. 10–11, 127–8.
97. Nicholson, *Catechism*, pp. 63–8, esp. p. 66.

distinct in the eyes of God, who pardons sinners solely on account of their being justified. But why had God decided to justify sinners?

In the scholastic terminology of sixteenth-century theologians, justification has three causes: the *formal* cause, which is what makes something what it is, the *meritorious* cause, and the *instrumental* cause. The formal cause of our justification was the imputation of Christ's righteousness to us. The meritorious cause was Christ's sacrifice and the instrumental cause was faith.

The Anglican divines of the Interregnum and Restoration broke with this orthodoxy on two related counts: first, their account of salvation made it difficult to distinguish justification from sanctification; and secondly, they demurred at the notion of the imputation of Christ's righteousness as the *formal* cause of justification.

Later seventeenth-century churchmen demanded some sign of sanctification, some evidence of amendment, before justification. In his *Practical Catechism*, Henry Hammond explained that 'the first part of sanctification, the beginning of a new life' must precede God's pardon or justification, but he then hedged this around with qualifications: 'in respect of time there is no sensible priority', that is we cannot perceive the chronology of God's pardon following our amendment; and where 'sanctification' is taken to mean holy living then that does follow our justification.[98] Repentance and amendment are, according to these divines, the 'necessary preservatives and qualifications to capacitate' us for grace; 'where a heart is possessed with lust, there can be no room for grace'.[99] William Sherlock stated quite plainly that the church taught that repentance, love of God, and sincere purposes of amendment 'are antecedently necessary to our justification'.[100]

John Tillotson imagined a querulous voice asking whether 'to say of ourselves we can repent and turn to God' is not Pelagianism? 'And who says we can *of ourselves* do this besides the *Pelagians?*' he countered:

> We affirm the necessity of God's grace hereto, and withal, the necessary of our *co-operating* with the grace of God. We say that without the powerful excitation and aid of God's grace, no man can repent and turn to God: but we say likewise, that God cannot be properly said to *aid* and *assist* those, who do nothing themselves.[101]

98. Hammond, I, pt. i, 36–8.
99. Littleton, II, 27–8.
100. Sherlock, *Defence*, pp. 312–13; cf. 273.
101. Tillotson, VI, 412.

God is in fact reconciled to us when he offers us the conditional promises of justification which we employ in our sanctification and when he extends grace to us. It is our obligation to pray for the grace to repent, and it is God's mercy to use his 'prevenient' grace to make us want to repent and his 'assisting' grace to help us actually repent.[102] The churchmen were wedded to the idea that God justifies men as unworthy sinners; 'there is no worth in our faith or repentance, or any poor weak grace of ours, to deserve God's favour to our persons, or pardon of what sins are past, or acceptation of our imperfect obedience for the future; 'tis his free grace to pardon, and accept us on such poor conditions as these, and this free grace purchased, and sealed to us by the death of Christ'.[103] 'Grace' and 'works' were terms 'at extreme opposition': works were required of a justified sinner, but not as a cause of justification: it is folly 'to bring in our inherent righteousness to join with grace, as if we were unwilling to be too far engaged to God's mercy'.[104] Nevertheless there has to be a motion on the part of the sinner towards the covenant of grace, for it is upon 'his embracing the overtures thereof, consenting to, and complying with the terms propounded therein, that is, sincerely believing, and seriously repenting', that God will dispense mercy and pardon, and receive him into grace.[105] The churchmen chose 'the middle, the royal way' between the Manichean and Pelagian errors, 'we suppose that with grace, but in subjection to it, the freedom of the will amicably unites.'[106]

There is no suggestion here that our own righteousness can justify us; but there is a tension, even a paradox. Adam Littleton spoke of 'moral actions' like repentance and amendment: 'on the one hand they virtuate our faith, and evidence grace in us, when once obtained, *after* a man's *conversion*; so on the other hand, they qualify us for the obtaining of grace, and are the forerunners of a true justifying faith *before conversion*.'[107] George Bull apparently referred to 'moral actions arising from the grace of the gospel'.[108] Although there were suspicions of such 'Pelagian tricks' as allegedly 'making a good work meritorious because it is of grace', most churchmen accepted that some form of 'cooperation', however one-sided, took place between

---

102. See Littleton, II, 50, 189, 259; Edward Fowler, *The Principles and Practices of Certain Moderate Divines of the Church of England* (1670), p. 115; South, II, 9; Tillotson, X, 399.
103. Hammond, I, pt i, 36; cf. Romans iv. 5; v. 8, 10.
104. Farindon, III, 581–2.
105. Barrow, IV, 310; cf. Farindon, III, 12, 176–7.
106. George Bull, *Harmonia apostolica* (1669: LACT, Oxford, 1844 edn cited), p. 217.
107. Littleton, II, 35.
108. Allison, *Rise of Moralism*, p. 122.

divine grace and human righteousness.[109] This cooperation was a concomitant of the conditional nature of the covenant of grace; God's promises of salvation 'were ever attended with an *if*', noted the vicar of Deptford. [110] The churchmen were 'very careful so to handle the doctrine of justifying faith, as not only to make obedience to follow it, but likewise to include a hearty willingness to submit to all Christ's precepts in the nature of it. . . . They also so state the doctrine of imputed, as to show the absolute necessity of inherent righteousness.'[111] The 'efficacy' of Christ's sacrifice and 'the necessity of our own personal righteousness do very well consist together,' explained Benjamin Calamy:

> Our Saviour's incarnation and perfect obedience even unto death, is the sole meritorious cause of our acceptance with God, and of our salvation. He alone purchased those great benefits for us, made atonement, paid our ransom, and procured this covenant of grace from God, wherein eternal life is promised to penitent sinners. But then these great advantages are not immediately and absolutely conferred upon us, but under certain qualifications and conditions of repentance, faith, and sincere obedience; for the performance of which the holy spirit is never wanting to sincere endeavours.[112]

And note Calamy's terminology: Christ's sacrifice was the 'meritorious cause' of our justification: our fruitful 'obediential' faith was clearly the instrumental cause. Adam Littleton preached of 'our victorious faith, which is the condition, or, if you will, taking the word in a moral sense, the instrument of justification'.[113] But what was the formal cause of justification in this scheme? Modern critics are surely correct in suggesting that it was the conditional covenant.[114] And this, of course, is precisely the theological innovation which they deplore and which seventeenth-century puritans denounced as heresy; but the innovators themselves were not in the least apologetic.

Later seventeenth-century doctrines of salvation were caught between two theological languages. The young Restoration divines were not at ease with the threefold scholastic distinction of formal,

---

109. Farindon, III, 582.
110. Evelyn, IV, 236.
111. Fowler, *Principles*, pp. 114, 115; also see idem, *The Design of Christianity* (1671), pp. 91–2.
112. Calamy, *Sermons*, p. 315.
113. Littleton, II, 77.
114. Allison, *Rise of Moralism*, p. 114.

meritorious and instrumental causes – Edward Fowler sneered at the use of the 'improper and obscure' word 'instrument' to describe the relationship of faith to justification.[115] Fowler and his like-minded brethren had shifted the formal cause of justification from the imputation of Christ's righteousness to the condition upon which one enters the covenant of grace. They had, as it were, reversed the orthodoxy. Instead of justification being the entrance into the covenant, entering into the covenant through the fulfilment of its conditions could be taken as justification. They looked at the problem not as sixteenth-century theologians, but as late seventeenth-century pastors and preachers, and from their perspective their notion of cooperation with divine grace was rational and beautiful. The beauty of the process by which God wished to save us was its retention of the principle that if we are saved we are saved by God, while if we are damned it is for our own impenitence and wickedness.

It is the Christian's righteousness which counts: the laity were urged to shun doctrines which preached comfort but not duty. Preachers were warned to 'beware that you play not the antinomian in this point, by taking away sorrow, whilst the just cause thereof, that is, confirmed habits of wickedness and vice still remain'.[116] In the forthright words of William Sherlock, Christ's righteousness 'was not an *imaginary imputed righteousness*, but *inherent and personal*; but what comfort is this to us, that Christ was righteous, if we continue wilful and incorrigible sinners?' Christ came to fulfil the law, not to abolish it (Matthew v. 17); he came to make it possible for man to fulfil the law: 'and therefore the gospel of our saviour must supply this defect, not by an *imputed righteousness*, but, by an addition of greater power to enable men to do that which is good, and to fulfil the external righteousness of the law by a sincere and spiritual obedience'.[117] 'Is Christ's death to excuse us from holy living?' asked Simon Patrick. No, it is to teach us to take up our cross and follow him.[118]

All men can take up their cross because the covenant of the gospel is open to all. Christ died for the sins of all mankind, so 'salvation is made attainable, and is really tendered unto all, upon feasible and equal conditions'.[119] 'For if each individual person cannot beassured that he is his saviour, and that he died for him; if he died not for all, nay, but for a few comparatively (as those say who deny that

---

115. Fowler, *Design*, p. 223.
116. MS Eng Th E 168, fo. 160v; James Arderne, *Directions concerning the Matter and Stile of Sermons* (1671), p. 59.
117. Sherlock, *Discourse*, pp. 234, 268.
118. Patrick, IV, 506; also see Calamy, *Sermons*, pp. 301–2; Evelyn, IV, 309.
119. Barrow, IV, 310.

he died for all) then what influence can the consideration of his death have upon the wills of men?' asked Edward Fowler.[120] But this did not mean that all men would be saved. 'Christ hanging on the cross looketh upon all; but all do not cast an eye, and look up in faith, upon him. He was delivered to deliver all; but all will not be delivered.'[121] Although Christ's sacrifice was the intended satisfaction for the sins of all men, it can only be the *effective* satisfaction for 'those that by faith apply him': man's side of the covenant is to meet the condition of faith and repentance. This is the doctrine of universal redemption. Throughout the 1640s and 1650s, a succession of Anglican divines had asserted that this was the doctrine of the Catholic Church;[122] and increasingly the Restoration Church of England identified herself with this soul-saving truth.[123]

The emphasis on the Christian's inherent righteousness and the teaching of universal redemption jeopardized the logical coherence of the traditional account of salvation. They disturbed traditional theological categories by offering a flawed account of the formal cause of justification, of what it is that justifies us in the eyes of God. But perhaps more disturbing to those brought up in the older, Reformed, tradition was the church's apparent failure to proclaim the good news of the gospel – believe and you will be saved. All responsibilities were now thrown back on to the individual Christian, and the new theology demanded of him a life of service, a taking up of the cross, a living up to the New Testament example of Christ himself, a constant unremitting whole duty of holy living. To the traditionalists this was mistaken on two counts: first, because it encouraged men to trust in their own efforts, and so could make salvation seem too easy; but second, because holy living was too daunting. The whole duty of man was a counsel of perfection which would inevitably awaken the fear of never being able to fulfil the requirements of the law.

The law is still in place, as all agreed, but Christ has freed us from its curse. The law has ceased to be our tyrant and tormentor, but remains our rule, guide and governor.[124] 'The grand intent of the

120. Edward Fowler, *Libertas evangelica* (1680), p. 83.
121. Farindon, I, 73.
122. Hammond, I, pt. i, 3, 138–9, 147; *Nineteen Letters*, ed. Peck, pp. 17–19, 31–4; J.W. Packer, *The Transformation of Anglicanism 1643–1660* (Manchester, 1969), pp. 54–5, 59–60; Wallace, *Puritans and Predestination*, p. 96; Clement Barksdale, *The Disputation at Winchcombe* (Oxford, 1653), p. 29.
123. See Farindon, I, 71–4; Patrick, VII, 205; George Bull, *Examen censurae* (1676; LACT, Oxford, 1844 edn cited), pp. 78–81; *Apologia* (1676; LACT, Oxford, 1844 edn), pp. 330–44; Calamy, *Sermons*, pp. 317–18; Littleton, II, 182–94, 223; Barrow, IV, 295, 310–15; Boughen, *Exposition of Church Catechism*, pp. 11, 23; Evelyn, III, 562; IV, 99, 344, 352, 385.
124. Barrow, IV, 361–2.

gospel being to make us partakers of an inward and real righteousness', the gospel enables man to fulfil the external righteousness
of the law by a sincere obedience.[125] Considered from this point
of view, any teaching which elevated grace at the expense of the
individual sinner's responsibility to obey the law was potentially
'antinomian'. Antinomianism is the doctrine that grace discharges
Christians from the obligation of the moral law. In the eyes of
seventeenth-century clergymen, this was 'the most pernicious heresy,
and most directly destructive of the great end and design of Christianity'; but like many other errors, antinomianism was principally
in the eye of the beholder.[126] Predestinarian Calvinist theology, for
example, stressed that justification was without conditions and was a
free act of God's grace from eternity; inevitably, for some, this
emphasis seemed to collapse justification into election, and to make
the antinomian assumption that God sees no sin in those whom he
saves. This was a very different proposition from the practical antinomianism of sects like the Ranters and, allegedly, the Quakers, who
maintained that whatever those in a state of grace do, it cannot be
'of sin'. The proponents of the new theology concentrated their fire
upon the pernicious effects of puritan teachings – such as the imputation of Christ's righteousness and the absolute predestination of
the elect and reprobation of the damned – and of puritan piety, that
'experimental', or experiential, religion which encouraged men to
believe that they were saved on the testimony of the spirit and their
inner experience. Yet the issue always returned to the nature of
justification; and the churchmen took every opportunity to identify
justification by faith alone, or 'solifidianism', with antinomianism.
The Roman apologists charged the Church of England herself with
teaching 'that if a man do but trust in Christ, that is, be but
confidently persuaded that he will save him and pardon him, this is
sufficient; and consequently he that is thus persuaded need not take
any farther care of his salvation, but may live as he list'. John
Tillotson admitted that this charge of 'solifidianism' would be undeniable 'unless we own holiness and obedience to be conditions of
our justification, as well as trust in Christ. I know no other middle
way between Popery and antinomianism.'[127] Skilfully, Tillotson had
turned his rebuttal of the Romanists so as also to tar Nonconformists
and sectaries with antinomianism.

The Restoration Church of England forged a 'middle way', a
primitive, Catholic, way in her theology. Although she would never

125. Fowler, *Design*, p. 226; also see Tillotson, X, 485.
126. Tillotson, VI, 367.
127. Tillotson, XI, 318–19.

renounce the Reformation, the church was candid about the harm done to religion by 'men's endeavours to be removed as far as they can from Rome'. Because Roman Catholics 'speak of justification differently from us, men are apt to live as though good works were a piece of popery'.[128] The sixteenth-century doctrine of justification by faith alone, without reference to repentance or obedience, was unknown to the Early Church or even to the Schoolmen; 'they did indeed, consider distinctly no such point of doctrine as justification, looking upon that word as used incidentally in some places of scripture, for expression of points more clearly expressed in other terms; wherefore they do not make much of the word, as some divines now do.'[129] As the Church of England had to recover for herself the Catholic doctrine of salvation, so had she to create the ethical system which answered to that doctrine. Obedience to the law requires careful instruction in the obligations of the law, the hazards of sin, and the resolution of dilemmas; in short, it requires a theology of moral instruction, a 'moral theology' in the proper sense of the term. When Jeremy Taylor, one of the pioneers of this Anglican moral theology, turned his mind to producing a much-needed book of 'cases of conscience', it soon became clear that the principles underpinning both Protestant and Roman Catholic moral theology were untrustworthy. So his first task was to show why it was necessary to live a holy life and then to demolish the errors of his opponents, who minimized sin either by their mortal–venial distinctions, penances and probabilism, or by antinomian doctrines like the imputation of Christ's righteousness. Hence the composition of *Unum necessarium*, his treatise on repentance – with its controversial opinions on original sin – before the writing of *Ductor dubitantum*, a manual of moral theology.[130]

The emergence of a body of Anglican moral theology in the mid-seventeenth century was an important indication of prevailing theological trends. Like the church's preaching on fasts and anniversaries, this moral theology contributed to a national sense of sin and guilt and to strict teaching in ethical matters.[131] Sin was always present in the world and the price of human free will was constant vigilance. The churchmen consciously adopted the strategy of convincing their

128. Patrick, I, 219.
129. Barrow, V, 149–50; cf. Tillotson, XI, 320–1.
130. Taylor, VIII, p. ccxliv (preface to *Unum necessarium*); Taylor wrote to Bishop Duppa explaining his motives, MS Tanner 52, fo. 93.
131. See H.R. McAdoo, *The Structure of Caroline Moral Theology* (1949); J. Mahoney, *The Making of Moral Theology – A Study of the Roman Catholic Tradition* (Oxford, 1987), p. 28.

congregations 'that they live in the practice of great sins, which they shall certainly suffer for, if they do not repent'.[132] The sermons recorded by John Evelyn were uncompromising in their assertion of the 'infinite danger of sin' and 'the necessity of crucifying all sinful desires of what sort soever, without the least indulgence to any' since all sins were an offence to God's justice.[133] Evelyn heard Tillotson on

> the exceeding difficulty of reforming habitual sins and making it next to impossible, from that of the Eithiops changing his skin, leopard his spots . . . like the camel going through the needle's eye, which our blessed Saviour makes only possible with God, to express the rich man's difficulty etc. It was a terrible and severe discourse, showing how it concerned sinners to serious repentance.[134]

In his sermon, Tillotson sought to emphasize the difficulty, but not the impossibility, of reforming and he expressed the hope that the simile of the camel passing through the needle's eye was 'somewhat hyperbolical'.[135] On moral questions, Anglican divines consistently took the harshest line – in continental terms, they were 'rigorists'. Their manuals of piety and their cases of conscience promoted the 'severest' life, the most holy and rigorous ascetic.[136] They trailed through their works the idea of Christian perfection; 'the end of the Christian is to be like unto Christ, that *where he is, he may be also* (John xiv. 3). That is his end, that is his perfection.' John Evelyn was told that ''twas not impossible not to sin; that true repentance was a thorough reformation of any known sin'. Yet at the same time, the churchmen taught that, in this life, the fallen Christian could never be pure of sin; he could, however, be as perfect as human frailty allows, through rigorous 'holy living', through the imitation of Christ, and through fulfilling the covenant of grace: 'we may please God evangelically, though not without infirmity'; we can perform our duty 'in such a measure as God will graciously accept, that is, in sincerity, though not in perfection'.[137]

132.   Edward Stillingfleet, *The Bishop of Worcester's Charge* (1691), p. 17.

133.   Evelyn, III, 326, 353, 403; IV, 435.

134.   Evelyn, IV, 240.

135.   Tillotson, II, 295.

136.   See *WAWD*, I, 90–1, 112–13, 120, 147–8.

137.   Farindon, I, 429; Evelyn, IV, 36; *WAWD*, I, 142. Also see Tillotson, VIII, 220–37; Taylor, VIII, 278–88, 293–7; Barrow, I, 527–8; II, 495–523. The idea of Christian perfection was central to the thinking of William Law, the Nonjuror, and of Wesley, who were both beneficiaries of the patristic legacy; see John Walsh, 'John Wesley and the Community of Goods', in *Protestant Evangelicalism*, ed. K. Robbins (SCH Subsidia 7, Oxford, 1990), pp. 32–3, 43–44. On perfection, see R.

The uneasy coexistence of a trust in mankind's moral potential and a conviction of the omnipresence of sin was as old as Christianity. Early Christianity had taken on a tinge of the Hellenic respect for the free will, dignity, reason and moral autonomy of natural man, as well as a thorough-paced Augustinianism.[138] Although largely submerged beneath the Augustinian and Pauline pessimism of the Protestant Reformation, this more inspiriting view of man had never been completely lost in seventeenth-century England, and the Restoration churchmen were heirs to both traditions.[139] They took an optimistic view of man's abilities and potential, but none of them believed that he could overcome sin without divine grace. Unhappily, their opponents, working from a different understanding of salvation, did not grasp the duality of the Anglican outlook; even more unfortunately, some later commentators have followed these opponents to the point of misunderstanding the church's 'moralism'. The 'moralism' of which the Restoration church was guilty, the specific offence of rearranging the formal cause of justification, is a very different issue from the vague phrases about 'moral preaching' misapplied by modern commentators in an attempt to describe the tone of Restoration Anglicanism. Restoration divines preached that doing good is a fundamental part of Christianity, that goodness is the great design of Christianity, and this was bound to mean the exaltation of charity, diligence, duties to self and neighbour, social virtues and public piety. A few clergymen went so far as to argue that the virtuous could reasonably expect to be rewarded. But to conclude, as some have, that the Restoration churchmen were peddling a merely utilitarian system of ethics, and promoting it through an appeal to self-interest and prudence, is a bizarre and highly selective interpretation of their views which takes little account of either the clergy's theology or the audiences at which the clergy aimed.

Newton Flew, *The Idea of Perfection in Christian Theology* (Oxford, 1934); N.P. Williams, *The Ideas of the Fall and Original Sin* (1927).

138. See J. Passmore, *The Perfectibility of Man* (1970): H. Baker, *The Dignity of Man* (Harvard, 1947).

139. A confidence in human nature can be discerned in Hooker, among the Great Tew group, in Socinian circles, among the Cambridge Platonists, and among the anti-Calvinists of Charles I's reign. See J. Morgan, *Godly Learning – Puritan Attitudes Towards Reason, Learning, and Education, 1560–1640* (Cambridge, 1986); C.A. Patrides (ed.), *The Cambridge Platonists* (1969); G.R. Cragg, *Freedom and Authority* (Philadelphia, 1975); T.H. Robinson, 'Lord Clarendon's Moral Code', *Huntington Library Quarterly*, 153 (1979–80); J.C. Hayward, 'New Directions in Studies of the Falkland Circle', *The Seventeenth Century*, 2 (1987); N. Tyacke, 'Arminianism and English Culture', *Britain and the Netherlands*, 7 (1981); McGee, *Godly Man in Stuart England*, pp. 107–13.

The churchmen believed that all men were potentially salvable, and so they spared no effort, and ignored no method, in their attempt to convert the entire nation to holy living; their message was addressed to the pious, to the apathetic, to the profane, and even to the unbeliever. John Wilkins's *Of the Principles and Duties of Natural Religion* deliberately sought to persuade men to become religious without invoking divine revelation – that is, without assuming what he was trying to demonstrate. Wilkins employed 'rational' arguments in order to show that, even if there was no revelation, there would still be good reason to be convinced, in Tillotson's words, 'that religion and happiness, our duty and our interest, are really but one and the same'. Confronted by 'reasoning atheists', the Restoration churchmen tried to prove the atheists and deists wrong in their own terms, and that is why they preached sermons with such titles as 'the wisdom of being religious'. When they heard the rationalist and the wit claim that piety was 'an enemy to profit', the diligent clerics promptly preached on 'the profitableness of piety'.[140] Hearing that 'living righteously is accounted dull' by many, that religion was seen as morose, tiresome, and a 'dumpish melancholy profession', they naturally portrayed holy living in its most attractive light, and dwelt upon its attainability and rewards.[141]

Holy living was not demanded for its own sake, but as a condition of salvation; and piety was not prudential or self-interested unless care of our salvation was to be counted self-interest. The soul, of course, 'deserves more care than all the things in the world besides, for . . . it is made after the image of God'. True self-love 'is the love and care of our souls' not the 'immoderate love of our own worldly interests and advantages'.[142] The doctrine of Christ is a doctrine of faith and manners, and 'is no way framed to serve the ends of ambitious and worldly men, or to help them in pursuing those ends by a pretence of religion'.[143] Indeed, the churchmen stressed that 'there neither is nor ever was any perfect and complete happiness in this life, but that there is, and of necessity both for the glory of God and the benefit of man, some affliction or imperfection interwoven and mingled among all sublunary enjoyments'.[144] Although riches are not in themselves harmful, men should recognize 'the preference of suffering in this life to a vicious prosperity, for the profitable effects thereof in bringing us to repentance, and to a disesteem of the

140. Barrow, I, 177.
141. Calamy, *Sermons*, p. 222; Littleton, II, 263; Tillotson, I, 152.
142. *WAWD*, I, sig. A, 146; cf. Tillotson, I, 169.
143. William Clagett, *Seventeen Sermons*, p. 56.
144. Evelyn, IV, 538.

vanities of this transitory world'.[145] The laity were exhorted to welcome afflictions for their spiritual benefits and endlessly reminded that 'the gain of godliness' exceeds 'all worldly traffic'.[146] John Evelyn heard Tillotson preach at least three times on Joshua xxiv. 15, 'showing the folly of sinful men's choice, the ease and happiness of a holy and temperate life, above that of the sensual [life]'.[147] 'The incomparable pleasure of true piety compared with worldly delights' was pointed out from every pulpit.[148]

The churchmen did not disguise that holy living was painful at the outset and strenuous thereafter. Entering upon religion, crucifying the old man of sin, repentance, mortification, and dying with Christ to a new life are a painful business, but they must be endured, for otherwise we perish eternally.[149] And thereafter the holy life is not calculated for the lazy or slothful, for those afraid of tribulation or persecution; it guarantees nothing in this life, but the unspeakable comfort of a future and eternal reward; 'so that you see Christianity is very aimiable even in its saddest dress, the inward comforts of it do far surpass all the outward tribulations that attend it, and that even in the instant, while we are in the state of warfare upon earth'.[150] 'The serious and the manly pleasures, the solid and substantial joys, are only to be found in the ways of religion and virtue'; the point to grasp was that holy living transforms our ideas of true happiness.[151] The commandments of Christ are not grievous (I John v. 3). But, as Tillotson said, for those who had 'never tried the experiment of a holy life' and simply measured the demands of religion by the reluctance of their degenerate senses, this must seem unlikely.[152] 'Prayer is a pleasant duty, but it is withal a spiritual one; and therefore if thy heart be carnal, if that be set either on the contrary pleasures of the flesh or dross of the world, no marvel, then, if thou taste no pleasantness in it.' [153] Holy living rectifies our reason, puts reason in the throne and vindicates the spirit from the tyranny of its vassal flesh.[154] A favourite text among Restoration preachers was Christ's exhortation *to take my yoke upon you . . . for my yoke is easy, and my burden is light* (Matthew xi. 29–30); 'his service

145. Ibid., 373.
146. Evelyn, III, 510; also see IV, 3, 195, 556.
147. Evelyn, IV, 371. Also see Tillotson, II, 247–69, 269–93; III, 394–437.
148. See Evelyn, IV, 52, 371, 504–5; III, 339–40, 478.
149. Tillotson, I, 165–6, 296.
150. *WAWD*, I, 147–8. Also see Barrow, I, 156, 186; Tillotson, I, 163; Evelyn, IV, 548.
151. Tillotson, I, 162.
152. Ibid., 153.
153. *WAWD*, I, 46; cf. 132, 139–40, 147.
154. Barrow, I, 161; Scott, *Works*, I, 19, 194–5.

does not bereave men of any true joy, but helps them to a great deal . . . there is in the practice of Christian duties a great deal of pleasant pleasure, and if we feel it not, it is because of the resistance our vicious and sinful customs make'. The churchmen did not minimize the duties of Christianity; all that they sought to show was 'the easiness of the Christian yoke and service of God, compared to the difficulty of other religions, etc, and most pleasures of sin'.[155] In comparison with the slavery of sin or the law of Moses, Christ's yoke was gentle, 'yet it was a yoke, as it had relation to the law of Christ; but such [a yoke] as was sweet and infinitely rewarded'.[156] It was not enough to live under 'Christ's easy yoke in respect of the law', said the churchmen, we should live 'in practic[al] obedience and take up the yoke'.[157]

The 'whole duty of man', as preached by the Restoration church, was a very severe ascetic: to profess Christianity was 'like a race . . . never to be at rest, but still proceeding'; 'Christian warfare' required 'all conditions to be striving for victory . . . by fasting, prayers, alms, against all luxury, avarice, Satan's temptations, etc'.[158] Far from demoting religion to the mere pursuit of virtue, 'holy living' required a rigorous pursuit of Christian perfection while asserting the impossibility of overcoming sin. Historians of the seventeenth century – perhaps mesmerized by Calvinism – have been slow to recognize this aspect of Restoration Anglicanism: it is those observers who look back from the Evangelical Revival of the eighteenth century who have most appreciated that Restoration Anglicanism was a demanding, if not daunting, system, virtually 'a system of religious terrorism'.[159] Yet this stern ascetic was sustained by a carefully balanced theology. Faith 'was not a strong persuasion only, but an assurance grounded on our obedience and [the] effects of our beliefs'. In practice, little distinction was possible between faith and 'obedential reliance on Christ'; and sometimes the clergy's message was, apparently, as stark as 'we are justified by faith and repentance'.[160] Anglican preachers spoke openly 'of the necessity of cooperating

155. Evelyn, IV, 183.
156. Ibid., 297.
157. Evelyn, III, 366; also see III, 308, 341, 401; IV, 40, 179, 277, 305, 489, 501; Fowler, *Design*, p. 305; Tillotson, I, 282; *WAWD*, I, 147, 226–7; McGee, *Godly Man in Stuart England*, p. 62.
158. Evelyn, IV, 134, 293; also see 61–2, 535; III, 271, 519, 552.
159. M.R. Watts, *The Dissenters* (Oxford, 1978), pp. 426–7, applies Lecky's phrase to the holy living school; also see *Diary of an Oxford Methodist – Benjamin Ingham, 1733–1734*, ed. R.P. Heitzenrater (Durham, N.C., 1985), pp. 28–38 (I am grateful to John Walsh for bringing this volume to my attention).
160. Evelyn, III, 336; IV, 630, 463.

with the grace of God', and although this raised all sorts of theoretical problems for those wedded to Reformed theology, it seemed eminently sensible to increasing numbers of clergymen and their parishioners. John Evelyn recorded a sermon by 'Dr Cradock at Whitehall on Phil. ii. 13, showing that though to will and to do were of God's good pleasure, yet he expected and received our cooperation with that grace through the abilities he had given us; and that it was not sufficient to pray for, but endeavour to live a life of grace and to work out our own salvation etc: an excellent discourse, as his always are, pious and clear and very sound divinity'.[161] To many this 'sound divinity' was psychologically plausible: it answered to their own spiritual and moral experience. This divinity taught the spiritual husbandry of grace, the improving of every small sign of divine mercy.[162] It is pointless, said the churchmen, to quibble over moral actions, or to split hairs over what what can be done of nature and what of grace: the crucial thing is to seize every opportunity to improve 'good motions'. 'Moral conversation did not come up to the exact height of gospel conversation,' they readily admitted, but 'we should not censure any walking soberly, since God only knew the heart'.[163]

'A New Theological World': Theology and Piety

> When I read it, I thought myself in a new theological world; believers appearing without their head for want of a mystical union, stripped and naked for lack of imputed righteousness; the full treasures of grace in Christ, which have supplied all the vessels of faith, emptied out of his sacred person, and transfused into the doctrine of the gospel; as if according to Pelagius all grace were in doctrine only.[164]

Edward Polhil's shocked reaction to William Sherlock's *Discourse concerning the Knowledge of Jesus Christ* (1673) conveys something of the incomprehension that greeted the new theological tendency within the Church of England. What seemed common sense to Sherlock was dangerous heresy to many Restoration Englishmen. 'People are very ill judges of error and heresy,' complained Sherlock.

161. Evelyn, IV, 196; cf. 4, where the same cleric preached on 'justified by free grace: incomparably well'.
162. *WAWD*, I, 63–4.
163. Evelyn, III, 490.
164. Edward Polhill, *An Answer to the Discourse of Mr William Sherlock* (1675), sigs. A4v–A5.

Some think everything heresy, but antinomianism; to persuade men to a good life, to tell them, that there are certain conditions annexed to the gospel-covenant; without the performance of which, we shall not be saved: that not an idle and notional, but an active and working faith justifies; that we are saved by Christ, not as a proxy, who has done all for us, but as a priest and sacrifice and mediator, who has expiated our sins by his death, and sealed the covenant of grace in his blood, and now powerfully intercedes for us with his father, and sends his spirit into the world to be a principle of a new life in us: these and such like doctrines are by some men reproached with the name of heresy; and upon their authority believed to be so by others . . .[165]

These novel views had caused a stir in 1669 when George Bull published his *Harmonia apostolica*. Bull's youthful attempt to reconcile St James and St Paul was designed as 'a timely antidote against this solifidianism, or rather libertinism, which some in these dregs of time teach openly and shamelessly, and which many, by incrusting it with empty distinctions in sermons and writings, have palmed upon their hearers and readers, and still do so'.[166] But the 'solifidianism' that Bull disparaged was the doctrine of justification by faith alone, a doctrine still close to the hearts of many Anglicans and Non-conformists – as Bull would soon find out.

The new school of which Bull was a member tended to obscure the theological distinction between justification and sanctification. In practice, most of their brethren did the same. In parish pulpits, the clergy had always asserted that, for all practical purposes, faith and works could not be distinguished; a 'working faith' justified the sinner and reconciled St Paul and St James.[167] But this pastoral concession to human frailty was clearly not permissible in a more academic or theological context. Bull's assertion that the faith which saves 'is not to be taken for one single virtue, but comprehends, in its complete sense . . . all the works of Christian piety', might have been acceptable from the pulpit, but when it was advanced at length and in Latin, it assumed the proportions of a theological challenge to the traditional view of the formal cause of justification.

The replies to the *Harmonia* came from a wide range of clergymen.

165. Sherlock, *Practical Discourse of Assemblies*, pp. 263–4.
166. Translation of *Harmonia* (LACT, Oxford, 1844), see pp. ix, 10, 21–2, 208. Two further parts, *Examen censurae* and *Apologia*, published in 1676, were translated (LACT, Oxford, 1844), see *Examen*, pp. 89–102, 144–54; the controversy can be followed in detail in Nelson's *Life of Bull*.
167. Littleton, II, 289; II, 133; A.E. McGrath, 'The Emergence of the Anglican Tradition on Justification', *Churchman*, 98 (1984), 37.

The response of John Tombes, a learned Calvinist and Baptist, was dismissed by Bull as 'a work, in which the self confidence of the author seems so much to vie with his ignorance, that it is difficult to say which is the greater'.[168] But Tombes had dedicated his work to Bishop Morley of Winchester. And Charles Gataker, the conformist son of a leading puritan divine, circulated his own strictures of the *Harmonia* among the bishops. A better-known churchman, Thomas Barlow, Lady Margaret professor of divinity at Oxford, lectured in the university against Bull's errors, and his attack was seconded from the press by Thomas Tully, principal of St Edmund Hall.[169] Tully's *Justificatio Paulina* (1674) was published with the support of George Morley and another, unknown, bishop, and the following year Tully was preferred to the deanery of Ripon.[170] It looked as though Bull had offended his own Anglican brethren as much as the Dissenters.

Yet Bull, too, found supporters both within and outside the church. When the Earl of Anglesey, who had 'turned of late a great divine', wrote 'a very shallow' book accusing Bull of perverting the Church of England's traditional 'episcopal Calvinist' teaching, Simon Patrick came to his defence.[171] Patrick argued that Anglesey and Bull were in full agreement that faith alone justifies and that all Christian virtues are connate with that faith;

> O but none of those virtues (you add) pass into the cause of justification; no, nor is faith itself any cause of it; not so much as an instrumental cause: and therefore you ought not to have quarrelled with Mr Bull about this matter, who detests any such thoughts as you impose on him, that our good words 'are required causally and antecedently to our justification'.[172]

Patrick was papering over the cracks here. Bull was indeed saying much the same as Sherlock later maintained, that repentance, love of

168. *Examen*, p. ix.
169. Barlow's lecture at the Oxford Act (the major occasion of the acadamic year), on 8 July 1671, was directed against Bull; see Wood, II, 166. Barlow himself wrote four MS volumes on the reconciliation of James and Paul; see N. Tyacke, 'Religious Controversy in Restoration England', in *The History of the University of Oxford: III The Seventeenth Century*, ed. N. Tyacke (forthcoming).
170. Nelson, *Life of Bull*, pp. 102, 211–27; *CSPD, 1673–75*, p. 400.
171. *The Letters of Humphrey Prideaux*, ed. E.M. Thompson (Camden Society, 15, 1875), pp. 57–8; Prideaux also reported that Sir Charles Wolseley's *Justification Evangelical* (1677) 'much offended' Anglesey and Barlow by opposing their view of justification. Also see Anglesey's MS letter in Barlow's copy of Wolseley's book, Bodleian copy, shelfmark 8⁰C 345 Linc.
172. Patrick, VI, 461.

God, and resolutions of amendment are antecedently necessary to our justification.[173] Patrick was concerned lest controversy over justification by faith, a doctrine upon which 'divines cannot well agree', should obscure the fact that justifying faith belongs as much 'to the plainest countryman' as to the scholar.[174] To complicate matters further, Patrick himself may well have thought that although justification did depend upon the righteousness of Christ, it was pastorally unwise to admit this to sinful man. It would not be the first nor the last time that a cleric had decided that certain truths should be kept from the vulgar both for their own sake and that of society at large.[175]

The new theological views did not always respect denominational boundaries, and on occasion they set churchman against churchman and Dissenter against Dissenter; Richard Baxter, for instance, was regarded as being in the same camp as George Bull.[176] The consequent alignments are unfamiliar and resist simple description or labelling. Several of the younger Anglican divines described themselves as 'moderate', 'rational', 'free' or 'new', or were described as 'mere moral men', 'latitude-men', or 'latitudinarians', but these terms were neither universal nor neutral, nor even very revealing.[177] In desperation, it is tempting to reach for those familiar labels 'Arminian' and 'Calvinist', and yet, while these are not inappropriate, they tell only half the story.

There never had been, nor ever would be, a time when all puritans were Calvinists and all episcopalians were Arminians. Arminianism was available to Restoration Nonconformists, just as Calvinism was to Restoration churchmen. Admittedly, for a while, the anxieties aroused by Archbishop Laud had driven Arminianism off the theological agenda, but during the 1640s, under the name of 'universal grace', it had once more become a tenable Protestant position, and with his *Aphorisms of Justification* of 1649, Richard Baxter presented a coherent, even persuasive, neo-Arminianism. Baxter became a standard bearer for a growing group of puritan Arminians – although neither he nor his followers would have called themselves such – during the 1650s.[178] They espoused a 'middle way' which

---

173. Sherlock, *Defence*, pp. 312–13.
174. Patrick, VI, 462–3.
175. See Patrick, IV, 376; D.P. Walker, *The Decline of Hell* (1964), pp. 4–8.
176. See Nelson, *Life of Bull*, pp. 257–76.
177. J. Spurr, ' "Latitudinarianism" and the Restoration Church', *HJ*, 31 (1988), 75–6.
178. See Packer, *Transformation*, pp. 164–5; W. Lamont, 'The Rise of Arminianism Reconsidered', *Past and Present*, 107 (1985); G.F. Nuttall on John Horne in *Christian Spirituality*, ed. P.N. Brooks (1975). On Baxter's complex theological position, a sort of 'hypothetical universalism' rather than simple Arminianism, see J.I. Packer,

continued to win support during the rest of the century; in addition, full-blown Arminianism had established itself at the very heart of Presbyterianism by the beginning of the next century.[179] And the Baptist movement had, of course, contained an Arminian wing throughout the later seventeenth century. During the Interregnum, the episcopalians were also active in the promotion of Arminianism. Books written in the heyday of the Laudian church, such as those by Samuel Harsnett, Samuel Hoard and Thomas Jackson, were reprinted, while apologists like Hammond and Heylyn restated their objections to the predestinarian scheme and strove to win their misguided brethren over 'to the genuine doctrines of the Church of England, now miscalled Arminianism'.[180] Yet the insurmountable differences between these 'prelatists' and those 'puritans who espoused a form of Arminianism prevented any cooperation between the two anti-Calvinist groups. It is noteworthy that while Richard Baxter himself had little time for Hammond, Pierce and other 'Grotian' divines, he was seen by one shrewd publisher as the ideal author to continue the good work against the 'increase of atheism, Popery and Socinianism' begun by the reissue of Thomas Jackson's books.[181]

On the other hand, the Church of England's strong Calvinist tradition did not die out in 1641, nor even in 1662. Despite its associations with Presbyterianism, rebellion and king-killing, Calvinist theology retained its hold over some Restoration churchmen. There were, for instance, several Calvinists on the bench of bishops and in university chairs, and presumably more in the lower reaches of the clergy.[182] In 1679 Thomas Smart was forced by the Oxford

'The Redemption and Restoration of Man in the Thought of Richard Baxter' (unpublished Oxford University D.Phil. thesis, 1954); Wallace, *Puritans and Predestination*, pp. 134–40, 143; B.G. Armstrong, *Calvinism and the Amyraut Heresy* (Madison, Wisconsin, 1969); W.M. Lamont, *Richard Baxter and Millennium* (1979), pp. 129–30. Adam Littleton denounced hypothetical universalism's crucial distinction between 'sufficient' and 'efficient satisfaction' as 'frigid and insignificant'; Littleton, II, 223.

179. See J.T. Spivey, 'Middle Way Men, Edmund Calamy and the Crisis of Moderate Nonconformity 1688–1732' (unpublished Oxford University D.Phil. thesis, 1986), pp. 51–72, 225–30; C.G. Bolam, J. Goring, H.L. Short, R. Thomas, *The English Presbyterians* (1968), pp. 135–7; Watts, *Dissenters*, pp. 371–82.

180. Peter Heylyn, *Certamen epistolare* (1658), p. 148. Heylyn's long controversy with Henry Hickman in 1658–61 produced some very clear formulations of the opposing positions; see J. Spurr, 'Anglican Apologetic and the Restoration Church' (unpublished Oxford University D.Phil. thesis, 1985), pp. 323–5.

181. DWL, Baxter Letters V, fo. 224 (Timothy Garthwait to Baxter, 20 April 1654).

182. Calvinists include George Morley, William Jane, John Hall, John Wallis, Robert South: see South, I, 55; II, 143; III, 77; Wallace, *Puritans and Predestination*, p. 144.

Heads of Houses to recant his intemperate preaching against Calvinism.[183] Thomas Barlow, Bull's opponent and eventually a bishop, was perhaps the leading figure in the campaign to prevent the University of Oxford 'from falling into Pelagianism' and Arminianism.[184] Of course, it was not politic to invoke the name of Calvin too often; and many of these so-called Calvinists were perhaps more anti-Arminian than anything else. Bishop John Hacket, for example, had a traditional view of justification, opposed Arminianism, but more than anything else he gloried in 'that impartiality and indifferency to truth which this happy Church of England hath maintained, not turning the scale either this way or that way, for Luther or Calvin's sake, or whomsoever else'.[185] Most Anglicans preferred to stress the independence, the uniqueness of the Anglican way, and to deny that the church owed any debt to Luther or Calvin or Arminius, 'having stood entirely upon her own bottom, used her own authority, and taken her own measures, in the glorious work of reformation'.[186] At the same time, the churchmen unanimously rejected 'those hard disputes about God's eternal decrees, and strange working of his grace . . . which will never cease, and never be decided'; 'how many by over-bold searches after the abstruse mysteries of faith, and hid decrees of God, have quite blinded themselves, and perplexed others?' Or as Sir Henry Yelverton put it,

> Some men are strangely mistaken when they would father the Calvinian doctrine on the Church of England in her articles, who hath most wisely left it undetermined; knowing that both learned and good men may differ in these sublime points, and that the church's peace ought not to be disturbed with such unnecessary determinations.[187]

In the mouths of the young, both Calvinism and Arminianism were unwieldy, old-fashioned terms. As a student, White Kennett 'held a conference with Mr Cheyney in defence of those tenets which he called Arminian'; by the 1680s, the churchmen were looking back to the distant, and rather distasteful, times 'when the contest ran high between the Presbyterians and Independents, the Arminians

183. Wood, II, 3, 448.
184. Ibid., 312, 166, 258.
185. John Hacket, *A Century of Sermons* (1675), pp. xliii, 862–72, 947.
186. Littleton, sig. b2; William Gould, *The Primitive Christian Justified* (1682), p. 11; also see Spurr, 'Latitudinarianism', 81–2.
187. John Hacket, *A Sermon Preached* (1660), pp. 20–1; Henry King, *A Sermon Preached at Lewes* (1663), p. 36; Yelverton's preface, sig. vii, to Thomas Morton, *Episkopos Apostolikos* (1670).

and Calvinists' and other outlandish groups.[188] In the universities, the young were fed on a wholesome diet of the practical works of Hammond, Sanderson, Cave, Patrick, Pearson, Fuller, Stillingfleet, Wilkins, and the author of *The Whole Duty of Man*.[189] In the parishes, the clergy and schoolmasters were sustained by the same authors.[190] The quarrels of the English church of the 1620s and 1630s were fast becoming incomprehensible to this generation. If, as has been said, Calvinism and Arminianism fed off each other, each nourished by the opposition of the other, then it was perhaps inevitable that once the antagonism cooled, both would begin to atrophy.[191] Survivors from an earlier age, like Thomas Barlow, could do nothing to stop the process, but Barlow's rage and sense of impotence is clear from the splenetic comments he scribbled in the margins of some of his books. He was outraged by the 'bold and ignorant' comments of John Goodman on the church's view of the Synod of Dort; on one page Barlow asked rhetorically, 'did not the Church of England, and all her obedient sons till 1626 or 1628 (both the universities) approve the doctrine of that synod'?[192]

However, the lack of clear labels for these new theological positions does not mean that the issues were unclear or unimportant. Those who resented and opposed the new theology were not simply reacting against innovative ideas, they were defending their own experience of religion, their own piety, against a real threat. Theology and its categories are often simply ways of expressing and explaining the psychological reality of religious experience. To cast doubt on a particular doctrine, therefore, may be to cast doubt on a particular religious experience. The mutual dependence of experience and doctrine has rarely been so plain as it was in the tradition of English puritanism. An obvious instance is the assurance of sal-

---

188. BL, MS Lansdowne 937, fos 27, 48; Scott in *Cases*, p. 246. Also see Patrick quoted at p. 322 below.

189. See MS Top Oxon F 31, fo. 101; J. Gascoigne, '"The Holy Alliance": The Rise and Diffusion of Newtonian Natural Philosophy and Latitudinarian Theology within Cambridge from the Restoration to the Accession of George III' (unpublished Cambridge University Ph.D. thesis, 1981), pp. 70–1; *The Flemings in Oxford*, ed. J.R. McGrath (Oxford Historical Society, 44, 1903; 62, 1913), I, 321, 239, 247, 262; II, *passim*; Salter, 'Books of a Curate'.

190. See *The Parochial Libraries of the Church of England* (Report to the Commission for the Care of Churches, 1959), pp. 18–19, 73–4, 79; *Catalogue of the Plume Library*, ed. S.G. Deed (Maldon, Essex, 1959).

191. G.R. Cragg, *From Puritanism to the Age of Reason* (Cambridge, 1950; 1966 edn cited), pp. 29–30.

192. Bodleian Library copy of Goodman, *A Serious and Compassionate Inquiry* (1674), shelfmark 8⁰A 43 Linc., p. 7.

vation given to so many English Protestants by the doctrine of justification by faith alone. The doctrine of justification by faith, by laying hold of Christ, matches an experience of inner renewing grace undergone by many Christians. This is what Sherlock's adversary Edward Polhill meant when he complained that grace had been reduced to 'doctrine only' and that believers had been denied 'a mystical union' with Christ.

Polhill simply could not square the new definition of faith with his own experience of faith: 'the whole is placed in believing and obeying the gospel: obedience, as I take it, is no part of faith. Works shew forth faith, *James* 2. and so are distinct from it; faith produces obedience, *Hebrews* 11. and surely it does not produce it self.'[193] It was essential to the older experience of religion that faith and works be kept separate: there could be no assurance of salvation if salvation depended upon our constant obedience, 'for that (by often sinning) is interrupted'.[194] Of course, once we are sure that we are saved, that is the greatest encouragement to obedience and to do good works. Thomas Barlow noted on his copy of Fowler's *Design of Christianity* that 'the *formale motivum*, for which God pronounces us just, is not the holiness of our life, nor the act or habit of faith it self, (which is only the hand which applies his righteousness) but the passion and merit of his beloved son, etc. Now of his satisfaction, or any righteousness of Christ's imputed for our justification Mr Fowler speaks not: nay he denies it': and Fowler indeed does say that this imputation 'consists in dealing with sincerely righteous persons, as if they were perfectly so, for the sake and upon the account of Christ's righteousness. The grand intent of the Gospel being to make us partakers of an inward and real righteousness, and it being but a secondary one that we should be accepted and rewarded as if we were completely righteous.'[195] His emphasis is all upon the righteousness, however defective, of the believer. Polhil correctly discerned the same tendency in Sherlock, who 'makes faith properly and as an act to justify; he makes the nature of faith to consist only in a firm assent: but I have before proved, that faith justifies as it receives Christ and his righteousness; and that justifying faith, over and above assent, includes in it a fiducial recumbency'.[196]

This whole notion of 'resting on' Christ, which some Anglicans attributed to William Ames (1576–1633), had become a plank of

193. Polhil, *Answer to Sherlock*, p. 5.
194. Barlow MS marginalia, Wolseley, *Justification Evangelical*, p. 109, Bodleian copy, shelfmark 8⁰C 345 Linc.
195. Fowler, *Design*, pp. 225–6.
196. Polhill, *Answer to Sherlock*, pp. 5, 387.

puritan piety.[197] Isaac Archer's spiritual struggles illustrate the importance of the 'fiduciary resting' on Christ for an assurance of salvation. As a young man Archer feared that he would be 'taken away' before he had made his peace with God, but his 'experienced' father

> judged that after I had been troubled about my condition I would make out for comfort and peace, and so I did; it was so with him, and others; some God went so far with and when they met with temptation they would go back to their assurance and peace and they would stay; this he thought a fine way, but his brother put him upon a way of faith, and recumbency rather then sensible assurance; and told him this relying, and hanging upon God's bare word of promise did most of all glorify him; my father was much addicted to that sensible way till God took him off; and wished me to go on in a way of faith, and leave it to God whether he would give peace or not.[198]

No wonder that Lewis Du Moulin complained of Simon Patrick's 'burlesquing upon the doctrine of imputative righteousness, and of the fiduciary relying and recumbency of a poor sinner upon the Lord Jesus Christ by faith'. Du Moulin concluded that 'to be short, Dr Patrick makes no other account of justification by faith, but of an hearty assent to the truth of the Gospel, and endeavouring to live according to it'.[199]

Anglicans did 'burlesque' upon the notion of 'fiducial recumbency' and all that lay behind it. In Simon Patrick's dialogue, *A Friendly Debate*, the churchman alleges that the Nonconformists are concerned only with the absolute promise of salvation for sinners 'in pursuance of which doctrines you persuade yourselves that assurance of God's love is not to be grounded upon any grace wrought in us; but only upon the testimony of the Spirit, persuading us that our persons are beloved, and that the promises are made to us'.

'This is antinomianism,' replies Patrick's Nonconformist.

'May be so; and your ministers may be antinomians, and yet not know it.'

'Call them what you please,' retorts the Nonconformist, he for one is resolved to follow them as the most 'experimental' preachers, or those who preach their own experiences in the ways of God.

Ha, exclaims the conformist, you mean those who preach their

---

197. See Barrow, V, 143–8.
198. CUL, Add. MS 8499, fos 35–6.
199. Du Moulin, *A Short and True Account*, pp. 31–4; cf. N.H. Keeble, *The Literary Culture of Nonconformity in Later Seventeenth-century England* (Leicester, 1987), pp. 177–8.

own fancies and conceits, and tell stories of God's 'withdrawings' and 'desertings', to pander to the melancholic in their congregations:

> If there be any that can be thought a sufficient ground of God's withdrawing himself, sure it must be some provoking sin which they have committed. And yet I see that they who cannot charge themselves with any voluntary act of sin, nor with any such omission neither, fall into these fancies (so I must still call them) of being forsaken by God. All the occasion that ever I could find for such black thoughts is but some such thing as this, that they have not such enlargements as they were wont; or cannot go to duty, as they speak, with the delight which formerly they took in it: which your ministers ought to teach them are no reasons, but only melancholic conceits. And if these be the things you call experiences, there are none of us but understand them as well as you, finding the same dullness and heaviness in ourselves. Only we are taught not to talk or complain of it, but to do our duty notwithstanding as well as we are able, and we shall find it will not last always.[200]

The churchmen had no ear for the scriptural cadences and spiritual metaphors of such preaching, they ridiculed this 'set of fantastical new-coined phrases, such as *laying hold of Christ, getting into Christ,* and *rolling themselves upon Christ*'. Worse still, the churchmen denounced 'the recumbency and rolling upon a naked Christ, than which (as the people understood it) never was a doctrine better fitted to cry down (or dispense with the neglect of) any great care of real holiness'.[201] Edward Fowler dismissed John Bunyan's notion of faith 'as a bare relying on the merits or righteousness of Christ, which any presumptuous wretch may do'; and claimed that 'the true Christian faith is such a belief of the doctrine of the gospel as implieth an hearty compliance with all its precepts; whereof that of relying on Christ's merits is one, and but one.'[202] Time and time again, Patrick and his brethren asserted that Nonconformity (and by implication traditional Calvinist churchmanship) not only pandered to melancholy, enthusiasm and spiritual pride, but fostered the dangerous delusion of antinomianism.

Nonconformity was not, of course, antinomian. Nonconformists, just like their puritan forebears, were staunch opponents of that error and keen to promote both tables of the decalogue; 'labour to get a saving change within, or else all external performances will be

200.   Patrick, V, 298–300.
201.   South, II, 157–8; *A Free and Impartial Inquiry* (1673), p. 93.
202.   [Edward Fowler] *The Dirt Wipt Off* (1672), p. 32.

to no purpose. And then study to show forth the power of godliness in the life ... piety, without charity, is but the half of Christianity, or rather impious hypocrisy. We may not divide the tables.'[203] Those Anglicans who knew the Reformed tradition would readily acknowledge that Luther and Calvin taught that the gospel contains a law of works as well as a law of faith.[204] Yet there can be no doubt that, by the Restoration, the fear of antinomianism had seriously distorted Anglican perceptions and representations of Calvinism. Although antinomianism as a theological digression from double decree predestinarianism was espoused by a mere handful in the 1640s, and although the practical antinomianism of the Ranters was mainly a bogeyman raised by their enemies, there was enough smoke for Anglicans to claim a Calvinist fire. After the Restoration, it became increasingly tempting for churchmen to bracket the fanatic with the sober Nonconformist and to portray Dissent as a single enthusiastic, schismatic sect with a common cant of extravagant antinomianism.

The doctrines of justification by faith alone and imputed righteousness were complemented by those of absolute predestination and limited atonement. These were reassuring, comfortable doctrines for those who espoused them. But to the new breed of churchmen, fullscale predestinarian teaching was inherently antinomian: the predestinarians employed a 'forked argument; if I be elected, I needs must, if otherwise, I cannot possibly use the means, and therefore still what need I trouble myself'.[205] Predestinarianism converted the Sermon on the Mount from 'a catalogue of holy duties' to 'a collection of promises', and so bred over-confidence in some sinners.[206] Evelyn recorded a sermon by William Clagett 'proving that there is no such thing as irresistible grace, and compulsory; but a disposition; that there would otherwise be no faith or need of obedience'.[207] On the other hand, the fixed number of the elect and the restricted scope of Christ's atonement sapped the faltering confidence of those who were unsure of their own salvation. The pragmatic evasions of those whose pastoral practice belied their theology were easy targets for the anti-Calvinists. Lawrence Womock accused the predestinarians of confuting the 'synodical and Calvinian principle' in the body of their popular sermons 'by an Arminian exhortation in your ap-

203. Josias Allaine, *A Most Familiar Exposition of the Assembly's Shorter Catechism* (1674), p. 168; also see Patrick, IV, 371 note 8; Wallace, *Puritans and Predestination*, pp. 134–8; Keeble, *Literary Culture*, pp. 220–1.
204. William Nicholson, *An Exposition of the Apostles Creed* (1661), Wing N1112, p. 422.
205. Walter Ralegh, *Reliquiae Raleighanae* (1679), p. 186.
206. Farindon, III, 278.
207. Evelyn, IV, 113.

plication' of the text.[208] Why exhort all men to repentance and faith from the pulpit if some are already and irretrievably excluded from the benefit of Christ's sacrifice on the cross? Polemicists like Robert Conold then twisted the knife by asking whether it mattered that Nonconformist preaching had been silenced by the Act of Uniformity when 'the decree of peremptory election' had long since fixed which souls were to be saved?[209] The churchmen mocked the arrogance of those who sought to penetrate God's secret decrees of predestination, 'which (besides the danger of it amongst the people for mistakes) nothing but unskilfulness could make any man confident enough to undertake the unfolding of'.[210] Thomas Pierce believed that 'amongst the clergy, there is not one in a hundred fit to speak of these mysteries; and amongst the laity not one in a thousand that's fit to hear them.'[211]

Yet the Church of England still believed and taught predestination: as Adam Littleton explained, the double decree predestinarians erred when they assumed that the covenant follows election; in reality, God elects the saved after the establishment of the covenant. Therefore election, although an act of God's free grace in Christ, is conditional in nature because founded upon a covenant.[212] In May 1682 Gilbert Burnet preached at the Rolls Chapel 'excellently well describing what was meant by election etc. viz, not the effect of any irreversible decree; but so called, because they embraced the gospel readily, by which they became elect or precious to God... It would be very needless to make our calling and election sure were they irreversible and what the rigid presbyterians pretend: no need of working out salvation with fear and trembling, were there no danger of relapses.'[213] The Restoration church preferred to propound universal redemption (but not, of course, universal salvation) and to concentrate upon the love rather than the justice of God. Simon Patrick was astounded when his use of Hammond's *Practical Catechism* with his pupils at Cambridge in the 1650s 'procured me with many the name of an Arminian, though I never made a controversy about those matters ... but preached God's love to mankind as the most evident truth'.[214]

'The goodness of God is a frequented theme,' admitted Isaac

208. Womock, *The Examination of Tilenus before the Triers* (1658), pp. 31, 79–81.
209. Robert Conold, *The Notion of Schism Stated* (1676; 1677 edn cited), p. 38.
210. John Goodman, *A Serious and Compassionate Inquiry* (1675), p. 23.
211. Pierce, *A Correct Copy of Some Notes* (1654), sig. B.
212. Littleton, II, 16–17.
213. Evelyn, IV, 282.
214. Patrick, IX, 425–6.

Barrow, 'to many perhaps it may seem vulgar and trite . . . but in truth neither can we speak too much upon this excellent subject, nor ought we ever to be weary in hearing about it'.[215] Convinced that their puritan rivals portrayed God as a tyrant who hated his creatures, the Restoration churchmen stressed 'the essential goodness of God, and his special benignity toward mankind' and deplored 'the injury we do to the justice and goodness of God by that doctrine of absolute reprobation'.[216] But, in truth, all Christians acknowledge the love of God, and where the Restoration Anglicans tipped the theological balance was not in their view of God, but in their estimation of mankind: man was moving to the centre of the stage in the new theological world of Restoration England.

The first time that Evelyn heard that 'person of extraordinary parts' Gilbert Burnet preach, he was 'explicating the nature and dignity of the human soul and new man; how to be made conformable to the image of God'.[217] That 'human nature doth somewhat resemble its excellent original, the nature divine' was a theme close to the churchmen's hearts. They pointed out that 'there do remain dispersed in the soul of human nature, divers seeds of goodness, of benignity, of ingenuity, which being cherished, excited, and quickened by good culture do, to common experience, thrust out flowers very lovely, yield fruits very pleasant of virtue and goodness'; 'there are particular excellencies scattered and dispersed among' the creatures, 'which are some shadows of the divine perfections'.[218] This optimistic vision of mankind was founded upon the ancient idea that there is an innate human impulse and capacity to grow towards the good, to become like God. As children grow like their parents, 'so is man improvable to more exact resemblance to God'; the Christian's duty 'is nothing else but virtue and goodness and holiness, which are the image of God, a conformity to the nature and will of God, and an imitation of the divine excellencies and perfections, so far as we are capable'.[219] Our love of God, in the words of Isaac Barrow, 'perfects and advances our nature, rendering it, in a manner and degree, divine, by resemblance to God (who is full thereof, so full that he is called love,) by approximation, adherence, and union, in a sort unto him'.[220]

Such statements are open to misinterpretation. They are too easily

---

215. Barrow, III, 490; also see Evelyn, IV, 29.
216. Barrow, II, 292; Evelyn, IV, 350, 72.
217. Evelyn, IV, 47–8, also see 92–3, 311.
218. Barrow, V, 227, 222; II, 328; Tillotson, I, 8.
219. Barrow, V, 227; Tillotson, I, 9; also see Evelyn, IV, 561; *WAWD*, I, 229.
220. Barrow, II, 288.

equated with the general trend towards the rehabilitation of 'natural man', and with the occasionally facile optimism about human nature, which were features of late seventeenth- and early eighteenth-century English thought.[221] This is not to deny that these Anglican views were a part of a widespread revulsion against theological and philosophical opinions and systems which appeared to rob man of his autonomy and dignity. There is no doubt that double decree predestinarianism and the determinism and egoistic psychology of Hobbes provoked some very strong statements of human free will and man's natural altruism, benevolence and sociability.[222] Voluntarist conceptions of morality also aroused Anglican ire. It had been the error of the 'rigid Calvinists' to argue – in a vain attempt to sustain the justice of absolute reprobation – that good and evil were simply what God arbitrarily chose them to be.[223] And a similar moral voluntarism was one of the more offensive tenets of Hobbism as both a political philosophy and a psychology. The churchmen believed that good and evil were fixed, that the world was governed by rational moral laws and discernible moral certainties, and that man's free will saved him from being a mere machine bound by the iron laws of necessity. Such convictions meant that the churchmen had no fear of the demand for a 'rational religion' – indeed they were in the vanguard of attempts to make the case for historical Christianity in terms of reason rather than revelation.[224]

The Restoration churchmen inhabited a world in which confidence about the natural rationalism, benevolence and sociablity of mankind was growing. They shared these sentiments, but only to a point. Mankind has potential: we are 'improvable'; it is our duty to imitate 'the divine excellencies and perfections, so far as we are capable'; but the churchmen recognized that the 'natural condition of mankind' is sin and transgression.[225] 'The fall of our first parents hath derived corruption and weakness upon the whole race and posterity of Adam.'[226] Men are weak, degenerate and irresolute: 'almost every man finds by his own frequent and sad experience,

221. For such equations see R.S. Crane, 'Suggestions toward a Genealogy of the "Man of Feeling"', *E[nglish] L[iterary] H[istory]*, I (1934); M.C. Jacob, *The Newtonians and the English Revolution 1689–1720* (1976); and for qualifications of these views see, respectively, D. Greene, 'Latitudinarianism and Sensibility: The Genealogy of the "Man of Feeling" Reconsidered', *Modern Philology*, 75 (1977), and Spurr, 'Latitudinarianism'.
222. See S.I. Mintz, *The Hunting of Leviathan* (Cambridge, 1970), pp. 142–6.
223. BL, MS Lansdowne 96, fos 58v–59.
224. See J. Spurr, '"Rational Religion" in Restoration England', *JHI*, 49 (1988).
225. Barrow, VII, 372, also see V, 402–4.
226. Tillotson, X, 401.

how inconstant his mind is to his own purposes, and how unfaithful and treacherous to his most solemn and severe resolutions'.[227] Even 'the most righteous are sinners'.[228] It was indeed fortunate then that God justifies sinners. Justification did not constitute a man 'intrinsically righteous' or infuse 'worthy qualities' into him, but rather was 'an act of God terminated upon a man as altogether unworthy of God's love, as impious, as an enemy, as a pure object of mercy'.[229] Their opponents clamoured that the churchmen must be making a claim for human capabilities since 'he, who denies imputed righteousness, must in the consequent deny Christ's satisfaction, nay, he must set up another satisfaction instead of it . . . our own inherent righteousness.'[230] But the new divines did not claim man's own righteousness was adequate satisfaction for sin. As we have seen, they argued that defective human righteousness was simply a condition required by God of all who would be saved; God will save any who embrace the new covenant and perform 'a faithful, though imperfect obedience, an obedience suitable to man's natural infirmity and frailty, and proportionable to the assistance afforded him'.[231] Trapped in the theological logic of their own system, Calvinist critics argued that the churchmen slighted the imputed righteousness of Christ and, by implication, the incarnation and atonement, and concluded that they were Socinians.[232] Socianianism was a double-edged accusation: just as Socinian views of the person of Christ undermined his atoning work, so doubts about the work of Christ were held to reflect upon his person. Yet the churchmen were, of course, staunch in their assertion of Christ as 'priest and sacrifice and mediator' for sinful mankind. 'God's detestation of sin was so great as he would never have pardoned it without the sacrifice of his son, repentance and contrition upon that account being only available', explained Sherlock.[233] The reality of sin was testimony enough to mankind's need for grace. Tillotson took John xv. 5, *without me ye can do nothing*, as a text: 'a man cannot make himself good, he cannot convert and change himself, nor by his own strength continue and

---

227. Ibid., 403.
228. Evelyn, IV, 221, also see 301, 370–1, 361; III, 155, 261, 351, 536.
229. Barrow, V, 170.
230. Polhill, *Answer to Discourse of Sherlock*, sigs. a3v–a4; *Free and Impartial Inquiry*, pp. 107, 111, (defending Fowler's *Design of Christianity*).
231. Barrow, IV, 311. Also see Evelyn, IV, 36, 236, 437.
232. Wallace, *Puritans and Predestination*, pp. 128–9, 145–6, 152–7, 176. To argue from this position, that they had already paved the way for full-blown deism, as Wallace does (pp. 167, 171), is not feasible; see G. Reedy, *The Bible and Reason* (Philadelphia, 1975); Spurr, 'Rational Religion'.
233. Evelyn, IV, 571.

hold out in a good course, we can do nothing of this, without the grace and assistance of Christ.'[234] At Deptford, Evelyn's vicar 'preached on Psalm v. 8, showing that the most righteous man has need of God's guidance and conduct, perstringing the Pelagians and other sects, who ascribed too much to our own will'.[235] The assumption then was that man has the capacity to be good, but needs to be 'awakened out of that drowsy state (which naturally in great measure hath seized upon all men)' by 'divine grace'.[236]

As always, the crux of the matter was the principle that 'supernatural grace and assistance does not exclude, but suppose the concurrence of our endeavours. The grace of God does not do all, without any concurrence on our part.'[237] The sinner can cooperate with grace; he can contribute to or prepare for it through a regime of piety; but it is still a divine gift.

> We may go to church, we may read and hear God's word, and upon the hearing of it may reflect upon the actions of our lives, and may be convinced of our sin and danger, and upon this conviction, may beg God's mercy and grace to reform and grow better. But this we cannot effect without supernatural grace and assistance.[238]

Once the penitent sinner embraces faith and grace is extended to him a gradual process of transformation begins. 'Faith doth purify our souls, and cleanse our hearts ... disposing them to an universal obedience and conformity to God's holy will ... for faith not only doth clear our understanding from its defects (blindness, ignorance, error, doubt) but it cleanseth our will from its vicious inclinations (from stubborn, froward, wanton, giddy humours).'[239] There is no instantaneous conversion, but a progressive and continual endeavour towards 'a nearer similitude to God'.[240] For the Restoration churchmen – as has been said of the Cambridge Platonists – grace liberates, not overpowers, human potential (a synergism they share with a wide range of other 'theological cousins').[241] The churchmen liked to think of grace renewing human nature: 'the free grace of God is infinitely more magnified in renewing our natures, than it could be

234. Tillotson, X, 398.
235. Evelyn, IV, 334.
236. Barrow, V, 228.
237. Tillotson, X, 405.
238. Ibid., 398.
239. Barrow, V, 90–1.
240. Ibid., 228.
241. See Patrides (ed.), *Cambridge Platonists*, p. 21; *Diary of an Oxford Methodist*, ed. Heitzenrater, pp. 33, 36–7.

in the bare justification of our persons'.[242] In short, it built upon the best of human nature and, like revelation, reinforced the duties of the law of nature.[243]

To concentrate, as this chapter has, upon the novel theology of some Restoration churchmen is to court several dangers. It distracts attention from the fact that in the seventeenth century theological innovation was *ipso facto* deviation from the truth; there was as yet no notion of doctrinal development, and Englishmen could only conceive of a single, immutable, revelation of divine truth. All theological endeavour was therefore cast in the mould of recovery rather than discovery, of renovation rather than innovation, of a return to the primitive truth of the first centuries rather than an advance to a deeper understanding. We also risk losing sight of the great silent mass of the clergy, many of whom may well have held on to older theologies – and here, for example, one has reason to be grateful to Thomas Barlow and his ilk for speaking up in defence of the Calvinist orthodoxy of an earlier Church of England. Not that the Nonconformists had any compunction about pointing out the church's theological change of heart:

> If Arminianism be the true genuine doctrine of the Church of England, how then comes it to pass that they who now follow Arminius did heretofore follow Calvin? The question is founded upon a probable supposition that that is the doctrine of the church which the generality of those who are members of the church are brought up in.[244]

The variety of theological opinion to be found in the Church of England had long been the butt of her opponents' jibes; as one poetaster asked of the chapter at Chichester under Bishop Peter Gunning,

> Is any church more catholic than we?
> Two prebends apostate Puritans there be,
> One perjur'd Protestant, the dean an atheist,
> And Peter the head thereof an arrant Papist.
> What a prodigious unity is there!
> Calvinist, Arminian, Roundhead, Cavalier,
> Protestant, papist, atheist, devil and all

---

242. Fowler, *Design*, p. 130.
243. See Tillotson, X, 485.
244. Henry Hickman, *Review of Certamen Epistolare* (Oxford, 1659), pp. 132–3.

Dryden put it more succinctly, if no less impolitely, when he dubbed the church 'a mere mock Queen of a divided herd'.[245] At times, the Dissenters seemed genuinely puzzled by the church's lack of doctrinal cohesion.

> So many of your ministers are so contrary one to another. Some are for the doctrine of predestination, and other against it; some are for justification by imputed righteousness, others not; some for a difference betwixt grace and morality, others oppose it: some for the divine right of episcopacy, others that the magistrate may appoint what form of government he please: in a word, some write or approve of such a book, that others of you think (as I have heard) fit to be burnt. Which of these shall we understand to be your church?[246]

But doctrinal unanimity was not the point. The Church of England had never been united by a detailed and explicit confession of faith: her Articles were short, often vague, and designed to foster unity rather than enforce orthodoxy. The church derived unity from other sources, from her Prayer Book and from her bishops: Henry Maurice believed that it was episcopal government which had saved the Church of England from following the European Reformed churches down the path of doctrinal fratricide.[247]

A further hazard of dwelling upon innovation, and upon the hostile reaction, is that of neglecting the common ground. In Restoration England, it was still just possible to assert that the church and Dissent were agreed on fundamental doctrines, and to mean it. Sober Nonconformists like Baxter and Matthew Henry claimed to derive much pleasure and profit from the sermons of 'moderate' churchmen like Stillingfleet and Tillotson. Perhaps theological differences are only seen in proportion when theology has been reinserted into its natural context of religious life, of piety, worship and practical religion. If, for example, the Nonconformists' theology is read alongside their devotional and practical literature, then many of

---

245. *The Character of the Church of Chichester* (1673), in *Poems on Affairs of State: I 1660–78*, ed. G. deF. Lord (New Haven and London, 1963), p. 312; Dryden, *The Hind and the Panther*, line 498 (in *Poems and Fables*, ed. J. Kinsley (Oxford, 1958), p. 367); also see p. 164 above.
246. *Separation Yet No Schisme* (1675), p. 60. Richard Baxter believed that the Anglican clergy were divided over, *inter alia*, Arianism, imputation and justifying faith, universal redemption, original sin, and the necessity of episcopacy to the being of a church.
247. Henry Maurice, *A Vindication of the Primitive Church, and Diocesan Episcopacy* (1682), p. 389.

the themes which I have discussed in connection with the Church of England – such as the necessity of works and faith, progress in grace through devotion and moral effort, the gradual nature of sanctification, even the attainment of evangelical perfection – appear to have been as prominent in Dissenting thought.[248] Certainly Protestants of all leanings were anxious to be assured of their salvation: John Evelyn had exactly the same forebodings about dying before he had 'worked out' his salvation as Isaac Archer and his father; Archer took the 'way of faith' and reliance on 'God's bare word of promise', while Evelyn took comfort from his vicar's preaching 'of the nature of divine hope, how little it differed from faith, rising from a life of holiness, how at last it arrives to assurance'.[249] But no one can doubt that there was little practical difference between these alternative routes to assurance.

Meanwhile, away from the theological controversies, most parish ministers spent most of their time propounding the essential saving truths of Christianity; English congregations did not suddenly hear new doctrines from the pulpits in 1660. The preachers continued along the familiar, homiletical paths. These were parish priests with a gospel to proclaim, a flock to bring to a sense of their sins; and their advice was that it was 'safer far to make ourselves fit to be justified, than too curiously to study how justification is wrought, in which study we are many times more subtle than wise: in a word, safer to make ourselves capable of favour and mercy'.[250] 'Justification was not by one single act, but continual progress,' explained the vicar of Deptford, 'so we must proceed in good life and works'.[251] The preacher's language was often still that of the Reformed tradition, full of references to 'sanctification' and 'justification', but its burden had changed: when Robert Breton preached 'of the necessity of appropriating faith in the free grace of Christ', he could be legitimately glossed by his congregation as teaching 'the necessity of good works for manifestation of our faith'.[252] The church's theological shift away from older notions of justification was probably experienced by the laity as a new emphasis upon repentance and 'the whole duty', as the promotion of a 'worthy reception' of the sacrament, and as a new attention to devotional life and liturgical

---

248. For example, the Christian life is a pilgrimage towards the heavenly city for both John Bunyan and Simon Patrick; see N.H. Keeble, *Literary Culture*, esp. pp. 12–14, 271–2.
249. See p. 319 above; Evelyn, IV, 47, 95.
250. Farindon, I, 21.
251. Evelyn, IV, 61–2.
252. Evelyn, III, 378, 379.

performance. As a prescription for holy living, the 'whole duty of man' sounds unremitting, austere and impossibly demanding, but it has to be seen it the light of its accompanying piety. The clergy offered the penitent a rich devotional life based on the church's liturgy and sacraments to sustain him through the rigours of holy living. The next chapter describes this piety, its formulation and promotion by the clergy, and its reception among the laity.

Chapter 7

'The Surest Foundation':
Anglican Piety

'Among all the duties prescribed to us by our religion, the rendering
due worship to God is in nature and for consequence the principal;
God thereby being most directly honoured and served, we from it
immediately deriving most ample and high benefits.'[1] In the Restoration church, worship was no subsidiary duty to be relegated to
a Sunday, but a constant obligation in the daily life of the Christian.
The life of prayer and a constant attendance upon the sacrament
of the Lord's Supper were essential parts of 'the whole duty of
man' as it was defined by the church. These were essential duties
because a fervent piety was at the same time a condition of individual salvation, an aid to repentance and regeneration, and the
fruit of a living faith. 'Do'st thou find at thy devotions and meditations that thy heart burns within thee, being set on fire with cel-
estial flames of zeal?' the penitent was asked by his minister: for
only a heartfelt piety offered that 'sensible' assurance of personal
union with Christ which all Christians craved.[2]

The piety of individuals also served communal or corporate ends.
The clergy of the Restoration church never tired of proclaiming
that the piety of her members was 'the surest foundation of the
church's peace'.[3] The piety of Anglicans would be the ultimate
vindication of the Church of England from the cavils and carpings
of her opponents. 'Did they see us frequent the public offices of
religion with an awful reverence and devotion, and exemplary in

1. Barrow, VII, 399.
2. Littleton, II, 87; Patrick, IV, 563.
3. Robert Grove, *A Short Defence of the Church and Clergy of England* (1681), p. 91: also see
   Richard Kidder, *Convivium coeleste* (1674), sig. A3; Richard West, *The Profitableness of
   Piety* (1671), p. 90; Richard Allen, *Insulae fortunatae* (1671), p. 11; John Goodman, *A
   Serious and Compassionate Inquiry* (1674; 1675 edn cited), p. 241; Roger Hayward, *A
   Sermon Preacht* (1673), pp. 24–5; Edward Fowler, *The Design of Christianity* (1671),
   pp. 303–5.

our lives for virtue and goodness, they would be induced to believe that we have a real concernment for religion, and that God is in us of a truth.'[4] It was the aim of the Church of England 'to be as like the primitive church in her zeal and devotion, as she is truly like her in her methods and constitutions'; 'primitive piety' would not only give 'sufficient check' to the papists, Dissenters and atheists, it would inspire the moral regeneration of English society.[5] For piety would bring moral reformation in its wake; 'we cannot think that profaneness, drunkenness, whoredom, thefts, robberies, and other enormities would so abound as they do, if persons were religiously bred up and the people everywhere accustomed to pious performances in the houses where they live.'[6] Another, more profound, relationship existed between individual piety and the church. The church existed to offer up a sacrifice of prayer and praise to God; when her laity consecrated their lives to worship they were fulfilling her deepest purpose. And the Church of England was particularly well equipped for the pursuit of the devout life. She could boast of a spiritual and theological resource second to none in the Book of Common Prayer. Anglicans gloried in their worship, in 'that virtuous mediocrity, which our church observes between the meretricious gaudiness of the Church of Rome and the squalid sluttery of fanatic conventicles'.[7] The Prayer Book occupied a central position in the life of the church; it had offered pious consolation during the Interregnum; and it formed the basis of the piety promoted by the church during the Restoration.

'Preces et lacrymae': The Power of Prayer

'Prayer as 'tis a high privilege, so 'tis the great duty we owe to God; comprehending in scripture language all religious worship.'[8] According to the churchmen, prayer was the summation of worship, 'the most noble, the most proper act of religion . . . by which we turn tenants to God, and own him as the donor of "every good and perfect gift"'.[9] Yet it was an obligation strangely slighted by the English: 'we make the pulpit our ark and chain all religion to it', lamented the churchmen; 'in these last and worst times some crafty

---

4. Samuel Crispe, *A Sermon Preached* (1686), p. 25.
5. Nathaniel Bisbie, *The Bishop Visiting* (1686), pp. 25–6.
6. *Domestick Devotions for the Use of Families and of Particular Persons* (1683), p. 73.
7. S.P., *A Brief Account of the New Sect of Latitude-men* (1662), p. 7.
8. Littleton, II, 55.
9. Hamon L'Estrange, *The Alliance of Divine Offices* (1659; LACT, Oxford, 1846 edn cited), p. 24.

men ... undervalue the administration of prayers and thanksgivings, which is the duty of the advocate or the priest. Hence sermons or prophesyings are extolled to the skies, sacraments and prayers are neglected.'[10] This was an error the clergy were determined to rectify and so they set about to portray prayer and its obligation in their true colours.

Prayer consists of thanksgiving, praise and supplication, but in Anglican accounts the last often seemed to loom largest.[11] Ask and you shall be given, knock and the door shall be opened, for prayer is the key which unlocks the treasures of heaven.[12] As the catechism teaches of the Lord's Prayer, 'all things that be needful both for our souls and bodies', including the grace to worship, serve and obey him, come from God 'of his mercy and goodness, through our Lord Jesus Christ'. Prayers and tears are 'the most prevailing methods of obtaining grace at God's hands for our selves and others'.[13] The 'convinced sinner' was urged to pray 'for converting grace'; 'O that the new nature did more strongly incline me to thee, and to thy service, than my corrupted nature inclineth me to the interest of carnal self and sense! O that I had a heart to believe in Christ as strongly as I know I should believe in him ... O give me thy holy spirit, through the mediation of my dear redeemer.'[14]

'Prayer prevails with God for the blessing that we pray for,' insisted Robert South,

neither by way of information, nor yet of persuasion, and much less by the importunity of him who prays, and least of all by any worth in the prayer itself, equal to the thing prayed for; but it prevails solely and entirely upon this account, that it is freely appointed by God, as the stated, allowed condition, upon which he will dispense his blessings to mankind.[15]

Prayer was another condition, another element in the whole duty of the Christian; it 'is an honour and benefit to us, and yet is accepted by God as our homage and the testimony of our observance'.[16]

10. Farindon, I, 471; *The Diary and Autobiography of Edmund Bohun*, ed. S.W. Rix (Beccles, 1852), p. 32; Evelyn, IV, 288.
11. Thomas Horne, *A Sermon Preached* (1685), pp. 27–8; cf. Barrow, I, 295; *WAWD*, I, 42–3; George Bright, *A Treatise of Prayer* (1678), ch. 1.
12. Littleton, II, 48, 56.
13. Ibid., 265.
14. C.P., *Christian Devotion* (1679), pp. 92–4. Also see Anthony Horneck, *The Fire of the Altar* (1683), pp. 132–4; John Gauden, *Whole Duty of a Communicant* (2nd edn, 1685), p. 118.
15. South, I, 317.
16. Comber, *A Companion to the Temple* (1684), I, 1.

Praying was also a technique of that regime of repentance and contrition which played such a major role in holy living. The very activity of prayer was beneficial and transforming: 'nothing alters us so much as serious prayer, which puts a new mind into us, and for the present makes us a quite another sort of creatures'.[17] 'Make use therefore of these private forms of devotion daily, and you shall (with God's blessing) soon perceive a happy and heavenly change in your souls.'[18]

Prayer was a single duty to be performed in several ways – in the privacy of the individual's closet or chamber, in the bosom of the family, and in public. Private prayer could be tailored most closely to the penitential needs of the individual, but public prayer was indispensable for salvation and was the due of God; it 'is an augustness and magnificence he is worthy of, nay it is infinitely below him, but it is all we can do'.[19] In private prayer 'we are to be more particular according to our particular needs, than in public it is fit to be' and to use our own words and forms of prayer; but in public or family worship, we are to use the public liturgy furnished us by 'the providence of God and the church'.[20] The Common Prayer, 'a store house of rare divinity', could edify us 'until at length we arrive at glory and perfection in the highest heavens'.[21] The liturgy wrought such changes in the individual through the coherence of its structure, its repetition of the creeds and the Lord's Prayer, its regular reading through the whole of scripture, and its construction from the words of the Bible: 'the very order of our service, and the returns of the fasts and great festivals are a perpetual catechism, and a constant motive to excite and quicken sober piety and true devotion.'[22] It was therefore important that the congregation should follow and understand the service; 'words do not work here as spells or charms, but as rational instruments that signify the belief and affections of our souls'.[23] But this did not mean that the Common Prayer was untouched by any sense of the transcendant or ineffable. Churchmen recognized that the worship of the church could stir deep emotions in the congregation; and, as we shall see, they sought to nurture and harness these pious emotions.

---

17. Patrick, IV, 652; also see Barrow, VII, 403–4.
18. *A Collection of Private Forms of Prayer . . . By the Author of the Weeks Preparation* (1690), sig. A5.
19. Bright, *Treatise of Prayer*, p. 106.
20. *WAWD*, I, 44–5, 149 (Preface to *Private Devotions*).
21. Taylor, I, 154; William Beveridge, *The Theological Works* (LACT, Oxford, 1842–8), VI, 398; Anthony Sparrow, *The Bishop of Exons Caution* (1669), p. 14.
22. Beveridge, *Works*, VI, 375–93; William Saywell, *A Serious Inquiry into the Means of an Happy Union* (1681), p. 27.
23. [Thomas Seymour], *Advice to the Readers of the Common Prayer* (1683), p. 3.

The obligation and consolation of prayer had been brought home to Anglicans during the Interregnum, when their public liturgy was prohibited, their church abolished, and God had 'snuffed our lamp so near, that it is almost extinguished'.[24] Prayers and tears had been their only weapons. From their Babylonian captivity, they petitioned God to

> shew the riches of thy goodness to thy desolate and persecuted church, that now sits mourning in her own dust and ruins; torn by schism, and stripped and spoiled by sacrilege. . . . Restore us once again the public worship of thy name, the reverent administrations of thy sacraments; raise up the former government both in church and state, that we may no longer be without king, without priest, without God in the world; but may once more enter into thy courts with praise, and serve thee with that reverence, that unity and order, as may be acceptable in thy sight . . . [25]

In these 'prayers of intercession for their use who mourn in secret', these 'mournful threnodies' composed and used by 'God's remembrancers and mourners in Sion', the dominant tone is one of lamentation, with long penitential litanies and confessions, composite psalms, and prayers of petition or intercession, all woven, as is the Common Prayer, from biblical texts, in particular from the Books of Lamentations, Jeremiah, Daniel, Isaiah, and of course the Psalms. Overshadowing all other concerns in these prayers was the execution of the King and the need to expiate the nation's guilt. For loyal churchmen were filled with foreboding that this wound might prove fatal, that the loss of their prince presaged the Lord's forsaking of the English, the removal of his candlestick and of all religion, and the nation's ruin. 'Blessed God, smite us not with a fatal and exterminating judgment,' prayed Jeremy Taylor:

> call not the watchmen off from their guards, nor the angels from their charges; let us not die by a famine of thy word and sacraments: if thou smitest us with the rod of a man, thou canst sanctify every stroke unto us, and canst bring good out of evil, and delightest to do so: but nothing can bring us recompense if thou hatest us, and sufferest the souls of thy people to perish.[26]

Yet, as Thomas Warmstry had written on the day after the regicide, 'there is no poison but have something medicinable in it, which

24. Taylor, VII, 284. Also see *Fragmentary Illustrations of the History of the Book of Common Prayer*, ed. W.C. Jacobson (1874), p. 10.
25. John Huit or Hewitt, *Prayers of Intercession for their Use who Mourn in Secret, for the Publick Calamities of the Nation. With an Anniversary Prayer for the 30th of January. Very Necessary and Useful in Private Families, as well as in Congregations* (1659), p. 16.
26. Taylor, XV, 339–40; also see *Prayers of Intercession*, p. 50.

the art of piety may draw forth of it.'[27] Tribulation from on high was intended as an Egypt on the way to Canaan, as a furnace to purge the heart of dross and corruption, and if only the people would use their divine scourges to become unfeignedly pious, then their eternal souls, although not their temporal fortunes, would be assured. The sufferings of the nation were designed to turn the English towards God in humility and repentance, trusting in no other. Before these afflictions might be lifted, God required serious mourning for the nation's transgressions, earnest supplications for forgiveness, and sincere resolutions of personal amendment. If the English Sion donned sackcloth and gave her time over to devotion then perhaps, hoped John Hewitt, the ark of the Lord might yet be recaptured from the Philistines.[28] In 1654 Bishop Joseph Hall proposed that

> we, the professed servants of our Lord Jesus Christ, orthodox and genuine sons of the Church of England, whose hearts are moved by the good spirit of God to a just resentment of our miseries and dangers, should firmly resolve, for the countermining of those engineers of hell and conspirers of our destruction, to enter into a safe, warrantable, holy fraternity of mourners in Sion; whose profession and work shall be a peculiarity of devotion: striving, with fervent prayers and tears, to obtain from heaven a seasonable redress of these our pressing calamities.[29]

Eventually their prayers were heard: as one preacher put it in 1660, 'amongst the means of the King's return, I shall in the last place mention, that which is not surely of the least efficacy, the prayers of the church, the lately persecuted ministers of the Church of England, and of the good people adhering to them'.[30] 'The court of heaven hath been solicited this many years *pro* and *con*, with much preaching, fasting, and crying to', pointed out the triumphant churchmen; 'now let the world judge whose prayers have been heard'.[31] But, in the main, the clergy were eager to portray themselves as 'both men of peace and men of prayers . . . our weapons are prayers and our message is peace'.[32] Once more the people

---

27. Thomas Warmstry, *A Hand-kirchife for Loyall Mourners* (1649), p. 4.
28. John Hewitt, *Repentance and Conversion the Fabrick of Salvation* (1658), sermon 7, p. 186.
29. Joseph Hall, *The Works*, ed. P. Wynter (Oxford, 1863), VII, 416. Hall was careful to add 'that here is no other design than merely spiritual; aiming at nothing, but religious transactions between God and our souls'.
30. Clement Barksdale, *The Kings Return* (1660), p. 9.
31. Gilbert Ironside, *A Sermon preached at Dorchester* (1660), pp. 13–14.
32. Henry Glover, *Exhortation to Prayer* (1663), p. 11.

could enter the courts of the Lord and serve him with 'reverence, unity and order' according to the rite of the Book of Common Prayer.

The Anglicans, who had been sustained by and who had 'suffered' for the Prayer Book, would not betray it when the church came into her own at the Restoration. Nonconformist objections to the Prayer Book were rejected, even though several of their precise criticisms had weight and were later recognized by the Church of England's own liturgical experts. It was complained that the Prayer Book's confession was too general; there were too many short and repetitive prayers; too much use of the doxology; many of the translations from scripture (most notably in the Psalms) were unsuitable or corrupt; readings from the Apocrypha had been included; and parts of the baptism and communion services and the vestiarian and ceremonial rubrics gave offence. Defensive church-men would not give way on such minor matters, however, because they were convinced that they were a smokescreen for a more fundamental Nonconformist objection to the imposition of any liturgy which subordinated the Nonconformist ministers' gifts for praying 'by the spirit' to a set form of worship. The Anglican arguments for a set form of public worship ranged widely. A self-proclaimed moderate opined that set forms were imposed 'not for any absolute necessity we put in them, but only for conveniency, to prevent schisms, stop errors, preserve order, unity and uniformity in the church'.[33] This was, of course, to rely upon the well-worn principle that these matters were *adiaphora* which became mandatory once instituted by those authorities whose decisions bind us. There is nothing 'more beautiful and becoming than uniformity' in the liturgy since Christians are obliged to dwell together in unity 'and to witness as much by their uniformity in the worship and service of God'.[34] A single liturgy was a hedge of order which sustained beauty and reverence in worship and purity and unity in religion: recent experience showed all too well what followed from the uprooting of this hedge.[35] 'Above all, a constant and complete liturgy mightily conduces to the edification and salvation as well as the unanimity and peace of the meaner sort of people.'[36]

33. Alan Carr, *A Peaceable Moderator* (1665), p. 10. Also see Fowler in *Cases*, p. 303; Richard Lytler, *The Reformed Presbyterian* (1662); John Pearson, *The Minor Theological Works*, ed. E. Churton (Cambridge, 1844), II, 97–111.

34. The opinion of the anonymous author of a tract with the guarded title of *Publick Devotion, and the Common Service of the Church of England Justified, and Recommended to all honest and well meaning, (however prejudiced) Dissenters* (1675), see pp. 28–9, 20–1.

35. Carr, *Peaceable Moderator*, pp. 67–8, 75–6, 20–1.

36. John Gauden, *Considerations touching the Liturgy* (1661), p. 11.

It was possible to extract a prescription of set forms of prayer from the authorities of scripture and the Early Church and from 'the concurrent testimony, experience, and practice of the universal church'.[37] Although the Bible contains no positive injunction to a single set form, it contains much that can be interpreted to that end. Thus particular instances of prayer and worship were taken as models and authority for set forms, for instance Christ's prescription of a form of prayer, the Lord's Prayer, to the disciples (Luke xi. 2).[38] The Acts of the Apostles and, above all, I Timothy ii. 1, 2, 'which text seems to be a platform, according to which the public service fitted for Christian assemblies was first framed upon', were seen as convincing evidence of Apostolic commitment to the principle that those with oversight of a church should impose a liturgy.[39] Such liturgies, it was claimed, existed in the sub-Apostolic church and were attributed to St Peter, St Mark and St James. The Early Church supplied the most convincing evidence and it was a simple matter to demonstrate that all subsequent churches, and especially those of the European Reformed tradition, had enjoyed set forms of worship. 'But what need I trouble myself with a long proof of this matter,' asked Simon Patrick, when those reverenced by the Dissenters themselves confess 'that there hath been no time wherein there was not a prescribed form of divine service?'[40]

Is it not more 'safe' and 'comfortable', asked the churchmen, for the 'truly pious to breathe out their desires in those wholesome public forms of devotion, than to trust to extemporary effusions, to the vain prattle and idle tautologies of those that pretend themselves gifted'?[41] The commandment was plain and easy: 'be not rash with thy mouth, and be not hasty to utter anything before God'.[42] The churchmen denigrated the 'wild, uncouth and fiery devotions' of the Nonconformists, which are 'so far from advancing real devotion and a holy worship (as is pretended they do) that they rather obstruct the most solemn devotion in prayer, and draw Christian people's minds from it, and feed them with empty husks of prayer'.[43] The Nonconformist ministers led their congregations

37. Beveridge, *Works*, VI, 371.
38. William Falkner, *Libertas ecclesiastica* (1674), pp. 91–101; Beveridge, *Works*, VI, 371–2.
39. Thomas Elborow, *The Reasonableness of our Christian Service* (1677), sig. A7v; cf. Falkner, *Libertas*, p. 109 (citing Hammond's *Paraphrase of the New Testament*); Taylor, VII, 355–62.
40. Patrick, IV, 762; he goes on to quote John Preston.
41. Littleton, II, 59.
42. Taylor, VII, 316, misquoting Ecclesiastes v. 2.
43. Edward Kemp, *Reasons for the Sole Use of the Churches Prayers in Publick* (1668), pp. 11, 9. Also see Evelyn, IV, 135.

in extempore prayer which conspicuously failed to meet the divine criteria of considered, reverent and brief worship. 'To invent the matter and words of prayer, is not to pray, but to study a prayer', and exhibits a pharisaical pride in the individual's 'gifts'. While the Nonconformists flattered themselves that 'those transports of passion, which are merely the effects of new and surprizing words striking briskly on their fancies', evidenced 'their piety and god-liness', the characteristic prolixity of extempore prayer was, in truth, a denial of divine omnipotence and hence an affront to God. Such worship was indeed an offering of that 'strange fire' (Numbers iii. 4) which would find no welcome with the Lord.[44] To be acceptable to the Lord, and to the Anglicans, public prayer had to be considered, reverent and unanimous. Minister and congregation were involved together. 'Ever since apostolical times', the English liturgy had been a 'mixed office ... wherein the priest or presbyter, and the people, jointly and interchangeably concur'. There was no barrier, as in the papists' Latin service or the Nonconformists' extempore prayer, between the Anglican celebrant and his congregation.[45] 'The church in general', not just individual members, was edified by the con-currence of 'devout and pious souls' in following a set form of public worship; and 'the welfare of the whole is to be preferred before the spiritual advantage of any particular member'.[46] 'The efficacy of the united prayers of a Christian congregation' was extolled by the clergy; it was 'a joint endeavour to bring public honour to their common Lord; and to forward their own salvation; who twist and combine their prayers and praises; and converse here with one another, as they hope to do hereafter in heaven'.[47]

Such a joint endeavour of prayer and praise, such truly *common* prayer, depended on a well-prepared congregation. Ideally, a con-gregation should assemble for common prayer 'every one of which hath lift up his heart privately unto him already, imploring his aid and assistance in the performance of so great a work, and so are all now ready to set about it'.[48] A set form of public worship was particularly useful because the devout could prepare themselves

44. Scott in *Cases*, esp. pp. 254, 260; South, I, 343–4, 348–51, 321–2.
45. Pearson, *Minor Theological Works*, II, 236; also see Scott in *Cases*, p. 258; South, I, 352–3; Falkner, *Libertas*, pp. 124–32; William Outram, *Twenty Sermons* (1682), pp. 135–6.
46. Beveridge, *Works*, VI, 373; John Williams in *Cases*, p. 121.
47. John Mapletoft, *A Perswasive to the Consciencious Frequenting the Daily Publick Prayers of the Church* (1687), pp. 18–19; Patrick, IV, 700.
48. Beveridge, *Works*, VI, 382; also see Thomas Horne, *Sermon*, pp. 30–1; Edward Wetenhall, *Two Discourses for the Furtherance of Christian Piety and Devotion* (1671), p. 306.

and study both the words and 'such affections as are suitable to them' before coming to church.

> Suppose the confession be that of our church's liturgy, wherein we begin with *almighty and most merciful father*; I can consider the meaning of these words before I come to church; and from the consideration of God's almighty and most merciful nature, excite my affections to an awful dread of his power, and an ingenuous sense of his mercy; by which when I come to joyn with these words in the public confession, I shall be duly affected with the sense of them, and my soul will be ready melted into all that filial sorrow and humiliation for my sin, which the consideration that I have offended by it an almighty and most merciful father suggests; and so if I consider, and apply beforehand all the rest of the confession, I shall thereby tune and set my affections to the sense and matter of each particular phrase and expression in it . . . [49]

For the Restoration churchmen, this opportunity to study and meditate upon the liturgy in the privacy of one's closet was the springboard into a life of piety and into common prayer. They recognized, however, that private devotion was somehow subordinate to public worship.

> God is much more honoured by our public addresses to him, than he can be, by anything we can do in private; not but we may, and ought to use private prayers suitable to our necessities, but we must not neglect his public worship, which the private ought not to hinder, but promote, because in truth, it is defective without public, being only worship, but not honour, glory, sacrifice and service. [50]

In recommending private devotion the church walked a tightrope, for on the one hand lay the advantage of strengthening the devout who already attended her worship, but on the other lay the danger of playing into the hands of the disaffected who preferred the 'privacy' of the conventicle. 'Private prayer' in this sense, whether at home or in public, was the 'life and soul' of schism within the church.[51] What the churchmen hoped for was a frequent recourse to both private and public prayer. 'One duty must not jostle out

49.   Scott in *Cases*, p. 257.
50.   *A Letter of Advice* (1688), p. 3 (citing Patrick's discourse on prayer; see Patrick, IV, 687); *domestick Devotions*, pp. 179–80; Henry Hammond, *Daily Practice of Devotion* (1684), pp. 67–8; C. P., *Christian Devotion*, sig. A4; Mapletoft, *Perswasive*, pp. 12–15.
51.   Richard Sherlock, *The Irregularitie of a Private Prayer in a Publick Congregation* (1674), p. 16; Richard Steward, *Several Short, but Seasonable Discourses* (1684).

another,' warned Matthew Bryan, 'the same God who commanded private has enjoined also public duties'.[52] The Restoration clergy saw the church as a fellowship of prayer which extended beyond her public worship into the household and private devotions of the laity. When the pious Anglican knelt in prayer in his closet, or led his family in worship, he was participating in and strengthening that fellowship.

'Enter into thy Closet': The Prayer Book, Private Devotion and a Worthy Receiving

I should not doubt to see such very considerable good effects in a short time, if you could and would either your self bestow, or prevail with any of your parishioners of ability to bestow, and disperse about the parish among your people copies of Dr Beveridge's excellent *Sermon concerning the Excellency and Usefulness of the Common Prayer*, (a sermon which now we have reprinted of the seventh edition) or the second edition of that devout laic Mr Seymour's most pious little book of *Advice to the Readers of the Common Prayer, and to the People attending the Same*; to which let me add that small piece, but very well and wisely designed, and lately published at Oxford, entitled, *The Common Prayer Book the Best Companion in the House and Closet as well as in the Temple, with a particular Office for the Sacrament*: which last collection, if it be once commonly received, and reverently used, will at the same time secure the keeping up sober religion in *private families*, and in *closets*, while it also brings the people to a good liking, pious using, and easily remembering of those same prayers, which at other times they shall hear read in your *churches*.[53]

Bishop Turner of Ely recommended these inexpensive tracts on the Common Prayer to his diocesan clergy because he had seen 'a world of good' come from their distribution among the laity. Although sure that his clergy already preached up the duty of private devotion, Turner especially commended to them Bishop Ken's single sheet of *Directions* from the catechism for use with the 'poorest and meanest' of their parish, and Ken's longer *Exposition* of the catechism for the more capable laymen. There was in fact an abundance of such pious tracts in Restoration England, some of them

52. Matthew Bryan, *A Perswasive to the Stricter Observation of the Lords Day* (1686), pp. 22–3.
53. Francis Turner, *A Letter to the Clergy of the Diocess of Ely from the Bishop of Ely. Before, and Prefatory to his Visitation* (Cambridge, 1686), pp. 14–15.

obviously dependent upon the Book of Common Prayer, other less so, but almost all of them designed to complement the public worship of the Church of England in some way.

Some of these devotionals described in great detail how to go about 'the exercises of godliness'. Edward Wetenhall's popular manual of 1666 explained its purpose and method on its title-page:

> *Enter into thy Closet: Or, a Method and Order for Private Devotion. A Treatise endeavouring a plain discovery of the most Spiritual and Edifying course of Reading, Meditation and Prayer; and so of Self-Examination, Humiliation, Mortification, and such most necessary Christian duties, by which we sue out the pardon of our sins from Heaven; and maintain an Holy Converse with God. Together with particular perswasives thereunto and helps therein.*[54]

Other Anglican authors offered prayers for the devout to use in the privacy of their own chamber or with their families during the daily round. There were prayers on waking – 'O Lord blot out, as a night mist, mine iniquities; and scatter my sins, as a morning cloud'[55] – and on going to bed; prayers or 'collects' for special graces or particular virtues; devotions suited to particular afflictions, blessings and seasons; *Domestick Devotions* and *Forms of Prayer for Every Day in the Week, Morning and Evening. Composed for the Use of Private Families.*[56] Prayers were added to every manual and catechism – the 'private devotions for several occasions' appended to *The Whole Duty* seem to have been especially influential. And these devotional works sold. Large numbers were printed, purchased, and even given away to parishioners by the clergy: according to William Crooke, the publisher, Lancelot Addison's *An Introduction to the Sacrament* (1682) – '24mo. Price bound 6d. Fitted for the pocket' – 'was so well liked by a great many ministers, that they gave them by dozens at a time to their poor parishioners, being found to be fittest and most plain to the meanest capacities; yet very useful to all who desire worthily to be partakers of the sacrament of the Lord's Supper'. In 1686, for the third edition, Addison added 'a collection of devotions'.[57]

Such a large and diverse literature cannot be easily or simply characterized, but two features do stand out: first, these devotionals were preoccupied with the repentance and self-examination which

---

54. This tract achieved a fourth edition in 1672 and a fifth in 1676: I cite the 1672 edition.

55. *Preparations to a Holy Life: Or Devotions for Families and Private Persons* (1684), p. 7.

56. *Domestick Devotions* (1683); John Meriton, *Forms of Prayer* (1682).

57. Lancelot Addison, *An Introduction to the Sacrament* (3rd edn, 1686), sig. A4.

figured so largely in the ideal of 'holy living'. A work like Weten-hall's *Enter into thy Closet* was a manual of penitence; *Preparations to a Holy Life* were primarily preparations for repentance, 'since the life of a Christian is a life of repentance, whose work it is, for ever to contend against sin'.[58] And just as the devotions attached to *The Whole Duty* were accompanied by brief heads for self-examination, so the devotions described in Brian Duppa's *Holy Rules and Helps to Devotion, both in Prayer and Practice* (1675) included self-examination: 'In your morning devotions you are to say within yourself, What shall I do this day which God hath given me? How shall I employ it? In the evening, What have I done this day? How have I spent it?'[59] The other salient characteristic of many of these tracts was that, although concerned with private and family piety, they as-sumed that church-going was at the heart of that piety. After com-pleting his private morning devotions, the devout Anglican was instructed: 'now repair unto the public service of the church. If not read the psalms for the day, and the first and second lessons, and the prayers.'[60] Prayers were supplied for those preparing to go to church, for use on arriving at church, and for use after leaving church. Meditations pertinent to holy days and festivals, to the Lord's Day and to communion days, were provided. Even Simon Patrick's *The Devout Christian Instructed How to Pray and Give Thanks to God; or a Book of Devotions for Families and for Particular Persons in most of the Concerns of Human Life* (1673) assumes that 'public service of God in his own house is to be preferred before the private devo-tion of families at home'.[61] Patrick constantly reminds his readers of the joys of worship in and on behalf of the church, and explicitly denies that his book is a rival to the Prayer Book, indeed he asserts that 'the reverence due to that book will be best preserved by em-ploying it only in the public divine service, or in private where there is a priest to officiate'.[62] Naturally, the connection between private devotion and public worship was made most explicit in the many devotionals which take the church's liturgy as their raw material. 'Frequent reading these holy offices by our selves and serious medi-tation thereon,' said the churchmen, 'would be a great help to our devotion, especially if we have such books as Dr Comber's excel-lent labours on the several offices of the Common Prayer to assist

58. *Preparations to a Holy Life*, p. 59.
59. Brian Duppa, *Holy Rules and Helps to Devotion, Both In Prayer and Practice* (1675), p. 126.
60. *A Weeks Preparation Towards a Worthy Receiving of the Lords Supper* (1679), p. 15.
61. Patrick, II, 109. Composed as part of a collaborative effort by the London clergy to 'most efficaciously promote true religion'; see Patrick, IX, 456.
62. Patrick, II, 11.

our meditations'.[63] The author of *The Common Prayer Book the Best Companion*, who had extracted from the liturgy a set of prayers for family and individual use, was predictably a staunch advocate of both public and private worship; 'neither can the doing of it in public atone for the neglect of it in private, nor the private performance on the other hand any way excuse the contempt of the public'.[64] Sancroft preached on the need for private prayer each morning 'as well as public devotion ... [so that] after David's example we might be continually praising God'.[65]

Public worship and personal piety reached an apogee in the Lord's Supper. The sacrament was, of course, a mystery; it sealed to the individual the covenant of grace which Christ had purchased and ratified by his death; but the obligation to receive the sacrament arose from its institution by Christ. So after explaining that the sacraments were signs, seals, pledges and means of grace, Restoration Anglicans shied away from defining how they operated, and even gloried in their mystery. The sacraments 'represent to us somewhat not subject to sense, and have a secret influence upon us; because what is intended by them is not immediately discernible by what is done, without some explication (their significancy being not wholly grounded in nature, but depending upon arbitrary institution ...)'.[66] Anxious that the sacrament of the Lord's Supper should not become a 'ball of contention', and confident that it was a symbol by which God accommodated his own complexity to the limited human mind, the clergy happily used a variety of metaphors to describe this commemoration, reconciliation, conveying of grace, sacrifice of praise, and 'feast of charity, and Christian love'.[67] The *effects* of the sacrament were what mattered because they were all that man could, or need, comprehend and admire:

> by means of this divine meat, the soul is united to the spouse: by this, the understanding is illuminated, the memory quickened, the will enamoured, the inward and spiritual taste delighted,

63. Thomas Seymour, *Advice* (1683 edn), p. 154; also see Granville, II, 43–4, 64–5, 154, 171.
64. William Howell, *The Common Prayer Book the Best Companion in the House and Closet as well as in the Temple* (1687), sig. A2.
65. Evelyn, IV, 53.
66. Barrow, VII, 501; cf. Daniel Brevint, *The Christian Sacrament and Sacrifice* (Oxford, 1673), pp. 42–4; Littleton, I, 329–30.
67. Anthony Horneck, *The Crucified Jesus* (1686), p. 83; Joseph Glanvil, *An Earnest Invitation to the Sacrament of the Lord's Supper* (1673; 1674 edn cited), p. 47. Also see Kidder, *Convivium*, p. 127; Patrick, I, 154; *A Devotionarie Book of John Evelyn*, ed. W.H. Frere (1936), pp. 7, 12–13; Brevint, *Christian Sacrament*, chs 6–8; Hammond, *Daily Practice*, pp. 130–3.

devotion increased, the good motions awaked, our weakness fortified; and by means of this divine meat, we receive strength to ascend up even to the hill of Almighty God.[68]

'To a well-prepared palate,' claimed Simon Patrick, the benefits of the sacrament 'afford a most sweet and delightsome relish'.[69] Anglicans were not encouraged to enquire into the mystery at the very heart of the sacrament, the presence of Christ. 'Lord, what need I labour in vain to search out the manner of thy mysterious presence in the sacrament, when my love assures me thou art there?' asked Bishop Ken, 'all the faithful who approach thee with prepared hearts, they well know thou art there'.[70] The church placed the emphasis squarely on the prepared heart and palate, on the need for spiritual preparation to feed on Christ in faith in the Lord's Supper.

The Restoration church taught that the sacrament only fed 'worthy receivers'. 'It is as clear as the sun that this sacrament is received by, and only by the faithful. Unbelievers may receive *panem domini*, the bread of the Lord: believers only *panem dominum*, the bread which is the Lord.'[71] The nature of Christ's presence in the sacramental bread and wine, or what actually happened to the elements at their consecration in the eucharist, was a question which the seventeenth-century Church of England had dodged repeatedly. One modern authority believed that the catechism and the 1662 Prayer Book 'require a belief in the reception of the body and blood of Christ by faithful communicants' and 'incline towards' the teaching that the body and blood are present at the consecration of the bread and wine.[72] Although the Roman Catholic doctrine of transubstantiation – the 'horrible doctrine' that man can 'create God' according to Taylor – was universally despised by English Protestants, some seventeenth-century churchmen had asserted a 'real presence' at the same time as they denied the popish dogma.[73]

68. *Weeks Preparation*, pp. 126–7; also see [Edward Bernard], *Private Devotion* (Oxford, 1689), ch. 13, section 3, ch. 14, section 1; Edward Pelling, *A Discourse of the Sacrament of the Lords Supper* (1685), ch. 6; *Domestick Devotions*, pp. 156–64, 256–63; John Rawlett, *The Christian Monitor* (1686), pp. 49–51.
69. Patrick, I, 288.
70. Thomas Ken, *An Exposition on the Church Catechism* (1685), pp. 75–6; cf. Patrick, II, 16.
71. William Nicholson, *An Exposition of the Catechism of the Church of England* (1655; LACT, Oxford, 1845), p. 185; also see Gauden, *Whole Duty of a Communicant*, p. 23.
72. Darwell Stone, *A History of the Doctrine of the Holy Eucharist* (1909), II, 344–5.
73. On the rejection of transubstantiation, see Pelling, *Discourse of Sacrament*, chs 7–9; Glanvil, *Earnest Invitation*, p. 107; C.W. Dugmore, *Eucharistic Doctrine in England from Hooker to Waterland* (1942), p. 84.

The intellectual difficulties of this stance had led by mid-century to the evolution of a 'central' position, in which worthy believers were held to have spiritually received the body and blood by faith.[74] Most Restoration churchmen believed that the body and blood of Christ were communicated only to those who received worthily, that they were real to faith rather than to the senses.[75] Some, however, preferred to understand the sacraments as conveying the benefits of the body and blood of Christ to the faithful communicant. *The Whole Duty*, for example, asserted that the sacrament 'is actually the giving of Christ and all the fruits of his death to every worthy receiver'.[76] The Restoration revision of the Prayer Book turned its back on all suggestions of a real presence independent of the worthy communicant, and its eucharistic prayers were very close to those of 1552. The suggestion in Convocation that the prayer of oblation might be moved to before the communion service (as it was in the 1637 Scottish Prayer Book), where it would indicate an 'offering up' or sacrifice of the body of Christ, fell on deaf ears. The prayer remained where it had been, with the emphasis firmly on the communicant's sacrifice of praise and of his holy life.[77]

The worthy communicant was an ideal of all seventeenth-century English Protestants.[78] But there had of late been 'a great dispute in the world' as to whether the sacrament was, like prayer and preaching, a 'converting ordinance'. Some Christians, notably the puritan divines, had come to believe that the sacrament was a privilege restricted to 'great and exemplary saints' and that it confirmed a prior conversion.[79] And many Restoration churchmen had to agree that, strictly speaking, this was so. 'This sacrament is not first designed to make us holy,' explained South, 'but rather supposes us to be so; it is not a converting, but a confirming ordinance: it is properly our spiritual food.'[80] 'Baptism and the holy eucharist

---

74. There was therefore no change in the consecrated bread and wine except for the sacred use to which they were put. The teachings of 'virtualism' and 'receptionism' are variants of this position; see Dugmore, *Eucharistic Doctrine*. Dugmore suggests that this doctrine of the 'real presence' contained several different interpretations such as a presence in the soul of the believer, or a spiritual reception of the body and blood in the soul of the worthy communicant, or a change in the elements.

75. Thomas Comber, *The Plausible Arguments of a Romish Priest Answered* (1686), p. 31.

76. *WAWD*, I, 23.

77. Patrick, I, 324.

78. See, for example, Jeremiah Dyke, *A Worthy Communicant* (1636; and many reprints); G.S. Wakefield, *Puritan Devotion* (1957), pp. 42–54; P. Lake, 'William Bradshaw, Antichrist and the Community of the Godly', *JEH*, 36 (1985), 582–3.

79. Benjamin Calamy, *Sermons Preached upon Several Occasions* (1687), p. 51.

80. South, I, 426.

do nothing for us,' alleged Taylor, in a paraphrase of St Cyprian, 'unless we do good works, and perfect them with a conjugation of holy duties, bringing forth fruits meet for repentance'.[81] On the other hand, the sacrament was not denied to those who were still striving towards godliness. Those who on self-examination found little evidence that the work of grace had yet begun in them, were urged to attend the sacrament and sermons, and were encouraged to humble themselves under a sense of their own wickedness, weakness and spiritual deadness of heart: when they had emptied themselves of 'self', then God would fill them with grace.[82] So the sacrament was a means to grace, a tool to conversion, if employed as a motive to repentance and reformation. Or, in other words, although the sacrament cannot of itself convert sinners, the work of spiritual preparation begins the process of conversion. The sacraments 'seal and assure us of the great mercies contained in God's covenant upon the performance of the conditions that God therein proposes . . . .It is not sealed to me by the two sacraments that I believe and repent which is the homage and conditions enjoined by God, but that if I believe and repent I shall be saved according to the tenor of God's merciful covenant.'[83] In the words of one prayer before receiving the Holy Communion:

let our souls be pardoned and our souls purged, let the testimony of our interest in Christ be manifested in our holy walking, by our holy warfare, and our strength received; let us give all diligence to make our calling and election sure; help us to improve our new birth, let it appear by our renewed life; let us as our Lord Jesus once grew, grow in the stature of grace; he did never sin, O let us therefore hate the spotted garment, the corrupt heart, and a walking and minding things that savour of the flesh; help us by faith to see him that sees us, and to walk with him and before him, striving to be as perfect as he who redeemed us was perfect.[84]

The Restoration church seems to have taken up spiritual preparation for a 'worthy receiving' of the sacrament on an unprecedented scale.[85] The available guides to a 'worthy receiving' ranged from the

81. Taylor, XV, 591.
82. Littleton, II, 88–9.
83. MS Eng Th E 168, fo. 131.
84. C.P., *Christian Devotion*, pp. 80–1.
85. On the need for preparation see Farindon, II, sermons 28, 29; South, I, 429 ff.; Littleton, II, 82 ff.; and among the devotional manuals, *WAWD*, I, 26–37; Edward Wetenhall, *Enter into thy Closet* (1666; 4th edn, 1673), pp. 176–214, 325 ff.; Bernard, *Private Devotion*, chs 11–14.

sixpenny volumes 'fitted for the pocket', such as Addison's *Introduction to the Sacrament*, to the bulky works of Jeremy Taylor; some
were rapturous meditations upon the Passion and sacrament, others
were mere heads of self-examination, or swollen catechisms, and
others offered a guide and commentary on the church's Office of
Holy Communion.[86] Thomas Comber argued

> that the illustration of this one part of liturgy will contain argu-
> ments to convince the negligent, instructions to teach the ignorant,
> and the properest method to prepare us for this sacrament, to
> assist us in receiving, and to confirm us in all holiness and virtue
> afterwards: Yea, I dare affirm, that he who will conscientiously
> practise by these measures, can neither be an ill man, an un-
> worthy receiver, or an enemy to that church which affords him
> such excellent means of salvation.[87]

Simon Patrick, who was regarded as the doyen of the devotional
writers on the sacrament, produced three substantial, and influential,
manuals and a treatise exhorting to more frequent communions.[88]
　Preparation took two forms; the 'habitual' preparation of holy
living; and 'actual' preparation – involving self-examination, confession, prayer, meditation and resolutions of amendment – which
'is, as it were, the furbishing or rubbing up of the former habitual
principle'.[89] Self-examination and repentance was the foundation
of the whole regime of preparation, whether actual or habitual;
without our mortification the sacrament would not charm away our
sins.[90] 'A good life in the discharge of our duties towards God and
man, is an habitual and constant preparation for the sacrament.'
The eucharist is a 'federal rite' and a heightened moment in what
should be a whole lifetime of acting out our part of the baptismal

86. See Jeremy Taylor, *The Worthy Communicant* (1660) in *Works*, XV, 391–695; Edward
　　Lake, *Officium eucharisticum* (1673; Oxford, 1843); Glanvil, *Earnest Invitation*; Kidder,
　　Convivium; anon., *A Weeks Preparation* (1679); John Kettlewell, *An Help and Exhortation
　　to a Worthy Communicating* (1683); Horneck, *Fire of the Altar*, and *The Crucified Jesus*
　　(1686); Pelling, *Discourse of Sacrament*; T.P., *A Guide to the Altar* (2nd edn, 1688).
87. Comber, *Companion*, III, epistle dedicatory.
88. These were *Mensa mystica* (1660), *The Book for Beginners* (1668), *The Christian Sacrifice*
　　(1670) (all in *Works*, I, 65–634), and *A Treatise on the Necessity and Frequency of
　　Receiving the Holy Communion* (1684) (*Works*, II). John Rawlett called them 'books for
　　which I have no words great enough to express my esteem', *Explication* (1679), p.
　　247. For other acknowledgements of Patrick's influence see Glanvil, *Earnest
　　Invitation*, pp. 119–20; Pelling, *Discourse of Sacrament*, sig. A3v; John Scott, *The
　　Christian Life* (1681), p. 381.
89. South, I, 427 and 424–9 passim.
90. Horneck, *Crucified Jesus*, pp. 86–7.

covenant.[91] We should exercise 'an everyday oversight over ourselves', and each evening, in the privacy of our chamber, assess our performance that day in the duties of the baptismal covenant, in the renunciation of the Devil and his works, in the belief of the articles of the Christian faith, and in adherence to the decalogue.[92] This was an opportunity to note down the details of our breaches of duty in preparation for the confession during the communion service.[93]

The devout Anglican did not lack for aids and techniques to make this crowning moment of his worship an edifying, satisfying and even overwhelming spiritual experience. From the devotional manuals we can reconstruct the ideal experience of the worthy Anglican communicant. During the week preceding his reception of the sacrament, the communicant prepared his soul with the help of daily meditations and prayers suggested in manuals like *A Weeks Preparation Towards a Worthy Receiving of the Lords Supper*. On Friday evening the communicant might arrive at the point of making a full confession of his sins to God, and this was followed, either immediately or upon the Saturday, by meditations upon the Passion.[94] When he rose on the Lord's Day, the chastened and penitent communicant threw himself into private prayer and then, still fasting, proceeded to church.[95] Pausing at the church door to reflect that 'surely the Lord is in this place', the communicant occupied himself with prayer and meditation while waiting for the service to begin.[96] But since 'your business there is to serve the Lord with your Christian brethren in public', the devout Anglican then put his private devotions aside to immerse himself in Morning Prayer and the communion service.[97] 'As soon as the sermon is ended', the communicant was instructed to 'approach the Lord's table,

91. Glanvil, *Earnest Invitation*, p. 73; also see Patrick, I, 77, 140–1, 184–5, 355, 381; Kidder, *Convivium*, p. 5; Rawlett, *Christian Monitor*, pp. 49–50; Scott, *Christian Life*, p. 380.

92. Patrick, I, 209, 597; Wetenhall, *Closet*, pp. 1–2; Littleton, II, 87; Horneck, *Fire*, pp. 16 ff.; Addison, *Introduction* (1686 edn), pp. 27 ff.

93. Patrick, I, 597–8. The catalogue of these breaches in *The Whole Duty* was much recommended; see Wetenhall, *Closet*, p. 243; Kidder, *Convivium*, p. 60; Lake, *Officium*, p. 8. Others either composed their own check-list or based them on the decalogue.

94. *Weeks Preparation*, pp. 78 ff.; and Lake, *Officium*, pp. 92, 7, 60, 41–2; T.P., *Guide*, pp. 80 ff.; Duppa, *Holy Rules*, pp. 156–8; Comber, *Companion*, III, 10.

95. Lake, *Officium*, pp. 61 ff.; *Domestick Devotions*, pp. 128–38, 236–44.

96. Steward, *Several Discourses*, IV, 7–11; and see *Weeks Preparation*, p. 107; anon., *Rules for Our More Devout Behaviour in Time of Divine Service in the Church of England* (1686; 1687 edn cited), pp. 50 ff.

97. Steward, *Several Discourses*, IV, 12.

place your self in a convenient place, and fall upon your knees'.[98]
It seems to have been imagined that those who were to receive
the sacrament would move from the nave into the chancel of the
church, for what was to all intents a separate service. When the
communicant penetrated this inner sanctum, he was to be confronted by a splendid theatre in which the drama of the eucharist
was about to take place. The floor might be a chequerwork of black-
and-white marble; the altar enclosed with rails, hung with sump-
tuously coloured cloths, frontals and tapestries, and bearing the
communion plate, a bound bible and perhaps a pair of candlesticks.
The altar could be under a canopy of marble or richly painted
wood, and behind it might be tablets inscribed with the Lord's
Prayer and the decalogue, or a tapestry, or even, as at Canterbury
cathedral, a magnificent gilt sun. Dazzled by the splendour of this
rarely seen part of the church, the communicant sank to his knees
and tried to follow the liturgy as it approached its climax. If his
mind began to wander or his devotion to falter, he might raise his
eyes to edifying texts inscribed upon the walls and ceiling or, even
better, use the pious 'ejaculations' and meditations prescribed by
the manuals for the moments before, while and after receiving the
blessed body and blood of Christ.[99] Thus fortified, with his good
resolutions and promises of amendment 'sealed', and his heart lifted
up in thanksgiving to his saviour, the ideal Anglican communicant
made his way home to spend the day in quiet contemplation and
works of piety, or if he was a family man to help his dependants
'digest what they have heard and received' at church 'by catechizing,
examining, meditation, conference, reading, singing of Psalms, and
prayer'.[100]

As portrayed in the devotional manuals, the clergy's ideal of private devotion and worthy reception was nothing if not ambitious.
They aimed high partly because they began from such a low point
of lay piety. To the clergy's eyes, the nation was sunk in spiritual
lethargy, the churches were half empty and the sacrament poorly
attended. Although the practice of piety will be discussed separately,
one contemporary explanation for the neglect of the sacrament ought

---

98. T.P., *Guide*, p. 123.
99. *Weeks Preparation*, pp. 16–18; *Rules for Our More Devout Behaviour*, pp. 67–9; C.P.,
     Christian Devotion, pp. 79 ff.; Addison, *Introduction*, pp. 109–12; Duppa, *Holy Rules*,
     pp. 180–3; Horneck, *Fire*, pp. 80, 82; Hammond, *Daily Practice*, pp. 141–8; Comber,
     Companion, III, 133–9.
100. Bryan, *Perswasive*, p. 22; *Weeks Preparation*, pp. 97, 121–33; Addison, *Introduction*,
     pp. 115–16; Kettlewell, *Help and Exhortation*, part 2, ch. 2; Horneck, *Fire*, p. 201;
     Hammond, *Daily Practice*, pp. 153–8. The devout, of course, returned to church for
     Evening Prayer.

to be noted here. It was alleged to be a legacy of 'the late distracted times' when the sacrament was laid aside 'for near twenty years together'.[101] Among the ill effects of 'our past confusions' was

that in many congregations of this kingdom Christians were generally disused and deterred from the sacrament, upon a pretence that they were unfit for it; and being so, they must necessarily incur the danger of unworthy receiving; and therefore they had better wholly abstain from it. By which it came to pass that in very many places this great and solemn institution of the Christian religion was almost quite forgotten . . .[102]

The excuse of 'unworthiness' was the obverse of the demand for a 'worthy' reception, and both came from the same source, the Apostle's warning, in I Corinthians xi. 29, against the participation of the 'unworthy' in the eucharist lest they eat and drink 'to damnation'. Simon Patrick deftly explained that this text referred not to eternal damnation, but to 'sicknesses, weaknesses, temporal death at the most'. Whether a man receives the sacrament or not has no bearing upon damnation; it is sin itself, the failure to obey God, which earns damnation:

He that eats irreverently is guilty by profaning of Christ's body, and so is he that eats not at all by despising of it, and preferring his lusts before him. As he eats damnation to himself, so doth the other by not eating judge himself in a damnable condition.[103]

The common Nonconformist scruple against receiving the sacrament in a 'mixed' congregation of sinners and saints turned upon the issue of 'worthiness'. Churchmen countered by citing I Corinthians xi, in which the godly at Corinth are told not to abstain from the communion of a tainted church, but by examination and preparation to take care that they are not as others are. No man can claim to be worthy to receive the sacrament on his own merits.[104] 'Unworthiness is the worst excuse,' preached Anthony Farindon, 'because we are bound to cast it off and we cannot dishonour the sacrament more than by not receiving it'.[105] While the benefits of

101. Patrick, II, 11; Thomas Smith, *A Sermon about Frequent Communion, preached before the University of Oxford, August the 17th. 1679* (1685), pp. 30–3; Pelling, *Discourse*, sig. A2v; Bisbie, *Bishop Visiting*, p. 25.
102. Tillotson, *A Perswasive to a Frequent Communion* (1683), p. 16.
103. Patrick, I, 598–9. The text is similarly interpreted in Kettlewell, *Help and Exhortation*, pp. 214 ff., and in the scripture commentaries of Joseph Hall, Jeremy Taylor and Daniel Whitby, but not those of Hammond, Thorndike or Farindon.
104. See Freeman in *Cases*, pp. 88–103, esp. p. 100.
105. Farindon, I, 461. Also see Calamy, *Sermons*, pp. 54–5.

the sacrament varied with the moral status of the recipient, reception itself was a duty incumbent upon all and abstention a denial of Christ and a repudiation of morality.[106] 'Unworthiness' was evidently a false scruple, an attempt by Satan to 'blind' men 'with the veil of humility',[107] yet it did place the churchmen in a dilemma. For it was part of their own strategy to constantly remind the laity of their unworthiness, of their need to be prepared before approaching the Lord's Table.

Although the clergy explained time and time again that what they said 'of the great danger of unworthy receiving is not to beat off or drive away any truly humbled and sincerely penitent sinners, how great soever their sins may formerly have been . . . but to keep off such as are unfit', the fear remained that the profane and hardhearted received with 'no sense of the danger', while the truly devout were daunted by the requirements of preparation.[108] The clergy did what they could to reassure them and to dispel the false scruple of unworthiness. The 'necessary knowledge' for a worthy reception 'is in few things, and those practical,' wrote Joseph Glanvil:

> If therefore thou art instructed in the main plain points of Christian doctrine and in the great rules of Christian life; if thou understandest the sacrament to be a remembrance of Christ, and a confirming our covenant with God; and knowest those easie things I have before set down about it: There is no reason then why thou shouldst plead ignorance in barr to thy duty and privilege.[109]

There was, very occasionally, a hint of clerical unease about the daunting and potentially superstitious apparatus of 'actual' preparation. In his only contribution to the literature promoting more frequent communion, John Tillotson struck a note of caution.

> The great necessity that lies upon men is to live as becomes Christians, and then they can never be absolutely unprepared. Nay, I think this to be a very good preparation; and I see not why men should not be very well satisfied with it, unless they intend to make the same use of the sacrament that many of the Papists do of confession and absolution, which is to quit with God once or twice a year, that so they may begin to sin again upon a new score.

---

106. Tillotson, *Perswasive*, p. 15; Lake, *Officium*, p. 2; Glanvil, *Earnest Invitation*, pp. 108, 85.
107. Evelyn, *Devotionarie Book*, p. 9.
108. MS Eng Th C 73, fos 132–3.
109. Glanvil, *Earnest Invitation*, pp. 80–1

Tillotson was not deprecating special preparation: 'the greater our actual preparation is, the better. For no man can examine himself too often.' His remarks were aimed at the negligent and at their excuses, for it is better to receive without any special preparation, than not to receive at all.[110]

Every Anglican writer agreed that 'a holy life is the true time for preparing our souls to be God's guests', while the duties of 'actual' preparation are merely 'sprucing up the soul'.[111] The worthy communicant uses these more immediate duties of preparation, the forms of prayer, confession, reading and meditation, as a *point d'appui* for making a perpetual sacrifice of his holy life.[112] Embarking upon a holy life is not easy, nor is it simply a matter of personal piety; one of the first steps on the path to holy living is to believe 'that the chiefest devotion consisteth in practice of virtues, without which there is neither solid piety, nor hope of salvation'. With practice, the holy life begins to sustain itself; 'use makes hard things easy, the chief, if not only difficulty in holiness, is want of practice, and a being accustomed to the contrary'. And soon, holy living becomes a joy: 'I pity all who will not make a thorough trial of the felicity of a holy life', announced Thomas Seymour.[113] However, the churchmen never made any pretence that holy living, offering up one's life as a sacrifice and one's heart as an altar, was of any worth when it came to salvation: 'it is not that I trust in mine own faith, but in thy faithfulness; not in mine own repentance, but in thy pardon; not in mine own preparation, but in thine acceptance, in thee, and in thy merits, in thy mercies do I trust.'[114] A stern and strenuous outlook lay behind the uplifting vision of Anglican piety promoted by the Restoration Church of England. The great question was whether this ideal was too stern and too onerous to win over the laity of Restoration England.

'The Practice of Piety'

On arriving at his new rectory of Chevening in March 1686, John Gaskarth was relieved to find that his parishioners were only negligent and not schismatic:

110. Tillotson, *Perswasive to Frequent Communion*, pp. 31–2; also see William Smythies, *The Worthy Non-Communicant* (1683), p. 109; cf. Patrick, I, 188–9.
111. Patrick, I, 181; also see Taylor, XV, 475–6, 653; Wetenhall, *Closet*, pp. 439 ff.
112. *Weeks Preparation*, p. 38; Patrick, I, 322; Brevint, *Christian Sacrament*, ch. 7; Gauden, *Whole Duty of a Communicant*, pp. 120–1.
113. *Preparations to a Holy Life*, p. 30; Addison, *Introduction*, pp. 126–7; Seymour, *Advice to Readers of Common Prayer*, sig. B2r.
114. *Weeks Preparation*, p. 6.

'tis only the common insensibility of most part of country people in the prayers of the church and the duty of saying their prayers in a joint assembly that they labour under, which I hope to work off in some time. I have already preached concerning prayer how it is the great and necessary definition of a Christian, or a creature to his creator, if we had no wants to be supplied, as also concerning the advantage of public prayer in the church, or consecrated place of God's worship, and the unanimous manner of a congregation, where charity, the mutual agreement and excitement from one another must needs add to the success of it, and I hope by this means, as also by recommending our liturgy, which I intend to do at large, I shall bring them to a true sense of their coming to church, that is to say their prayers together and not hear a sermon only, and so be more frequent there.[115]

These, then, were some of the limitations under which the practice of Anglican piety laboured: the 'common insensibility' of country folk towards the public prayers of the church; the belief that the sermon was the pivot of worship; and the glaring omission of any reference to the sacrament. We still lack 'a true sense' of the seventeenth century's 'coming to church': although the devotional works tell us what the clergy hoped for from their congregations, we know little about what went on in the parish churches. What form did the Sunday service normally take and how did the laity participate in it? Such questions are especially pertinent in view of various recent suggestions that Prayer Book worship had 'almost by an osmotic process' contributed to the creation of a 'Protestant consciousness', that the liturgy 'had earthed itself into the Englishman's consciousness and had sunk deep roots into popular culture', or alternatively that 'the Interregnum had completed a process of alienation between the liturgy and the people which was probably well advanced even before 1640'.[116] Only the most tentative answers can be offered to these questions.

It seems that the usual Sunday service comprised the Morning Prayer, then the litany, followed by the communion service – with a sermon – up to and including the prayer for the Church Militant.[117]

115.   MS Tanner 31, fo. 296.
116.   P. Collinson, 'The Church and the New Religion', in *The Reign of Elizabeth I*, ed. C. Haigh (1984), p. 179; J.S. Morrill, 'The Church in England, 1642–9', in *Reactions to the English Civil War, 1642–1649*, ed. J.S. Morrill (1982), p. 113; N. Temperley, *The Music of the English Parish Church: I* (Cambridge, 1979), p. 86.
117.   This part of the communion service is known as the antecommunion. Temperley suggests that the prayer for the Church Militant was often omitted; see *Music of Parish Church*, p. 124.

The Elizabethan Injunctions of 1559 allowed for Psalms or hymns to be sung before or after service, but it appears they were some-times sung before or after the sermon, or between the litany and the ante-communion, or in some churches after the second lesson, and since they were sung at an excruciatingly slow tempo, they caused a considerable interruption in the service, which gave the minister time to absent himself or to change his gown for the sermon. Nor were the Psalms sung well; it was 'sad to hear what whining, toting, yelling, or skreeking there is in many country congregations'.[118] Another witness recorded that the singing of the Psalms 'is custo-marily omitted in parish churches, for want of skill as I conceive'.[119] Evening Prayer on Sundays and holy days included the instruction and examination of children in the catechism, or a second sermon which was often described as 'a catechetical lecture'.[120] But what did laity contribute to worship besides the caterwauling of Psalms? What was expected of them?

It was the clergy's view that, in public, the minister 'prays as the common mouth of the congregation'.[121] The congregation said the confession and the Lord's Prayer after the minister, they recited alternate petitions in the service and the litany, and 'the custom is, more or less in most places' for the people to 'recite the Psalms and other godly hymns with the minister by way of answering in turns'.[122] In reality it was more often the parish clerk who made the responses. It was the clerk's function to lead the congregation in their part of the liturgy and in their singing.[123] However, con-gregations could not always follow the clerk since, unlike modern churches, the Restoration parish church was lucky to possess two clean copies of the Prayer Book, one for the minister and one for the clerk. It was recorded of the woefully dilapidated parish of Budbrooke, Worcestershire, in 1674 that 'they have but one Book of Common Prayer, and if they had two there could be no person procured in the parish to be clerk that could read, the person that hath served that office for these twenty years being illiterate'.[124]

118. Temperley, *Music of Parish Church*, pp. 87–8, 90–2, 123–4.
119. William Clagett in *Cases*, p. 291. Also see F. Thompson, *Lark Rise to Candleford* (Harmondsworth, 1973), pp. 210–11.
120. *Bishop Fell and Nonconformity*, ed. M. Clapinson (Oxfordshire Record Society, 62, 1980), p. 19.
121. Scott in *Cases*, p. 256.
122. Clagett in *Cases*, p. 291.
123. On the clerk's musical function see Temperley, *Music of Parish Church*, pp. 88–90; for the practice of 'lining out' or reading each line of the psalm before the congregation sang it, see p. 82.
124. *Inspections of Churches and Parsonage Houses in the Diocese of Worcester in 1674, 1676, 1684, and 1687*, ed. P. Morgan (Worcestershire Historical Studies, 12, 1986), p. 48,

So unless literate parishioners brought their own copy of the Prayer Book to church with them – and this seems unlikely – they would have to rely upon their memory and follow the clerk as best they could. The result was that the laity's contribution 'is in a manner lost to some of the congregation, since in the confused murmur of so many voices nothing can be distinctly heard'.[125]

At the Restoration, the Dissenters asked that the repetitions, responsals and readings, 'which cause a confused murmur in the congregation, whereby what is read is less intelligible, and therefore unedifying, may be omitted'. The same issue was taken up again in later comprehension proposals: 'in churches where many cannot read, let the minister read all the Psalms himself: because the confused voice of the multitude is seldom intelligible'.[126] In response, the clergy rushed to the defence of the liturgy. 'I grant, that which is uttered in the congregation ought to be understood,' wrote William Clagett. 'But then those verses of the Psalms which are uttered by the congregation may be well enough understood by every one that has a book, or who is acquainted competently well with the Psalms themselves. I need not say much in answer to this objection, because it may be removed by every one that makes it, if he can read, and will bring a book along with him.' As for those who could not read,

> I must needs say, that it is not so hard as is pretended for them also to take those verses which are uttered by those that are near them, if they will carefully attend. And I have been credibly informed, that some devout people that could never read, have attained to an ability of reciting most of the Psalms without book, by often hearing them in those churches where they are alternately recited; which shews that the murmur is not so confused, but that the words may be heard distinctly enough to be understood, if one has a mind to it. And then they that cannot read may by this means be more quickened, than otherwise they would be, to learn to read; however to attend, and to learn the Psalms without book, that they also may bear their part vocally with the congregation in God's praises.

also see pp. 6–7, 19–20, 70; *Notes on Visitations in the Archdeaconry of Essex*, ed. W.J. Pressey, (Transactions of the Essex Archaeological Society, 19, 1930; 20, 1930–1; 21, 1933–4; 22, 1936–40; 23, 1942); *Churchwardens' Presentments: II Archdeaconry of Lewes*, ed. H. Johnstone (Sussex Record Society, 50, 1948–9), pp. 17, 20, 21, 33, 35.

125. Clagett in *Cases*, p. 291.
126. Edward Cardwell, *A History of Conferences and Other Proceedings Connected with the Revision of the Book of Common Prayer* (3rd edn, Oxford, 1849), p. 305; *RB*, III, 33.

Clagett added 'that for the most part the Psalms are recited alternately in those churches only, where it may be reasonably presumed that the whole congregation can read, very few excepted. For by the way, this method of reading the Psalms is not commanded, but every parish church is left at liberty to observe her own custom about it. In the country parishes the minister generally recites all, (which way I do not think so convenient as that of responsals).'[127] But when not on the defensive, the clergy too admitted that the people's responses were often 'little heard'.[128]

There is scant evidence of literate, book-bearing congregations in Restoration England, and what there is suggests that they carried the Bible not the Prayer Book; in 1668 the churchwardens of Grimstead complained that the church windows were too small 'to let in sufficient light for the congregation to make use of their Bibles'.[129] That some congregations were familiar with the liturgy is suggested by their complaints that the minister or clerk garbled or omitted parts of the service; the vicar of Lockington, Leicestershire was taken to task for reading the prayers 'in such a mumbling and low tone of speech and irreverent manner, that few or none of the parishioners then assembled to hear divine service would or could understand what he read'. At Highworth some parishioners were seated so far from desk and pulpit 'that they are deprived thereby not only of hearing the word, but joining with [the minister] in that great worship'.[130] In London, the vestry of St Giles Cripplegate ordered the clerk's and reader's desks to be moved 'whereby the congregation may better hear them'.[131] It is quite possible that the illiterate did learn their part in the liturgy aurally, but this cannot have involved much understanding or recognition on their part. For instance, in the 1650s George Bull, then a young curate, delivered a Prayer Book service from memory and was subsequently complimented upon his powers of extempore prayer by his uncom-

127. Clagett in *Cases*, p. 291.
128. Thomas Seymour, *Advice to Readers of Common Prayer*, p. 20; Temperley, *Music of Parish Church*, p. 86.
129. E.A.O. Whiteman, 'The Episcopate of Dr Seth Ward, Bishop of Exeter (1662 to 1667) and Salisbury (1667 to 1688/89)' (unpublished Oxford University D.Phil. thesis, 1951), p. 277.
130. J.H. Pruett, *The Parish Clergy Under the Later Stuarts – The Leicestershire Experience* (Urbana, Illinois, 1978), p. 125; D.A. Spaeth, 'Parsons and Parishioners: Lay–Clerical Conflict and Popular Piety in Wiltshire Villages, 1660–1740' (unpublished Brown University Ph.D. thesis, 1985), pp. 149, 185; Whiteman, 'Ward', pp. 298–9.
131. Vestry Minute Book, August 1682, Guildhall Library, London, MS 6048/1, fo. 89v.

prehending puritan parishioners.[132] Nor was having the liturgy by heart any guarantee of piety, as a Georgian church-goer's diary reveals:

> I could not help looking at Mrs Alworthy, who has a strange roving eye. I thought it was very comical to see her looking about her and seemingly entirely unconcerned about what passed in the pulpit and at the desk, and yet to see her lips continually moving in the repetition of the prayers and joining in the form of worship with her mouth.[133]

This was of course exactly the 'formality' for which the Nonconformists condemned the Prayer Book. Appreciation of and familiarity with the Prayer Book were unlikely to be deepened by haphazard and partial attendance at church: 'some few coming it may be after the lessons are read; others at latter end of prayers or the first service, and others not till the sermon begins or is ready to begin, and all these but few of the whole parish', reported one Oxfordshire curate in 1682.[134] Despite the lack of conclusive evidence, it is tempting to concur with the authority who sees seventeenth-century congregations increasingly becoming 'mere spectators to a performance by the minister, assisted by the parish clerk'.[135] It is suggestive, and it may be significant, that seventeenth-century Englishmen habitually referred to 'hearing' the service and their clergy talked of 'reading' the liturgy.

One eager new incumbent planned 'every day in the week in summer-time they shall have morning prayers in the church, in the wintertime, only on litany days and festivals, on Sunday morning a sermon and the church catechism explained to the children and concluded with a practical meditation for those of riper years in the afternoon'.[136] If only they had been diligently performed and well attended, the Prayer Book services of Morning and Evening Prayer 'daily throughout the year' would have been an invaluable channel for a regime of private devotion and public piety. However, for all the good resolutions of the clergy and the constant exhortations of the hierarchy, a daily sacrifice of prayer and thanksgiving was uncommon in the nation's churches. 'If I require a constant diligence in offering the daily sacrifice of prayer for the people,'

132. Robert Nelson, *The Life of Dr George Bull* (1713), pp. 39–40; cf. *WR*, p. 152 (Forbench).
133. *The Diary of Dudley Ryder, 1715–1716*, ed. W. Matthews (1939), p. 191; cf. Pepys, V, 356.
134. *Fell*, ed. Clapinson, p. 22.
135. Temperley, *Music of Parish Church*, p. 86.
136. MS Carte 77, fo. 538.

complained Bishop Fell, 'the usual answer is, they are ready to do their duty, but the people will not be prevailed with to join with them'.[137] The rector of Clayworth obviously thought that he was being conspicuously pious when he resolved to read prayers on Wednesdays and Fridays during Lent.[138] Pepys was surprised to find daily prayers read at St Dunstan's in Fleet Street in 1664.[139] Yet two decades later the situation in London was rather different. A tract of 1683 listed five parish churches in the city with a single daily service, seven with Morning and Evening Prayer, and eight chapels with daily services. In 1680 daily services at 6 a.m. and 7 p.m. had been established at St Paul's, Covent Garden; these were in addition to the services at 10 a.m. and 3 p.m. which were funded by an association of pious persons. By 1687 there were nearly thirty parish churches in London offering daily prayers.[140] Archdeacon Granville of Durham attributed the improvement to the example of his own diocese:

> the daily homage that is offered unto God in our parish churches (a thing I fear more rare in other dioceses) hath preached a long time very successfully to the nation, and may have contributed, in all probability, to that good order, which some other places are now advancing to.[141]

But when the services were read daily, they could attract only small congregations. The laity, who expected to work on weekdays, could rarely be brought to church on holy days and there was even less chance that they would attend daily devotions.[142] Nevertheless, Bishop Turner of Ely exhorted the clergy to persevere with reading the daily services however mean a congregation of widows, schoolchildren or even their own families attended, because their example would inspire others.[143] The clerical vision of Prayer Book piety was based on the laity's full participation in the church's public worship. The Prayer Book was not the priest's office, but the corporate praise of the whole church, yet it is plain that many

137. MS Tanner 31, fo. 156.
138. *The Rector's Book, Clayworth*, ed. H. Gill and E.L. Guilford (Nottingham, 1910), p. 40.
139. Pepys, V, 202–3. There were daily morning prayers at St Christopher-le-Stocks in 1670; *The Account Book of the Parish of St Christopher Le Stocks*, ed. E. Freshfield (1895), p. 52.
140. See Seymour, *Advice to Readers of Common Prayer*, p. 168; Patrick, IX, 476; *Rules for Our More Devout Behaviour* (2nd edn, 1687), pp. 78–82.
141. Denis Granville, *Advice concerning Strict Conformity* (1684), p. 6.
142. D.A. Spaeth, 'Common Prayer?', in *Parish, Church and People*, ed. S.J. Wright (1988), pp. 139–40; Whiteman, 'Ward', pp. 301–2.
143. Turner, *Letter to Clergy of Ely*, pp. 12–13.

of the laity were simply onlookers rather than participants in the public worship of the Restoration Church of England.

A similar disparity between the clergy's ideal and the laity's practice was evident in the matter of the sacrament. As always, 'primitive Christianity' was the rule against which the 'slight and perfunctory performances' of Restoration England were measured.[144] The primitive Christians communicated every day or at least every Lord's Day, yet 'we judge of them perhaps by ourselves, and think that it was superstition rather than religion made them so forward to this office; and by casting a blot upon their piety, we hope in this frozen age to be accounted pious.'[145] Henry Hammond recognized that the daily or weekly communions of the first age of the Church had now declined to monthly communions, but he abhorred the suggestion that reception of the sacrament a mere three times a year – the stipulated minimum – was adequate.[146] Indeed the devotional manuals generally assumed that the devout Anglican was making a monthly communion.[147]

The rubric at the end of the Order for Communion stipulated that 'every parishioner shall communicate at least three times in the year, of which Easter to be one', yet it seems unlikely that many of the English, especially the young and those in service, even fulfilled this requirement, never mind the clergy's ideal.[148] In many parishes the eucharist was celebrated only at Christmas, Easter and Whitsun, although at Easter in particular a series of communions were held so that the whole parish was able to receive the sacrament.[149] At St Nicholas, Durham, for instance, there were communions on Palm Sunday, Maundy Thursday, Good Friday, Easter Sunday and the following Sunday. Whereas four quarts of wine

---

144. Smith, *Sermon*, pp. 18, 14–16; also see Wetenhall, *Closet*, p. 335; Brevint, *Christian Sacrament*, p. 76; Comber, *Companion*, p. 73.

145. Patrick, I, 217.

146. Hammond, *Daily Practice*, pp. 138–9; also see John Scott, *Christian Life*, pp. 383–4, but cf. Evelyn, *Devotionarie Book*, p. 7.

147. See Lake, *Officium*, p. 92; Horneck, *Crucified Jesus*, p. 359; Patrick, I, 218, 411; Kettlewell, *Help and Exhortation, passim*; Taylor, XV, 629–35.

148. An obligation repeated in Canons 21 and 22 and most visitation articles. Also see Whiteman, 'Ward', pp. 294–6; J.L. Salter, 'Warwickshire Clergy, 1660–1714' (unpublished Birmingham University Ph.D. thesis, 1975), pp. 100–102; Spaeth, 'Parsons and Parishioners', pp. 48–76; Pruett, *Parish Clergy*, p. 121. For the young and servants, see *Episcopal Visitation Returns for Cambridgeshire*, ed. W.M. Palmer (Cambridge, 1930), p. 105; *Notes of the Episcopal Visitation of the Archdeaconry of Ely in 1685*, ed. H. Bradshaw (Cambridge Antiquarian Society Communications, 3, Cambridge, 1879), p. 341.

149. See *Rector's Book, Clayworth*; *Visitation Returns for Cambridgeshire*, ed. Palmer, pp. 96, 92, 109.

or less were adequate for each of the communions celebrated at other times of the year, the Easter communion required twenty-four quarts.[150] At Christmas 1684 William Sampson of Clayworth 'added to the communion of this day, the two Sundays next following and so resolved to do at Whitsuntide communion; that so having three times three communions (that is nine in all) there might be opportunity for all to communicate'.[151] This ancient pattern of three communions a year, with most parishioners only receiving at Easter, was probably ingrained in the English. Many of them expected and wanted no more. Edmund Bohun, a pious Anglican, who took great pains to prepare his soul before the Lord's Supper, received on only two or three occasions a year, and does not appear to have felt that his devotion was being denied a full expression by the paucity of communions.[152] But many of the English expected no fewer than three communions. It seems that the interruption of the sacrament during the Interregnum was resented: in 1663 there had been no sacrament 'for about 20 years last past' in Chippenham and the newly appointed vicar realized 'twas expected now'.[153] And those Restoration parishioners who suffered a neglect would often 'invite' their minister to celebrate the Lord's Supper or complain to the bishop.[154] There is some evidence, too, that monthly celebrations were not unheard of in London during the 1660s and 1670s. At St Bartholomew Exchange, London in 1673, the vestry debated reviving the office of 'lecturer to preach a preparation sermon for the better taking of the sacrament of the Lord's supper monthly'.[155] The famous preacher Anthony Horneck used to administer the sacrament on the first Sunday of each month at the Savoy Chapel and to preach a preparation sermon on the preceding Friday.[156]

150. *Durham Parish Books* (Surtees Society, 84, 1888), pp. 229–30 and *passim*. At St Nicholas there were, besides the Easter communions, celebrations of the sacrament at New Year, in early June and at Michaelmas. In John Kettlewell's parish in Warwickshire there were eight or nine celebrations a year, according to Kettlewell's entry in the *DNB*.
151. *Rector's Book, Clayworth*, p. 66.
152. Bohun, *Autobiography*, pp. 51, 52, 54–6, 58–60.
153. CUL, MS Add. 8499, fo. 81.
154. MS Rawlinson D 399, fo. 279.
155. *The Vestry Minutes of St Bartholomew Exchange*, ed. E. Freshfield (1890), pp. 121–2. Also see Nathaniel Hardy, *The Royal Commonwealthsman* (1668), p. 34; Horneck, *Crucified Jesus*, sig. A3; J. Wickham Legg, *English Church Life from the Restoration to the Tractarian Movement* (1914), ch. 2; *Account Book of St Christopher Le Stocks*, ed. Freshfield, pp. 7, 8, 37–8, 40; and beyond London, see *Durham Parish Books*, pp. 335–6; Humphrey Henchman, Bishop of Salisbury, *Visitation Articles* (1662), I. 10.
156. See R. Kidder, *The Life of Anthony Horneck* (1698), pp. 9–10.

When the devout Anglican had the opportunity to receive the Lord's Supper, the surroundings were often a far cry from the vision of dignity and reverence offered by the devotional manuals or the cathedrals.[157] Even the near exemplary church of Hungry Hatley, Cambridgeshire was a good deal plainer than the ideal. The Hatley churchwardens provided a full description of their church in response to Bishop Wren's enquiries of 1662:

> A convenient and decent communion table, with a carpet of decent green saye which cost twelve shillings, and is at this time worth ten shillings, continually laid thereon at time of divine service, and a fair linen cloth which cost ten shillings and is now worth eight shillings and is continually laid thereon at time of administering the communion, and our communion table is so conveniently placed that the minister may be well heard in his administration and the greatest number may reverently communicate standing at the east end of the chancel and the ends thereof are placed north and south, with steps and ascents thereunto. There are none in our parish that do use it unreverently by leaning or sitting on it, throwing hats or writing on it nor any profane use, we have also a decent rail of wood placed handsomely about the steps before the holy table near one yard high reaching from the north wall to the south with a convenient door before the same table, with pillars and ballisters close.[158]

But not all of Bishop Wren's diocese was so conformable. That eminently puritan parish, Dry Drayton, boldly replied that the sacrament was celebrated three times a year with the communion table in the body of the church, its ends facing east and west, a position in which – throwing the words of the bishop's enquiry back in his teeth – 'the communicants may best hear the minister at the administration and the greatest number may reverently communicate'.[159] For all the efforts of the hierarchy, in many Restoration churches the communion table had not yet been placed 'altarwise' against the east wall and railed off, but remained in the middle

---

157. For an impression of cathedral furnishings see MS Tanner 44, fo. 66 (Lichfield); BL, MS Harleian 3785, fo. 1 (the consecration of the chapel at Auckland Castle); Legg, *Church Life*, pp. 127, 136–8; V. Staley, *Hierurgia Anglicana* (1902–4), vol. II; G.W.O. Addleshaw and F. Etchells, *The Architectural Setting of Anglican Worship* (1948); R.A. Beddard, 'Cathedral Furnishings of the Restoration Period; A Salisbury Inventory of 1685', *Wiltshire Archaeological Magazine*, 66 (1971).
158. *Visitation Returns for Cambridgeshire*, ed. Palmer, p. 80 and pp. 78–91.
159. *Visitation Returns for Cambridgeshire*, ed. Palmer, pp. 92, 96. For Dry Drayton's puritan heritage, see M. Spufford, *Contrasting Communities* (Cambridge, 1974), pp. 327–8.

of the chancel, often surrounded by benches or seats for the communicants. In 1697, the Nonconformist Miss Fiennes was gratified to observe that in the church at Hull 'their altar stood table-wise for the communion just in the middle of the chancel, as it was in the primitive times before popery came in'.[160] It was reported from Impington in 1666 that there was a 'sacrament four times a year. Some (who can conveniently place themselves), do receive the sacrament in the chancel, the rest do receive in their seats, all receive reverently and kneeling.'[161] Other churches fell far short of the ideal: some even lacked a communion table.[162] Not every chancel was floored in marble, some were still strewn with rushes or 'old peas-straw'.[163] Many churches were, like Hungry Hatley, adorned with edifying texts: 'the ten commandments are set up in our parish church where the people may read them, and other chosen sentences are written upon the walls of our said church in places convenient' – such texts, probably painted in 1683, can still be seen at the church of St John Baptist, Stokesay, Shropshire. But in many Restoration churches these texts needed repainting, and at least one preacher believed that 'not one in forty minds' the faded, familiar 'scripture sentences written upon the wall in country churches'.[164] The communion table was covered with a 'carpet' and during times of divine service with a fair linen or damask cloth. Few churches

160. *The Journeys of Celia Fiennes*, ed. C. Morris (1947), p. 89. It is not clear that the rubrics, injunctions and Canons of the church did warrant the 'altar-wise' position for the table, but the insistence of the hierarchy and the resistance of many parishes are apparent in several sets of Restoration visitation returns; see *Notes on Visitations in Essex*, ed. Pressey, *passim*; *Inspections of Churches ... in Diocese of Worcester*, ed. Morgan, pp. 19–20; *Visitation Returns for Cambridgeshire*, ed. Palmer, pp. 92, 96. Further evidence of altars still in the old position is to be found in *Churchwardens Accounts of S. Edmund and S. Thomas, Sarum 1443–1702*, ed. H.J.F. Swayne (Wiltshire Record Society, 1896), pp. xxxix, 238; *The Parish of St Paul's, Covent Garden* (The Survey of London, 36, 1970), p. 105; MS Tanner 30, fo. 49; BL, MS Egerton 3358; Evelyn, III, 317; IV, 132. It seems likely that the situation changed quickly after 1688, see F.C. Mather, 'Georgian Churchmanship Reconsidered: Some Variations in Anglican Worship 1714–1830', *JEH*, 36 (1985), 264–5.
161. *Visitations Returns for Cambridgeshire*, ed. Palmer, p. 113.
162. *Churchwardens' Presentments ... Lewes*, ed. Johnstone, p. 6.
163. *Inspections of Churches ... in Diocese of Worcester*, ed. Morgan, pp. 50, 51; *Durham Parish Books*, pp. 223, 225, 228.
164. Anthony Horneck, *The First Fruits of Reason* (1686), p. 43; for the disrepair of the texts see *Visitation Returns for Cambridgeshire*, ed. Palmer, pp. 80, 106; *Inspections of Churches ... in Diocese of Worcester*, ed. Morgan, pp. 11, 69–70; *Notes on Visitations in Essex*, ed. Pressey, 22 (1936–40), pp. 321, 325, 327; G. Cobb, *London City Churches* (1977 edn), pp. 80–1. For the case of Moulton where the texts were whitewashed and replaced with images of SS Peter and Paul and the Holy Ghost, see Thomas Barlow, *Several Cases of Conscience* (1692), pp. 3–25.

possessed a pair of candlesticks, and many still used pewter plates for the communion bread. It was, however, rare for a church to be in the position of Lower Pillarton and have 'no chalice, so that when the communion is administered they usually make use of a borrowed pewter cup'.[165] Those who enquired into the state of churches were always very interested to know if the utensils were sufficient for the communion. Many English churches received gifts of plate during the Restoration, possibly to replace losses sustained during the Civil War and Interregnum.

In the early 1680s, when the world had once more been made safe for the church, the clergy led a drive for more frequent celebration of the sacrament. The indefatigable Denis Granville, archdeacon and subsequently dean of Durham, campaigned from about 1680 for stricter adherence to the rubrical requirement of weekly celebration in the cathedrals. He lobbied for support in person and by letter, he marshalled authorities, distributed tracts, badgered bishops and even button-holed the King. Although the dean's hectoring did not endear him to his own bishop, Nathaniel Crew, it won him the support of clergymen such as Barnabas Oley, Isaac Basire, Francis Turner, Daniel Brevint, Thomas Comber and William Beveridge.[166] The efforts of Granville and others, who 'have lately laboured hard' to convince the nation of the importance of the sacrament,[167] finally bore fruit in Archbishop Sancroft's circular of 1684 ordering weekly communions in all the cathedrals. The circular was welcomed by the clergy; Simon Patrick began a sermon series at Peterborough which became his *Treatise on the Necessity and Frequency of Receiving* and a delighted Granville rushed into print to stir up the parish clergy to imitate 'an example so pious and worthy of their high station, by celebrating the holy communion more frequently, than of late hath been accustomed in parish churches'.[168] But practical difficulties soon emerged: at York Minster, Dean Comber greeted the instruction with enthusiasm, but setting up

165. *Inspections of Churches ... in Diocese of Worcester*, ed. Morgan, p. 55. On lack of utensils, see *Churchwardens' Presentments ... Lewes*, ed. Johnstone, pp. 44 ff.
166. See Granville, I, 174–83; II, 45–6, 48–62, 73–82, 85–92, 121–32; MS Rawlinson Letters 93, fo. 192. For Granville's lobbying see Granville, II, 107–119; I, 164–74; Granville, *Compleat Conformist* (1684); C.E. Whiting, *Nathaniel Lord Crewe Bishop of Durham (1674–1721)* (1940), pp. 139–41.
167. Pelling, *Discourse of Sacrament*, sig. A3.
168. Patrick, II, 11; Granville, *Compleat Conformist*, dedication, and the appended *Letter of Advice to the Clergy*, pp. 1, 10–11. The circular emerged from a meeting of the bishops in 1683, see *Concilia*, IV, 612–14; cf. MS Rawlinson Letters 93, fo. 192; J. Mackay, 'John Tillotson, 1630–1694' (unpublished Oxford University D. Phil. thesis, 1985), p. 156; E. Carpenter, *The Protestant Bishop – Being the Life of Henry Compton* (1956), p. 226.

the weekly communions there was a slow business; while Bishop Lloyd of St Asaph, who had been so eager the previous year, now tried to excuse his own cathedral on the grounds of poverty.[169] In the London parishes, however, the celebration of weekly eucharists, like the reading of daily prayers, was gaining ground during the 1680s.[170] Edward Fowler, vicar of St Giles Cripplegate, wrote to Sancroft in November 1685 that 'God hath blessed mine and my assistant's endeavours here, with not only as numerous and regular a congregation as is perhaps to be found in England, but also very comfortable weekly communions.'[171] Elsewhere in the country, away from the thronged parishes of London, the zealous advocate of weekly communion and daily public prayer might even encounter opposition from the clergy; John Foster, curate of Holdenhurst, Sussex, who set himself 'to repair the public worship of God in the daily service and weekly communion', was disappointed 'that so many of my brethren are otherwise minded'.[172]

But in the spring of 1686 there was a further remarkable development. From Lichfield, Dean Lancelot Addison reported, 'the clergy assure me they have had very great store of communicants this Easter, and that people begin to regard the sacrament more than they have done'.[173] Bishop Lloyd of Norwich estimated that the number of communicants in his diocese had trebled in the first months of 1686 and ascribed the increase to the strict enforcement of the penal laws.[174] Edmund Bohun's diary for Easter 1686 confirms the bishop's impression of an increase in communicants, but offers a different explanation:

> April 4th. I received the holy communion, in the parish church at Westhall, at the hands of Isaac Girling the present vicar there; when I had the blessed satisfaction of seeing three score of the inhabitants of that parish receive at one time; having scarce ever seen twenty, at any one time, before. This was owing principally, to the pious care of the present bishop of Norwich, Dr Lloyd; who had issued out a circular letter to all his diocese, that all that were above sixteen years of age should receive the Lord's supper in the beginning of this Lent; and next, to Mr Girling, who is a

169. MS Tanner 32, fos 47, 176, 213; for Lloyd see *Concilia*, IV, 608–10; A.T. Hart, *William Lloyd* (1952), p. 77; and for similar hesitancy at St Paul's see Carpenter, *Protestant Bishop*, pp. 243–4.
170. A.T. Hart, *The Life and Times of John Sharp* (1949), p. 76.
171. MS Tanner 31, fo. 225.
172. MS Tanner 32, fo. 106.
173. MS Tanner 30, fo. 26.
174. Ibid., fo. 37 (Lloyd to Sancroft, 21 May 1686).

good man and a good preacher, and very much beloved by his people.[175]

Isaac Archer was another minister in Lloyd's diocese who took notice of his bishop's 'strict order about the sacrament: I gave my parish notice a month before and expounded on Lord's Days; and privately instructed the younger sort, finding them very serious, so that I hope my pains will not be in vain'.[176] The importance of an energetic bishop, like Lloyd – who had earlier achieved impressive results by decreeing an obligatory 'general sacrament' throughout the diocese of Peterborough – is undeniable;[177] but the developing policies of James II may also have played a part in driving the people back into the arms of the church in 1686.

Too much should not be read into such exceptional surges of popular enthusiasm for the sacrament, for the general picture is far from impressive. In 1685, Simon Patrick could still complain that the sacrament was 'not so frequently administered, much less attended, as it ought to be'.[178] Nor, according to Barnabas Oley, were the citizens of Worcester eager to take advantage of the weekly communions celebrated at the cathedral.[179] Bishop Lloyd of Peterborough observed that 'the parishioners in most parishes of the diocese were strangely averse to the liturgy and sacrament of the Lord's Supper', before he resorted to coercion;[180] while a newly arrived minister in Sussex also found it 'strange' that his docile and respectable parishioners 'are generally very awkward to the sacrament. In Shropshire I was fain to drive away, here I must use the hook and change my bait.'[181]

Are we to conclude, then, that lay practice did not measure up to the ideal of a Prayer Book piety tied to a worthy reception of the sacrament and the holy life? No, such a conclusion would be rash, for there were laymen who had the time and the temperament to pursue the clergy's vision of Anglican piety; 'that devout laic', Thomas Seymour was 'bred to the exercise of piety in another way', but was won over to Prayer Book piety and became one of its propagandists.[182] Leisured ladies filled notebooks with their meditations and 'pious reflections upon certain sermons', and

175. Bohun, *Autobiography*, pp. 74–5.
176. CUL, MS Add. 8499, fo. 208.
177. MS Rawlinson D 1163, fos 17–18.
178. Patrick, IV, 615–16.
179. Granville, II, 61.
180. MS Rawlinson D 1163, fo. 16.
181. MS Eng Letters E 29, fo. 176 v.
182. Seymour, *Advice to Readers of Common Prayer*, sig. B2v.

earnest gentlemen drew up elaborate manuscript 'collections of godly prayers to be used before and after receiving the holy sacrament'.[183] These personal commonplace books of prayers and meditations are not, however, unequivocal evidence of Anglican piety; the complexity of human motivation repeatedly clouds the picture. John Evelyn, an undoubted Anglican, composed a manuscript devotional, which dwelt upon the need for frequent communion, and included in it his own service of 'mental communion' drawn from the Prayer Book and apparently used during the Interregnum when the sacrament had been unavailable. But even the pious Evelyn found his devotional life taking some strange directions during his intense relationship with Margaret Godolphin.[184] Another conforming Anglican and practitioner of the holy life, Mary Rich, Countess of Warwick, had first been converted in a puritan household in 1647 and her subsequent devotional regime drew upon the puritan tradition as much as the church.[185] The private piety of the Restoration elite often contained (or perhaps retained) more than a hint of the plain puritanical devotions of an earlier generation of godly gentry.[186] The evidence, such as it is, suggests that the piety of those lower down the social ladder may have been even more sluggish or resistant to change. Lay piety can be very slow to respond to the nuances of clerical exhortation, especially when, as in this case, the clergy are only pressing for a subtle shift of attitude, a re-evaluation of prayer and the sacrament, rather than for any drastic renewal or reformation of religion.

As John Gaskarth complained, many of the country people thought of going to church only to hear a sermon and were scarcely conscious of their duty to pray or celebrate the sacrament together. The Church of England was much troubled by those who 'never come to their parish church until the common prayers be ended, and come only to the preaching'. Her visitation articles still enquired 'are there any among you that come only to the preaching, and not to the

183. The collection cited is by Benjamin Carpenter, dated 1681, and heavily dependent upon the Prayer Book, MS Carte 272. Also see Mrs Delaval's 'meditations and prayers', MS Rawlinson D 78; MS Carte 265 (possibly by Sir Leoline Jenkins); MS Add. C 304b, fos 54–69, in which appears material by Taylor, Patrick and Andrewes; Evelyn, IV, 152.

184. See Evelyn, *Devotionarie Book*; W.G. Hiscock, *John Evelyn and Mrs Godolphin* (1951); W.G. Hiscock, *John Evelyn and his Family Circle* (1955), chs 5–7.

185. See Anthony Walker, *The Virtuous Woman Found* (1678); S.H. Mendelson, *The Mental World of Stuart Women: Three Studies* (Brighton, 1987), ch. 2, esp. pp. 85, 93–6.

186. See Bohun, *Autobiography*, pp. 58–62; Warwickshire Record Office, CR 136, B413, fos 9, 16 (Bishop Fell to Richard Newdigate).

common prayers of the church?'[187] But even the diligent conformists tended to see the sermon as the centre of their religious life: sermons were noted in diaries, judged as performances, and those in print were read over at home. The English, opined Halifax, 'generally place their religion in the pulpit, as the papists do theirs upon the altar'.[188] Dean Granville looked 'upon it as a huge decay of Christian piety, to place all, or most of our religion in hearing of a sermon, ushered in with a private prayer, which among some is valued above the church's public devotion, and to which many are so passionately addicted that they will not endure to be present at our assemblies till that prayer be begun'.[189] The clergy were not immune to this preference for preaching. On the evidence of his autobiography, Isaac Archer was, for much of his life, typical of those who believed that the core of religion lay in a proper understanding, exposition and application of the Word. As a young and only partially conforming Anglican minister, he 'read as little as was possible' of the liturgy to his congregation, 'and sometimes in the short and cold days none at all but the psalms and the lessons'; and although, before his arrival, the congregation 'had the ceremonies to the height', they did not murmur at his omissions for he used the extra time to preach, 'which they liked better'.[190]

Ideally, sermon, sacrament and prayer should dovetail together in a complete piety: 'we must neither divide praying from preaching, nor preaching from praying, but we must join them both together'.[191] Preaching the Word was a mark of the true Church, the duty of God's ministers, the means to confute atheism and error, and a vital weapon in the campaign to persuade the people to a better prepared and more frequent reception of the Lord's Supper. There were weekday sermons in several cathedrals during Lent and Advent to help the laity prepare for communion. It had been the ambition of the sixteenth-century Reformers to turn the cathedrals into preaching centres, from which the Word might be spread into the surrounding countryside. The subsequent attempts of the Laudians to revive the cathedrals' life of prayer or their role as liturgical

187.   *Churchwardens' Presentments: I Archdeaconry of Chichester*, ed. H. Johnstone (Sussex Record Society, 49, 1947–8), p. 131; *Fell*, ed. Clapinson, p. 22; [Bishop Robert Sanderson] *Visitation Articles for Lincoln* (1662), IV, 4; [Dean Thomas Pierce] *Visitation Articles for Sarum* (Oxford, 1675), IV, 4; [Bishop William Lloyd] *Visitation Articles for Peterborough* (1683), IV, 4.

188.   *The Life and Letters of Sir George Savile, Bart, first Marquis of Halifax*, ed. H.C. Foxcroft (1898), I, 467 (letter to the Earl of Chesterfield, 20 July 1686).

189.   Granville, II, 73–4.

190.   CUL, MS Add. 8499, fo. 94.

191.   MS Eng Th D 59, p. 18; also see *Weeks Preparation*, p. 56.

exemplars had met with little success; and in the later seventeenth century, the cathedrals, short of resident clergy and unsure of their role in the church, offered a poor liturgical example to the parishes.[192] Nor did newly built churches offer any clear lead in worship during the Restoration. St James's, Piccadilly, opened in 1684, was a typical Wren 'preaching box' designed for 'all to hear the service, and both to hear distinctly, and see the preacher'. Yet it was the altar which caught John Evelyn's attention:

> I went to see the new church, St James's, elegantly indeed built, especially adorned was the altar, the white marble enclosure curiously and richly carved, and the flowers and garlands about the walls by Mr Grinling Gibbons in wood, a pelican with her young at her breast just over the altar in the carved compartment and bordure, environing the purple velvet, richly fringed with IHS most richly embroidered, and most noble plate . . . [193]

John Evelyn's diary for Good Friday 1687 perhaps affords the best available example of how sermon, private devotion and the sacrament could work together as they were supposed to to create an effective piety. At St Martin-in-the-Fields, Evelyn heard Tenison preach 'a most pathetical discourse, describing how our blessed Saviour had our sins transferred on him'. When Tenison described 'the infinite charity of God in sending his Son for this end and our ingratitude in being no more affected with it, he drew tears from many eyes: the holy sacrament followed, of which I participated after a very solemn preparation and to my extraordinary comfort: the Lord make me mindfull and thankfull'.[194]

The country folk, poorly educated and hidebound, were far from irreligious, but their religion was customary and idiosyncratic, shot through with suspicion of authority and hatred of innovation. 'I find many of the people have, at the bottom, an ill affection for the prayers and governors of the church, really judging the worship tainted with popery', concluded the curate of Ibstone in Oxfordshire.[195] At Pewsey in Wiltshire, 'of the greater number upon Sundays few continue all the time of divine service in the church, the most hasting out before the second service begins, as apprehending some superstition in it'.[196] Popular religious sensibilities may have followed patterns established long before the Restoration: the

---

192. See *A History of York Minster*, ed. G.E. Aylmer and R. Cant (Oxford, 1979), pp. 234–7.
193. Evelyn, IV, 397. Also see Addleshaw and Etchells, *Architectural Setting*.
194. Evelyn, IV, 544–5, also see 64, 543.
195. *Fell*, ed. Clapinson, p. 22.
196. Whiteman, 'Ward', p. 297.

ordinary people still read the older classics of Protestantism, Bayly, Ball and Dent, and if contemporary writers wished to address them then they had to adopt the black letter of the penny godlies.[197] Illiteracy was a perennial and insuperable obstacle to the clergy's aspirations for lay piety: they urged the illiterate – 'the number of which will be every day fewer I hope' – to learn by heart from their parents or others the Lord's Prayer and the decalogue in prayer form.[198]

Popular piety was able to express itself in forms other than those laid down by the clergy. The social significance of quasi-pious or para-liturgical associations, such as societies of the natives of certain counties, societies of bell-ringers, and the village choirs, cry out for further study.[199] Above all, the 'religious societies' which came to prominence in London and elsewhere in the 1690s attest to a powerful current of popular lay piety in the Church of England. It was later said that these had begun in about 1678 when a group of young London men applied to Anthony Horneck, the devotional writer and preacher at the Savoy, for spiritual direction. Horneck drew up rules for their weekly meetings and regular communions. This pious initiative was a result of Horneck's 'awakening' sermons and 'Mr Smithies' Sunday morning lectures, 'chiefly designed for the instruction of youth', at St Michael's Cornhill.[200] The lecturer William Smythies (also curate to Edward Fowler at St Giles Cripplegate), found himself the target of Roger L'Estrange's venom in 1684 for allegedly praying, reading and catechizing in a 'private meeting' or 'club' in Ave-Mary Lane, off Ludgate Hill. Smythies was indignant:

> 'Tis true, that there are some young persons that are my morning auditors, who meet once a month at a club, and always give somewhat to the poor, which I have had the disposal of. They

197. See M. Spufford, *Small Books and Pleasant Histories* (Cambridge, 1981), ch. 8; E. Duffy, 'The Godly and the Multitude in Stuart England', *The Seventeenth Century*, 1 (1986); I.M. Green, '"For Children in Yeeres and Children in Understanding": The Emergence of the English Catechism under Elizabeth and the Early Stuarts', *JEH*, 37 (1986); idem, 'The Changing Form and Content of Religious Instruction in Early Modern England' (unpublished paper).

198. Bright, *Treatise of Prayer*, p. 387; also see Howell, *Common Prayer Book the Best Companion*, sig. A5.

199. For bell-ringers see E. Morris, *The History and Art of Change Ringing* (1931). Temperley, *Music of Parish Church*, is helpful on choirs and town bands, but Spaeth, 'Parsons and Parishioners', ch. 5, is the best study of the religious implications of choirs.

200. See Legg, *Church Life*, pp. 291–3, 308–9; Josiah Woodward, *An Account of the Rise and Progress of the Religious Societies in the City of London* (2nd edn, 1698), pp. 34–5; J. Spurr, 'The Church, the Societies, and the Moral Revolution of 1688', in *From Toleration to Tractarianism: The Church of England, 1689–1833*, ed. C.M. Haydon, S. Taylor and J.D. Walsh (forthcoming).

have made an order amongst themselves, that no disloyal person shall come amongst them, nor any but those that are communicants. But that I, or any clergyman, ever came amongst them to pray, read, etc., or ever was but one half hour with them at their club, is utterly false.[201]

Despite the danger of being misrepresented as a dissident conventicle, other such religious societies had been formed. In 1681 the 'devout young men' of St Martin-in-the-Fields drew up articles of association, restricting membership to those who 'frequent our parish church' and who have received the sacrament or declared 'they will do it as they have opportunity', and 'if any person shall neglect coming to the holy sacrament three times together without a very good reason, he shall be excluded'. The society met at five o'clock every third Sunday of the month, 'in decent order with our hats off', their 'monitor' read 'some prayer as shall be useful for our purpose', the stewards read a chapter out of the Bible, and then any of the society repeated the heads of a sermon 'or anything else that is useful for us'. The other purpose of their meeting was to take a collection for the poor to be distributed by 'the Doctor', presumably Dr Thomas Tenison, rector of St Martin's.[202] These associations apparently continued to grow during the reign of James II, when Horneck and Beveridge, rector of St Peter's Cornhill, 'had the chief direction of the religious societies'.[203]

To conclude that Anglican piety was not practised during the Restoration, or at least not on the scale of which the clergy dreamt, does not diminish its significance for our understanding of the churchmen and their church. The Restoration's vision of the consecrated life of the laity was not new; it had been variously foreshadowed in the Henrican primers, in the works of Andrewes, Cosin, Laud and Bayly, and in the devotional writings of Donne, Herbert and Traherne; it also had much in common with the puritan devotional writers of the late sixteenth and seventeenth centuries, and with works of Restoration Nonconformity such as Thomas Doolittle's *Treatise concerning the Lord's Supper* (1665) or Oliver Heywood's *Closet Prayer* (1671). It is undoubtedly true that works of piety are 'grounded in the major acceptances of their day' and that they therefore often transcend denominational boundaries; the works of George Herbert were, for instance, immensely popular among

201. William Smythies, *A Letter to the Observator* (1684), p. 7.
202. BL, MS Add. 38693, fo. 137.
203. Thomas Birch, *The Life of the Most Reverend John Tillotson* (2nd edn, 1753), p. 214; cf. Woodward, *Account of Religious Societies*, pp. 39–40.

Nonconformists.[204] Some of the common ground and the differences between churchmen and Dissenters are revealed by comparing two works of 1679, J.B.'s *Directions for the Right Receiving of the Lords Supper* and the anonymous *A Weeks Preparation Towards a Worthy Receiving of the Lords Supper*. The former, by John Bartlett, an ejected Non-conformist minister, was a Calvinist catechism originally intended for the 'citizens of Exeter', while the latter was almost certainly a product of a 'High Church' circle around Sancroft. Bartlett defined faith as 'a special, and supernatural gift of God, wrought by the spirit, through the ministry of the Word, in the hearts of the elect, whereby we come to know, assent unto, take, and rely upon the Lord Jesus Christ for salvation'; while *A Weeks Preparation* asserts 'that all the perfection of a Christian life consists in the imitation and following of the virtues of our saviour Christ'.[205] Bartlett's account of 'habitual' preparation is far longer than his sketch of 'actual' preparation or 'stirring up the graces'; *A Weeks Preparation* is devoted to actual preparation for the sacrament. While the *Directions* is focused on the Lord's Supper, it naturally makes no mention of what is performed at church or of the liturgy. *A Weeks Preparation*, on the other hand, is built around the liturgy: preparation begins when the minister announces in church that the communion will be celebrated on the following Sunday; and the communicant is to 'repair to the public service of the church' every day of the intervening week, or failing that to privately read the day's Psalms, Lessons and prayers from the Prayer Book. Yet beneath these differences, the two works are akin; they are both uncompromising in their disdain for the worth of human efforts; they are both unequivocally Protestant.[206]

The Restoration Church of England had not, however, isolated herself from all Roman Catholic influence; there are many examples of Anglican interest in, and borrowings from, Roman Catholic devotional authors such as à Kempis or de Sales; and an English market existed for Roman Catholic works, especially those which had been adapted to suit Protestant sensibilities.[207] Who is to say

---

204. See H.C. White, *English Devotional Literature [Prose] 1600–1640* (Madison, Wisconsin, 1931), p. 163 and *passim*. Also helpful on this subject are C.J. Stranks, *Anglican Devotion* (1961); G.S. Wakefield, *Puritan Devotion* (1957); N.H. Keeble, *The Literary Culture of Nonconformity in Later Seventeenth-century England* (Leicester, 1987).

205. [Bartlett], *Directions*, p. 16; *Weeks Preparation*, p. 84.

206. *Weeks Preparation*, p. 6.

207. See L.L. Martz, *The Poetry of Meditation* (New Haven and London, 1962); J.M. Blom, *The Post–Tridentine English Primer* (Catholic Record Society Monograph 3, 1982), pp. 137–62; J.M. Blom, 'A German Jesuit and his Anglican Readers: The Case of Jeremias Drexelius 1581–1638', in *Studies in Seventeenth-century English Literature, History and Bibliography*, ed. G.A.M. Janssens and F.G.A.M. Aarts (Amsterdam, 1984).

that the Salesian ideal of a devout life lived fully in the world did not contribute to the enthusiasm with which some Anglican divines pursued 'holy living'; certainly, there were few churchmen who had not read or did not possess a copy of de Sales's *Introduction to the Devout Life*.[208] A minor, but striking, instance of the mingling of several different pious traditions is afforded by the popularity of the motif of Christian pilgrimage: John Bunyan's *The Pilgrim's Progress* appeared in 1678, some time after Simon Patrick's *The Parable of the Pilgrim* (1665); Patrick's parable had been suggested by a short piece with the same title which appeared in *Sancta Sophia* (1657), a collection prepared from the manuscripts of Augustine Baker by his fellow Benedictine Serenus Cressy, but Baker's piece was in fact an extract from a fourteenth-century work, Walter Hilton's *The Scale of Perfection*.[209]

Yet there was a distinctively 'Anglican' quality to the piety envisioned and promoted by the Restoration church. This quality was composed of several elements. First, it was low key. The devotional writings of Allestree and Patrick do not evoke the rapturous and mystical union of the soul with God; not even Taylor, Horneck or Ken can be compared with St Teresa, de Sales or Ignatius as devotional writers. Broadly speaking, Anglican piety emphasized the unworthiness of sinners, the prospect of damnation, the atoning sacrifice of Christ, and his redemption of sinners; it offered little on the felicity to which the sinner was admitted by redemption, on the parousia, or on the creation. Nevertheless, this low-key quality should not be confused with lukewarmness. It has been asserted that 'in contrast to the sober moralizings' of *The Whole Duty* and Tillotson's sermons, the Nonconformists' pious literature 'welcomes the transporting power of feeling; it delights in the amorous and sensory ... it offers a model of the religious life which demands the full responsiveness of emotional and sentient beings'.[210] Without disputing what is essentially a subjective judgement, a word should be said in defence of the Restoration churchmen. It has been one of the principal contentions of this and the preceding chapter that *The*

---

208. On the Salesian tradition in English Catholicism, see E. Duffy, ' "Poor Protestant Flies": Conversions to Catholicism in Early Eighteenth-century England', *SCH*, 15 (1978), esp. 293–4; Duffy, 'The English Secular Clergy and the Counter-Reformation', *JEH*, 34 (1983). For Anglican interest in de Sales, see *Catalogus librorum . . . Gulielmi Outrami* (1681), p. 58, item 689; *A Catalogue of Books . . . of the Library of the Rev. Mr William Sill, late Prebendary of Westminster* (1687), p. 5, item 99, p. 6, item 144; and, for the early seventeenth century, see Martz, *Poetry of Meditation*, pp. 144–9, 249–59.

209. See Patrick, IV, preface to *The Parable of the Pilgrim*; and on Baker, D. Lunn, *The English Benedictines 1540–1688* (1980), pp. 202–17.

210. Keeble, *Literary Culture*, p. 213.

Whole Duty of Man was part of a much more complex theological and devotional enterprise than has been recognized. The context of these Anglican works of sober morality needs to be reinstated; that is, these works need to be reinserted into the rigorous Anglican theology of salvation and the pious regime of penitence, prayer and sacrament, if we are to recapture their full meaning. When they are read in their theological and pious context, the commitment of Restoration Anglicanism to a religious life which awakens and stimulates the heart as much as the intellect becomes apparent. The Restoration church was never going to adopt the language of 'recumbency on Christ', of 'heart religion' or enthusiasm, but within her carefully chosen limits she strove to offer a model of the religious life which aroused a response from the *whole* individual.

Anglican piety was also distinguished from Nonconformist piety in ways which reflected and reinforced the ecclesiological differences between the two camps. It has been said that puritan piety tends to see the Christian's union with Christ as the beginning of the Christian life.[211] Faith was the means by which this union was achieved; and so puritan piety resounded with 'calls to the unconverted' and 'alarms for sinners', it was full of predestination and election, and could not help but elevate the role of the saving Word of God. The gospel was the key to the sinner's union with Christ; and the Church of Christ was built up of those born to new life in Christ through faith. Among Restoration Anglicans, however, the view was beginning to prevail that 'our union with Christ's Church is the medium of our union with Christ'.[212] In other words, the Christian life *culminated* in union with Christ. It would be a caricature of these ecclesiological differences to suggest that they formed a sharp antithesis; all too often the arguments were unresolved or deliberately evasive. But there is a clear, and revealing, distinction in the case of Anglican and Nonconformist understandings of the Pauline term 'edification'. The Nonconformist or puritan view was that the individual's 'edification' or growth in grace constituted the edification or building of the church. However, the churchmen, assuming that individuals could only grow in grace through the church, took 'edification' for a corporate exercise of the whole communion. Edification was easily equated with the church's common life of prayer and praise. Thus the practice of piety, the worship of the church, and the celebration of her sacraments were part of the edification or building of the church; in this basic ecclesiological

211. Wakefield, *Puritan Devotion*, p. 160.
212. William Sherlock, *A Discourse concerning the Knowledge of Jesus Christ* (1674), pp. 165–6.

sense, her liturgy and sacraments contributed to the Restoration Church of England's understanding of how she was constituted as a church; and the piety based upon them was by definition 'Anglican'. The suggestion that her worship and sacraments played a part in constituting and nourishing the church was of great significance to the Church of England. Lacking a strong doctrinal definition of herself, the English church was beginning to appreciate how her liturgy and piety contributed to her identity. We have seen the same process in action in earlier chapters, perhaps most clearly in the description of how episcopacy came to be seen as a source of unity for the Church of England. Anglican piety can now be put into place, alongside episcopacy, the theology of holy living, the campaign against national sin, and the principle of national religious uniformity, to complete our picture of Restoration Anglicanism.

Chapter 8

The Church of England and Restoration Anglicanism

The Restoration Church of England was the creation of one revolution and the victim of another. The 'Glorious Revolution' of 1688–9
precipitated a crisis of identity and authority in the Church of
England which did much to obscure the achievements of the preceding decades.

Not the least of the glories of 1688–9, to modern eyes, is the
admission of the cherished, and long-delayed, civil right of religious
liberty. Yet to most contemporaries the revolution principally ensured
liberty from popery; the Toleration Act was a generally unwelcome,
and slightly disreputable, compromise born out of political deadlock.
In fact, the 'Toleration Act' is a misnomer. Contemporaries called
it the 'indulgence', which is what it was. Protestant Dissenters from
the Church of England were simply 'indulged' or exempted by the
Act from the penalties of a long list of statutes, all of which remained
in force. To qualify even for these exemptions laymen had to register
and take the new oaths of allegiance and supremacy and the 1678
Test against transubstantiation, while Nonconformist clergy took the
oaths, the Test and subscribed to all but four of the Thirty-Nine
Articles. Only registered congregations were free to worship, and
then only if the doors of their meeting houses were propped open.
Roman Catholics, of course, gained nothing from the Act. And the
string of civil disabilities borne by non-Anglicans remained. Nor
was the permanence of even this 'toleration' guaranteed: Parliament
considered limiting the Act's life to seven years; and the Occasional
Conformity Act of 1711 and the Schism Act of 1714 represented
serious reversals of the principle of toleration for Protestant Dissenters. It was, perhaps, the repeal of these two statutes in 1718
that marked the firm legal establishment of religious toleration in
England.[1]

1. See R.B. Barlow, *Citizenship and Conscience* (Philadelphia, 1962). In 1714 a one-year
   indemnity removed some of the civil disabilities of non-Anglicans; this concession
   was repeated in 1727 and more frequently thereafter.

The Church of England was nevertheless outraged by the Toleration Act, by its genesis, and its effects. That a lay Parliament had
presumed to revise the religious settlement rankled with many
churchmen: 'I never knew these grey-coated ecclesiastics reform to
any good purpose', wrote one divine; for these laymen believe the
government of the church is as alterable as that of the state 'and
that presbyterian orders may become valid by an almighty vote to
knights and burgesses'.[2] Another, less temperate, cleric denounced
MPs as 'a company of irreligious wretches who cares not [*sic*]...
what becomes of the church... if they can but get their hawks,
hounds and whores, and the sacred possessions of the church'.[3] The
decision, in the spring of 1689, to shelve the comprehension bill,
while pressing on with the toleration, 'makes all sober men amazed
here,' wrote one provincial gent, 'not knowing what they would be
at'.[4] Confronted with a harsh choice, the church's 'false friends' in
Parliament had preferred to sacrifice the church's interests rather
than surrender the Anglican monopoly on office and power.

The Church of England took her demotion from 'the national
church' to 'an established church' badly. Many churchmen continued to preach against toleration and insisted that, whatever
Parliament might enact, the Dissenters remained guilty of the sin
of schism: 'there is not one of a thousand among them that knows
what schism means,' reported one Lincolnshire parson of his errant
parishioners, 'or will believe that they are guilty of the crime, since
they are freed by the laws from the penalty of it'.[5] Objectively
viewed, however, the church had lost little: in the 'public realm' of
ideology, law and politics, she still enjoyed an hegemony.[6] The
church retained a presence in every parish in the land, her clergy
continued to perform and record the vast majority of baptisms,
marriages and burials; she still controlled the universities, and her
bishops still sat in the House of Lords; there were few Dissenters and

2. MS Ballard 30, fo. 26, quoted by G.V. Bennett, 'Loyalist Oxford and the
   Revolution', in *History of the University of Oxford: V The Eighteenth Century*, ed. L.S.
   Sutherland and L.G. Mitchell (Oxford, 1986), p. 25.
3. *The Diary of Abraham de la Pryme*, ed. C. Jackson (Surtees Society, 54, 1870), quoted in
   C. Holmes, *Seventeenth-century Lincolnshire* (Lincoln, 1980), p. 259
4. MS Rawlinson Letters 48, fo. 98.
5. Lambeth Palace Library, MS 933, item 9, p. 3 (Edward Bowerman to Tenison, 17
   December 1692).
6. For some reflections on whether eighteenth-century England was a 'confessional
   state', and on what this might mean, see J.C.D. Clark, 'England's ancien regime',
   Past and Present, 17 (1987), 199–200; idem, 'England's ancien regime as a
   Confessional State', *Albion*, 21 (1989), 458, 461–2. For a different view of the weight
   of the civil disabilities, see D.L. Wykes, 'Religious Dissent and the Penal Laws: An
   Explanation of Business Success?', *History*, 75 (1990).

no Catholics in Parliament; those who held office under the Crown or in corporations were obliged to take the sacramental test. And behind these legal privileges lay a cast of mind peculiar to those who believe themselves to enjoy an unquestionable superiority. As Dudley Ryder observed of Anglican attitudes towards Dissenters in 1715: 'there are too many of the churchmen [i.e., Anglican laymen] who are not Tories nor for downright persecuting them and yet think they have no right to have anything to do with government. Even the Whigs themselves that are churchmen have not all got over their prejudices. They look upon themselves as persons in a higher rank, of a superior degree and therefore grudge them all the privileges that they have. Think that they are born to something above them.'[7]

Contrary to Anglican prophecies, Dissent had not swamped the land after the Toleration Act: between 1689 and 1709 licences were taken out for 4,000 congregations, and reliable estimates put the number in 1715–18 at 1,845 meetings, or perhaps 338,000 Dissenters out of a nation of 5.4 million. One can safely conclude that even in the early eighteenth century, fewer than one in ten of the population attended something other than the Church of England.[8] More significant, however, was the number of English men and women who attended no form of worship. As one Anglican clergyman expostulated,

> in a short time it [the Toleration Act] will turn half the nation into downright atheism. I do not find . . . that conventicles have gained anything at all thereby, but rather they have lost. But the mischief is, a liberty being now granted, more lay hold of it to separate from all manner of worship to perfect irreligion than go to them; and, although the Act allows no such liberty, the people will understand it so, and, say what the judges can at the assizes, or the Justices of Peace at their sessions, or we at our visitations, no churchwarden or constable will present any for not going to church, though they go nowhere else but the alehouse, for this liberty they will have.[9]

The nation sank further into vice, apathy and non-attendance; in 1699 one Worcestershire curate reported that he often had no congregation at all, 'no not upon a sacrament day, but returned home without saying service'.[10] Atheism and apathy, rather than any brand of religion, appeared to be the true victors of 1689.

7. *The Diary of Dudley Ryder, 1715–1716*, ed. W. Matthews (1939), p. 65.
8. W.A. Speck, *Stability and Strife: England 1714–60* (1978), p. 112
9. *The Letters of Humphrey Prideaux*, ed. E.M. Thompson (Camden Society, 15, 1875), p. 154.
10. Quoted in G.A. Holmes, *The Trial of Dr Sacheverell* (1973), p. 25.

The Revolution had compromised the fundamental principles of the Restoration Church of England. The Restoration ideal of a single, all-inclusive, national church had been repudiated; and the vision of the complete Christian life, which had complemented that ideal, had been tarnished and diminished. The ecclesiological consensus of the Restoration church – her sense of being both Reformed and Catholic and her refusal to follow through the implications of her own episcopalianism – faltered and, with the departure of the Nonjurors, began to collapse. The Revolution had set in train the eventual fragmentation of Anglicanism: it is only fitting that we should briefly trace this process through to its culmination in the early nineteenth century.

Almost as soon as James II had fled, the Church of England began to disintegrate into clerical parties. With Sancroft refusing to act, the protection of the church's interests fell to an assortment of London clergy and others, under the leadership of Tillotson and the Earl of Nottingham. Thus it was that moderate Tory churchmen received preferment and that, following the deprivation of the Nonjurors, the episcopal promotions and appointments of 1691 also went to moderates like Stillingfleet, Patrick and Sharp. In 1689 Tillotson and Nottingham dangled before William the prospect of Anglican concessions towards a comprehension, and accordingly a royal commission was erected in September to consider reform of the liturgy, Canons, ecclesiastical courts, clerical discipline, and lay manners. Many churchmen, however, were in no mood for concession. Resentful of the Toleration Act and the abolition of Scottish episcopacy, suspicious of the motives and even legality of the commission, they resolved to oppose the new direction in which the church was being led. Several of those appointed to the Ecclesiastical Commission did not appear, others withdrew, and a pamphlet campaign, directed from the University of Oxford, was waged against revision of the terms of communion.[11] When Convocation met on 21 November 1689, the representatives of the discontented parish clergy – doubtless manipulated by politicians like Rochester and bishops like Compton – refused to contemplate any change of the laws governing the Church of England, and the assembly was swiftly prorogued. Thereafter the paths of the two clerical parties quickly diverged.[12]

11. See T.J. Fawcett, *The Liturgy of Comprehension 1689* (Alcuin Club, Southend, 1973).
12. A satisfactory modern account of the eighteenth-century Church of England is still to be written, but much can be learned from N. Sykes, *Church and State in England in the Eighteenth Century* (Cambridge, 1934); W.K. Lowther Clarke, *Eighteenth Century*

Many in the upper echelons of the clergy readily identified themselves with the needs of government and adapted to the changing political and ecclesiastical circumstances brought about by the Revolution. But this did not mean that they were the placemen of the new rulers: for most of the 1690s, under the leadership of first Tillotson and then Tenison, and with the aid of the commission for ecclesiastical appointments, major church preferment was kept out of the arena of party politics.[13] Meanwhile the parish clergy found the going hard as church attendance dwindled, vice and irreligion blossomed, and the new land tax ate into clerical incomes. These disgruntled ministers began to look to opposition to restore their fortunes. The Tory opposition which cohered around Nottingham, the Hyde brothers, and Bishops Compton, Trelawney and Sprat, became known as the 'High Church' party – while 'latitudinarian', an old, and almost redundant, epithet from the 1660s, was dusted off and applied by controversialists to those who seemed to have accommodated themselves a little too eagerly to the new regime.[14]

The High Church opposition found a platform in the campaign for a Convocation, which had not met since 1689. The first blow was struck by Francis Atterbury's *A Letter to a Convocation Man* (1697), which detected 'an universal conspiracy amongst a sort of men under the style of Deists, Socinians, latitudinarians, deniers of mysteries, and pretending explainers of them, to undermine and overthrow the catholic faith', and demanded that Convocation deal with this heresy. But Atterbury went further to claim that Convocation had a right to sit and be heard without royal licence, rather as if the clergy's synod was a counterpart of the House of Commons. While the campaign was principally a stick to beat Archbishop

Piety (1944); S.C. Carpenter, *Eighteenth Century Church and People* (1959); G.F.A. Best, *Temporal Pillars* (1964); G.V. Bennett, *The Tory Crisis in Church and State* (Oxford, 1975); idem, 'Conflict in the Church', in *Britain After the Glorious Revolution 1689–1714*, ed. G. Holmes (1969); idem, 'Loyalist Oxford', and 'University, Society and Church', in *History of University of Oxford: V*; G.A. Holmes, *Augustan England* (1982); E.G. Rupp, *Religion in England, 1688–1791* (Oxford, 1986); P. Virgin, *The Church in an Age of Negligence* (Cambridge, 1988); H.D. Rack, *Reasonable Enthusiast – John Wesley and the Rise of Methodism* (1989).

13. See G.V. Bennett, 'William III and the Episcopate', in *Essays in Modern English Church History*, ed. G.V. Bennett and J.D. Walsh (1966).

14. 'High' in its common seventeenth-century sense of 'extreme' is occasionally found in Restoration religious polemic, but its application to a clerical party dates from the 1690s; see G. Every, *The High Church Party 1688–1718* (1956); its modern association with ritualism and sacramentalism is a legacy of nineteenth-century terminology. Also see J. Spurr, '"Latitudinarianism" and the Restoration Church', *HJ*, 31 (1988); idem, 'Anglican Apologetic and the Restoration Church' (unpublished Oxford University D.Phil. thesis, 1985), pp. 314–15.

Tenison and the episcopal supporters of the Whig Junto, the High Church Tory divines also yearned for the lost harmony of church and state, when Moses and Aaron had cooperated in maintaining religious and social discipline, and the church ostensibly incorporated the whole nation. They believed that only the exaction of strict conformity from Anglican clergy and laity, and limiting the Dissenters to the strict letter of the Toleration Act, could prevent further religious anarchy and moral degeneration. While remaining true to her principles of loyalty and passive obedience, the national church should conduct her own affairs through Convocation and exercise her own discipline through the spiritual courts. It was her duty to preserve the priestly dignity, the Apostolical succession of the ministry, and order and decency in ritual. Such attitudes betray the growing influence of the Nonjurors on the High Church Anglican clergy. Forced out of the church by their own scruples about the oaths of allegiance to William and Mary, the Nonjurors had since busied themselves in creating a churchmanship to justify their separation. Nonjuring apologists like Charles Leslie, Henry Dodwell and George Hickes argued for a complete distinction between the spiritual and temporal powers, denying the right of secular rulers to depose bishops, and claiming for bishops an independent ecclesiastical jurisdiction in matters spiritual; in short, they developed the earlier, Cyprianic, notions of the role of the bishop into the foundation of the church's independence as a divine society – and then reintroduced these views into the Church of England.[15]

In 1701, when the Tories came to power, Convocation finally met and embarked upon a decade of guerrilla warfare against the bishops and the governments of the day. Although the 1701 Act of Settlement established that henceforth the monarch would be a communicant member of the Church of England, it could not guarantee that monarchs or their ministers would favour High Churchmen above moderates or even latitudinarians. So, throughout the reign of Queen Anne, the High Church party was at odds with the ruling ministries, crying that the church was 'in danger' whenever the Whigs were in power, and grumbling that too little was

15. See Rupp, *Religion in England*, ch. 1; H.D. Rack, ' "Christ's Kingdom Not of this World": The Case of Benjamin Hoadly versus William Law Reconsidered', *SCH*, 12 (1975), 277; J.C. Findon, 'The Nonjurors and the Church of England, 1689–1716' (unpublished Oxford University D.Phil. thesis, 1978), esp. pp. 92–4, 152–82; M. Goldie, 'The Nonjurors, Episcopacy, and the Origins of the Convocation Controversy', in *Ideology and Conspiracy: Aspects of Jacobitism 1689–1759*, ed. E. Cruickshanks (Edinburgh, 1982); R. Sharp, 'New Perspectives on the High Church Tradition: Historical Background 1730–80', in *Tradition Renewed*, ed. G. Rowell (1986).

being done to curb Dissent and reinvigorate the church under Tory governments. The High Churchmen demanded that the wings of Dissent should be clipped by legislation against occasional conformity – by which practice hypocritical Nonconformists qualified themselves for office – and against Dissenting schools and academies. Meanwhile the church should be restored to her glory days of the early 1680s. In 1710 Atterbury unveiled proposals to restore the authority of the church courts, give the bishops power to license all schools, tackle heresy with statutory censorship, protect clerical incomes, ease the creation of new parishes, and build new churches in the capital. But the High Church movement foundered on the shoals of Augustan party politics, and its only legacies were the Act for the Building of Fifty New Churches in London (1711) and an embittered parish clergy.

The nostalgic goals of the High Church party are easily summarized; but not so the aims of their allegedly 'Whig' and 'latitudinarian' opponents in the church. Their outlook has been characterized as a willingness to accept on the part of the church 'the place in English society of a basically voluntary body working within the legal conditions of the establishment' or, in other words, to recognize that religious pluralism was here to stay and the church's coercive machinery was gone for good.[16] But was this any more than an ability to make the best of the fluid political situation, where a partial victory for the church such as the Act of Settlement might be swiftly followed by a defeat, such as the Act of Union (which allowed Scotland to retain Presbyterianism and thus produced the anomaly of two established religions in one kingdom)? It was the clerical pragmatists, able to adapt to yet another change in dynasty, who won high office in the Hanoverian church, and who became, after the suppression of Convocation in 1717, the main voice of the Church of England.[17] These pragmatists should not, however, be mistaken for mere timeservers. Admittedly, they were Whig political appointees – preferment was closely controlled by Walpole's 'Pope', Bishop Gibson of London, and later by the Duke of Newcastle – and the bishops' parliamentary duties consumed much of their time and energy. Admittedly, no eighteenth-century bishop was going to assert the spiritual independence of his office. Yet few had any time for the blatant Erastianism of the notorious Bishop Hoadly. The principle of churchmen like Bishop Gibson was to maintain 'the Protestant succession, the church establishment,

---

16.   Bennett, 'Conflict in Church', p. 165.
17.   See P. Langford, 'Convocation and the Tory Clergy, 1717–61', in *Jacobite Challenge*, ed. E. Cruickshanks and J. Black (Edinburgh, 1988).

and the toleration; as wisely fixed and bounded at the Revolution'; Gibson was a keen enough defender of the church's rights and constitution to be lampooned as a successor to Laud, and in 1736 he finally broke with Walpole over the question of exempting Quakers from the tithe.[18] The episcopate as a whole has long since been acquitted of the charges of pastoral negligence, spiritual torpor, 'infidelity and secularity'.[19] Pragmatic and prosaic, the leaders of the eighteenth-century church increasingly set the tone for the lower clergy, and with Whig predominance ensured under the Hanoverians, the fire went out of clerical quarrels, rather as it did out of political life.[20]

'The eighteenth century witnessed a steady and progressive laicisation of religion, which is the keynote of its ecclesiastical development', wrote Dean Sykes, insisting that 'laicisation' rather than 'secularisation' was the most accurate description of this trend.[21] By the time of George III, the Church of England enjoyed a greater identity of interest and outlook with the politically powerful, landed classes than she had since before the Civil War.[22] The Georgian layman's interest and involvement in the church stands in marked contrast to the Restoration laity's suspicion and distance; but Restoration attitudes were a long time dying. The different forms of lay antipathy towards the clergy, church and organized Christianity each subsided at its own pace. The historian of atheism suggests that unbelief had its heyday in Restoration England and that it had dwindled by the mid-eighteenth century, while it is clear that Restoration 'wit' and debauchery went out of fashion even earlier.[23] Yet even under the Hanoverians, there was a constant sniping at 'priestcraft', principally by the deists, but also by those rational, moderate men, many of them Dissenters, who admired Locke's

18. See S. Taylor, 'Sir Robert Walpole, the Church of England, and the Quaker Tithe Bill of 1736', *HJ*, 28 (1985), 52.
19. See Sykes, *Church and State*, p. 413, and *passim*; A. Warne, *Church and Society in Eighteenth-century Devon* (1969), p. 34; E.A.O. Whiteman, 'The Church of England 1542–1837', *Victoria County History of Wiltshire*, 3 (1956), p. 50; Taylor, 'Walpole and Church'; F.C. Mather, 'Georgian Churchmanship Reconsidered: Some Variations in Anglican Worship 1714–1830', *JEH*, 36 (1985); M.G. Smith, *Fighting Joshua – A Study of the Career of Sir Jonathan Trelawney* (Redruth, 1985); W.M. Marshall, 'Episcopal Activity in the Hereford and Oxford Dioceses, 1660–1760', *Midland History*, 8 (1983).
20. But the eighteenth-century church was far from Erastian; see Sharp, 'New Perspectives on High Church', and P. Nockles, 'The Oxford Movement: Historical Background 1780–1833', in *Tradition Renewed*, ed. G. Rowell (1986).
21. Sykes, *Church and State*, p. 379.
22. Best, *Temporal Pillars*, p. 70.
23. D. Berman, *A History of Atheism in Britain* (1988), p. 48.

views on toleration and resented the 'absurdity and inconvenience and unreasonableness' of an established church.[24] A series of 'anti-clerical' measures on tithes, church rates and ecclesiastical courts were mooted in Parliament in the 1730s; and there were, of course, always plenty of parochial squabbles to remind the clergy that their authority was not unquestioned.[25] On the other hand, the eighteenth-century clergy enjoyed a developing material affinity with the English upper classes as the clerical profession slowly became more prosperous and attracted men of a higher social standing into its ranks. The growth of clerical prosperity occurred at a different rate for curates and for the dignified clergy, and for those beneficed in southern, central or northern England, but it was a discernible trend across the ministry. In a variety of ways, the eighteenth-century Church of England seems to have maintained her cultural and religious presence by accommodating herself to the prevailing concerns of the society of which she was a part. The fox-hunting, brandy-swigging 'squarson', indistinguishable in dress and manners from other gentleman farmers, was a familiar figure in the provinces.[26] Other clerics were at home in the 'polite and commercial' world of the metropolis and the provincial towns. They were just as susceptible as their congregations to the new fashions and fads, just as anxious to be thought 'rational', just as eager to partake in the new cult of the polite, with its values of sociability, benevolence and good conversation, and just as suspicious of anything that smacked of 'enthusiasm'.

In the increasingly sophisticated worlds of the gentry, the mercantile elites, the provincial towns and the cities, religious duties, sermon-tasting and church-visiting took their place as leisure activities alongside coffee-houses, political clubs, self-improving societies, newspapers, plays and taverns. While the authors of polite literature sought to form taste and mould lay conduct, scientists and philosophers were making the intellectual running. The clergy attempted, often with real success, to embrace science, philosophy and 'reason' within their Christian outlook. Their interest in natural theology was complemented by Newtonian science, which they in turn popularized through the Boyle Lectures. The clergy's rationalism was demonstrated to good effect by their refutation of deism, which never recovered from Bishop Butler's rational demonstration

24. See *Diary of Dudley Ryder*, pp. 210, 172, 82.
25. Taylor, 'Walpole and Church'; Clark, 'Confessional State', 467–74
26. See Virgin, *Church in Age of Negligence*, pp. 70–4; J.H. Pruett, *The Parish Clergy Under the Later Stuarts – The Leicestershire Experience* (Urbana, Illinois, 1978), p. 156; Best, *Temporal Pillars*, chs 2, 4; E.J. Evans, 'The Anglican Clergy of Northern England', in *Britain in the First Age of Party*, ed. C. Jones (1987), p. 230.

that natural religion was as full of doubt as was revealed religion. The churchmen resolutely refused to concede the weapon of reason to their opponents, arguing, as they always had, that Christianity and the Church of England could commend themselves on grounds of rationality. It seems likely that this Anglican rationalism was one reason why the English Enlightenment – unlike that of other countries – could pursue 'enlightened' goals within, rather than in opposition to, organized religion and piety.[27]

Occasionally, the churchmen overreached themselves in trying to reconcile revealed religion and reason, as they did during the trinitarian controversy of the 1690s and 1700s. In 1689, Arthur Bury, rector of Exeter College, Oxford, published *The Naked Gospel*, an unequivocal statement that Arian opinions of the person of Christ were sufficient to salvation. Bury had hoped to contribute to Convocation's discussion of comprehension, but he had clearly misjudged his brethren – amid howls of protest, his opinions were condemned and his book burnt by the University of Oxford, and a war of words was unleashed. Casting caution and Restoration practice to the winds, the church broke ranks and succumbed to a bout of fratricidal controversy which exposed the divergent trinitarian thinking among the churchmen: William Sherlock was accused of tritheism by Robert South, and replied with a charge of Sabellianism, while 'Stephen Nye scattered his fire, charging South as a Socinian, Wallis as a Sabellian, Sherlock as a tritheist, and even including Cudworth and Hooker among the heretics.[28] Despite a royal prohibition of further debate, the controversy rumbled on to claim more victims: in 1710 William Whiston lost his Cambridge Chair of Mathematics on account of his Arianism; and in 1714 Samuel Clarke, rector of St James's, Westminster, was disciplined by Convocation for his *Scripture Doctrine of the Trinity* (1712), which had conclusively shown that no theory of the trinity had scriptural support.[29] Thereafter the controversy died down, but the church had been left in disarray, and doubts about the doctrine of the trinity would surface again among her clergy. It was anti-trinitarianism of various sorts which lay behind the Anglican campaign of the 1770s for a relaxation of the terms of subscription to the Prayer Book and the Thirty-Nine Articles.

The eighteenth-century Anglican clergy's growing affinity with

27. See R.S. Porter, 'The Enlightenment in England', in *Enlightenment in National Context*, ed. R.S. Porter and M. Teich (1981).
28. Rupp, *Religion in England*, p. 248; also see R.N. Stromberg, *Religious Liberalism in Eighteenth-century England* (1954), ch. 4.
29. Stromberg, *Religious Liberalism*, pp. 42–4; M.R. Watts, *The Dissenters* (Oxford, 1978), pp. 372–3.

many sections of the English laity doubtless had some connection with the style and substance of their ministry. 'The predominant tone' of their sermons 'was that of moderation, and their content was rational and ethical rather than emotional, dogmatic, or mystical'.[30] The clergy got on with their jobs in a passably efficient way, generally not treading on lay toes by either an excess of zeal or a striking negligence; they preached a gospel which was practical if a little prosaic; and they displayed a degree of pastoral enterprise in the field of catechetics and household piety.[31] The specifically Anglican piety envisaged by the Restoration churchmen does not seem to have taken root and flourished in the Augustan and Hanoverian church; by the later eighteenth century, daily service was rare, while monthly communions were uncommon – a situation which has been attributed to the reluctance of the laity. The overall picture is one of great variety in liturgical practice. It has been established that a 'sacramental' piety, a 'High Church' piety as we might now call it, survived in pockets, where it often had an invigorating local influence.[32] These were the exceptions, however; the tenor of the age and the desires of the laity tended towards the dilution of ritual and the informality of worship.

A minor but revealing instance of this laicization of church life was the increasing use of cathedrals and churches for the public performance of secular music; new events like the Three Choirs Festival, founded in about 1718, suggest that the church was coming to play a part in the cultural life as much as the sacramental life of the laity. Lay membership of the various reforming, educative and devotional societies also suggests a trend towards the laicization of church life. The Religious Societies, which were principally lay Anglican devotional groups, and the Societies for the Reformation of Manners, which were non-denominational pressure groups goading the lay magistracy to the prosecution of vice and profanity, flourished from the 1690s until the 1730s. The Society for the Propagation of Christian Knowledge (founded in 1698), and its offshoot the charity school movement, sought to Christianize the English, while the Society for the Propagation of the Gospel (founded in

---

30. Sykes, *Church and State*, p. 283.
31. On institutional efficiency see Warne, *Devon*, ch. 5; Evans, 'Anglican Clergy of Northern England', pp. 236–8; M. Kinner, 'The Correction Court in the Diocese of Carlisle, 1704–1756', *Church History*, 59 (1990); and the forthcoming work of Jan Albers. Jeremy Gregory's forthcoming Oxford D.Phil. thesis indicates the clergy's pastoral enterprise in the diocese of Canterbury.
32. These comments draw heavily on Mather, 'Georgian Churchmanship'; also see Sharp, 'New Perspectives on High Church'; J. Wickham Legg, *English Church Life from the Restoration to the Tractarian Movement* (1914); Lowther Clarke, *Eighteenth Century Piety*.

1701) concentrated on spreading the message overseas. These voluntary initiatives represent the response of English Protestants, lay and clerical, Anglican and Dissenter, to the new situation of religious pluralism and liberty; and they hint at the growing irrelevance of the church's own institutional machinery of discipline. Moreover, as many have observed, those who governed eighteenth-century England often interpreted their duty to the church in terms of suppressing wickedness and vice rather than maintaining true religion and virtue.[33]

The Church of England's old foes no longer seemed as threatening as they had in the later seventeenth century. At the beginning of the eighteenth century, Defoe found Durham 'full of Roman Catholics who live peaceably and disturb nobody, and nobody them'; the nation's small, quiescent, seigneurial Roman Catholic community seems to have slowly grown from its Restoration figure of about 60,000 to perhaps 80,000 by the 1770s. But the practical toleration enjoyed by Catholics was always precarious: anti-popery was never far from the surface of political life; invasion scares and Jacobite risings led to harassment; and it was the suggestion of relief from the penal laws which provoked the Gordon riots of 1780. Meanwhile Protestant Dissent had its own troubles. Nonconformist attempts to cooperate and unite in the aftermath of the Toleration Act came to grief as theological disagreements forced the Dissenting denominations apart. Presbyterians suspected Independents of antinomianism and Independents accused Presbyterians of Arminianism; and, in 1719, a conference at Salters' Hall revealed that the Dissenting clergy were split down the middle over the same trinitarian questions which had recently caused such contention in the Church of England. The ground was set for the Presbyterians and General Baptists to move gradually towards Unitarianism and rationalism, leaving their former brethren far behind.[34] This theological reconfiguration of Dissent was accompanied by a startling numerical decline from approximately a third of a million in about 1720 to 250,000 or less thirty years later.[35] The decay of Dissent was spiritual too. There was a perceptible decline in zeal and relaxation of discipline as these originally dynamic 'sects' settled down into 'denominations' catering for the formal worship and religious preferences of predominantly urban and commercial congregations.[36]

33. See M.G. Smith, *Pastoral Discipline and the Church Courts* (Borthwick Papers, 62, York, 1982), pp. 8–11.
34. Watts, *Dissenters*, pp. 373–7, 464–78.
35. Ibid., pp. 267–76, 490–510.
36. Ibid., pp. 382–93; Wykes, 'Religious Dissent and Penal Laws'; A.D. Gilbert, *Religion and Society in Industrial England: Church, Chapel and Social Change 1740–1914* (1976).

In the 1730s and 1740s churchmen exulted that the numbers of Dissenters in their parishes had 'of late years considerably decreased', while Dissenting clergy and students conformed to and then ascended within the Church of England. The next threat to the church was to arise from among her own ranks.

The Evangelical Revival began in the 1730s as a reversion within the Church of England to Reformation theology and piety.[37] A number of 'awakened' clergy who had experienced 'conversion' sought to evangelize the nation by preaching of man's total depravity, justification by faith alone, the necessity of conversion, and the supremacy of scripture, all within an Augustinian or moderately Calvinist theology. Scattered in parts of Wales, Cornwall and Yorkshire, these Evangelical churchmen found no welcome from the bishops who were reluctant to prefer them to benefices or to ordain their sympathizers. Historically, they have been overshadowed by the followers of John Wesley and George Whitefield, who eventually seceded from the Church of England to form the Methodist church. But we should be wary of distinguishing Methodism as a separate denomination too early in its history; for much of the eighteenth century, it was unclear whether the Methodists were Dissenters or aberrant members of the Church of England. Evangelical churchmen tried to cooperate pastorally with peripatetic Methodist preachers; the autocratic Wesley, who found it impossible to repudiate the church of his youth, insisted that Methodist worship should not conflict with Anglican services; and Methodism won followers from among Anglicans, Dissenters and the ungodly.[38]

The Evangelical Revival was one of the forces which would convulse the Church of England, and the whole political establishment, in the late eighteenth and early nineteenth centuries. The industrial revolution, a population explosion and urbanization were transforming society, and religion with it; Methodism was one beneficiary of these changes, and Roman Catholicism was another. The Catholic community was swollen, and its character changed, by Irish immigration in the 1790s, and inevitably the pressure began to grow for the repeal of the Test Acts.[39] Meanwhile the rural Church of England was being deserted – a group of Lincolnshire clergy reported that only a third of parishioners attended church in 1800,

---

37. The Revival had, of course, an important international context; see Rack, *Reasonable Enthusiast*, pp. 161–70; Watts, *Dissenters*, pp. 394–6.
38. See Rack, *Reasonable Enthusiast*, pp. 551–2; Warne, *Devon*, pp. 109–10, 126–7; Watts, *Dissenters*, pp. 442–7. J. Kent, *The Unacceptable Face* (1987), pp. 110–11, raises the possibility that the Revival was merely a rearrangement of the existing religious subcultures.
39. See Kent, *Unacceptable Face*, pp. 127–8, 158–61.

while the number of communicants in Oxfordshire may have fallen by 25 per cent between 1738 and 1802.[40] Towards the end of the century, the clamour for the abolition of the Tests and lifting of civil disabilities from non-Anglicans grew steadily louder. But in the age of the American and French Revolutions, such campaigns were almost bound to provoke a Tory Anglican backlash. 'Church and King' mobs tore down Nonconformist meeting houses; Edmund Burke reminded the nation that 'in a Christian commonwealth the church and the state are one and the same thing, being different integral parts of the whole'; Bishop Horsley of St Asaph tarred Methodists as 'Jacobins' and proclaimed that 'the principles of a Nonconformist in religion and a republican in politics are inseparably united'. Horsley was a spokesman for the 'Hackney Phalanx', a 'High Church' pressure group of laymen and clerics which attempted to 'educate the poor in the principles of the established church' and which, during Lord Liverpool's ministry, exercised considerable influence on church preferment and won funds for building new churches. At the same time, on the other side of London, around Clapham Common, lived the upper middle-class laymen whose support for the Evangelical party made the first decades of the nineteenth century the golden age of the Evangelical wing of the church. The 'Clapham sect' threw themselves into the reformation of manners, the abolition of the slave trade, and numerous missionary societies.

Such energetic lay participation in the life and work of the church could not disguise the fact that the church was approaching a crisis. Just as reform of the constitutional and electoral arrangements of the old political order was overdue, so too was reform of the Church of England's finances and administration. The problems of pluralism, inadequate stipends, insufficient churches, and all the other inequalities and anomalies which had dogged the church since the sixteenth century could only be resolved by Parliament. Finally, in the 1830s, the hierarchy grasped the nettle, and acceded to the commissions of inquiry which began to overhaul the church. So while the constitutional revolution of 1828–32 was weakening the connection between church and state by sweeping away the Test and Corporation Acts and emancipating Roman Catholics, Parliament was also busy restructuring the church. Such lay interference smacked of Erastianism to some churchmen; and some form of clerical reaction was predictable. It finally came in 1833, when, in an assize sermon at Oxford, John Keble denounced the government's

---

40. Rack, *Reasonable Enthusiast*, p. 319; Gilbert, *Religion and Society*, p. 71.

proposal to suppress ten Irish bishoprics as 'national apostasy'. The Oxford Movement had been born.

Unlike the High Church lobby or the Evangelical tendency, the Oxford Movement was, from the start, an organized party, with a base in Oxford, a mouthpiece in the *Tracts*, and a leader in J.H. Newman; and although the movement had reached its zenith by the late 1830s, just before Newman and others seceded to the Church of Rome, its repercussions on the Church of England have been immense. The Catholic revival precipitated the fragmentation of the Church of England: 'the Church of England seemed to dissolve into its constituents and ecclesiastical parties began to take their identity more from the particular insight or emphasis that they had contributed to the common vision, than from that comprehensive vision itself. Each tended to absolutise aspects of the total inheritance that had until now formed the ingredients of a synthesis.'[41] This hardening of the church into antagonistic, and mutually uncomprehending, parties was, at least in part, a result of the Tractarians' avowed intention to 'unprotestantize' the Church of England, to undo the Reformation, and to return to the Apostolical faith: Newman aimed at nothing less than 'a second Reformation: – a better reformation, for it would be a return, not to the sixteenth century, but to the seventeenth'.[42] Paradoxically, the Anglo-Catholic 'rediscovery' of the seventeenth-century Church of England put paid to the seventeenth century's ideal of a single Anglicanism and a national episcopal Church of England. From the 1830s, the Church of England's history becomes a story of sectarian fragmentation, of adapting to modern, primarily secular, thought, of coming to terms with the slow but irresistible decay of institutional Christianity, and of the emergence of a corresponding ecumenical impulse. The problems and preoccupations of the Restoration Church of England have been left far behind. To all intents and purposes, our story comes to an end with the controversies of the early nineteenth century.

The world of the Restoration Church of England is obscured from our view by the events of the intervening three centuries and by the use made of the Restoration church in those centuries. Just as no period of the church's history is truly discrete or self-contained, so no period is proof against later interpretation and portrayal. After 1689, the Restoration church acquired new lustre from a comparison with the divided and disheartened Augustan and Hanoverian church. The Restoration church was mined for her apologetical riches: new

41. P.D.L. Avis, *Anglicanism and the Christian Church* (Edinburgh, 1989), p. 158.
42. J.H. Newman, *Apologia pro vita sua*, ed. M.J. Svaglic (Oxford, 1967), p. 50.

folio editions of the *Cases to Recover Dissenters* appeared in 1694, 1698 and 1718;[43] while in 1738 Bishop Gibson published *A Preservative Against Popery* in three folio volumes drawn from Restoration polemic against Rome – a work which was reissued with supplements in eighteen volumes in 1848–9. Others were eager less to celebrate the Restoration as a golden age for the Church of England than to subject the period to partisan reinterpretation. The Nonjurors, for instance, sought evidence of a deep-laid plot among the Restoration clergy to betray the church. In 1695, the Nonjuror George Hickes accused Gilbert Burnet of misrepresenting Luther in his *History of the Reformation* 'to serve the popular design of comprehension . . . to the endangering of everything that hath been received for catholic and fundamental in Christianity in the purest ages of the church'; John Tillotson was charged with pandering to atheism, deism and Socinianism, and promoting 'treaties of comprehension with Dissenters upon such terms as are not consistent with the catholic and apostolic tradition concerning episcopacy and episcopal ordinations'.[44] These accusations of betraying the church would scarcely have been possible before 1689; they would have been suppressed, as were the similar charges made by Parker and Lowth, in order to preserve the façade of Anglican unity, a façade which had to be maintained not least because the Restoration church's view of episcopacy was still deeply ambiguous.[45] From other ideological directions came the partisan historical accounts of *Reliquiae Baxterianae* (1696) and Burnet's *History of My Own Time* (1724–34). The effect of these narratives was to read later divisions back into the Restoration, to see the Restoration Church of England as divided between contending High Church and latitudinarian parties, when, as we have seen, for all its tensions, the Restoration church strove to create and maintain a clerical consensus.

Partisan misrepresentation of the Restoration church was obviously pernicious; more subtle, but equally harmful, was the curious alchemy by which Restoration churchmanship was transmuted into something far more acceptable to enlightened England. Here again we encounter the 'laicization' of the church and of English religious life in the eighteenth century. Polite culture, and especially polite literature, had come to rival the sermon and the religious tract as a shaper of lay opinion and conduct; there could be no doubting that,

43. The *Cases* were also 'digested' into one volume, *An Answer to the Dissenters Plea for Separation* (Cambridge, 1700), by Thomas Bennet.
44. George Hickes, *Some Discourses upon Dr Burnet and Dr Tillotson* (1695), pp. 21–2, 65.
45. See Findon, 'Nonjurors and Church', pp. 159–60; J.T. Spivey, 'Middle Way Men, Edmund Calamy and the Crisis of Moderate Nonconformity 1688–1732' (unpublished Oxford University D.Phil. thesis, 1986), ch. 7.

for many Englishmen, Mr Spectator, for example, exercised a moral influence on a par with that of their own parson. *The Spectator* recorded that Sir Roger de Coverley's chaplain preached from the published sermons of Bull, South, Sanderson, Barrow and Tillotson, as well as those of younger authors. This was not simply a reflection of contemporary taste in sermons, it was also a positive recommendation of these sermons by that great opinion-former *The Spectator*.[46] Moreover, periodicals like *The Spectator* did not just offer guidance on what to read, but on how to read it. They helped to create the intellectual context in which Restoration sermons were read in the eighteenth century; a context which differed markedly from that in which they had been first preached and which inevitably wrenched their theological teaching out of shape.

This process is visible in the diary of Dudley Ryder, who deliberately read *The Tatler* and *The Spectator* 'to improve my style and manner of thinking' and who was a keen critic of sermons at church and meeting house. Among his diary entries are:

> Read part of a sermon by Tillotson. I am more and more pleased with his manner of writing. I am only vexed with myself that what I hear or read in the way of religion has no more effect upon my life to assist my conduct, teach me to govern my passions, conquer my unruly inclinations and live by the rule of reason.

> Reading Tillotson's sermon about regeneration, it put me in mind of the advantage of a good and sober education. I don't know but the religion of people and their sobriety is much more owing to that than anything of their own reason.[47]

To reduce the regeneration of sinners to an effect of their upbringing in this manner was a far cry from Tillotson's intentions; other readers, however, took his intended message to heart. On the evening of 8 October 1756, Thomas Turner

> read one of Tillotson's sermons and which I think a very good one. Oh! may the God of all goodness give me the grace to mind what I read, that the same may sink deep into my heart and mind, and that I may every day become a better Christian. Oh! how weak and feeble are my best resolutions .... Daily and hourly do I sin, my own righteousness being but filthy rags ... and may the God of all goodness pour into my heart his holy spirit that I may

46. *The Spectator*, ed. D.F. Bond (Oxford, 1965), I, 144–2 (2 July 1711).
47. *Diary of Dudley Ryder*, pp. 117, 219, 293; but also see pp. 275, 351, 358, 362.

live by faith and not rely on my own works, which are vain, and that I may work out my own salvation with fear and trembling.[48]

In the eighteenth century there was a vogue for the sermons of 'the immortal Tillotson' (as Samuel Wesley described him), 'the most eminent and useful author of the age we live in', according to *The Tatler*; Thomas Turner, who read his entire sermons at least twice, commented, 'so far as I am a judge I think them to be a complete body of divinity, they being wrote in a plain familiar style, but far from what may be deemed low.'[49] It was the style of Tillotson's sermons, which read like the polite essays of the new journalists and moralists, that enabled avid readers like Turner to get through several at a sitting. For every reader like Turner, there were many more who heard, or indeed preached, an adulterated version of Tillotson's gospel. When 'adapted to the ears of rustic auditors' by plain country parsons, Tillotson's message of divine benevolence and of the present pleasure and future rewards of Christianity was too often sundered from his explanation of how rigorous holy living and the pursuit of Christian perfection transforms sinners and their notions of pleasure. As we have seen, this adulteration provoked no less a churchman than Bishop Gibson to protest against the misreading of Tillotson and other 'of our most eminent divines' of the Restoration.[50]

The reputation of the Restoration Church also suffered at the hands of the Evangelical Revival. Whitefield's denunciation of Tillotson as knowing no more of the gospel than Mahomet is but an extreme example of Evangelical disdain for the 'moralism' of the Restoration divines.[51] The first generation of Evangelicals and Methodists believed that they had virtually rediscovered the doctrine of justification by faith for themselves; and there can be no doubt that the Restoration church had played down the doctrine, preferring to hold faith and works in a fruitful tension as part of her soteriology. The soteriology of the Restoration churchmen was suspect in Evangelical eyes, and *The Whole Duty of Man* was the *bête noire* of many awakened Christians, despite abundant evidence that it had sparked the conversions of Methodists like Howell Harris and Evangelicals like Charles Simenon. A *New Whole Duty of Man* was

48. *The Diary of Thomas Turner*, ed. D. Vaisey (Oxford, 1984), p. 65.
49. Ibid., p. 125.
50. See *The Tatler*, ed. D.F. Bond (Oxford, 1987), II, 122; N. Sykes, *From Sheldon to Secker* (Cambridge, 1959), pp. 176–8; L.G. Locke, *Tillotson – A Study in Seventeenth-century Literature* (Anglistica 4, Copenhagen, 1954), chs. 4, 5; and for Gibson's protest, p. 296 above.
51. See Locke, *Tillotson*, p. 157; Rack, *Reasonable Enthusiast*, pp. 174, 278.

produced in the 1740s, with additional doctrinal matter, and in 1763 the Evangelical Henry Venn published *A Complete Duty of Man* to establish a 'proper foundation' of faith and grace in the Christian reader. But these works could not supersede the original, which Wesley defiantly republished in abridgement, and as late as 1837 Evangelicals are to be found pleading for the suppression of *The Whole Duty of Man*.[52] The Revival also raises a much larger question for the historian since the very notion of religious 'revival' or 'renewal', whether Evangelical in the 1730s or Catholic in the 1830s, inevitably prejudges the era preceding that revival. In fact, the Evangelical assumption that the Church of England had been sunk in spiritual lethargy and 'moralism' since the heroic age of mid-seventeenth-century puritanism was no more true than the Oxford Movement's claim that the church had been Erastian since 1688.

The Oxford Movement has long dictated modern perceptions of the seventeenth-century Church of England. Newman had written of the need to systematize the Church of England's inheritance: 'our champions and teachers have lived in stormy times: political and other influences have acted upon them variously in their day, and have since obstructed a careful consolidation of their judgments. We have a vast inheritance, but no inventory of our treasures. All is given in profusion; it remains for us to catalogue, sort, distribute, select, harmonize and complete.'[53] What such 'consolidation' might mean can be seen in Newman's sweeping claim to have followed 'Bramhall, then Laud, Field, Stillingfleet, Beveridge, and others of the same school'; or in his later reference to 'Anglicanism, the religion of Andrewes, Laud, Hammond, Butler and Wilson'.[54] But Newman does not bear the full responsibility for forming the Anglo-Catholic view of the seventeenth-century church. He came to the 'Caroline divines' by way of the Fathers, and what he valued in the seventeenth-century Anglicans was their patristic teaching and the support they offered his own views. In the 1820s, there were already signs of growing interest in the seventeenth century among High Churchmen, and it tended to be the High Churchmen in the Oxford Movement, men like Keble, Hook and Churton, to whom the notion of a *grand siècle* of Anglican theology was deeply attractive, who disseminated the notion of the 'Caroline divines'. By far the

---

52. See Watts, *Dissenters*, pp. 425–7; Carpenter, *Church and People*, pp. 225, 235; Rack, *Reasonable Enthusiast*, p. 22; Lowther Clarke, *Eighteenth Century Piety*, p. 144.

53. Newman, *Lectures on the Prophetical Office of the Church* (1837), pp. 29–30.

54. See T.M. Parker, 'The Rediscovery of the Fathers in the Seventeenth-century Anglican Tradition', in *The Rediscovery of Newman*, ed. J. Coulson and A.M. Allchin (1967), p. 32; Newman, *Lectures on Prophetical Office*, p. 21; cf. *Apologia pro vita sua*, p. 71.

most important agency for this view of the seventeenth-century church was the 'Library of Anglo-Catholic Theology', which reprinted 88 volumes of works by seventeenth-century Anglican divines between 1841 and 1863.[55] These volumes are indispensable to a study of the seventeenth-century Church of England, and their indispensability is in itself part of the problem they present: for, although the editorial rules were exemplary, the selection of authors and texts, the absence of historical contextualization in the form of introductions or notes, the fortuitous omission of certain works, and the frame of reference brought to bear – especially the assumption of the coherence of the notion of the 'Caroline divines' – has had a profound effect on how these seventeenth-century authors are read and understood. Where, for instance, are the works of William Sherlock, an author who was on the original list of candidates, who exemplifies the Anglo-Catholic approach in the Restoration church, and who has never been reprinted? Why does Herbert Thorndike receive such massive attention when his contorted writings were regarded with deep suspicion by contemporaries? More importantly, is it just to gather up Andrewes and Laud with Bull and Beveridge, Bramhall with the Nonjurors, as if the years and the cataclysmic events which separate them were of no account? Nor is the slight unease with which any student of the Restoration church approaches these volumes diminished by other Tractarian uses of the sixteenth- and seventeenth-century church; for instance, Keble's rather desperate attempts, in the introduction to his edition of Richard Hooker's *Laws of Ecclesiastical Polity*, to force Hooker into the mould of Tractarian episcopalianism.[56]

This temptation to anachronistic readings of the Stuart church has persisted into our own century – albeit in more subtle ways. In his article on the 'Caroline Divines' in Ollard and Crosse's *Dictionary of English Church History* (1912), W.H. Hutton claimed that 'the common bond which unites them [the Caroline divines] is a consciousness that the Catholicity rather than the Protestantism was the decisive feature of the English church'; Hutton emphasized their closeness to the Church of Rome, especially in their eucharistic thinking. But such magisterial assertions do not sit easily with the picture of the Restoration Church of England presented in this book; the Rome-centred conception of catholicity seems at odds with

---

55. Newman and Pusey were far more concerned with the 'Library of the Christian Fathers'; see S.L. Ollard, *A Short History of the Oxford Movement* (1915), pp. 209–11; F.L. Cross, *The Oxford Movement and the Seventeenth Century* (1933), pp. 7–14.

56. See editor's preface to *The Works of . . . Richard Hooker*, ed. J. Keble *et al.* (7th edn, Oxford, 1888); S.W. Sykes and S.W. Gilley, 'No Bishop. No Church!', in *Tradition Renewed*, ed. G. Rowell (1986), pp. 122–3.

the robust anti-Romanism and self-conscious 'Anglicanism' of the Restoration churchmen. P.E. More and F.L. Cross's *Anglicanism*, an SPCK volume of 1935, was designed 'to present the genius of Anglicanism as it found expression in the seventeenth century', but it wore its Anglo-Catholicism on its sleeve or, rather, on its title-page since Newman's *Lectures on the Prophetical Office* supplied the epigraph. More and Cross held the seventeenth century to run from 1594 to 1691, from Hooker to the Nonjurors, which was when 'first the Anglican communion was made aware of itself as an independent branch of the church universal, neither Roman nor Calvinist, but with a positive doctrine and discipline of its own and a definite mission in the wide economy of grace'.[57] On the other hand, modern theological imperatives are just as inescapable: some ecumenicals, for instance, have detected in the Church of England especial powers of reconciliation and synthesis; these powers are derived from an Anglican ecclesiology which locates the foundation of the church in holy baptism and the baptismal faith.[58]

The common strand of all such interpretations of the Church of England's history is the belief in an enduring quality called 'Anglicanism'. Some have discerned an 'Anglican principle' or 'spirit' at work in the seventeenth-century Church of England. This Anglicanism, it is said, is not a system, but an approach; the Church of England has no systematic theology, but a 'theological method'; Anglicanism is inherently pragmatic. I would not wish to dispute these theologically based judgements, but to the historian's eye, which tends to be focused on change, there seem to have been several 'Anglicanisms' across the centuries. The years between 1646 and 1689 saw the invention of one 'Anglicanism', which then formed a heritage to be reappropriated, cannibalized, or transformed into other 'Anglicanisms'. As a necessary consequence, the Anglicanism of the Restoration has been obscured by these later versions, but it is that Anglicanism, and the Church of England in which it was created, that are the subject of this book, and it is high time we returned to the subject.

The Restoration Church of England was a many-sided institution, a communion of overlapping interests and ambitions; she was the creation of her clergy and, to a lesser extent, of her laity; and the Anglicanism to which she gave birth was an amalgam of their preoccupations, aspirations and speculations.

57. P.E. More and F.L. Cross (eds), *Anglicanism* (1935), p. xix.
58. A modern ecumenical such as Dr Avis follows this Anglican thread from the work of F.D. Maurice and others back to Richard Hooker.

As we have seen, the Church of England was defined by her scholars, champions and teachers, by the eminent churchmen whose names still live, men like Henry Hammond, Jeremy Taylor, Edward Stillingfleet, Isaac Barrow, Robert South and John Tillotson. But the names that live on were not necessarily those most familiar to or most honoured by contemporaries: influential churchmen like Simon Patrick or Adam Littleton have been unduly neglected since the seventeenth century, while other churchmen, now lionized, were far from admired by contemporaries. The hard-headed Sheldon shed no tears over the death of Jeremy Taylor in 1667. 'I am glad he left no more trouble behind him, he was of a dangerous temper apt to break out into extravagancies, and I have had, till of late years, much to do with him to keep him in order, and to find diversions for him – now those fears are at an end.'[59]

Sheldon, too, was a creator of Restoration Anglicanism, even if he left only a single sermon in print, for his was a legacy of institutional recovery and political promotion. The Sheldonian Theatre and the Conventicle Acts were as much a part of the Restoration church as Stillingfleet's apologetics and Patrick's devotionals. So, too, was the great census of religious affiliation conducted by the energetic and efficient Bishop Compton in 1676. As John Evelyn had presciently remarked on hearing Compton preach at court in 1673, 'this worthy person's talent is not preaching; but he is like to make a grave and serious good man'.[60] There was room in the Restoration church for men of all talents and qualities.

While Compton and other dignitaries guided the political fortunes of the church, she was also sustained by the day-to-day preaching of obscure country parsons. All those unpublished, much repeated, derivative sermons on the fundamental duties and comforts of Christian belief, all those catechetical series on the Lord's Prayer, the creed and the sacraments – the sort of plain, practical preaching which Ralph Josselin described as 'my affectionate strivings to recover sinners out of Satan's and their hearts snare' – were the stuff of Restoration Anglicanism.[61] We are fortunate that we can leaf through John Evelyn's diary to gain an impression of what the layman might have heard from Restoration Anglican pulpits and of the message of repentance, piety and trust which he might have taken away from church. But the Restoration church did not live by preaching alone: the Book of Common Prayer was her staff both in adversity and in prosperity. Far from being a constant in English

---

59. MS Carte 45, fo. 222.
60. Evelyn, IV. 9.
61. Josselin, p. 558.

religious life, the Prayer Book's influence has ebbed and flowed across the centuries; during the Restoration, it was brought to a new prominence as the matrix of a pious life by Anglican devotional authors and preachers.

It would be unrealistic to expect a body such as the Restoration Church of England to think as one at all times and on all issues. The church contained a spectrum of opinion on the question of clerical conformity; as Francis Turner remarked, 'we have our enthusiasts too. Their [i.e., the Dissenters'] fanatics or weak judgements think our ceremonies unlawful, ours think them necessary.'[62] The associated problem of how to treat sober Dissenters was equally divisive; while some Anglican clergy rejoiced in the name of 'moderate' and sighed over the excesses of the persecuting zealots, others were convinced that the episcopal church was being undermined by such lax and hypocritical fifth columnists.[63] Opponents were quick to exploit the situation, as one churchman complained:

> Some are counted moderate men and friends to Dissenters, whilst others, that believe these to be schismatics, and the church to have given them no cause of displeasure, and therefore strictly observe the orders of the church, and seek to bring the Dissenters to repentance and a return to their duty, they are branded as popishly affected, persecutors and High Church men, are many ways rendered contemptible to the vulgar.[64]

More unusually in the seventeenth century, the English church allowed her clergy and her laymen a generous latitude in theological matters. This lack of interest in doctrinal uniformity and orthodoxy tended to dismay or baffle all of those, whether Nonconformists or not, brought up in and wedded to the Word-centred Reformed tradition. For instance, when Isaac Archer was examined before ordination by Dr Boldero, chaplain to Bishop Wren of Ely, two opposing conceptions of the church came into conflict. 'I told him that the witness of the Holy Ghost was the best argument to prove that the scriptures were God's Word,' recorded Archer, 'but he still urged me to tell him the argument, as he called it, at last I said the authority of the church was a good outward argument, when he told me it was the best argument, quoting St Augustine who said he would not believe the scriptures to be the scriptures except the church had said so'.[65] Even allowing for exaggeration, Boldero

62. MS Rawlinson Letters 99, fo. 104.
63. See Spurr, 'Anglican Apologetic', pp. 317–19.
64. Thomas Seymour, *Advice to Readers* (1682), pp. 122–3.
65. CUL, MS Add. 8499, fos 73–4.

represented a growing trend in the Church of England. Restoration churchmen found it increasingly difficult to disguise their conviction that the church and her sacraments were the surest, and possibly the only, path to salvation.

The church did not renounce her Protestantism, however; the churchmen were not prepared to concede their 'great contest' with Nonconformity about 'who stick closest to the interest of Protestant religion, and to the Reformation'.[66] As they repeatedly told the Roman Catholics when repudiating Rome's claim to decide on matters of faith: 'the truth is not built upon the church, but the church upon the truth'.[67] What makes a church truly Catholic is her profession of Apostolic doctrine. The Church of England could take a stand on 'scripture and the catholic consent of antiquity', on her own role as 'a witness and keeper of holy writ' and an upholder of the truth.[68] But as everyone knew – and some like Dr Boldero were apparently prepared to admit – the scriptural truth was not without its ambiguities. Scripture could not resolve many of the important incidental questions about church order, worship or even doctrine. Moreover, scripture was not enough to sustain an 'Anglican' identity for the Church of England. Created by royal fiat in the 1530s, the church had had an identity imposed upon her from without, when she became the territorial church of a godly Protestant prince. But in the seventeenth century, the ideal of a national church constituted by a godly prince was wearing dangerously thin. It was while defending their national church against Rome's overbearing claims, Presbyterian usurpation and sectarian anarchy that Anglican apologists argued for the autonomy of a national church under her own bishops and metropolitans. A principle of unity, an identity, had at last begun to emerge from within the church, rather than being imposed upon her. Obviously the principle of episcopal autonomy was in conflict with the idea of a national church – there was no *intrinsic* reason why bishops should be organized on national basis – and eventually this episcopalianism would challenge the principle of a national church. But during the Restoration, the Church of England managed to balance the ideals of a national and the Catholic church, to reconcile the principles of royal supremacy and episcopal authority.

In effect, Restoration Anglican ecclesiology retained both the Catholic and the Reformed models of a church rather than being

66. Henry Hesketh, *A Sermon, Preached ... September the 9th* (1684), p. 18.
67. John Sudbury, *A Sermon preached before the King* (1676), p. 21.
68. Edward Cardwell, *A History of Conferences and Other Proceedings Connected with Revision of the Book of Common Prayer* (3rd edn, Oxford, 1849), p. 338; Article 20; Patrick, VI, 475–6.

torn between the two. In the Anglican account of the constitution of a national church, the Catholic Church now became as important as the Word, and Apostolical continuity now began to balance the Apostolical faith. There is no denying that this balance was precarious and depended upon a broad degree of latitude allowed to churchmen and laity in their views of such potentially divisive matters as episcopacy. Yet a generous consensus based on the 'moderation' of the Church of England was in turn a sufficient basis for the adumbration of a distinct Anglicanism. Indeed, as each of the constituent parts fell into place, it reinforced the others. This process can be illustrated from the Anglican insistence on religious unity and uniformity. That all Christians should be members of their local church and that there could only be one church in one place were ecclesiological principles. As the clergy defended religious unity and uniformity, they inevitably argued for the authority of the bishops, for the beauty and utility of Common Prayer, and for the necessity of a worthy reception of the sacrament. And as they argued these points, they began to appreciate how a church could be constituted not only by doctrine, but also by her episcopal government and liturgy. The churchmen realized that not all religious truths could be expressed as intellectual propositions, for some were best expressed symbolically through worship and sacraments.

Although these are all shifts in a Catholic direction, the Church of England was a Reformed church; and her clergy exhibited the characteristics of a Protestant preaching ministry. Like other Protestant churches, she was committed to a rationalism which allowed her no room for manoeuvre against the rational objections of deism and atheism. Convinced that the English were caught up in some providential contest with God, the clergy struggled to reclaim the nation from error, vice and apathy. In response to past 'misuse' of the theology of grace and salvation, they refashioned theology to give practical support to human efforts and virtues. But while this practical theology broke with the older Calvinist-Arminian framework, it was not a repudiation of the Covenant of Grace, nor a renunciation of saving faith – it remained a distinctly Protestant account of the path to salvation. Restoration Anglican theology was complemented by the church's moral and reformist preaching and demanded a constant attention to the whole duty of man. The whole duty of man in turn required a life of pious devotion, a life of private prayer, public worship and reverent reception of the sacrament. Anglican theology and piety reflected popular distaste for enthusiasm and fanaticism, suspicion of speculation about predestination, and a preference for straight-forward practical duties; yet it would be a mistake to write this off as prudent social ethics or to overlook its context of strongly providential, reformist preaching against national vice and impiety. The Restoration clergy and their flocks lived in a puritan century, and the church propounded a severe regime of repentance, a demanding piety and a rigorous theology.

The purpose of all this preaching, teaching and controversy was the purpose of the Christian ministry through the ages: to unite the believer with his saviour. What the Restoration Church of England brought to this endeavour was a pronounced sense that this union was achieved through membership of the church and full participation in her life; that Christian communion begins with the church and ends in Christ, and 'the union of particular Christians to Christ is by means of their union to the Christian church'.[69] The union with Christ depended on the church, in the form of either the parish church with its common prayer, its sacraments and preaching; or the national church under the government of her bishops and prince; or the church purchased by Christ's blood, the church which 'cannot be preserved, much less promoted, but by a due regard to those who are over us in the Lord; and by adhering closely to such an authentic constitution as that of this church: which is the genuine offspring of the apostles; declaring nothing to the people but the true sense of the ancient apostolic church throughout the world. Which always had such governors of a superior order and degree to other ministers, as we have; such prayers, such hymns; in a word, such a face of religion as is here seen in this our Church of England.'[70]

69. William Sherlock, *A Discourse concerning the Knowledge of Jesus Christ* (1674), pp. 143–4; also see Edward Hyde, *Christ and His Church* (1658), p. 395; J. Spurr, 'Schism and the Restoration Church', *JEH*, 41 (1990), 422–3.
70. Patrick, IV, 767.

Select Bibliography

The select bibliography is intended as a guide to the principal materials used in the composition of this book. It would not be practical to list all of the sources consulted over a decade of research, nor indeed all of the primary and secondary sources cited above, but this bibliography indicates the wealth of material available.

Readers should note that, in order to save space, I have cited collected editions wherever possible: in the cases of *A Collection of Cases and other Discourses Written to Recover Dissenters to the Communion of the Church of England* and Edmund Gibson (ed.), *A Preservative against Popery*, this has had the unfortunate effect of obscuring the contribution of several Anglican authors, most notably, Michael Altham, William Cave, Robert Grove, Gregory Hascard, William Sherlock and John Williams. Those in search of further bibliographical guidance might consult various works listed under 'secondary sources', especially Wing's *Short-Title Catalogue*.

Whenever I have consulted and cited anything other than the first edition of a work, I give the date of the later edition after that of the first. All works were published in London unless otherwise stated.

Primary Sources

A Note on Manuscript Sources

References are given in the footnotes for all manuscript citations. The unpublished sources for the study of the Church of England and her clergy in the later seventeenth century are spread far and wide. Parish records, clerical diaries, letters, commonplace books, and notes of sermons heard or preached survive in abundance. Although some sources such as Richard Baxter's correspondence or Roger Morrice's 'Entring Books' (both in Dr Williams's Library) are well known to historians, others such as Isaac Archer's diary (Cambridge University Library, MS Add. 8499) have been little used. I have consulted and cited manuscript collections in several libraries and archives, including the Guildhall Library, London; Doctor Williams's Library, Gordon Square, London; Lambeth Palace Library; Cambridge University Library; Warwickshire County Record Office; Leicestershire County Record Office. The two most significant collections for the study of the Restoration church are those of the British Library and the Bodleian Library, Oxford. In the case of Archbishop Sheldon's letter books a single source has been split between these two libraries: Bodleian Library, MS Add. C 308 is the archbishop's letter book for 1664 to 1669 and British Library, MS Harleian 7377 is its successor; for further details see E.A.O. Whiteman, 'Two Letter Books of Archbishops Sheldon and Sancroft', *Bodleian Library Record*, 4 (1953). The British Library holdings include material on Anglicanism in the 1640s and 1650s (MS Harleian 6942, much of which was printed by Pocock) and the personal correspondence of William Sancroft (MSS Harleian 3783–5). White Kennett's commonplace book and correspondence (MSS Lansdowne 960 and 937) are helpful on clerical opinion in the 1680s. I have drawn most heavily upon the rich collections of the Bodleian Library. The Tanner Manuscripts must be at the heart of any study of this sort. Useful material is scattered throughout this diverse collection of documents and correspondence, much of which was gathered by Sheldon and Sancroft, but MSS Tanner 28–49, 51–9 are arranged chronologically and provide a virtual narrative for our period. The papers of the Duke of Ormonde (MS Carte 45), Lord Wharton (MSS Carte 77 and 81) and Francis Turner (MSS Rawlinson Letters 91–2) are illuminating in their different ways. Much miscellaneous information about churchmen and church affairs can be gained from MSS Add. C 302, 304, and the Rawlinson D, Eng Letters, Eng Th and Eng Misc collections.

Printed Sources

Sources are listed alphabetically by author, editor or title. Some documents dealing with a particular place, such as churchwardens' presentments or visitation records, are listed under that place.

T.A., *Religio clerici* (1681)

Lancelot Addison, *An Introduction to the Sacrament* (1682)

Lancelot Addison, *A Modest Plea for the Clergy* (1671)

Lancelot Addison, *The Primitive Institution* (1674)

Richard Allen, *Insulae fortunatae* (1675)

[Richard Allestree], *The Causes of the Decay of Christian Piety* (1667)

Richard Allestree, *Forty Sermons*, 2 vols (Oxford, 1684)

[Richard Allestree], *The Whole Duty of Man* (1658)

[Richard Allestree], *The Works of the Learned and Pious Author of the Whole Duty of Man* (Oxford, 1684)

John Allington, *The Reform'd Samaritan* (1678)

John Allington, *The Regal Proto-Martyr* (1672)

Vincent Alsop, *Anti-Sozzo* (1675)

Vincent Alsop, *Melius inquirendum* (1678)

Vincent Alsop, *The Mischief of Impositions* (1680)

An Answer to Two letters of T.B. By the Author of the Vindication of the Clergy (1673)

James Arderne, *Directions concerning the Matter and Stile of Sermons* (1671)

James Arderne, *A Sermon Preached at the Visitation* (1677)

George Ashwell, *De Socino et socinianismo dissertatio* (Oxford, 1680)

George Ashwell, *Fides apostolica* (Oxford, 1653)

William Assheton, *The Cases of Scandal and Persecution* (1674)

William Assheton, *The Danger of Hypocrisie* (1673)

William Assheton, *Toleration Disapprov'd and Condemn'd* (Oxford, 1670)

W.B., *Corporal Worship Discuss'd and Defended* (1670)

Edward Bagshaw, *A Brief Enquiry* (1662)

Peter Bales, *Infirmity Inducing to Conformity* (1650)

Matthew Barker, *The Faithful and Wise Servant* (1657)

Matthew Barker, *Natural Religion* (1674)

Clement Barksdale, *The Disputation at Winchcombe Nov. 9. MDCLIII* (Oxford, 1653)

Clement Barksdale, *The Kings Return* (1660)

Clement Barksdale, *A Sermon Preached upon the Fifth of November 1679* (Oxford, 1680)

Thomas Barlow, *Brutum fulmen* (1680)

Thomas Barlow, *The Genuine Remains of . . . Dr Thomas Barlow* (1693)

Thomas Barlow, *Several Cases of Conscience* (1692)

John Barnard, *Censura cleri, or, A Plea against Scandalous Ministers* (1660)

Miles Barne, *A Discourse concerning the Nature of Christ's Kingdom* (Cambridge, 1682)

Miles Barne, *A Sermon Preached before the King* (1675)

Miles Barne, *A Sermon Preach'd before the University of Cambridge on the 9th of September* (Cambridge, 1683)

John Barrett, *The Rector of Sutton Committed with the Dean of St Paul's* (1680)

Isaac Barrow, *The Theological Works*, ed. A. Napier, 9 vols (Cambridge, 1859)

Vestry Minutes of St Bartholomew Exchange, ed. E. Freshfield (1890)

J[ohn] B[artlett], *Directions for the Right Receiving of the Lords Supper* (1679)

John Barwick, *ΙΕΡΟΝΙΚΗΣ or the Fight, Victory and Triumph of St Paul* (1660)

Isaac Basire, *The Ancient Liberty of the Britannick Church* (1661; original Latin edn, Bruges, 1656)

The Correspondence of Isaac Basire, ed. W.N. Darnell (1831)

William Bates, *The Divinity of the Christian Religion* (1677)

Michael Batt, *A Sermon preached at Bury St Edmunds . . . at the Primary Visitation* (1686)

[Richard Baxter], *The Nonconformists Plea for Peace* (2 parts, 1679, 1680)

Richard Baxter, *Reliquiae Baxterianae*, ed. M. Sylvester (1696)

Richard Baxter, *Richard Baxters Answer to Dr Edward Stillingfleet's Charge of Separation* (1680)

Richard Baxter, *Sacrilegious Desertion of the Holy Ministry Rebuked* (1672)

Aphra Behn, *The Uncollected Verse of Aphra Behn*, ed. G. Greer (Stump Cross, Essex, 1989)

[Edward Bernard], *Private Devotion* (Oxford, 1689)

Nicholas Bernard, *Devotions of the Ancient Church* (1660)

William Beveridge, *The Theological Works of William Beveridge*, 12 vols (LACT, Oxford, 1842–8)

Thomas Bilson, *The Perpetual Government of Christ's Church* (1593; Oxford, 1842)

Thomas Birch, *The Life of the Most Reverend John Tillotson* (2nd edn, 1753)

Nathaniel Bisbie, *The Bishop Visiting* (1686)

Nathaniel Bisbie, *The Modern Pharisees* (1683)

Nathaniel Bisbie, *Prosecution no Persecution* (1682)

Zachary Bogan, *A Help to Prayer both Extempore and by a Set Forme* (1660)

Edmund Bohun, *The Diary and Autobiography of Edmund Bohun*, ed. S.W. Rix (Beccles, 1853)

Samuel Bolde, *A Plea for Moderation towards Dissenters* (1682)

Samuel Bolde, *A Sermon Against Persecution. Preached March 26* (1682)

William Bolton, *Core redivivus* (1684)

Joshua Bonhome, *The Arraignment and Conviction of Atheism* (1679)

Joshua Bonhome, *A New Constellation* (1675)

Robert Boreman, *Paideia-Thriambas. The Triumph of Learning over Ignorance* (1653)

Edward Boughen, *A Short Exposition of the Catechism of the Church of England* (1646; 1673)

Thomas Bradley, *Comfort from the Cradle* (Oxford, 1650)

Thomas Bradley, *A Sermon ad clerum* (York, 1663)

John Bramhall, *The Works of the Most Reverend Father in God, John Bramhall*, 5 vols (LACT, Oxford, 1842)

Sir John Bramston, *Autobiography*, ed. Lord Braybrooke (Camden Society, 32, 1845)

Daniel Brevint, *The Christian Sacrament and Sacrifice* (Oxford, 1673)

Francis Bridge, *A Sermon Preached before the . . . Lord Mayor . . . 5 November 1684* (1685)

George Bright, *A Treatise of Prayer* (1678)

Philip Browne, *The Observation of Holy Days Justified* (1684)

Philip Browne, *The Sovereign's Authority, and the Subject's Duty* (1682)

Matthew Bryan, *A Perswasive To the Stricter Observation of the Lords Day* (1686)

Episcopal Visitation Book for the Archdeaconry of Buckinghamshire 1662, ed. E.R.C. Brinkworth (Buckinghamshire Record Society, 7, 1947)

George Bull, *Apologia* (1676) LACT, Oxford, 1844)

George Bull, *Examen censurae* (1676; LACT, Oxford, 1844)

George Bull, *Harmonia apostolica* (1669; LACT, Oxford, 1844)

Richard Burd, *A Sermon Preached . . . May 29. 1684* (1684)

Gilbert Burnet, *A History of My Own Time*, ed. M.J. Routh, 6 vols (Oxford, 1833)

Gilbert Burnet, *A History of My Own Time*, ed. O. Airy, 2 vols (Oxford, 1897–1900)

Gilbert Burnet, *A Supplement to Burnet's History of My Own Time*, ed. H.C. Foxcroft (Oxford, 1902)

Gilbert Burnet, *A Modest Survey* (1676)

Gilbert Burnet, *Some Passages of the Life and Death of the Right Honourable John, Earl of Rochester* (1680)

Gilbert Burnet, *Some Unpublished Letters of Gilbert Burnet*, ed. H.C. Foxcroft (Camden Society, 11, 1907)

Gilbert Burnet, *A Vindication of the Ordinations of the Church of England* (1677)

Hezekiah Burton, *Several Discourses*, 2 vols (1684–5)

Arthur Bury, *The Bow* (1662)

Arthur Bury, *The Constant Communicant* (1681)

Seth Bushell, *A Warning-Piece for the Unruly* (1673)

Samuel Butler, *Prose Observations*, ed. H. De Quehen (Oxford, 1979)

Benjamin Calamy, *Sermons Preached upon Several Occasions* (1687)

Calendar of the State Papers Domestic, Charles II, ed. M.A.E. Green *et al.* (HMSO, 1860–1938)

Calendar of the State Papers Domestic, James II, no editor (HMSO, 1960–77)

Episcopal Visitation Returns for Cambridgeshire, ed. W.M. Palmer (Cambridge, 1930)

Edward Cardwell (ed.), *Documentary Annals of the Reformed Church of England 1546–1717*, 2 vols (2nd edn, Oxford, 1844)

Edward Cardwell, *A History of Conferences and Other Proceedings Connected with the Revision of the Book of Common Prayer* (3rd edn, Oxford, 1849)

Alan Carr, *A Peaceable Moderator* (1665)

Thomas Carter, *Non-Conformists No Schismaticks, No Rebels* (1670)

Meric Casuabon, *Of Credulity and Incredulity; In Things Divine* (1670)

A Catalogue of the Discourses for and against Popery, ed. T. Jones, 2 vols (Chetham Society, 48 and 64, 1859 and 1865)

John Cave, *A Sermon Preached in a Country-Audience . . . January 30* (1679)

William Cave, *Antiquitates Christianae* (1675)

William Cave, *A Dissertation Concerning the Government of the Ancient Church* (1683)

William Cave, *Primitive Christianity* (1673)

Zachary Cawdrey, *A Discourse of Patronage* (1675)

Zachary Cawdrey, *A Preparation for Martyrdom* (1681)

Certain Considerations Tending to Promote Peace (1674)

The Character of a Town Gallant (1680)

Stephen Charnock, *Works*, 2 vols (1684)

J[ohn] C[heney], *The Conforming Nonconformist* (1680)

Churchwardens' Presentments: I Archdeaconry of Chichester, ed. H. Johnstone (Sussex Record Society, 49, 1947–8)

The Account Book of the Parish of St Christopher Le Stocks, ed. E. Freshfield (1895)

Nicholas Clagett, *A Sermon Preached at St Edmunds Bury . . . at the . . . Visitation* (1686)

William Clagett, *Eleven Sermons* (1693)

William Clagett, *The Present State of the Controversie* (1687)

[William Clagett], *A Reply to a Pamphlet called the Mischief of Impositions* (1681)

William Clagett, *Seventeen Sermons* (1689)

The Rector's Book, Clayworth, ed. H. Gill and E.L. Guilford (Nottingham, 1910)

A Collection of Cases and Other Discourses Written to Recover Dissenters to the Communion of the Church of England / By Some Divines of the City of London (issued separately in 1683, as a collection in 1685, and as a single folio volume in 1694; reprinted 1698)

A Collection of Private Forms of Prayer . . . By the Author of the Weeks Preparation (1690)

Thomas Comber, *The Autobiographies and Letters of Thomas Comber*, ed. C.E. Whiting, 2 vols (Surtees Society, 156 and 157, 1941 and 1942)

Thomas Comber, *The Church Catechism with a Brief and Easie Explanation* (1681)

Thomas Comber, *A Companion to the Temple* (1684)

Thomas Comber, *The Plausible Arguments of a Romish Priest Answered* (1686)

Thomas Comber, *Religion and Loyalty* (1683)

Thomas Comber, *Short Discourses upon the Whole Common Prayer* (1684)

Henry Compton, *The Bishop of London's Eighth Letter to His Clergy* (1692)

Henry Compton, *Episcopalia* (1686)

John Conant, *Sermons* (1693)

Malachi Conant, *Urim and Thummim* (Oxford, 1669)

Concilia Magnae Britannae et Hiberniae, ed. D. Wilkins, 4 vols (1737)

Robert Conold, *The Notion of Schism Stated* (1676; 1677)

Records of the Northern Convocation (Surtees Society, 113, 1907)

John Copleston, *Moses next to God, and God next to Moses* (1661)

John Cosin, *The Works of the Right Reverend Father in God, John Cosin*, 4 vols (LACT, Oxford, 1843–51)

Zachary Cradock, *A Sermon Preached before the King* (1678)

Hugh Cressy, *Fanaticism Fanatically Imputed* (1672)

Samuel Crispe, *A Sermon Preach'd at the Primary Visitation* (1686)

Herbert Croft, *The Legacy of the Right Reverend Father in God, Herbert, Lord Bishop of Hereford* (1679)

[Herbert Croft], *The Naked Truth* (1675)

Herbert Croft, *A Short Discourse Concerning the Reading his Majesties Late Declaration* (1688)

[Sir Thomas Culpeper], *Essayes or Moral Discourses on Several Subjects* (1671)

The Diaries and Papers of Sir Edward Dering, ed. M.F. Bond (1976)

The Parliamentary Diary of Sir Edward Dering 1670–73, ed. B.D. Henning (New Haven and London, 1940)

Documents Relating to the Settlement of the Church of England by the Act of Uniformity of 1662, ed. George Gould (1862)

Henry Dodwell, *A Discourse concerning the One Altar and the One Priesthood* (1683)

Henry Dodwell, *Separation of Churches from Episcopal Government . . . proved Schismatical* (1679)

Domestick Devotions for the Use of Families and of Particular Persons (1683)

John Dryden, *Poems and Fables*, ed. J. Kinsley (Oxford, 1958)

James Duport, *Three Sermons preach'd in St Maries Church in Cambridge* (1676)

The Correspondence of Bishop Brian Duppa and Sir Justinian Isham 1650-1660, ed. G. Isham (Northamptonshire Record Society, 17, 1950–1)

Brian Duppa, *Holy Rules and Helps to Devotion, both in Prayer and Practice* (1675)

[Brian Duppa], *Private Forms of Prayer* (Oxford, 1645)

Durham Parish Books (Surtees Society, 84, 1888)

John Eachard, *The Grounds and Occasions of the Contempt of the Clergy* (1670)

John Eachard, *Mr Hobbs's State of Nature* (1672)

John Eachard, *Some Observations upon the Answer to an Enquiry* (1671)

Robert Elborough, *London's Calamity by Fire Bewailed and Improved* (1666)

Thomas Elborow, *The Reasonableness of Our Christian Service* (1677)

James Ellesby, *The Doctrine of Passive Obedience* (1685)

Clement Ellis, *The Gentile Sinner* (1661)

Clement Ellis, *The Scripture Catechist*, ed. J. Veneer (1738)

[Clement Ellis], *The Vanity of Scoffing* (1674)

Notes of the Episcopal Visitation of the Archdeaconry of Ely in 1685, ed. H.

Bradshaw (Cambridge Antiquarian Society Communications, 3, 1879)

[Edmund Elys], *Justifying Faith* (1679)

Notes on Visitations in the Archdeaconry of Essex, ed. W.J. Pressey, (Transactions of the Essex Archaeological Society, 19, 1930; 20, 1930–1; 21, 1933–4; 22, 1936–40; 23, 1942)

The Essex Correspondence, ed. C.E. Pike (Camden Society, 24, 1913)

George Etherege, *Letters of Sir George Etherege*, ed. F. Bracher (Berkeley, 1974)

John Evans, *Moderation Stated* (1682)

John Evelyn, *A Devotionarie Book of John Evelyn*, ed. W.H. Frere (1936)

John Evelyn, *The Diary of John Evelyn*, ed. E.S. de Beer, 5 vols (Oxford, 1952)

John Evelyn, *The History of Religion*, ed. R.M. Evanson, 2 vols (1850)

Fair-Warning (1663)

William Falkner, *Christian Loyalty* (1679)

William Falkner, *Libertas ecclesiastica* (1674)

Anthony Farindon, *The Sermons of the Rev. Anthony Farindon*, ed. J. Nichols, 4 vols (1849)

James Fawkett, *An Account of George Seignior* (1681)

Bishop Fell and Nonconformity: Visitation Documents from the Oxford Diocese, 1682–83, ed. M. Clapinson (Oxfordshire Record Society, 62, 1980)

John Fell, *The Character of the Last Daies* (Oxford, 1675)

[John Fell], *Of the Unity of the Church ... written ... by Cyprian Bishop of Carthage and Martyr* (Oxford, 1681)

John Fell, *A Sermon preached before the House of Peers on December 22 1680* (Oxford, 1680)

Henry Ferne, *Certain Considerations* (1653)

Henry Ferne, *A Compendious Discourse* (1655)

Henry Ferne, *Of the Division between the English and Romish Church upon the Reformation* (1652; 1655)

Thomas Fettiplace, *The Sinner's Tears* (1653)

Celia Fiennes, *The Journeys of Celia Fiennes*, ed. C. Morris (1947)

A Form of Prayer to be used on Wednesday November the Thirteenth (1678)

Edward Fowler, *The Design of Christianity* (1671)

Edward Fowler, *Dirt Wipt Off* (1672)

Edward Fowler, *A Discourse of Offences* (1683)

Edward Fowler, *Libertas evangelica* (1680)

Edward Fowler, *The Principles and Practices of Certain Moderate Divines of the Church of England* (1670)

Fragmentary Illustrations of the History of the Book of Common Prayer, ed. W. Jacobson (1847)

A Free and Impartial Inquiry into the Causes of that very great Esteem and Honour that the Nonconforming Preachers are generally in with their Followers (1673)

Samuel Freeman, *A Plain and Familiar Discourse* (1687)

Thomas Fuller, *The Collected Sermons of Thomas Fuller*, ed. J.E. Bailey and W.E.A. Axon, 2 vols (1891)

Francis Fullwood, *The Case of the Times* (1683)

Francis Fullwood, *The Necessity of Keeping Our Parish Churches* (1672)

Francis Fullwood, *Roma ruit* (1679; Oxford, 1847)

Francis Fullwood, *Toleration Not to be Abused* (1672)

Richard Gardiner, *XVI Sermons* (1659)

Samuel Gardner, *A Sermon Preached at the Visitation* (1672)

John Gaskarth, *A Sermon preached before the Right Reverend Father in God John [Lake], Lord Bishop of Bristol* (1685)

John Gauden, *Causa dei* (1659)

John Gauden, *Considerations touching the Liturgy of the Church of England* (1661)

John Gauden, *Ecclesiae Anglicanae suspiria* (1659)

·John Gauden, *Gods Great Demonstrations* (1660)

John Gauden, *Hieraspistes* (1653)

John Gauden, *A Petitionary Remonstrance* (1659)

John Gauden, *Slight Healings of Publique Hurts* (1660)

John Gauden, *Whole Duty of a Communicant* (2nd edn, 1685)

Edward Gee, *A Catalogue of all the Discourses* (1689)

Edward Gee, *Veteres vindicati* (1687)

Charles Gibbes, *XXXI Sermons* (1677)

Edmund Gibson, *The Bishop of London's Three Pastoral Letters* (1732)

Edmund Gibson (ed.), *A Preservative against Popery*, 3 vols (1738)

Joseph Glanvil, *An Earnest Invitation to the Sacrament of the Lord's Supper* (1673; 1674)

Joseph Glanvil, *Essays on Several Important Subjects in Philosophy and Religion* (1676)

Joseph Glanvil, *Some Discourses, Sermons and Remains* (1681)

Joseph Glanvil, *The Zealous, and Impartial Protestant* (1681)

Henry Glover, *An Exhortation to Prayer for Jerusalems Peace* (1663)

John Goodman, *The Interest of Divine Providence* (1683)

John Goodman, *The Old Religion* (1684)

John Goodman, *A Serious and Compassionate Inquiry* (1674; 1675)

John Goodman, *A Sermon Preached before the ... Mayor* (1685)

John Goodman, *A Visitation Sermon* (1677)

William Gould, *Conformity according to Canon Justified* (1674)

William Gould, *The Primitive Christian Justified* (1682)

Richard Gove, *The Saint's Honeycomb* (1652)

Denis Granville, *The Compleat Conformist* (1684)

Denis Granville, *The Remains of Denis Granville*, ed. G. Ornsby, 2 vols (Surtees Society, 37 and 47, 1860 and 1865)

John Gratton, *A Journal of the Life of that Ancient Servant of Christ, John Gratton* (1720)

Robert Grove, *A Short Defence of the Church and Clergy of England* (1681)

Robert Grove, *A Vindication of the Conforming Clergy* (1676)

Peter Gunning, *Lex talionis* (1676)

Peter Gunning, *The Paschal Fast* (1662)

John Hacket, *A Century of Sermons* (1675)

John Hacket, *A Sermon Preached before the Kings Majesty [22 March 1660–1]* (1660)

George Hall, *A Fast Sermon, Preached to the Lords* (1666)

George Hall, *God Appearing for the Tribe of Levi* (1655)

Joseph Hall, *The Works of Joseph Hall D.D.*, ed. P. Wynter, 10 vols (Oxford, 1863)

Henry Hammond, *Of the Daily Practice of Devotion* (1660; 1684) [*Spiritual Sacrifice* (1676), Wing S5001, is the same work]

Henry Hammond, *Nineteen Letters of the Truly Reverend and Learned Henry Hammond*, ed. F. Peck (1739)

Henry Hammond, *The Works*, ed. W. Fulman, 4 vols (1684)

Robert Hancocke, *A Sermon preached before the ... Lord Mayor* (1680)

Nathaniel Hardy, *The Apostolical Liturgy Revived* (1661)

Nathaniel Hardy, *The Hierarchy Exalted and Its Enemies Humbled* (1661)

Nathaniel Hardy, *Lamentation, Mourning and Woe* (1666)

Nathaniel Hardy, *A Loud Call* (1668)

Nathaniel Hardy, *The Royal Commonwealthsman* (1668)

Nathaniel Hardy, *A Sad Prognostick* (1658)

James Harwood, *A Plea for the Common Prayer Book* (1657)

Gregory Hascard, *A Sermon preached upon the Fifth of November, 1678* (1678)

Roger Hayward, *A Sermon Preached before the King* (1676)

Roger Hayward, *A Sermon Preacht before the King* (1673)

Matthew Henry, *The Life of the Rev. Philip Henry*, ed. J.B. Williams (1825)

George Herbert, *A Priest to the Temple*, ed. Barnabas Oley (1671)

Henry Hesketh, *A Sermon, Preached... On September the 9th* (1684)

Henry Hesketh, *A Sermon Preached... 26 July 1685* (1685)

Henry Hesketh, *A Sermon Preached... September the 2nd 1682* (1682)

John Hewitt, *Prayers of Intercession for their Use who Mourn in Secret* (1659)

John Hewitt, *Repentance and Conversion the Fabrick of Salvation* (1658)

Peter Heylyn, *Certamen epistolare* (1658)

Peter Heylyn, *Cyprianus Anglicus* (1668)

Peter Heylyn, *Ecclesia restaurata* (1661)

Peter Heylyn, *Ecclesia vindicata* (1657)

Peter Heylyn, *Historia quinqu-articularis* (1660)

Peter Heylyn, *A Sermon preached... May 29th 1661* (1661)

Oliver Heywood, see Joseph Hunter, *The Rise of the Old Dissent Exemplified in the Life of Oliver Heywood* (1842)

Edmund Hickeringill, *The Horrid Sin of Man-Catching* (1680)

George Hickes, *A Sermon Preached before the Lord Mayor... 30th of January 1681/2* (1683)

George Hickes, *Some Discourses upon Dr Burnet and Dr Tillotson* (1695)

George Hickes, *The Spirit of Enthusiasm Exorcized* (1680)

George Hickes, *The True Notion of Persecution Stated* (1681)

[Henry Hickman], *Plus ultra* (1661)

[Henry Hickman], *Speculum Sherlockianum* (1674)

Samuel Hill, *The Catholic Balance* (1687)

[Samuel Hill], *The Necessity of Heresies Asserted and Explained* (1688)

Samuel Hinde, *Englands Prospective-Glasse* (1663)

Historical Manuscripts Commission:
8th Report, part 1, appendix, House of Lords MSS
9th Report, part 2, appendix, House of Lords MSS
11th Report, appendix 2, House of Lords MSS
12th Report, appendix 7, Le Fleming MSS
13th Report, appendix 2, Portland II, Harley MSS
14th Report, appendix 2, Portland III, Harley MSS
15th Report, appendix 4, Portland VIII, Harley MSS
Ormonde MSS, new series, III–VII
Finch MSS, I–II

Thomas Hodges, *The Necessity, Dignity and Duty of Gospel Ministers* (1685)

Thomas Hodges, *A Scripture Catechisme* (Oxford, 1658)

Thomas Hodges, *Sions Halelujah* (1660)

Henry Holden, *The Analysis of Divine Faith* (Paris, 1658)

Richard Hollingworth, *An Account of the Penitence of John Marketman* (1680)

Richard Hollingworth, *Christian Principles* (1681)

Richard Hollingworth, *A Modest Plea for the Church of England* (1676)

Richard Hooker, *The Works*, ed. J. Keble et al. (7th edn, Oxford, 1888)

Thomas Horne, *A Sermon Preached* (1685)

Anthony Horneck, *The Crucified Jesus* (1686)

Anthony Horneck, *The Fire of the Altar* (1683)

Anthony Horneck, *The First Fruits of Reason* (1686)

Anthony Horneck, *The Great Law of Consideration* (1677)

Anthony Horneck, *The Happy Ascetick* (1681)

[John Howe], *An Answer to Dr Stillingfleets Mischief of Separation* (1680)

William Howell, *The Common Prayer Book the Best Companion in the House and Closet as well as in the Temple* (1687)

[William Howell], *Prayers in the Closet* (Oxford, 1689)

William Howell, *A Sermon Preached at the First Visitation* (1675)

William Hughes, *A Discourse of Pluralities* (1680)

William Hughes, *Two Sermons Preach'd on the Ninth of September 1683* (1684)

John Humfrey, *The Peaceable Design* (1675)

Edward Hyde, *Christ and his Church* (Oxford, 1658)

Henry Hyde, *The Correspondence of Henry Hyde, Earl of Clarendon*, ed. S.W. Singer, 2 vols (1828)

D.I., *Hieragonisticon* (1672)

Gilbert Ironside, *A Sermon preached at Dorchester* (1660)

William Jackson, *Of the Rule of Faith* (Cambridge, 1675)

John James, *Ad clerum* (1678)

William Jane, *A Sermon preached at the Consecration of Henry, Lord Bishop of Oxford* (1675)

William Jane, *A Sermon preached on the Day of the Publick Fast* [11 April 1679] (1679)

William Jegon, *The Damning Nature of Rebellion* (1685)

Thomas Jekyll, *Popery a Great Mystery of Iniquity* (1681)

John Jewel, *The Works of John Jewel*, ed. J. Ayre, 4 vols (Parker Society, Cambridge, 1845–50)

Ralph Josselin, *The Diary of Ralph Josselin 1616–1683*, ed. A. Macfarlane (1976)

Edward Kemp, *Reasons for the Sole Use of the Churches Prayers in Publick* (Cambridge, 1668)

Thomas Ken, *An Exposition on the Church Catechism* (1685)

[Thomas Ken], *Ichabod; Or the Five Groans of the Church* (Cambridge, 1663)

[White Kennett], *A Complete History of England*, 3 vols (1706)

John Kettlewell, *A Discourse Explaining the Nature of Edification* (1684)

John Kettlewell, *An Help and Exhortation to a Worthy Communicating* (1683)

Richard Kidder, *Convivium coeleste* (1674)

Richard Kidder, *The Life of Anthony Horneck* (1698)

Richard Kidder, *The Life of Richard Kidder D.D. Bishop of Bath and Wells Written by Himself*, ed. A.E. Robinson (Somerset Record Society, 37, 1922)

Henry Killigrew, *A Sermon Preach'd before the King* (1666)

Henry King, *A Sermon preached at Lewes in the Diocess [sic] of Chichester* (1663)

S.L., *Remarques on the Humours and Conversation of the Gallants of the Town* (2nd edn, 1673)

Sir Edward Lake, *Memoranda* (1662)

Edward Lake, *Officium eucharisticum* (1673; Oxford, 1843)

Thomas Lamplugh, *A Sermon preached before the House of Lords on the Fifth of November* (1678)

Benjamin Laney, *Five Sermons* (1668)

Benjamin Laney, *A Sermon Preached Before the King* (1675)

William Langley, *The Persecuted Minister* (1656)

Paul Lathom, *God Manifested by his Works* (1678)

Thomas De Laune, *De Laune's Plea for the Nonconformists* (1704 edn)

Sir Peter Leicester, *Charges to the Grand Jury at Quarter Sessions 1660–1677*, ed. E.M. Halcrow (Chetham Society, 5, 1953)

Henry Leslie, *The Martyrdome of King Charles* (The Hague and London, 1649)

Hamon L'Estrange, *The Alliance of Divine Offices* (1659; LACT, Oxford, 1846)

Sir Roger L'Estrange, *Toleration Discussed* (1663)

A Letter of Advice to all the Members of the Church of England, To come to the Divine Service Morning and Evening Every Day (1688)

Churchwardens' Presentments: II Archdeaconry of Lewes, ed. H. Johnstone (Sussex Record Society, 50, 1948–9)

Adam Littleton, *Sixty-one Sermons*, 3 vols (1680)

John Lloyd, *A Treatise of the Episcopacy, Liturgies, and Ecclesiastical Ceremonies of the Primitive Times* (1661)

[William Lloyd], *Papists No Catholicks* (1679)

William Lloyd, *A Sermon Preached before the House of Lords on November 5 1680* (1680)

William Lloyd, *A Sermon Preached before the King* (1679)

John Locke, *Epistola de tolerantia*, ed. and trans. R. Klibansky and J.W. Gough (Oxford, 1968)

Thomas Lodington, *The Honour of the Clergy Vindicated* (1674)

Thomas Long, *The Character of a Separatist* (1677)

Thomas Long, *A Sermon against Murmuring* (1680)

Thomas Long, *The Unreasonableness of Separation: The Second Part* (1682)

James Lowde, *The Reasonableness of the Christian Religion* (1684)

Roger Lowe, *The Diary of Roger Lowe*, ed. W.L. Sachse (1938)

Simon Lowth, *Catechetical Questions* (1673)

Simon Lowth, *A Letter to Edward Stillingfleet* (1687)

Simon Lowth, *Of the Subject of Church Power*, (1685)

Sir John Lowther, *Memoir of the Reign of James II*, ed. T. Zouch (York, 1808)

Richard Lucas, *Unity and Peace* (1683)

William Lucy, *A Treatise of the Nature of a Minister* (1670)

Richard Lytler, *The Reformed Presbyterian* (1662)

A.M., *Plain-Dealing* (1675)

[Thomas Manningham], *A Short View of the Most Gracious Providence of God in the Restoration and Succession* (1685)

[Thomas Manningham], *A Solemn Humiliation for the Murder of King Charles I* (1686)

John Mapletoft, *A Perswasive to the Consciencious Frequenting the Daily Publick Prayers of the Church* (1687)

John March, *A Sermon Preached before the ... Mayor ... of Newcastle ... 30th of January 1676/7* (1677)

Thomas Marshall, *The Catechism Set Forth* (Oxford, 1679)

Edward Martin, *Doctor Martin, Late Dean of Ely, His Opinion* (1662)

John Martin, *Go in Peace* (1674)

[Andrew Marvell], *An Account of the Growth of Popery and Arbitrary Government* (1677)

[Andrew Marvell], *Mr Smirke, or the Divine in Mode* (1676)

Andrew Marvell, *The Poems and Letters of Andrew Marvell*, ed. H.M. Margoliouth, 2 vols (3rd edn, Oxford, 1971)

[Andrew Marvell], *The Rehearsal Transpros'd* (1672; ed. D.I.B. Smith, Oxford, 1971)

Henry Maurice, *The Antithelemite* (1685)

Henry Maurice, *A Sermon Preached before the King ... on January the 30th* (1682)

Henry Maurice, *A Vindication of the Primitive Church, and Diocesan Episcopacy* (1682)

Jasper Mayne, *A Sermon against Schism* (1652)

Jasper Mayne, *A Sermon Preached at the Consecration of the Right Reverend Father in God Herbert [Croft], Lord Bishop of Hereford* (1662)

John Meriton, *Curse not the King* (1660)

John Meriton, *Forms of Prayer for every Day in the Week, Morning and Evening* (1682)

John Milton, *Of True Religion*, in *Complete Prose Works of Milton: VIII* (New Haven and London, 1982)

John Milward, *The Diary of John Milward*, ed. C. Robbins (Cambridge, 1938)

Giles Moore, *The Journal of Giles Moore*, ed. R. Bird (Sussex Record Society, 68, 1971)

George Morley, *Several Treatises* (1683)

Thomas Morton, *Episkopos apostolikos* (1670)

Thomas Morton, *A Sermon Preached at St Paul's* (1642)

Robert Mossom, *An Apology in the Behalf of the Sequestered Clergy* (1660)

Lewis Du Moulin, *A Short and True Account of the Several Advances the Church of England hath made towards Rome* (1680)

N.N., *An Account of the Late Proposals of the Archbishop of Canterbury, with some other Bishops to his Majesty* (1688)

Robert Nelson, *The Life of Dr George Bull* (1713)

Henry Newcome, *The Autobiography of Henry Newcome*, ed. R. Parkinson (Chetham Society, 26–7, 1852)

Samuel Newton, *The Diary of Samuel Newton*, ed. J.R. Foster (Cambridge Antiquarian Society, 23, 1890)

William Nicholson, *An Exposition of the Apostles Creed* (1661; Wing N1112)

William Nicholson, *An Exposition of the Catechism of the Church of England* (1655; LACT, Oxford, 1845)

John Norris, *A Discourse concerning the Pretended Religious Assembling in Private Conventicles* (1685)

Order to the Sessions of Peace at Ampthill, 14 January 1684 [1684/5]

Francis Osborne, *Advice to a Son* (Oxford, 1656)

Thomas Otway, *The Works*, ed. J.C. Ghosh, 2 vols (Oxford, 1932)

William Outram, *Catalogus librorum ... Gulielmi Outrami* (1681)

William Outram, *Twenty Sermons* (1682)

John Overing, *Hadadrimmon* (1670)

The Oxinden and Peyton Letters, 1642–1670, ed. D. Gardiner (1937)

C.P., *Christian Devotion* (1679)

S.P., *A Brief Account of the New Sect of Latitude-Men* (1662)

T.P., *A Guide to the Altar* (2nd edn, 1688)

John Paradise, *Hadadrimmon* (1660)

Samuel Parker, *The Case of the Church of England* (1681)

Samuel Parker, *A Demonstration of the Divine Authority of the Law of Nature* (1681)

Samuel Parker, *A Discourse of Ecclesiastical Politie* (1670)

The Parliamentary History of England, ed. W. Cobbett and J. Wright, 36 vols (1806–20)

Richard Parr, *Christian Reformation* (1660)

Richard Parr, *The Judges Charge* (1658)

Richard Parr, *The Life of Archbishop James Ussher* (1668)

A Pastoral Letter from the Four Catholic Bishops to the lay Catholics of England (1688)

Simon Patrick, *The Works of Simon Patrick,* ed. A. Taylor, 9 vols (Cambridge, 1858)

[Edward Pearse], *The Conformists Plea for the Nonconformists* (1681) [Second and third 'Pleas' appeared in 1682 and a fourth in 1683]

John Pearson, *An Exposition of the Creed* (1659)

John Pearson, *The Minor Theological Works of John Pearson,* ed. E. Churton (Cambridge, 1844)

Edward Pelling, *A Discourse of the Sacrament of the Lords Supper* (1685)

Edward Pelling, *The Good Old Way* (1680)

Edward Pelling, *The True Mark of the Beast* (1685)

Samuel Pepys, *The Diary of Samuel Pepys,* ed. R.C. Latham and W. Matthews, 11 vols (1970–83)

Richard Perrinchief, *Samaritanism Revised and Enlarged* (1669)

Richard Perrinchief, *A Sermon Preached before the Honourable House of Commons at St Margaret's Westminster on 7 November* (1666)

[Pete]R [Pet]T, *A Discourse concerning Liberty of Conscience* (1661)

The Petty–Southwell Correspondence 1676–1687, ed. Marquis of Lansdowne (1828)

Thomas Pierce, *A Collection of Sermons upon Several Occasions* (Oxford, 1671)

Thomas Pierce, *A Correct Copy of Some Notes* (1654)

Thomas Pittis, *A Private Conference* (1670)

A Plea for the Non-conformists Tending to Justifie Them Against the Clamorous Charge of Schism (1674)

Josias Pleydell, *Loyalty and Conformity Asserted* (1682)

Robert Plot, *The Natural History of Oxfordshire* (Oxford, 1676)

Nicholas Pocock (ed.) 'Illustrations of the State of the Church During the Great Rebellion', *The Theologian and Ecclesiastic,* VI–XV (1848–54)

Poems on Affairs of State: I 1660–1678, ed. G. deF. Lord (New Haven and London, 1963)

Edward Polhill, *An Answer to the Discourse of Mr William Sherlock* (1675)

[Edward Polhill], *The Samaritan* (1682)

Walter Pope, *The Life of the Right Reverend Father in God Seth [Ward], Lord Bishop of Salisbury* (1697)

Preparations to a Holy Life: Or Devotions for Families and Private Persons (1684)

Humphrey Prideaux, *The Letters of Humphrey Prideaux,* ed. E.M. Thompson (Camden Society, 15, 1875)

Private Forms of Prayer, Fitted for the late Sad Times (1660) [Wing H597]

Publick Devotion, and the Common Service of the Church of England Justified, and Recommended to all honest and well meaning, (however prejudiced) Dissenters (1675)

Timothy Puller, *The Moderation of the Church of England* (1679)

Walter Ralegh, *Reliquiae Raleighanae* (1679)

William Ramsay, *The Julian Ship* (1681)

The Rawdon Papers, consisting of letters . . . to and from Dr John Bramhall, ed. E. Berwick (1819)

John Rawlett, *The Christian Monitor* (1686)

John Rawlett, *A Dialogue betwixt two Protestants* (1685)

John Rawlett, *An Explication of the Creed, the Ten Commandments and the Lords Prayer* (1672; 2nd edn, 1679)

Reasons Why a Protestant Should Not Turn Papist (1687)

A Representation of the State of Christianity (1674)

John Reresby, *The Memoirs of Sir John Reresby*, ed. A. Browning (Glasgow, 1936)

Edward Reynolds, *The Author and Subject of Healing in the Church* (1660)

Edward Reynolds, *Divine Efficacy* (1660)

Edward Reynolds, *Joy in the Lord* (1655)

Edward Reynolds, *The Misery of a Deserted People* (1659)

Edward Reynolds, *The Pastoral Office* (1663)

Edward Reynolds, *The Peace of Jerusalem* (1657)

Edward Reynolds, *The Preaching of Christ* (1662)

Edward Reynolds, *Sion's Praises* (1657)

John Riland, *Doom's-day Books Opened* (1663)

Matthew Robinson, *The Autobiography of Matthew Robinson*, ed. J.E.B. Mayor (Cambridge, 1856)

[Samuel Rolle], *A Sober Answer to the Friendly Debate* (1669)

Rules for Our More Devout Behaviour in the Time of Divine Service in the Church of England (1686; 2nd edn, 1687)

George Rust, *A Discourse of the Use of Reason in Matters of Religion* (1683)

Dudley Ryder, *The Diary of Dudley Ryder, 1715–1716*, ed. W. Matthews (1939)

W.S., *An Answer to a Letter of Enquiry, into the Grounds and Occasions of the Contempt of the Clergy* (1671)

Andrew Sall, *The Recantation of Andrew Sall, A Jesuit of the Fourth Vow* (1674)

Peter Samwaies, *Devotion Digested* (1652)

Richard Samwaies, *England's Faithfull Reprover* (1653)

William Sancroft, see G. D'Oyly, *The Life of William Sancroft*, 2 vols (1821)

Robert Sanderson, *The Works of Robert Sanderson, D.D.*, ed. W. Jacobson, 6 vols (Oxford 1854)

Churchwardens' Accounts of S. Edmund and S. Thomas, Sarum, ed. H.J.F. Swayne (Salisbury, 1896)

George Savile, *Halifax – Complete Works*, ed. J.P. Kenyon (Harmondsworth, 1969)

William Saywell, *Evangelical and Catholick Unity* (1680)

William Saywell, *The Reformation of the Church of England Justified* (Cambridge, 1688)

William Saywell, *A Serious Inquiry into the Means of an Happy Union* (1681)

John Scott, *The Christian Life* (1681)

John Scott, *A Sermon Preached . . . 2 September 1686* (1686)

John Scott, *The Works of John Scott*, 2 vols (1718)

A Seasonable Treatise (1678) [Wing S2246]

George Seignior, *God, the King and the Church* (1670)

George Seignior, *Moses and Aaron* (Cambridge, 1670)

Separation yet no Schisme (1675)

Edward Sermon, *The Wisdom of Public Piety* (1679)

[Thomas Seymour], *Advice to the Readers of the Common Prayer* (1683)

John Sharp, *Sermons*, 7 vols (1735–48)

R[obert] S[harrock], *De finibus virtutis Christianae* (Oxford, 1673)

John Shaw, *No Reformation of the Established Reformation* (1685)

John Shaw, *Origo Protestantium* (1677)

Joseph Shaw, *Parish Law* (1733)

Gilbert Sheldon, *David's Deliverance and Thanksgiving* (1660)

Richard Sherlock, *The Irregularitie of a Private Prayer in a Publick Congregation* (1674)

Richard Sherlock, *Mercurius Christianus: The Practical Christian* (1673)

Richard Sherlock, *The Principles of Holy Christian Religion* (1656)

William Sherlock, *A Continuation and Vindication of the Defence* (1682)

William Sherlock, *A Defence and Continuation of the Discourse concerning the Knowledge of Jesus Christ* (1675)

William Sherlock, *A Discourse about Church Unity* (1681)

William Sherlock, *A Discourse concerning the Knowledge of Jesus Christ* (1674)

William Sherlock, *A Practical Discourse of Religious Assemblies* (1681; 1682)

William Sherlock, *A Short Summary of the Principal Controversies* (1687)

William Sill, *A Catalogue of Books . . . of the Library of the Rev. Mr William Sill, late Prebendary of Westminster* (1687)

Thomas Smith, *A Sermon about Frequent Communion, preached before the University of Oxford, August the 17th. 1679* (1685)

Thomas Smith, *A Sermon of Conforming and Reforming* (Cambridge, 1662)

Thomas Smith, *A Sermon of the Credibility of the Mysteries of the Christian Religion* (1675)

William Smyth, *The Safe Way to Glory* (1656)

William Smythies, *A Letter to the Observator* (1684)

William Smythies, *The Norfolk Feast* (1671)

William Smythies, *The Worthy Non-Communicant* (1683)

Robert South, *The Sermons of Robert South D.D.*, 5 vols (Oxford, 1842)

Edward Sparke, *Scintillula altaris* (1678 edn)

Anthony Sparrow, *The Bishop of Exons Caution* (1669)

Anthony Sparrow, *A Collection of Articles, Injunctions, Canons* (1661)

Anthony Sparrow, *A Rationale upon the Book of Common Prayer* (1655; 1661)

Thomas Sprat, *A Sermon preached at the Anniversary Meeting of the Sons of the Clergy* (1678)

Thomas Sprat, *A Sermon preached before the . . . Commons* (1678)

Thomas Sprat, *A Sermon Preached before the King* (1677)

Thomas Sprat, *A Sermon Preached before the King* (1678)

Richard Steward, *Several Short, but Seasonable Discourses* (1684)

John Stileman, *A Peace-offering* (1662)

John Stileman, *A View of Church Government* (1663)

Edward Stillingfleet, *A Discourse concerning the Idolatry practiced in the Church of Rome* (1671)

Edward Stillingfleet, *Origines Sacrae: Or a Rational Account of the Grounds of Natural and Revealed Religion* (1662: Oxford, 1797)

Edward Stillingfleet, *A Rational Account of the Grounds of Protestant Religion* (1664; Oxford, 1844)

Edward Stillingfleet, *The Works of Edward Stillingfleet*, ed. R. Bentley, 6 vols (1710)

George Stradling, *A Sermon Preach'd before the King . . . Jan. 30. 1674/5* (1675)

George Stradling, *Sermons and Discourses* (1692)

John Sudbury, *A Sermon Preached at the Consecration of . . . the Bishops of London, Sarum, Worcester, Lincoln and St Asaph* (1660)

John Sudbury, *A Sermon Preached before the King* (1676)

John Sudbury, *A Sermon Preached before the King* (1677)

Jeremy Taylor, *The Whole Works*, ed. R. Heber, 15 vols (1828)

John Templer, *The Reason of Episcopall Inspection* (Cambridge, 1676)

Thomas Tenison, *The Difference Betwixt the Protestant and Socinian Methods* (1687)

Terms of Accommodation (1661) [Wing T756]

William Thomas, *An Apology for the Church of England* (1679)

Herbert Thorndike, *The Theological Works*, 6 vols (LACT, Oxford, 1854)

Thurloe State Papers, ed. T. Birch, 5 vols (1742)

John Tillotson, *The Protestant Religion Vindicated* (1680)

John Tillotson, *Sermons*, 12 vols (1757)

Thomas Tomkins, *The Modern Pleas for Comprehension* (1675)

[George Touchet], *Historical Collections* (1674)

Gabriel Towerson, *An Explication of the Catechism of the Church of England*, 4 vols (1676–87)

Francis Turner, *Animadversions on the Naked Truth* (1676)

Francis Turner, *A Letter to the Clergy of the Diocess of Ely from the Bishop of Ely* (Cambridge, 1686)

John Turner, *A Sermon Preached at Epsom upon the 9th of September* (1683)

Thomas Turner, *The Diary of Thomas Turner*, ed. D. Vaisey (Oxford, 1984)

Sir Roger Twysden, *An Historical Vindication of the Church of England in point of Schism* (1657)

James Ussher, *Works*, ed. C.R. Elrington, 17 vols (1864)

George Villiers, *The Genuine Works of His Grace George Villiers, Duke of Buckingham* (Edinburgh, 1754)

A Vindication of the Clergy from the Contempt Imposed (1672)

The Voice of the Nation (1675)

William Wake, *A Continuation of the Present State of the Controversy* (1688)

John Ward, *The Diary of the Rev. John Ward, A.M.*, ed. C. Severn (1849)

Seth Ward, *An Apology for the Mysteries of the Gospel* (1673)

Seth Ward, *Six Sermons* (1672)

Thomas Warmstry, *A Box of Spikenard* (1660, 3rd edn)

Thomas Warmstry, *A Hand-Kirchife for Loyall Mourners* (1649)

Thomas Warmstry, *Suspiria ecclesiae & republicae anglicanae* (1648)

[Albert Warren], *An Apology for the Discourse of Humane Reason* (1680)

Jeffry Watts, *A Scribe, Pharisee, Hypocrite* (1657)

Thomas Watts, *The Christian Indeed, and Faithful Pastor* (1714)

A Weeks Preparation Towards a Worthy Receiving of the Lords Supper (1679)

Richard West, *The Profitableness of Piety* (1671)

Edward Wetenhall, *Enter into thy Closet* (1666; 4th edn, 1673)

Edward Wetenhall, *Miserere cleri* (1668)

Edward Wetenhall, *The Protestant Peace-Maker* (1682)

Edward Wetenhall, *A Sermon against Neutrality* (1663)

Edward Wetenhall, *Two Discourses for the Furtherance of Christian Piety and Devotion* (1671)

Peniston Whalley, *The Civil Rights and Conveniences of Episcopacy* (1661)

Daniel Whitby, *The Protestant Reconciler* (1682; 2nd edn, 1683)

Daniel Whitby, *Three Sermons Preach'd at Salisbury* (1685)

Thomas Willis, *The Excellency of Wisdom* (1676)

John Wilmot, *The Complete Poems of John Wilmot, Earl of Rochester*, ed. D.M. Vieth (New Haven and London, 1968)

Theophilus Wodenote, *Eremicus theologus* (1654)

Sir Charles Wolseley, *The Reasonablenesse of Scripture-Belief* (1672)

Sir Charles Wolseley, *The Unreasonablenesse of Atheism* (1669)

Laurence Womock, *The Examination of Tilenus before the Triers* (1658)

Laurence Womock, *Moses and Aaron* (1675)

Anthony Wood, *Athenae Oxonienses*, ed. P. Bliss (1813–20)

Anthony Wood, *The Life and Times of Anthony Wood*, ed. A. Clark, 5 vols (Oxford Historical Society, 19, 21, 26, 30, 40, 1891–1900)

Josiah Woodward, *An Account of the Rise and Progress of the Religious Societies in the City of London* (2nd edn, 1698)

Inspections of Churches and Parsonage Houses in the Diocese of Worcester in 1674, 1676, 1684 and 1687, ed. P. Morgan (Worcestershire Historical Studies, 12, 1986)

John Worthington, *A Form of Sound Words* (1674)

Edward Young, *A Sermon Preached at Lambeth January the 25th* (1685)

Secondary Sources

W.M. Abbott, 'The Issue of Episcopacy in the Long Parliament, 1640–1648: The Reasons for Abolition' (unpublished Oxford University D.Phil. thesis, 1981)

G.R. Abernathy, 'The English Presbyterians and the Stuart Restoration, 1648–1663', *Transactions of the American Philosophical Society*, 55, pt. 2 (1965)

G.W.O. Addleshaw, *The High Church Tradition* (1963)

G.W.O. Addleshaw and F. Etchells, *The Architectural Setting of Anglican Worship* (1948)

J. Addy, *Sin and Society in the Seventeenth Century* (1989)

C.F. Allison, *The Rise of Moralism – The Proclamation of the Gospel from Hooker to Baxter* (1966)

B.G. Armstrong, *Calvinism and the Amyraut Heresy* (Madison, Wisconsin, 1969)

C.D. Atkins, *The Faith of John Dryden* (University of Kentucky Press, 1980)

P.D.L. Avis, *Anglicanism and the Christian Church – Theological Resources in Historical Perspective* (Edinburgh, 1989)

P.D.L. Avis, *The Church in the Theology of the Reformers* (1981)

J. Axtell, 'The Mechanics of Opposition: Restoration Cambridge v. Daniel Scargill', *BIHR*, 38 (1965)

G.E. Aylmer, 'Unbelief in Seventeenth-Century England', in *Puritans and Revolutionaries*, ed. D. Pennington and K.V. Thomas (Oxford, 1978)

G.E. Aylmer and R. Cant (eds), *A History of York Minster* (Oxford, 1979)

J. Barry, 'The Parish in Civic Life: Bristol and its Churches, 1640–1750', in *Parish, Church and People*, ed. S.J. Wright (1988)

J. Barry, 'The Politics of Religion in Restoration Bristol', in *The Politics of Religion in Restoration England*, ed. T. Harris, P. Seaward and M. Goldie (Oxford, 1990)

F. Bate, *The Declaration of Indulgence 1672* (1908)

R.A. Beddard, 'Bishop Cartwright's Death-Bed', *Bodleian Library Record*, 11 (1984)

R.A. Beddard, 'Cathedral Furnishings of the Restoration Period; A Salisbury Inventory of 1685', *Wiltshire Archaeological Magazine*, 66 (1971)

R.A. Beddard, 'The Character of a Restoration Prelate: Dr John Dolben', *Notes and Queries*, 17 (1970)

R.A. Beddard, 'Church and State in Old St Paul's', *Guildhall Miscellany*, 4 (1972)

R.A. Beddard, 'The Church of Salisbury and the Accession of James II', *Wiltshire Archaeological Magazine*, 67 (1972)

R.A. Beddard, 'The Commission for Ecclesiastical Promotions, 1681–84: An Instrument of Tory Reaction', *HJ*, 10 (1967)

R.A. Beddard, *A Kingdom without a King – The Journal of the Provisional Government in the Revolution of 1688* (Oxford, 1988)

R.A. Beddard, 'Of the Duty of Subjects: A Proposed Fortieth Article of Religion', *Bodleian Library Record*, 10 (1981)

R.A. Beddard, 'The Privileges of Christchurch, Canterbury: Archbishop Sheldon's Enquiries of 1671', *Archaeologia Cantiana*, 87 (1972)

R.A. Beddard, 'The Restoration Church', in *The Restored Monarchy, 1660–1688*, ed. J.R. Jones (1979)

R.A. Beddard, 'Sheldon and Anglican Recovery', *HJ*, 19 (1976)

R.A. Beddard, 'Vincent Alsop and the Emancipation of Restoration Dissent', *JEH*, 24 (1973)

R.A. Beddard, 'Wren's Mausoleum for Charles I and the Cult of the Royal Martyr', *Architectural History*, 27 (1984)

G.V. Bennett, 'Conflict in the Church', in *Britain After the Glorious Revolution 1689–1714*, ed. G.A. Holmes (1969)

G.V. Bennett, 'Loyalist Oxford and the Revolution', in *History of the University of Oxford: V The Eighteenth Century*, ed. L.S. Sutherland and L.G. Mitchell (Oxford, 1986)

G.V. Bennett, 'Patristic Tradition in Anglican Thought, 1660–1900', *Oecumenica* (Gütersloh, 1972)

G.V. Bennett, 'The Seven Bishops: A Reconsideration', *SCH*, 15 (1978)

G.V. Bennett, *The Tory Crisis in Church and State* (Oxford, 1975)

G.V. Bennett, 'University, Society and the Church 1688–1714', in *History of the University of Oxford: V The Eighteenth Century*, ed. L.S. Sutherland and L.G. Mitchell (Oxford, 1986)

G.V. Bennett, 'William III and the Episcopate', in *Essays in Modern English Church History*, ed. G.V. Bennett and J.D. Walsh (1966)

D. Berman, *A History of Atheism in Britain from Hobbes to Russell* (1988)

G.F.A. Best, *Temporal Pillars – Queen Anne's Bounty, the Ecclesiastical Commissioners and the Church of England* (1964)

J.M. Blom, *The Post-Tridentine English Primer* (Catholic Record Society Monograph 3, 1982)

R.S. Bosher, *The Making of the Restoration Settlement 1649–62* (1951)

J. Bossy, *The English Catholic Community 1570–1850* (1975; 1979)

P.F. Bradshaw, *The Anglican Ordinal* (Alcuin Club, 1971)

L.I. Bredvold, *The Intellectual Milieu of John Dryden* (Chicago, 1934)

L. Brockliss, G. Harriss and A. Macintyre, *Magdalen College and the Crown* (Oxford, 1988)

J. Buckroyd, *Church and State in Scotland 1660–1681* (Edinburgh, 1980)

E. Carpenter, *The Protestant Bishop – Being the Life of Henry Compton* (1956)

S.C. Carpenter, *Eighteenth Century Church and People* (1959)

P.J. Challinor, 'Restoration and Exclusion in the County of Cheshire', *Bulletin of the John Rylands Library*, 64 (1982)

J.A.I. Champion, 'The Ancient Constitution of the Christian Church – The Church of England and its Enemies 1660–1730' (unpublished Cambridge University Ph.D. Thesis, 1989)

R. Clark, 'Anglicanism, Recusancy, and Dissent in Derbyshire, 1603–1670' (unpublished Oxford University D.Phil. thesis, 1979)

R. Clark, 'Why was the Re-establishment of the Church of England Possible? Derbyshire: a Provincial Perspective', *Midland History*, 8 (1983)

W.K. Lowther Clarke, *Eighteenth Century Piety* (1944)

A.M. Coleby, *Central Government and the Localities: Hampshire, 1649–1689* (Cambridge, 1987)

P. Collinson, *The Religion of Protestants* (Oxford, 1982)

J.S. Coolidge, *The Pauline Renaissance in England – Puritanism and the Bible* (1970)

J.I. Cope, *Joseph Glanvill, Anglican Apologist* (St Louis, 1956)

G.R. Cragg, *Freedom and Authority* (Philadelphia, 1975)

G.R. Cragg, *From Puritanism to the Age of Reason* (Cambridge, 1950; 1966)

G.R. Cragg, *Puritanism in the Period of the Great Persecution* (Cambridge, 1957)

R.S. Crane, 'Suggestions toward a Genealogy of the "Man of Feeling"', *E[nglish] L[iterary] H[istory]*, 1 (1934)

C. Cross, *The Royal Supremacy in the Elizabethan Church* (1969)

F.L. Cross, *The Oxford Movement and the Seventeenth Century* (1933)

G. Cuming, *The Godly Order* (Alcuin Club, 1983)

C.E. Davies, 'The Enforcement of Religious Uniformity in England, 1668–1700, with Special Reference to the Dioceses of Chichester and Worcester' (unpublished Oxford University D.Phil. thesis, 1982)

A Dictionary of English Church History, ed. S.L. Ollard and G. Crosse (1912)

The Dictionary of National Biography, ed. L. Stephens and S. Lee, 63 vols (1885–1900)

E. Duffy, 'The English Secular Clergy and the Counter-Reformation', *JEH*, 34 (1983)

E. Duffy, 'The Godly and the Multitude in Stuart England', *The Seventeenth Century*, 1 (1986)

E. Duffy, '"Poor Protestant Flies": Conversions to Catholicism in Early Eighteenth-century England', *SCH*, 15 (1978)

E. Duffy, 'Primitive Christianity Revived: Religious Renewal in Augustan England', *SCH*, 14 (1977)

C.W. Dugmore, *Eucharistic Doctrine in England from Hooker to Waterland* (1942)

P. Elmen, 'Richard Allestree and *The Whole Duty of Man*', *The Library*, 6 (1951–2)

G. Every, *The High Church Party 1688–1718* (1956)

T.J. Fawcett, *The Liturgy of Comprehension 1689* (Alcuin Club, Southend, 1973)

J.C. Findon, 'The Nonjurors and the Church of England, 1689–1716' (unpublished Oxford University D.Phil. thesis, 1978)

A. Fletcher, 'The Enforcement of the Conventicle Acts 1664–1679', *SCH*, 21 (1984)

A. Fletcher, *Reform in the Provinces: the Government of Stuart England* (New Haven and London, 1986)

G.C.F. Forster, 'Government in Provincial England under the Later Stuarts', *TRHS*, 33 (1983)

R.H. Fritze, 'Root or Link? Luther's Position in the Historical Debate over the Legitimacy of the Church of England, 1558–1625', *JEH*, 37 (1986)

I.J. Gentles and W.J. Sheils, *Confiscation and Restoration: The Archbishopric Estates and the Civil War* (Borthwick Papers, 59, York, 1981)

M. Goldie, 'Danby, the Bishops and the Whigs', in *The Politics of Religion in Restoration England*, ed. T. Harris, P. Seaward and M. Goldie (Oxford, 1990)

M. Goldie, 'John Locke and Anglican Royalism', *Political Studies*, 31 (1983)

M. Goldie, 'The Nonjurors, Episcopacy, and the Origins of the Convocation Controversy', in *Ideology and Conspiracy: Aspects of Jacobitism 1689–1759*, ed. E. Cruickshanks (Edinburgh, 1982)

M. Goldie, 'Sir Peter Pett, Sceptical Toryism and the Science of Toleration in the 1680s', *SCH*, 21 (1984)

I.M. Green, 'Career Prospects and Clerical Conformity in Early Stuart England', *Past and Present*, 90 (1981)

I.M. Green, 'The Changing Form and Content of Religious Instruction in Early Modern England', unpublished paper given in Oxford, January 1987

I.M. Green, '"For Children in Yeeres and Children in Understanding": The Emergence of the English Catechism under Elizabeth and the Early Stuarts', *JEH*, 37 (1986)

I.M. Green, 'The First Five Years of Queen Anne's Bounty', in *Princes and Paupers in the English Church 1500–1800*, ed. R. O'Day and F. Heal (Leicester, 1981)

I.M. Green, 'The Persecution of "Scandalous" and "Malignant" Parish Clergy during the English Civil War', *EHR*, 104 (1979)

I.M. Green, *The Re-establishment of the Church of England, 1660–1663* (Oxford, 1978)

D. Greene, 'Latitudinarianism and Sensibility: The Genealogy of the "Man of Feeling" Reconsidered', *Modern Philology*, 75 (1977)

P. Hammond, 'Thomas Smith: A Beleaguered Humanist of the Interregnum', *BIHR*, 56 (1983)

A.T. Hart, *The Life and Times of John Sharp* (1949)

A.T. Hart, *William Lloyd, 1627–1717* (1952)

P. Harth, *Swift and Anglican Rationalism* (Chicago, 1961)

F. Higham, *Catholic and Reformed* (1962)

D. Hirschberg, 'Episcopal Incomes and Expenses, 1660–*c*.1760', in *Princes and Paupers*, ed. R. O'Day and F. Heal (Leicester, 1981)

C. Holmes, *Seventeenth-century Lincolnshire* (Lincoln, 1980)

G.A. Holmes, *The Trial of Dr Sacheverell* (1973)

H. Horwitz, *Parliament, Policy and Politics in the Reign of William III* (Manchester, 1977)

H. Horwitz, 'Protestant Reconciliation in the Exclusion Crisis', *JEH*, 15 (1964)

J.J. Hughes, 'The Missing "Last Words" of Gilbert Burnet in July 1687', *HJ*, 20 (1977)

M. Hunter, *John Aubrey and the Realm of Learning* (1975)

M. Hunter, 'The Problem of "Atheism" in Early Modern England', *TRHS*, 5th series, 35 (1985)

M. Hunter, 'Science and Heterodoxy: an Early Modern Problem Reconsidered', in *Reappraisals of the Scientific Revolution*, ed. D.C. Lindberg and R.S. Westman (Cambridge, 1990)

M. Hunter, *Science and Society in Restoration England* (Cambridge, 1981)

J.J. Hurwich, 'Dissent and Catholicism in English Society: a Study of Warwickshire, 1660–1720', *Journal of British Studies*, 16 (1976)

R. Hutton, *Charles the Second* (Oxford, 1989)

R. Hutton, *The Restoration: a Political and Religious History of England and Wales, 1658–1667* (Oxford, 1985)

P.W. Jackson, 'Nonconformists and Society in Devon 1660–1689' (unpublished Exeter University Ph.D. thesis, 1986)

M.D.W. Jones, 'The Ecclesiastical Courts before and after the Civil War: The Office Jurisdiction in the Dioceses of Oxford and Peterborough, 1630–1675' (unpublished Oxford University B.Litt. thesis, 1977)

M.G. Jones, 'Two Accounts of the Welsh Trust, 1675 and 1678(?)', *Bulletin of the Board of Celtic Studies*, 9 (1939)

N.H. Keeble, *The Literary Culture of Nonconformity in Later Seventeenth-century England* (Leicester, 1987)

J. Kent, *The Unacceptable Face – The Modern Church in the Eyes of the Historian* (1987)

J.P. Kenyon, *The Popish Plot* (1972; Harmondsworth, 1984)

J. King, 'The Episcopate during the Civil Wars, 1642–1649', *EHR*, 83 (1968)

P. King, 'The Reasons for the Abolition of the Book of Common Prayer in 1645', *JEH*, 21 (1970)

D.R. Lacey, *Dissent and Parliamentary Politics in England, 1661–1689* (New Brunswick, 1969)

P. Lake, *Anglicans and Puritans? Presbyterianism and English Conformist Thought from Whitgift to Hooker* (1988)

P. Lake, 'Presbyterianism, the Idea of a National Church and the Argument from Divine Right', in *Protestantism and the National Church in Sixteenth-century England*, ed. P. Lake and M. Dowling (1987)

P. Lake, 'The Significance of the Elizabethan Identification of the Pope as Antichrist', *JEH*, 31 (1980)

P. Lake, 'William Bradshaw, Antichrist and the Community of the Godly', *JEH*, 36 (1985)

W.M. Lamont, *Richard Baxter and the Millennium* (1979)

W.M. Lamont, 'The Rise of Arminianism Reconsidered', *Past and Present*, 107 (1985)

J. Wickham Legg, *English Church Life from the Restoration to the Tractarian Movement* (1914)

S.E. Lehmberg, *The Reformation of the Cathedrals – Cathedrals and English Society 1485–1603* (Princeton, 1988)

H.R. McAdoo, *The Spirit of Anglicanism* (1965)

H.R. McAdoo, *The Structure of Caroline Moral Theology* (1949)

J.S. McGee, *The Godly Man in Stuart England* (New Haven and London, 1976)

A.E. McGrath, 'The Emergence of the Anglican Tradition on Justification', *Churchman*, 98 (1984)

A.E. McGrath, *Iustitia Dei – A History of the Doctrine of Justification: II* (Cambridge, 1986)

J. MacKay, 'John Tillotson, 1630–1694: A Study of his Life and of his Contribution to the Development of English Prose' (unpublished Oxford University D.Phil. thesis, 1952)

D.F. McKenzie, 'Bibliography and History in Seventeenth-century England', unpublished Lyell Lectures, University of Oxford, 1988

H.J. McLachlan, *Socinianism in Seventeenth-century England* (1951)

J. Marshall, 'The Ecclesiology of the Latitude-Men 1660–1689: Stillingfleet, Tillotson, and "Hobbism"', *JEH*, 36 (1985)

W.M. Marshall, 'Episcopal Activity in the Hereford and Oxford Dioceses, 1660–1760', *Midland History*, 8 (1983)

L.L. Martz, *The Poetry of Meditation* (New Haven and London, 1962)

F.C. Mather, 'Georgian Churchmanship Reconsidered: Some Variations in Anglican Worship 1714–1830', *JEH*, 36 (1985)

A.G. Matthews, *Calamy Revised* (Oxford, 1934)

A.G. Matthews, *Walker Revised* (Oxford, 1948)

T.F. Mayo, *Epicurus in England* (Dallas, 1934)

A.C. Miller, 'Herbert Astley, Dean of Norwich', *Norfolk Archaeology*, 38 (1982)

J. Miller, *Popery and Politics in England 1660–1688* (Cambridge, 1973)

A. Milton, 'The Laudians and the Church of Rome *c.* 1625–1640' (unpublished Cambridge University Ph.D. thesis, 1989)

S.I. Mintz, *The Hunting of Leviathan* (Cambridge, 1962)

W.F. Mitchell, *English Pulpit Oratory from Andrewes to Tillotson* (1932)

P.E. More and F.L. Cross, *Anglicanism* (1935)

J. Morgan, *Godly Learning – Puritan Attitudes Towards Reason, Learning and Education, 1560–1640* (Cambridge 1986)

J.S. Morrill, 'The Attack on the Church of England in the Long Parliament, 1640–1642', in *History, Society and the Churches*, ed. D. Beales and G. Best (Cambridge, 1985)

J.S. Morrill, 'The Church in England, 1642–9', in *Reactions to the English Civil War 1642–1649*, ed. J.S. Morrill (1982)

J.S. Morrill, 'The Religious Context of the English Civil War', *TRHS*, 34 (1984)

E. Morris, *The History and Art of Change Ringing* (1931)

P.J. Norrey, 'The Restoration Regime in Action: The Relationship between Central and Local Government in Dorset, Somerset and Wiltshire, 1660–1678', *HJ*, 31 (1988)

G.F. Nuttall, 'The First Nonconformists', in *From Uniformity to Unity, 1662–1962*, ed. G.F. Nuttall and O. Chadwick (1962)

G.F. Nuttall, 'John Horne of Lynn', in *Christian Spirituality*, ed. P.N. Brooks (1975)

R. O'Day, 'Anatomy of a Profession: the Clergy of the Church of England', in *The Professions in Early Modern England*, ed. W. Prest (1987)

S.L. Ollard, *A Short History of the Oxford Movement* (1915)

P.H. Osmond, *Isaac Barrow* (1944)

D.M. Owen, *The Records of the Established Church of England* (1970)

J.I. Packer, 'The Redemption and Restoration of Man in the Thought of Richard Baxter' (unpublished Oxford University D.Phil. thesis, 1954)

J.W. Packer, *The Transformation of Anglicanism 1643–1660 (with special reference to Henry Hammond)* (Manchester, 1969)

T.M. Parker, 'The Rediscovery of the Fathers in the Seventeenth-century Anglican Tradition', in *The Rediscovery of Newman*, ed. J. Coulson and A.M. Allchin (1967)

J. Passmore, *The Perfectibility of Man* (1970)

C.A. Patrides (ed.), *The Cambridge Platonists* (1969)

K.F. Paulson, 'The Reverend Edward Stillingfleet and the "Epilogue" to Rochester's *A Satyr against Reason and Mankind'*, *Philological Quarterly*, 50 (1971)

H.B. Porter, *Jeremy Taylor – Liturgist* (Alcuin Club, 1979)

R.S. Porter, 'The Enlightenment in England', in *Enlightenment in National Context*, ed. R.S. Porter and M. Teich (1981).

A. Powell, *John Aubrey and his Friends* (1963 edn)

J.H. Pruett, *The Parish Clergy Under the Later Stuarts – The Leicestershire Experience* (Urbana, Illinois, 1978)

H.D. Rack, *Reasonable Enthusiast – John Wesley and the Rise of Methodism* (1989)

H.W. Randall, 'The Rise and Fall of a Martyrology: Sermons on Charles I', *Huntington Library Quarterly*, 10 (1946–7)

J. Redwood, *Reason, Ridicule and Religion* (1976)

G. Reedy, *The Bible and Reason* (Philadelphia, 1975)

C.F. Richardson, *English Preachers and Preaching 1640–1670* (1928)

I. Rivers, 'Grace, Holiness, and the Pursuit of Happiness: Bunyan and Restoration Latitudinarianism', in *John Bunyan Conventicle and Parnassus*, ed. N.H. Keeble (Oxford, 1988)

E.G. Rupp, *Religion in England, 1688–1791* (Oxford, 1986)

J.L. Salter, 'Warwickshire Clergy, 1660–1714' (unpublished Birmingham University Ph.D. thesis, 1975)

G. Schochet, *Patriarchalism in Political Thought* (Oxford, 1975)

A.A. Seaton, *The Theory of Toleration under the later Stuarts* (Cambridge, 1911)

P. Seaward, *The Cavalier Parliament and the Reconstruction of the Old Regime, 1661–1667* (Cambridge, 1989)

P. Seaward, 'Gilbert Sheldon, the London Vestries, and the Defence of the Church', in *The Politics of Religion in Restoration England*, ed. T. Harris, P. Seaward and M. Goldie (Oxford, 1990)

B.J. Shapiro, *John Wilkins 1614–1672* (Berkeley and Los Angeles, 1969)

I. Simon (ed.), *Three Restoration Divines – Barrow, South and Tillotson*, 2 vols (Paris, 1967, 1976)

W.G. Simon, *The Restoration Episcopate* (New York, 1965)

M.D. Slatter, 'The Records of the Courts of Arches', *JEH*, 4 (1953)

H.F.R. Smith, *The Theory of Religious Liberty in the Reigns of Charles II and James II* (Cambridge, 1911)

M.G. Smith, *Fighting Joshua – A Study of the Career of Sir Jonathan Trelawney* (Redruth, 1985)

M.G. Smith, *Pastoral Discipline and the Church Courts: the Hexham Court 1680–1730* (Borthwick Papers, 62, York, 1982)

M.G. Smith, 'A Study of the Administration of the Diocese of Exeter during the Episcopate of Sir Jonathan Trelawney, bart., 1689–1707' (unpublished Oxford University B.D. thesis, no year)

C.J. Sommerville, *Popular Religion in Restoration England* (Gainesville, 1977)

J.P. Sommerville, 'The Royal Supremacy and Episcopacy "Jure Divino", 1603–1640', *JEH*, 34 (1983)

M.R. Sommerville, 'Richard Hooker and his Contemporaries on Episcopacy: an Elizabethan Consensus', *JEH*, 35 (1984)

D.A. Spaeth, 'Common Prayer?', in *Parish, Church and People*, ed. S.J. Wright (1988)

D.A. Spaeth, 'Parsons and Parishioners: Lay–Clerical Conflict and Popular Piety in Wiltshire villages, 1660–1740' (unpublished Brown University Ph.D. thesis, 1985)

W.A. Speck, *Reluctant Revolutionaries – Englishmen and the Revolution of 1688* (Oxford, 1988)

W.M. Spellman, *John Locke and the Problem of Depravity* (Oxford, 1988)

J.T. Spivey, 'Middle Way Men, Edmund Calamy and the Crisis of Moderate Nonconformity 1688–1732', (unpublished Oxford University D.Phil. thesis, 1986)

M. Spufford, *Contrasting Communities* (Cambridge, 1974)

M. Spufford, *Small Books and Pleasant Histories* (Cambridge, 1981)

J. Spurr, 'Anglican Apologetic and the Restoration Church' (unpublished Oxford University D.Phil. thesis, 1985)

J. Spurr, 'The Church of England, Comprehension and the Toleration Act of 1689', *EHR*, 104 (1989)

J. Spurr, '"Latitudinarianism" and the Restoration Church', *HJ*, 31 (1988)

J. Spurr, '"Rational Religion" in Restoration England', *JHI*, 49 (1988)

J. Spurr, 'Schism and the Restoration Church', *JEH*, 41 (1990)

J. Spurr, '"Virtue, Religion and Government": The Anglican Uses of Providence', in *The Politics of Religion in Restoration England*, ed. T. Harris, P. Seaward and M. Goldie (Oxford, 1990)

V. Staley, *Hierurgia Anglicana* (1902–4)

S. Staves, *Players' Scepters – Fictions of Authority in Restoration England* (Lincoln, Nebraska, 1979).

B.S. Stewart, 'The Cult of the Royal Martyr', *Church History*, 38 (1969)

D. Stone, *A History of the Doctrine of the Holy Eucharist* (1909)

C.J. Stranks, *Anglican Devotion* (1951)

C.J. Stranks, *The Life and Writings of Jeremy Taylor* (1952)

R.N. Stromberg, *Religious Liberalism in Eighteenth-century England* (1954)

P. Styles, *Studies in Seventeenth-century West Midlands History* (Kineton, 1978)

N. Sykes, *Church and State in England in the Eighteenth Century* (Cambridge, 1934)

N. Sykes, *From Sheldon to Secker* (Cambridge, 1959)

N. Sykes, *Old Priest and New Presbyter* (Cambridge, 1956)

S. Sykes and J. Booty (eds), *The Study of Anglicanism* (1988)

N. Temperley, *The Music of the English Parish Church: I* (Cambridge, 1979)

R. Thomas, 'Comprehension and Indulgence', in *From Uniformity to Unity, 1662–1962*, ed. G.F. Nuttall and O. Chadwick (1962)

R. Thomas, 'The Seven Bishops and their Petition, 18 May 1688', *JEH*, 12 (1961)

D. Trotter, 'Wanton Expressions', in *Spirit of Wit*, ed. J. Treglown (Oxford, 1982)

N.R.N. Tyacke, *Anti-Calvinists – The Rise of English Arminianism, c. 1590–1640* (Oxford, 1987)

G.S. Wakefield, *Puritan Devotion* (1957)

D.P. Walker, *The Decline of Hell* (1964)

D.D. Wallace, *Puritans and Predestination – Grace in English Protestant Theology 1525–1695* (Chapel Hill, 1982)

A. Warne, *Church and Society in Eighteenth-century Devon* (1969)

M.R. Watts, *The Dissenters* (Oxford, 1978)

H.C. White, *English Devotional Literature [Prose] 1600–1640* (Madison, Wisconsin, 1931)

E.A.O. Whiteman, 'The Church of England 1542–1837', *Victoria County History of Wiltshire*, 3 (1956)

E.A.O. Whiteman (ed.), *The Compton Census of 1676* (1986)

E.A.O. Whiteman, 'The Episcopate of Dr Seth Ward, Bishop of Exeter (1662 to 1667) and Salisbury (1667 to 1688/89) with Special Reference to the Ecclesiastical Problems of his Time' (unpublished Oxford University D.Phil. thesis, 1951)

E.A.O. Whiteman, 'The Re-establishment of the Church of England, 1660–1663', *TRHS*, 5 (1955)

E.A.O. Whiteman, 'The Restoration of the Church of England', in *From Uniformity to Unity, 1662–1962*, ed. G.F. Nuttall and O. Chadwick (1962)

E.A.O. Whiteman, 'Two Letter Books of Archbishops Sheldon and Sancroft', *Bodleian Library Record*, 4 (1953)

C.E. Whiting, *Nathaniel Lord Crewe Bishop of Durham (1674–1721)* (1940)

C.E. Whiting, *Studies in English Puritanism from the Restoration to the Revolution* (1931)

J.H. Wilson, *The Court Wits* (Princeton, 1948)

D. Wing (ed.), *Short-Title Catalogue of Books Printed in England ... 1641–1700*, 3 vols (New York, 2nd edn, 1972–88)

H.F. Woodhouse, *The Doctrine of the Church in Anglican Theology 1547–1603* (1954)

A.B. Worden, 'Literature and Political Censorship in Early Modern England', in *Too Mighty to be Free* (Zutphen, 1988)

A.B. Worden, 'Toleration and the Cromwellian Protectorate', *SCH*, 21 (1984)

Index

Names and subjects in the text, and the authors of all quotations, are indexed: other material in the footnotes is not indexed. The following abbreviations are used: abp = archbishop; adn = archdeacon; bp = bishop; dn = dean; Nc = Nonconformist; RC = Roman Catholic; r = rector; v = vicar. Dates given after an office or preferment are the date of appointment. All of the Restoration bishops of each see are listed chronologically under the diocese. Any further references will be found under the names of the individual bishops. Parliamentary bills and statutes are listed under 'Statutes'.